Lecture Notes in Computer Science 4761

Commenced Publication in 1973
Founding and Former Series Editors:
Gerhard Goos, Juris Hartmanis, and Jan van Leeuwen

Roman Obermaisser   Yunmook Nah
Peter Puschner   Franz J. Rammig (Eds.)

Software Technologies for Embedded and Ubiquitous Systems

5th IFIP WG 10.2 International Workshop, SEUS 2007
Santorini Island, Greece, May 7-8, 2007
Revised Papers

 Springer

Volume Editors

Roman Obermaisser
Peter Puschner
Vienna University of Technology, Real-Time Systems Group
Treitlstr. 3/182-1, 1040 Wien, Austria
E-mail: {romano, peter}@vmars.tuwien.ac.at

Yunmook Nah
Dankook University, Department of Electronics and Computer Engineering
Hannam-dong, Yongsan-gu, Seoul 140-714, Korea
E-mail: ymnah@dku.edu

Franz J. Rammig
University Paderborn, Design of Parallel Systems
Fürstenallee 11, 33102 Paderborn, Germany
E-mail: franz@uni-paderborn.de

Library of Congress Control Number: 2007936568

CR Subject Classification (1998): C.2, C.3, D.2, D.4, H.4, H.3, H.5

LNCS Sublibrary: SL 3 – Information Systems and Application, incl. Internet/Web
and HCI

ISSN   0302-9743
ISBN-10   3-540-75663-9 Springer Berlin Heidelberg New York
ISBN-13   978-3-540-75663-7 Springer Berlin Heidelberg New York

Springer is a part of Springer Science+Business Media

springer.com

© IFIP International Federation for Information Processing 2007
Printed in Germany

Typesetting: Camera-ready by author, data conversion by Scientific Publishing Services, Chennai, India
Printed on acid-free paper   SPIN: 12174065   06/3180   5 4 3 2 1 0

Preface

The workshop on Software Technologies for Future Embedded and Ubiquitous Systems (SEUS) started as an IEEE event in 2003 but was reborn as an IFIP event during 2006-2007. The SEUS series will be one of the few flagship events of the newly formed IFIP WG10.2. The Steering Committee of the new SEUS series is chaired by Franz Rammig, the chairman of IFIP TC10. This workshop continued the tradition of the first, second, third, and fourth IEEE SEUS workshops held in Hakodate (Japan), Vienna (Austria), Seattle (USA), and Gyeongju (Korea), respectively. It was our great honor and pleasure to hold SEUS 2007 on Santorini, the most famous island for its stunning caldera view among the Cyclades cluster in Greece.

The application domain of both embedded computing and ubiquitous systems have had explosive growth over the past few years. Given the advances in these fields, and also those in the areas of distributed computing, sensor networks, middleware, etc., the area of ubiquitous embedded computing is now being envisioned as the way of the future. The systems and technologies that will arise in support of ubiquitous embedded computing will undoubtedly need to address a variety of issues, including dependability, real-time, human-computer interaction, autonomy, resource constraints, etc. All of these requirements pose a challenge to the research community. The purpose of SEUS 2007 was to bring together researchers and practitioners with an interest in advancing the state of the art and the state of practice in this emerging field, with the hope of fostering new ideas, collaborations and technologies.

SEUS will now be even more of an elite event where new trends will be discussed based on a very selective set of contributions. One of its unique characteristic is that some of the papers are presented by invited world-class research leaders, and we have 23 such contributions in this workshop. This year we received 102 regular submissions for the technical program and finally accepted 35 papers, including 31 full papers and 4 short papers, with an acceptance rate of 34%. We owe a great deal of thanks to the members of the Program Committee and the reviewers. The success of this year's SEUS would not be possible without their hard work. We are also grateful to all the members of the Steering Committee for their advice and support. We would also like to thank the organizers of ISORC 2007 for their help in organizing the workshop. Finally, we would like to thank all the authors for their contributions, which made the workshop a success.

June 2007
Yunmook Nah
Roman Obermaisser

Organization

General Co-chairs

Moon Hae Kim   Konkuk University, Korea
Franz J. Rammig   University of Paderborn, Germany
Peter Puschner   Vienna University of Technology, Austria

Program Co-chairs

Yunmook Nah   Dankook University, Korea
Roman Obermaisser   Vienna University of Technology, Austria

Publicity Co-chairs

Tei-wei Kuo   National Taiwan University, Taiwan
Seongje Cho   Dankook University, Korea

Program Committee

Uwe Brinkschulte   University of Karlsruhe, Germany
Lynn Choi   Korea University, Korea
Paul Couderc   IRISA, France
Wilfried Elmenreich   Vienna University of Technology, Austria
Sebastian N. Fischmeister   University of Pennsylvania, USA
Kaori Fujinami   Tokyo University of Agriculture and
                            Technology, Japan
Petr Grillinger   TTTech, Austria
Minyi Guo   University of Aizu, Japan
Jan Gustafsson   Mälardalen University, Sweden
Hwansoo Han   Korea Advanced Institute of Science and
                            Technology, Korea
Tei-Wei Kuo   National Taiwan University, Taiwan
Dongman Lee   Information and Communication University,
                            Korea
Istvan Majzik   Budapest University of Technology and
                            Economics, Hungary
Yukikazu Nakamoto   University of Hyogo and Nagoya University,
                            Japan

Michael Paulitsch   Honeywell AES Centers of Excellence, USA
Philipp Peti   General Motors Europe, Germany
Taehyung Wang   California State University Northridge, USA

Sponsoring Institutions

The Aerospace Coorporation
TTTech Computertechnik AG

Table of Contents

Validation of Embedded and Ubiquitous Systems

Ubiquitous Computing Applications

Scheduling and Non Functional Properties

Self-organization and Reconfiguration

Service Discovery and Development Platform

Wireless Networks

Middleware Architectures and Virtualization

Environment Interaction

An Efficient Method to Create Business Level Events Using Complex Event Processing Based on RFID Standards*

Byung-Kook Son, Jun-Hwan Lee, Kyung-Lang Park, Cheong-Ghil Kim,
Hie-Cheol Kim, and Shin-Dug Kim

Department of Computer Science, Yonsei University,
Seoul, Korea
{ssonkk, jhlee, lanx}@parallel.yonsei.ac.kr,
{Tetons, sdkim}@yonsei.ac.kr
School of Computer and Communication Engineering, Daegu University,
Daegu, Korea
hckim@daegu.ac.kr

Abstract. RFID systems should be designed to process a large number of RFID data in real time. Therefore, there have been much research and company studies regarding RFID data processing. One of methods is CEP (Complex Event Processing), which can provide a method to process RFID data efficiently. However, previous work is just focused on raw RFID data processing, such as data filtering, the elimination of duplicated data, and the aggregation of data. Also, it creates primitive events based on just one physical or logical reader. Therefore, processing overhead for complex events may increase. And it cannot provide business level events. Therefore, we propose a method that can reduce processing overhead and create business level events by using CEP. Proposed method provides two primitive events that are defined by using the relationship of two readers. Thus, when any pattern of events is matched for a specific complex event, business level events can be generated and execution time can be reduced comparing with other mechanisms without those events. And, execution time can be reduced by about 57% as compared to others.

1 Introduction

RFID (Radio Frequency Identification) systems are constructed as four major components, i.e., the tags with unique ID, the RFID readers that identify any tags by using RF frequency, the middleware that can process raw RFID data, and the applications. Recently, EPCglobal [1] leads to standards for the components of RFID systems such as, tag data, air interface for communication, RFID middleware, and so on.

RFID systems should be designed to process many data in real time. Those data is processed by the RFID middleware.

* This research was supported by the UPLUS project of Ministry of Commerce, Industry and Energy.

R. Obermaisser et al. (Eds.): SEUS 2007, LNCS 4761, pp. 1–10, 2007.

Therefore, the role of RFID middleware is important in RFID systems. A standard of RFID middleware is proposed by EPCglobal as ALE (Application Level Event) [2]. However, RFID middleware based on ALE just provides pure RFID data. As a result, RFID applications have to include some logics to process business events. Although EPCglobal proposes the EPCIS (Electronic Product Code Information Service) [3] to provide business level events, that is incomplete standard that does not define many specific parts. And to apply the EPCIS in RFID systems, agreement is required for partners.

Therefore, we propose a CEP based on ALE to provide business level events. Especially, primitive event types in our proposed method are defined based on relationship of two readers. That is, most of business events occur when a certain tag moves between any two or more readers. For example, we can assume a situation that a customer pays for some items in a counter with RFID reader after taking out those from a shelf with RFID reader in the market. In this situation, when a customer takes out an item from the shelf, a business event for "SELL" can be started. And when a customer pays for an item at the counter, a business event for "SELL" can be completed. Our proposed event model can be expressed as "RelativeObservation" by considering relationship of two readers. And that event model can specify the starting of business level event (take out an item from the shelf) as "PredictedObservation". Thus, when any pattern of events matched for complex event to generate business level events, execution time can be reduced comparing with other mechanisms without those events and many effective business level events can be provided. When we use our method, execution time can be reduced by about 57% comparing with other mechanisms.

2   Related Works

Event processing technology has been studied in active database [4 - 6] for long time. Especially, it has been studied to process real-time stream data including sensor and RFID data. Also it is important to improve the performance of RFID systems. Therefore, in [7], several methods for RFID data management are introduced. In [9], temporal-based data model and rule-based RFID data transformation are introduced for RFID data processing. However, it does not provide any simple query to get high level events. And in [9], to get high level information, complex query has to be used, because it is not suited for handing RFID events. Therefore, CEP is introduced to process RFID data efficiently. Especially, in [10], to process RFID data, CEP is considered in RFID systems. However, it does not provide any information about detailed architecture of CEP. In [8], CEP is also applied to process RFID data. In that work, components of CEP are discussed including primitive event types, event operators, RFID rules, and complex event detection algorithm. It also introduces the algorithm that can detect non-spontaneous events. However, it is only focused on raw RFID data processing, such as the elimination of duplicated data, and the aggregation of data.

3   Proposed Complex Event Processing

Basically, we can consider two kinds of events in CEP. One is primitive event and another is complex event. Primitive events are basically composed to create complex events. Also, complex event can be created when one or more primitives are matched with any special pattern or when one or more complex events show any special pattern.

3.1 Primitive Event

In RFID systems, previous CEP techniques are focused on raw RFID data processing in the RFID middleware, elimination of duplicated data, and aggregation of data. For that reason, a primitive event in previous work [8] is defined based on the tag identified by just one reader as physical or logical. However, we propose primitive events based on the tags identified between two readers.

Observation(r, o, t). Observation event type occurs when a reader identifies a tag. This primitive event type is equal to that in previous work. However, our event type can be considered unique RFID tag data because based on ALE. In the format of Observation(r, o, t), where r represents logical reader, o represents the EPC of object, t represents timestamp when the object is identified by reader.

PredictedObservation(r, o, t). The PredictedObservation event occurs when a tag disappears from any reader. That is, a tag disappeared from any reader may appear again to other readers some time. In the format of PredictedObservation(r, o, t), r represents a logical reader, the o represents the EPC of object, t represents timestamp when this object disappears from the reader.

RelativeObservation(o, r1, t1, r2, t2). RelativeObservation event occurs when a tag disappeared from any reader is identified by another reader. RelativeObservation means that an object is currently identified by r2 after it is identified by r1 first. In the format of RelativeObservation(o, r1, t1, r2, t2), o represents the EPC of object, r1, r2 represents logical reader, t1 represents relative time(after/before) between two readers, and t2 represents timestamp when this object is identified by reader2.

3.2 Event Operators

As mentioned above, a complex event can be created through detecting any specific pattern of primitive events or complex events by using event operators. In CEP, the role of event operators is to define any pattern of complex events. Event operators can be classified into temporal and non-temporal operators [8]. However in this paper, the definition of temporal operator is not required, because we cannot predicate the time when any business event occurs.

So, we have to define new operators for creating the business level events. These are causal operators that can express any casual relationship. In the market, if we assume "SELL" event by considering only events occurred at the counter reader, this may cause any misleading situation. Because, when a worker takes an item to the counter, this case may predicate a "SELL" event. Therefore, to predicate a correct business event, we have to check any causing event activated first for this business event. After then, we can predicate correct event by checking the result activated. For that reason, causal operators and the relationship of events are important for creating business level event.

3.2.1 Proposed Operator for Business Level Event

Table 1 shows operators for creating business level events in this proposed method.

Table 1. Event operator for complex event processing

Operator	Meaning	Usage
AND($\wedge$)	Conjunction of two events E1 and E2 occur when both E1 and E2 occur without occurrence order	(E1 $\wedge$ E2)
OR($\vee$)	Disjunction of two events E1 or E2 occur when either E1 or E2 occur without occurrence order	(E1 $\vee$ E2)
NOT($\neg$)	Negation of E1 event occur when E1 never occur	($\neg$E1)
SEQ (;)	Sequence of two events E1 and E2 occur when both E1 and E2 occur with occurrence order	(E1;E2)
CASUAL($\rightarrow$)	Cause of two event E1 and E2 occur when E1 is cause E2	(E1$\rightarrow$E2)

3.3 Event Rule

We have to detect any complex event by using any given event pattern.

```
ON PredictedObservation(r, o, t)
IF Condition
      DEFINE RelativeObservation(o, r1, t1, r2, t2)
      ON Event
      IF Condition
            DO Action
```

Fig. 1. Event rule definition for complex event

So a method that detects the complex event is required. To detect any complex event efficiently, a rule should be defined. Traditionally, rule definition to composite events has been studied based on ECA (Event Condition Action) model. ECA model can used to detect any event easily and simply. Therefore, we use modified ECA model to express PredictedObservation and RelativeObservation as shown in Figure 1.

4 CEP Architecture and Operation Flow

Until now, we explain about the components of CEP. In this section, the architecture to process complex events will be presented. And we will explain the operation flow of architecture to create complex events.

4.1 Architecture and Operation Flow

Figure 2 shows the proposed architecture for CEP. Proposed method is based on ALE. Application will request monitoring about business events defined in section 3.3 according to rule definition. Query analyzer receives application requests and analyzes them. And query analyzer sends those to the rule matcher. Rule matcher tries to search its rule repository to check whether same rule exist or not. If there is no match, rule matcher needs to register that in the rule repository.

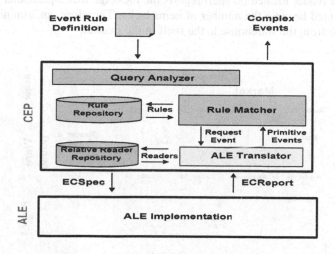

Fig. 2. Proposed architecture of complex event processing

After that, the rule matcher sends a message to ALE translator. The ALE translator makes the ECSpec to creating primitive event. And the ALE translator requests ECReport message by the ECSpec through ALE API. ALE translator waits for the ECReport. If ALE translator receives the ECReport from the ALE, it may generate primitive events based on ECReport. ALE translator may search the relative reader repository for checking relationship of reader registered to crate the RelativeObservation event. If the incoming event is not related with the registered reader, ALE translator may generate the Observation or PredictionObservation events depending on whether the tag is disappeared from the readers or not. The rule matcher checks whether primitive events generated by ALE translator matches with any complex event pattern or not. If primitive events match with any complex event pattern, the rule matcher may generate complex events.

5   Examples of Complex Event Detection

In this chapter, an example that creates the business level events by using primitive events, event operators, and event rules is shown. We assume two scenarios. One is that a customer is shopping as shown in Figure 3. Another one is that an object is moving along fixed path as shown in Figure 6.

5.1   Scenario 1 (Shopping in the Market)

Figure 3 shows shopping scenario in the market. A customer with shopping cart enters the gateway with RFID reader. When he passes the gateway, the RFID reader identifies the tag on shopping cart. After that, he is walking around shelves to find some items. When he finds item needed, he takes out the item from shelf. After he finishes shopping, he pays for some items at the counter with RFID reader. On the other hand, a reader located on shelf reports the message that a particular item has to be supplemented because the number of items lacks. Therefore, an administrator supplies the item from the warehouse to the shelf in the market.

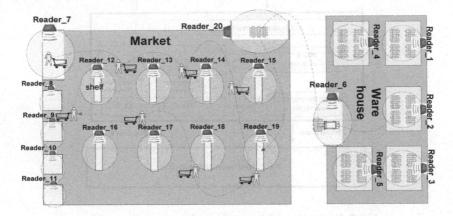

Fig. 3. A customer pays for items, after taking out some items

Table 2 shows the logical readers named by the role of physical readers in the market.

Table 2. Logical readers definition in avobe scenario

Logical Reader	Physical Readers	Role of Readers
BSectionReader	Reader_1 ~ Reader_5	Identify items that exist in the warehouse
BGatewayReader	Reader_6	Identify items that take out from warehouse
SEnteranceReader	Reader_7	Identify the people that enter in the market
SGatewayReader	Reader_20	Identify the items that income in the market
SCalculationReader	Reader_8 ~ Reader_11	Identify the items at the counter
ShelfReader	Reader_12 ~ Reader_19	Identify the items that exist at the shelves

When considering the business events occurred by a customer in the market, those events may be caused by shopping, selling, robbery, and refund. And events occurred by a administrator may be caused by incoming of products, outgoing of products, and supply of products in the shelf. All business events defined above can be expressed by our proposed method. Figure 4 shows complex event definition about "SELL". When an item on the shelf with RFID readers disappears, PredictedObservation event may occur as soon as possible. At that time, another reader waits for a tag disappeared from that reader. If the tag is identified by readers in the counter, system may create the action as "SELL".

```
ON PredictedObservation(ShelfReader, EPC, T1)
IF True
        DEFINE E1 = RelativeObservation(EPC, ShelfReader, AFTER,
                            SCalculationReader, T2)
        ON E1
        IF True
                DO "SELL"
```

Fig. 4. The complex event definition of "SELL"

Figure 5 shows the complex event definition about "THEFT". When an item on the shelf with RFID readers disappears, PredictedObservation event may occur as soon as possible. If the PredictedObservation event occurs in one reader, another reader in the store waits for a tag disappeared from that reader. If the tag is identified by reader in the gateway rather than reader at the counter, the system creates this action as "THEFT".

```
ON PredictedObservation(ShelfReader, EPC, T1)
IF True
        DEFINE E1 = RelativeObservation(EPC, ShelfReader, AFTER,
                            SCalculationReader, T2)
        DEFINE E2 = RelativeObservation(EPC, ShelfReader, AFTER,
                            SEnteranceReader, T3)
        ON ( ¬E1 AND E3)
        IF True
                DO "THEFT"
```

Fig. 5. The complex event definition of "THEFT"

5.2 Scenario 2 (Recognition of Right Path)

Another example, recognition of right path, can be performed in our proposed method as follows. This scenario shows that a tag is moving along any fixed path formed by many readers. Figure 6 shows the situation that checks whether any tag X is moving along its correct fixed path or not. We amuse that the fixed path is specified as A->C ->D->E->G->H. In this case, if we use any event model that do not define any relation ship among readers, although tag X arrives at the reader H after reader A, C, D, E, F, G , and H, the system may create a complex event that tag X was moved within the correct fixed path. However, tag X is moved incorrectly, because tag X passes through the

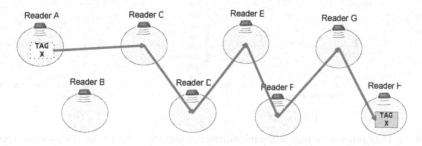

Fig. 6. The recognition of right path

reader F undefined in the path. If we use our event model, tag X has to pass through the reader G after reader E without any other reader between them.

If the path to move is defined as A->C->D->E->G->H, the system may create complex event that tag X is moved along the incorrect path. Figure 7 shows the complex event definition about "RIGHT PATH".

```
ON PredictedObservation(Reader A, X, T1)
IF True
        DEFINE E1=RelativeObservation(X, Reader A, AFTER, Reader C, T2)
        DEFINE E2=RelativeObservation(X, Reader C, AFTER, Reader D, T2)
        DEFINE E3=RelativeObservation(X, Reader D, AFTER, Reader E, T2)
        DEFINE E4=RelativeObservation(X, Reader E, AFTER, Reader G, T2)
        DEFINE E5=RelativeObservation(X, Reader G, AFTER, Reader H, T2)
        ON (E1 → E2 → E3 → E4 → E5)
        IF True
                DO "RIGHT PATH"
```

Fig. 7. The complex event definition of "RIGHT PATH"

6   Experience Results

In this chapter, we will show experiment results when using our CEP to create complex events. We examine the performance of proposed method by using CEP simulator. Performance of CEP is compared with those without any PredictedObservation and RelativeObservation events for equal test conditions. As a test condition, the number of tags is increased by 100 each time. And we assume that 50% of tags are moved fro one reader to another reader. After that, event processing time is measured required to create complex events.

Figure 8(a) shows total event processing time to create complex events when the number of tags increases by 100 each time. Most of time is spent to check whether primitive events satisfy any predefined complex event pattern or not. Therefore, if we can reduce the number of primitive events used in pattern match processing, we may reduce the overall event processing time. Actually, when we reduce the number of primitive events by using PredictedObservation and RelativeObservation events, we can obtain the result as shown in Figure 8(a).

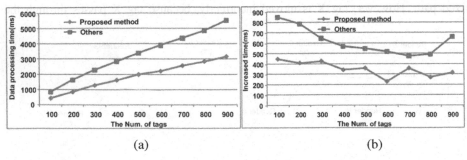

(a)   (b)

Fig. 8. (a) Data processing time when the number of tags increase, (b) Increased data processing time when the number of tags increase

Figure 8(b) shows the increased time required to process events, when the number of tags increases by 100 each time. As mentioned above, to create complex events, pattern matching is needed. Therefore, the more tags increase, the more event processing times increase. However, the number of events is increased in the proposed method less than others because of using two primitive events. Therefore, the proposed method can reduce the time to process events when the number of tags increases by 100 each time.

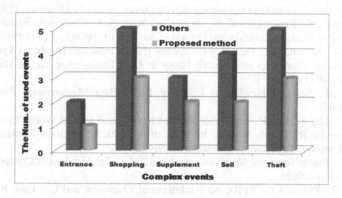

Fig. 9. The number of used events for creating complex events

Figure 9 shows the number of used primitive events to create complex events in the proposed method and other CEP. Proposed method generates a primitive event based on the relationship of two readers. Also, it can express the direction of moving tags. Therefore, when proposed method and other define equal complex events, the number of used primitive events can be reduced significantly.

7 Conclusion

In this paper, we propose a method that can apply CEP based on RFID standards to RFID systems. Especially, we introduced new primitive events that are PredictedObservation and RelativeObservation, because most of business level events occur when any tag moves between any two or more readers. And we propose a method that can create business level events by using those. And we could confirm the facts that when any pattern of events matched for complex event to generate business level events, execution time can be reduced comparing with other mechanisms without those events and many effective business level events can be provided. When we use our method, execution time can be reduced by about 57% comparing with other mechanisms. In addition, we can check whether any tag moves along the correct route in fixed path or not.

However, in the paper, we just consider RFID data for complex event processing. Therefore we will consider not only RFID data but also other sensor data in future work. Also we will design new primitive event type, event operator, and event rule definition for use these data in complex event processing.

References

1. EPCglobal, http://www.epcglobalinc.org/
2. EPCglobal Proposed Specification, The Application Level Events (ALE) Specification Version 1.0, EPCglobal (2005)
3. Working Draft Version, EPC Information Services (EPCIS) Version 1.0 Specification, EPCglobal (2005)
4. Gatziu, S., Dittrich, K.R.: SAMOS: an Active Object-Oriented Database System. IEEE Quarterly Bulletin on Data Engineering, Special Issue on Active Databases (1992)
5. Chakravathy, S., Krishnaprasad, V., Anwar, E., Kim, S.-k.: Composite Events for Active Databases: Semantics, Contexts and Detection. In: VLDB, pp. 606–617 (1994)
6. Gatziu, S., Dirtrich, K.R.: Detecting Composite Events in Active Databases Systems Using Petri Nets. In: Workshop on Research Issues in Data Engineering: Active Database Systems, pp. 2–9 (1994)
7. Palmer, M.: Seven Principles of Effective RFID data Management. Progress Software (2004)
8. Wang, F., Liu, S., Liu, P., Bai, Y.: Bridging Physical and Virtual World: Complex Event Processing for RFID data Streams. In: Proc. of the 10th International Conference on Extending Database Technology, Munich Germany (2006)
9. Wang, F., Peiya: Temporal Management of RFID data. In: 31st VLDB Conference, Tondheim Norway (2005)
10. Trigg, J.B.: Progress for RFID: An Architectural Overview and Use Case Review. Progress Software (2005)

Physical/Cyber Objects Management Framework for Multiple-Area Detectable RFID

Masayuki Iwai, Ryo Osawa, Suzuki Kei, Takuya Imaeda, and Hideyuki Tokuda

Graduate School of Media and Governance, Keio University
5322 Endo, Fujisawa, Kanagawa, 252-8520, Japan
{tailor,ryo,suzuk,che,hxt}@ht.sfc.keio.ac.jp
http://www.ht.sfc.keio.ac.jp/smart-furoshiki

Abstract. Recently, there is lots research for tangible objects which enables to support users everyday's life. However, due to the high price of sensors , end-users hesitate to attach such devices to physical objects. Even worth, batteries of embedded devices should despoil the living environment. Therefore, the low-price system to detect users' phisical objects without battery is needed. We will propose a novel hardware platform using cheap RFID tags which can attach on any everyday physical objects. We have designed and implemented two size of RFID systems which have flexible multiple area antennas to support manage users' physical objects. This paper describes details of Smart-Furoshiki system and its applications.

Keywords: RFID, Multiple-area Detection, Physical Objects Management.

1 Introduction

Nowadays, number of researchers which have proposed ubiquitous systems to detects physical objects in users' everyday life are increasing. These systems use lots of embedded computers and sensors to detects human activities [6][10]. As in our past projects, we have been creating non-export DIY ubiquitous system, for example smart furniture [3,12,4] without thinking the cost of back-end system.

However, it is difficult to setup all of devices for users who are unfamiliar with computing technology. To make matters worse, buying many of sensors is too expensive to end users. Most of research has ignored such economical cost and users' maintainability. To give an actual example, documents using at a weekly meeting should be not worth to attach sensor-embedded devices which costs more than 15$. Even worth, batteries of sensor-embedded devices should despoil the earth environment. Therefore, the low-priced system to support users' daily life without battery is needed. We will propose a novel hardware platform using low cost RFID tags which can attach on any everyday items. We have design and implemented two size of RFID system which has flexible multiple area antennas to support accumulation of users' context.

Our reaseach goal is to develop software and harware which enable non-expert users to create smart objects without battery in cheaper way . We use RFID tags, which is less than 10cents and they are easy to attach to any kinds of phisical objects.

R. Obermaisser et al. (Eds.): SEUS 2007, LNCS 4761, pp. 11–19, 2007.

Fig. 1. Furoshiki: traditional Japanese wrapping cloth

We propose a novel hardware called Smart-Furoshiki which is a sensorized cloth for supporting office and home activities. "Furoshiki" is a type of traditional Japanese wrapping cloth that can were frequently used to transport clothes, gifts, or other goods(see Figure 1). As Furoshiki is so flexible and simple, it can use lots of porpose. For example it can wrap any type of shapes from bottles to box. It also can cover on the important things, or spread under cloth.

Smart-Furoshiki has more than 4 passive RFID antennas and a tiny RFID reader. Beause of it's flexbility, Smart-Furoshiki can be used universally for the porpose of table-cloth, tapestry and cover. Users can easily use Smart-Furoshiki without configuring computers, sensors and networks inside each Smart-Furoshiki. This paper describes details of Smart-Furoshiki and its software framework of phisical objects managemenet system.

2   Hardware Architecture

In this section, we describe the harware system architecture of Smart-Furoshiki.For the popose of adapting lots of usage, we have develop two type of Smart-Furoshiki, large size and mobile size.

2.1   Desktop-Size Furoshiki

Desktop-size version can use in a office and home environment. This type can detect not only RF-IDs of objects but also the existence area ID. By using these two type of ID, the system can detects the context information. An example scenario is that a userfs car key and her/his wallet are always put nearside on the Smart-Furoshiki.

Hardware of Desk-Top Size Furoshiki. Figure 2 and 3 leftside show the architecture of Smart-Furoshiki. Smart-Furoshiki has 8 RFID antennas and 8 tags. RFID reader uses 8 antennas on timesharing system due to avoid the radio wave collisions between antennas. The reader is special model Takaya TR3-D002C-8 which has 8 antenna channels. Each antenna is made by conductive fabric[11] for the purpose of bending it flexibly

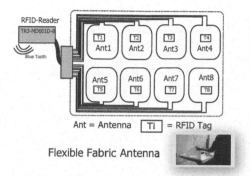

Ant = Antenna | Ti | = RFID Tag

Flexible Fabric Antenna

Fig. 2. Architecture of the Smart-Furoshiki and Flexible Fabric Antenna

as shown in Figure2. The material of fabric antenna has special film of metal. It has a thickness of 0.125mm. The density is 72g per m^2. According to the tag size, the reading distance is from -18cm to 18cm.

The 13.56 MHz tags are stitched into the Furoshiki at the center of each antenna. Every antenna is unified as the cable to the 8 port RFID reader. The Smart-Furoshiki is separated in to 8 areas, which is cover Furoshikic range of RFID antenna. To simplify the explanation, we user Ant_1-Ant_8 as the name of antennas and T_1-T_8 as RFID tags. T_i is placed at the center of Ant_1 and always detected by Ant_i.

Figure 3 right side shows the middleware screen shot of Smart-Furoshiki. Smart-Furosiki can read multiple objects ID in multiple areas unlike other RFID system. The middleware has also has application repository and multicast data transition architecture to support applications developers.

2.2 Mobile-Size Furoshiki

Users carry many kinds of everyday objects including books, papers, cell phone, magazines, DVDs, wallet, and music player. Furthermore, they have needs both to reduce things left behind the bag and not to lose something important work related on the something on the bags. To satisfy these needs, we have developed mobile type of Smart-

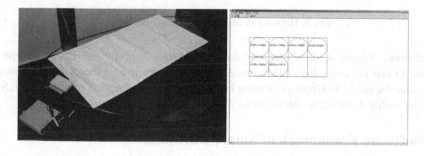

Fig. 3. Exterior of Smart-Furoshiki

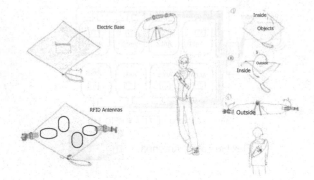

Fig. 4. Use Case of Mobile Size Furoshiki

Furoshiki. All the electric devices, such as bluetooth communication module, RFID reader, and antenna much condenser circuits, and battery, are accumulate into a small electric box(see Figure 5).

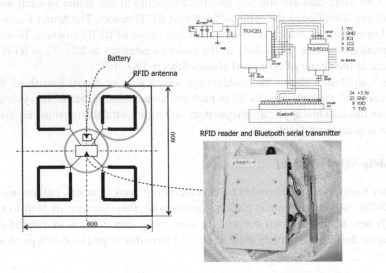

Fig. 5. Harware of Mobile size Smart-Furoshiki

Hardware. Figure 4 show the use case of Mobile-Size Furoshiki. This type of Furoshiki can put everyday objects inside and can carry it anyplace. The system can recognize the users' belongings, a thing left behind and the duration time to bring. System can gather these users context even if users are outside of office.

3   Software Framework of Smart-Furoshiki

In this section, we describe the software framework to manage phicical objects in Smart-Furoshiki system.

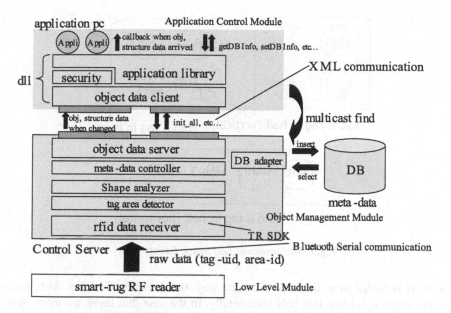

Fig. 6. Middleware Framework of Smart-Furoshiki

3.1 Total Framework of Smart-Furoshiki Middleware

Smart-Furoshiki Middleware are separated into 3 modules as shown in Figure 6. Smart-Furoshiki Middleware are separated into 3 modules as shown in Figure 6. First one is most low level software which only detects RFID numbers eventually.This module send data to Object Management Layer eventually using bluetooth communication Second module is Object Management Layer which analyze structure of Smart-Furosihki. Analyzing structure is mentioned in next subsection. This Object Management Layer has a meta-data DB which is mapping between tag-ID and physical objects. This meta-data DB also obtain the applications' meta information to launch. Object Management Layer send detected/detached RFID tag information to upper layer using multicast network communication.

Third module, most upper layer, is on the client side as shown in Figure6. This Application Control Modules try to control suitable application for users using information from Object Management Layer. Application Control Modules, which are implemented in windows DLL, are always communicate to the Object Management Layer. This layer also controls the relations of tags which must detect in the same time to support secure applications.

3.2 Algolism of Shape Recognition

Smart furoshiki is so flexible that it can be folded into any shape. To recognize the shape of Smart-Furoshiki, we are using below algorisms.

When Ant_1 detects T_4, the shape of Smart-Furoshiki is folded in to half as figure 7. When Ant_2 detects T_1 and Ant_3 detects T_4 simultaneously, the shape of Smart-

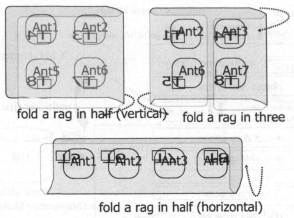

fold a rag in half (vertical)   fold a rag in three

fold a rag in half (horizontal)

Fig. 7. Mechanism of Self Shape Recognition

Furoshiki is folded in to three. In the same way, the detection T_2 from Ant_1 means that the shape is folding into half horizontal. In the case that there are more than 2 Smart-Furoshikis, We can estimate physical overlapping of Furoshikis by reading the neighbor's tags. Thus, the Smart-Furoshiki can detects tags' ID, detected area on it, and physical shape of Furoshiki.

4 Applications

To assume the usage in office environment of Smart-Furoshiki middleware, We have 3 applications based on the affordance of Smart-Furoshiki, laying, covering, and hanging.

4.1 Supporting Collaborative Works by Laying Smart-Furoshiki on A Desk

Currently, the number of documents and data which are treated in cyber space is increasing. However, cyber desktop management systems can not recognize objects on a physical desktop area, correctly. (ex. Books, DVD jackets, pens, papers, lights, electrical appliances ,room sensors) On the other hand, physical objects can not recognize either cyber object which used by same person. This Smart-Furoshiki is a novel hardware and desktop management system which can handle both cyber and physical objects.

The users can lay Smart-Furoshiki on a desk. The Smart-Furoshiki supports cooperation between objects on it. Objects on Smart-Furoshiki are identified by RF-ID. Figure 8 shows it. When computers are brought close, those computers share directories each other. When the users edit the same file on those computers, the changes are immediately updated on the editors each other (1). Also Smart-Furoshiki supports cooperation between computers and objects. For example, the users place a music CD near a computer, and the music data in CD is copied to the computer (2). Besides, Smart-Furoshiki supports cooperation between objects. The users can see the movies on the display putting the movie DVD near the display (3).

Fig. 8. Supporting Collaborative Works by Laying Smart-Furoshiki on A Desk

4.2 Managing Objects Covered with Smart-Furoshiki

Users can manage the users' objects covered with Smart-Furoshiki. The scenario is showed in Figure 9. First, the user attaches an RF-ID tag to the user's objects and registers it to Smart-Furoshiki (1). When the user puts the user's object that is registered before, the user is authenticated and login the PC on the desk. The authenticated user can work at the desk(2). When the user leaves the desk, by covering the objects with Smart-Furoshiki the user visually hide them and log off the PC (3). When the user wants to uncover the objects hidden by Smart-Furoshiki, the user must put the user's object. If a user that is not authenticated put off Smart-Furoshiki, the Furoshiki informs the home security system of the theft. Also, Smart-Furoshiki reminds a user of the object left behind on it. For example, when a user always brings the user's cell phone, watch and wallet together Smart-Furoshiki remembers this practice. When the user left the watch behind although the user brought cell phone and wallet Smart-Furoshiki warns the user.

4.3 Wall Type Task Schedular Using Smart-Furoshiki

The third example is the application to manage users' tasks. The scenario is shown in Figure 5. Smart-Furoshiki hangs on a wall. The wall is separated into some areas. The area means the priority of tasks, such as "Emergency task" and "Pending task". First, a user writes a memo pad about the user's task with an electronic pen that is able to convert handwriting to digital data [7], and pins that memo pad to Smart-Furoshiki (1). The application registers a task content written on this memo pad as pinned areas' @meaning (2). Furthermore, when a user removes the pin, the application deletes the pinned task.

Fig. 9. Managing objects Covered with Smart-Furoshiki

Fig. 10. 1:Writing memo pad 2:Pinned tasks 3:Timeline viwer

The pinned tasks are shared in the group, and also the user can check the tasks wherever the user can connect the network. Finally, these task histories are referenced on a PC by Timeline viewer (3). Users can see the task histories, and retrieve before tasks easily.

5   Related Work

There is a research that aims to realize a smart carpet that identifies things on it[2]. However the size is too large to be used as a tablecloth or a tapestry like Smart-Furoshiki. bYOB developed at MIT media Lab is a smart bag with embedded sensors [5]. bYOB is built in antenna of RF reader. Our Smart-Furoshiki is made from a conductive textile and can work as the antenna itself. Therefore Smart-Furoshiki is thinner and cheaper than that of bYOB. Other research [1] [9] are also using sensorized fabrics. The aim of these research is to obtain biometrics information at wearable environment. Our research target, on the other hand, is for collaborative work at office environment.. Electronic Tablecloth made from E-broidery [8] is an electronic conductive textile can read an RF-ID tag. However the usage of it is limited to tablecloth. Smart-Furoshiki has more flexibility.

6   Conclusion

We have developed a cloth-like RFID system called "Smart-Furoshiki" that allows users to manage phisical objects in inexpensive and environment-aware way. We also provide a software framework for management RFID information and application control called Smart-furoshiki Middleware. Smart-Furoshiki Middleware can recognize the changing its own shape autonomously through combination of detecting RFID tags and antennas. Moreover, Smart-Furoshiki's flexibility allows to turn fold this into any shape. Using these features, Smart-Furoshiki can be based on a lots of applications. To show the utilization of Smart-Furoshiki for the various purposes at office environment, we implemented demonstrations based on three scenarios. First one is the collaboration between mobile PCs on the laying Smart-Furoshiki At the second demo by using Smart-Furoshiki for covering objects, users can keep privacy in easy way. As the third application Smart-Furoshiki, hanged on a wall, helps tasks management between cyber and physical memo papers. Secondly, to accumulate context information even when users outside environment, we provide mobile-seize Smart-Furoshiki. We proved two type of Furoshiki. Large size Smart-Furoshiki can detect objects ID and place using 8 RFID antennas which are made from flexible fabric. Mobile-size has 4 RFID antennas, chargeable battery, tiny RFID readers, and Bluetooth communication module. By using two type of Smart-Furoshiki, ubiquitous applications can accumulate users' context easily and contentiously.

Acknowledgement

This research has been conducted as part of Ubila Project supported by Ministry of Internal Affairs and Communications, Japan.

References

1. De Rossi, D., Santa, A., Mazzoldi, A.: Dressware: wearable piezo- and thermoresistive fabrics forergonomics and rehabilitation. In: Engineering in Medicine and Biology society, 1997. Proceedings of the 19th Annual International Conference of the IEEE, 5th edn, pp. 1880–1883 (1997)
2. Fukumoto, M., Shinagawa, M.: Carpetlan: A novel indoor wireless(-like) networking and positioning system. In: Beigl, M., Intille, S.S., Rekimoto, J., Tokuda, H. (eds.) UbiComp 2005. LNCS, vol. 3660, pp. 1–18. Springer, Heidelberg (2005)
3. Kohtake, N., Ohsawa, R., Yonezawa, T., Matsukura, Y., Iwai, M., Takashio, K., Tokuda, H.: u-Texture:Self-organizable Universal Panels for Creating Smart Surroundings. In: Beigl, M., Intille, S.S., Rekimoto, J., Tokuda, H. (eds.) UbiComp 2005. LNCS, vol. 3660, pp. 19–36. Springer, Heidelberg (2005)
4. Kohtake, N., Yonezawa, T., Ohsawa, R., Matsukura, Y., Takashio, K., Tokuda, H.: Creating pervasive services with self-organizable universal boards. In: Gellersen, H.-W., Want, R., Schmidt, A. (eds.) PERVASIVE 2005. LNCS, vol. 3468, pp. 187–192. Springer, Heidelberg (2005)
5. Nanda, G., Michael Bove, J.V., Cable, A.: byob (build your own bag):a computationally-enhanced modular textile system. In: Davies, N., Mynatt, E.D., Siio, I. (eds.) UbiComp 2004. LNCS, vol. 3205, Springer, Heidelberg (2004)
6. Muller-Tomfelde, C., Streitz, N., Tandler, P., Konomi, S.: Roomware: Towards the next generation of human-computer interaction based on an integrated design of real and virtual worlds. In: Carroll, J. (ed.) Human-Computer Interaction in the New Millenium, pp. 553–578. Addison-Wesley, Reading
7. Pentel. Pentel airpen, http://www.airpen.jp/
8. Post, E.R., Orth, M., Russo, P.R., Gershenfeld, N.: E-broidery: design and fabrication of textile-based computing. IBM Syst. J. 39(3-4), 840–860 (2000)
9. Sensatex, I.: Smart textile, http://www.sensatex.com/
10. Intille, S.S., Larson, K., Tapia, E.M., Beaudin, J.S., Kaushik, P., Nawyn, J., Rockinson, R.
11. Tanaka, M., Jang, J.-H.: Wearable microstrip antenna for satellite communications. In: IEICE Transaction on Communications (August 2004)
12. Yanagihara, T., Sakakibara, H., Ohsawa, R., Ideuchi, M., Kohtake, N., Iwai, M., Takashio, K., Tokuda, H.: A self configurable topology-aware network for smart materials. In: IWSAWC 2005 (June 2005)

A Task Decomposition Scheme for Context Aggregation in Personal Smart Space

Hoseok Ryu, Insuk Park, Soon J. Hyun, and Dongman Lee

School of Engineering, Information and Communications University,
119, Munjiro, Yuseong-gu, Daejeon, 305-732, Korea
{hsryu, ispark, shyun, dlee}@icu.ac.kr

Abstract. In context-aware computing, the context aggregation is an important function of the context management. In an infrastructure-based smart space, a centralized context management system need not concern about its resource consumption for context aggregation. However, in a personal smart space which consists of only resource-constrained mobile devices, not only global resource consumption of the personal smart space but also that of the device which plays a role of a context manager (coordinator) must be minimized. In this paper, we propose a task decomposition scheme in which heavy context aggregation tasks to be imposed on a centralized coordinating device are decomposed and distributed to all the participating mobile devices (clients) in a mobile smart space. By decomposing and distributing the heavy aggregation operations the processing overhead upon the coordinating device can be minimized while providing equivalent context aggregation capability for applications, but maintaining the total amount of processing of all devices not to be significantly increased.

Keywords: Ubiquitous computing, Context awareness, Personal smart space, Context aggregation, Task distribution.

1 Introduction

In recent years, most existing context-aware services are offered in an infrastructure-based smart space like a smart home or an office. A centralized context management system on a powerful, resource-rich machine gathers, processes, aggregates, and disseminates the context information. Context-aware services request and get notified of context information from the centralized context management system.

As a user carries several mobile devices, it composes a personal area network (PAN). The PAN environment with context management configures a new type of smart space, called a personal smart space [1], [2]. Each personal smart space includes a coordinator device and zero or more client devices. Each device may include several sensors and corresponding context providers which capture context information from them. Additionally, a coordinator device which has relatively more resource than client devices provides additional capabilities such as rule-based

R. Obermaisser et al. (Eds.): SEUS 2007, LNCS 4761, pp. 20–29, 2007.

context aggregation, and managing context information and a list of context providers.

A context aggregation method such as logic inference requires high resource consumption [4], [5]. If a coordinator device is wholly responsible for context aggregation in a personal smart space, its processing overhead is significantly increased and its battery is exhausted. As a result, the personal smart space can last no longer. To solve this problem, the distribution of context aggregation has been proposed. By distributing the aggregation function, EDCI [6] focuses on reducing processing time taken in context reasoning, and Solar [7] focuses on increasing the reusability of existing context providers. However, none of them considers mobile ad-hoc settings. A recent work presents a middleware for context provisioning in a mobile environment which consists of resource-constrained devices. However, it does not consider resource consumption caused by context aggregation [3].

In this paper, we propose an efficient context aggregation scheme which avoids overburdening the coordinator device with context aggregation by distributing sub tasks of high level context in the client devices. The proposed scheme decomposes an aggregation task into several sub tasks based on the placement of the context providers on mobile devices in order for the sub tasks not to incur the wasteful network transmission. The evaluation results shows that the processing overhead of the coordinator device decreases about 70 percent while maintaining that of each client device is increased by only 8 percent, comparing with the total amount of processing in previous work.

The rest of the paper is organized as follows. Section 2 explains the motivation of the proposed scheme. Section 3 introduces the requirements for context aggregation in personal smart space. We discuss design consideration and describe the context management architecture for a personal smart space in Section 4. The implementation details of the proposed scheme are described in Section 5. Section 6 shows the performance analysis of our approach. The related work is presented in Section 7. Finally, conclusion follows in Section 8.

2 Motivation

We develop an example scenario for an over running status. In that scenario, Mr. Kim carries a cell-phone, a smart watch, a MP3 player, and a PDA. Each device has its sensors and their corresponding context providers as shown in Fig 1. The example scenario is as follows.

Mr. Kim is exercising on the running machine in a fitness center. While running continuously, Mr Kim's pulse and blood pressure may exceed his normal status and he may be wet with his sweet during his exercising. If his physical condition excesses beyond normal values, he is on the over running status which has to be taken care of. Therefore, his PDA alerts to Mr. Kim about adjusting the level of exercise, and shows the current physical condition information about him on PDA. To support this example scenario, there is an aggregation rule and ECA policy rule. Aggregation rule and ECA policy rule included in the context-aware exercise assistant application are represented as shown in Table 1 and 2, respectively. A mobile device can include several condition rules for an aggregation task. In this case, the centralized context aggregation may delay the context aware service not provided on a right time and cause the concentration of computational overhead on a coordinator device. It is inefficient to conduct the execution of aggregation processing on every context change only in a coordinator device.

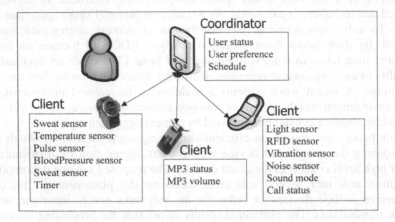

Fig. 1. An example of context information in a personal smart space

Table 1. The aggregation rule for example scenario

Condition rules:	
a) Vibration(Kim, Running) ^	Provided by cell-phone
b) Pulse(Kim, Over 140) ^	Provided by smart watch
c) BloodPressure(Kim, Over 160) ^	Provided by smart watch
d) Sweat(Kim, Wet) ^	Provided by smart watch
e) -> Status(Kim, OverRunning)	On PDA

Table 2. The ECA rule of context-aware exercise assistant application

On(Status(Kim, OverRunning))
   If(true)
   Do(start(service set2))
   { Alert to Kim for adjusting amount of exercise,
     Show the health information on PDA   };

3   Requirements for Context Aggregation in Personal Smart Space

To provide the function of context aggregation in resource limited personal smart space, we introduce two main requirements of context management.

First, in personal smart space, constrained resource on each mobile device means that load balancing is an important issue for the context aggregation. Centralized context aggregation can cause the failure of coordinator device by exhausting the battery resource and the delay of context aware service by over-loaded aggregation processing on a coordinator. Therefore, to perform context aggregation effectively on resource limited environment, the aggregation processing requires small processing overhead, and the aggregation task has to be distributed. To deal with these issues, we use simple inference mechanism instead of heavyweight ontology based inference engine, and we propose decomposition scheme for the distribution of aggregation task.

Second, the reliability of the context aware system is also an important issue. There are two kinds of aspects for reliability. One aspect is the reliability of a personal smart space. To deal with this aspect, Mobile Gaia [2] proposes election algorithm to select suitable coordinator when previous coordinator dies or disappears. Another aspect is the reliability of context event subscription. A personal smart space is configured with several devices including a coordinator device in an ad-hoc manner. Ad-hoc connectivity among devices can cause the change of network environment. In that case, it is not impossible to define all possible context event subscription for sub task rule according to network change. Therefore, characteristics of dynamic network change require flexible and adaptive context event subscription based on dynamic operating conditions varying over time and space.

4 Context Management Architecture for Personal Smart Space

To achieve the decomposition of context aggregation tasks, we need to consider three issues. First, we have to consider how to decompose an aggregation task into several sub tasks. As mentioned in Section 3, a large number of network transmissions can cause more processing overhead. Therefore, we decompose an aggregation task into several sub tasks based on the locality of context provider. If a client device processes a sub task locally, it is possible to reduce the number of network transmission. In personal smart space, locality is the most important consideration of any other factors. Second, it can be possible that a device has two context providers of same type. In that case, decomposition mechanism must select a suitable provider. Except for locality of context provider, there are other considering factors to select a suitable provider like frequency, accuracy, and granularity of context. Third, we also deal with the reusability of current sub tasks in personal smart space. It is wasteful that a coordinator delivers existing sub task to the same device every decomposition time. This fact makes our mechanism require the reusability of current sub task.

4.1 System Architecture

Fundamental functionalities of the context management are gathering, reasoning, and delivery of context information. We define five components as follows. **Context Widget** abstracts the raw sensor data and provides abstract context information. **Context Aggregator** provides high-level context information from low-level contexts according to aggregation rules. In our architecture, to provide small processing overhead, we use composite event detection mechanism [11] as an inference mechanism instead of logic based inference engine. **Context Interpreter** keeps track of the context in which the user is interested and notifies to application when one of contexts is set to true. **Context Aware Application** implements context sensitive application policy, which is ECA policy performing action according to context event change. **Context Manager** has the role of context repository and includes minimal context ontology.

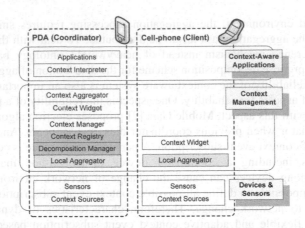

Fig. 2. Context management architecture for a personal smart space

In addition to these components, our efficient aggregation mechanism requires some extra components to provide the task decomposition scheme. Details of additional components are as follows. **Context Registry** manages the list of context providers. All context providers register themselves to context registry. Moreover, it supports to lookup the provider with the combination of context name and type. Moreover, it has the context properties for all existing context providers. **Decomposition Manager** receives decomposition requests and applies decomposition algorithm to generate context event subscription tree and sub task rule tree. After configuring two kinds of trees, decomposition manager adds sub task rules to the local aggregator and adds composite event rule to context aggregator. **Local Aggregator** detects that a certain sub task rule is satisfied and generates composite event. Then it notifies composite event change generated from sub task rules to context aggregator. And all devices in personal smart space have a local aggregator. Fig 2 shows an overall architecture of the context management in personal smart space depending on the role of devices.

4.2 Decomposition Algorithm

Decomposition algorithm uses aggregator name as an input parameter. In a personal smart space, several context aggregators can function as the status aggregator. A context aggregator includes one or more context aggregation rules. When a context provider appears or a context aggregator requests the decomposition of context aggregator, the decomposition manager gets aggregation rules from a context aggregator, and gets the device list currently available in a personal smart space from the context registry. This algorithm generates two kinds of trees: the one represents context event subscription and the other composite event rules and sub task rules. For a context aggregation rule, decomposition algorithm generates a sub task rule tree with the result rule of the duplicated random value. Each result rule of a sub task is represented as RDF triple, SubTaskRule(ip, random value). And after finishing above sequences, sub task rules are inserted into sub task rule table, and a subscription tree is generated for a context aggregator.

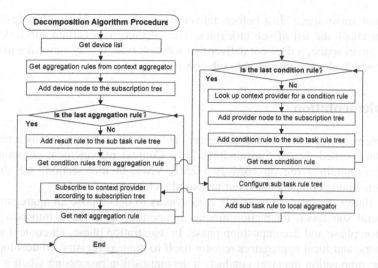

Fig. 3. Flowchart of task decomposition algorithm

Fig 3 shows the algorithm for task decomposition. In this algorithm, there are some mechanisms to select context provider of same type and to increase the reusability of existing sub task rules. We explain later in detail about these issues.

4.2.1 Selection of Suitable Context Provider

If there are several context provider of same type on the same device, we need to select more suitable provider among them. The function of *selectProvider (possibleProviderList)* provides the mechanism for selection of suitable provider. When a context provider list is registered to Context Registry, some considering factors like frequency of context change, accuracy of context, and granularity of context are also registered as the form of ContextProperties class. Then we measure the utility value from the result of utility function. Fig 4 shows the utility function for a suitable context provider.

Each factor has its weight value according to developer's policy. This algorithm calculates utility values for every possible provider, and selects the appropriate provider which has the highest utility value.

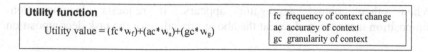

Utility function	fc frequency of context change
Utility value = $(fc*w_f)+(ac*w_a)+(gc*w_g)$	ac accuracy of context
	gc granularity of context

Fig. 4. Utility function for selection of context provider

4.2.2 Reusability of Existing Sub Task Rules

Reuse of existing sub task rules makes it possible to avoid the delivery of a new sub task rule. Before adjusting the function of *addSubTaskRule()*, Decomposition Manager checks that a certain sub task rule exists or not in personal smart space. Decomposition manager on coordinator device has the list of sub task rules provided in personal smart space. Just before delivering a sub task rule to other device, this algorithm check the list of sub task rules. Then if there is a certain sub task rule in personal smart space, it does not deliver that sub task rule. It only subscribe to context provider which already has reusable sub task rule.

5 Implementation

We implement the proposed architecture as part of our ubiquitous computing middleware, called Active Surroundings [10]. Context management components in Active Surroundings run on IBM J9 (J2ME VM). In this section, we show the interaction among components in our proposed architecture.

Fig 5 shows the interaction among components to decompose an aggregation task into several sub tasks. Interaction among components is divided into two phases: registration phase and decomposition phase. In registration phase, all context widgets, aggregators, and local aggregators register itself to context registry. In decomposition phase, decomposition manager conducts a decomposition processing when a context aggregator or context registry requests decomposition. The overall interaction procedure among components works as follows.

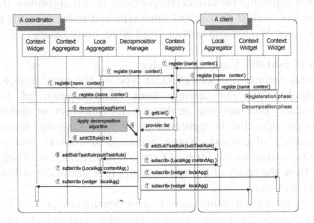

Fig. 5. Interaction among components for task decomposition

When other context aggregator appears, it requests decomposition to decomposition manager, and repeat the above procedure of the task decomposition.

6 Performance Analysis

In this section, we show how decomposition scheme reduces processing overhead for context aggregation. We expect that computational overhead for context aggregation is distributed in personal smart space. In the experiments, we measure the aggregation processing time on both coordinator and client devices and compare them with total processing time taken in the previous approach.

The over-running scenario in Section 2 is used for the experiments. We generate 100 context event changes randomly. Then we compare two cases: processing time in the previous and our approach. Total processing time for two cases is derived from the sum of processing time on coordinator, processing time on clients, and network transmission time for delivery context change events as shown in Equation (1).

$$PT(total) = PT(coor) + PT(cli) + NTT \qquad (1)$$

PT(total) represents total processing time, PT(coor) represents processing time on coordinator device, PT(cli) represents processing time on clients, and NTT represents network transmission time, respectively. We use two PDAs, HP rx3715(Processor speed: 400MHz, Installed RAM: 152MB), and their operating system is Microsoft Windows Mobile Pocket PC 2003. We use IBM J9 as the VM to run our systems.

Fig 6 shows the result of the experiments considering four metrics: PT(total), NTT, PT(coor), and PT(cli).

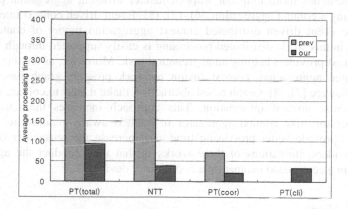

Fig. 6. The processing time and network transmission time on coordinator and clients

As Fig 6 shows, NTT takes the most part of PT(total). It means that network transmission affects the processing overhead for context aggregation significantly. Additionally, in case of our scheme, processing overhead only on client device is larger than that of previous work. However, processing overhead on client devices is slight to be ignored, comparing with the network transmission overhead.

The previous approach requires more PT(total) because it notifies context event to other device for every context change. On the contrary, our approach notifies the context change event only when a sub task rule is satisfied. In this way, the proposed scheme reduces the processing time for context aggregation. By reducing the aggregation processing overhead, it is possible to provide context aware services more efficiently and minimize the resource usage in personal smart space.

7 Related Works

Previous research projects present infrastructure based context management architecture in typical smart space. Ontology based context aware middleware approaches like SOCAM, Context aware middleware in Gaia, and Cobra provide context information in resource plentiful environment [3], [4]. However, as a new concept of personal smart space appears, context aware systems need to consider limited resources on each device.

To provide context information in resource constrained mobile devices, Contory presents a context factory middleware for context provisioning on smart phone [5]. It supports three kinds of context provisioning methods including distributed context in ad hoc networks. The flexibility on switching one method to another at run time allows optimizing the utilization of computing and communication resources. However, unfortunately, it does not consider the processing overhead concentrating on a coordinator device for context aggregation.

Some researches motivating our works consider efficient aggregation processing by distributing a context aggregation. [6], [7], [8]. Event driven context interpretation presents the event driven distributed context aggregation model of context aware system [6]. In this work, distributed processing is easily supported through the use of several context providers helping an aggregation task. Moreover, as another approach for distributed aggregation, context fusion network presents graph based context aware middleware [7], [8]. Graph based abstraction make it easy to collect, aggregate, and disseminate context information. This approach increases the reusability of existing operators like context aggregator in context aware middleware. Although these works provide better processing time and increase the reusability of existing context providers, limitations of these works is that they conduct the aggregation processing in a centralized manner on a coordinator device.

8 Conclusion

We propose a resource efficient context aggregation scheme in personal smart space. We present the context management architecture to distribute aggregation tasks without predefined sub task rule in personal smart space. With this approach, we achieve reducing the processing overhead on a coordinator device by distributing an aggregation task into several sub tasks.

In this approach, we propose a lightweight context aggregation mechanism using composite event detection. Although it can reduce the aggregation processing overhead, the lightweight aggregator limits to support semantic context reasoning. We have a plan to consider providing semantic context information.

Moreover, as an extension of this work, we plan to consider multi-user environment where all devices are connected in an ad-hoc manner without coordinator device. Currently, we only support personal smart space considering single user environment and including a coordinator. With multi-user environment, we are also investigating some more complex scenarios and planning to present context management architecture in ad-hoc environment.

Acknowledgments. This research was partially supported by the Ubiquitous Computing and Network (UCN) Project, the MIC(Ministry of Information and Communication) 21st Century Frontier R&D Program and the KT-ICU Joint Research Center in Korea.

References

1. Karypidis, A., Lalis, S.: Automated context aggregation and file annotation for PAN-based computing. In: Personal and Ubiquitous Computing(PUC 2006), Oct. 2006 (2006)
2. Chetan, S., Al-Muthadi, J., Campbell, R., Mickunas, M.D.: Mobile Gaia: A Middleware for Ad-hoc Pervasive Computing. In: IEEE Consumer Communications & Networking Conference (CCNC 2005), Jan. 2005 (2005)
3. Riva, O.: Contory: A Middleware for the Provisioning of Context Information on Smart Phones. In: Riva, O. (ed.) the Proceedings of the ACM/IFIP/USENIX 7th International Middleware Conference (Middleware'06) (2006)
4. Gu, T., Pung, H.K., Zhang, D.Q: A Service-Oriented Middleware for Building Context-Aware Services. Journal of Network and Computer Applications (JNCA) 28(1), 1–18 (2005)
5. Ranganathan, A., Campbell, R.H.: An Infrastructure for Context-Awareness based on First Order Logic. Personal and Ubiquitous Computing 7 (2003)
6. Tan, J.G., Zhang, D., Wang, X., Cheng, H.S.: Enhancing Semantic Spaces with Event-Driven Context Interpretation. In: Gellersen, H.-W., Want, R., Schmidt, A. (eds.) PERVASIVE 2005. LNCS, vol. 3468, Springer, Heidelberg (2005)
7. Chen, G., Kotz, D.: "Context Aggregation and Dissemination in Ubiquitous Computing Systems", Dartmouth Computer Science Technical Report TR, -420 (2002)
8. Chen, G., Li, M., Kotz, D.: Design and Implementation of a Large-Scale Context Fusion Network. In: Proceedings of the First Annual International Conference on Mobile and Ubiquitous Systems: Networking and Services (MobiQuitous 2004) (2004)
9. Dey, A.K., Salber, D., Abowd, G.D.: A Conceptual Framework and a Toolkit for Supporting the Rapid Prototyping of Context-Aware Applications. Anchor article of a special issue on context-aware computing in the Human-Computer Interaction (HCI) Journal (2001)
10. Lee, D., Han, S., Park, I., Kang, S., Lee, K., Hyun, S.J., Lee, Y.-H., Lee, G.: A Group-Aware Middleware for Ubiquitous Computing Environments. In: ICAT (2004)
11. Pietzuch, P.R., Shand, B., Bacon, J.: Composite Event Detection as a Generic Middleware Extension. In: IEEE Network Magazine, Special Issue on Middleware Technologies for Future Communication Networks (2004)
12. Chen, H., Finin, T., Joshi, A.: An Ontology for Context-Aware Pervasive Computing Environments. The Knowledge Engineering Review(2003)

Distributed k-NN Query Processing
for Location Services

Jonghyeong Han, Joonwoo Lee, Seungyong Park,
Jaeil Hwang, and Yunmook Nah

Department of Electronics and Computer Engineering, Dankook University, Hannam-dong,
Yongsan-gu, Seoul, 140-714, Korea
{jhhan, jwlee, sypark}@dblab.dankook.ac.kr,
hwangjaeil@yahoo.co.kr, ymnah@dku.edu

Abstract. The architecture named the GALIS is a cluster-based distributed computing system architecture which has been devised to efficiently handle a large volume of LBS application data. In this paper, we propose a distributed k-NN query processing scheme for moving objects on multiple computing nodes, each of which keeps records relevant to a different geographical zone. We also propose a hybrid k-NN scheme, which utilizes range queries instead of k-NN queries for the neighboring overlapped nodes, thus resulting in 30% reduction of query processing cost. Through some experiments, we show the efficiency of hybrid k-NN scheme over naïve k-NN scheme.

Keywords: k-NN query processing, distributed databases, GALIS, location-based services.

1 Introduction

Recent advances in location navigation technology and wide distribution of mobile devices have caused rapid growth of interests in Location Based Services (LBS). But, most of the current research activities related with LBS systems are single node-oriented, making it difficult to handle the extreme situation that must cope with a very large volume, at least millions, of moving objects. The architecture named the GALIS (Gracefully Aging Location Information System) is a cluster-based distributed computing system architecture which consists of multiple computing nodes, each dedicated to keeping records relevant to a different geographical zone and a different time-zone [1,2,3]. The GALIS consists of SLDS (Short-term Location Data Subsystem) controlling current location information of moving objects, and LLDS (Long-term Location Data Subsystem) controlling past location information.

To realize location services, we have to support item-based queries, range queries, and k-NN (k-Nearest Neighbor) queries. For a k-NN query, the user specifies a point and the system has to return k closest moving objects. There has been lots of research efforts to efficiently handle k-NN queries, especially for the centralized computing environments [6,7,8,9,10,11,12]. In this paper, we propose a naïve distributed k-NN query processing scheme for moving objects geographically spread over multiple

R. Obermaisser et al. (Eds.): SEUS 2007, LNCS 4761, pp. 30–39, 2007.

computing nodes. The proposed scheme runs k-NN query for the current node, modifies the query points for overlapped neighboring nodes, and then executes k-NN queries for neighboring nodes. We have implemented a single node k-NN query processing scheme, by utilizing R-trees [13,14]. We also propose a hybrid k-NN scheme, which utilizes range queries instead of k-NN queries for the neighboring overlapped nodes, thus resulting in 30% reduction of query processing cost.

We propose a naïve method for distributed k-NN query processing on multiple computing nodes in section 2 and a hybrid k-NN query processing scheme in section 3. Some experimental results related with performance and precision of each query processing scheme are shown in section 4. Finally, section 5 concludes the paper.

2   A Naïve Scheme for Distributed Processing of k-NN Queries

The two-dimensional space of interest is divided into n spatial regions and the one-dimensional time axis is divided into p time zones. A region (or partition) of the geographical area dealt with by the LBS system is called a *macro-cell*. Each macro-cell covers a square-shaped region, of which the default unit length is 25.6km but can be set differently. The regions covered by different macro-cells may be of different sizes. With respect to keeping records on current (most recently observed) locations, moving items in a spatial region are covered by a SDP node. With respect to keeping location histories, moving items in a spatial region are handled by up to p LDP nodes. Here, p means the number of time zones (or temporal regions).

2.1   Overall Scheme

A k-NN query can be performed on a single node, as shown in Figure 1(a). For multiple nodes, as shown in Figure 1(b), moving objects for neighboring overlapped nodes have to be considered.

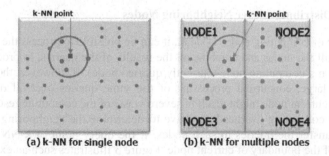

(a) k-NN for single node   (b) k-NN for multiple nodes

Fig. 1. Comparison of k-NN query on single node and on multiple nodes

We first run the given k-NN query on the current node. If the circle, whose center is the query point (indicated as k-NN point in Figure 1) and whose radius is the distance between the query point and k-th closest point in the current node, is overlapped with neighboring nodes, as shown in Figure 1(b), we have to decide the necessity of broadcasting the queries to the neighboring nodes.

The query processing system to handle k-NN queries consists of Index Creator, Query Analyzer, Query Checker and Query Creator. The structure of the query processing system for the case of 4 computing nodes is illustrated in Figure 2.

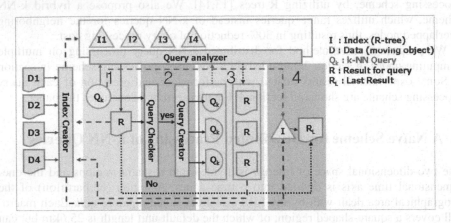

Fig. 2. Query processing system structure for multiple nodes

The Index Creator configures index structures by making use of location information of moving objects stored in each node. The Query Analyzer processes the given queries using appropriate index structures. The Query Checker checks the neighboring nodes based on the query result from the current node, to determine the necessity of transferring the queries to the neighboring nodes. The Query Creator creates a partial query for the target neighboring nodes and sends that partial query to the neighboring nodes. All the query processing results from neighboring nodes are combined and a temporary R-tree index structure is created by the Index Creator. The k-NN query is finally processed by using the final R-tree and its result is returned to user.

2.2 Query Distribution over Neighboring Nodes

If the number of computing nodes is small, it can be possible to process the same k-NN queries over all the nodes and combine all the results of the queries, to process a given k-NN query on a computing node (currently queried node). If, however, the number of the nodes is large, concurrent processing of the same queries over all of the nodes including the current node might result in severe waste of the computing resources.

To reduce computing overhead, we have to determine the neighboring overlapped nodes and transfer the queries to such nodes, if the query point of k-NN query is in the vicinity of the boundary of current node. Figure 3 illustrates such an example of k-NN query on Node 1, where k = 4. In this figure, the object P_2 of Node 2 and the object P_1 of Node 3 can be nearer than the k-NN candidate points between P_{k-3} and P_k on the current node. This means that it is required to send queries to neighboring overlapped nodes and compare candidate locations and related locations to finalize true k-NN points, considering all the nodes. It is expected that enlarging an arc section of the resultant area for the given k-NN query to a round section causes overlapping of certain part of the area over neighboring nodes.

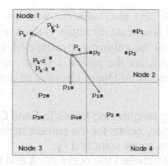

Fig. 3. Necessity of transferring queries to neighboring overlapped nodes

After running the k-NN query on the current node, the neighboring overlapped nodes, which can contain closer points than the current node, can be determined by using the query point and the query results on the current node.

Figure 4 illustrates the procedure to determine the necessity of transferring queries to the neighboring overlapped nodes. Let R be the distance between the query point P_q and the result position P_k (the location of k-th closest object), as shown in Figure 4(a). Let N, S, E, W be the distances between the query point P_q and the boundary points in each direction, P_{bn} (north boundary point), P_{be} (east boundary point), P_{bs} (south boundary point) and P_{bw} (west boundary point), respectively, also as shown in Figure 4(a). The neighboring nodes located in the directions with distances (N, S, E, W) shorter than R, are target nodes to send queries.

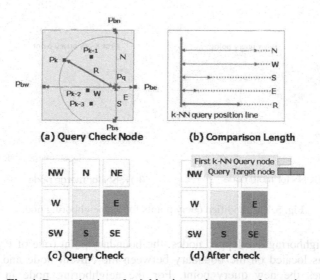

Fig. 4. Determination of neighboring nodes to transfer queries

In Figure 4(b), therefore, the neighboring nodes in south and east direction to the current node are the appropriate nodes to further process the given k-NN query. We also have to transfer queries to the neighboring node located in the diagonal position to the current node and also adjacent with the selected target nodes. In Figure 4(d), the node in the southeast direction is such a node. Therefore, among 8 neighboring nodes, the final neighboring overlapped nodes, which will further process the given k-NN query, are the nodes in south, east and southeast direction. Algorithm 1 shows the procedure of Query Checker to determine neighboring nodes to send queries.

Algorithm 1. Determining Neighboring Nodes to Send Queries ( )
// P_{bn}, P_{be}, P_{bs}, P_{bw} : boundary points for the current node
// R : distance between the query point and P_k
// N, S, E, W: the distance between the query point and the boundary points
                in each direction
// T: target node list
begin
  if (N<R) **then**
      add north node to T;
      if (E<R) add east node and northeast node to T;
      if (W<R) add west node and northwest node to T;
  else if (S<R) **then**
      add south node to T;
      if (E<R) add east node and southeast node to T;
      if (W<R) add west node and southwest node to T;
  else if (E<R) then add east node to T;
  else if (W<R) then add west node to T;
  else add empty node to T;
    endif
end.

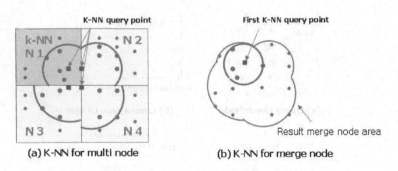

(a) K-NN for multi node   (b) K-NN for merge node

Fig. 5. The modified query points for the neighboring nodes

For the neighboring overlapped nodes, the boundary point (one of P_{bn}, P_{be}, P_{bs} and P_{bw}), which is located on the boundary between the current node and the neighbor node, becomes the new query point. For the neighboring node in the diagonal position, one of the corner point of the current node, facing the neighbor node, becomes the new query point. In Figure 5(a), P_{be} becomes the query point for N2, P_{bs} becomes the query point for N3, and the southeast corner point of N1 becomes the query point for N4. Figure 5(b) shows the typical query shape for the proposed distributed k-NN query processing.

3   Hybrid k-NN Query Processing

By utilizing range queries instead of k-NN queries for the neighboring overlapped nodes, we can reduce the entire query processing time, while obtaining the exactly same query result. We call this slightly modified scheme as the hybrid k-NN query processing scheme. In this hybrid scheme, the Query Checker of the query processing system converts the k-NN query into range queries.

We again use the value R, which is the distance between the query point P_q and the result position P_k (the location of k-th closest object). Let R_n (radius north), R_w (radius west), R_s (radius south) and R_e (radius east) be the same distance with R to the corresponding directions. Let P_{qn} (north query point), P_{qw} (west query point), P_{qs} (south query point) and P_{qe} (east query point) be the virtual points each located in the corresponding direction with distance R. Algorithm 2 shows the procedure of Query Checker to create range queries.

Algorithm 2. Range Query Creation (d direction_of_neighbor_node)
// P_{bn}, P_{be}, P_{bs}, P_{bw} : boundary points for the current node
// P_{qn}, P_{qw}, P_{qs}, P_{qe} : shifted query points to the corresponding direction
//   with distance R
begin
    if (d=north) **then** create query with range $(P_{qw}(x), P_{qn}(y), P_{qe}(x), P_{bn}(y))$;
    if (d=south) **then** create query with range $(P_{qw}(x), P_{qs}(y), P_{qe}(x), P_{bs}(y))$;
    if (d=east) **then** create query with range $(P_{qe}(x), P_{qn}(y), P_{be}(x), P_{qs}(y))$;
    if (d=west) **then** create query with range $(P_{qw}(x), P_{qn}(y), P_{bw}(x), P_{qs}(y))$;
end.

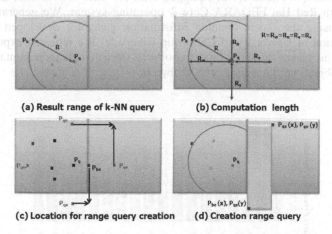

(a) Result range of k-NN query   (b) Computation length

(c) Location for range query creation   (d) Creation range query

Fig. 6. Range query creation example in the east direction

Figure 6 illustrates the procedure to create the range query for the neighbor node located in the east direction compared to the current node. In this case, the coordinate $(P_{qe}(x), P_{qn}(y))$ becomes the upper right corner and the coordinate $(P_{be}(x), P_{qs}(y))$ becomes the lower left corner for the query range.

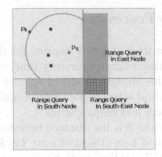

Fig. 7. Query range shape example in hybrid k-NN scheme

The lower part of the query range in the east direction crosses over the node boundary of Node 2. Also, the right part of the range query in the south direction crosses over the node boundary of Node 3. These two out of node query ranges meet at the node in the diagonal direction, Node 4. Therefore, the query range for the diagonal node can be determined from the overflowed portion of one of the neighboring nodes. In our experiment, we use the right or left side neighboring nodes in such cases. Figure 7 shows the query range for the hybrid k-NN scheme.

4 Experiments

Four nodes are configured on a single system for excluding communication delay among the nodes. We used a PC, equipped with 3.0 GHz D-processor and 1 Gbyte memory, with Red Hat FEDARA Core 4 operating system. We generated moving objects by using the object location information generator developed by Marios Hadjieleftheriou of University of California-Riverside. We repeated experiments 18 times, while increasing number of moving objects in each node incrementally, starting from 1,000 objects until reaching 50,000 objects.

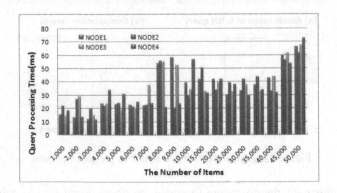

Fig. 8. Naïve k-NN query processing time

To compare query processing times, we measured the processing time of each query 5 times and used the average of 3 measured values, excluding highest and lowest values.

The value k was fixed as 10. Figure 8 shows the query processing time of the naïve k-NN scheme and Figure 9 shows the query processing time of the hybrid k-NN scheme.

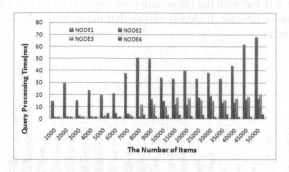

Fig. 9. Hybrid k-NN query processing time

Figure 10 compares the query processing time of naïve k-NN query processing scheme and hybrid k-NN query processing scheme. The query processing times of Node 1 of both methods are the same, because both use the normal k-NN query processing algorithm. But, in other nodes, the query processing time of hybrid scheme is faster than the query processing time of naïve scheme, because the hybrid scheme utilizes range queries instead of k-NN queries for the neighboring overlapped nodes.

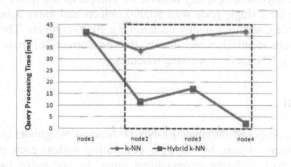

Fig. 10. Comparison of query processing time between naïve and hybrid scheme

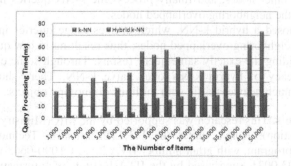

Fig. 11. Comparison of maximum query processing time

Figure 11 compares the maximum query processing times (worst cases) of both schemes. Figure 12 compares the minimum processing time (best case) of naïve k-NN query processing scheme with the maximum processing time (worst case) of hybrid k-NN query processing scheme. It clearly shows that the hybrid scheme is always better than the naïve scheme.

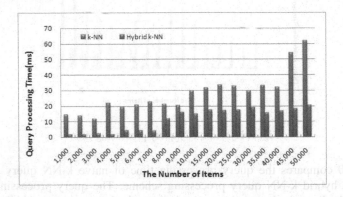

Fig. 12. Comparison of the minimum processing time of naive k-NN query processing scheme with the maximum processing time of hybrid k-NN query processing scheme

To show the correctness of query results, we compared the query results of k-NN query processing on a single node with 80,000 objects and naïve scheme and hybrid scheme on multiple computing nodes, each having 20,000 objects. The final results of three methods were identical, which means that no correct object is omitted by the naïve and hybrid k-NN query processing schemes.

5 Conclusion

In this paper, we proposed distributed k-NN (k-Nearest Neighbor) query processing schemes for moving objects on multiple computing nodes, each of which keeps records relevant to a different geographical zone. In our naïve method, we first process the k-NN query on the target node, then decide whether the query region is overlapped with other nodes, and finally process the k-NN queries from the shifted query points for the neighboring overlapped nodes.

We also proposed a hybrid k-NN, which utilizes range queries instead of k-NN queries for the neighboring overlapped nodes, thus resulting in low query processing cost, while providing the exactly same query results. Through some experiments, we show the efficiency of hybrid k-NN over naïve k-NN. There should be further experiments on much heavier traffic with millions of moving objects.

Acknowledgments. This research was supported by the MIC(Ministry of Information and Communication), Korea, under the ITRC(Information Technology Research Center) support program, with grant number IITA-2006-C1090-0603-0006 and IITA-2006-C1090-0603-0031, supervised by the IITA(Institute of Information Technology Assessment).

References

1. Nah, Y., Kim, K.H., Wang, T., Kim, M.H., Lee, J., Yang, Y.K: GALIS: A Cluster-based Scalable Architecture for Location-based Service Systems. Database Research, 18(4). KISS SIGDB, 66–80 (2002)
2. Nah, Y., Kim, K.H., Wang, T., Kim, M.H., Lee, J., Yang, Y.K: A Cluster-based TMO-structured Scalable Approach for Location Information Systems. In: Proc. WORDS 2003 Fall, pp. 225–233. IEEE Computer Society Press, Los Alamitos (2003)
3. Kim, M.H., Kim, K.H., Nah, Y., Lee, J., Wang, T., Lee, J., Yang, Y.K: Distributed Adaptive Architecture for Managing Large Volumes of Moving Items. In: IDPT. Society for Design and Process Science, vol. 2, pp. 737–744 (2003)
4. Saltenis, S., Jensen, C.S., Leutenegger, S.T., Lopez, M.A.: Indexing the Positions of Continuously Moving Objects. In: Proc. ACM SIGMOD, pp. 331–342 (2000)
5. Zhang, J., Zhu, M., Papadias, D., Tao, Y., Lee, D.: Location-Based Spatial Queries. In: Proc. ACM SIGMOD, pp. 467–478. ACM Press, New York (2003)
6. Hjaltason, G.R., Samet, H.: Ranking in Spatial Databases. In: Egenhofer, M.J., Herring, J.R. (eds.) SSD 1995. LNCS, vol. 951, pp. 83–95. Springer, Heidelberg (1995)
7. Cheung, K.L., Fu, A.W.-C: Enhanced Nearest Neighbor Search on the R-tree. SIGMOD Record 27(3), 16–21 (1998)
8. Iwerks, G.S., Samet, H., Smith, K.P.: Continuous k-Nearest Neighbor Queries for Continuously Moving Points with Updates. In: Proc. VLDB, pp. 512–523 (2003)
9. Dasarathy, B.V.: Nearest Neighbor (NN) Norms: NN Pattern Classification Techniques (1991)
10. Song, Z., Roussopoulos, N.: K-Nearest Neighbor Search for Moving Query Point. In: Proc. SSTD, pp. 79–96 (2001)
11. Hadjieleftheriou, M., Hoel, E.G., Tsotras, V.J.: SaIL: A Spatial Index Library for Efficient Application Integration. GeoInformatica 9(4), 367–389 (2005)
12. Shakhnarovish, Darrell, Indyk (eds.): Nearest-Neighbor Methods in Learning and Vision. MIT Press (2005)
13. Guttman, A.: R-Trees: A Dynamic Index Structure for Spatial Searching. In: Proc. ACM SIGMOD, pp. 47–57. ACM Press, New York (1984)
14. Beckmann, N., Kriegel, H.-P., Schneider, R., Seeger, B.: The R*-Tree: an Efficient and Robust Access Method for Points and Rectangles. In: Proc. ACM SIGMOD, pp. 322–331. ACM Press, New York (1990)

Ontology Based Context Alignment
for Heterogeneous Context Aware Services

Seungkeun Lee

INRIA Rhône-Alpes
Montbonnot Saint-Martin, France
Seung-Keun.Lee@inrialpes.fr

Abstract. In a pervasive environment, context aware services are necessary to enable collaborate and communicate with others in order to provide proper service to users. Each service can be designed with individual context information which represents different perspective over the context. This paper proposes an advanced context management model with context alignment among heterogeneous context aware services. This model enable the interaction between context information producer devices and context information consumer devices and as well as their insertion in an open environment. And this paper show how this model can be used in context aware middleware.

Keywords: Context Aware, Context Alignment, Ubiquitous Computing.

1 Introduction

The context aware computing systems are being studied and many prototypes have been implemented [1,2,3,4,5]. The popularity of context aware computing research indicates that systems that can identify the user's context and that of the surrounding environment have the profound potential to provide services that are much more user specific. Context information can be retrieved from a wide diversity of sources such as user profiles, location system, sensors, devices.

However, conventional context modeling approaches based on ontology bear several problems. First, a context awareness service must share the context ontology with the context awareness system in the designing phase. In turn, when a context awareness service is dynamically added to or deleted from the system, the new context awareness service cannot share the context ontology with the system under the circumstances where other context awareness services are not affected. In addition, the problem of context uncertainty, which can arise in the process of deducing the data acquired from the sensor into the context information based on the dynamic modification of the context ontology, must be resolved. This study proposes the dynamic context management by context alignment between the context awareness services.

We have built a context alignment manager for test the proposed model. The designed manager can align between context aware services and manage the alignment relation. This alignment relation is used for context aware service to cooperate with others.

R. Obermaisser et al. (Eds.): SEUS 2007, LNCS 4761, pp. 40–46, 2007.

2 Relative Works

In this dynamic pervasive environment, each context manager manages context information of its device. To express its context model, its needs or its capabilities, we use semantic web languages described below. They ensure interoperability between these heterogeneous devices. The ground language for the semantic web is RDF (Resource Description Framework [5]). It enables expressing assertions of the form subject-predicate-object. The strength of RDF is that the names of entities (subjects, predicates or objects) are URIs (the identifiers of the web that can be seen as a generalization of URLs: http://www.w3c.org/sw). This opens the possibility for different RDF documents to refer precisely to an entity (it is reasonable to think that a URI denotes the same thing for all of its users).

The OWL language [6], has been designed for expressing « ontologies » or conceptual models of a domain of knowledge. It constrains the interpretation of RDFgraphs concerning this domain. OWL defines classes of objects and predicates and makes it possible to declare constraints applying to them (i.e., that the « output » of a « thermometer » is a « temperature »). The context model that we will use at that stage is very simple: a context is a set of RDF assertions. Interoperability is guaranteed through considering that context-aware devices are consumer and producer of RDF. However, this is not precise enough and devices might want to extract only the relevant information from context sources. For that purpose, a language like RDQL [7] is useful for querying or subscribing to context sources. In order to post the relevant queries to the adequate components, it is necessary that components publish the OWL classes of objects and properties on which they can answer.

3 Context Alignment Model

A context awareness service must be able to exchange context information based on identical understanding of the content among the user, devices and services. This chapter presents a method for dynamically modifying the context information required by the context awareness services operated from the context awareness middleware, as well as the hierarchical context ontology management and context uncertainty resolution methods in order to deliver the changes in the middleware so that the corresponding context information can be received from the middleware.

3.1 Hierarchical Context Ontology

The context information managed by the middleware is constructed into the domain context information that is delivered to all services in the middleware and the individual context information defined for each service. All of the context information is defined by ontology. If a service is newly allocated in the middleware, the middleware must be able to integrate the existing domain context information and the individual context information separately defined in the service for operation. Here, the correlation between the two sets of context information must be guaranteed, for which purpose the common context information layer is located between the two context information layers. The common context information defines the basic elements required for the context awareness application as the Person, CompEntity, Location, Environment and Activity, and the domain context information and the individual context information are designed by inheriting the common context information. By providing correlation among sets of context information inherited from an identical parent class, the information is used to integrate the two sets of context information in the middleware. Fig 1 displays the hierarchical context ontology designed in this paper.

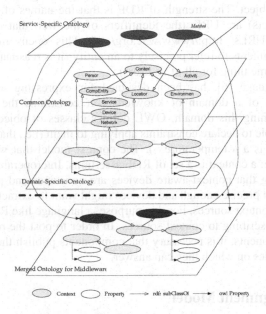

Fig. 1. Hierarchical Context Information

Every type of ontology is inherited from the context class for creation. The common ontology comprises Person, CompEntity, Location and Environment and Activity Class inherited from the highest Context class, as well as Service, Device and Network inherited from CompEntity. Context may include multiple attributes to describe the corresponding situation, as well as other situations as properties. For example, in home network ontology, if there is a Room context inherited from the Location class and a Temperature context inherited from the Environment class, the Temperature context can be used as the property of the Room context.

3.2 Context Alignment

We identify one-to-one context alignment between two context aware services using lexical resemblance between concept names and then inference. The lexical alignment identifies shared concepts across context information based on lexical similarity between concept names. Both preferred concept names and synonyms are used in the lexical alignment process. Lexical similarity is assessed through exact match. Concepts exhibiting similarity at the lexical level across context are called alignment, as they could be be used as reference concepts in the structural validation and for comparing associative relationship. Additional alignment provided a definition of the alignment structure so as to be able to use and reuse it in various situations. Given two contexts C_1 and C_2, alignments are made of a set of correspondences (called mappings when the relation is oriented) between pairs of (simple or complex) entities e_1, e_2 belonging to C_1 and C_2 respectively. A correspondence is described as a quadruple:

$$<e_1, e_2, R>$$

e_1, e_2 are the entities (e.g., formulas, terms, classes, individuals) between which a relation is asserted by the correspondence. R is the relation, between e_1 and e_2, asserted by the correspondence. For instance, this relation can be a simple set-theoretic relation (applied to entities seen as sets or their interpretation seen as sets), a fuzzy relation, a probabilistic distribution over a complete set of relations, a similarity measure, etc. These relationships are *subClassOf, TransitiveProperty, subPropertyOf,* disjointWith and inverseOf

Having extracted the relations explicitly represented in the ontologies, we then normalize the representation of the relations in each ontology in order to facilitate structural comparisons across contexts. We first complement the hierarchical relations represented explicitly with their inverses as necessary. Implicit semantic relations are then extracted from various combinations of hierarchical relations (inference). Inference generates additional semantic Inference generates additional semantic relations by applying inference rules to the existing relations in order to facilitate the comparison of paths between anchors across ontologies. These inference rules, specific to this alignment, are listed in Table 1.

Table 1. Infence Rule

Relation	Inference Rule
subClassOf	(?A rdfs:subClassOf ?B),(?B ?rdfs:subClassOf ?C) -> (?A rdfs:subClassOf ?C)
TransitiveProperty	(?P rdf:type owl:TransitiveProperty), (?A ?P ?B),(?B ?P ?C) ->(?A ?P ?C)
subPropertyOf	(?A rdfs:subPropertyOf ?B) $\wedge$ (?B rdfs:subPropertyOf ?C) -> (?A rdfs:subPropertyOf ?C)
disjointWith	(?A owl:disjointWith ?B) $\wedge$ (?X rdf:type ?C) $\wedge$ (?Y rdf:type ?D) -> (?X owl:differentFrom ?Y)
inverseOf	(?A owl:inverseOf ?B) $\wedge$ (?A ?X ?Y) -> (?Y ?B ?X)

4 Experiment

This chapter explains the process of conducting tests by implementing a smart home network to evaluate the functions and performance of the context awareness middleware proposed in this paper. The server used for the home network service was IBM eServcer X206, 2.8GHz, 512MB RAM, and it was operated with Windows Server 2003 using the

44   S. Lee

OSGi framework Knopflerfish 1.3.3 and HP Semantic web toolkit Jena2[8,9]. Fig 2 displays the home network environment implemented for the test.

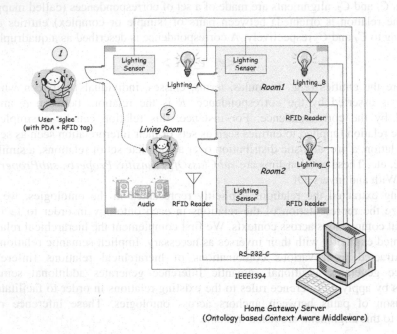

Fig. 2. Prototype of Smart HomeNetwork

The test scenario involved creating context information that is generated when a user comes into the house, and the information was delivered to the context awareness service. The light control service is a context awareness service that automatically turns on the light nearest to the user if the lighting is too dim. The light control service uses the information acquired by the illumination intensity sensor to recognize the brightness of each location. In order to assess the level of illumination in the house, light sensors are installed in Room1, Room2 and LivingRoom.

The sensor in each location detects the light intensity and expresses it in 10 bits, creating a value between 0 and 1023. The context is deduced to be "dim" if the value is below 512, and "bright" otherwise. The light control service defines the independent contexts of the "user location dim" and the "light must be turned on" as in List 1.

List 1. The Rule for Context Inference

```
(?LightSensor locateIn ?place), (?LightSensorValue
bigger 512) -> (?place lightLevel "Bright")

(?LightSensor locateIn ?place), (?LightSensorValue
smaller 512) -> (?place lightLevel "Dim")

(?user locatedIn ?place), (?place lightLevel "Dim") ->
(?place needed "lighting")
```

When the user "sglee" moves from location 1 to 2 in Fig 4, the RFID reader 3 reads the user ID from the RFID tag attached to the user. The RFID reader delivers the data to the RFID management service, which parses the corresponding data to forward the user ID value to the middleware. Then the basic context generator creates the information ("sglee" locatedIn "LivingRoom"). The generated basic context information is delivered to the ontology deduction engine, as well as the light control context service.

The illumination intensity in each room and the living room is regularly checked using the sensors, and the values are delivered to the middleware. According to List 2, the middleware generates the context "bright" for a sensor value acquired in each location greater than 512 and "dim" otherwise. Fig 5 describes the process of deducing the complex context information using the data obtained from the light sensors.

The values acquired by the sensors were ("Room1" lightingValue 284), ("Room2" lightingValue 653) and ("LivingRoom" lightingValue 327), which created the basic contexts ("Room1" lightLevel "Dim"), ("Room2" lightLevel "Bright") and ("Livin-gRoom" lightLevel "Dim"). The contexts are delivered to the deduction engine, which used the knowledge ("sglee" locatedIn "LivingRoom"), (?user locatedIn ?place) and (?place lightLevel "Dim") -> (?place needed "lighting") to deduce the complex con-text information ("LivingRoomg" needed "lighting"). The deduced complex context is delivered to the light control service that has registered the context through the event broker.

Since the context awareness service can dynamically register the context ontology, the middleware proposed in this paper has the ontology integration overhead in addition to the time required for loading the ontology to the memory. As a result of measuring the overhead, the integration time was not a significant burden compared to the loading time as indicated in Fig 5. Moreover, the amount of increase in the integration time was not substantial compared to the amount of increase of the domain context ontology value and the developed context ontology value. Therefore, due to the time required for integrating the context information, it can be suggested that the middleware proposed in this study is not adequate for the real-time service platform, but useful for general application services.

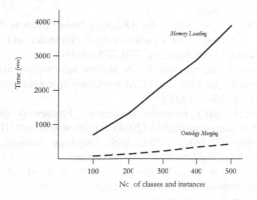

Fig. 3. Overhead of Merging Context Ontology

5 Conclusion

We specifically addressed the problem of adaptability of context management to an ever-evolving world. This is achieved by providing distributed component based architecture and by using semantic web technologies. Components enable the addition, at any moment, of new devices that can provide information about the context of applications. The use of RDF and OWL ensures interoperability between components developed independently by taking advantage of the open character of these technologies. Moreover, using ontology alignment modules allows dealing with the necessary heterogeneity between components. The proposed approach relies on a minimal commitment on basic technologies: RDF, OWL, and some identification protocol. Functions and performance of the middleware were evaluated through the test, and it was confirmed that the overhead of the proposed hierarchical context ontology management model makes the middleware unfit for the hard real-time ubiquitous computing environment. However, it was determined that the model can be applied to the general ubiquitous computing environment. It can be concluded that the ontology based context awareness middleware proposed in this paper can be applied in the service gateway for various ubiquitous environments such as the home network, telematics and smart office for providing context awareness services.

Acknowledgement

This work was supported by the Korea Research Foundation Grant funded by the Korean Government(MOEHRD)" (KRF-2006- D00163).

References

1. Lee, S., Lee, J.: Dynamic Context Aware System for Ubiquitous Computing Environment. In: Shi, Z.-Z., Sadananda, R. (eds.) PRIMA 2006. LNCS (LNAI), vol. 4088, Springer, Heidelberg (2006)
2. Hung, N.Q., Lee, S.Y., Hung, L.X.: A Middleware Framework for Context Acquisition in Ubiquitous Computing Systems. In: Proceedings of the Second International Conference on Computer Applications (2004)
3. Gu, T., Pung, H.K., Zhang, D.Q.: An Ontology-based Context Model in Intelligent Environments. In: Proceedings of Communication Networks and Distributed Systems Modeling and Simulation Conference, pp. 270–275 (2004)
4. Euzenat, J., Pierson, J., Ramparany, F.: A contex information manager for pervasive computing environments. In: Proc. 2nd ECAI workshop on contexts and ontologies (C&O), Riva del Garda (IT), pp. 25–29 (2006)
5. Klyne, G., Carroll, J. (eds.): Resource Description Framework (RDF): Concepts and Abstract Syntax, W3C Recommendation (2004), http://www.w3.org/TR/rdf-concepts
6. Dean, M., Schreiber, G. (eds.): OWL Web Ontology Language: Reference, W3C Recommendation (2004), http://www.w3.org/TR/owl-ref
7. Seaborne, A.: RDQL — A Query Language for RDF, W3C Member submission (2004), http://www.w3.org/Submission/2004/SUBM-RDQL-20040109/
8. Open Services Gateway Initiative. http://www.osgi.org
9. Knopflerfish. http://www.knopflerfish.org

Community Computing Model Supporting Community Situation Based Strict Cooperation and Conflict Resolution*

Youna Jung, Jungtae Lee, and Minkoo Kim

Graduate School of Information and Communication Engineering, Ajou University,
Suwon, Republic of Korea, 443-749
{serazade,jungtae,minkoo}@ajou.ac.kr

Abstract. Community computing is a new computing environment where ubiquitous services are provided by cooperation between existing smart object. In these days, it is studied by many researchers but works on community computing are still at an early phase. To design and describe cooperation effectively, in this paper, we propose the community situation based cooperation model. In addition, we introduce conflict resolution scheme for community computing. Consequently, we propose the community computing model supporting the community situation based cooperation and conflicts resolution. Case studies are also tried to examine the proposed community computing model.

1 Introduction

In recent years, 'Community Computing' has been suggested as a new technical environment. For an instance, Jonathan Murray, Microsoft's chief technology officer for the EMEA (Europe, Middle East and Africa) region, expressed his vision about community computing in InfoWorld magazine [1]. He said, "We are moving from a world where we just have my own personal device that runs my own applications to a new world where we are sharing other device's computing capacity and resources". Microsoft Company called such a new environment as community computing. In fact, the idea is not totally new. By several projects such as PICO [2] and GAIA [3], community concept had been introduced. Yet despite these interests, a number of fundamental questions about community computing remained unanswered. In particular, a formal model and development process for community computing system were not well defined. In order to find an answer, we have researched on the model for community computing and a development process to generate a community computing application system. As a progress, we proposed an early version of community computing model and a development process using MDA approach [4] .

However, in the previous model, there is no cooperation model. At that time, we didn't have an idea to abstract cooperation, thus we just described a specific

---

* This research is supported by the ubiquitous Autonomic Computing and Network Project, the Ministry of Information and Communication (MIC) 21st Century Frontier R&D Program in Korea.

R. Obermaisser et al. (Eds.): SEUS 2007, LNCS 4761, pp. 47–56, 2007.

procedure of cooperation just like pseudo codes in protocol description part. Such description style didn't help to intuitively design cooperation of community at all. By the difficulties in cooperation design, we have tried to find a cooperation model for community computing. In addition, in the previous model, we assumed a conflict-free circumstance but, in practice, conflicts are exists. Accordingly, we have also tried to find a solution of conflicts.

In this paper, the major contribution is that we proposed the community situation based cooperation model for community computing. By the cooperation model, each member of a community cooperates with other members according to a community situation. Additionally, we analyzed conflicts which can be happened in community computing systems, and make up policies for conflict resolution. Using the cooperation model and policies, we improve the previous community computing model.

The rest of the paper is organized as follows. In section 2, we introduce some related works, and then we propose the community situation based cooperation model and conflicts resolution scheme in section 3. In Section 4, community computing models supporting the community situation based cooperation model and conflicts resolution scheme are proposed. Case studies are presented in section 5. Finally, section 6 is dedicated to the conclusion and future works.

2 Related Works

2.1 Previous Community Computing Model

In our work, community computing is a computing technology to offer ubiquitous services by exploiting the cooperation between smart objects. To design and develop a community computing system effectively, we surveyed several existing models. In particular, we concentrated on abstraction models for multi-agent systems such as GAIA [3] because of agent's flexible and autonomous problem solving behavior. However, the existing multi-agent based models focus on what agents are needed to satisfy the requirements of a system, while community computing focuses on how to meet requirements of a ubiquitous system using cooperation between given ubiquitous objects. In other middleware approach projects such as Active Space [5] and PICO [2], a vision is similar with ours but there are no formal models. Therefore, we proposed a community computing model [4] as an abstraction model for community computing systems. In the previous community computing model, a community computing system is abstracted as a society, and a society is composed of members and communities. A community, a proactive organization consisting of members, is represented by its goals, protocols, and necessary roles. A member is a ubiquitous object, which can play a certain role in a community. At the runtime, if a goal arises dynamically, ubiquitous objects are selected for each role then a community is instantiated. After creation of a community, each member cooperates with other members to attain a goal according to protocol description. When the goal is finally achieved, the community is disorganized.

2.2 Existing Cooperation Models

In the previous community computing model, cooperation between members is considered as a predefined procedure. It means that a designer should know which task should be executed in which order. However, in case of a huge and complex cooperation, it is not easy that a designer lay out a whole cooperation procedure in once. Therefore, we considered a cooperation model should be necessary to intuitively design the cooperation. To find an appropriate cooperation model, we surveyed existing cooperation models. In many systems, infrastructures, and cooperation models, cooperation is used and described.

First of all, in 1997, a refined formal cooperation model for ARCHON was proposed [6]. In this model, cooperation is represented just as a recipe, a set of predefined tasks. AGDRSCOM [7] is an agent cooperation model which member agents are able to adjust own cooperative tasks according to the changes of environment and the feedbacks from other members. In AGDRSCOM, an idea of adaptive cooperation is introduced but the detailed mean of adaption is not proposed. Cooperation is just represented as a programming element in a skill description. In the cooperation model of MAPFS [8], a cooperation process is also procedural described by actions and instructions. In 2006, Ji Gao is proposed the hybrid cooperation using recipes, policies, and advertisements [9]. In this model, policy is the obligations and restrictions that agents should comply to, and advertisement is the record of interests of other agents. However, the fundamental cooperation process is also represented by a recipe.

In most cooperation models, as you can see, cooperation is described as a predefined static pseudo program called as recipe, plan, or skill. In many systems, infrastructures, and cooperation models, means of realizing cooperation were introduced but the mean of designing cooperation itself was not concerned. Therefore, we arrived at a decision that we needed a new cooperation model to design cooperation of community intuitively.

3   Community Situation Based Cooperation Model

In order to design cooperation of community, we proposed the community situation based cooperation model as a new cooperation model, especially for community computing [10]. The idea is that cooperation is executed according to community situation. If community's situation is changed then tasks of each member are also changed. That is, tasks which each member should perform are decided by the community situations. At this time, the final situation of a community should be a goal achievement situation. Since the proposed cooperation model is based on the community situations, we define the community situation first.

3.1   Community Situation Model

In order to define the community situations, we proposed the community situation model. In this model, a community situation is determined by situations of specific members. At this time, a member situation is decided by attribute values of the member. The definition of a community situation is as follows.

In this version of community situation model, a community situation is represented as a logical association of attributes. However, the expression power of the community situation model can be improved. If the power of community situation model then the cooperation model is also improved.

Definition 1. Community Situation Model

```
<community-situation>::= <situation-name> = <community-situation>
<community-situation>:: = <single-community-situation> | <conjunctive-community-situation> |
    <disjunctive-community-situation>
<single-community-situation>::= [<quantifier>] <role-name>.<role-situation>
<quantifier>::= ∀ | ∃ , <role-name>::=<string>, <role-situation>::=<member-situation>
<conjunctive-community-situation>::=(<community-situation>AND<community-situation>)
<disjunctive-community-situation>::=(<community-situation>OR<community-situation>)
<member-situation>::= <single-member-situation> | <conjunctive-member-situation> |
    <disjunctive-member-situation>
<single-member-situation>::=<attribute>,<attribute>::=(<attribute-name> <operator><attribute-value>)
<attribute-name>::= <string> , <attribute-value>::= <value>
<operator>::= >| < | >= | <= | = | !=  ,<value>::=<number>|<string>|<symbol>|TURE|FALSE
<conjunctive-member-situation>::=(<member-situation>AND<member-situation>)
<disjunctive-member-situation>::= (<member-situation> OR <member-situation>)
```

3.2 Community Situation Based Strict Cooperation Model

Using the proposed community situation model, we define the cooperation for community computing. Before the definition the community situation based cooperation model, let you know some promises of this model.

Assumptions. The community situation based cooperation model is founded on following strong promises.
1) Certainty of community situation
2) All members of a community are aware of community situations and know own tasks to do according to each community situation
3) In a community situation, each member can perform more tasks than one in sequential order
4) Although tasks of members are not completely finished in a community situation, community situation can be changed
5) Community situation is dynamically changed, but finally reached the situation of goal achievement

Definition 2. Community Situation based Cooperation Model

```
<community-cooperation>::= <goal-name> = {<cooperation-block>}⁺
<cooperation- block >::=<community-situation>=>{<role-task>}⁺,<role-name>::=<string>
<role-task>::=<role-name>:{<role-action-name>}⁺,<role-action-name>::= <string>
```

When a member performs own actions in a certain community situation, conflicts with other actions of the member or another member can occur. Such conflicting actions may be executed to play another role for a different community or be not finished in a previous community situation. In both case, we should resolve conflicts.

First of all, we defined that tasks of a member in a certain community situation are executed by one thread, thus we do not need to worry about conflicts on a thread. Accordingly, what we should consider is conflicts between threads. These conflicts are happened when a member cannot execute actions or when more than two members try to execute conflicting actions simultaneously. To handle such conflicts, we classify conflicting actions into two types, mutual exclusive conflict type and time dependent conflict type. In case of the mutual exclusive conflict type, if a conflict occurs then one among conflicting actions should be terminated. In case of the time dependent conflict type, one among conflicting actions should be executed first and then another action is executed. For handling conflicts in runtime, a community manager has an action-conflicts list about conflicts between own actions of a member or actions of different members. The list represents types of action conflicts. At this time, conflicts between same actions can be included in the list. For example, assume that a member performs action a_2 in community situation S_1. Then a situation is changed to S_2, although a_2 is not finished. After that, a situation is changed again to S_3 and the member should perform a_2 in a situation S_3. However, a_2 executed in previous situationS_1 is still operating.

Definition 3. Action-conflicts List

```
<action-conflict-list-in-community>::= { <mutual-exclusive-action-conflicts-in-community> |
    <time-dependent-action-conflicts-in-community>}*
<mutual-exclusive-action-conflicts-in-community-in-community>::= MEC(<role-name>.
    <remained-action-name>,<role-name>.<killed-action-name>)
<time-dependent-action-conflicts-in-community-in-community> ::= TDC(<role-name>.
    <precedent-action-name>,<role-name>.<following-action-name>)
<remained-action-name>::= <action-name> , <killed-action-name>::= <action-name>
<precedent-action-name>::=<action-name>,<following-action-name>::=<action-name>
    <action-name>::= <string>
```

4 Community Computing Models with Community Situation Based Strict Cooperation

In order to design the community computing system, we had proposed the community computing model called as CCM. In addition, to systematically develop community computing systems, we had also proposed a development process [4]. Since the process is based on MDA (Model Driven Architecture) approach, we had generated more detailed models than CCM, CIM-PI (Platform Independent Community Computing Implementation Model) and CIM-PS (Platform Specific Community Computing Implementation Model). Using the proposed models and development process, we could create a community computing system fast and conveniently.

However, as we mentioned above, the previous models did not concern about cooperation model [4]. In those models, cooperation was just described like a procedural pseudo codes. Although the previous models aimed to abstract a cooperation system, an idea of cooperation was not involved. In order to make up the defect, we generated the community situation based cooperation model [10]. Thus, in this paper, we applied the cooperation model to the previous community computing models. As a result of that, we propose the improved community computing models, the community situation based community computing models. In this section, we introduce the community situation based CCM, the community situation based CIM-PI, and the community situation based CIM-PS. The differences from the previous models are as follows.

- Community situation based cooperation between members
- Conflict Resolution in a community computing system

4.1 The Community Situation Based Community Computing Model

The community computing model, called as CCM, is the most high-level abstraction model for a community computing system. The objective of the CCM is to describe the requirements and the boundary of a system. In order to do, a community comput-ing system is represented as a society, and a society consists of community types and member types. The major difference between the previous CCM and the community situation based CCM is in the cooperation description part. In the improved CCM, a cooperation of a community is represented by community situations and description about each role's tasks in a certain situation. In Fig.1, an example of the community situation based CCM is shown.

```
Society COEX_Mall {
 Community Type Description {
  Community Patrol_COEX{
   Role Patrol_Robot : 1 ~ 10 {
    Attribute:POWER={ON|OFF};
     LOCATION={location_type};MODE={BUZY|ORDINARY};
     Action:Area_Assign();Patrol();
     Cast : POWER=ON; LOCATION= IN.COEX_Mall;}
   Role Patrol_Manager : 1~ 2{
    Attribute:STATUS={ON DUTY| OFF DUTY};
     LOCATION={location_type};
     Action:Patrol_Management();
     Cast : STATUS=ON DUTY; LOCATION=IN.COEX_Mall;}
   Role Guide : 1~ 5{ ... }
  Goals Patrol_COEX(Patrol_Robot, Patrol_Manager, Guide){
    PATROL_AREA_ASSIGN: Areas of All patrol_ robots,
     guides, and patrol_manager is assinged
    PATROL_BEGIN: Start up a patrol service at COEX
    PATROL_END: Shut up a patrol service at COEX, and
     disorganize an instance of 'Patrol_COEX' community}
  Ontology : Patrol_COEX_Ontology; }
 Community Find_Person{
   Role Patrol_Robot: 1 ~ 10 {
    Attribute:POWER={ON|OFF};
LOCATION={locaton_type};

    Action: Area_Assign();Patrol();Broadcast_Info();
     Find_Person();Guide_To();
    Cast : POWER=ON; LOCATION= IN.COEX_Mall; }
   Role Guidian_of_Lost_Person: 1 {
    Attribute:LOCATION={locaton_type};
CONTACT={OMD_ID};
    Action:
Cast:LOCATION= IN.COEX_Mall; }
   Role Guide : 1~ 5 {
    Attribute : STATUS={ON DUTY| OFF DUTY};
     LOCATION={location_type};
    Action:Patrol();Find_Person();Guide_To();Report_Police();
     Cast : STATUS=ON DUTY; LOCATION=IN.COEX_Mall;}
   Role Salesman: 1~1000{ ...}
  Goals Find_a_lost_person(Patrol_Robot,
     Guidian_of_Lost_Person, Guide, Salesman){
    READ_PROFILE_OF_PERSON:Read a profile of a lost per-
son
    FIND_PERSON: Broadcast the profile, and try to find a
person
    PERSON_FOUNDED : The person is founded
    PERSON_NOT_FOUNDED : The person is founded}
   Ontology : Patrol_COEX_Ontology; } }
 Member Type Description {
  Member Siociety_Member{
    Attribute : LOCATION={locaton_type};
    Cast : LOCATION= IN.COEX_Mall; } }
```

Fig. 1. An example of community situation based CCM

4.2 The Community Situation Based Platform Independent Community Implementation Model Supporting Conflict Resolution

CIM-PI is a more detailed model than CCM. Its objective is to describe the implemen-tation using given ubiquitous objects without knowledge of specific platforms. In order to do, in CIM-PI, descriptions of society, community types, and member types are more expanded and detailed. First of all, in the community type description, mapping information between role and member types is added to represent which member types can play which role. Secondly, description of cooperation is detailed. In particular, tasks to be executed by a member shaped up as a sequence of actions of the member, and the definition of community situations is also specified. In third, conditions of community creation are described. To initiate a community instance, two ways are allowed: a member requests an initiation to a society manager or a community man-ager requests an initiation as a part of cooperation. Finally, policies are added to man-age conflicts during the lifetime of a community. In the present version, member cast-ing policy, member secession policy, and action conflicts list (see Definition.3) are defined. The member casting policy represents a rule about member selection such as distant dependent casting or response-time dependent casting. In the member secession policy, treatments for sudden secession of a member are specified. For examples, if a member disappears, then we can initialize a cooperation process with a new member, continue cooperation with a new, or terminate the cooperation. In the member type description part, all member types are described and hierarchy of member types is also defined using the *extends* keyword. In addition, member situations are specified as a logical association of attribute's values. Finally, policies for a member are also described. When a member performs tasks to play one or more than one role, conflicts between own tasks can occur. To resolve such conflicts, we define an action conflicts list (see Definition.3) and represent it in member policy description. In society description, society policy is additionally described. In society policy description, precedence of communities and exclusive communities are defined. When a society manager takes more than one requests for community creation, these policies are used to select one. In Fig.2, an example of the community situation based CIM-PI is shown.

Fig. 2. An example of community situation based CIM-PI

4.3 The Community Situation Based Platform Specific Community Implementation Model Supporting Conflict Resolution

In a community situation based CIM-PS, combines the description in the CIM-PI with the details that specify how that system uses a particular platform. In improved CIM-PS, descriptions about attribute acquisition, action mapping, and member configuration are added. In attribute acquisition part, we describe where values of each attribute derived from. The source of attribute values can be a kind of sensor or action. In action mapping description, we describe how to realize actions of members. In case of using existing programmed objects, we should make a connection between actions in model and programmed actions in an existing object. On the other hand, in case that we should program a ubiquitous member object, we use action names in models to program a member. In member configuration part, components of each member are described.

```
Society COEX_Mall {                                    Read_Personal_Profile():Read_RFID(person_RFID);
Community Type Description { ... }                       Broadcast_Info( ∀ Patrol_Robot and ∀ Guide and
Member Type Description { ...                              ∀ Resident, "Find a person", profile): BroadCast
  Member ARGUS extends Robot {                          (towhom, msg); Find_Person(profile):Search_Obj(Info);
    Attribute : ...                                      Announce( ∀ Patrol_Robot and ∀ Guide and
    Actions ...                                           ∀ Resident, "Person is founded", location):Notify
    Member Situation {................}                  (towhom,msg);Guide_To(founded person, information
    Member Configuration={                              office):GuideServie(who,where);Announce("Person is
      Vision_Sonsor_v3; Samsung_Location_Sensor_v1;}    not founded", ∀ Patrol_Robot):Notify(msg,towhom);}
    Attribute Acquisition {                             Member Policy {
      TAKE_REQUEST_FIND_PERSON:Vision_Sonsor_v3;}         Exclusive Actions={
    Action Mapping {                                       (Patrol(COEX_Mall), END_Patrol_Service()); } } }
      Area_Assign(COEX_Mall, Patrol_Robot):Set_patrol_  ...}
      range(location); Patrol(COEX_Mall):CyberCap(patrol); Society Policy { ... }
    END_Patrol_Service():CyberCap(patrolstop);
```

Fig. 3. An example of community situation based CIM-PS

5   Case Study

In a huge shopping mall, several robots exist. These robots have various functionalities such as move, vision sensing, alarm, voice recognition, information search, and so on. At the ordinary time, each robot offers its own services such as guide service or information presentation. Sometime, robots compose a community to achieve a community's goal. Each robot can take multiple roles, depending on its ability.

Level-1 Cooperation: When a shopping mall is opened, a *Patrol_COEX* community is initiated by casing all robots and guides. Area to patrol is assigned to all robots and guides as soon as a community is created, then each robot and guide patrols assigned area. When a robot or guide cannot patrol because of too much load or sudden interruptions, they request to reassign.

Level-2 Cooperation: When a robot is on patrol as a member of a *Patrol_COEX* community, the robot is asked for finding a lost child by child's mother. The robot generates *TAKE_REQUEST_FIND_PERSON* member situation, and then requests a creation of *Find_Person* community to a society manager. The society manager, which supervises the COEX-Mall Community computing system, creates a community manager for *Find_Person* community, and then the community manger initiates a

Find_Person community by casting necessary members. The robot taking a request sends child's profile to all robots, guides, and salesman in COEX-Mall. After robots get the profile, they start to find the child while patrolling. At this time, each robot takes at least two roles in *Patrol_COEX* community and *Find_Person* community.

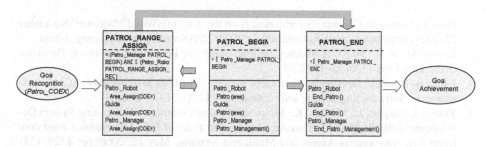

a) Community Situation based Cooperation for *Patrol_COEX* community

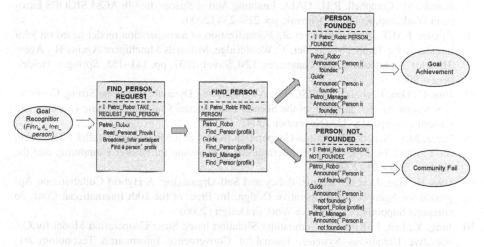

b) Community Situation based Cooperation for *Find_Person* community

Fig. 4. Community Situation based Cooperation for level-1 case and level-2 case

6 Conclusion

In this paper, we proposed the community situation based cooperation model and conflict resolution scheme for community computing. Using the cooperation model and policies, we improved the previous community computing model. In addition, to examine the improved community computing model, we introduced case studies. However, our proposal leaves space for further works as follows.

- Improvement of power of community situation based cooperation model and situation model. – This version of community situation based cooperation model is based on strict assumptions.

- Improvement of conflict resolution scheme
- Various case studies

References

1. Blau, J.: Microsoft: Community computing is on the way. InfoWorld Magazine (November 22, 2005), http://www.infoworld.com/article/05/11/22/HNcommunitycomputing_1.html
2. Kumar, M., et al.: PICO: A Middleware Framework for Pervasive Computing. Pervasive Computing 1268-1536, 72–79 (2003)
3. Jennings, R., et al.: Developing Multiagent Systems: The Gaia Methodology. ACM Transactions on Software Engineering and Methodology 12(3), 317–370 (2003)
4. Youna, J., Jungtae, L., Minkoo, K.: Multi-agent based Community Computing System Development with the Model Driven Architecture. In: Proc. of Fifth International Joint conference on Autonomous Agents and Multiagent Systems, May 12, 2006, pp. 1329–1331 (2006)
5. Román, M., Campbell, R.H.: GAIA: Enabling Active Spaces. In: 9th ACM SIGOPS European Workshop, Kolding, Denmark, pp. 229–234 (2000)
6. Brazier, F.M.T., Jonker, C.M., et al.: Formalization of a cooperation model based on joint intentions. In: Tambe, M., Müller, J., Wooldridge, M.J. (eds.) Intelligent Agents II - Agent Theories, Architectures, and Languages. LNCS, vol. 1037, pp. 141–155. Springer, Heidelberg (1996)
7. Hua, C., Gao, J., et al.: AGDRSCOM: A complicated Dynamic Real-time Strong Cooperation System Model. In: Proc. of the Second International Conf. on Machine Learning and Cybernetics, pp. 318–323 (November 2003)
8. Perez, M.S., Sanchez, A., et al.: Cooperation Model of a Multiagent Parallel File System for Clusters. In: Proc. of IEEE International Symposium on Cluster Computing and the Grid, pp. 595–601 (2004)
9. Guo, H., Gao, J., et al.: Recipe, Policy and Self-Organizing: A Hybrid Collaboration Approach for Agent-based Cooperative Design. In: Proc. of the 10th International Conf. on computer Supported Cooperative Work in Design (2006)
10. Jung, Y., Lee, J., Kim, M.: Community Situation based Strict Cooperation Model for Cooperative Ubiquitous Systems. Journal of Convergence Information Technology 2(1) (2007)

Advancements in Dependable Time-Triggered Communication

Wilfried Steiner

TTTech Computertechnik AG
Vienna, Austria
wilfried.steiner@tttech.com

Abstract. When developing strategies for future research directions it may be a wise decision to reflect on the development in the respective area during the last few years. As to future applications of embedded systems, we consider a concise solution for interconnecting embedded systems to be one of their core requirements. In particular, we focus on the development of dependable communication.

Our paper recapitulates progress in research and development of dependable time-triggered communication protocols as done by the Institute for Computer Engineering at the Vienna University of Technology and by TTTech Computertechnik AG over the last five years. We provide an overview of the current situation and discuss the ongoing research and development directions.

1 Introduction

Dependable communication infrastructures are required in various applications that ensure the standards of our daily life. Such applications range from flight-control systems in aircrafts to distributed control systems in nuclear power plants. The basis of a dependable communication infrastructure is the communication protocol and the properties that it provides. Determinism and predictability are desired properties for communication protocols as they support the reasoning about the system during the development process as well as during the application process of a respective system. Protocols that implement the time-triggered paradigm provide determinism and predictability.

Time-triggered protocols are suitable for the x-by-wire market, for example fly-by-wire in avionics or steer-by-wire in the automotive sector. While time-triggered technology is used in the avionics market for quite some time, it is an emerging technology for the automotive market and is about to hit the market in form of FlexRay[TM][Fle05]. Furthermore, as embedded systems are evolving from stand-alone solutions to distributed embedded systems, there is a potential for dependable distributed embedded systems in markets adjacent to the traditional safety-critical ones. Examples of future applications that require dependable communication are distributed implants, human robotics, or novel games. Fault tolerance is a key mechanism in these examples. Assume a distributed

R. Obermaisser et al. (Eds.): SEUS 2007, LNCS 4761, pp. 57–66, 2007.
© IFIP International Federation for Information Processing 2007

implant that consists of a distributed embedded system with sensors and actuators placed in several organs; it shall not happen, e.g., that a "stuck message"[1] causes an overdose of adrenaline. Similar scenarios can easily be constructed for human robotics and novel games, where corrupted communication may lead to significant economic loss, or loss of fun respectively. At a glance, such thinking may appear to be science fiction, and this might be true for the examples above. However, a low-cost dependable communication infrastructure with accompanying novel software technologies is an enabler for such applications.

Time-triggered protocols have been intensively studied over 25 years at the Technical University of Vienna and at TTTech Computertechnik AG since its establishment in 1998. We give an overview on time-triggered communication in Section 2. It is a vision of TTTech to offer a product line of time-triggered protocols that supports a wide range of dependable distributed embedded systems including the traditional safety-critical ones as well as emerging and future systems. One step towards this goal is a layering of protocol services to make it configurable to a customer's needs. This approach has resulted in the Layered Time-Triggered Protocol (LTTP), a TTP research derivative. We discuss LTTP in Section 3. One particular fault-tolerance mechanism that has been studied intensely over the last years are central guardian instances; we give an overview of the central guardian concepts in Section 4. Ongoing research and development is concerned with bridging the gap between the Ethernet world and dependable time-triggered communication. This research trend is sketched in Section 5. This paper concludes with Section 6.

2   Time-Triggered Communication

In a distributed system where each of the components has access to a local clock, the states of the local clocks can be brought into agreement, that is, the clocks can be *synchronized*. For this purpose there are two types of algorithms: clock-synchronization algorithms and startup algorithms. Clock-synchronization algorithms are used to maintain the quality of the synchronization once a certain threshold is reached. The startup algorithm has to ensure that such a threshold is reached within an upper bound in time. This separation of the synchronization problem into the subproblems of startup and clock synchronization is not always done in the literature and there are clock-synchronization algorithms that solve both subproblems at once. Many of these algorithms, however, either assume a reliable transmission of messages between the nodes *per se* or are of a probabilistic nature.

Furthermore, in a computer system, there is no action that starts *by itself*. An action needs a trigger to be executed. We can distinguish two basic types of triggers: event-triggers and time-triggers. Event-triggers are external triggers that are received by a component either via the communication channels or from the environment. Time-triggers (are triggers that) arise when a clock, to which the component has access to, has reached an action state. These action states

---

[1] This is a message that is continually re-sent by a communication participant, e.g. imposed by a faulty controller.

can either be defined *a priori*, and be therefore explicitly known to the system's designer, or can evolve from the execution of certain algorithms on a component. An example for an a priori defined action state would be the start of a Task A: *schedule task A at time 12:00*, where *12:00* is the action state of the component's clock. An example for an evolved action state would be the start of a Task B: *schedule Task B after Task A*, where the action state evolves depending on the execution time of Task A.

Synchronization of the local clocks of the components allows action states to be defined throughout the distributed system, such that it is guaranteed that these action states are reached within the precision Π, an off-line calculable parameter. Hence, it is possible to implement synchronized time-triggers, that allow the components to operate as a coordinated whole. Synchronized time-triggers can be used for the communication strategy: we off-line specify the action states when a node is allowed to access the shared medium. If all nodes adhere to this schedule, a fair distribution of bandwidth is guaranteed. Faulty nodes that do not restrict their sending behavior to the specification have to be blocked by additional guardian instances. We call a communication strategy that is based on synchronized time-triggers a time-triggered communication strategy, whereas communication strategies that use unsynchronized (event- or time-) triggers are called event-triggered communication strategies. The communication schedule for time-triggered communication is generated off-line. The time it takes to process through the schedule table once is called a TDMA round (Time-Division Multiple-Access).

A fine property of time triggered communication is the time-triggered broadcast property that supports agreement algorithms.

From Reliable to Atomic to Time-Triggered Broadcast: A set of processes communicates by exchanging messages and each of these processes produces local output based on the messages exchanged. Informally spoken, reliable broadcast is a mechanism that guarantees that all processes generate the same unordered set of messages as their local outputs.

The broadcast problem introduces two functional primitives: `broadcast()` and `deliver()`. Each process uses the `broadcast()` primitive to distribute messages to all the other processes. Each process uses the `deliver()` function to generate output. Thus, with progress of time, the `deliver()` primitive generates a sequence of messages. A set of processes solves the reliable broadcast problem if it provides [HT94]:

- Validity: if a correct process broadcasts m, it eventually delivers m.
- Agreement: if a correct process delivers m, all correct processes eventually deliver m.
- Integrity: for any message m, every correct process delivers m at most once, and only if m was previously broadcast by a correct sender.

Atomic broadcast is defined as reliable broadcast that fulfills the following additional ordering property:

- Total Order: if correct processes p and q both deliver messages m and m', then p delivers m before m' if and only if q delivers m before m'.

Informally spoken, atomic broadcast guarantees that not only the set of messages is equal within the set of correct processes, but also the delivery order of the messages.

The time-triggered broadcast makes the implementation of the `broadcast()` primitive on a shared medium trivial: each node uses the shared medium in its assigned time slot. Time-triggered broadcast even enhances the atomic broadcast property in that the delivery order of messages is *a priori* known.

3   Layered Time-Triggered Protocol (LTTP)

The prime design goal of LTTP was a clean separation of the communication layer from higher-layer mechanisms. A membership service is for example a higher-layer mechanism. The encapsulation of the communication layer resulted in a more robust protocol state machine including an enhanced fault-tolerant startup algorithm and clique resolution algorithm.

The LTTP protocol distinguishes several protocol phases that can be grouped as follows: the startup phases, which consists of the INIT, INTEGRATION, and COLDSTART phase, the synchronized operation phase, which consists of the SYNC phase, and the external synchronization phase, which consists of the PAUSE_SYNC and the EXTERNAL_STARTUP phase. The phases are depicted in Figure 1.

3.1   Protocol Startup

After power-on (that is, after the node is initialized) the node starts the INTEGRATION phase. Each slot in the communication schedule is assigned to a sending node and each message carries the identifier of its sender. Hence, the node listens to the communication channels and has to identify, based on the messages

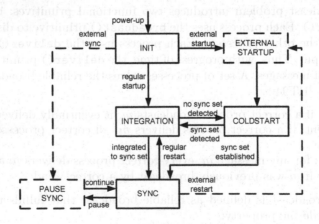

Fig. 1. Protocol Phases

received, if there is a sufficient number of nodes communicating synchronously. If such a set exists, the node integrates into this set and becomes synchronized. If such a sufficient set does not exist, the node enters the COLDSTART phase.

In the COLDSTART phase, the node waits for coldstart signals that are used as starting signal for schedule processing. Such coldstart signals are sent by nodes when a local timer expires (only a subset of nodes may be configured to send a coldstart signal). A node that receives a coldstart signal will start to proceed through the schedule and reply in its assigned slot. The nodes are able to acquire the number of nodes that react to the coldstart signal by counting the replies. The COLDSTART phase ends when a sufficient set of nodes has been synchronized. In general it may also happen that only a subset of nodes in coldstart will reach synchronous operation. For this reason the LTTP startup algorithm defines conditions for a re-transition to the INTEGRATION phase, such that nodes that did not reach the sync phase are able to integrate to the established synchronous communication.

In the SYNC phase the node has reached synchronous operation (but not necessarily steady state). If synchronization is lost, the nodes restart the startup process with the INTEGRATION phase.

The transitions between the different phases of the startup strategy can be taken either by the expiration of timeouts or by the reception of a sufficiently long sequence of messages per TDMA round. It is highly important that a faulty node or channel cannot be able to spread such a sequence of messages (e.g. by masquerading a number of different nodes) that will cause a non-faulty node to take an incorrect transition between startup phases.

To speed up the startup process, LTTP allows using a dedicated TDMA schedule during coldstart. This dedicated schedule may only consist of four slots of minimum size. A more detailed discussion of the startup of time-triggered communication is given in [SK06].

3.2   Synchronized Operation

In LTTP a single node may occupy more than one sending slot in the communication schedule. Furthermore, LTTP introduces the mechanism of "sender-dynamic slots". These slots are scheduled off-line but not statically assigned to a particular node. Instead, the nodes execute an arbitration protocol during run-time to assign the sender-dynamic slots to a particular node. The information for this arbitration protocol is transmitted with the messages in slots that are statically assigned to the nodes. The arbitration protocol used is not part of the LTTP specification; it could be, for example, a sophisticated agreement algorithm to ensure fault-tolerant arbitration or a simple client-server algorithm.

3.3   External Synchronization

LTTP may be used as a sub-bus in a high-speed network. For such and similar purposes LTTP is equipped with provisions to synchronize to external sources. This external synchronization can be achieved in two ways: LTTP can be put into a PAUSE_SYNC phase or into an EXTERNAL_STARTUP phase. In the PAUSE_SYNC phase the communication is halted and operation is resumed either after a given duration or upon an external event. In the EXTERNAL_STARTUP phase LTTP awaits an external startup event upon which the regular coldstart will be executed.

Also, these mechanisms support a global synchronization if several LTTP systems (so called clusters) are connected together to form an LTTP multi-cluster.

3.4 Clique Resolution Algorithms

A potential threat to time-triggered communication protocols is the establishment of a cliques scenario. Cliques are then established, when two sets of disjoint nodes are synchronized within their respective set but the two sets are unsynchronized to each other. In our opinion an assumption that cliques will never form is not acceptable for safety-critical systems as multiple transient failures or faulty communication channels may cause their establishment. Hence, appropriate algorithms to resolve cliques scenarios are required.

TTP uses a so-called clique avoidance algorithm: as the node cyclically proceeds through the communication schedule it classifies each message it receives as correct or incorrect and increases a respective counter. When the node reaches its sending slot in the TDMA round (in TTP each node occupies only one slot per TDMA round) it checks the counters. The node detects cliques when the number of incorrect received messages is higher than the number of correct messages. Hence, this algorithm is based on the relative number of correct messages.

A drawback of this approach is that a node may not receive all incorrect messages, as communication is performed via half-duplex communication links. As a result, depending on the communication schedule configuration there is a probability that cliques scenarios are not diagnosed. In LTTP we propose a clique resolution algorithm that is not based on the relative number of correct messages received, but on the absolute number [SPK06]. If the number of received messages falls beyond an off-line calculable threshold for a given duration, cliques are detected. The threshold is a function of either the number of nodes in the system, or of a dedicated subset of nodes.

3.5 Formal Analysis of (L)TTP Services

Several services, such as the clock-synchronization service and the membership service [Pfe03], have been formally verified by means of theorem proofing using PVS. Rushby gives an overview of formal analysis activities in the time-triggered architecture in [Rus02]. Lately, the TTP and the LTTP startup algorithms have been subject to model-checking studies [SRSP04, SK06] using SAL[2]. Due to the performance of the SAL model checker it was possible to assess the startup algorithms by means of exhaustive failure simulation.

---

[2] PVS and SAL are developed by SRI International.

4 The Central Guardian Concept

For the discussion of fault-tolerance methods we define fault-containments regions (FCRs), that are regions that are impacted by a fault and fail as a whole. In distributed embedded networks each node computer and each communication channel forms such an FCR.

When multiple FCRs share a common resource, as in our case a shared broadcast channel, it is necessary to protect that shared resource via additional, independent FCRs. If such a protection mechanism is not implemented, a faulty FCR bears the potential danger to monopolize the shared resource and to render it unusable for other, correct FCRs. Temple introduced the concept of "local guardians" in [Tem99]: a node will not access a shared broadcast channel directly but will communicate with a local guardian which may or may not relay the send attempt to the shared broadcast channel, depending if the local guardian classifies the sending attempt correct or faulty. To tolerate the failure of one local guardian or of one shared broadcast channel itself, the local guardian, as well as the channel, have to be duplicated. This results in a number of $2 * n$ local guardians in a system of n nodes with two replicated channels. To justify the independence argument of FCRs it is required to implement the node and local guardians on separated silicon which makes the local guardian solution economically unattractive. Indeed, the first implementations of the local guardian concept (for TTP) placed the local guardians and the node on the same chip, thus weakening the requirements on a FCR. Fault-injection studies showed that this implementation of local guardians leads to error propagation scenarios [ABST03].

With the movement from a bus topology to a star topology, the promising concept of central guardians was introduced [BFJ+00]: instead of implementing the guardian FCRs locally at the node's side, the guardians are placed at the hubs of the star network. The economic benefit of this solution is obvious, instead of $2*n$ local guardians only two central guardians are necessary in a two-channel system for any number of nodes. The first proof of concept for central guardians [BKS03] basically places a passive node, that is a node without hardware units for message generation, at the hub that executes the same protocol as the regular nodes. The hub controls the dataflow according to the passive node. From a conceptual point of view, this solution is elegant: a node and the central guardian temporally form a self-checking pair, that is, the central guardian is able to transform the arbitrary behavior of a faulty node to a detectably-faulty behavior (with respect to protocol execution). Thus, no semantically faulty messages will pass the central guardian and the fault tree of the system can be kept at a minimum. In particular this first generation of central guardians required following mechanisms:

– the guardian has to execute a semantic filter, that is, certain fields of a messages are analyzed by the guardian and, if a semantic failure is detected, the message is transformed into a syntactically faulty message, by truncation of the message,

- the centralized guardian instances have to use interlinks which are unidirectional direct connections between the two centralized guardians, such that a centralized guardian receives the messages transmitted on the respective other channel, and
- any one non-faulty guardian has to be powered on before any non-faulty node starts to transmit messages.

Another central guardian strategy is a minimum strategy that aims at keeping the state in a central guardian as small as possible. This strategy has certain benefits for reasoning about the fault behavior of the central guardian itself, since we have to argue that even a faulty central guardian will not create valid messages. Such a minimum state strategy for a central guardian was selected for the LTTP protocol. This second generation of central guardians allows dismissing the above listed requirements, although they may be implemented for performance reasons.

5   Dependable Communication on Ethernet

There are several approaches to equip standard Ethernet with real-time capabilities [Fel05]. Probably most notable beyond all is the IEEE activity in form of the IEEE 1588 standard [IEE04]. IEEE 1588 specifies a clock synchronization protocol on top of Ethernet.

An orthogonal approach to IEEE 1588 is Time-Triggered Ethernet (TTE) [KAGS05]. TTE fundamentally distinguishes between foreground time-triggered traffic and background event-triggered traffic, while both traffic classes conform to the Ethernet frame format. Foreground traffic is scheduled *a priori* and prioritized in the TTE switch. A prototype switch [Ste06] developed by the Vienna University of Technology implements a "preemption" mechanism. This mechanism will preempt ongoing transmission of event-triggered messages whenever a time-triggered message has to be relayed. This mechanism provides a high quality on transmission delay and transmission jitter of a time-triggered message. Preempted event-triggered messages will be relayed after the time-triggered message.

However, as IEEE 1588, as well as the synchronization protocol in TTE, are master-slave based protocols, their fault-tolerance capabilities may not be accurate for dependable communication. It is a research activity of TTTech to design a fault-tolerant TTE. One possible solution is to incorporate the (L)TTP services into TTE.

6   Conclusion

Time-triggered technology is successful for dependable communication in well-established markets such as avionics, it is likely to be implemented in emerging markets for dependable communication like, for example, the automotive market, and it is promising and even an enabler for future markets. The LTTP protocol together with the developed guardian instances provide the basis for a robust dependable communication infrastructure and, hence, is suitable to a wide range of applications. On the other side, TTTech is developing Ethernet-based time-triggered protocols with a focus on dependability.

Acknowledgments

Many thanks to the colleagues from the Institute of Computer Engineering, for their hospitality and discussions of many topics. This work was supported by the European Project DECOS (IST-2-511764).

References

[ABST03] Ademaj, A., Bauer, G., Sivencrona, H., Torin, J.: Evaluation of fault handling of the time-triggered architecture with bus and star topology. In: Proc. of International Conference on Dependable Systems and Networks (DSN 2003), San Francisco (June 2003)

[BFJ+00] Bauer, G., Frenning, T., Jonsson, A.K., Kopetz, H., Temple, C.: A centralized approach for avoiding the babbling-idiot failure in the time-triggered architecture. In: ICDSN, New York (June 2000)

[BKS03] Bauer, G., Kopetz, H., Steiner, W.: The central guardian approach to enforce fault isolation in a time-triggered system. In: Proc. of 6th International Symposium on Autonomous Decentralized Systems (ISADS 2003), Italy, pp. 37–44 (April 2003)

[Fel05] Felser, M.: Real-time ethernet - industry prospective. Proceedings of the IEEE 93, 1118–1129 (2005)

[Fle05] FlexRay Communications System - Protocol Specification - Version 2.1. FlexRay Consortium (2005), Available at http://www.flexray.com

[HT94] Hadzilacos, V., Toueg, S.: A modular approach to fault-tolerant broadcasts and related problems. Technical Report TR94-1425 (1994)

[IEE04] IEEE, INC. IEEE 1588 – Precision clock synchronization protocol for networked measurement and control systems (2004)

[KAGS05] Kopetz, H., Ademaj, A., Grillinger, P., Steinhammer, K.: The time-triggered ethernet (tte) design. In: 8th IEEE International Symposium on Object-oriented Real-time distributed Computing (ISORC), Seattle, Washington (May 2005)

[Pfe03] Pfeifer, H.: Formal Analysis of Fault-Tolerant Algorithms in the Time-Triggered Architecture. PhD thesis, Universität Ulm (2003)

[Rus02] Rushby, J.: An Overview of Formal Verification for the Time-Triggered Architecture. In: Damm, W., Olderog, E.-R. (eds.) FTRTFT 2002. LNCS, vol. 2469, pp. 83–105. Springer, Heidelberg (2002)

[SK06] Steiner, W., Kopetz, H.: The startup problem in fault-tolerant time-triggered communication. In: International Conference on Dependable Systems and Networks (DSN 2006), (June 2006)

[SPK06] Steiner, W., Paulitsch, M., Kopetz, H.: The tta's approach to resilience after transient upsets. Real-Time Systems 32, 213–233 (2006)

[SRSP04]   Steiner, W., Rushby, J., Sorea, M., Pfeifer, H.: Model checking a fault-
tolerant startup algorithm: From design exploration to exhaustive fault
simulation. In: The International Conference on Dependable Systems and
Networks (DSN 2004) (June 2004)
[Ste06]   Steinhammer, K.: Design of an FPGA-Based Time-Triggered Ethernet System. PhD thesis, Technische Universität Wien, Institut für Technische Informatik, Treitlstr. 3/3/182-1, 1040 Vienna, Austria (2006)
[Tem99]   Temple, C.: Enforcing Error Containment in Distributed Time-Triggered
Systems: The Bus Guardian Approach. PhD thesis, Technische Univer-
sität Wien, Institut für Technische Informatik, Treitlstr. 3/3/182-1, 1040
Vienna, Austria (1999)

On Distributed Real-Time Scheduling in Networked Embedded Systems in the Presence of Crash Failures

Binoy Ravindran[1], Jonathan S. Anderson[1], and E. Douglas Jensen[2]

[1] ECE Dept., Virginia Tech, Blacksburg, VA 24061, USA
andersoj@vt.edu, binoy@vt.edu
[2] The MITRE Corporation, Bedford, MA 01730, USA
jensen@mitre.org

Abstract. We consider the problem of scheduling distributable real-time threads in networked embedded systems that operate under run-time uncertainties including those on thread execution times, thread arrivals, and node failure occurrences. We present a distributed scheduling algorithm called CUA. We show that CUA satisfies thread time constraints in the presence of crash failures, is early-deciding, has an efficient message complexity of $O(fn)$ (where f is the number of crashes that actually occur and n is the number of nodes), and is time-optimal with a time lower bound of $O(D + fd + nk)$ (where D is the message delay upper bound, d is the failure detection bound, and k is the maximum number of threads). In crash-free runs, the algorithm constructs schedules within $O(D + nk)$, and yields optimal total utility if nodes are also not overloaded. The algorithm is also "best-effort" in that a high importance thread that may arrive at any time has a very high likelihood for feasible completion (in contrast to classical admission control algorithms which favor feasible completion of admitted threads over admitting new ones, irrespective of thread importance).

1 Introduction

In distributed systems, action and information timeliness is often end-to-end—e.g., a causally dependent, multi-node, sensor to actuator sequential flow of execution in networked embedded systems that control physical processes. Such a causal flow of execution can be caused by a series of nested, remote method invocations. It can also be caused by a series of chained, publication and subscription events, caused due to topical data dependencies—e.g., publication of topic $\mathcal{A}$ depends on subscription of topic $\mathcal{B}$; publication of $\mathcal{B}$, in turn, depends on subscription of topic $\mathcal{C}$, and so on. Designers and users of distributed systems, networked embedded systems in particular, often need to dependably reason about — i.e., specify, manage, and predict — end-to-end timeliness.

Many emerging networked embedded systems are dynamic in the sense that they operate in environments with dynamically uncertain properties (e.g., [1]). These uncertainties include transient and sustained resource overloads (due to context-dependent activity execution times), arbitrary activity arrivals, and arbitrary node failures. Reasoning about end-to-end timeliness is a very difficult

R. Obermaisser et al. (Eds.): SEUS 2007, LNCS 4761, pp. 67–81, 2007.

and unsolved problem in such dynamic uncertain systems. Another distinguishing feature of motivating applications for this model (e.g., [1]) is their relatively
long activity execution time magnitudes—e.g., milliseconds to minutes. Despite
the uncertainties, such applications desire the strongest possible assurances on
end-to-end activity timeliness behavior.

Maintaining end-to-end properties (e.g., timeliness, connectivity) of a control
or information flow requires a model of the flow's locus in space and time that
can be reasoned about. Such a model facilitates reasoning about the contention
for resources that occur along the flow's locus and resolving those contention to
optimize system-wide end-to-end timeliness. The *distributable thread* programming abstraction which first appeared in the Alpha OS [2] and subsequently in
Mach 3.0 [3] (a subset), MK7.3 [4], Real-Time CORBA 1.2 [5], and Sun's emerging Distributed Real-Time Specification for Java (DRTSJ) [6] directly provide
such a model as their first-class programming and scheduling abstraction. A distributable thread is a single thread of execution with a globally unique identity
that transparently extends and retracts through local and remote objects.

A distributable thread carries its execution context as it transits node boundaries, including its scheduling parameters (e.g., time constraints, execution time),
identity, and security credentials. The propagated thread context is intended to
be used by node schedulers for resolving all node-local resource contention among
distributable threads such as that for node's physical (e.g., processor, I/O) and
logical (e.g., locks) resources, according to a discipline that provides application-
specific, acceptably optimal, system-wide end-to-end timeliness. Figure 1 shows
the execution of four distributable threads. We focus on distributable threads as
our end-to-end control flow/programming/scheduling abstraction, and hereafter,
refer to them as *threads*, except as necessary for clarity.

When overloads
occur, meeting time
constraints of all
threads is impossi-
ble as the demand
exceeds the supply.
The urgency of a
thread is sometimes
orthogonal to the
relative importance
of the thread—-e.g.,
the most urgent
thread may be the
least important, and
vice versa; the most
urgent may be the
most important, and

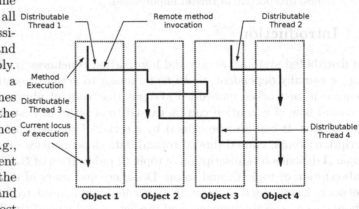

Fig. 1. Four Distributable Threads

vice versa. Hence when overloads occur, completing the most important threads
irrespective of thread urgency is desirable. Thus, a distinction has to be made

between urgency and importance during overloads. (During underloads, such a distinction generally need not be made, especially if all time constraints are deadlines, as optimal algorithms exist that can meet all deadlines—e.g., EDF [7].)

Deadlines cannot express both urgency and importance. Thus, we consider the *time/utility function* (or TUF) timeliness model [8] that specifies the utility of completing a thread as a function of that thread's completion time. We specify a deadline as a binary-valued, downward "step" shaped TUF; Figure 2 shows examples. A thread's TUF decouples its importance and urgency—urgency is measured on the X-axis, and importance is denoted (by utility) on the Y-axis.

When thread time constraints are expressed with TUFs, the scheduling optimality criteria are based on maximizing accrued thread utility—e.g., maximizing the total thread accrued utility. Such criteria are called *utility accrual* (or UA) criteria,

Fig. 2. Example Step TUF Time Constraints

and sequencing (scheduling, dispatching) algorithms that optimize UA criteria are called UA sequencing algorithms (see [9] for example algorithms).

UA algorithms that maximize total utility under downward step TUFs (e.g., [10,11]) default to EDF during underloads, since EDF satisfies all deadlines during underloads. Consequently, they obtain the optimum total utility during underloads. During overloads, they inherently favor more important threads over less important ones (since more utility can be attained from the former), irrespective of thread urgency, and thus exhibit adaptive behavior and graceful timeliness degradation. This behavior of UA algorithms is called "best-effort" [10] in the sense that the algorithms strive their best to feasibly complete as many high importance threads — as specified by the application through TUFs — as possible.[1] Consequently, high importance threads that arrive at any time always have a very high likelihood for feasible completion (irrespective of their urgency). Note also that EDF's optimal timeliness behavior is a special-case of UA scheduling.

Contributions: Assured Thread Timeliness in the Presence of Failures. In this paper, we consider the problem of scheduling threads in the presence of the previously mentioned uncertainties, focusing particularly on (arbitrary) node failures. Past efforts on thread scheduling (e.g., [2, 12, 13]) consider a paradigm broadly called *independent node scheduling*, where threads are scheduled at nodes using propagated thread scheduling parameters and without any interaction with other nodes (thereby not considering node failures during scheduling). Fault-management is separately addressed by *thread integrity protocols* [14] that run concurrent to thread execution. Thread integrity protocols detect failures of the thread abstraction, delivering failure-exception

---

[1] Note that the term "best effort" as used in the context of networks actually is intended to mean "least effort."

notifications [2, 13]. This approach avoids the overhead of inter-node communication, and is therefore message-efficient and tractable (solely from the thread scheduling standpoint). However, the approach poses theoretical difficulties in establishing end-to-end timing assurances, due to the complex (and concurrent) interaction between thread scheduling and thread fault-management mechanisms.

We consider instead *collaborative scheduling*, where nodes explicitly cooperate to construct system-wide thread schedules, anticipating node failures. Of course, doing so incurs message overhead costs, and thus raises fundamental questions including a) what upper bounds can be established for such message costs, and b) what are the consequent payoffs.

We answer these questions. We present an algorithm called *Consensus-based Utility accrual scheduling Algorithm* (or CUA). The algorithm considers distributable threads that are subject to TUF time constraints. Threads may have arbitrary arrival behaviors, may exhibit unbounded execution time behaviors (causing node overloads), and may span nodes that are subject to arbitrary crash failures. For such a model, we consider the scheduling objective of maximizing the total thread accrued utility.

CUA is a distributed algorithm that consists of a set of node schedulers that cooperate to realize the algorithm's logic. Node schedulers invoke themselves at events of interest (e.g., thread arrival, failure-suspicion), construct local schedules, broadcast schedules, and arrive at consensus on system-wide schedules, despite failures. We show that CUA satisfies thread time constraints in the presence of crash failures, is early-deciding (i.e., its decision time is proportional to the actual number of crashes), has an efficient message complexity of $O(fn)$ (where f is the number of crashes that actually occur and n is the number of nodes), and is time-optimal with a time lower bound of $O(D+fd+nk)$ (where D is the message delay upper bound, d is the failure detection bound, and k is the maximum number of threads). Note that early-deciding consensus algorithms in the continuous-time synchronous model (where processes do not execute in lock-step rounds) have an optimal time lower bound of $O(D + fd)$ [15]. In crash-free runs, CUA constructs schedules within $O(D+nk)$, and yields optimal total utility if nodes are also not overloaded. The algorithm also retains the fundamental best-effort property of UA algorithms—i.e., a high importance thread that may arrive at any time has a very high likelihood for feasible completion. To the best of our knowledge, this is the first algorithm to provide these properties.

The rest of the paper is organized as follows: In Section 2, we discuss the models of our work and state the algorithm objectives. Section 3 presents CUA. We establish the algorithm's properties in Section 4. We conclude the paper in Section 5.

2 Models

2.1 Distributable Thread Abstraction

Threads execute in local and remote objects by location-independent invocations and returns. A thread begins its execution by invoking an object operation. The object and the operation are specified when the thread is created. The portion of a thread executing an object operation is called a *thread segment*. Thus, a thread can be viewed as being composed of a concatenation of thread segments.

A thread's initial segment is called its *root* and its most recent segment is called its *head*. The head of a thread is the only segment that is active. A thread can also be viewed as being composed of a sequence of *sections*, where a section is a maximal length sequence of contiguous thread segments on a node. A section's first segment results from an invocation from another node, and its last segment performs a remote invocation. Further details of the thread model can be found in [2, 5, 16].

Execution time estimates of the sections of a thread are assumed to be known when the thread arrives. A section's execution time estimate is the execution time estimate of the contiguous set of thread segments that starts from the operation of the object invoked on the node (i.e., the first thread segment executed on the node) and ends with the first remote invocation made from the node. The time estimate includes that of the section's normal code and its exception handler code, and can be violated at run-time (e.g., due to context dependence, causing processor overloads).

The sequence of remote invocations and returns made by a thread can typically be estimated by analyzing the thread code (e.g., [17]). The total number of sections of a thread is thus assumed to be known a-priori.

The application is thus comprised of a set of threads, denoted $\mathbf{T} = \{T_1, T_2, T_3, \ldots\}$. The set of sections of a thread T_i is denoted as $[S_1^i, S_2^i, \ldots, S_k^i]$.

2.2 Timeliness Model

We specify the time constraint of each thread using a TUF. A thread T_i's TUF is denoted as $U_i(t)$. A classical deadline is unit-valued—i.e., $U_i(t) = \{0, 1\}$, since importance is not considered. Downward step TUFs generalize classical deadlines where $U_i(t) = \{0, m\}$. We focus on downward step TUFs (e.g., Figure 2), and denote the maximum, constant utility of a TUF $U_i(t)$, simply as U_i. Each TUF has an initial time I_i, which is the earliest time for which the TUF is defined, and a termination time X_i, which, for a downward step TUF, is its discontinuity point. $U_i(t) > 0, \forall t \in [I_i, X_i]$ and $U_i(t) = 0, \forall t \notin [I_i, X_i], \forall i$.

2.3 System and Failure Models

Our system and failure models follow that of [15]. We consider a system model where a set of processing components, generically referred to as *nodes*, denoted by the totally-ordered set $\Pi = \{1, 2, \ldots, n\}$, are interconnected via a network. We consider a single hop network model (e.g., a LAN), with nodes interconnected through a hub or a switch. The system is assumed to be (partially) synchronous in that there exists an upper bound D on the message delivery latency. A reliable message transmission protocol is assumed; thus messages are not lost or duplicated. Node clocks are assumed to be perfectly synchronized, for simplicity in presentation. The CUA algorithm, however, can be extended to clocks that are nearly synchronized with bounded drift rates.

As many as f_{max} nodes may crash arbitrarily. The actual number of node crashes is denoted as $f \leq f_{max}$. Nodes that do not crash are called *correct*.

Each node is assumed to be equipped with a perfect failure detector [18] that provides a list of nodes that are deemed to have crashed. If a node q belongs to such a list of node p, then node p is said to *suspect* node q. The failure detection time [19] $d \leq D$ is assumed to be bounded. Similar to [15], for simplicity in presentation, we assume that D is a multiple of d. Failure detectors are assumed to be (a) *accurate*—i.e., a node suspects a node q only if q has previously crashed; and (b) *timely*—i.e., if a node q crashes at time t, then every correct node permanently suspects q within $t + d$.

2.4   Scheduling Objectives

Our primary objective is to design a thread scheduling algorithm that will maximize the total utility accrued by all the threads as much as possible. Further, the algorithm must provide assurances on the satisfaction of thread termination times in the presence of (up to f_{max}) crash failures. Moreover, the algorithm must exhibit the best-effort property of UA algorithms (described in Section 1).

3   The CUA Algorithm

3.1   Rationale and Design

In the absence of crash failures, there is no compelling motivation for nodes to collaborate for constructing a system-wide schedule.[2] Thus, we consider crash failures and first establish the premise for collaboration—i.e., why thread scheduling in the presence of crash failures should consider node collaboration. We first define the notion of a thread's *current head node* and *future head nodes*:

Definition 1 (Current Head Node). *The current head node of a thread T_i is the node where T_i is currently executing (i.e., where T_i's head is currently located).*

Definition 2 (Future Head Nodes). *The future head nodes of a thread T_i are those nodes where T_i will make remote invocations in the future.*

The crash of a node p affects other nodes in the system in three possible ways: (a) p may be the current head node of one or more threads; (b) p may be the future head node of one or more threads; and (c) p may be the current and future head node of one or more threads.

If p is only the current head node of one or more threads, then all nodes in the system which are future head nodes of those threads are immediately affected, since they can now release the processor time for scheduling those future heads

---

[2] One motivation for such a collaboration would be to construct an optimized system-wide schedule — one that can result in greater timeliness (e.g, total accrued utility) than what would be possible without collaboration. We do not consider such a node collaboration as that is outside the scope of this work.

and use it for scheduling other threads. If p is only the future head node of one or more threads, all nodes in the system which are (also) future head nodes of those threads are affected, since they can now similarly release the processor time for scheduling other threads. There may be a set of nodes which are not future head nodes of p's threads. Only those nodes are unaffected.

This implies that when a node p crashes, a system-wide decision must be made (by all those nodes which are affected by p's crash) regarding which set of threads are eligible for execution in the system—referred to as an *execution-eligible thread set*—and which are not. Furthermore, this decision must be made in the presence of failures, since nodes may crash while that decision is being made. We formulate this problem as a *consensus* problem [20] with the following properties: (a) If a correct node decides an eligible thread set T, then some correct node proposed T; (b) Nodes (correct or not) do not decide different execution-eligible sets (*uniform agreement*); (c) Every correct node eventually decides (i.e., termination).

Observe that the first property is stronger than the uniform validity property of the (uniform) consensus problem specification. Uniform validity states that if a node decides a value, then some node previously proposed that value. For the thread scheduling problem, this would mean that it would be possible for correct nodes to decide on an execution-eligible thread set that was previously proposed by a node, which later crashed. Consequently, this will result in an invalid system-wide execution-eligible thread set. Thus, we qualify the uniform validity property with *correct*.

Now that a premise for node collaboration is established, we need to determine how a node can propose a set of threads that should be eligible for execution. Since the task model is dynamic—i.e., when threads will be created is entirely arbitrary and statically unknown, future scheduling events cannot be considered at a scheduling event.[3] Thus, the execution-eligible thread set must be constructed solely exploiting the current system knowledge. Since the primary scheduling objective is to maximize the total thread accrued utility, and it may not be possible to meet all thread termination times due to overloads, a reasonable heuristic for determining the execution-eligible thread set is a "greedy" strategy: Favor "high return" threads over low return ones, and complete as many of them as possible before thread termination times.

The potential utility that can be accrued by executing a thread section on a node defines a measure of that section's "return on investment." We measure this using a metric called the *Potential Utility Density* (or PUD). On a node, a thread section's PUD measures the utility that can be accrued per unit time by immediately executing the section on the node.

Thus, each node (that is a current head node for one or more threads) examines thread sections in its local ready queue for potential inclusion in a feasible schedule for the node in the order of decreasing section PUDs. For each section, the algorithm examines whether that section can be completed early enough, allowing successive sections of the thread to also be completed early enough, to

---

[3] A "scheduling event" is an event that invokes the scheduling algorithm.

allow the entire thread to meet its termination time. We call this property, the feasibility of a section. If the section is infeasible (due to schedule overload), it is rejected. The process is repeated until all sections are examined, yielding a local schedule of feasible sections.

To determine section feasibility, we assign termination times for each section of a thread (derived from the thread's termination time) in a way that allows the thread's termination time to be met if each of the section termination times are met. The termination time that a section must meet to allow the thread to meet its termination time is simply the thread termination time if the section is the last section; otherwise, it is the latest start time of the section's successor section minus the communication delay upper bound. The latest start time of a section is the section's termination time minus its estimated execution time. Thus, the section termination times of a thread T_i with k sections are given by:

$$S_j^i.tt = \begin{cases} T_i.tt & j = k \\ S_{j+1}^i.tt - S_{j+1}^i.ex - D & 1 \le j \le k - 1 \end{cases} \tag{1}$$

where $S_j^i.tt$ denotes section S_j^i's termination time, $T_i.tt$ denotes T_i's termination time, and $S_j^i.ex$ denotes the estimated execution time of section S_j^i.

Thus, the local schedule constructed by a node p is an ordered list of a subset of sections in p's ready queue that can be feasibly completed, and will likely result in high local accrued utility (due to the greedy nature of the PUD heuristic). The set of threads, say T_p, of these sections included in p's schedule is proposed by p as those that are eligible for system-wide execution, from p's standpoint. However, not all threads in T_p may be eligible for system-wide execution, because the current and/or future head nodes of some of those threads may crash. Consequently, the set of threads that are eligible for system-wide execution is that subset of threads with no absent sections from their respective current and/or future head node schedules.

3.2   Algorithm Description

The CUA algorithm that we present is derived from Aguilera *et. al*'s time-optimal, early-deciding, uniform consensus algorithm in [15]. A pseudo-code description of CUA on each node i is shown in Algorithm 1.

The algorithm is invoked at a node i at the scheduling events including 1) creation of a thread at node i and 2) inclusion of a node k into node i's suspect list by i's failure detector.

When invoked, a node i first constructs the local section schedule by invoking ConstructLocalSchedule() (line 3). This procedure accepts i's (unordered) local ready queue of sections σ_r^i and returns a schedule (an ordered list) σ_i. The node then sends this schedule (σ_i, i) to all nodes (line 4). This message contains a header that indicates that consensus will start within $2D$ time units of the sender's message transmission—i.e., one D for the sender's message and one D for the recipients to respond (line 5). Recipients are expected to immediately respond by constructing their local section schedules and sending them to all

---

Algorithm 1. CUA: Code for each node i

```
1: input: σ_r^i; output: σ_i; // σ_r^i: unordered ready queue of node i's
       sections; σ_i: schedule
2: Initialization: Σ_i = ∅; ω_i = ∅; max_i = 0;
3: σ_i = ConstructLocalSchedule(σ_r^i);
4: send(σ_i, i) to all;
5: upon receive (σ_j, j) until 2D do // After time 2D, consensus begins
6:     Σ_i = Σ_i ∪ σ_j;
7:     ω_i = DetermineSystemWideFeasibleThreadSet(Σ_i);
8: upon receive (ω_j, j) do
9:     if j > max_i then max_i = j; ω_i = ω_j;
10: at time (i − 1)d do
11:    if suspect j for any j : 1 ≤ j ≤ i − 1 then
12:        ω_i = DetermineSystemWideFeasibleThreadSet(Σ_i \ σ_j);
13:        send(ω_i, i) to all;
14: at time (j − 1)d + D for every j : 1 ≤ j ≤ n do
15:    if trust j then decide ω_i;
16: UpdateSectionSet(ω_i, σ_r^i);
17: σ_i = ConstructLocalSchedule(σ_r^i);
18: return σ_i;
```

---

nodes. When node i receives a schedule (σ_j, j), it includes that schedule into a schedule set Σ_i (line 6). Thus, after $2D$ time units, all nodes have a schedule set containing all schedules received.

A node i then determines its consensus decision (i.e., system-wide execution-eligible thread set) by calling procedure `DetermineSystemWideFeasible ThreadSet()`. This procedure accepts i's schedule set Σ_i and determines that subset of threads with no absent sections from their respective (current head and/or future head) node schedules in Σ_i. Node i uses a variable ω_i to maintain its consensus decision. Node i now starts the consensus process.

The algorithm divides real-time in consecutive rounds of duration d each, where node i's round (or round i) corresponds to the time interval $[(i-1)d, id)$. At the beginning of round i, node i checks whether it suspects *any* of the nodes with a smaller node ID. If so, it sends (ω_i, i) to all nodes (line 11). Note that for $i = 1$, node i will send $(\sigma_1, 1)$ to all nodes (if i does not crash), since no nodes have an ID lower than 1. Also, note that the messages sent in a round could be received in a higher round since $D > d$.

Each node i maintains a variable max_i that contains the ID of the largest-ID node from which it has received a consensus proposal (max_i is initialized to zero). When a node i receives a proposed execution-eligible thread set (ω_j, j) that is sent from another node j with an ID that is larger than max_i (i.e., $j > max_i$), then i updates its consensus decision to thread set ω_j and max_i to j (line 9).

At times $(j-1)d + D$ for $j = 1, \ldots, n$, node i is guaranteed to have received potential consensus proposals from node j. Thus, at these times, i checks whether

j has crashed; if not, i arrives at its consensus decision on the thread set ω_i (line 15).[4]

Node i then updates its ready queue σ_r^i by removing those sections whose threads are absent in the consensus decision ω_i. The updated ready queue is used to construct a new local schedule σ_i, which is returned by the algorithm. The head section of this schedule is subsequently dispatched for execution.

3.3   Constructing Section Schedules

We now describe the algorithm ConstructLocalSchedule(). To describe this algorithm, we first define a few auxiliary functions. Since this algorithm is not a distributed algorithm per se, we drop the suffix i from notations σ_r^i (input unordered list) and σ_i (output schedule), and refer to them as σ_r and σ, respectively. Similarly, sections are referred to as S_i, for $i = 1, 2, \ldots$, except when reference to their distributable threads is needed.

- sortByPUD(σ) returns a schedule ordered by non-increasing section PUDs. If two or more sections have the same PUD, then the section(s) with the largest execution time estimate will appear before any others with the same PUD.
- Insert(S_i, σ, I) inserts section S_i in the ordered list σ at the position indicated by index I; if entries in σ exists with the index I, S_i is inserted before them. After insertion, S_i's index in σ is I.
- Remove(S_i, σ, I) removes section S_i from ordered list σ at the position indicated by index I; if S_i is not present at the position in σ, the function takes no action.

Algorithm 2. Algorithm ConstructLocalSchedule()

```
1: input: σ_r; output: σ;
2: Initialization: t := t_cur, σ := ∅;
3: for each section S_i ∈ σ_r do
4:     if S^i_{j-1}.tt + D + S^i_j.ex > S^i_j.tt then
       // If j = 1, then S^i_{j-1}.tt = 0
5:         abort(S_i);
       else
6:         S_i.PUD = U_i (t + S_i.ex) /S_i.ex;

7: σ_tmp := sortByPUD(σ_r);
8: for each section S_i ∈ σ_tmp from head to tail do
9:     if S_i.PUD > 0 then
10:        Insert(S_i, σ, S_i.tt);
11:        if ScheduleFeasible(σ)=false then
12:            Remove(S_i, σ, S_i.tt);
13:    else break;
14: return σ;
```

---

[4] If node i receives a proposed execution-eligible thread set (ω_j, j) from another node j at times $(i-1)d$ or $(j-1)d + D$, we assume that the node executes line 8 before it executes line 10 or line 14 (similar to [15]).

Algorithm 2 describes the local section scheduling algorithm. When invoked at time t_{cur}, the algorithm first checks the feasibility of the sections. If the earliest predicted completion time of a section is later than its termination time, it can be aborted (line 4). Otherwise, the algorithm calculates the section's PUD (line 6).

The sections are then sorted by their PUDs. In each step of the *for*-loop from line 8 to 13, the section with the largest PUD is inserted into σ, if it can produce a positive PUD. The schedule σ is maintained in the non-decreasing order of section termination times. Thus, a section S_i is inserted into σ at a position that corresponds to S_i's termination time $(S_i.tt)$ in σ's non-decreasing termination time order.

After inserting a section S_i, the schedule σ is tested for feasibility (line 11; Algorithm 3). If σ becomes infeasible, S_i is removed. After examining all sections, the ordered list σ is returned.

Algorithm 3. Algorithm `ScheduleFeasible()`

1: **input**: σ; **output**: true or false;

2: *Initialization*: $CumExecTime = 0$;

3: **for** *each section* $S_j^i \in \sigma$ **do**

4:      $\quad CumExecTime = CumExecTime + S_{j-1}^i.tt + D + S_j^i.ex;$ // If $j = 1$, then $S_{j-1}^i.tt = 0$

5:      $\quad$ **if** $CumExecTime > S_j^i.tt$ **then return** false;

6: **return** true;

Algorithm 3 determines the feasibility of a schedule σ. A schedule σ is feasible if the predicted completion time of each section S_i in σ, denoted $S_i.ct$, does not exceed S_i's termination time $S_i.tt$ (line 5). $S_i.ct$ is the time at which S_i is released on its node plus the sum of the execution times of all sections that occur before S_i in σ and S_i's execution time $S_i.ex$. Note that except for current thread head nodes, Algorithm 1 is invoked before sections are actually released on future thread head nodes. Thus, we calculate a section S_i's release time as the termination time of S_i's predecessor (i.e., $S_{j-1}^i.tt$) plus the message delay upper bound D, since that is the latest time by which S_i must be released on its node.

Algorithm 2 therefore seeks to include those sections in the schedule that are likely to result in high total utility (due to the greedy nature of the PUD heuristic). Further, since the invariant of schedule feasibility is preserved throughout the examination of sections, the output schedule is always a feasible schedule. Thus, during underloads, schedule σ will always be feasible in line 11 (Algorithm 2), the algorithm will never reject a section, and will produce a schedule which is the same as that produced by EDF (where deadlines are equal to section termination times). Consequently, this schedule will meet all section termination times during underloads.

During overloads, the algorithm will reject one or more sections to construct a feasible schedule. Due to the algorithm's greedy nature, the rejected sections

78   B. Ravindran, J.S. Anderson, and E.D. Jensen

are less likely to contribute a total utility that is larger than that contributed by the accepted sections.

Asymptotic Complexity. The cost of Algorithm 2 is dominated by the *for*-loop (line 8 to 13) which iterates at most k times for a ready queue with k sections. The cost of this loop is dominated by Algorithm 3, which costs $O(k)$ to test the feasibility of a schedule with k sections. Thus, Algorithm 2's asymptotic cost is $O(k^2)$.

4 Algorithm Properties

We first describe CUA's timeliness property under crash-free runs:

Theorem 1. *If all nodes are underloaded and no nodes crash (i.e., $f_{max} = 0$), CUA meets all thread termination times, yielding optimum total utility.*

Proof. From the discussion in Section 3.3, if a node is underloaded, Algorithm 2 will meet all section termination times at the node. Thus, if all nodes are underloaded and $f_{max} = 0$, all section termination times are met. If all sections of a thread meet their termination times, then the thread will meet its termination time by virtue of Equation 1. Theorem follows.

Theorem 2. *CUA achieves (uniform) consensus (i.e., uniform validity, uniform agreement, termination) on the system-wide execution-eligible thread set in the presence of up to f_{max} failures.*

Proof. This is self-evident from the algorithm description and follows from [15].

Theorem 3. *CUA's time complexity is $O(D+fd+nk)$ and message complexity is $O(fn)$.*

Proof. If the maximum number of sections at a node is k, then ConstructLocal Schedule costs $O(k^2)$. Procedure DetermineSystemWideFeasibleThreadSet will cost $O(nk)$ to examine at most n schedules sent by n nodes, with each schedule containing at most k sections. Thus, lines 3-7 of Algorithm 1 has an actual time cost of $2D + \delta_1$, where δ_1 measures the actual cost of $O(k^2) + O(nk)$. These steps will involve n messages, one for each schedule sent by a node in line 4.

Lines 8–15 has an actual time cost of $D + fd$ and will involve $(f + 1)n$ messages [15]. Line 12, executed at most f times adds computational cost $O(fnk)$, and UpdateSectionSet will remove at most k sections in its schedule, costing $O(k)$, and ConstructLocalSchedule costs $O(k^2)$, resulting in a combined actual cost of a constant, say δ_2.

Thus, Algorithm 1 has an actual time cost of $2D + \delta_1 + D + fd + \delta_2$, or $3D+\delta+fd$, and will involve $n+(f+1)n$, or $(f+2)n$ messages. The corresponding asymptotic costs are $O(D + fd + nk)$ and $O(fn)$, respectively (for $n \geq k$ and $f \geq 2$). When $f = f_{max}$, the algorithm thus constructs schedules in at least $3D + \delta + f_{max}d$ time, or $O(D + f_{max}(d + nk))$. When $f_{max} = 0$ (i.e. crash-free), the algorithm constructs schedules in time $3D + \delta$, or $O(D + nk)$.

From Theorems 2 and 3, we obtain the algorithm's early-deciding property:

Theorem 4. *CUA is a time-optimal, early-deciding algorithm that achieves consensus on the system-wide execution-eligible thread set.*

Proof. From Theorem 3, CUA decides in time proportional to f. From Theorem 2, the algorithm achieves consensus on the system-wide execution-eligible thread set. From [15], no early-deciding algorithm (in the continuous-time synchronous model, where processes do not execute in lock-step rounds) has a time bound lower than $D + fd$. Theorem follows.

We now establish CUA's timeliness property in the presence of failures.

Theorem 5. *If $n - f$ nodes (i.e., correct nodes) are underloaded, then CUA meets the termination times of all threads in its (consensus decision of) execution-eligible thread set.*

Proof. From Theorem 4, $n - f$ nodes arrive at the same decision on the system-wide execution-eligible thread set, say $\mathcal{T}$. If these nodes are under-loaded, then CUA meets the termination times of all threads in $\mathcal{T}$, per Theorem 1.

To establish the algorithm's best-effort property (Section 1), we first define the concept of a *Non Best-effort time Interval* (or NBI):

Definition 3. *Consider a distributable thread scheduling algorithm $\mathcal{A}$. Let a thread T_i be created at a node at a time t with the following properties: (a) T_i and all threads in $\mathcal{A}$'s execution-eligible thread set at time t are not feasible (system-wide) at t, but T_i is feasible just by itself; and (b) T_i has the highest PUD among all threads in $\mathcal{A}$'s execution-eligible thread set at time t. Now, $\mathcal{A}$'s NBI, denoted $NBI_\mathcal{A}$, is defined as the duration of time that T_i will have to wait after t, before it is included in $\mathcal{A}$'s execution-eligible thread set. Thus, T_i is assumed to be feasible at $t + NBI_\mathcal{A}$.*

We now describe the NBI of CUA and other distributable thread scheduling UA algorithms including DASA [11], LBESA [10], and AUA [13] under crash-free runs. Note that DASA, LBESA, and AUA are thread scheduling algorithms that belong to the independent node scheduling paradigm (i.e., they make their scheduling decisions using propagated thread scheduling parameters and without collaborating with other nodes). Since we focus on crash-free runs, the presence of a thread integrity protocol that these algorithms use for thread fault-management can be ignored.

Theorem 6. *Under crash-free runs (i.e., $f_{max} = 0$), the worst-case NBI of CUA is $3D + \delta$, DASA's and LBESA's is δ, and that of AUA is $+\infty$.*

Proof. CUA will examine T_i at t, since the arrival of a new thread is a scheduling event. Since T_i has the highest PUD and is feasible system-wide, the algorithm will arrive at a consensus decision on an execution-eligible thread set that includes T_i in time $3D + \delta$ when $f_{max} = 0$, per Theorems 2 and 3.

DASA and LBESA will examine T_i at t (at the node where T_i was created), since a thread arrival is also a scheduling event for them. Further, since T_i has the highest PUD and is feasible, they will include T_i's first section in their feasible (local) schedules at t, yielding a worst-case NBI of δ, the time constant involved for the algorithm to arrive at the local decision. This cost δ will be the same as that of CUA, since DASA's and LBESA's asymptotic computational costs are the same as that of CUA (i.e., $O(k^2)$).

AUA will examine T_i at t, since a thread arrival at any time is also a scheduling event under it. However, AUA is a TUF/UA algorithm in the classical admission control mould (e.g., [21]) and will reject T_i in favor of previously admitted threads, yielding a worst-case NBI of $+\infty$.

5   Conclusions and Future Work

We presented a distributed real-time scheduling algorithm called CUA. The algorithm considers distributable threads with TUF time constraints, arbitrary thread arrival behaviors, thread execution overrun behaviors causing overloads, and arbitrary crash failures. We showed that CUA satisfies thread time constraints in the presence of crash failures, is early-deciding, has an efficient message complexity of $O(fn)$, and is time-optimal with a time lower bound of $O(D + fd + nk)$. In crash-free runs, the algorithm constructs schedules within $O(D + nk)$, and yields optimal total utility if nodes are also not overloaded. We also showed that the algorithm has a tightly bounded non-best-effort time interval, which implies that a high importance thread that may arrive at any time has a very high likelihood for feasible completion.

Our work just scratched the surface of a very rich problem space, and so many directions exist for immediate and long-term study. Example directions include considering asynchronous models (e.g., [22,23]), allowing synchronization dependencies between threads (e.g., due to mutually exclusive sharing of non-processor resources), considering ad hoc network infrastructures (e.g., mobile, wireless networks), and developing non-deterministic (e.g., probabilistic) timing assurances.

References

1. CCRP: Network centric warfare. http://www.dodccrp.org/ncwPages/ncwPage.html
2. Northcutt, J.D.: Mechanisms for Reliable Distributed Real-Time Operating Systems — The Alpha Kernel. Academic Press, London (1987)
3. Ford, B., Lepreau, J.: Evolving Mach 3.0 to a migrating thread model. In: Ford, B., Lepreau, J. (eds.) USENIX Technical Conference, pp. 97–114 (1994)
4. The Open Group: MK7.3a Release Notes. The Open Group Research Institute, Cambridge, Massachusetts (October 1998)
5. OMG: Real-time CORBA 2.0: Dynamic scheduling specification. Technical report, Object Management Group (September 2001)

6. Jensen, E.D., Wellings, A., Clark, R., Wells, D.: The distributed real-time specification for Java: A status report. In: Proceedings of The Embedded Systems Conference (2002)
7. Horn, W.: Some simple scheduling algorithms. Naval Research Logistics Quaterly 21, 177–185 (1974)
8. Jensen, E.D., et al.: A time-driven scheduling model for real-time systems. In: Jensen, E.D. (ed.) IEEE RTSS, pp. 112–122. IEEE Computer Society Press, Los Alamitos (1985)
9. Ravindran, B., Jensen, E.D., Li, P.: On recent advances in time/utility function real-time scheduling and resource management. In: IEEE ISORC, pp. 55–60. IEEE Computer Society Press, Los Alamitos (2005)
10. Locke, C.D.: Best-Effort Decision Making for Real-Time Scheduling. PhD thesis, CMU (1986)
11. Clark, R.K.: Scheduling Dependent Real-Time Activities. PhD thesis, CMU (1990)
12. Kao, B., Garcia-Molina, H.: Deadline assignment in a distributed soft real-time system. IEEE TPDS 8(12), 1268–1274 (1997)
13. Curley, E., Anderson, J.S., Ravindran, B., Jensen, E.D.: Recovering from distributable thread failures with assured timeliness in real-time distributed systems. In: IEEE SRDS, pp. 267–276. IEEE Computer Society Press, Los Alamitos (2006)
14. Goldberg, J., Greenberg, I., et al.: Adaptive fault-resistant systems (chapter 5: Adpative distributed thread integrity). Technical Report csl-95-02, SRI International (January 1995), http://www.csl.sri.com/papers/sri-csl-95-02/
15. Aguilera, M.K., Lann, G.L., Toueg, S.: On the impact of fast failure detectors on real-time fault-tolerant systems. In: Malkhi, D. (ed.) DISC 2002. LNCS, vol. 2508, pp. 354–370. Springer, Heidelberg (2002)
16. Anderson, J., Jensen, E.D.: The distributed real-time specification for Java: Status report. In: JTRES (2006)
17. Maynard, D.P., Shipman, S.E.,;et al.: An example real-time command, control, and battle management application for Alpha. Technical Report Archons Technical Report 88121, CMU CS Dept (December 1988)
18. Chandra, T.D., Toueg, S.: Unreliable failure detectors for reliable distributed systems. J. ACM 43(2), 225–267 (1996)
19. Chen, W., Toueg, S., Aguilera, M.K.: On the quality of service of failure detectors. IEEE Transactions on Computers 51(5), 561–580 (2002)
20. Lynch, N.: Distributed Algorithms. Morgan Kaufmann (1996)
21. Bestavros, A., Nagy, S.: Admission control and overload management for real-time databases. In: Real-Time Database Systems: Issues and Applications, Kluwer Academic Publishers, Dordrecht (1997)
22. Fetzer, C., Schmid, U., Susskraut, M.: On the possibility of consensus in asynchronous systems with finite average response times. In: ICDCS '05: Proceedings of the 25th IEEE International Conference on Distributed Computing Systems (ICDCS'05), pp. 271–280. IEEE Computer Society Press, Washington, DC (2005)
23. Hermant, J.F., Widder, J.: Implementing reliable distributed real-time systems with the theta-model. In: Anderson, J.H., Prencipe, G., Wattenhofer, R. (eds.) OPODIS 2005. LNCS, vol. 3974, pp. 334–350. Springer, Heidelberg (2006)

Probabilistic Optimization and Assessment of Voting Strategies for X-by-Wire Systems

Markus Kucera[1] and Hans Mauser[2]

[1] University of Applied Sciences, Regensburg
markus.kucera@informatik.fh-regensburg.de
[2] Siemens AG, München
hans.mauser@siemens.com

Abstract. Signal voting of redundant sensor values and communication channels is of central importance in today's X-by-wire systems. The required degree of sensor redundancy, the type of redundancy, and finally the voting strategy must be designed to meet the system's dependability requirements. These design decisions depend on an analysis of the probabilities and effects of all underlying fault scenarios. Given a probabilistic fault model and a communication model, the voting step can be formally stated as a maximum-likelihood estimation of the correct input signal. With an example of an X-by-wire system we show how GTEFT can be used to derive the failure probabilities of different fault scenarios for various systems architectures and different voting strategies. Thus the capability of GTEFT to support system development and system assessment is demonstrated.

Keywords: Fault-tolerance, Dependability, Voting, Embedded System, Automotive.

1 Introduction

The driving innovation force in today's cars has become the area of Information Technology. Powerful new vehicle systems like Brake-by-Wire, Steer-by-Wire, or Park-Assistant are not viable without powerful functionality in software and electronics [1]. This increase in functionality comes together with an increase in system complexity.

Complexity is thus one major challenge to face when dealing with future embedded systems.

The increasing ubiquitous use of embedded systems directs many applications into an area where problems regarding human health and life emerge. This leads to the topic of dependability and safety in particular. Safety has become a topic of special importance in the automotive area, where system cost, penetration rates, and short innovation cycles are the driving factors.

Thus, meeting dependability requirements whilst meeting cost targets and development schedule is the second major challenge to face in that area.

R. Obermaisser et al. (Eds.): SEUS 2007, LNCS 4761, pp. 82–92, 2007.
© IFIP International Federation for Information Processing 2007

The idea to support dependability assessment by tools is not new. Many approaches exist to evaluate dependability figures for distributed systems [7-10]. However, two main problems remain when dealing with above mentioned challenges:

(1) countering the state space explosion problem
(2) efficient integration into a product development cycle to allow for professional use

In [3] an approach is presented that synthesizes dynamic fault trees from UML System Models. The author's main motivation to use UML as modelling and specification language was to integrate into their sponsor's development toolchain. In [4] another approach is presented, that aims at efficient integration into the product development cycle. For that purpose Matlab/Simulink is used for system modelling. Both approaches provide semi-automatic fault tree synthesis for reliability assessment. In [6] Grunske and Kaiser present an approach that offers the possibility for automatic fault tree generation by providing a special Transformation Notation between interacting components. The state space explosion problem, however is not countered following above presented approaches.

In [11] a method is presented that relieves the problem of state space explosion by combining formal and informal techniques. Amari et al. [5] propose a method to analyze dynamic fault trees in order to find the best strategy for avoiding or minimizing the state space explosion problem. The problem of efficient integration into the product development cycle, however is not solved following these methods.

In contrast to these approaches, we presented GTEFT in [2]. GTEFT is an approach that solves both of above mentioned challenges. To do so, we combine simulative and analytic techniques. GTEFT makes use of a COTS GUI (Matlab/Simulink) for efficient integration into the product development cycle. For dependability evaluation GTEFT makes use of classical Markov theory. The problem of state space explosion is avoided by means of a dependability module that uses locality traversing. GTEFT not only allows to derive reliability figures for a given system architecture automatically. It also generates and analyses all failure sequences possible in a given system. New system development or system optimisation is thus strongly supported.

Voting strategies are a central part of today's safety related systems. In general, voting strategies, and thus voting decisions, can be classified as exact, or probabilistic. The distinction between probabilistic and exact voting decisions depends on the underlying fault-model. If the fault-model contains complex faults like conspiracy scenarios, then every voting strategy can be corrupted and exact voting decisions become impossible.

For safety-related systems the question whether a voting strategy can guarantee exact decisions for a reasonable fault-model is crucial.

On the other hand, the questions whether probabilistic voting decisions can be applied, and what error-probabilities are acceptable, depend on the system under investigation. In some cases probabilistic voting decisions are acceptable as a last resort to make best-effort decisions in the presence of severe fault scenarios. If the system and consequently the voter output has a safe state, it is advisable to vote ambiguous input signal combinations to the safe-state signal.

In this paper we present a way to derive probabilistic voting strategies with GTEFT. Given a probabilistic fault model and a communication model, the voting step is formally stated as a maximum-likelihood estimation of the correct input signal. This estimation can then be exploited in order to develop a suitable voting strategy.

2 Signal Voting

We show the usefulness of exhaustive fault-state-space enumeration in the context of the generation and analysis of voting strategies. The necessity of voting arises in redundant systems, when input signals are transmitted over several independent communication channels. Ultimately, the redundant communication signals have to be voted into one authoritative signal that drives an actuator.

We state the voting problem as a channel-decoding problem as follows:

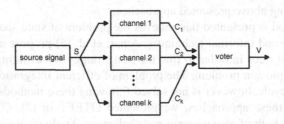

A source signal S is generated by a sensor, by manual input or by an automated control system and has to be transmitted to an actuator which reacts upon the value of the signal. In order to achieve fault-tolerance, the source signal S is split and communicated redundantly over k independent communication channels. The outputs of these channels are denoted $C_1 \ldots C_k$ and are processed by a voter which generates an output V. In the fault-free case all signals S, $C_1 \ldots C_k$ and V agree. We assume that faults can affect the communication channels, such that the voter input signals $C_1 \ldots C_k$ can differ from S. In this case the voter has to make its decision based on faulty input data. The voter decision is correct if the value of the output signal V is identical to S. A voting strategy is a function $V(C_1, \ldots, C_k)$ that maps all possible input signal values to a voted output signal.

We classify the voting decisions for a given input signal combination $C_1, \ldots, C_k$ as follows:

- **exact voting decisions:** The value of the source signal S can be inferred with absolute certainty from the voter input. This means that no fault-combination will cause the voting strategy to make a wrong decision.
- **Probabilistic voting decisions:** The combination of input signals does not allow to infer the correct source signal with absolute certainty. Based on the values of the input signals, however, the correct value of the source signal can be reconstructed with a high probability. The decision involves an error-probability which should be small.

Note that even in the case of probabilistic voting decisions, the voting strategy remains a deterministic function.

The distinction between probabilistic and exact voting decisions depends on the underlying fault-model. If the fault-model contains complex faults like conspiracy scenarios between independent communication channels, then every voting strategy can be corrupted and exact voting decisions become impossible. Conversely, by adding redundant communication channels the voting strategy can be made more robust to communication faults and more combinations of input signals can be voted by an exact voting decision.

In the following we present a general approach that employs exhaustive fault-state-space exploration to automatically generate voting strategies for a given system architecture. For every input-signal combination an optimal voting decision is found. Furthermore, for every voting decision we derive whether the decision is exact or calculate the conditional probability of the voting decision being correct given the correct value of the source signal.

3   System Description

We present a simple system architecture as a case study for constructing and analyzing the voting strategy. The example was chosen to be simple enough for an exhaustive treatment, yet to contain the key elements and features of a real-world system.

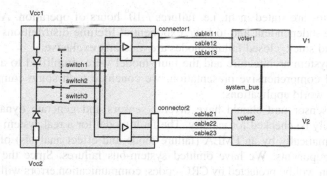

The system has a typical dual-channel architecture as is frequently employed in X-by-wire applications. A switch unit generates the source signal from a mechanical input by an array of three redundant switches. The switches have normally-closed (NC) contacts, the switch unit has redundant power supply. The three redundant signals from the switches are transmitted to two independent actuators, which react upon the signals after a voting decision has been made. The input stages of the voters are assumed to have pull-down resistors so that open input lines are read as logical 0. The independent actuators also communicate over a system bus and transmit their individual input signal over the system bus to each other. Hence, the voter receives 6 input signals: Three input signals S_1, S_2, S_3 directly from the switch unit and three signals R_1, R_2, R_3 relayed from the peer voter.

For the system we consider the following fault model:

fault identifier	fault description	failure-rate [fit]
vcc1_down	voltage supply from channel one insufficient	10
vcc2_down	voltage supply from channel two insufficient	10
switch1_stuck_open	the switch has always disconnected terminals	4
switch1_stuck_closed	the switch has always connected terminals	1
switch2_stuck_open	... same for other switches	4
switch2_stuck_closed		1
switch3_stuck_open		4
switch3_stuck_closed		1
connector1_disconnected	the connector1 disconnects all cables	5
connector2_disconnected	the connector2 disconnects all cables	5
cable11_disconnected	cable11 is open	5
cable12_disconnected	cable12 is open	5
cable13_disconnected	cable13 is open	5
cable21_disconnected	cable21 is open	5
cable22_disconnected	cable22 is open	5
cable23_disconnected	cable23 is open	5

The failure rates are stated in fit, i.e. failures / 10^9 hours of operation. All faults are assumed to be independent and to have exponential lifetime distributions. Obviously stuck_open and stuck_closed failure modes are mutually exclusive.

Since the system architecture and the fault-model were simplified to allow a self-contained and comprehensive presentation, we conclude with some comparative remarks on real-world applications:

Usually a sensor unit should have diverse sensors and generate dynamic signals which can easily be checked for validity. The fault model for a real system must be developed systematically by an FMEA (failure mode and effect analysis) of the system and all its components. We have omitted system-bus failures. Since the system-bus communication will be protected by CRC-codes, communication errors will be detected with a high probability. The voter would then have to process detectably unavailable signals at its input. Though this poses no conceptual problem, it increases the set of possible input combinations. Shorted communication lines were also omitted.

4 Automatic Generation of Voting Strategies

In order to construct a voting strategy, we explore the failure-state-space exhaustively and analyse how the different failure-scenarios affect the communication of the source signal to the voter input. This allows to determine which failure combinations can affect the communication in such a way that a given input signal combination arrives at the voter.

We have presented efficient methods for enumerating the failure states and calculating their corresponding time-dependent probabilities in [2]. The method is based on a depth-first exploration of all possible component-fault-sequences beginning from the global intact state, where all components are intact.

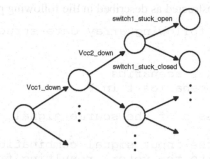

The diagram shows a part of the generated state space. Nodes represent failure states, edges represent component faults and are labelled with the fault identifier. By replacing the edge labels with the associated failure rates, the event graph can be analysed as a Markov-Chain to calculate the state probabilities.

Brute-force attempts at exhaustive state-space exploration suffer from the problem of state-space explosion. It is necessary to define reasonable truncation criteria where the exploration of further fault-events is aborted. The following truncation criteria are useful:

- If we reach a failure state where the continued operation of the system becomes impossible, we can truncate the depth-first search, because the system will have to be repaired immediately and therefore will not encounter further faults before the repair.
- It is reasonable to limit the length of considered fault-sequences. This is possible because long fault-sequences have small probabilities and can therefore be neglected in the sense of a rare-event-approximation. Also to meet a specified safety and integrity level it suffices to consider fault sequences up to a required length.

With these truncation criteria it is possible to analyse a realistic fault model with several hundred single component faults up to a reasonable search depth.

For the example model we have analyzed all fault-sequences of length up to three and calculated their time-dependent probabilities. What we get from this analysis is a set of fault scenarios $F = \{f_1, f_2, \ldots, f_n\}$ and their associated probabilities $P(f_1)$, $P(f_2)$, $\ldots P(f_n)$. Since X-by-wire systems usually have to survive a given mission time without repair, the probabilities $P(f_i)$ are calculated for the time at the end of the mission assuming that all components were intact at the beginning of the mission and that there was no repair during the mission. Reasonable mission times can be inspection periods, maintenance periods or for non-safety-critical systems warranty periods. For the purpose of this study we have chosen a mission time of 2 years of continued operation.

Note that the correct procedures for calculating the probabilities $P(f_i)$ depend on the system under investigation. Alternative methods and assumptions for calculating $P(f_i)$ can be perfectly suited for other systems and do not affect the following procedure for constructing voting strategies.

Given the set of considered fault scenarios F and the associated probabilities $P(f_i)$, the voting strategy is constructed as described in the following pseudo code:

```
Initialize the following array data-structures to zero:
n[s, C₁, …, Cₖ]
p[s, C₁, …, Cₖ]
// traverse fault scenarios
For all fault scenarios f in F
  {
   For all values s of the source signal
     {
      Calculate the input signal combination
      (C₁, …, Cₖ) to the voter, resulting from
      f and s.
      increment n[s, C₁, …, Cₖ] by 1
      increment p[s, C₁, …, Cₖ] by P(f)
     }
  }
// output voting strategy
For every input signal combination (C₁, …, Cₖ)
  {
   if (0 < n[s, C₁, …, Cₖ]
       and for all t != s: 0 == n[t, C₁, …, Cₖ]
      )
     {
      The exact voting decision is s
     }
   else if (for all t != s:
            p[t, C₁, …, Cₖ] < p[s, C₁, …, Cₖ]
           )
     {
      The probabilistic voting decision is s
     }
   else
     {
      No voting decision possible
     }
  }
```

The values of the arrays can be readily interpreted:

- $n[s, C_1, …, C_k]$
  represents the number of considered fault scenarios that cause the input signal combination $C_1, …, C_k$ to appear at the voter input given the condition that s is the correct input signal. This is used to make exact voting decision by ruling out all possible source signal values but one.

- $p[s, C_1, ..., C_k]$
  is the conditional probability that the input signal combination $C_1, ..., C_k$ appears at the voter input given the condition that s is the correct input signal. This is used to make probabilistic voting decisions by maximum likelihood estimation of the true source signal value. This maximum likelihood decision is optimal, if we make no a priori assumptions on the probability of the source signal values.

The above procedure includes the possibility that for a given input combination $C_1, ..., C_k$ to the voter no well-justified voting decision can be made. This can be the case if:

- The input combination $C_1, ..., C_k$ does not arise for any source signal s and any considered fault scenario f.
- The input combination $C_1, ..., C_k$ is equally likely for different values of the source signal. This can occur if the system architecture shows a certain degree of symmetry.

If no voting decision can be made, we recommend to refine the fault model or to set the voter output to a safe state for unresolvable voter inputs.

For the example system model we show the complete voting table. Since the voters are symmetric their voting strategies will be identical up to the naming convention of the input signals. The constructed voting table can easily be coded into software or hardware for a real system implementation.

The analysis has been explicitly carried out for first-fault scenarios, double-fault scenarios and triple-fault scenarios separately.

For the source signal the signal values 0 and 1 have the following interpretation:
0: button released, i.e. switches closed
1: button applied, i.e. switches open

For the communication signals s_i, r_i the values 0 and 1 have the following interpretation:

0: signal from switch unit connected to ground.
1: signal from switch unit connected to Vcc.

The following values are reported in the table:

$n(0)$ corresponding to $n[0, C_1, ..., C_k]$
$n(1)$ corresponding to $n[1, C_1, ..., C_k]$
$p(0)$ corresponding to $p[0, C_1, ..., C_k]$
$p(1)$ corresponding to $p[1, C_1, ..., C_k]$

The column 'exact' marks all exact voting decisions with the label 'exact' and all probabilistic decisions with '-'.

Note in interpreting the $n(0)$, $n(1)$ values that our implementation counts all permutations of a fault sequence individually.

	voter input							single component fault scenarios					double component fault scenarios					triple component fault scenarios				
#	s1	s2	s3	r1	r2	r3	V	n(0)	p(0)	n(1)	p(1)	exact	n(0)	p(0)	n(1)	p(1)	exact	n(0)	p(0)	n(1)	p(1)	exact
0	0	0	0	0	0	0	1	0		13	1,26E-03	exact	4	3,83E-08	169	1,26E-03	-	178	3,84E-08	1975	1,26E-03	exact
1	0	0	0	0	0	1	1	0		0			0		4	3,07E-09	exact	30	2,60E-12	106	3,07E-09	-
2	0	0	0	0	1	0	1	0		0			0		4	3,07E-09	exact	30	2,60E-12	106	3,07E-09	-
3	0	0	0	0	1	1	0	0		0			4	1,38E-08	0		exact	106	1,38E-08	6	2,68E-14	-
4	0	0	0	1	0	0	1	0		0			0		4	3,07E-09	exact	30	2,60E-12	106	3,07E-09	-
5	0	0	0	1	0	1	0	0		0			4	1,38E-08	0		exact	106	1,38E-08	6	2,68E-14	-
6	0	0	0	1	1	0	0	0		0			4	1,38E-08	0		exact	106	1,38E-08	6	2,68E-14	-
7	0	0	0	1	1	1	0	1	8,75E-05	0		exact	17	8,75E-05	0		exact	185	8,75E-05	0		exact
8	0	0	1	0	0	0	1	0		0			0		4	3,07E-09	exact	30	2,60E-12	106	3,07E-09	-
9	0	0	1	0	0	1	1	0		1	1,75E-05	exact	2	4,91E-09	17	1,75E-05	-	56	4,91E-09	179	1,75E-05	-
10	0	0	1	0	1	0	1	0		0			0		0			6	5,37E-13	0		exact
11	0	0	1	0	1	1	0	0		0			2	6,13E-09	0		exact	44	6,14E-09	6	2,68E-14	-
12	0	0	1	1	0	0	0	0		0			0		0			6	5,37E-13	0		exact
13	0	0	1	1	0	1	0	0		0			2	6,13E-09	0		exact	44	6,14E-09	6	2,68E-14	-
14	0	0	1	1	1	0	0	0		0			0		0			6	6,71E-13	0		exact
15	0	0	1	1	1	1	0	0		0			2	7,66E-09	0		exact	32	7,67E-09	0		exact
16	0	1	0	0	0	0	1	0		0			0		4	3,07E-09	exact	30	2,60E-12	106	3,07E-09	-
17	0	1	0	0	0	1	0	0		0			0		0			6	5,37E-13	0		exact
18	0	1	0	0	1	0	1	0		1	1,75E-05	exact	2	4,91E-09	17	1,75E-05	-	56	4,91E-09	179	1,75E-05	-
19	0	1	0	0	1	1	0	0		0			2	6,13E-09	0		exact	44	6,14E-09	6	2,68E-14	-
20	0	1	0	1	0	0	0	0		0			0		0			6	5,37E-13	0		exact
21	0	1	0	1	0	1	0	0		0			0		0			6	6,71E-13	0		exact
22	0	1	0	1	1	0	0	0		0			2	6,13E-09	0		exact	44	6,14E-09	6	2,68E-14	-
23	0	1	0	1	1	1	0	0		0			2	7,66E-09	0		exact	32	7,67E-09	0		exact
24	0	1	1	0	0	0	0	0		0			4	1,38E-08	0		exact	106	1,38E-08	6	2,68E-14	-
25	0	1	1	0	0	1	0	0		0			2	6,13E-09	0		exact	44	6,14E-09	6	2,68E-14	-
26	0	1	1	0	1	0	0	0		0			2	6,13E-09	0		exact	44	6,14E-09	6	2,68E-14	-
27	0	1	1	0	1	1	0	1	7,00E-05	0		exact	15	7,00E-05	2	3,07E-10	-	129	7,00E-05	32	3,07E-10	-
28	0	1	1	1	0	0	0	0		0			0		0			6	6,71E-13	0		exact
29	0	1	1	1	0	1	0	0		0			2	7,66E-09	0		exact	32	7,67E-09	0		exact
30	0	1	1	1	1	0	0	0		0			2	7,66E-09	0		exact	32	7,67E-09	0		exact
31	0	1	1	1	1	1	0	1	8,75E-05	0		exact	11	8,75E-05	0		exact	65	8,75E-05	0		exact
32	1	0	0	0	0	0	1	0		0			0		4	3,07E-09	exact	30	2,60E-12	106	3,07E-09	-
33	1	0	0	0	0	1	0	0		0			0		0			6	5,37E-13	0		exact
34	1	0	0	0	1	0	0	0		0			0		0			6	5,37E-13	0		exact
35	1	0	0	0	1	1	0	0		0			0		0			6	6,71E-13	0		exact
36	1	0	0	1	0	0	1	0		1	1,75E-05	exact	2	4,91E-09	17	1,75E-05	-	56	4,91E-09	179	1,75E-05	-
37	1	0	0	1	0	1	0	0		0			2	6,13E-09	0		exact	44	6,14E-09	6	2,68E-14	-
38	1	0	0	1	1	0	0	0		0			2	6,13E-09	0		exact	44	6,14E-09	6	2,68E-14	-
39	1	0	0	1	1	1	0	0		0			2	7,66E-09	0		exact	32	7,67E-09	0		exact
40	1	0	1	0	0	0	0	0		0			4	1,38E-08	0		exact	106	1,38E-08	6	2,68E-14	-
41	1	0	1	0	0	1	0	0		0			2	6,13E-09	0		exact	44	6,14E-09	6	2,68E-14	-
42	1	0	1	0	1	0	0	0		0			0		0			6	6,71E-13	0		exact
43	1	0	1	0	1	1	0	0		0			2	7,66E-09	0		exact	32	7,67E-09	0		exact
44	1	0	1	1	0	0	0	0		0			2	6,13E-09	0		exact	44	6,14E-09	6	2,68E-14	-
45	1	0	1	1	0	1	0	1	7,00E-05	0		exact	15	7,00E-05	2	3,07E-10	-	129	7,00E-05	32	3,07E-10	-
46	1	0	1	1	1	0	0	0		0			2	7,66E-09	0		exact	32	7,67E-09	0		exact
47	1	0	1	1	1	1	0	1	8,75E-05	0		exact	11	8,75E-05	0		exact	65	8,75E-05	0		exact
48	1	1	0	0	0	0	0	0		0			4	1,38E-08	0		exact	106	1,38E-08	6	2,68E-14	-
49	1	1	0	0	0	1	0	0		0			0		0			6	6,71E-13	0		exact
50	1	1	0	0	1	0	0	0		0			2	6,13E-09	0		exact	44	6,14E-09	6	2,68E-14	-
51	1	1	0	0	1	1	0	0		0			2	7,66E-09	0		exact	32	7,67E-09	0		exact
52	1	1	0	1	0	0	0	0		0			2	6,13E-09	0		exact	44	6,14E-09	6	2,68E-14	-
53	1	1	0	1	0	1	0	0		0			2	7,66E-09	0		exact	32	7,67E-09	0		exact
54	1	1	0	1	1	0	0	1	7,00E-05	0		exact	15	7,00E-05	2	3,07E-10	-	129	7,00E-05	32	3,07E-10	-
55	1	1	0	1	1	1	0	1	8,75E-05	0		exact	11	8,75E-05	0		exact	65	8,75E-05	0		exact
56	1	1	1	0	0	0	0	1	8,75E-05	0		exact	17	8,75E-05	0		exact	185	8,75E-05	0		exact
57	1	1	1	0	0	1	0	0		0			2	7,66E-09	0		exact	32	7,67E-09	0		exact
58	1	1	1	0	1	0	0	0		0			2	7,66E-09	0		exact	32	7,67E-09	0		exact
59	1	1	1	0	1	1	0	1	8,75E-05	0		exact	11	8,75E-05	0		exact	65	8,75E-05	0		exact
60	1	1	1	1	0	0	0	0		0			2	7,66E-09	0		exact	32	7,67E-09	0		exact
61	1	1	1	1	0	1	0	1	8,75E-05	0		exact	11	8,75E-05	0		exact	65	8,75E-05	0		exact
62	1	1	1	1	1	0	0	1	8,75E-05	0		exact	11	8,75E-05	0		exact	65	8,75E-05	0		exact
63	1	1	1	1	1	1	0	5	4,02E-04	0		exact	23	4,02E-04	0		exact	65	4,02E-04	6	5,37E-15	-

5 Analysis of the Voting Strategy

The derived voting strategy can make exact voting decisions for all single component fault scenarios. This means that no single fault from our fault-model can defeat the voting strategy.

In the columns for double component fault scenarios we find some input signal combinations were the voting strategy cannot make exact decisions. This could be expected, since the degree of redundancy of our system is two with respect to power supply and connectors and the degree of redundancy is three with respect to switches.

By probabilistic voting the voter can, however, make a best-effort decision for all input signal combinations.

Note that the voting strategy makes exact decision, where a simple majority voter would have failed: In line number 24 the majority of four input signals has value 0 indicating that the button of the switch unit is applied. The exact voting result, however, is 0, indicating a released button.

The columns for the triple component fault scenarios show that the voter can still make exact decisions for half the input signal combinations.

The error probability of the derived voting strategy can be analyzed by summing up the probability of all states were the voter makes wrong decisions for either value of the source signal. For the example model the time-dependent error probabilities are plotted in the following diagram. The voter output shows a bias towards the applied switch position (voter output v = 1). Obviously there are more fault combination which simulate an applied switch than a released switch. An inspection of the critical fault sequences shows that identical stuck-at faults at two switches defeat the voting strategy. In addition, the voter_stuck_at_1 error can also be caused by double faults in the power supply (Vcc1_down, Vcc2_down) or in the two connectors (connector1_disconnected, connector2_disconnected).

Replacing the normally-closed switches by normally-open switches would allow to shape the error probabilities.

Since the error-probabilities approach 0 for short mission times, the total failure rate of the system can be kept acceptably low by enforcing short inspection and maintenance intervals to detect and remove first component faults.

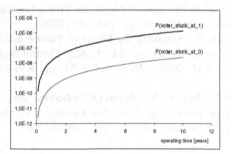

6 Conclusion

This paper presented a practical approach to develop and assess voting strategies that make use of probabilistic voting decisions. For safety-related systems the question whether a voting strategy can guarantee exact decisions for a reasonable fault-model is crucial. In systems where probabilistic voting decisions are acceptable such decisions could be used, e.g. as a last resort to make best-effort decisions in the presence of severe fault scenarios.

References

[1] Kucera, M.: Drive-By-Wire Applications for future vehicles (in German). 20. Tagung Elektronik im Kraftfahrzeug, Haus der Technik, Essen (Juni 2000)

[2] Kucera, M., Mauser, H.: Semi-Automatic Reliability Assessment of Safety Related Embedded Systems. In: Proceedings of the 18th IASTED International Conference on Parallel and Distributed Computing and Systems, 13-15 November 2006, pp. 495–502 (2006)

[3] Pai, G.J., Dugan, J.B: Automatic synthesis of dynamic fault trees from UML system models. In: Proceedings of the 13th International Symposium on Software Reliability Engineering, ISSRE 2002, 12-15 November 2002, pp. 243–254 (2002)

[4] Papadopoulos, Y., Grante, C.: Techniques and tools for automated safety analysis & decision support for redundancy allocation automotive systems. In: Proceedings of the 27th Annual International Computer Software and Applications Conference, COMPSAC 2003, 3-6 November 2003, pp. 105–110 (2003)

[5] Amari, S., Dill, G., Howald, E.: A new approach to solve dynamic fault trees. In: Proceedings of the annual Reliability and Maintainability Symposium, 27-30 January 2003, pp. 374–379 (2003)

[6] Grunske, L., Kaiser, B.: Automatic generation of analyzable failure propagation models from component-level failure annotations. In: Fifth International Conference on Quality Software (QSIC 2005), 19-20 September 2005, pp. 117–123 (2005)

[7] Johnson, A., Malek, M.: Survey of Software Tools for Evaluating Reliability, Availability, and Serviceability. ACM Computing Surveys 20(4) (December 1988)

[8] Sheldon, Greiner, Benzinger: Specification, Safety and Reliability Analysis Using Stochastic Petri Net Models. In: Proceedings of the 10th International Workshop on Software Specification and Design (IWSSD'00), p. 123 (2000)

[9] Feng, Z., Dearden, R., Meuleau, N., Washington, R.: Dynamic Programming for Structured Continuous Markov Decision Problems. In: Proceedings of the 20th Conference on Uncertainty in Artificial Intelligence, pp. 154–161 (2004)

[10] Sheldon, F.T., Jerath, K.: Assessing the Effect of Failure Severity, Coincident Failures and Usage-Profiles on the Reliability of Embedded Control Systems. In: Handschuh, H., Hasan, M.A. (eds.) SAC 2004. LNCS, vol. 3357, pp. 826–833. Springer, Heidelberg (2004)

[11] Karlsson, D., Eles, P., Peng, Z.: Validation Of Embedded Systems Using Formal Method Aided Simulation. In: Proceedings of the 8th Euromicro Conference on Digital System Design, 30 August-3 September 2005, pp. 196–199 (2005)

Application of Safety Analyses in Model Driven Development

Javier Fernández Briones, Miguel Ángel de Miguel, J.P. Silva, and Alejandro Alonso

Department of Telematics Engineering, Technical University of Madrid (UPM),
Ciudad Universitaria s/n, 28040 Madrid, Spain.
jfbriones@dit.upm.es

Abstract. Some high integrity software systems require the rigorous validation of safety properties. Assessing whether software architectures are able to meet these requirements is of great interest: to avoid the risk that the implementation does not fulfill requirements due to a bad design, and, to reduce the development cost of safety critical parts of the system. Safety analyses like FMECA and FTA are two methods used during preliminary safety assessments. We have implemented tools to automatically generate safety analyses from the models of the architecture: a UML profile for safety, modeling languages to express safety analyses, and a model transformation chain. Safety analysts can use these tools to annotate the models, analyze the architecture, and recommend system engineers mitigation means to apply for improving the architecture.

1 Introduction

Even though software already inundates many industries and human activities, there is still interest in constructing, using complex software, more pervasive systems with safety requirements. Some features have been requested to the development of such systems, to highlight: a better reuse, new solutions for managing complexity, and enhanced ways for undertaking safety concerns in complex software systems.

Component-based development and model-driven architecture (MDA) are two relatively new methods for software development which tackle the problem of reusability and complexity. With the former, software architectures are assembled with components potentially from a variety of sources, written in different programming languages and running on several platforms. The latter takes software models as leitmotiv in a development process based on continuous model transformations; converting representations of the structure and functionality of an application into implementation models dependent of a specific platform.

Software analysis aims to provide information about the behavior of the software during all phases of the development, whilst formal methods are of more application during the implementation phase. Software safety analyses are an important requisite in the stage of certification, but also, its use at the early phases of the development claims to be a means for reducing costs, keeping the system assessed as safe. FMECA (Failure Mode Effects and Criticality Analysis [8], [10]) and FTA (Fault Tree Analysis [9], [10]) are two ways to analyze the safety and reliability of a system.

R. Obermaisser et al. (Eds.): SEUS 2007, LNCS 4761, pp. 93–104, 2007.

Safety analysis models are classically created within a safety tool or just using an office suite application, but they clearly depend on system elements which are usually expressed in a development modeling language. The isolation of both approaches, analysis and design, creates inconsistencies and duplicates efforts. We convincingly consider that some safety analyses are subject of automation.

- Those that extensively use information stored in a uniform way by requiring that safety characteristics are produced using a modeling language.
- Those where we learn from the results of the analysis (an organized table, a graph, or some meaningful ciphers) more than from the process.

We are carrying out our work ([4], [5], [6], [7]) in the context of air navigation systems (ANS) where a component and model-driven based development is suitable and where safety needs are significant. Eurocontrol works to create regulatory requirements (ESARR) and guidelines to improve the safety of air navigation. One of these guidelines is the EATMP Safety Assessment Methodology (SAM [2]) which does not address certification issues but prepares and supports a certification process as intends to be a means of compliance to ESARR 4. In a cyclic and evolutionary process like the one proposed by SAM, automation could be of great importance given that the same safety analyses have to be reworked several times.

The purpose of our work is to aid safety and software engineers to find the quality software architecture that best meets cost and safety concerns taking into consideration the trade-off between them. We propose that safety and software teams work with the same models, the ones of the model-driven approach, but now including safety characteristics. Working with the same models improves the communication between them by having the same vocabulary but also avoids the need to keep model consistency. Safety engineers can see one or more "safety views" of the architecture necessary for their analyses, while software engineers can work with the same models they were using, but with the recommendations of the safety engineers. Automatic safety analyses allow for the evaluation of the architecture at zero-cost so that the safety team can propose means to eliminate or prevent hazards at any time. Both teams will choose the architecture and the combination of mitigation means that best fulfill safety constraints with the minimum cost. Due to the use of software models as the starting point for the integration we get the extra benefit that the relationship between models and code could be established.

This paper introduces the tools we developed to support safety analyses of architectures. Further clarifications about safety are detailed in [7]. Section 2 gives an overview about the use of safety analyses during the specification of the architecture in a MDA. Section 3 describes how to create analyzable architectures by annotating development models. Section 4 illustrates the languages for modeling FMECA and FTA. The model transformation to create safety analysis models from annotations is presented in section 5, whilst section 6 briefly shows the current implementation.

2 Application of Safety Analyses in Model-Driven Development

Safety engineers can support software engineers in the election of an architecture that fulfils safety requirements with the minimum cost; and they can do it all along the process of architecture specification. Performing safety analyses from the beginning of the architecture specification has the following goals:

- Assess the safety of a system architecture form the beginning,
- Reduce the development cost of safety critical parts of the system.

Consequently, safety analyses proposed here do not have the (sometimes only) objective traditional safety analyses have of demonstrating the assurance of a system to a certification authority, even though they can prepare and support a certification process. Safety analyses in this paper must be considered in the bounds of preliminary safety assessments. This sort of assessments cope with the risk that system implementations do not fulfill safety requirements because of a bad design, but they can also be used to deal with the trade-off always found between safety and cost by supporting the identification of the architecture which achieves the best balance.

The process starts after system engineers have modeled a prototype of the architecture. Safety engineers can annotate this prototype with safety goals of the system (safety objectives), restrictions the system has to fulfill (safety requirements), ways some parts of the system can fail (failure modes), etc. They have to make the annotations in a formal manner to allow a later export of data. Automatic generation of safety analyses from the models of the architecture is the key of the process to avoid building the safety analyses each time he wants to assess the last version of the architecture. Safety analyses have to be presented in a way familiar to safety engineers given that they can be used in documents for safety certification. Both, system and safety engineers, can communicate using the same "documents", the models of the architecture, to propose improvements if the architecture does not fit the requirements in terms of cost and safety. It is convenient that results of the analyses are incorporated back into the architecture as, again, formal annotations. This process can be automatic as well, but for the moment has not been implemented. The whole process is a cyclic procedure that ends when the architecture is evaluated as able to meet all the requirements (functional, non-functional, cost and safety).

2.1 Using MDA in the Process

Automatic generation of safety analyses from UML models requires the integration of at least two tools: a modeling tool (where the architecture is expressed) and another tool used to perform safety analyses. For many reasons, the best way to perform the integration is with the support of MDA standards, processes, and guidelines. Fig. 1 shows Meta Object Facility (MOF [12]) modeling stacks which represent the integration.

The architecture (Air Traffic Management models) is defined based on the UML meta-model and a safety profile. On the other hand, the safety analysis models (Fault Tree Analysis and Failure Modes, Effects, and Criticality Analysis) are based on a safety analysis meta-model. Both meta-models can be expressed in MOF. Since we are working with a component-based architecture, the instances of the system are components in execution. In contrast, instances of safety analysis models are failures of the system, if they unfortunately happen. A key transformation is necessary to convert safety-annotated system models into safety analysis models. These two types of models represent completely different concepts, hence its difficulty and

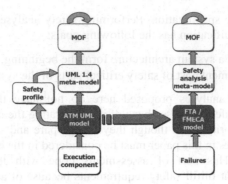

Fig. 1. MDA Rationale

importance. Other transformations are required to adapt integration models to models usable within the tools (modeling and safety).

3   Creation of Safe-Aware Architectures

The set of annotations we introduce in this section assumes: software architectures based on components, models of the architecture that include the capabilities supported in the system, each capability is supported by a set of logical components, and each logical component is supported by a set of physical components. Furthermore, we assume the existence of modeling facilities to support traceability among previous elements.

To model safety concepts we have preferred to integrate safety properties in the general description of software architecture rather than to create specific views or models for the safety analyses. This enables us to readily relate software models and safety properties. To support this approach we have reused standard profiles ([4], [11]) and we have created a UML profile that directly represents safety concepts.

3.1   Safety Concepts

Safety concepts identified so far are pretty tailored to our aim of applying safety analyses in a preliminary safety assessment like the one proposed by Eurocontrol. The following are the main concepts we need for creating such safety analyses. Future work will provide more general concepts to be able to apply other safety analyses to software architectures, and thus serves as more general assistance.

- A **safety objective** is resulted from hazard analyses and defines a safety goal. When the goal is broken a hazard occurs, the effects of which reveal a severity. Indicators used to discern the severity of the effects are: exposure (exposure time, and number of aircraft exposed), recovery (annunciation, detection, contingency measures, and diagnosis), rate development of the hazardous condition, etc.
- A **safe-aware capability** is a software capability with safety objectives associated or that can affect some of them indirectly.
- **Safe-aware component**s represent logical and physical components that support safe-aware capabilities. A safe-aware component has a software assurance level

(SWAL) used to establish the level of confidence that its implementation needs to accomplish. A good level of confidence means a disciplined process that limit the likelihood of development faults that could impact safety.

- A **safety dependency** is a safety-related relationship of cause-effect between two model elements. They can be used to assert, as proposed in [7], that a safe-aware component affects the safety of another safe safe-aware component, that a safe-aware component affects the safety of a safe-aware capability or that a safe-aware capability affects the safety of another safe-aware capability.
- **Mitigation means definition.** Mitigation means allows avoidance, detection, propagation control or mitigation of failure effects. The definition of a mitigation mean characterizes it independently of its application, according to: the phase where it has to be applied (topic), the type of mitigation (failure control), and the level where it has to be applied (application level).
- **Mitigation means application.** The application of mitigation means on safe-aware components provides a way to reduce the risk considering component's failure modes and the particular mitigation mean applied. The combination of a specific set of mitigation mean in a component produces a specific risk reduction.

4   Safety Analysis Meta-models

Two modeling languages have been defined so far: a FMECA and a FTA meta-model. Models created based on them are agnostic to any specific implementation of these types of analyses in a safety tool.

4.1   FMECA

Failure Modes, Effects, and Criticality Analysis is an inductive approach to system design and reliability. It identifies each potential failure within a system or manufacturing process and uses severity classifications to show potential hazards associated with theses failures. There are 3 main elements in a FMECA analysis:

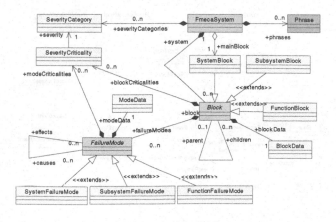

Fig. 2. FMECA safety analysis meta-model

- FmecaSystem. FMECA is constructed as a hierarchy of blocks. FMECA system holds all the properties global to the analysis and the main block of the system.
- A Block represents every component in the hierarchy. Blocks are specialized as SystemBlock, SubsystemBlock, and FunctionBlock. This specialization is done because the same parameters in different blocks can have different meaning; i.e. a severity in a block can be input or result of the analysis.
- FailureMode. Each block can have associated several failure modes. These failure modes can be primary or derived from a cause-effect relationship. Primary failure modes are represented with the class FunctionFailureMode, while derived ones are usually represented with SubsystemFailureMode. End-effects are the last step in the process of derivation of failure modes and they are represented with the class SystemFailureMode.

4.2 FTA

Fault Tree Analysis is used during the safety assessments to represent the logical interaction and the probabilities of occurrence of component failures in a system. It provides quantitative information (probability theory is used), and qualitative (in the way of minimal cut sets: combinations of events leading to failure of the system). We can recognize 3 main classes in the diagram: FtaSystem, Gate, and Event.

- FtaSystem. A FTA system holds all the properties global to the system. The first thing to be done when starting a fault tree analysis is to define the hazard to be analyzed, which is represented as the TopEvent.
- Gate. A gate is a logical function of some inputs. Typical logical functions are AND, OR and VOTE. The output of a gate is a derived event of its inputs: either PrimaryEvents or the output of other gates (DerivedEvent).
- Event. Main events in a fault tree analysis are the PrimaryEvents. Primary events have associated a failure model. The most typical failure model is RateFailureModel created from a constant failure and repair rate.

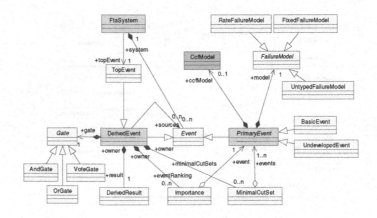

Fig. 3. FTA safety analysis meta-model

5 Safety Analyses

There is no single way to perform a safety analysis from safety characteristics identified such as hazards, failure modes, mitigation means, etc. Even two safety analysts can perform FMECA or FTA in different ways according to their purposes, contrasting with other fields like in real time system where the purpose is clear: "make the system schedulable". Our purposes for safety analyses, framed in a general process of a preliminary safety assessment, are: to evaluate how an architecture can cause some hazards to occur, to estimate whether the architecture can fulfill the safety objectives of the system, to allocate SWALs to software components to accomplish these objectives, and to discover mitigation means for preventing hazards to occur.

For the creation of safety analyses models from safety annotations in UML we convert (Fig. 1) development models into safety analysis models. We designed this transformation using a set of rules. Next subsections will describe succinctly how it converts UML entities (system elements and safety annotations) into safety analysis meta-models entities (for instance blocks and failure modes for FMECA and events and gates for FTA).

5.1 FMECA Models Creation

Safe-aware capabilities and safe-aware components from system models shape the structure of a FMECA model by constituting the FMECA blocks. A function block can only represent a bottom-level safe-aware component (that one which does not depend on any other). A top-level safe aware capability (that one with at least one safety objective associated directly) is represented by a top-level sub-system block. The only way to include a mitigation mean in a FMECA model is in unison with the safe-aware component it is affecting. A safety objective is an invariant that the system must fulfill, so that when it is not fulfilled we identify a failure mode of the system (the system block). In a preliminary safety assessment failure modes of safe-aware components are hard to identify, and we use some common keywords like corruption, loss, and error; even though other schemes are valid. In FMECA, a dependency among blocks is a parent-child relationship whilst a dependency among failure modes is a cause-effect relationship (limited from a child to its parent). In system models, safe-aware elements are interrelated by means of safety dependencies which we use to create the hierarchy of the analysis model. This makes necessary to replicate FMECA model elements in some cases; for instance, when a safe-aware component affects two safe-aware capabilities we create two blocks for the safe-aware component.

5.2 FTA Models Creation

FTA models should start by defining a hazard. As we said for FMECA, the non-fulfillment of a safety objective constitutes a hazard. Consequently, it seems obvious that a different FTA model has to be created for each safety objective in the system, so we will end up with several FTA models for only one system. In FTA it can be reasonable to create a FTA model from a lower-level hazard although this is not supported by our FTA model generation. Primary events will represent the failure of a bottom-level safe-aware component. The other important element in FTA, gates, will represent the failure of a higher level safe-aware component or capability. Since there is not more information included in safety dependencies we must suppose the worst case and use the OR gate; a gate will produce true if one of the components supporting it fails. Mitigation means impede failure propagation in a degree according to the risk reduction, so that they are represented as AND gate. Only those failure modes, declared in the mitigation mean definition, will be mitigated.

5.3 Example

We will study a simple but comprehensive example with only one capability, "Consult SFPL (System Flight Plan)", by which an ATC controller request information about a flight plan. This capability needs to fulfill a safety objective, "SO_1: The probability of detected and undetected corruption for greater than 5 minutes shall be no greater than 10-5 per hour". The capability is hypothetically supported by a single component, "FDM (Flight Data Management)". In order to achieve the safety goal the safety engineers have allocated a mitigation mean to this component "MM_1: Processing servers are replicated on different nodes". Fig. 4 illustrates how, with the help of the safety profile, the constraint SO_1 is linked to the capability Consult SFPL expressed as a use case. We represent the component as a package annotated with the stereotype SafeAwareComponent. A constraint with stereotype MMApplied indicates the application of MM_1.

The model transformation currently automates our particular proposal for the construction of FMECA and FTA. Previous annotations constitute the input of the transformation, whilst Fig. 4 shows the output for a FTA after been imported into a safety (and graphical) tool. This analysis will assess the safety objective SO_1 which is transformed into a TopEvent. "Consult SFPL" and "FDM" are mapped into DerivedEvent resulted from OR gates, whereas "Error" and "Loss" failure modes of

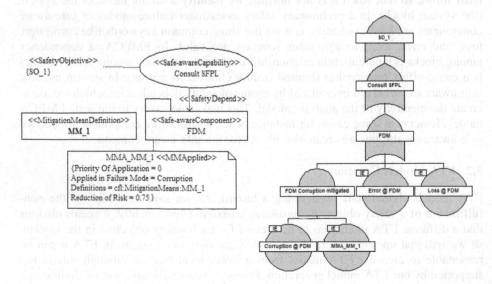

Fig. 4. Development model and annotations on the left. FTA in the safety tool on the right.

FDM into BasicEvents. Since the failure mode "Corruption" has been mitigated, an AND gate is used to create a reduction of the failure mode's probability. This means that the corruption of FDM will only show up at system level when both the failure mode occurs and the mitigation mean does not impede its propagation.

This is a simple example with a few elements and thus one could easily create manually the FTA within the safety tool. The potential of the automatic generation of safety analyses becomes apparent when the system model grows or/and when there is real benefit to maintain consistency between system models and safety analyses. During validation we tested the analyses generation with a large safety model: 21 safe-aware capabilities, 19 safe-aware components, 5 mitigation mean definitions and 9 mitigation mean applications were found in a system model much larger. The inherent evolutionary property of PSSA make of this environment an ideal test.

5.4 Results

The last step of the process would be the assessment of the analyses by the safety staff within the safety tool. This tool will provide tables (FMECA), trees (FMECA) and diagrams (FTA) depicting the models. Safety analysts can now inspect them to see how the elements of the architecture related with safety work together. FMECA can indicate the severity of function failure modes by setting the severity of system failure modes. FTA can provide us the list of minimal cut sets, i.e. the combinations of bottom-level failures leading to a hazard when happening together; we should specially address combinations with only one element.

One of our final aspirations with the safety analyses is to allocate SWAL to safe aware components. Reducing the SWAL of a component means reducing the cost of its development. Naturally it cannot be done arbitrarily and justification material has to be provided, such as safety analyses and mitigation means. Allocating a SWAL to a component does not imply calculating a failure rate for software; hence SWALs cannot be used by safety assessment process as can hardware failure rates. In case of hardware, we could map components' SWAL to failure rates in safety analysis models, and thus the safety tool could provide quantity results.

The methodology provided by Eurocontrol ([2], succinctly explained in [7]) strictly forbids allocating a failure rate to the software and we have to assume that software fails. Allocation of SWALs is accomplished by looking at the overall system design in its operational environment. Therefore, it is considered as key to keep the link from the safe-aware component to the end effect and its maximum tolerable frequency of occurrence. Development models provide the link between a safe-aware component and the hazard but not to the end effect, it can be easily obtained from other documents though. We have worked on the safety analysis creation to provide quantity results by automating some hand-made processes ([7]). Quantity values can be used to derive SWALs.

6 Current Implementation Scenario

As previously mentioned, two tools had to be integrated (see Fig. 5): a UML modeling tool and a safety tool. Current implementation uses Eclipse Modeling

Framework (EMF [3]) as common framework: to create meta-models, instance repositories, and to implement transformations. We use a UML modeling tool (it could be either a UML 1.X tool or a UML 2.0 tool) to create ATM models, to define and deploy profiles, and to export models to EMF. Finally, we also use FMECA and FTA modules of a safety tool to perform analysis calculations, create reports, etc.

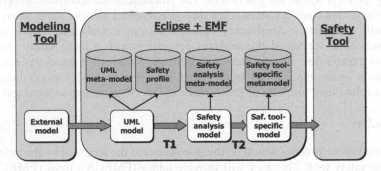

Fig. 5. Implementation Scenario

7 Related Work

Other approaches exist for integrating safety engineering into the software development cycle. Most of them agree to highlight the benefits of applying safety techniques early in the development cycle and the drawbacks of its appliance at code level in large scale systems. Some of the approaches are based on development models. [14] explores the features, within UML, applicable to the development of a safety case for a product under development. After comparing formal methods and a rigorous process, the paper pragmatically decides not to introduce truly formal methods in the development cycle because of the additional complexity without tangible benefit. However we demonstrate how to get some benefits in preliminary safety assessments without affecting complexity.

Precisely modeling safety semantics is required to later analyze safety. The UML profile for quality of service and fault tolerance [11] includes some notations for the description of risk assessment, but it limits the scope to safety mitigation means and fault tolerance. There are also similarities between our work and the UML profile from SAE Architecture Analysis & Design Language (AADL) [13]. AADL is a language used to design and analyze the software and hardware architecture of real-time systems and their performance-critical characteristics. The UML profile for AADL expresses AADL concepts in UML, whilst we directly express safety concepts in UML. AADL integrates reliability and safety analysis methods, by equipping components with reliability models, which are Markov chains that relate fault events and error states. Jürjens [17] include safety requirements in the UML models for a later analysis of requirement satisfaction. Some other work in York University [18] present very useful concepts for expressing safety constraints using OCL.

Few (if any) safety standards utilize visual modeling techniques provided by UML, so formal methods and safety analyses are necessary to fulfill standards. Pai and Dugan propose UML extensions for the description of software redundancy, reliability dependencies, and reconfigurations; they also tackle the transformation of UML models into Fault-Tree Analysis (FTA) models [16]. These notations are useful for the analysis of systems that mitigate risk with redundancy methods but they do not consider other mitigation means. The extensions are used to annotate deployment modeling elements and not architectural modeling elements such as components. Other works use UML activity, sequence and state diagram to generate FTA [19].

8 Summary and Discussion

We think safety and software engineers can work together to complete the specification of the software architecture with the tools presented in this paper. Automatic safety analyses are fundamental to succeed since the architecture evolves during this stage and safety analyses need to be reworked for each evolution, nevertheless some potential issues may arise as a consequence of the way humans interact with automation. For instance, safety analysts need to learn how to formalize safety parameters in the architecture with the UML profile.

We consider that separation of safety and safety analysis modeling is a must. Some safety analyses can be considered as different arrangements of elements from a well-known safety vocabulary (hazard, fault, failure, failure propagation, etc.). Safety analysis meta-models enable to model safety analyses. Our UML profile is a suitable instrument to model safety, rather tailored to Eurocontrol although can be extended.

Modeling and characterizing safety vocabulary enables to transform safety models into safety analysis models. The way we create the analyses can be fairly general to an MDD development in the duty of evaluating high-level models; nevertheless, work may be necessary to adapt the creation of safety analyses to our needs. Safety engineers could assist in this transformation. Having safety analysis meta-models independent of a specific tool offers us the possibility to change the safety tool with less effort and knowledge of safety than if we directly map from the safety meta-models to the safety tool.

Data for safety analyses could arise from system model elements, for instance functional dependencies between components. Although it is not a trivial task it could be automatically detected when a functional dependency is a safety dependency as well. Two safety concepts could be seen as trivially considered in this work: component failure modes and safety dependencies. Failure modes might be fully described whilst token words used instead are only clues for their identification. Depends-on relationships among components used here cannot be enough to find mitigation means to stop propagation. Nevertheless these two concepts can be enough for a preliminary safety assessment.

Acknowledgements. The work presented here has been co-funded by the European Commission under the IST 6th FP 2002-2006 (MODELWARE project [1]), and by the Spanish Ministry of Education (TIC2005-08665-C03). We would like to thank our partners, especially Thales ATM. This paper reflects only the author's views.

References

1. Modelware Web Page: http://www.modelware-ist.org/
2. European Organization for the Safety of Air Navigation, Air Navigation Systems Safety Assessment Methodology, http://www.eurocontrol.int
3. Budinsky, F., et al.: Eclipse Modeling Framework. Addison Wesley Professional (2003)
4. de Miguel, M., Pauly, B., Person, T., Briones, J.F.: Model-Based Integration of Safety Analysis and Reliable Software Development," words. In: 10th IEEE International Workshop on Object-Oriented Real-Time Dependable Systems WORDS, pp. 312–319. IEEE Computer Society Press, Los Alamitos (2005)
5. Silva, J.P., de Miguel, M., Briones, J.F., Alonso, A.: Safety Metrics for the Analysis of Software Architectures. In: Workshop on Visual Modeling for Software Intensive Systems (VMSIS) at the 2005 IEEE Symposium on Visual Languages and Human-Centric Computing (VL/HCC), IEEE Computer Society Press, Los Alamitos (2005)
6. de Miguel, M., Briones, J.F., Silva, J.P., Alonso, A.: Model Based Integration of Safety Analysis and Development. In: 9th IEEE International Symposium on Object and component-oriented Real-time distributed Computing ISORC, IEEE Computer Society Press, Los Alamitos (2006)
7. Briones, J.F., de Miguel, M., Silva, J.P., Alonso, A.: Integration of Safety Analysis and Software Development Methods. In: 1st IET Conference on System Safety (June 2006)
8. MIL-STD-1629. A Military Standard, Procedures for Performing A Failure Mode, Effects and Criticality Analysis (1980)
9. NUREG-0492. Fault Tree Handbook, U.S. Nuclear Regulatory Commission (1981)
10. Levenson, N.: Safeware: System Safety and Computers. Addison Wesley (1995)
11. Object Management Group. UML Profile for Modeling Quality of Service and Fault Tolerance Characteristics and Mechanisms, OMG document number ptc/2005-05-02 (2005)
12. Object Management Group. Meta Object Facility (MOF) Core Specification, OMG document number formal/2006-01-01 (2006)
13. AADL. SAE Architecture Analysis & Design Language. http://www.aadl.info/
14. ARTiSAN Software Tools. Safety in the Loop (2002)
15. Khan, K., Han, J.: Composing Security-Aware Software. IEEE Software (January 2002)
16. Pai, G., Dugan, J.: Automatic Synthesis of Dynamic Fault Trees from UML System Models. In: International Symposium on Software Reliable Engineering, IEEE Computer Society, Los Alamitos (2002)
17. Jürjens, J.: Developing Safety-Critical Systems with UML. In: Stevens, P., Whittle, J., Booch, G. (eds.) «UML» 2003 - The Unified Modeling Language. Modeling Languages and Applications. LNCS, vol. 2863, Springer, Heidelberg (2003)
18. Conmy, P., Paige, R.: Using UML, OCL and MDA to support development of Modular Avionics Systems. In: Baar, T., Strohmeier, A., Moreira, A., Mellor, S.J. (eds.) Workshop on Critical Systems Development with UML at UML 2004. LNCS, vol. 3273, Springer, Heidelberg (2004)
19. Towhidnejad, M., Wallace, D., Gallo, A.: Validation of Object Oriented Software Design with Fault Tree Analysis. In: Software Engineering Workshop, 28th Annual NASA Goddard, IEEE Computer Society Press, Los Alamitos (2003)

Mission Modes for Safety Critical Java

Martin Schoeberl

Institute of Computer Engineering
Vienna University of Technology, Austria
mschoebe@mail.tuwien.ac.at

Abstract. Java is now considered as a language for the domain of safety critical applications. A restricted version of the Real-Time Specification for Java (RTSJ) is currently under development within the Java Specification Request (JSR) 302. The application model follows the Ravenscar Ada approach with a fixed number of threads during the *mission* phase. This static approach simplifies certification against safety critical standards such as DO-178B. In this paper we extend this restrictive model by mission modes. Mission modes are intended to cover different modes of a real-time application during runtime without a complete restart. Mission modes are still simpler to analyze with respect to WCET and schedulability than the full dynamic RTSJ model. Furthermore our approach to thread stopping during a mode change provides a clean coordination between the runtime system and the application threads.

1 Introduction

The Real-Time Specification for Java (RTSJ) [1] was a first and successful attempt to enable Java based real-time application development. The RTSJ is a quite dynamic environment reflecting the dynamic nature of Java and aimed at soft real-time applications. Soon after the RTSJ was published, suggestions to restrict the RTSJ for high-integrity applications have been proposed [2,3]. The restrictions are based on the Ravenscar profile for Ada [4].

The basic idea of the proposed profiles is to divide the application into an *initialization* phase and a *mission* phase. During initialization all threads are created and data structures for communication are allocated. In the mission phase a fixed number of threads are scheduled. The profile disallows garbage collection to provide time predictable scheduling of the real-time threads. Only a restricted version (no sharing between threads) of scoped memory areas is allowed for simple dynamic memory management.

1.1 A Safety Critical Java Profile

The Java Specification Request (JSR) 302 builds on those profiles to define a standard for safety critical Java [5]. The intention of this JSR is to provide a profile that supports programming of applications that can be validated against safety critical standards such as DO-178B level A [6]. In [7] we have defined a simple safety critical Java profile based on the former work. Our extension includes, besides a more natural way to define the scheduling requirements by deadlines instead of priorities, a clean way to shutdown the application.

R. Obermaisser et al. (Eds.): SEUS 2007, LNCS 4761, pp. 105–113, 2007.
© IFIP International Federation for Information Processing 2007

```
package javax.safetycritical;

public abstract class PeriodicThread
        extends RealtimeThread {

    public PeriodicThread(RelativeTime period,
        RelativeTime deadline,
        RelativeTime offset, int memSize)

    public PeriodicThread(RelativeTime period)
}

public abstract class SporadicThread
        extends RealtimeThread {

    public SporadicThread(String event,
        RelativeTime minInterval,
        RelativeTime deadline, int memSize)

    public SporadicThread(String event,
        RelativeTime minInterarrival)

    public void fire()
}
```

Fig. 1. Classes for periodic and sporadic real-time events

The profile contains *periodic* and *sporadic* threads. The periodic threads represent the main application logic. Sporadic threads handle software and hardware events (i.e. interrupts). Figure1 shows the simplified classes that represent periodic and sporadic threads.

Both classes extend RealtimeThread (shown in Figure 2) that contains properties common to periodic and sporadic threads. Note that RealtimeThread is not the RTSJ version of a RealtimeThread. We do not inherit from java.lang.Thread to avoid problematic constructs (e.g. sleep()). Furthermore, our thread abstraction does not contain a start() method. All threads are started together at mission start. We extend the profile in this paper to start threads also on a mode change.

The run() method is different from an RTSJ or java.lang thread. It is abstract to enforce overriding in a sub-class. Method run() has to return a boolean value. This value indicates that a periodic task is ready for shutdown or for stopping during a mode change.

In contrast to the RTSJ scheduling parameters are defined by time values (deadlines) instead of priorities. Deadlines represent application requirements more natural than priorities. An implementation on top of a priority based scheduler can map the deadlines to priority values by a deadline monotonic order [8]. This mapping is part of the runtime system and does not have to be done by the application developer. The distinction between an initialization and a mission phase (with static threads) simplifies

```
package javax.safetycritical;

public abstract class RealtimeThread {

    protected RealtimeThread(RelativeTime period,
        RelativeTime deadline,
        RelativeTime offset, int memSize)

    protected RealtimeThread(String event,
        RelativeTime minInterval,
        RelativeTime deadline, int memSize)

    abstract protected boolean run();

    protected boolean cleanup() {
        return true;
    }
}
```

Fig. 2. The base class for all schedulable entities

the generation of the mapping. The mapping is performed only once at the start of the mission. Furthermore, the definition of deadlines as the main scheduling parameter allows switching to an EDF scheduler in the middleware without changing the application logic.

1.2 Mission Modes

Although a static approach to the development of safety critical applications simplifies (or even enables) certification, the model of a single mission with a fixed number of threads is quite restrictive. Safety critical applications often consist of different modes during runtime, e.g. take off, cruse, and landing of an airplane. During those different modes different tasks have to be performed. In this paper we evaluate different forms to implement mode changes: At the application level, with dynamic thread creation, and with static mission modes. The main idea is to provide a restricted form of dynamic application change without the hard to analyze dynamic creation and stopping of real-time threads. Just stopping a real-time task can be a dangerous action. We build on [7] to enable a coordinated stopping of real-time tasks during a mode change.

2 Mode Changes

Several safety critical applications have different modes of operation. Imagine a part of an avionic application: takeoff, cruse, and landing are typical modes where different tasks are necessary. Several tasks will run during all modes and several are only needed during a specific mode. When a mode change occurs the continuous tasks should not be disturbed by the mode change.

Tasks that are *stopped* shall have a chance to shutdown in a clean way, i.e. run till all actuators are in a safe position. Furthermore the tasks shall be able to perform some form of cleanup. In [7] we introduced the coordinated shutdown for the whole real-time application. We use the proposed mechanism for the shutdown of threads that belong to a specific mode in this proposal.

Switching between different modes does not only represent different tasks to be executed but also reusing of resources. We can distinguish between CPU time and memory resources that can be reused. With respect to reuse three forms of mode change frameworks are possible:

1. Mode changes at the application level do not reuse memory; CPU budgets are reused, but hard to analyze
2. Dynamic created threads can reuse memory with mission scoped memory and CPU resources
3. Predefined modes do not reuse memory. CPU budgets are reused and simple to analyze

2.1 Application Level

A simple form of mode changes can be implemented at the application level – a form of *poor man's* mode changes. All threads that are needed in all modes of the mission are started. The actual application logic is only executed at the modes needed as following example shows:

```
public void run() {

    if (State.mode==State.TAKE_OFF) {
        takeOffTask();
    }
}
```

In this example the run() method represents a periodic task. This form fits well for the static approach to start all threads during mission start. However, it leaves the handling of different missions at the application programming and complicates clean mission changes. Furthermore it complicates WCET analysis and incorporation of those WCET values into schedulability analysis for different modes.

2.2 Dynamic Threads

A real-time system that allows dynamic creation of threads during the mission phase can easily reuse CPU budgets and memory. This is the model that the RTSJ proposes. However, this dynamic thread creation is hard to analyze and will hamper certification of the safety critical application.

A more restrictive model will group threads belonging to missions or mission phases. Those groups can share a scoped memory that can be recycled when all threads of the group are not needed anymore. However, no coordinated shutdown of threads that belong to a mission phase is part of the RTSJ framework.

2.3   Predefined Modes

Our approach is to define different mission modes at the initialization phase. All threads are still created in this phase and no dynamic thread creation during mission phase is necessary. Each mode contains the list of threads that have to run in this mode. Therefore we can still build all the scheduling tables before the mission starts. The static assignment of threads to mission modes also simplifies schedulability analysis.

We do not reuse any memory that is used for communication between threads for different modes. All those structures are still allocated at the initialization phase. However, threads itself can use scoped memories for intermediate data structures during their execution. We assume that the amount of memory that is used for thread communication is not that high and we would gain little from reusing part of it for different modes.

3   Implementation

The different modes are represented by a simple class that contains the list of threads belonging to the mode:

```
public class MissionMode {

    public MissionMode(RealtimeThread rt[]) {
        // immutable MissionMode object
    }
}
```

Class MissionMode provides just the constructor with the list of real-time threads to implement immutable mode objects. An immutable mode guarantees that the mode cannot be changed at runtime.

The class RealtimeSystem represents the real-time runtime system and is shown in Figure 3. Method start() performs the mission start. Compared to [7] it contains now the mission mode as a parameter. That mode is the one which is used as the first one. Method changeMod() performs the change to the new mission mode. Method stop() performs shutdown of the whole real-time application.

3.1   Shutdown

Before we discuss mode changes we give a brief description of the shutdown process. The same mechanism is used to shutdown individual threads for a mode change.

In [7] we provide an additional phase for the real-time application: *Shutdown*. This phase is intended to provide a safe termination of the real-time system. All threads have a chance to bring actuators into a safe position.

The shutdown phase is initiated similar to the start of the mission phase, by invoking stop() from RealtimeSystem. However, we cannot simply stop all threads, but need a form of cooperation. All real-time threads return a boolean value from the run() method. This value indicates: *I'm ready for a shutdown*. When a thread is in a critical operation, where a shutdown is not allowed, the thread just returns false to delay the shutdown

```
package javax.safetycritical;

public class RealtimeSystem {

    /**
     * This class is uninstantiable.
     */
    private RealtimeSystem()

    public static void start(MissionMode m)

    public static void changeMode(MissionMode m)

    public static void stop()

    public static boolean modeChangePending()

    public static int currentTimeMicros()
}
```

Fig. 3. The representation of the real-time system with mission modes

process. The runtime system waits for *all* threads to be ready for shutdown before actually performing the shutdown.

During the shutdown the cleanup() method is scheduled periodically (with the same period) *instead* of the run() method. The cleanup method itself also returns a boolean value to signal *shutdown finished* with true. In that case the thread is not scheduled anymore.

3.2 The Mode Change

When switching from mode *A* to mode *B* all threads that belong to both modes just continue to be scheduled. Threads part of mode *A* and not part of mode *B* have to be stopped. We reuse our approach to a clean shutdown of periodic threads, as described before, to perform the mode change. All threads that have to be stopped go through the same phases as during a shutdown. That means that the application logic of a single thread does not need to be changed when extending the single mode profile to a multi-mode system.

A current mode change can be queried by the application threads with RealtimeSystem.modeChangePending(). An application task should query this state before performing a long lasting state change where the application thread cannot be stopped. This query is not mandatory. However, it can help to perform the mode change in less time.

When all to-be-stopped threads have performed their cleanup function the threads that are part of mode *B* and not part of mode *A* are *added* according to their release parameters to the schedule table. As this table is known at the initialization phase it is easily built in advance and this *adding* is just a switch between different tables. Performing this switch is the last step in the mode change.

```
public class MissionExample {

    static MissionMode modeTakeOff;
    static MissionMode modeCruise;
    static MissionMode modeLand;

    public static void main(String[] args) {

        PeriodicThread watchdog = new PeriodicThread(
                new RelativeTime(1000, 0)) {

            protected boolean run() {
                // do the watchdog work
                return true;
            }
        };

        PeriodicThread takeoff = new PeriodicThread(
                new RelativeTime(100, 0)) {

            boolean finished;
            protected boolean run() {
                doWork();
                if (finished) {
                    RealtimeSystem.changeMode(modeCruise);
                }
                return true;
            }
            protected boolean cleanup() {
                // we need no cleanup as we triggered
                // the mode change
                return true;
            }
            private void doWork() {
                // the periodic work
                // sets finished to true when done
            }
        };

        RealtimeThread mto [] = { watchdog, takeoff };
        modeTakeOff = new MissionMode(mto);
        RealtimeThread mcr [] = { watchdog, cruise };
        modeCruise = new MissionMode(mcr);
        RealtimeThread mld [] = { watchdog, land };
        modeTakeOff = new MissionMode(mld);

        RealtimeSystem.start(modeTakeOff);

    }
}
```

Fig. 4. An example of an application with three mission modes

3.3   An Example

Figure 4 shows a simple example using the mission modes. We define three modes: takeoff, cruise, and landing. For each mode we have a periodic task that performs the operation. Only thread takeoff is shown in the example. Furthermore, the task watchdog is part of all three modes.

For each mode we create a MissionMode object and add all threads that belong to the mission with the constructor during the initialization phase. The mission is started with the takeoff mode with RealtimeSystem.start(modeTakeOff). When this phase is finished a mode change is triggered by the takeoff thread with changeMode(modeCruise). During this mode change takeoff is stopped and cruise is started. The thread watchdog just continues to run during the mode change and in the new mode.

4   Discussion

The example showed that the API for different application modes is quite simple and intuitive to use. The proposed solution provides some form of dynamic application change during runtime within the static framework for safety critical Java.

4.1   Analysis

The restricted form of dynamic application change with different modes simplifies WCET and schedulability analysis. For each mode all threads that will be scheduled are known in advance. During the mode change all not anymore used threads are stopped first before new threads from the new mode are started. In that case we do not need additional schedulability analysis for the mode changes.

During stopping of a thread the cleanup() method is invoked instead of the run() method at the same period. We only have to use the larger WCET value from the two methods for schedulability analysis.

The analysis of different modes is slightly more complex than the analysis of a single mission phase. However, it is still simpler than fully dynamic thread creation in the mission phase. We assume that the proposed modes provide enough dynamics in safety critical applications without hampering certification.

4.2   Runtime Overhead

A runtime system that provides a single mission phase with statically created threads can be implemented very efficient. During the start of the mission all relevant scheduling parameters (e.g. priorities ordered deadline monotonic) can be calculated. As a result a single scheduling table can be built. As this table does not change during runtime an efficient array instead of a list can be used. For a full dynamic system a list of threads that can be changed during runtime has to be used. Therefore, scheduling decisions at runtime are more complex.

The proposed approach of static modes is slightly more complex than the single mission solution. However, as all modes and the resulting scheduling tables are known before the mission start the tables can still be built in advance. At the end of the mode change (when the new threads are released) just the scheduling table has to be set to the precalculated one for the new mode. Scheduling decisions during runtime are as complex as for the single mission system.

The mode change itself, with stopping some threads and scheduling their cleanup method, is as complex as the shutdown process in the former proposal.

5   Conclusion

In this paper we have proposed an enhancement of safety critical Java to cover different modes during the runtime of a real-time application. The intention is to keep the system still simple in order to certify it according to standards such as DO-178B level A [6]. The WCET and schedulability analysis for a single mode is identical to the analysis of a single mission. Our proposal for mode changes also includes a coordinated shutdown of threads that are not used anymore in a new mode.

We believe that the slightly more complex analysis is outweighed by the benefits from reusing CPU budgets for different modes and providing a simple framework for the application to perform those mode changes. As a next step we will evaluate the proposal with a real-world example. When this evaluation is positive we will suggest this framework to the JSR 302 expert group for inclusion in the future standard of Safety Critical Java Technology.

References

1. Bollella, G., Gosling, J., Brosgol, B., Dibble, P., Furr, S., Turnbull, M.: The Real-Time Specification for Java. Java Series. Addison-Wesley (June 2000)
2. Puschner, P., Wellings, A.J.: A profile for high integrity real-time Java programs. In: 4th IEEE International Symposium on Object-oriented Real-time distributed Computing (ISORC), IEEE Computer Society Press, Los Alamitos (2001)
3. Kwon, J., Wellings, A., King, S.: Ravenscar-Java: A high integrity profile for real-time Java. In: Proceedings of the 2002 joint ACM-ISCOPE conference on Java Grande, pp. 131–140. ACM Press, New York (2002)
4. Burns, A., Dobbing, B., Romanski, G.: The ravenscar tasking profile for high integrity real-time programs. In: Asplund, L. (ed.) Ada-Europe 1998. LNCS, vol. 1411, pp. 263–275. Springer, Heidelberg (1998)
5. Java Expert Group: Java specification request JSR 302: Safety critical java technology. Available, at http://jcp.org/en/jsr/detail?id=302
6. RTCA/DO-178B: Software considerations in airborne systems and equipment certification (December 1992)
7. Schoeberl, M., Sondergaard, H., Thomsen, B., Ravn, A.P.: A profile for safety critical java. In: 10th IEEE International Symposium on Object/component/service-oriented Real-time distributed Computing (ISORC 2007), IEEE Computer Society Press, Los Alamitos (2007)
8. Audsley, N.C., Burns, A., Richardson, M.F., Wellings, A.J.: Hard real-time scheduling: The deadline monotonic approach. In: Proceedings 8th IEEE Workshop on Real-Time Operating Systems and Software, Atalanta, IEEE Computer Society Press, Los Alamitos (1991)

Safety Property Analysis Techniques for Cooperating Embedded Systems Using LTS

Woo Jin Lee[1], Ho-Jun Kim[1], and Heung Seok Chae[2]

[1] EECS, Kyungpook National University, Sangyeok-dong, Buk-gu, Daegu, South Korea
woojin@knu.ac.kr, sisqo00@nate.com
[2] Department of Computer Science and Engineering, Pusan National University,
30 Changjeon-dong, Keunjeong-gu, Busan, 609-735, South Korea
hschae@pusan.ac.kr

Abstract. Safety issues of cooperating embedded systems are very important since they are closely related to our living. In this research, modeling techniques and safety analysis techniques for cooperating embedded systems are provided. Behaviors of embedded systems and safety properties are described by Labeled Transition Systems (LTS). For convenient and effective analysis, we provide a slicing method of the state space of a system according to a property. Based on the slice models, we provided an equivalence algorithm of LTS models and a compositional analysis technique of safety properties.

Keywords: safety property analysis, embedded system, LTS, slice model.

1 Introduction

Recently, cooperating embedded systems via internets have been widely used in our lives. The main task of embedded software is to engage the physical world, interacting directly with sensors and actuators in distributed processing nodes. Since even a simple failure of software may lead to severe consequences, safety properties of embedded software should be checked before delivery.

Various static analysis techniques have been proposed for verifying properties of distributed systems, which include model checking [1], inequality-necessary conditions analysis [2], data flow analysis [3,4], explicit state enumeration [5,6,7,8], and compositional reachability analysis[9, 10]. Among these analysis techniques, our approach focuses on compositional reachability analysis techniques, especially based on property automata [10] due to its scalability.

In this paper, we propose an efficient approach to verifying safety properties of cooperating embedded systems using Labeled Transition Systems (LTS). We introduce a slice model concept for easily checking behavioral equivalence between a system model and safety properties. After LTS models and safety properties are transformed into slice models, respectively, safety analysis for each property is performed in the incremental and iterative manner.

The remainder of the paper is organized as follows. Related works for LTS modeling and compositional analysis techniques are described in Section 2. Section 3

R. Obermaisser et al. (Eds.): SEUS 2007, LNCS 4761, pp. 114–124, 2007.

provides a description technique of system behaviors and safety properties by LTS. Section 4 presents a slice model concept and an algorithm for checking equivalence between two LTS models using slice models. In Section 5, a compositional safety analysis technique and its procedure are described. Section 6 evaluates the generated state space in the compositional safety analysis. Conclusion and future work appear in Section 7.

2 Related Works

LTS computation model has been widely used for specifying and analyzing distributed systems. To perform analysis based on LTS, it is necessary to construct the whole behavior model from the specification of the primitive processes. The whole behavior of the system can be described by the composite LTS which is constructed by composing the LTS1, LTS2, ..., and LTSn of its constituent processes. This approach is generally known as reachability analysis. A major problem with reachability analysis is that the search space involved can grow exponentially with the increase in the number of concurrent processes.

To cope with this problem reduction techniques have been proposed by reducing the search space. These reduction techniques can be categorized into two classes; reduction by partial ordering and reduction by compositional minimization. In the reduction techniques by partial ordering, the search space is reduced by excluding the paths formed by the interleaving of the same set of transitions [6]. In techniques by compositional minimization, also known as compositional reachability analysis, the search space is reduced by compositionally constructing the composite LTS where globally observable actions are abstracted out [9,11,12,13].

We will adopt and extend the compositional reachability analysis since it is amenable to automation and can reflect the architecture of distributed software. In the compositional safety analysis method [10], safety properties are described by state machines, called a property automata, which is augmented with a special undefined state (π). A property automata is automatically transformed to its corresponding image property automata by adding the π state for capturing potential violation of safety properties. For example, we want to check a safety property which an event 'on' should be followed by event 'off' in all cases. Fig. 1 (b) and (c) show examples of a property automata and its image property automata, respectively.

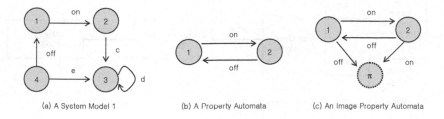

(a) A System Model 1   (b) A Property Automata   (c) An Image Property Automata

Fig. 1. Examples of compositional safety analysis

Fig. 1 (a) shows a simplified system model, whose main behaviors include on → c → d*. In the example system, behaviors of the system do not have the safety property. However, the violations of the safety property in the model are not detected by the image property automata. For rigorously checking safety properties, the equivalence checking between safety properties and the system model should be enforced.

3   Modeling System Behaviors and Properties

Suppose that we have a gas oven that can be remote-controlled at home or outside using mobile devices. This remote control system may be useful for turning off the gas oven when we forgot to turn it off at going outside or when we want to control the oven remotely at home. However, it is unsafe to control a gas oven remotely since we can not check its status such as gas leakage and inflammable materials on it. Therefore, for safety, we need some complementary devices such as a flame detection sensor, which can be monitoring the status of the gas oven. Fig. 2 shows the overall structure of the gas oven that can be remote-controlled. Now, is the gas oven system safe ?

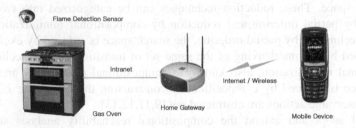

Fig. 2. An example of remote-controlled gas oven system

Fig. 3 represents a block diagram of the remote-controlled gas oven system. For simplicity, we abstractly describe only core components. The gas oven system is composed of a gas oven controller, a valve controller, a flame sensor, a communication media, and mobile devices.

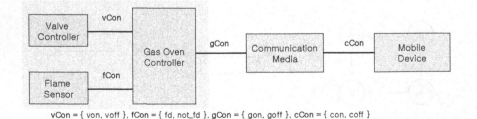

vCon = { von, voff }, fCon = { fd, not_fd }, gCon = { gon, goff }, cCon = { con, coff }

Fig. 3. A block diagram of the remote-controlled gas oven system

Each component of the block diagram is described by LTS. Fig. 4 shows the LTS models of the remote-controlled gas oven system. Communicating channels between components such as vCon and cCon are described by shared labels. In a LTS, all the states are considered as accepting states. The parallel composition of two LTS models, denoted by P ‖ Q, models the synchronized behavior of shared labels. Local events behave independently while the shared labels should be synchronized.

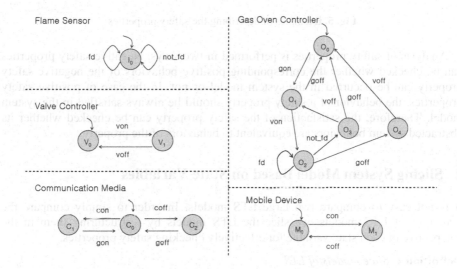

Fig. 4. The LTS models of the gas oven system

Safety properties can be represented by a sequence of events or be related with system states. And they can be described in positive form or negative form. In this paper, we support a state-based property and an event-based property in both the descriptions by extending property automata description technique [10]. Safety properties are also represented by LTS. But, a safety property model has several accepting states not all accepting ones. Followings are two types of safety properties: a state-based one and an event-based one.

- State-based safety property: safety properties are described based on state variables.
  Safety Property 1 (SP1): When the valve controller component is in the "V_1" state, the event "con" must not be occurred (!(State(V_1) $\rightarrow$ con))
- Event-based safety property: safety properties are described as a sequence of events.
  Safety Property 2 (SP2): After a gas valve is opened, it should be closed (von $\rightarrow$ voff).

Fig. 5 represents the safety property models of SP1 and SP2. In the figure, double circled states means the accepting states.

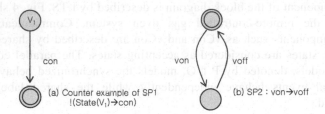

Fig. 5. Examples of describing the safety properties

Analysis of safety properties is performed in two ways. Negative safety properties can be checked whether the corresponding positive behaviors of the negative safety property can be occurred in the system model or not. In the case of positive safety properties, the behavior of a safety property should be always satisfied in the system model. Therefore, the satisfaction of the safety property can be checked whether its abstracted system behaviors are equivalent to behaviors of the property.

4 Slicing System Model Based on State Variables

It is not easy to compare two large LTS models. In order to simply compare the structures of LTS models, we slice the LTS models by restructuring them in the perspective of each state variable for effectively checking safety properties.

Definition 1. *Slice models of LTS*
A slice model of LTS is an LTS model that has only two boolean system states related and their related transitions, which has only four types of transitions (00, 01, 10, 11).

Fig. 6 shows an example of representing a slice model in a graphical and a tabular form, which represents the valve controller component shown in Fig. 4.

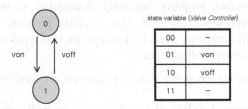

Fig. 6. Graphical and tabular representations of the slice models

For transforming an LTS model into the slice models, the states in the LTS model are represented by state variables. For each state variable, one or more slice models can be generated. If a state variable has several enumerated values, it is represented by several slice models. Followings show the steps for transforming a LTS model into the slice models.

Step 1: If there are the same labels in a LTS model, rename all the same transitions for differentiating all the transitions. For example, the 'voff' transition that appears severally in the gas oven controller component is renamed into $voff_1$, $voff_2$, and $voff_3$.

Step 2: For each transition in the LTS model, record the transition label in the each pattern of changes for each state variable in the slice models. As shown in Fig. 7, the 'con' transition from the state O_0 to the state O_1 is transformed into the '10' transition of S_0, the '01' transitions of S_1, respectively.

Fig. 8 shows the slice models of the communication media component. There are two state variables: GON(command on) and GOFF(command off). The equivalence of an original LTS model and the composition of the slice models can be easily checked. Since we assume that all the transitions in the LTS model are different, there is one-to-one and onto mapping between two transition sets. The transition information between the corresponding transitions is equivalent since the transition rules preserve the transition information. The memory space for representing slice models in the tabular form is equivalent to the original LTS representation.

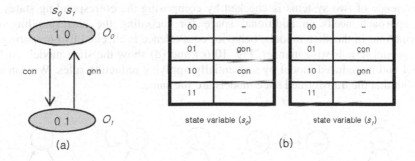

00	–
01	gon
10	con
11	–

state variable (s_0)

00	–
01	con
10	gon
11	–

state variable (s_1)

(a)   (b)

Fig. 7. An example for transformation rules

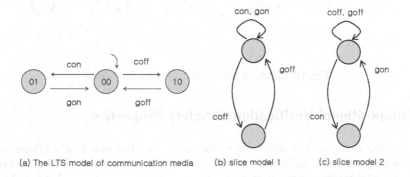

(a) The LTS model of communication media   (b) slice model 1   (c) slice model 2

Fig. 8. Two slice models of the communication media component

Fig. 9 shows simple reduction rules for slice models. The event which is always occurred at any state can be reducible since it has no effects in enabling the other events.

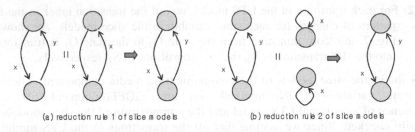

(a) reduction rule 1 of slice models   (b) reduction rule 2 of slice models

Fig. 9. Reduction rules for the slice models

Checking equivalence of two finite state machines is generally not easy since it is difficult to find the corresponding parts between different models. As shown in Fig. 10 (a) and (b), two finite state machines have the same equivalent behavior. But, their structures are different. In the observation equivalence [15], the behavioral equivalence of two systems is checked by composing the corresponding states. But, this approach needs an additional space for recording the corresponding states information. In the slice models, behavior equivalence is checked by comparing each slice model in pair-wise manner. Fig. 10 (c) and (d) show the slice models of LTS2 model and its reduced model by sequentially applying reduction rules. We can easily find out that the transformed slice models are the same.

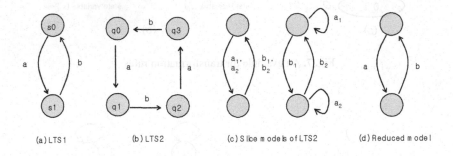

(a) LTS1   (b) LTS2   (c) Slice models of LTS2   (d) Reduced model

Fig. 10. Checking equivalence of two LTS models

5   Compositional Verification of Safety Properties

For effective analysis, it is important to minimize the state space of a system model by localizing and reducing features unrelated to the safety property. During making an reduced model by the compositional approach, local transitions are abstracted by the λ elimination rules of transformations from the λ–acceptor to the λ–free machine [14]. Fig. 11 shows the overall procedure of our algorithm. In the start of analysis procedure, the system model and the safety property are composed since we need the same reference points between two models for easily finding corresponding ones. During reduction procedure, the state variables and transitions of the property model are preserved.

Safety properties are categorized into a positive form and a negative form. Safety analysis is differently performed according to its form. Followings are overall explanation of two safety analysis approaches.

- Negative safety property: A safety property in the negative form describes that a situation should not be occurred. For checking these properties, we check whether the reversed positive situation is occurred in the system model or not. If the situation occurs, the property is not satisfied.
- Positive safety property: A safety property in the positive form means that the property should be always satisfied in the system model. In this case, we check the equivalence of the property model and the abstracted system model against the property model.

Main analysis procedure is performed on the slice models. Therefore, the reduced system model and the property model are transformed to the slice models. Inclusion of two models is decided by checking whether each slice model of the property model is equivalent to the corresponding slice model of the system model. Equivalence of two models is checked by the equivalence of all the corresponding slice models.

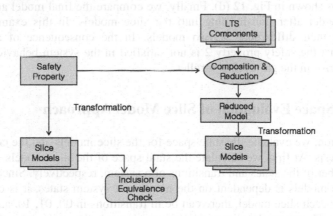

Fig. 11. Safety analysis procedure of LTS models

Fig. 12 shows the analysis steps of the safety property (SP2) using the compositional analysis technique. Fig. 12 (a) shows the abstract model of (communication media ‖ mobile device), called C1. Fig. 12 (b) represents the composed model of C1 and the gas oven controller component. In Fig. 12 (b), local transitions such as gon and goff are transformed into the λ transition and eliminated by the λ-elimination rules [14] such as the λ-loop elimination and the λ-transition reduction ($q_0 = \lambda => q_t -s->q_1$ ➔ $q_0 -s-> q_1$) to become the model shown in Fig. 12 (c). Through several composition and reduction steps, the final composed model C4 is

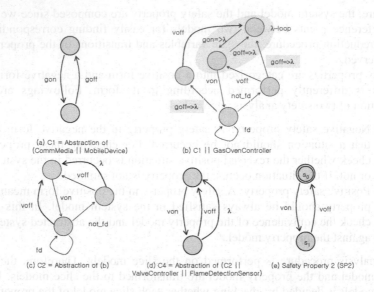

(a) C1 = Abstraction of
(CommMedia || MobileDevice)

(b) C1 || GasOvenController

(c) C2 = Abstraction of (b)

(d) C4 = Abstraction of (C2 ||
ValveController || FlameDetectionSensor)

(e) Safety Property 2 (SP2)

Fig. 12. Analysis steps of the safety property SP2

generated as shown in Fig. 12 (d). Finally, we compare the final model and the safety property model after transforming into the slice models. In this example, we can easily find their differences of two models. In the consequence of analysis, we conclude that the safety property 2 is not satisfied in the system behavior due to the modeling error in the gas oven controller.

6   State Space Evaluation of Slice Model Approach

In this section, we evaluate the state space for the slice models and the compositional safety analysis. At first, we calculate the state space of the slice models. Let n and m be the number of the states and transitions of a system, respectively. Since the number of the slice models is dependent on the number of system states, it is calculated by $\log_2(n)$. For each slice model, there can be m transitions in 00, 01, 10, and 11 slots at worst cases. Therefore, the slice model approach needs the state space of $\log_2(n) * m * 2$ (bits for identifying 4 transition slots). This number is the same to that of the FSM approach in which, for each transition, the source and destination states information ($\log_2(n)$) should be recorded.

Next, we consider the state space for performing equivalence checking based on the slice models. In the observational equivalence approach, additional state space (the same or more size of the original model) is needed since the mapping information between corresponding states in two models should be recorded, while the slice model approach needs no additional space due to pair-wise comparison of each slice model.

Table 1 shows the generated state spaces for checking the safety property SP2. As shown in Table 1, the compositional approach is more efficient than the FSM approach. Our compositional safety analysis method can fully utilize these merits of the compositional approach.

Table 1. The generated analysis spaces for checking the safety property SP2

Approaches Composed models	State diagrams (number of states and transitions)	Compositional approach		
		Original Models	Reduced Models	Reduction Rates (%)
C1 = S1 ‖ S2	4 (4)	3 (4)	3 (2)	0.0 (50.0)
C2 = C1 ‖ S3	10 (19)	5 (8)	3 (6)	40.0 (25.0)
C3 = C2 ‖ S4	10 (19)	3 (6)	2 (3)	33.3 (50.0)
C4 = C3 ‖ S5	14 (23)	2 (3)	2 (3)	0.0 (0.0)
Total	38 (65)	13 (21)	10 (14)	23.1 (33.3)

Legends: S1: Communication Media, S2: Mobile Device, S3: Gas Oven Controller, S4: Flame Detection Sensor, S5: Valve Controller.

7 Conclusion and Future Work

Safety issues are very important in the embedded system literature. In this paper, cooperating embedded systems such as the remote-controlled embedded system are described and analyzed by LTS. For convenient and effective compositional analysis of safety properties, we provide a slicing method of the system state space based on the system property, which is obtained by restructuring the LTS model. Based on the slice models, we provided an equivalence algorithm of LTS models and a compositional analysis technique of safety properties.

Currently, we are developing a modeling and analysis tool that helps to describe LTS models and to automatically partition a LTS model into the slice models. In future work, we will add timing concepts in our analysis approach.

Acknowledgments. This research was supported by the MIC (Ministry of Information and Communication), Korea, under the ITRC (Information Technology Research Center) support program supervised by IITA (Institute of Information Technology assessment).

References

1. McMillan, K.L.: Symbolic model checking. Kluwer Academic Publishers, Dordrecht (1993)
2. Avrunin, G.S., et al.: Automated analysis of concurrent systems with the constrained expression toolset. IEEE trans. software engineering 17(11), 1204–1222 (1991)
3. Cheung, S.C., Kramer, J.: Tractable dataflow analysis for distributed systems. IEEE trans. software engineering 20(8), 579–593

4. Dwyer, M.B., Clarker, L.A.: Data flow analysis for verifying properties of concurrent programs. In: Proc. of the 2nd ACM SIGSOFT Symposium on the foundation of software engineering, pp. 62–75. ACM Press, New York (1994)
5. Cheung, S.C., Kramer, J.: Context constraints for compositional reachability analysis. ACM trans. software engineering and methodology 5(4), 334–377 (1996)
6. Godefroid, P., Wolper, P.: Using partial orders for the efficient verification of deadlock freedom and safety properties. In: Proc. of the 3rd international conference on computer aided verification (1991)
7. Long, D., Clarke, L.: Task interaction graphs for concurrency analysis. In: Proc. of the 11th ICSE, pp. 44–52 (1989)
8. Valmari, A., et al.: Putting advanced reachability analysis techniques together: The 'ARA' tool. In: Larsen, P.G., Woodcock, J.C.P. (eds.) FME 1993. LNCS, vol. 670, pp. 597–616. Springer, Heidelberg (1993)
9. Yeh, W.J., Young, M.: Compositional reachability analysis using process algebra. In: Proc. of ACM SIGSOFT, pp. 49–59 (1991)
10. Cheung, S.C., Kramer, J.: Checking Safety Properties using Compositional Reachability Analysis. In: ACM TOSEM, pp. 49–78 (1999)
11. Malhotra, J., et al.: A tool for hierarchical design and simulation of concurrent systems. In: Proc. of the BCS-FACS workshop on specification and verification of concurrent systems, pp. 140–152 (1988)
12. Sabnani, K.K., et al.: An algorithmic procedure for checking safety properties of protocols. IEEE trans. communication 37(9), 940–948 (1989)
13. Tai, K.C., Koppol, P.V.: An incremental approach to reachability analysis of distributed programs. In: Proc. of the 7th international workshop on software specification and design, pp. 141–150 (1993)
14. Denning, P.J., et al.: Machines, Languages, and Computation. Prentice-Hall, Englewood Cliffs (1978)
15. Milber, R.: Communication and Concurrency. Prentice Hall, Englewood Cliffs (1989)

Testing Embedded Control Systems with TTCN-3

An Overview on TTCN-3 Continuous

Ina Schieferdecker[1,2] and Jürgen Großmann[1]

[1] Technical University Berlin, Franklinstr. 28/29, D-10623 Berlin
[2] Fraunhofer FOKUS, Kaiserin-Augusta-Allee 31, D-10589 Berlin

Abstract. TTCN-3 has gained increasing significance in recent years. Originally developed to fit the needs for testing software-based applications and systems in the telecommunication industry, TTCN-3 has shown its applicability to a wide range of other industrial domains in the mean time. TTCN-3 provides platform-independent, universal and powerful concepts to describe tests — especially for discrete, interactive systems — on different levels of abstraction. However, TTCN-3 addresses systems with discrete input and output characteristics only. In the automotive industry — as well as in other industries that deal with highly complex software-based control systems — this is not sufficient. Control systems often interact with their environment trough sensors and actuators using continuous signals. A test environment that adequately supports the specification, execution and evaluation of tests for embedded control systems has to provide concepts to handle this kind of signals. Moreover it has to support the test engineer with suitable abstractions that ease signal specification and signal evaluation.

1 Introduction

Embedded systems play an ever increasing role for the realization of complex control functions in many industrial domains — resulting in a big variety of requirements with respect to their functionality and reliability. Especially software-based control systems have specific characteristics, which — at least in their combination — are unique: they are typically embedded, interact with the environment using sensors and actuators, supervise discrete control flows, obtain and process simple and complex structured data, communicate over different bus systems and have to meet high safety and real time requirements. While different, model-based development processes and methods for embedded systems exist, a generally recognized test technology for the analysis and evaluation of these systems, which lead to qualitatively high-quality, safe and reliable systems, is missing. Such a test technology has to address the different aspects of embedded systems and it has to enable the testing of discrete behaviors for the communication sequences, continuous behaviors for the regulation sequences, and hybrid (i.e. combinations of discrete and continuous) behaviors for the control sequence in interaction with sensors/actuators, with other system components and the user.

R. Obermaisser et al. (Eds.): SEUS 2007, LNCS 4761, pp. 125–136, 2007.

TTCN-3 provides a standardized test environment that was originally tailored to satisfy the requirements of testing systems in the telecommunication industry, including also embedded systems. In order to use however the full potential of TTCN-3 to test embedded systems also, it needs to be extended. This paper presents concepts especially dedicated to the testing of embedded, hybrid control systems in the automotive domain.

We start with the overall definition of requirements for an integrated test environment that is viable for the automotive domain in section 2. Section 3 provides the respective TTCN-3 integration and section 4 presents an example application as a proof of concepts. A summary concludes the paper.

2 Testing Automotive Control Systems

Test processes in the automotive industry are tool-intensive and affected by technologically heterogeneous test infrastructures. The established test tools from e.g. dSPACE [1], Vector [2], MBtech [3] etc. are highly specialized, rely on proprietary languages and technologies and are closed in respect to portability, extension and integration. In recent years the application of model-based specifications in development and the establishment of powerful code generators have led the development process to be noticeably more effective, automated, and reaching a higher level of abstraction. Due to the availability of executable models, tests and analytical methods can be applied early and integrated into subsequent development steps. The positive effects — early error detection and early bug fixing — are obvious.

Nevertheless, model based approaches have to be integrated into existing development processes and combined with existing methods and tools. Hence, in the industrial practice an embedded control system has to pass several test levels such as Model-in-the-Loop- (MIL), Software-in-the-Loop- (SIL) and Hardware-in-the-Loop- (HIL) tests. Normally, different test systems are used for this purpose and almost each test system has its individual requirements on methods, languages and concepts. Moreover the whole development process is highly distributed and fragmented. The OEM, i.e. the system integrator and solution provider, is responsible for specification and integration whereas software and hardware of the control systems are normally provided by different suppliers.

However, to keep the whole development and test process efficient and manageable, the definition of an integrated and seamless approach is required. Such an approach especially addresses the subjects of test exchange, autonomy of infrastructure, methods, and platforms and the reuse of tests. The basis constitutes a domain specific test language, that is executable and that unifies tests of communicating, software-based systems in all of the automotive subdomains (telematics, power train, body electronics etc.), and that unifies the test infrastructure as well as the definition and documentation of tests.

TTCN-3 has the potential to serve as such a testing middleware. It provides concepts for local and distributed and for platform- and technology-independent testing. A TTCN-3 based test solution can be adapted to concrete testing environments and to concrete systems to be tested by means of an open test execution environment with well-defined interfaces for adaptation. However as mentioned before: while the testing of discrete controls is well understood and available in TTCN-3 [4], concepts for specification-based testing of continuous controls and for the relation between discrete and the continuous system parts are not. TTCN-3 lacks especially concepts for specifying tests for continuous and hybrid behavior.

3   Continuous TTCN-3

To enhance the core language to the requirements of testing continuous behavior we introduce[1]:

- the notions of streams, stream ports and stream variables,
- the notions of time represented by a global clock and its sampling in test behaviors, and
- the definition of control flow structures to support the guided provisioning and evaluation of continuous behaviors (in combination with discrete behaviors).

3.1   Type Definitions

TTCN-3 provides a complex type system to define data structures and the structured assembly of testing components. To interact with the environment, TTCN-3 uses the notion of ports and distinguishes different communication characteristics for ports. To support continuous system testing we supplement TTCN-3 with so called *stream ports*. A stream port is a named variable with a history that — unlike message-based and procedure-based ports — receives a value at every step defined by the sample time. We are able to access current values and the history of a stream by using the operators @ and []. With x_1@timevalue we access the allocation of x_1 at a certain point in time and with x_1[i] we access the ith value written to x_1. Example stream port type definitions and their usage in component type definitions for stream ports are shown in listing 1.1.

Listing 1.1. TTCN-3 Stream Port Definition

```
type port FloatOut stream {out float}
type port FloatIn stream {in float}

type component MyComponent {
  port FloatOut x_1,x_2,x_3;                                    5
  port FloatIn y_1,y_2,y_3;
}
```

In addition to stream ports we also allow the definition of *stream variables* and *stream constants*. Whereas a port represents a connection to the outside world, stream variables and constants are the in memory representation of streams. Listing 1.2 shows the declaration of stream variables and constants and the definition of their respective types.

---

[1] We already presented parts of the approach shown below in previous articles [5,6].

Listing 1.2. Stream Variables and Constants

```
type stream of float FStrm;
type stream of boolean BStrm;
                                                                    3
var FloatStrm myStrm_1;

const FStrm referenceStrm_1(t):={1.0}; // 1.0 for all t
const FStrm referenceStrm_2(t):={sin(t)}; // sinus of t
const BStrm referenceStrm_3(t):={t>10.0 ? true : false};        8
    // true for all t larger 10.0, otherwise false
```

Besides the basic access operators we additionally provide arithmetic operations on streams. We allow to calculate with streams (e.g. `myStrm_1+myStrm_2`), to directly compare streams (e.g. `myStrm_1>reference`) and the assignments of streams to other streams and stream ports (e.g. `x_1:=myStrm_1`).

3.2   Control Flow Structure for Continuous Behavior

TTCN-3 is a computational language. Test behavior is defined by computational algorithms that typically assign messages to ports. The evaluation at ports is realized using statements that obey the TTCN-3 snapshot semantics [4,7]. Whereas the snapshot semantics provide means for a pseudo parallel evaluation of ports, there is no notion of simultaneous stimulation and sampled evaluation on ports.

The *carry-until-statement* serves as an environment that provides a local time property t, sampling, and enables pseudo simultaneous stimulation and evaluation. Listing 1.3 shows the base structure of the carry-until construct.

Listing 1.3. Carry Until Construct

```
carry name_1{
  statement_1;
  statement_2
}
until {                                                         5
  [] event_1 {statement_3}
  [] event_2 {statement_4; repeat}
}

carry name_2{                                                  10
  statement_3
}
until {
  [] event_3 {statement_5; name_1()}
  [] event_4 {statement_6; goto name_1}                        15
}
```

The statements enclosed by the carry block are executed iteratively, once at every step defined by the sampling rate. This repeats as long as no event is triggered in the until block. When events are triggered, the execution of the carry block is stopped and the statement block that is defined in conjunction with the triggered event specification is executed.

The carry-until construct can be named (similar to functions and test cases in TTCN-3). The name may be used as a label, so that it may serve as a destination for goto statements. This provides the ability for more complex control flow specifications (see listing 1.3). The concise semantics of carry-until are best explained using terms of existing TTCN-3 statements. Listing 1.4 shows the mapping result of the first carry-until-statement defined in listing 1.3.

Listing 1.4. Carry Until Mapped to TTCN-3 Constructs

```
label:=cu_name_1;
var boolean continue:= true;
var float t:=0;
timer step;                                                          4
do {
    step.start(sample_rate);
    statement_1;
    statement_2;
    alt {                                                           9
    [] event_1 {
                statement_3;
                continue:= false;
            }
    [] event_2 { statement_4; }                                    14
    }
    step.timeout();
    t:= t+sample_rate;
} while continue;
```

We can use the carry-until construct to realize equation systems with TTCN-3. We are able to simultaneously assign new values to stream ports. Usually this is done inside the carry part by using the assignment operator (e.g. `port@t:=2*t` or `port@t:=var@(t-10)` etc.). We can also evaluate ports. The latter is done inside the until part by using compare operations (e.g. `[]port@t>var@t`). The symbol `t` represents the current execution time and is updated according to the definition in listing 1.4. For the evaluation of inputs at ports we consider delayed effectiveness, i.e. each assignment to an output port is available for input not before the next iteration. This condition holds if for every t, the values of the output ports are defined by use of the values of the input ports for $t' \leq t$ and by use of the values of the output ports for $t' < t$ only. For more details on the power and expressiveness of the carry-until construct see [5,6].

3.3   Construction of Streams

The most elementary form of a stream definition is given by an expression over time. The expression my contain a property called `t` to express time progress. The property `t` represents the local time of a stream (it starts with the value `0.0` whenever a stream is started). For stream expressions, we use the full range of TTCN-3 expressions including the use of variables, functions and the newly introduced concepts defined above (e.g. streams and stream access operators). Listing 1.5 presents the definition of a constant integer stream and of two time dependant float streams.

Listing 1.5. Simple Streams

```
myFirstStrm:=4;
mySecondStrm:=sin(t)+100.0;
myThirdStrm:=mySecondStrm@(t-10.0)*4.0;
```

Furthermore, we allow the part-wise definition of streams. In principle, this is similar to the definition of $\langle m_k \rangle$ by use of an TTCN-3 array (see listing 3.3). Concerning the large amount of data normally necessary to represent a sampled signal, this approach is not feasible for signals with a significant length. To forgo the explicit specification of each individual value, we enable the definition of larger structures called substreams here. To define substreams we use the range expression — normally used to express template values in TTCN-3 — to address a multitude of numeric or time-related index values. For example, myStrm@(0..100):=4 denotes the assignment of the value 4 to the first 101 time steps (and indices) of stream m̈yStrm.

Part-wise Definition of Streams

```
myFirstStrm:={1,2,45,66,223};
// finite stream with 5 values
mySecondStrm:={
    @(0..100)              :=sin(t)*100.0,
    @(100..2000)          :=4.0,                              5
    @(2000..infinity)  :=4.0+sin(t/20.0)}
// infinite stream with 3 phases
myThirdStrm:={
    [0..100]              :=sin(t)*100.0,
    [100..2000]          :=4.0,                              10
    [2000..infinity]  :=4.0+sin(t/20.0)}
// the same as mySecondStrm only if the sampling rate is 1
```

In order to concatenate multiple stream assignments into one individual stream we use the shorthand notation for ranges presented in listing 3.3.

3.4   Stream Templates

In TTCN-3, especially for the definition of reference values, the use of templates is encouraged. A template describes a pattern that is used to characterize values. An arbitrary value is either matched by a template or not. We extend the notion of streams to include also streams of template matches, where every match or mismatch is represented by a Boolean true or false. Besides for numerical values, TTCN-3 encourages the use of templates for values of each type: for base types as well as for user defined types. We apply the notion of templates to streams, but restrict it to *stream templates* for numerical streams and to the definition of upper and lower ranges for the stream value only. More complex stream templates will be subject to further research.

A stream template defines a pattern that characterizes a stream or a multitude of streams. The most elementary stream template is an individual stream itself (see listing 3.4). Such a template matches only if the stream that serves as template definition is exactly the same as the one the template is compared with.

Stream Templates

```
type stream of float FS;
template FS t_1:=100.0*t;
template FS t_2:=(100.0..200.0);                              3
template FS t_3:=(sin(t)+100.0
                  .. sin(t)-100.0);
```

Similar to scalar value templates for numerical types (e.g. `float`, `integer`), we allow the definition of stream templates that denote the upper and lower bounds for numerical streams. Listing 3.4 presents example stream templates. The template `t_1` is defined by a stream itself, template `t_2` is defined by a range with the constant lower bound `100.0` and the constant upper bound `200`, and template `t_3` uses dynamic evolving boundaries defined by stream expressions.

Moreover, ranges — especially in the field of signal processing — are often used to indicate tolerances, either as a fixed value tolerance or a relative (percentage) value tolerance. To express tolerances explicitly, we introduce an additional syntactical construct for range definitions. With (`strmval|tol`) we denote a range with a fixed value tolerance `tol` and with (`strmval|tol%`) we express percentage value tolerances `tol%`. Example template definitions are shown in listing 1.6 and their application is shown in section 4.

Listing 1.6. Tolerance Templates

```
template FS t_4:=(100.0|5.0);
template FS t_5:=((sin(t)+100.0)|5%);
template FS t_6:=(template1,(4.0|4%));
```

In order to apply stream templates on streams received via stream ports, we use the match operator already known in TTCN-3. A match expression can either be applied to a complete stream (e.g `match(t_2, strmval)`) or to single values on a certain point in time (e.g.
(`match(t_2@t,strmval@t)`). For usage within the carry-until construct, we propose `x_2.match(t_2)` as a shorthand to apply the current template value of `t_2` to the current value at a stream port `x_2`.

4 Case Study

In order to demonstrate the usage of the introduced concepts and to show their applicability to automotive test tasks, we provide a small case study that represents a TTCN-3 realization for testing an *Adaptive Cruise Control* (ACC[8]).

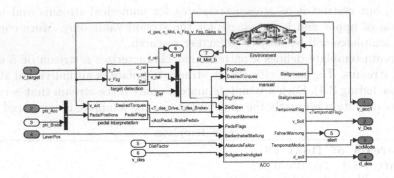

Fig. 1. Simulink Model of an Adaptive Cruise Control

4.1   The System Under Test

An ACC is a cruise control that automatically detects vehicles running ahead
and — in the case of a slow vehicle ahead (the target) — it adjusts the actual
speed (v_acc) so that a safe distance to the detected vehicle is guaranteed (the
distance control mode). When there is no vehicle ahead, an ACC works like
any other cruise control (the velocity control mode). Today there are different
variants of ACC's available. We use a simplified example here (see Figure 1)
that does not match the requirements of a real product but that is sufficient to
demonstrate the new features that we have introduced for TTCN-3.

The ACC consists of three major parts. The ACC-control unit provides the
main functional behavior. It is responsible to calculate the desired velocity
(v_soll), the destination distance to the vehicle ahead (d_des) and it provides
a warning signal to inform the driver when the safe distance is violated. The
ACC-control is supplemented by the target detection unit that preprocess sensor information on the velocity of the vehicle ahead (v_target) and the pedal
interpretation unit that preprocess the driver's input (phi_brake, phi_gas). For
testing purposes we use the test interface specified in table 1.

Table 1. ACC Test Interface

symbol	dir	unit	datatype
v_target	in	m/s	double
phi_gas	in	%	double
leverpos	in	-	enumeration
v_des	out	m/s	double
d_des	out	m/s	double
accMode	out	-	boolean
v_acc	out	m/s	double

4.2   The Informal Test Specification

In this example we test the changeover between distance control mode — when there is a slow vehicle ahead — and velocity control mode — without any vehicle ahead. This forms one of the more complex tasks of an ACC and can be tested by the following test behavior (for a similar test specification see [8]).

1. **Init:** Accelerate the vehicle `phi_gas:=100` until velocity `v_acc` rises to more than 40 m/s. Than switch on the cruise control `leverpos:=HOLD_ACC`.
2. **Activate ACC:** Now, we introduce a vehicle ahead by setting the target velocity to `phi_target:=35+sin(t)` m/s. The initial distance `d_init:=90` m is set using the parameter interface that is out of scope here. The ACC should switch to distance control mode after a few seconds. The safe distance to the vehicle ahead can be calculated with `v_acc/2*df`. The symbol `df` represents a distance factor that is set to the value of 2 here.
3. **Accelerate Target:** To test whether the ACC switches back to velocity control mode, we accelerate the target vehicle using a smooth ramp. The ACC should now adjust the actual velocity according to the vehicle ahead as long as the velocity excess 40 m/s. We allow a tolerance of 10% here. Afterwards, the ACC should switch back to velocity control mode.

4.3   The TTCN-3 Test Specification

We use TTCN-3 and the concepts specified in section 3 on page 127 to implement the test case. We start with the specification of the test system architecture and the test interface. Please note that TTCN-3 uses a test system centric perspective, i.e. system inputs are declared as outputs here and system outputs as inputs. We declare continuous stream ports to cover the velocity (v_des, d_des, v_target), the pedal output (phi_gas), and the input of the actual acc status (accMode). To set the lever position we choose a port with a message based communication characteristics.

Listing 1.7. Test Architecture

```
type port FloatOut stream {out float};
type port FloatIn stream {in float};
type port BoolIn stream {in boolean};

type enumerated Lever { MIDDLE, HOLD_ACC,               5
                        HOLD_DEC, OFF };
type port LeverOut message
  { out Lever };


                                                        10
type component ACCTester {
  port FloatOut v_target,phi_gas;
  port FloatIn v_des,d_des, v_acc;
  port BoolIn accMode;
  port LeverOut leverpos;                               15
}
```

After the definition of the structural setup, we define constant values and streams that are used for the stimulation of the system later on.

Listing 1.8. Constants and Stream Constants used during Stimulation

```
type stream of float FS;
const integer INIT_SPEED:=40;
const integer INIT_T_SPEED:=35;
const integer KICKDOWN:=100;                                    4
const integer TIMEOUT:=20000;

const FS target_speed:=INIT_T_SPEED+sin(t);
const FS accelerate_slow:=t/1000.0;
```

For the evaluation of system behavior we define stream templates. The template `s_dist_fail` covers an essential safety requirement. The desired distance shall never under-run the minimal safety distance. The template `v_des_fail` will be used later on to monitor the destination velocity in proportion to the velocity of the target.

Listing 1.9. Template Definitions

```
template FS s_dist_fail(integer df,
                        float vel):=
   complement(vel/2*df..infinity);

template FS v_acc_fail(float vel ):=            5
   complement( vel|10%);
```

Similar to the altstep-construct already available in TTCN-3, we use the untilstep-construct to define reusable evaluation statements that are activated as defaults and so applied to multiple carry-until statements in the following.

Listing 1.10. Definition of an Untilstep

```
untilstep tout_and_safety runs on ACCTester{
  [] d_des.match@t(s_dist_fail(df,v_acc@t)){
    setverdict(fail)}
  [] t>TIMEOUT {                                4
    setverdict(fail)}
}
```

Now we are able to define the test case itself. We start with the init phase and activate the ACC when INIT_SPEED is reached.

Listing 1.11. The Test Case Definition

```
testcase ACC_Mode_Test() runs on ACCTester
  setverdict(pass);
  var integer df :=2;

  carry init{                                             5
    phi_gas@t:=KICKDOWN;
  }
  until{
    [] v_acc@t>INIT_SPEED{
      leverpos.send(ON)                                   10
    }
  }
...
```

In the following we activate the untilstep defined in listing 1.10. This guarantees the detection of safe distance violation and timeouts. For test behavior we use carry-until to introduce the vehicle ahead (`v_target:=target_speed@t`). We also check for the beginning of the distance control mode (`[]acc_mode@t==true`).

Listing 1.12. Test ACC Mode Activation

```
var default safety_default :=
  activate(tout_and_safety);

carry activate_acc{
  v_target@t:=target_speed@t;                             5
}
until{
  [] acc_mode@t==true{};
}
...                                                       10
```

In the end, we check whether the ACC holds the correct velocity during the acceleration of the target and switches back to velocity control mode when the destination velocity is reached again.

Listing 1.13. Test ACC Mode Deactivation

```
carry accelerate_target{
  v_target:=v_target@t+accelerate_slow@t;
}
until{
  [] acc_mode==false{}                                    5
  [] v_acc@t.match(v_acc_fail(v_target@t))
    {setverdict(fail)}
}
  deactivate(safety_default);
}//testcase                                               10
```

Occurring errors were detected during test execution and logged using the setverdict(fail) statement. After the test execution we are able to obtain the test result by examining the verdict value provided by the test case.

5   Summary and Conclusions

This paper reviews the general requirements for a test technology for embedded systems, which use both discrete signals (i.e. asynchronous message-based or synchronous procedure-based ones) and continuous flows (i.e. streams). It compares the requirements with the only standardized test specification and implementation language TTCN-3 (the Testing and Test Control Notation [4]). While TTCN-3 offers the majority of test concepts, it has limitations for testing systems with continuous aspects.

Hence, this paper introduces basic concepts and means to handle continuous real world data in digital environments. Therefore, we introduce streams that can be created, calculated and examined by means of continuous and potentially discretized data. Moreover, TTCN-3 is being extended with the concepts of stream-based ports, sampling, equation systems, and additional control flow structures to be able to express continuous behavior. The paper demonstrates the feasibility of the approach by providing a small example. In future work, the concepts will be completed, implemented and applied to real case studies in the field of automotive software engineering and the development of ECUs (electronic control units).

References

1. dSpace AG: Web pages of the dSpace corporation (2005)
2. Vector Informatik GmbH: Web pages of the Vector Informatik GmbH (2007)
3. MBtech Group: Web pages of the MBtech Group (2007)
4. ETSI: ES 201 873-1 V3.1.1: Methods for Testing and Specification (MTS). The Testing and Test Control Notation Version 3, Part 1: TTCN-3 Core Language (2005)
5. Schieferdecker, I., Großmann, J.: Testing of Embedded Control Systems with Continous Signals. In: 2nd Dagstuhl-Workshop MBEES 2007: Model based Development of Embedded Systems (2006)
6. Schieferdecker, I., Großmann, J., Bringmann, E.: Continuous TTCN-3: Testing of embedded control systems. In: 3rd International ICSE workshop on Software Engineering for Automotive Systems (2006)
7. International Organization for Standardization: Information technology - Open systems interconnection — Conformance testing methodology and framework - Part 3: The Tree and Tabular combined Notation (TTCN), ISO/IEC 9646-3, 2nd edn. (1998)
8. Conrad, M.: Modell-basierter Test eingebetteter Software im Automobil. PhD thesis, TU-Berlin (2004)

Cross-Platform Verification Framework for Embedded Systems*

Ingomar Wenzel, Raimund Kirner, Bernhard Rieder, and Peter Puschner

Institut für Technische Informatik
Technische Universität Wien
Treitlstrasse 3/182-1
1040 Vienna, Austria
{ingo, raimund, bernhard, peter}@vmars.tuwien.ac.at

Abstract. Many innovations in the automotive sector involve complex electronics and embedded software systems. Testing techniques are one of the key methodologies for detecting faults in such embedded systems.

In this paper, a novel cross-platform verification framework including automated test-case generation by model checking is introduced. Comparing the execution behavior of a program instance running on a certain platform to the execution behavior of the same program running on a different platform we denote cross-platform verification. The framework supports various types of coverage criteria. It turned out that end-to-end testing is of high importance due to defects occurring on the actual target platform for the first time.

Additionally, formal verification can be applied for checking requirements resulting from the specification using the same model generation mechanism that is used for test data generation. Due to a novel self-assessment mechanism, the confidence into the formal models is increased significantly.

We provide a case study for the Motorola embedded controller *HCS12* that is heavily used by the automotive industry. We perform structural tests on industrial code patterns using a wide-spread industrial compiler. Using our technique, we found two severe compiler defects that have been corrected in subsequent releases.

1 Introduction

The last years have seen significant advances in electronic control systems. Such systems replace more and more conventional control systems. Driven by the increased flexibility resulting from the use of microprocessors in control systems, increasing functionality is integrated into electronic control units (ECUs) causing higher complexity of the control applications. This causes an increase in the number of safety-critical electronic control systems. Safety-criticality means that a failure of such systems may result in catastrophic consequences [1].

---

* This work has been partially supported by the FIT-IT research project "Systematic test case generation for safety-critical distributed embedded real time systems with different SIL levels (TeDES)" and the FWF research project "Compiler-Support for Timing Analysis" (CoSTA).

R. Obermaisser et al. (Eds.): SEUS 2007, LNCS 4761, pp. 137–148, 2007.

For instance, the automotive industry is one of the key drivers pushing these developments. Today, new cars contain about 80 ECUs. According to current figures of the Austrian automobile association ÖAMTC, about 27% of all car breakdowns are directly related to defects of car electrics and electronics [2].

Thus, the correct operation of safety-critical systems has to be ensured. This confidence is established by validation and verification [3,4]. Validation denotes checking the specification, verification refers to whether a system fulfills given requirements. Within verification, testing is a method for getting evidence of the absence of faults.

High-level development tools like *Matlab/Simulink*[1] supporting model-based development help shortening product cycles. Especially code generators boost software development cycles for embedded systems. In such development environments C-code targeting specialized embedded hardware is generated automatically from *Matlab/Simulink* models.

Input to the verification framework is C-source code performing a specified function in the embedded system. This source code is compiled for the target platform and expected to behave according to its specification. The notion of the cross-platform verification framework allows to verify embedded systems software by comparing the execution of the software on the target platform with an alternative execution platform (denoted as host platform). To allow an semantics-equivalent execution of software, it is necessary to transform the program for proper operation on the host platform.

1.1 Contribution

First, the notion of cross-platform verification is introduced. Target-specific C-code is parsed and platform-semantics-equivalent models are generated that are used for test-data generation. These models can also be used for formal verification purposes.

Second, a verification framework has been developed. Instrumented test files are produced and it is checked whether the generated test data fulfill their purpose in the execution scenario.

Third, cross-platform checks using the actual system-under-test allow to determine if the target implementation operates semantically equivalent to the generated test data of the reference implementation. This increases the confidence in the generated models. We found out that this novel self-assessment mechanism helps to identify severe errors within the system development processes. This mechanism allows strengthening the confidence in the overall framework.

Fourth, using this method we found two severe bugs in a widely used commercial cross-platform compiler. For legal reasons, the company name is not published.

1.2 Structure of This Paper

The paper is structured as follows: First, basic concepts including verification, testing, model checking and platform behavior are introduced (Section 3). Then, individual patterns used in testing are formulated and composed into the novel concept of cross-platform verification (Section 4). In Section 5, the implementation of the cross-platform verification framework is presented. Subsequently, we present experimental results

---

[1] http://www.mathworks.com

exercising the framework for an embedded system (Section 6). Finally, Section 7 concludes this paper.

2 Related Work

To the best of our knowlegde there is no scientific research that addresses cross-platform verification as a tool to verify a program instance running on a certain platform by comparing its behavior with another program instance running on a different platform.

A research area related to our approach is test case generation using formal methods, which is an active area of research. Chlipala et al. [5] describe how to test reachability using the model checker BLAST. Rayadurgam et al. [6] have worked on generating test of MC/DC coverage using model checkers to comply with the standard DO-178B [4]. The use of model checking to create test cases for mutation testing is described by Ammann et al. [7]. Hamon et al. present results on using the model checker SAL to generate tests for complete state and transition coverage of Stateflow models [8].

3 Basic Concepts

Verification denotes the process of checking whether a system fulfills given properties called verification conditions [1]. Some people consider testing and verification as alternative strategies for increasing the dependability of computer systems. However, in the following, a classification of verification techniques is presented that is based on work of Laprie et al. [1]. The highest level classification criterion is whether the system is exercised or not. If a system is verified without actually executing it, this is called *static verification*. When a system is verified by executing it, this is referred to as *dynamic verification*

If static verification is based on analyzing *the code itself*, we distinguish between *static analysis* (inspections, walk-through, abstract interpretation, etc.) and *theorem proving*. If verification is performed on a *model* of the system behavior (whereby the model usually is a state transition system represented by finite or infinite state automata), this is called *model checking* [9].

When using dynamic verification, the system is exercised by providing inputs to the system. These inputs can be symbolic in case of *symbolic execution* or concrete in case of *testing*.

The cross-platform verification framework is designed for supporting *testing* and *model checking*. Thus, in the following, these two techniques are introduced.

4 Cross-Platform Verification

In this section we introduce the basic verification patterns that are instantiated within our verification framework. Most of these patterns are already used in practice; however, due to the lack of a conceptional description in research literature the respective key concepts are formulated explicitly.

Beside these patterns, functional equivalence between two different platforms is required in order to ensure that the target semantics are equivalent to the host semantics.

Especially, this is required for the formal model that is automatically built and used within the framework.

Subsequently, the combination of the concepts of remote testing, cross-platform testing, reference-platform testing, formal verification, and functional equivalence leads to our cross-platform verification framework is outlined in detail.

4.1 Remote Testing

A scenario where the test-control software and the software under test run on different components is called *remote testing*.

When testing embedded systems, the component of the embedded system to be tested is called *target*; the component where the testing control software runs is called *host*. When testing embedded software using automatic test data generation, the host and target are typically different components, i.e., forming a remote testing scenario. Remote testing is used in this case due to resource limitations at the target.

In case of our verification framework we verify the automatically generated test data in a first step on the host where it is generated. In order to verify the correctness of the generated test data, it is verified in a first step on the host where it is generated. Then, in the next step the verified test data are converted and sent to the target platform. This technique increases the confidence of test data significantly. It ensures that the test data fulfills exactly its purpose.

4.2 Cross-Platform Testing

Cross-platform testing aims at performing tests on two or more different platforms with semantically equivalent code and test data.

The concept of cross-platform testing is shown in Figure 1(a). The software is tested on platform 1 and 2, using the same test cases. The intended output of the test cases may need to be transformed differently for platform 1 and 2 to compute the test verdict.

Cross-platform testing has to be used to verify safety-critical systems in the case that important parts of the system are computed with diversity on either hardware or software level.

4.3 Reference Platform Testing

Reference platform testing is a technique to achieve automatic test verdicts even if only input test data instead of complete test cases are available. The input test data are processed on two different components, where one of it is typically called *reference platform*.

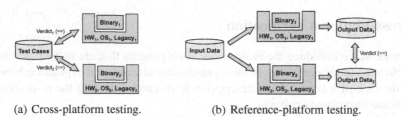

(a) Cross-platform testing.   (b) Reference-platform testing.

Fig. 1. Cross-platform vs. reference-platform testing

As shown in Figure 1(b), the test data are applied on both components and the test verdict is obtained by comparing the observed output of both components.

If the two components provide different execution platforms, it is in general necessary to transform the program code of the reference platform to obtain the same intended behavior as of the other platform.

4.4 Functional Equivalence Between Two Platforms

When doing cross-platform verification, one has to keep in mind that the program semantics may include properties not only of the target hardware, but also of a program transformer, e.g., a C compiler. In case of the ANSI C programming language, the program semantics of a sequential C program does not even completely describe the program behavior in the value domain [10]. We call a sequential program's semantics of the value domain *functional semantics*.

Thus, verifying a platform by comparing its behavior in the value domain with a reference platform has the problem that both platforms may behave differently.

Our way to resolve this is to transform the program before executing it on the reference platform (B), such that it exhibits the same functional semantics on the reference platform as on the target platform (A) (functional equivalence between platforms).

4.5 Verification of Embedded Systems

Our verification framework [11] allows to analyze embedded software both, by testing and formal verification. It allows to dynamically test the program and to formally verify the software using the identically generated models. The key idea is that the test data required for testing are generated by model checking. To do this, a formal model of the program is required as input to the model checker. When this model has been built, it can be used for the test data generation using model checking and for formal verification. Thus, in the framework two platforms are supported: the host platform involving the model for the model checker and the target platform (the embedded system). The test data that have been generated using model checking are subsequently used to exercise the program running on the target hardware. During these test runs, it is checked whether the test data produce correct results (both, test data and results have to be transformed to ensure functional equivalence between the platforms). One of the core contributions of this framework is that this way of using the formal model increases the confidence in the model. If any faults are observed within these executions, the reasons have to be investigated: the cause can be located within the framework (i.e., erroneous model transformation) or within the execution platform (i.e., hardware, compiler). Thus, the presented framework forms a kind of intelligent self-assessment mechanism helping to create correct formal models and to ensure the correctness of the applied transformations.

Testing Framework. Besides the above mentioned formal model representing the core of the verification framework, reference platform testing is supported. The transformed target program can be executed on the host which yields execution traces. These traces are recorded and compared to executions performed on the target hardware. It is also possible to use test data generated by model checking to exercise the transformed target program on the host in order to obtain a preflight check of the generated data. On the first glance, this may look a little bit strange, however, in practical use it turned out that each of these components is very useful.

Formal Verification. As we use a formal model of the software under test, it is possible to use the same model for formal verification. We can extract this formal model directly from the software. However, formal verification is not sufficient to ensure correct behavior of the software. This is because the behavior of a component is defined by the software as well as its execution platform and it is practically infeasible to model and analyze the PSS of the execution platform in full detail.

However, we have to model the PSS at least partially, since as introduced in Section 4.4, the PIS of ANSI C source programs in general is not enough to get the behavior of the software in the value domain.

5   Cross-Platform Verification Framework

The verification framework uses model-based testing to generate test cases. Since we use model checking for our test case generation, it is relatively easy to derive test cases that feature a specific coverage criteria. As with conventional testing, using such a framework does not permit to apply the ideal testing metrics of path coverage. And of course, achieving even more comprehensive coverage like state coverage is far from feasible. In practice, coverage-based testing is reduced to coverage metrics that cover local structures of the control flow graph, e.g., statement coverage or branch coverage.

Our testing framework provides additional flexibility as it allows us to decompose the program into segments of parametric size and achieve path coverage within each of these segments. The verification based on such a segmentation is used to verify the execution platforms of our measurement-based WCET analysis [12].

As a feature of our framework, we utilize the same formal model for both, formal verification and testing. The key drivers for the architecture of our verification framework are:

1. **Automated test data generation:** Test data should be generated completely automatically. We use bounded model checking for this purpose.
2. **Extendability:** The extension to new test cases (formal verification and cross-platform testing) as well as to new target platforms should be easily possible. This flexibility is achieved by using ANSI-C as language for applications subject to test.
3. **Cross-platform testing:** Due to faults in the build environment or hardware configuration, end-to-end testing is necessary even for unit testing.

5.1   Overview

In Figure 2 the architecture of the framework is illustrated. The big gray shaded background arrows show processing that is performed completely automatically by the framework. There are no user interactions required. Following, we present an overview about each step performed by the framework.

The C-code passed to our tool is strongly dependent on the actually used target platform.

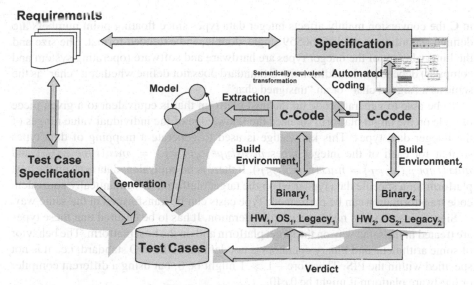

Fig. 2. Verification framework

Thus, in the first step the code for the target platform is transformed to a semantically equivalent C-code for the host platform. The transformed code is used as a "reference implementation" for testing hardware and compiler effects.

Further, from this C-code we extract models with respect to the test case specification, i.e., depending on the actual test case specification modifications are automatically applied to the source code (e.g., adding additional constraints from the specification required by the test case).

These modified source codes are passed to the CBMC model checker [13]. The model checker generates the desired test data by deriving a counter-example. Failures occuring in this step indicate possible contradictions in the test case specification. For instance, when generating data for simple C1 coverage (basic block coverage), test data can always be provided as long as the code is reachable. Whenever no test data can be found, the program may contain unreachable code.

Finally, the resulting test data and reference results are delivered to the execution environments. This is a two phase process: first the sample data is issued to the host platform to verify the generated test data. Usually this process finishes successfully. Then in the second step, the respectively converted test data is provided to the target platform execution environment. Finally, the results calculated on the target platform are compared with the results on the host platform, resulting in a final verdict.

Section 5.2 outlines the process of code transformation in more detail. Section 5.3 explains the test data generation process.

5.2 Code Transformation

A code transformation is performed to generate code for the host platform with exactly the same behavior like the original code on the target platform. For applications written in C the conversion mainly affects integer data types since floating point numbers are defined according to the IEC 60559 single, double, and extended format. The size and the binary layout of the integer types are hardware and software (operating system and compiler) dependent. In addition the C Standard does not define whether a "char" is the same as a "signed char" or an "unsigned char".

To be able to generate code on the host platform that is equivalent to a given piece of code on the target platform we need the knowledge of the individual value ranges of the integer data types. This knowledge is used to generate a mapping of data types so that for each of the integer types $min(type_{TARGET}) = min(type_{HOST})$ and $max(type_{TARGET}) = max(type_{HOST})$. If there is no equivalent data type on the host platform for a specific data type used on the target platform, no semantically equivalent code transformation can be performed. Type casts can be transformed in the same way.

Signed integer types need special consideration. It has to be ensured that these types are treated in the same way on the target platform and on the host platform. The behavior of some arithmetic and binary operators is not defined in the ISO standard, i.e., it is not specified within the PIS. Therefore $-1 \gg 1$ might be 0, but using a different compiler or hardware platform it might be $0x40$.

The behavior of bit fields is undefined. The ISO standard does not state if an implementation has to restrict variable values to fit the width given in the declaration. If a is declared as "struct { unsigned int a : 3; }" then a should be in the range from zero to seven. The ISO standard does not describe the behavior for the case that a value outside this range is assigned to a. The same behavior on the target platform and on the host platform has to be ensured.

There are some compiler or platform specific extensions like #pragma directives or _near or _far modifiers, whose influence on the code semantic has to be examined individually. Modifiers like _near or _far that influence neither data types nor control flow can be expected to conserve the semantics of the application.

Target-specific hardware has to be available or to be emulated on the host platform if it is used in the examined application. If neither is possible, then no semantically equivalent code transformation can be performed.

When a code transformation is performed the target platform code is parsed into a syntax tree. Based on this tree, the host platform code is generated. However, integer types have to be modified according to the rules given above. If there are any constructs that cannot be converted safely, the transformation has to stop with an error message.

Figure 3 shows the code on the target platform (with a word size of 16 bit) and the semantically equivalent code generated for the i386 platform. In this case the transformation from the target to the host architecture has been accomplished by converting the int data type on the target to the short data type on the host.

5.3   Test Data Generation

The target platform code cannot only be transformed into semantics-equivalent code for the host platform. It is used to generate a semantics-equivalent application model that can be used with a model checker. The complexity of this task depends on the model checker syntax and semantics. For model checkers like CBMC [13], which uses

```
 1  int max (int a, int b)
 2  {
 3      int max;
 4      if (a>b) {
 5          max = a;
 6      } else {
 7          max = b;
 8      }
 9      return max;
10  }
```

```
 1  short max(short a, short b)
 2  {
 3      short max;
 4      if (a>b) {
 5          max = a;
 6      } else {
 7          max = b;
 8      }
 9      return max;
10  }
```

Fig. 3. Target code vs. host code

models specified in C, the implementation effort is much lower compared to other model checkers like SAL, whose input language strongly differs from C.

In the described testing framework, model checking is performed within an external module which allows to use either CBMC or SAL depending on the size and complexity of the examined application. Since model checkers often use exact math in contrast to C which uses residue classes for arithmetic operations, the behavior of C arithmetic operations has to be simulated on this model checkers.

For this purpose, we implemented two different model checking backends for our framework. One for the symbolic model checker SAL and another one for the ANSI-C model checker CBMC [13]. In case of the SAL backend the C-code is converted to semantics-equivalent code of the model checker input language.

Depending on the selected coverage criteria, different models are generated. Currently, branch coverage (C1) and path coverage (C2) for program segments is supported. The detailed model generation mechanism is described in [11]. The generated test data are stored in a XML repository.

5.4 Communication and Test Data Representation

As already described, differences in the platform-specific semantics have to be considered when transforming the programs between platforms. We decided to choose the host platform as base platform.

Test data are stored platform independent in XML repositories, the respective values are represented as logical integer numbers. When test data is exchanged across platform boundaries, the corresponding transformations are carried out completely automatically by the framework, which has to be aware of the host and the target platform properties. Important properties are the data size and layout which may be either big or little endian.

An important issue is, where the data conversion from XML to platform specific binary values takes place. Since the targets are likely limited in resources the conversions are performed on the host. The host automatically generates stubs for the target that receive the platform specific test data via a RS232 or USB link, writes the data to the variables (local variables are also placed within the stub) and executes the target code. The stub traces the program execution using callback functions and writes the results back to the host where they are checked for correctness.

6 Experiments

In this section we describe the setup of our experiments. We perform cross-platform testing for selected applications.

In order to show the cross-platform testing mechanism, we decided to perform basic block coverage cross-platform testing. In this experiment, the generated and verified test data is used for structural tests on a Motorola HCS12 evaluation board with its respective build environment (using the commercial C compiler).

As benchmark sample we used three C-code files (like before each containing one function that is subject to our test). Function F5 is a simple demo function, function F11 and F12 contain industrial code.

We summarized the results in Figure 4. When applying structural basic block coverage test to the more complex applications we got very surprising results.

Function Name	Characteristics					Testing Time				Result		
	Industrial code	Lines of code	# Basic blocks	# Basic blocks reachable	Complexity (# paths)	Testdata generation (m)	Target verification (m)	Total (m)	Time / basic block (m)	# Basic blocks reached correctly	Correctness %	Error reason
Function F5	no	46	30	30	72	1,2	2,8	4,0	0,13	30	100%	None
Function F11	yes	274	54	54	97	4,5	5,3	9,8	0,18	54	100%	None
Function F12	yes	1150	171	165	1,90E+11	124,7	21,5	146,2	0,85	159	96%	Compiler defect

Fig. 4. Experimental Results

```
1   typedef signed short int T_INT16;
2   typedef signed long int T_INT32;
3
4   T_INT32 in_32;
5
6   void test(void) {
7     T_INT32 Aux_S32;
8
9     Aux_S32 = (T_INT16) ((T_INT32)in_32 / (T_INT16)3);
10
11    // Aux_S32 = ((T_INT32)in_32 / (T_INT16)3);
12    // Aux_S32 = (T_INT16) Aux_S32;
13  }
14
15  void my_frame(void) {
16    in_32 = 0x8000001E;  // -2147483618
17    test();
18  }
```

Listing 1.1. Code for defect D1

```
1   typedef signed short T_INT16;
2   typedef signed long T_INT32;
3
4   volatile T_INT32 t;
5   volatile T_INT32 t1;
6   volatile T_INT32 c1 ;
7
8   void test2(void) {
9     t1 = (T_INT32) ((T_INT16) ((T_INT32)c1 /
10                              ((T_INT16) 0x4000 )));
11
12    t = (T_INT32) ((T_INT16) ((T_INT32)0x8001 ));
13  }
14
15  void ingo_test(void) {
16    c1 = 0x20007FFF;
17    test2();
18  }
```

Listing 1.2. Code for defect D2

First, there is some difference between the number of basic blocks and the number of reachable basic blocks. With basic blocks that are proved by the model checker being not reachable may seem to be something wrong. However, the reason for this is that code generators assign fixed values to some parameters. Thus, there is some code that cannot be executed at runtime. Second, when cross-platform testing is applied some basic blocks could not be reached correctly as on the reference platform where test data have been already verified. The reason for this problem turned out to be some compiler defect. We found 3 other industrial applications where similar compiler errors occurred.

Due to the fact that the code of function F12 (respectively the other industrial applications) is proprietary and it is hard to see the defect, we constructed smaller examples D1 and D2 showing these problems.

Defect D1 is illustrated in Listing 1.1. The calculation of the variable Aux_S32 should result in 0x00005560 on both platforms. However, on the HCS12 platform it yields 0xFFFF8000 (using version 4.6a of the compiler). When the statement is rewritten in an alternative form as shown at lines 11 and 12 in Listing 1.1, the computed result is correct. After we reported this bug to the compiler manufacturer, the bug was committed and few weeks later a version was provided having this bug fixed.

However, after installing the new compiler version and re-running the tests, we found another problem referred to as D2. The simplified example code is depicted in Listing 1.2. In the correct case the calculation of t1 and t yields 0xFFFF8001. However, on the HCS12 platform t1 yields 0x00008001 and t equals 0xFFFF8001. In line 9 the division results in the intermediary result 0x00008001. It seems that in this expression the cast to INT16 is simply omitted by the compiler (although all optimizations are disabled). A few weeks after the second bug has been submitted to the manufacturer, a corrected version has been delivered where no further faults have been detected.

7   Summary and Conclusion

We introduced the notion of cross-platform verification for embedded systems. Based on a target source code, a semantics-equivalent model is generated for a host computer. By model checking, respective test data are generated that are self-checked on the host. As practice has shown, this self-check is very useful to verify whether the test data (and the models behind) are correct (self assessment mechanism). Then, these data are used to exercise the actual execution platform and the results are compared with those on the host computer (reference platform testing). Due to our experience, it is highly important to include the whole execution platform involving the compiler, linker, target loader, and the hardware itself to exhaustively test embedded systems (end-to-end testing).

The model generation mechanism that is used for test data generation can be also used for formal verification. This has the advantage that the confidence into the models is increased as the same mechanisms are used. From our experience, the joint use of formal models and test data obtained from them seems promising.

In the future, we plan to add new platforms and so – by platform diversification – more faults can be detected in execution platforms. Further, it is easily possible to extend the framework to support other coverage criteria.

In our experiments, we have shown that by using this method even compiler faults can be detected.

Acknowledgments. Our tool uses the CBMC model checker developed by Daniel Kroening and Edmund Clarke at Carnegie Mellon University. Further, we use the SAL model checker developed by Leonardo Demura at SRI Labs.

References

1. Laprie, J.C., Randell, B.: Basic concepts and taxonomy of dependable and secure computing. IEEE Trans. Dependable Secur. Comput. (Fellow-Algirdas Avizienis and Senior Member-Carl Landwehr) 1(1), 11–33 (2004)
2. Lackner, K.: Bordelektronik im Zwielicht Economy Austria - Printausgabe (25 August 2006)
3. Commission, I.E.: Functional safety of electrical / electronic / programmable electronic safety-related systems. IEC standard 61508 (1998)
4. Software considerations in airborne systems and equipment certification. RTCA/DO-178B (1992)
5. Beyer, D., Chlipala, A.J., Henzinger, T., Jhala, R., Majumdar, R.: Generating tests from counterexamples. In: Proc. 26th International Conference on Software Engineering (ICSE), Edinburgh, Scotland, UK, pp. 326–335. IEEE Computer Society Press, Los Alamitos (2004)
6. Rayadurgam, S., Heimdahl, M.P.E.: Coverage based test-case generation using model checkers. In: Proc. 8th IEEE International Conference and Workshop on the Engineering of Computer Based Systems (ECBS '01), IEEE Computer Society Press, Washington, DC (2001)
7. Ammann, P., Black, P.E., Majurski, W.: Using model checking to generate tests from specifications. In: Proc. 2nd IEEE International Conference on Formal Engineering Methods, Brisbane, Queensland, Australia, pp. 46–54. IEEE Computer Society Press, Los Alamitos (1998)
8. Hamon, G., deMoura, L., Rushby, J.: Generating efficient test sets with a model checker. In: 2nd International Conference on Software Engineering and Formal Methods, Beijing, China, pp. 261–270. IEEE Computer Society Press, Los Alamitos (2004)
9. Clarke, E., Grumberg, O., Peled, D.: Model Checking. MIT Press, Cambridge (1999)
10. Koenig, A.: C Traps and Pitfalls. Addison-Wesley, Reading (1988)
11. Wenzel, I.: Measurement-Based Timing Analysis of Superscalar Processors. PhD thesis, Technische Universität Wien, Institut für Technische Informatik, Treitlstr. 3/3/182-1, 1040 Vienna, Austria (2006)
12. Wenzel, I., Rieder, B., Kirner, R., Puschner, P.: Automatic timing model generation by CFG partitioning and model checking. In: Design, Automation and Test in Europe, 2005. Proceedings, pp. 606–611 (2005)
13. Clarke, E., Kroening, D.: Hardware verification using ANSI-C programs as a reference. In: Proceedings of ASP-DAC 2003, pp. 308–311. IEEE Computer Society Press, Los Alamitos (2003)

Experimental Analysis on Time-Triggered Power Consumption Measurement with DVS-Enabled Multiple Power Domain Platform

Songah Chae[1], Doo-Hyun Kim[1,*], Changhee Jung[2], Duk-Kyun Woo[2], and Chaedeok Lim[2]

[1] Embedded S/W and Sensor (Essens) Lab.
Konkuk University, Seoul, Korea
{sachae, doohyun}@konkuk.ac.kr
[2] Embedded S/W Research Division, ETRI, Taejon, Korea
{chjung, dkwu, cdlim}@etri.re.kr

Abstract. Recently, the battery and low-power H/W technologies for mobile and wearable computing devices have been advanced rapidly. But on the other hand the computation and communication demands of the embedded applications are increasing more rapidly. Therefore, the application developers are still required to develop their codes to utilize the available energy as efficient as possible. The provision of software power measurement with reasonable accuracy, consistency and low overhead is an indispensable factor for software power engineering. In this paper, we present a time-triggered mechanism for providing energy consumption profiles in the level of C functions. The similar mechanisms have already been introduced at the previous researches such as PowerScope and ePRO. Instead, we, in this paper, introduce our efforts to extend these researches to incorporate power domains and DVS(Dynamic Voltage Scaling), then interpret these mechanisms as the view of time-triggered approach for better understanding to the relationships among timer interrupt, context switching, DAQ triggering, multi-channel DAQ delay, and etc. From our experimental results, we could conclude that the time-triggered approach for the function level energy measurement properly worked with low overheads and produced consistent energy consumption profiles on the DVS-applied program codes running upon the platforms supporting multiple power domains.

Keywords: Embedded Software, Power Consumption Measurement, Dynamic Voltage Scaling.

1 Introduction

Power aware computing is becoming fundamentally important with the proliferation of portable, battery operated systems, such as PDA, cellular phones, MP3 player,

---

* Corresponding author: New Millennium Hall 1203, School of Internet and Multimedia Engineering, Konkuk University, Kwangjin-Gu, Seoul, 143-701, Korea.

R. Obermaisser et al. (Eds.): SEUS 2007, LNCS 4761, pp. 149–158, 2007.

PMP(Portable Media Player), and etc. In order to support the low power management, there has been variety of research areas in wide levels of spectrum including compiler, OS, system architecture, microprocessor, circuit and other H/W component as well as power consuming applications. Among these areas, the microprocessors have been mainly focused on providing low power functionalities such as DVS(Dynamic Voltage Scaling) and DFS(Dynamic Frequency Scaling). For example, Intel's PXA27x processor family is providing six power modes for enabling more efficient power management than the previous XScale processor family. Although such low-power H/W and battery technologies have been recently advanced rapidly, the computation and communication demands of such embedded applications are increasing more rapidly. Therefore, the application developers are still required to develop their codes to utilize the available energy as efficient as possible; consequently, the provision of software power measurement with reasonable accuracy, consistency and low overhead is an indispensable factor for software power engineering.

In this paper, we present a time-triggered mechanism for providing energy consumption profiles in the level of C functions of the applications using dynamic voltage scaling. The time-triggered mechanism uses periodic timer interrupts for activating DAQ(Data Acquisition) instrument, which is installed outside of the target device, to acquire the power from the concerned power domains such as processor core and memory. In addition, the timer interrupt handler records the instruction counter at the same moment. The stored trail of power and instruction counters is combined by referencing symbol table, generated at the compile time, to produce accumulated energy for each function in the application codes.

The similar mechanisms were already introduced at the previous researches such as PowerScope[7] and ePRO[9]. Instead, we, in this paper, introduce our efforts to extend these researches to incorporate power domains and DVS, then interpret these mechanisms as the view of time-triggered approach for better understanding to the relationships among timer interrupts, context switching, DAQ triggering, multi-channel DAQ delay, and etc. We also present our experimental results as an experimental validation of these time-triggered approaches in the presence of power domain and DVS.

The chapter 2 will provide background for the power estimation of software and introduce related researches and our own efforts. The chapter 3 will be focused on introducing our facilitations for the domain-wise power measurement of DVS-related applications. The section 4 will present our experimental results with our interpretation in the view of consistency and overhead. The section 4 will conclude this paper with suggestions for further research directions such as imposing our efforts into other time-triggered engines like TMO (Time-triggered and Message-triggered Object) [3].

2   Backgrounds and Related Works

2.1 Power Consumption of Software

According to the elaborated research results [1], while the instruction level current consumption in SA-1100 has a variation of about 38%, the variation of the current consumption in programs is much less, that is, 8% in maximum. This means that the current consumption depends on the operating voltage and frequency of the processor rather than a piece of code. But, as mentioned in [1], it might be significant in datapath dominated processors.

Also, the microprocessors have been mainly focused on providing low power functionalities with such as DVS and DFS. There is a quadratic dependency on the voltage with power consumption. This means that halving the voltage reduces the power consumption to one-fourth its original value. Meanwhile, reducing the power to one-fourth its original value only halves the maximum frequency since the maximum frequency is roughly linear in the voltage [2]. Thus, if the codes run at different frequency and different voltage by using DVS capabilities in certain situations, then the same codes lead different power consumptions.

In addition, the Intel PXA27x, for example, provides ten power domains such as VCC_CORE, VCC_MEM, VCC_LCD, and etc, as well as it allows DVM(Dynamic Voltage Management). In conjunction with PMIC(Power Manage Integrated Circuit), it provides six power modes such as IDLE, DEEP IDLE, and STANBY modes of which each mode requires different levels of voltage in each power domain[4-7]. So, the behavior of codes can also significantly affect the usage of power by changing power modes. Accordingly, it is necessary to allow application software developers to analyze the power consuming behavior of his/her program codes in details in the presence of DVS and power domains as well as in the view of the whole behaviors.

2.2 Software Power Measurement Tool

Software power measurement tool is the indispensable factor in leading application software developers to develop their software with the awareness on the power consumption. For this purpose, the tools are required to support several key factors such as the accuracy, consistency, low overhead, usability as well as DVS and power domains. The accuracy is supposed to depend on various aspects such as the usage of instrumental equipments for DAQ, the delay and jitter engaged with the channel multiplexing in DAQ instrument, and timer interrupt regularity.

The consistency is also important factor to the developers in the process of power optimization. The tools have to provide dependable measurements by providing consistent results with reasonable minor ratio of deviations for the same codes and same situations even in case of using time-sharing and multi-tasking platforms. The low overhead requirement is also important since some part of power measurement mechanism potentially intervenes the execution of the concerned application. As a sort of software engineering tools, the power measurement tool has interactions with users, i.e., software developers, hence, is necessarily required to provide decent multilateral views with proper presentation schemes.

2.3 Related Works

There were several research works related to this paper, including PowerScope[8], SES[9], ePRO[10], Arun[11] and Esto[12]. PowerScope[8] uses digital multimeter for DAQ with the support of triggering from OS running in the target system. It does not need to impose extra hardware into the target system. PowerScope maps energy consumption acquired from the external multimeter to program structure to determine the energy consumption of different procedures within a program. SES [9] collects energy consumption data in cycle-by-cycle resolution and maps the data into program structure to provide higher accuracy and resolution. But, SES needs extra acquisition module with measurement circuit, profile controller and acquisition memory, and hence, it may not be applied to ordinary target systems not equipped with the modules.

While it uses similar techniques used in PowerScope and SES, the ePRO [10] does not need extra instrumentation like SES and provides performance profiling as well as energy profiling. As its experimental target system, ePRO uses a commercial toolbox using PAX255 which enables performance profiling by using PMU(Performance Monitoring Uint) provided at architecture level. These previous research works gave many inspirations and technical details to our works. However, those are not dealing with the situations using DVS, nor considering simultaneous acquisitions from separate multiple power domains. The work from Arun Thomas[11] deals with DVS in their measurement platform. But it measures only the power of the overall laptop system with extra external circuits, and does not support function level energy profile.

Esto [12] is a visual IDE(Integrated Development Environment), based on Eclipse 3.0, for the embedded applications running on Qplus Embedded Linux[12]. It supports optimization techniques by transforming loop structure of source code, such as loop distribution, loop interchanging, loop unrolling, and scalarization. This paper is related to enable Esto to provide energy profiling, using Intel Mainstone [4] as a primary target toolbox with DVS and power domains.

3   Time-Triggered Power Measurement

3.1   Architectural Mechanism

As illustrated in Figure 1 and Figure 2, our system consists of target system, host system and DAQ board with a connector block. For the DAQ, we use NI-PCI-6251[13] that can be plugged into PCI slot of the host system. The connector block, SCC-2345[14], enables connections between NI-PCI-6251 and pins from power domains in the target system microprocessor, PXA270A. The NI-PCI-6251 provides simultaneous acquisitions from multiple power domains through channels. For the target system, we use the Intel Mainstone toolbox [4-7] installed with Qplus embedded Linux [12] enhanced with kernel level low power management module, called Harmonia. By using the Harmonia API, application program codes can change the frequency of the processor properly according to the situations of execution. Then, the Harmonia maps the requested frequency to the proper voltage. The host system is just normal desktop Linux computer installed with the device driver for the NI-PCI-6251.

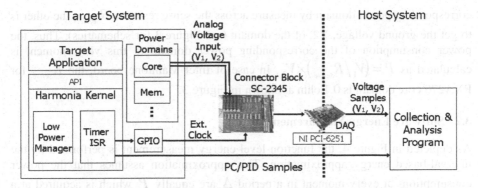

Fig. 1. Overall Architecture of Target System and DAQ facilitation

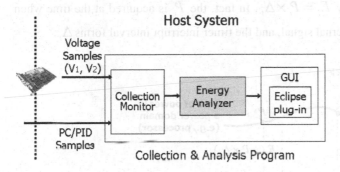

Fig. 2. Overall Architecture of Host System

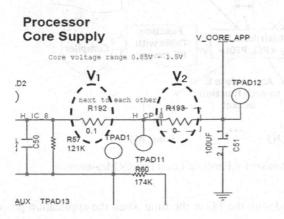

Fig. 3. Schematic around header for Core (excerpted from [5])

Simultaneously with the start of target application, the timer starts to generate timer interrupt to activate its corresponding ISR (Interrupt Service Routine). For our experiment, the timer interrupt interval was set-up with 2ms. Whenever the timer ISR is activated, it generates external signal through GPIO for invoking NI-PCI-6251 to acquire voltages from each concerned power domain through the SC-2345 connector block. In addition, the ISR also records program counter (PC) of the application process that has been suspended due to the timer interrupt. These records are used for deriving function level energy consumption profiles later at the host system.

The Intel Mainstone toolbox provides pairs of two outer pins of each power domain. Among these two pins of a pair, one is to get voltage drops, V1, of the corresponding power domain by measure across the sense resistor, R_{sense}, the other is to get the ground voltage, V2, of the domain (see Figure 3 for schematics). Thus, the power consumption of the corresponding power domain at this very moment is calculated as $P = (V_1/R_{sense}) \times V_2$. In case of Intel Maintone board, the R_{sense} for PXA270 core domain is 0.1 ohm as shown in Figure 3.

3.2 Software Energy Measurement

As depicted in Figure 4, the function level energy measurement is performed by the interval-based energy approximation. This approximation assumes that the power consumptions at every moment in a period Δ_t are equally P_i which is acquired at a single moment during the period. Thus, the energy consumption E_i during an interval Δ_t is obtained by $E_i = P_i \times \Delta_t$. In fact, the P_i is acquired at the time when the ISR generates the external signal, and the timer interrupt interval forms Δ_t.

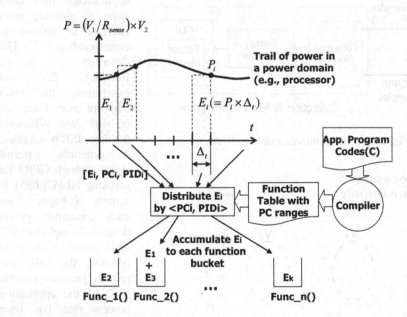

Fig. 4. Overall Mechanism for Function Level Energy Measurement

Each E_i is also accompanied with the PC at the time when the application process is interrupted. By using both of this PC and the function table generated at compile time, each E_i can be indexed and accumulated to the energy bucket corresponding to the function in the application program codes.

In the course of this indexing process, we have another assumption that the process in attention does not suffer any significant interventions from other processes. This assumption sounds quite unrealistic, but we could get quite consistent experimental data by simply not executing other processes during the measurement.

The above two assumptions necessarily affect the accuracy and consistency of the measurement. At first, the granularity of timer interrupt intervals mainly affects the density of the data acquisitions and eventually does the accuracy of the interval-based approximation. In fact, the regularity of timer interval is related to both of the accuracy and consistency of the measurement. It is true that the drifting of the timer interrupt intervals is rarely avoidable in time-sharing system, and if it goes over a reasonable range, then the accuracy can not be guaranteed. And also, if the irregularity happens, then the results of each measurement become inconsistent and consequently not dependable.

3.3 Timing Analysis

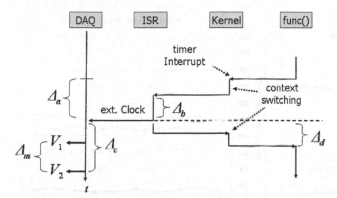

Fig. 5. Timing relationship diagram

Another important view point related the accuracy and consistency is the racing situation between the DAQ instrument and the target system. Immediately after the target system releases a external signal through GPIO, the target system continues remained works for finishing ISR and returning to the interrupted process. On the other hand, once the DAQ gets the signal from the target system, the DAQ starts off with scanning the channels. Fundamentally the time needed for a single acquisition should be negligible. But, in case when the DAQ instrument is required to perform multiple acquisitions from multiple channels, then it has to do multiplexing among channels, which takes relatively a while, i.e. Δ_m, compared to the speed of the target system processor. The SC-2345 and NI-DAQ-6251 need around 10 microseconds for acquiring both the V_1 and V_2 by multiplexing [13, 14]. Although these two values are from the different channel, these should be used simultaneously to get the single value of $P = (V_1/R_{sense}) \times V_2$. Thus, it takes at least the time for multiplexing delay in acquiring a single digital value P at a single moment. Therefore, as shown in Figure 5, there may exist a racing situation between Δ_c and Δ_d. In case of $\Delta_d \geq \Delta_c$, the measurement loses its validation since the DAQ instrument only acquires the power that the ISR uses. But, normally, the situation is

$\Delta_d < \Delta_c$ since the Δ_m which holds the most part of Δ_c is usually in the range of microseconds, while the processor takes at most few nanoseconds[1] for Δ_d.

4 Experimental Analysis

Figure 6 shows that the variance among measurements was insignificant when we repeated the same experiment ten times with the same program codes. The standard deviations were 1.03 mJ for 104MHz mode and 1.38mJ for 416MHz mode. This program simply performs a loop of integer multiplications ten million times with different frequencies. In addition, the overhead, $\Delta_a + \Delta_d$, mainly induced by the ISR for timer interrupt was only 0.3% which is relatively insignificant.

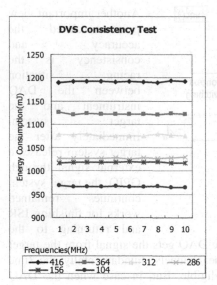 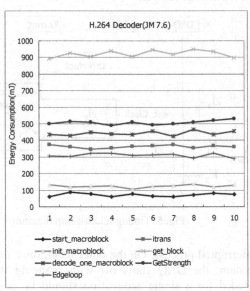

Fig. 6. Energy Consumption for same operations with different DVS

Fig. 7. Energy Consumption of major functions in H.264 Decoder (JM 7.6)

Figure 7 shows our experimental results when we applied our measurements to the JM Ver. 7.4, the open source S/W for H.264 decoder[15, 16]. Seeing the figure, it is consistent and clear that the meaningful functions in the decoder such as get_block(), GetStrength(), and decode_one_block() consume more energy than others like start_macroblock() which only initiates decoding of one block.

---

[1] The 624 MHz PXA270 is reported to perform 800 MIPS (http://en.wikipedia.org/wiki/Intel_XScale).

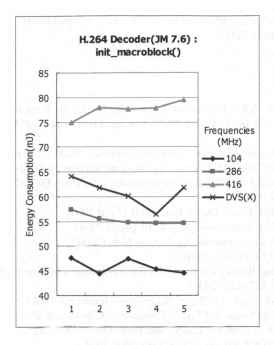

H.264 Decoder(JM 7.6) :
init_macroblock()

Frequencies
(MHz)
- 104
- 286
- 416
- DVS(X)

Fig. 8. Power Consumption of init_macroblock() with different DVSs

Figure 8 shows the results when we applied DVS into the init_macroblock() function so it is executed at 104MHz, 286MHz, and 416MHz modes. It also shows consistently that the same codes can consume more energy when executed with higher frequency, and vice versa. These two experiments on the H.264 decoder imply that it would be effective to elaborate upon the get_block() and change the power modes properly according to the picture types like I, P, B as the previous works [17]. This implication is also meaningful in that the time-triggered approach for the function level energy measurement properly works and gives consistent energy consumption profiles on the DVS-applied program codes running upon the platforms supporting multiple power domains.

5 Conclusions

The provision of software power measurement with reasonable accuracy, consistency and low overhead is indispensable factors for software power engineering. In this paper, we presented the time-triggered mechanism for providing energy consumption profiles in the level of C functions. The similar mechanisms were already introduced at the previous researches such as PowerScope and ePRO[8-11]. Instead, we introduced our efforts to extend these researches to incorporate the platform capabilities such as power domains and DVS, and interpreted these mechanisms as the view of time-triggered approach for better understanding to the relationships among timer interrupts, context switching, DAQ triggering, multi-channel DAQ delay, and etc. From our experiments, we could conclude that the time-triggered approach for the function level energy measurement properly worked with low overheads and produced consistent energy consumption profiles on the DVS-applied program codes running upon the platforms supporting multiple power domains.

Fundamentally, the time-triggered approach depends on the timer interrupts, thus, this approach can be imposed into or integrated with other time-triggered systems such as TMO [3]. The TMO uses clock interrupts for scheduling and dispatching the processor to SpM's and SvM's in TMO objects. If we add our time-triggered energy measurement mechanism into the clock interrupt hander of the TMO engine, then we might expect that the energy consumption behaviors of TMO objects can be analyzed in the level of SpM and SvM. This work is remained as our further research direction.

Acknowledgement. This paper was partially supported by ETRI, ITRC project from MIC, Korea, and Seoul R&BD Program in 2007.

References

1. Sinha, A., Ickes, N., Chandrakasan, A.P.: Instruction Level and Operating System Profiling for Energy Exposed Software. IEEE Tr. on VLSI Systems 11(6), 1044–1057 (2003)
2. Mudge, T.: Power: A First-class Architectural Design Constraint. Computer, 52–58 (2001)
3. Kim, K.H., Ishida, M., Liu, J.Q.: An Efficient Middleware Architecture Supporting Time-Triggered Message-Triggered Objects and an NT-based Implementation. In: Proc. ISORC '99, St. Malo, France, pp. 54–63 (May 1999)
4. Intel PXA27x Processor Developer's Kit, User's Guide, Rev. 4.001 (April 2004)
5. Intel PXA27x Processor Developer's Kit, Schematics, Rev. 4.001 (April 2004)
6. Intel PXA27x Processor Family Power Requirements, Application Note (2004)
7. Intel PXA27x Processor DVK PMIC(LDO) Card (2004)
8. Flinn, J., Satyanarayanan, M.: Managing Battery Lifetime with Energy-Aware Adaptation. ACM Tr. on Computer Systems 22(2), 137–179 (2004)
9. Shin, D., Shim, H., Joo, Y., Yun, H.-S., Kim, J., Chang, N.: Energy-Monitoring Tool for Low-Power Embedded Programs. IEEE Design and Test of Computers (July-August 2002)
10. Baek, W., Kim, Y.-J., Kim, J.: ePRO: A Tool for Energy and Performance Profiling for Embedded Applications. In: Proc. of ISOCC'04, pp. 372–375 (October 2004)
11. Thomas, A.: A Measurement Platform for DVS Algorithm Development and Analysis. TCC 402, Unversity of Virginia (2003)
12. Qplus, Electronics and Telecommunications Research Institute. http://qplus.or.kr/english/
13. Series, D.M: User Manual - NI 622x, NI 625x, and NI 628x Devices, National Instruments Corp (2006). http://www.ni.com/pdf/manuals/371022g.pdf
14. SCC-AI Series Isolated Analog Input Modules, User Guide, National Instrument Corp. http://www.ni.com/pdf/manuals/371066c.pdf
15. H.264/AVC Reference Software. http://iphome.hhi.de/suehring/tml/
16. Wiegand, T., Sullivan, G.J., Bjontegaard, G., Luthra, A.: Overview of the H.264/AVC Video Coding Standard. IEEE Tr. On Circuits and Systems for Vider Technology 13(7), 560–576 (2003)
17. Choi, K.W., Dantu, K., Cheng, W.C., Pedram, M.: Frame-Based Dynamic Voltage and Frequency Scaling for a MPEG Decoder. In: Proc. of 2002 IEEE/ACM Int'l conference on Computer-aided design, San Jose, CA, pp. 732–737 (2002)

A Framework for Hardware-in-the-Loop Testing of an Integrated Architecture

Martin Schlager[1], Roman Obermaisser[2], and Wilfried Elmenreich[2]

[1] TTTech Computertechnik AG
Schoenbrunner Strasse 7, 1040 Vienna, Austria
martin.schlager@tttech.com
[2] Vienna University of Technology
Treitlstrasse 3, 1040 Vienna, Austria
{romano,wil}@vmars.tuwien.ac.at

Abstract. In this paper we present a distributed Hardware-in-the-Loop (HiL) simulation approach that supports the verification and validation activities in an integrated architecture as recently developed in DECOS (Dependable Embedded COmponents and Systems), an integrated project within the Sixth Framework Programme of the European Commission. Focusing on the interconnection between the simulated environment and the Integrated System Under Test (ISUT), our approach involves the concept of a Smart Virtual Transducer (SVT) that replaces the physical transducers of the ISUT without a probe effect on the ISUT. Our approach enables a complexity reduction for setting up an HiL simulation and supports a well-designed scalable interface to an integrated architecture. Furthermore, we support non-intrusive, deterministic interaction between the environment simulation system and the ISUT in order to guarantee reproducible test-runs. We show an exemplary application of the proposed concept by tailoring the generic components of the proposed simulation approach to an automotive park assistant system.

1 Introduction

The increasing number of electronic functions in future automobiles requires a change from the traditional "one function – one Electronic Control Unit (ECU)" concept to integrated architectures that support bundling several functions in one ECU. Such an *integrated system architecture* must provide means to handle the complexity of distributed applications while supporting efficient integration of functions into the shared hardware.

An example for an integrated system architecture is the DECOS Integrated Architecture [1], which builds upon the validated architectural services of a time-triggered core architecture. A distributed time-triggered computer system provides a physical network as a shared resource for the communication activities of more than one application subsystem. Other integrated architectures are AUTOSAR [2] and IMA [3].

Integrated architectures pose also a challenge to the HiL test procedure, a standard method for testing of an embedded controller before its deployment [4].

R. Obermaisser et al. (Eds.): SEUS 2007, LNCS 4761, pp. 159–170, 2007.

HiL simulation is a technique where parts of a real system are replaced by a simulation, i. e., a mathematical model of these real system parts [5]. HiL simulation offers increased realism of the simulation because access to hardware features is provided that would not be available in a pure software simulation. In an integrated system, applying the HiL test procedure requires finding adequate interfaces between the simulator and the ISUT.

In this paper we present a distributed HiL simulation approach for the DECOS Integrated Architecture. The interaction between the simulated environment and the ISUT involves the concept of an SVT [6] that replaces the physical transducers of the ISUT without a probe effect on the ISUT. Thus, an ISUT as part of an integrated architecture can be connected to the HiL simulator in a non-intrusive way. Each SVT communicates with other components of a distributed environment simulator via a standardized time-triggered digital interface. Furthermore, an SVT emulates a transducer-specific interface. The proposed concept enables a complexity reduction for setting up a HiL simulation and supports a well-designed scalable interface to an integrated architecture.

The rest of the paper is structured as follows: Section 2 reviews related work in the area of HiL simulation. Section 3 describes structure and features of the integrated system architecture that is used in our approach. Section 4 elaborates on the architecture of the environmental simulation system and discusses the implications on reproducibility of simulation results. We present a case study based on an exemplary prototype application in Section 5. The paper is concluded in Section 6.

2   Related Work

HiL simulation involves physical hardware components, i. e., nodes, of a real-time system. Hence, HiL simulation requires the construction of an environment simulator in order to emulate the environment of these nodes [7]. In case only a subset of nodes of a distributed real-time system exists, non-existing nodes must be simulated by a cluster simulator as discussed in [8,9,10].

HiL simulators are constructed for a wide range of different applications. For instance in [11], real-time HiL simulation of vehicle and mobile robots is proposed to avoid extensive formal analysis of these systems. In the traffic control domain, system integrators are confronted with frequent changes of signal timing plans implemented in traffic controllers. These signal timing plans are provided by sub-suppliers as closed Intellectual Property (IP) software modules. Hence, HiL simulation is proposed in order to fine-tune these signal timing plans while at the same time protecting the IP of the individual sub-suppliers [12].

Commercially available HiL simulation systems range from simple simulators that target at testing a single ECU to complex simulators that are capable of testing large distributed real-time systems. *DSP Builder* [13] by Altera[1] and *Tanto2 Test* by Hitex[2] are examples for simple HiL simulators, where a single

---

[1] http://www.altera.com
[2] http://www.hitex.de

hardware target (i. e., an FPGA, or a single ECU) is directly connected to a development PC that executes an environment simulation.

Several vendors offer solutions for more complex HiL simulators. Regarding such complex HiL simulators, we can basically distinguish between monolithic and distributed HiL simulators.

A modular, component-based, monolithic HiL simulator, uses a single device that is configured to offer all required interfaces for a particular SUT. Monolitic HiL simulators are offered for instance by dSpace[3] (*Simulator Mid-Size, Simulator Full-Size*), The Mathworks[4] (*xPC Target*[14]), National Instruments[5] (*LabVIEW*), and Pi Technology[6] (*Pi Autosim*). These simulator products can be equipped with a range of modular I/O boards and processor boards in order to be tailored to a particular HiL simulation system. I/O hardware solutions include analog and digital I/O, CAN, PWM, dynamic signals, motion control, image acquisition as well as FPGA modules.

In contrast to a monolitic HiL simulator, a distributed HiL simulator consists of several interacting nodes that are capable of executing a distributed simulation model. Each of these nodes can be equipped with application-specific I/O hardware. Distributed HiL simulators are provided by Applied Dynamics International (ADI)[7] (*ADI rtX simulator*), Opal-RT[8] (*RT-LAB*), and RTDS Technologies[9] (*RTDS Simulator*). These distributed simulators interact either by the exchange of data that is visible at the interfaces of the SUT (*emulated electronic interfaces*), or by the exchange of data that is part of the simulation model and that is not visible at the SUT's interfaces (*virtual interfaces*) [15]. Communication via the virtual interfaces, i. e., interaction between different nodes of a distributed simulator is either realized by the implementation of an event-triggered protocol (e. g., Ethernet, SCRAMNet, FireWire, or INFINIBAND) or by a common communication backplane as for the RTDS Simulator, that links all processing nodes in parallel.

Although all HiL simulators are designed for real-time execution of a simulation model, the existing solutions lack a scalable approach for deterministic interaction between HiL simulator components. Moreover, none of the existing solutions target at HiL simulation in an integrated architecture.

3   Integrated System

Many large applications (e. g., in the automotive or aerospace domain) consist of a number of nearly independent application systems. We call such an application subsystem a Distributed Application Subsystem (DAS). A DAS provides a major part of the overall application and is composed of smaller functional elements

---

[3] http://www.dspace.com
[4] http://www.mathworks.com
[5] http://www.ni.com
[6] http://www.pitechnology.com
[7] http://www.adi.com
[8] http://www.opal-rt.com
[9] http://www.rtds.com

called *jobs*. In the automotive domain, the powertrain subsystem, the comfort subsystem, and the multimedia subsystem are examples for DASs. Examples of DASs in a present-day avionic application are the cabin pressurization system, the fly-by-wire system, and the in-flight entertainment system.

The proposed framework for HiL simulation is designed for integrated architectures, i. e., a single distributed computer system serves as the execution platform for multiple DASs. Each node computer of the distributed computer system contains jobs of one or more DASs (cf. Figure 1). Likewise, the communication network that interconnects the node computers serves the transport of messages between jobs of more than one DAS.

In the following, we will discuss the structural elements of the DECOS architecture (i. e., network, nodes, environment), because this system architecture will be used for the construction of the framework for HiL simulation.

3.1   Communication Network

The communication network of the integrated architecture executes a time-triggered protocol (e. g., TTP [16], FlexRay [17]). The rationale behind choosing a time-triggered communication protocol is the suitability for ultra-dependable systems [18]. Time-triggered communication protocols are characterized by a guaranteed message transport with low jitter, error containment between node computers, and a fault-tolerant distributed global clock service.

3.2   Node Computers

A node computer provides an execution environment for multiple collocated jobs of one or more DASs as shown in Figure 1. Each job implements a part of the

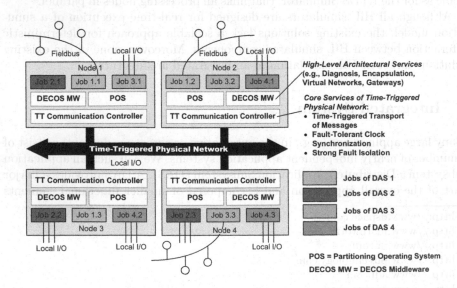

Fig. 1. Distributed System in the DECOS System Architecture

application functionality and is within the responsibility of a single organizational entity (e. g., a specific supplier).

The allocation of computational resources (e. g., memory, CPU time) to jobs occurs using a partitioning operating system with support for fault isolation and modular certification [19,20]. The partitioning operating system implements mechanisms for spatial and temporal partitioning in order to encapsulate the individual jobs. The scheduling of jobs needs to ensure that a timing failure of a job, such as a worst-case execution time violation, does not affect the CPU time available to other jobs. In analogy, the spatial partitioning mechanisms of the partitioning operating system enforce memory protection between jobs (e. g., with a memory management unit).

The interaction with other jobs occurs through the services provided by the DECOS middleware. The DECOS middleware offers high-level architectural services, which serve as a baseline for the development of applications. These services constitute the interface for the jobs to the underlying platform. Among the high-level services are gateway services, virtual network services, encapsulation services, and error detection services. On top of the time-triggered physical network, different kinds of virtual networks are established and each type of virtual network can exhibit multiple instantiations. Gateway services selectively redirect messages between virtual networks and resolve differences with respect to operational properties and naming. The encapsulation services control the visibility of exchanged messages and ensure spatial and temporal partitioning for virtual networks in order to obtain error containment.

Below the DECOS middleware, each node computer in Figure 1 contains the communication controller. The communication controller executes a time-triggered communication protocol as required for accessing the network. It provides so-called core architectural services (i. e., time-triggered transport of messages, fault-tolerant clock synchronization, strong fault isolation), which are used as the basis for the implementation of the high-level architectural services in the DECOS middleware.

The rationale for distinguishing between core architectural services and high-level architectural services is the ability to exploit existing time-triggered communication protocols for the construction of an integrated architecture. For example, it has been demonstrated by formal analysis [21] and experiments [22] that the Time-Triggered Protocol (TTP) is appropriate for the implementation of applications in the highest criticality class in the aerospace domain according to RTCA DO-178 B Level A.

3.3   Input/Output

In order to perform integration tests that involve the interaction between a given distributed computer system and its environment, the framework needs to simulate the physical surroundings of the computer system, i. e., the controlled object(s) and the operator. In a real-world system, the interaction between the computer system and the environment occurs via transducers, i. e., sensors and actuators. These transducers can either be connected directly or interfaced via a fieldbus. The latter approach simplifies the installation from a logical and a physical point of view and is extendable but might introduce higher cost and increased latency of sensory information and actuator control values.

4   Environmental Simulation

4.1   Simulator Architecture

HiL simulation of an ISUT involves a simulation of the environment of this ISUT by means of an environment simulator. The environment simulator is linked to the ISUT via the ISUTs Controlled Object Interface (COI) [23] which can either be a standardized digital transducer interface or an arbitrary transducer-specific interface (e. g., an analog interface).

In the following we introduce a development approach with generic components that can be tailored to establish the coupling between an HiL simulator and a specific ISUT. Hence, we separate between those components that emulate the COI, e. g., via a 4-15mA interface, a fieldbus, or direct I/O, and those components that are used to execute part of a distributed simulation model but do not directly interact with the ISUT.

Following this separation, our HiL simulation framework involves a distributed environment simulator consisting of a set of *Frontend Simulation Components (FSCs)* that control the physical interaction between the environment simulation and the ISUT, as well as a set of *Backend Simulation Components (BSCs)* that are used to execute (part of) the environment simulation model. Additionally, a time-sync master component is employed in the HiL simulation framework. The time-sync master component is part of the environment simulator, i. e., it triggers the individual FSCs and BSCs according to a pre-defined schedule. Furthermore, the time-sync master is a (passive) member of the ISUT, i. e., it

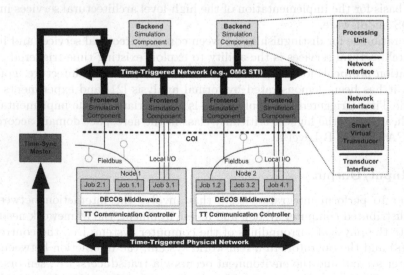

Fig. 2. HiL Simulation with an Integrated System

synchronizes its time-base with the time-base of the ISUT. Hence, the time-sync master establishes synchronism between the ISUT and the environment simulator without a probe effect with respect to the ISUTs execution.

As depicted in figure 2, the interaction of nodes of an ISUT with their environment is realized via an arbitrary transducer interface including value/time-depen dent analog and/or digital direct I/O as well as standardized fieldbus interfaces. An FSC connects to nodes of the integrated system for the purpose of interacting with these nodes via a particular transducer interface. FSCs and BSCs collectively execute the distributed simulation model of the environment of the ISUT.

An FSC requires updates of simulation values that are provided by one or several BSCs. Based on these simulation values, the FSC determines the I/O signal that is to be provided to the ISUT. Both the control logic that calculates the required I/O signal based on the simulation values and the physical wiring are part of the FSC. Thus, a change in the interface specification of the ISUT directly affects the FSC, but not necessarily the BSC as long as the FSCs can be provided with simulation values in time.

The availability of separate FSCs in an HiL simulation is particularly advantageous when it comes to incremental testing of an integrated system. Starting with a single node, a stepwise inclusion of jobs of the integrated system in the HiL simulation is required. At each step, the environment model of the real-time system is simulated (by BSCs) and the coupling between this simulation and the actual ISUT is established with FSCs. With separate FSCs it is possible to scale the HiL simulation from a small ISUT (e.g., a single node with only one job) up to a complete integrated system by adding additional FSCs as required.

FSCs of the environment simulator are realized by SVTs (cf. Figure 3). An SVT implements two interfaces – a standardized digital interface to a time-triggered transducer network (e.g., the Smart Transducer Interface of the Object Management Group [24]) and a transducer-specific interface. The digital interface is used to interact with the BSCs and with other SVTs (i.e., FSCs). The transducer-specific interface resembles the interface of a sensor or actuator element for coupling the SVT with direct I/O of the ISUT. Furthermore, an SVT can implement a certain fieldbus interface. In that case, the SVT would act as a gateway between the environment simulator and a fieldbus of the ISUT.

An SVT consists of a processor core, memory, a UART, as well as the digital and analog I/O necessary to emulate a specific transducer of the ISUT. The

Fig. 3. Smart Virtual Transducer (SVT)

prototype given in figure 3 includes an Atmel ATMega168 microcontroller and an Analog Devices 8-Bit DA converter (AD5330).

4.2 Reproducibility of Simulation Results

Deterministic interaction between the environment simulator (i. e., network of FSCs and BSCs) and the respective ISUT is important in order to guarantee reproducible results of an HiL simulation run. Thereby, deterministic interaction relates to the functional (i. e., message value or signal size) and the temporal domain (i. e., instant of interaction).

In order to achieve reproducible results in our proposed architecture, the following requirements have to be fulfilled:

1. The HiL simulator must share a common time base with the ISUT and have *a priori* knowledge about the time when a sensor is read or an actuator is set by the ISUT.
2. The values exchanged across interfaces between HiL simulator and ISUT must be deterministic.
3. The ISUT and the HiL simulator may not exhibit intrinsic sources of indeterminism, e. g., by suffering from race conditions.

The proposed architecture can satisfy the first requirement by sharing its existing global timebase with the HiL simulator. Furthermore, the DECOS architecture supports a time-triggered action model the allows the prediction of the instants of accessing a sensor's or actuator's value.

The second requirement depends on the employed interfaces. While the digitalization of a pure analog value, e. g., by an ADC, always constitutes a possible source of indeterminism, a DAC – ADC system may behave deterministically, when (i) there is no sampling while the current value is changing to a new one and (ii) each value generated by the DAC can be interpreted by the ADC in a non-ambiguous way. (i) is already solved by the synchronization mechanisms and the temporal determinism of our architecture while (ii) in general requires a careful design of the analog path. For sensor types with only few detection results, e. g., a binary on/off detector, (ii) can be easily fulfilled.

Regarding the HiL simulator, we can establish deterministic behavior due to the usage of a time-triggered communication and execution scheme. Deterministic construction of the ISUT lies outside the sphere of control of the HiL simulator and requires a deterministic architecture. Our proposed case study builds on a time-triggered architecture that avoids sources of indeterminism by design and thus fully satisfies the third requirement.

5   Case Study

5.1   Exemplary Application Using the Integrated Architecture

The case study used to exemplify the HiL simulation environment includes two automotive DASs (which are part of a larger automotive electronic system):

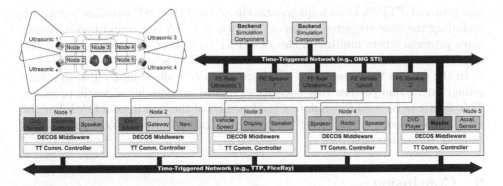

Fig. 4. Exemplary Integrated System with Environmental Simulation

- **Multimedia DAS.** Today's luxury cars contain multimedia functionality such as DVD players, high-end audio systems, and GPS navigation systems. In addition, voice control and hands-free speaker phones relieve the driver of concentrating on multimedia devices instead of traffic.
- **Park assist DAS.** This DAS implements a parking aid with ultra-sonic sensors. In case a threshold for a minimum distance is exceeded, the DAS produces an acoustic alarm signal. Therefore, the park assist DAS encompasses four jobs reading inputs from ultra-sonic distance sensors. In addition, the DAS contains an obstacle detector job, which reads the distance measurements from the four other jobs and determines whether an alarm signal should be produced. In this case, the acoustic alarm signal is transferred via a gateway to the speaker jobs of the multimedia DAS.

Figure 4 depicts a possible realization of these DASs using the DECOS architecture. Each node computer hosts multiple jobs, which can belong to different DASs (such as the multimedia or park assist DAS).

5.2 Exemplary Environmental Simulation

In the scope of the case study we exemplarily focused on two kinds of transducers, namely ultra-sonic sensors for distance measurement of the park assist DAS and loudspeakers of the multimedia DAS. Hence, the interaction between the environment simulation and the integrated system (i. e., the ISUT) across the COI involves SVTs that emulate the behavior of an ultra-sonic sensor as well as SVTs that capture and process the signals provided by the audio system jobs of the ISUT.

As depicted in figure 4, the setup of the environment simulation system additionally involves an FSC that receives the actual vehicle speed from the ISUT (i. e., *FE vehicle speed*) and a master node that controls the operation of the involved SVTs (i. e., *Master*) and that synchronizes the time-base of the environment simulation to the time-base of the ISUT.

Within the prototypical realization of the environment simulation system, we use TTP/A [25] to interconnect the deployed SVTs. The time-triggered fieldbus protocol TTP/A is an implementation of the OMG ST interface standard, including the time-triggered transport service. TTP/A is a round-based master slave protocol where multiple nodes of a TTP/A cluster arbitrate a shared bus according to a *time division multiple access (TDMA)* scheme.

In the current implementation we prototypically realized an SVT with a simplified interaction pattern that consists of digital samples for acoustic pressure. This SVT can be used to emulate a loudspeaker of the multimedia DAS. For the ultra-sonic sensors we realized SVTs that emulate a Polaroid 6500 series sonar ranging transducer [26].

6 Conclusion

In this paper we outlined a distributed HiL simulator that consists of FSCs and BSCs that are interlinked by a standardized digital transducer interface, e. g., the OMG STI. For the realization of the FSCs we propose to use SVTs that replace the physical transducers of the ISUT.

Besides showing an exemplary application of the proposed concept in the automotive domain, we discussed the prerequisites to achieve reproducible results in our proposed architecture.

Our approach supports the verification and validation activities in an integrated architecture, e. g., DECOS, IMA, AUTOSAR and supports deterministic interaction between an HiL simulator and an ISUT in order to guarantee reproducible test results. Moreover, this approach offers the possibility to test an integrated system at the physical interface. Hence, it is possible to perform non-intrusive (black box) tests which is particularly important for an integrated system where different vendors provide closed IP software or hardware/software components.

Acknowledgments

This work has been supported in part by the European IST project ARTIST2 under project No. IST-004527, the European IST project DECOS under project No. IST-511764, and DOC [DOKTORANDENPROGRAMM DER ÖSTERREICHISCHEN AKADEMIE DER WISSENSCHAFTEN]. We would like to thank Bernhard Wenzl for proofreading an earlier version of this paper.

References

1. Obermaisser, R., Peti, P., Huber, B., El Salloum, C.: DECOS: An integrated time-triggered architecture. e&i journal (Journal of the Austrian professional institution for electrical and information engineering) 3 (March 2006)
2. AUTOSAR GbR. AUTOSAR - Technical Overview V2.0.1 (June 2006)
3. Aeronautical Radio Incorporated (ARINC), Annapolis, MD, USA. ARINC Specification 651: Design Guide for Integrated Modular Avionics (November 1991)

4. National Instruments Corporation. LabVIEW FPGA in hardware-in-the-loop simulation applications, (July 2003)
5. Wu, X., Lentijo, S., Deshmuk, A., Monti, A., Ponci, F.: Design and implementation of a power-hardware-in-the-loop interface: a nonlinear load case study. In: Applied Power Electronics Conference and Exposition (APEC) 2005, pp. 1332–1338. IEEE Computer Society Press, Los Alamitos (2005)
6. Schlager, M., Elmenreich, W., Wenzel, I.: Interface design for hardware-in-the-loop simulation. In: Proceedings of the IEEE International Symposium on Industrial Electronics (ISIE'06), Montréal, Canada, pp. 1554–1559 (July 2006)
7. Schütz, W.: Testing distributed real-time systems: An overview. Research Report 12/1995, Technische Universität Wien, Institut für Technische Informatik, Treitlstr. 1-3/182-1, 1040 Vienna, Austria (1995)
8. Fleisch, W., Ringle, T., Belschner, R.: Simulation of application software for a TTP real-time subsystem. In: European Simulation Multiconference (ESM), Istanbul, Turkey (June 1997)
9. Galla, T.: Cluster Simulation in Time-Triggered Real-Time Systems. PhD thesis, Technische Universität Wien, Institut für Technische Informatik, Treitlstr. 3/3/182-1, 1040 Vienna, Austria (1999)
10. Schlager, M.: A simulation architecture for time-triggered transducer networks. In: Proceedings of the First Workshop on Intelligent Solutions for Embedded Systems (WISES'03), Vienna, Austria, pp. 39–49 (June 2003)
11. Papp, Z., Dorrepaal, M., Verburg, D.J.: Distributed hardware-in-the-loop simulator for autonomous continuous dynamical systems with spatially constrained interactions. In: Proceedings of the IEEE International Parallel and Distributed Processing Symposium, Nice, France (April 2003)
12. Li, Z., Kyte, M., Johnson, B.: Hardware-in-the-loop real-time simulation interface software design. In: Proceedings of the IEEE Intelligent Transportation Systems Conference, Washington, D.C., USA, pp. 1012–1017 (October 2004)
13. Altera Corporation. DSP Builder - user guide (April 2006), Available at www.altera.com
14. Burns, D.J., Rodriguez, A.A.: Hardware-in-the-loop control system development using MATLAB and xPC. Report, Department of Electrical Engineering, Center for System Science and Engineering, Arizona State University (May 2002)
15. Applied Dynamics International. Distributed HIL simulation (2005), Available at www.adi.com
16. TTTech Computertechnik AG, Schönbrunner Strasse 7, A-1040 Vienna, Austria. Time-Triggered Protocol TTP/C - High Level Specification Document (July 2002)
17. FlexRay Consortium. BMW AG, DaimlerChrysler AG, General Motors Corporation, Freescale GmbH, Philips GmbH, Robert Bosch GmbH, and Volkswagen AG. FlexRay Communications System Protocol Specification 2.1 (May 2005)
18. Suri, N., Walter, C.J., Hugue, M.M.: Advances In Ultra-Dependable Distributed Systems. ch. 1. IEEE Computer Society Press, Los Alamitos (1995)
19. Schlager, M., Herzner, W., Wolf, A., Gründonner, O., Rosenblattl, M., Erkinger, E.: Encapsulating application subsystems using the DECOS core OS. In: Górski, J. (ed.) SAFECOMP 2006. LNCS, vol. 4166, pp. 386–397. Springer, Heidelberg (2006)
20. Huber, B., Peti, P., Obermaisser, R., El Salloum, C.: Using RTAI/LXRT for partitioning in a prototype implementation of the DECOS architecture. In: Proc. of the Third Int. Workshop on Intelligent Solutions in Embedded Systems (2005)

21. Rushby, J.: An overview of formal verification for the time-triggered architecture. In: Damm, W., Olderog, E.-R. (eds.) FTRTFT 2002. LNCS, vol. 2469, pp. 83–105. Springer, Heidelberg (2002)
22. Ademaj, A., Sivencrona, H., Bauer, G., Torin, J.: Evaluation of fault handling of the time-triggered architecture with bus and star topology. In: Proc. of Int. Conference on Dependable Systems and Networks, pp. 123–132 (2003)
23. Kopetz, H., Fuchs, E., Millinger, D., Nossa, R.: An interface as a design object. In: 2nd IEEE International Symposium on Object-Oriented Real-Time Distributed Computing (ISORC '99), 2-5 May 1999, IEEE Computer Society Press, Los Alamitos (1999)
24. OMG. Smart Transducers Interface. Specification ptc/2002-05-01, Object Management Group, (May 2002). Available at http://www.omg.org/.
25. Kopetz, H., Holzmann, M., Elmenreich, W.: A universal smart transducer interface: TTP/A. International Journal of Computer System Science & Engineering 16(2), 71–77 (2001)
26. Wirz, B.: Technical specifications for 600 series instrument grade electrostatic transducer (1997), Available at
    controls.ae.gatech.edu/gtar/electronics/6500.pdf

An Embedded Integration Prototyping System Based on Component Technique

Youngjin Jung[1], Jeongbae Lee[1], Jinbaek Kwon[1],
Keewook Rim[1], and Sangyoung Cho[2]

[1] Department of Computer Science, Graduate School, Sunmoon University,
Kalsan-ri, Tangjeong-myeon, Asan-si, ChungNam, 336-840, Korea
[2] Department of Computer Science and Engineering, Hankuk University of Foreign Studies,
89, Wangsan-ri Mohyun, Yongin-si, Kyounggi-do, 449-791, Korea
yjjung.kr@gmail.com, {jblee, jbkwon, rim}@sunmoon.ac.kr,
sycho@san.hufs.ac.kr

Abstract. Nowadays in the development of embedded system, cutting-edge embedded system products are quickly disappearing from the markets because of their short product development period which shortens the product life cycle. Therefore, strengthening its competitiveness and minimizing its development cost can be said to be one of the most important factors. For this motive, an Embedded Integration Prototyping (IP) system based on Component Technique was designed and implemented through this paper. The system is composed of Physical Prototyping (PP) providing the environment in which the product can be tested by using Actuator(Motor), Sensor and reusable Blocks, and Virtual Prototyping (VP) in which visual test on the product can be carried out by applying various components and libraries based on technique related to the computer. And, IP System was built in order to mutually compensate for drawbacks latent in both of physical and virtual prototyping environment by making use of component module. The module will be able to enhance the product competitiveness, through spending less time in developing kinds of the component owning almost same features, using it again for different embedded system products, and accordingly minimizing spent cost and time for developing the component.

Keywords: Component, Embedded System, Integration Prototyping (IP), Physical Prototyping (PP), Virtual Prototyping(VP), Simulation.

1 Introduction

The Embedded System has been widely used in a diversity of industry fields including military affairs, aerospace, information appliance, etc. In general, it is the complicated combination of hardware and software equipped with unique operation environment, independent architecture, special interface, and so on. And, because embedded products applying latest technology have short life and development cycle for them, they are disappearing from the market in fast speed, after their launch into the market.

R. Obermaisser et al. (Eds.): SEUS 2007, LNCS 4761, pp. 171–180, 2007.

As result of these reasons, prototyping technology used for developing embedded system product was needed to strengthen its competitiveness, with lessening the cost to be spent for initial development stage, as well as applying Time-to-Market shorter than before [1]. And, any problematic matters or errors possibly to take place at built-in function and hardware after product's launching into the market can be found in advance by using prototyping technology and applying it in the product's features and function from the stage of designing hardware. Besides, such found errors can be immediately modified at found time points to carry out test on them again. Like this, prototyping technology enables product to have higher level of reliability and performance until its launch by gradually repeating these series of process. Prototyping technology already known until present includes: PP in whose technology real embedded system built in factory automation system, vending machine, washing machine, mobile phone, etc is tested and produced by using Embedded System Prototyping Suit (ESPS)[2]; VP in whose technology using computer-related technology 3D model product can be visually created by providing libraries and various components; IP under currently active research in whose technology physical and virtual prototyping can be integrated. But, PP technology can't support diverse components and libraries to closely control small-sized appliances built with embedded system. On the other hand, VP technology can't support practical test environment for embedded system, even if it is possible for the system to execute virtual simulation with using computer technology. IP system at current times is implemented to give and receive only simple data, by using communication technology between physical and virtual prototyping. Besides, to be troublesome, it needs additional tasks initializing and declaring data set up in actuator and sensor to let the system operate.

To solve these problems, Component-based IP system was designed and developed at this paper in order to make it easier and promptly to reuse actuator and sensor built in currently developed IP system to different embedded systems. This system set up Double Rock Spin (DRS) system built in embedded system as its target, and constructed PP environment using ESPS, while it made use of RapidPLUS[3] tool visually providing 3D object to carry out simulation, and constructed VP environment. The remainder of this paper is structured as follows. In the next section, we discuss related works on embedded system prototyping. In section 3, we describe the design of our integration prototyping component system. Section 4 presents the implementation of integration prototyping component system for DRS, and section 5 provides a final discussion on our work and plans for future research.

2 Related Works

2.1 Physical Prototyping

A Prototype is miniature or real sized model product made during product development prior to production. A prototype is applied to test product's appearance and performance before its launch, and belongs to the part of production. As computer technology is developing in recent days, the process in which testable prototype equal to real product is created by applying advanced visual and engineering technology based on computer is called "Prototyping" [4-6]. PP can produce and test practically embedded product such as model of factory automation system or vending machine. To do so, PP supports operation environment similar to target model, by modifying real-time operation system, Real-Time(RT) Linux kernel and producing board and device driver for turning the product into drive. And, it can be applied as a tool of promoting mutual understanding among professional developers in various fields required due to the characteristic of embedded system in order to work together and to invent efficient solution to settle problems. Using PP allows hardware and software developers to carry out respective tasks at the same time in the middle of development stage, and allows problems possibly occurring (if software may be applied) to be directly communicated to hardware developer in order to solve them, as well as allowing developers to improve in their mutual understanding. In addition, it guarantees end product's quality from its development stage. This PP enables smooth communication among developers, together with lessening cost, and thus has merit in product's price competitiveness, whereas it can strengthen ability of coping with any faults in hardware found at the stage of developing software. But, PP environment can not completely support various components or fully controlling libraries of small information appliance product equipped with embedded system program, unlike VP environment can do. Lots of development tools have been studied and developed, as importance has been put on this PP concept in recent years.

2.2 Virtual Prototyping

VP using computer technology provides varied components and libraries. It supports visually simulating real product with visual 3D modeling on the computer in order to allow for the convenience in design modification and full control. Accordingly, with technology development and application expansion related to computer, engineers currently make use of VP technology in developing complicated systems. Current physical prototype needs new prototype in order to change product's appearance and adding another function, but virtual prototype can easily change design by using modeling method on GUI on condition that the design still exists on the computer. And it also can add new function without difficulty, because a function is linked to appearance expressed in formal specifications. But, it can not guarantee certainty of correct simulation in embedded system environment, because it adopts visual simulation with sense of sight using computer technology. VP like this is utilized in developing appliance, designing car audio system, building visual factory, designing airport's control system, other validation field, etc, and is expected to enhance productivity by developing product through it in most of production realm, afterwards. Tools of developing it includes RapidPLUS, ASADAL[7], Rahpsody[8] and Virtio-made Virito[9].

3   The Design of Integration Prototyping Component System

This section explains the architecture built up in component-based IP system to be applied to various embedded system fields. Because this component module exists in the middle of physical and virtual prototyping environment, it can add, delete, or modify actuator and sensor component's data and property set through TCP/IP Socket. Data values set in component module and API(Application Programming

Interface) already produced for actuator and sensor are used in PP environment. User-Defined Object (UDO) and RapidPLUS are used to be applied to values set in component module in VP environment. Fig. 1 shows the architecture of component-based IP system.

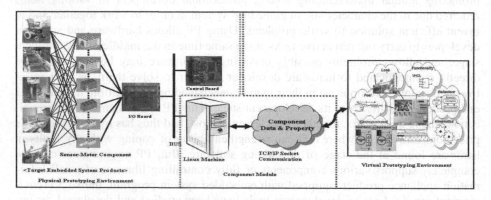

Fig. 1. The Architecture of IP Component System

3.1 The Design of Physical Prototyping

This section explains architecture of PP environment required for IP component system. This system constructed simulating environment turning actuator and sensor into operate, by using ESPI-API and data set in Component Module. Fig. 2 below displays the architecture of device driver and API for controlling several SMC(Sensor Motor Controll) devices. Each SMC device driver acts like real-time task for operating each device in RTLinux environment. This device drivers control sensor and motor to operating via I/O port, Interrupt and DMA to be assigned to each oneself. Also, each device driver communicate with user layer, higher-layer via RT-FIFO. And SMC API has Application Programming Interface for using easier device driver of user application.

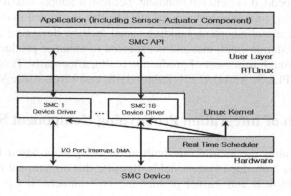

Fig. 2. The Architecture of Device Driver and API

Fig.3 describes the role of device driver and API for PP. In user level, ESPS-API carries out its role in connecting RT-Task and Linux process. RT-Task in RT kernel carries out its role as device driver. RT-FIFO is needed as method of communicating to this device driver. ESPS-API existing in kernel level executes its communication to RT-Task, by internally using FIFO. ESPS-API was developed so that user could easily control LEGO board. ESPS-API can directly call LEGO device's driver task from kernel level. It is available for precise control, but has difficulty in programming.

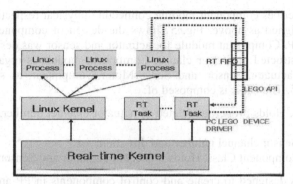

Fig. 3. The Role of Deice Driver and API for PP

3.2 The Design of Virtual Prototyping

This section explains the construction of VP environment, by using RapidPLUS - tool available for simulating embedded system product on User Interface (UI). Target product is designed with RapidPLUS, as the process steps below.
① Placement: Place various objects provided for the appearance of targeted embedded system product, dependent on the Layout.
② Design: Use objects to create Product appearance, and then design Mode, Transition, Trigger, Activity, etc to turn product into work.
③ As final step, use prototype provided in VP environment to test former process and simulate product with debugged errors and problems.
   Fig.4 expresses the relationship between application and UDO for constructing VP component to be built in IP component system. It is possible to create/control actuator and sensor in PP environment by setting up component in VP environment using UDO.

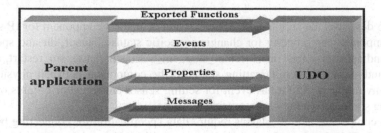

Fig. 4. The Relationship between Application and UDO

- Exported Functions: Sole function usable from other application
- Events: UDO reports its status change to parent application.
- Properties: Some types of data on object held.
- Messages: Able to send message to both of UDO and parent application by defining its structure type.

3.3   The Design of Component Module

This section describes component module connecting physical respective PP and VP components designed as above. Fig. 5 shows the design of component module between PP and VP. Component module for actuator and sensor was designed by using PP and VP constructed in former clause. Component module is organized by each class including actuator, sensor, and SensorMotor Component, as shown in class diagram in Fig. 5. The Class is composed of:

- Actuator Class: Holds properties related to actuator channel number, direction, and speed;
- Sensor Class: Sensor channel number and direction;
- SensorMotor Component Class: Holds objects of Actuator and Sensor Class.

This system was designed to create and control components in PP and VP environment, by using three classes set up in component module.

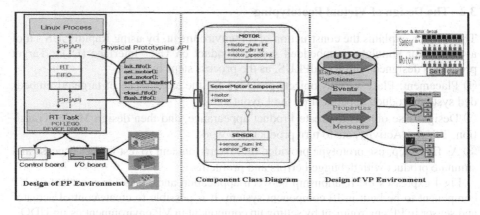

Fig. 5. The Design of Component Module between PP and VP

Fig. 6 describes the architecture of sensor and actuator's component for IP system. This component has property for changing specific status(channel, dir and speed) of sensor and actuators and interface(sm_stop, sm_start, sm_pause, sm_restart, and set motor, and so on) for setting/getting status of the component between physical and virtual environment. And it has event for setting sensor and actuator's status or using or calling some information from outside.

Also, component module classes require data specification for connecting between PP and VP. This data specification is shown in Table 1. The data specification is classified by Component, Function and Property for Actuator and Sensor.

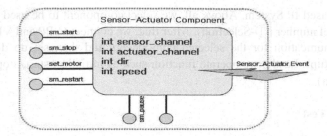

Fig. 6. The Architecture of Sensor and Actuator for IP System

Table 1. The Data Specification of Component Module for IP System

Type	Factor	Definition
Component	Actuator/Sensor	Select Actuator/Sensor Component
Function	Initialize	Initialize properties of Actuator and Sensor
	Start/Stop	Set up Start/Stop Function
	Order	Set up Auto/Manual Mode
Property	Num	Set up Actuator/Sensor's Channel
	Dir	Set up Actuator/Sensor's Direction
	Speed -	Set up Actuator's Speed

4 The Test and Evaluation of Integration Prototyping Component System

This section describe the implementation of PP and VP for setting up targeted product as DRS among embedded system products, and implementation of IP component system through designing component-based system. We also describe the results using component-based IP System in this section. Fig. 7 shows the test scenario for

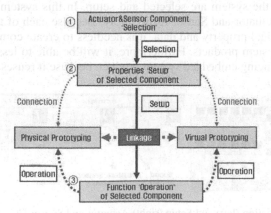

Fig. 7. The Test Scenario

component-based IP System. Above all, we select component to be used and component's channel number (①-Selection). After that, we connect to PP and VP each using socket communication for the selected components and then set up direction and speed (②-Setup). Lastly, we operate function such as initialize, start, stop, and pause (③-Operation).

4.1 System Test

(1) Physical Prototyping Side
Fig. 8 below displays PP for DRS already developed toward IP component system. In this PP, four actuators are used, and they are operated by ESPS–API. Actuators included here works so that DRS can revolve inward and outward. And sensors are used to control work of the above defined motors.

Fig. 8. The DRS PP

(2) Virtual Prototyping Side
For DRS, VP can more easily and faster implements UI than PP, by realizing it with using computer technology. Besides, it can test functions like almost real product, and can easily find and modify problems. Fig. 9 describes functions of Actuator and Sensor Component UI and shows that actuator and sensor components of VP environment required for the system are selected and setup. In this system, we use channel number 1, 2 for Actuator and Sensor respectively. Because each of these components has its own individual property and data, it is needless to create component again, for other embedded system products. Furthermore, it will be able to lessen time and cost to be spent in producing embedded system product, because it reuses components.

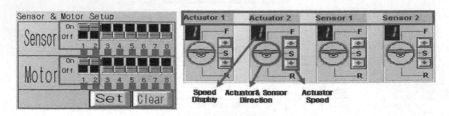

Fig. 9. Selection (left) and Setup (right) Actuator and Sensor Component UI

4.2 Evaluation

Table 2 below defines value, property and function of used actuator and sensor component in IP System. We use two motors and two sensors to handle the motor work in this system. And this system initializes value of defined actuator and sensor component's property. It also defines Start/Stop/Pause functions about work of the system and function of order operation such as Auto and Manual Mode.

Table 2. The Used Simulation Data in IP System

Type	Factor	Descriptions (Value)
Component	Sensor	Select Sensor Component
	Motor	Select Motor Component
Function	Initialize	Initialize values of the above Actuator and Sensor (4)
	Start/Stop	Set up Start/Stop (1/2)
	Order	Set up Manual Mode (2)
Property	Num	Set up available Sensor/Motor's Channel(1,2/1,2)
	Dir	Set up selected Sensor/Motor's Direction (0,1)
	Speed	Set up selected Motor's Speed (0x0, ..., 0xF)

The result of simulated data shows that components implemented between PP side and VP side are synchronized. And we can simulate fast and easily component-based IP system to handle operation and change direction and speed of selected component using setting Actuator and Sensor components.

5   Conclusion and Future Studies

Previously, IP system was an interlocking system to simulate target product in virtual and physical environment. In developing embedded system, strengthening its competitiveness and minimizing its development cost can be said to be one of the most important factors. For this motive, Component-based IP System was designed and implemented through this paper. Implementing component-based system using sensor and actuator that is highly reusable could make it possible to easily and fast implement IP systems for various embedded system products. Reliable embedded system products pertinent to Time-to-Market will be able to be launched into markets, by applying component-based IP system. In addition to it, it will make contribution to strengthening product competitiveness, too.

Implemented component-based IP system will be made in formal specification to expand its application to more industry fields, and debugger finding and then modifying any errors will be additionally developed, afterwards. And, further studying the method of assessing functionality built in embedded system product is for future study plan.

Acknowledgment. This study was supported by the Ministry of Information and Communication of Korea under the Information Technology Research Center Support Program supervised by the Institute of Information Technology Assessment (IITA-2006-C1090-0603-0020).

References

1. Gaver, B., Dunne, T., Pacenti, E.: Cultural Probes. Interactions 6(1), 21–29 (1997)
2. ESPS, http://www.artsystem.co.kr
3. RapidPLUS, http://www.e-sim.com
4. Song, J.-H.: Institute of Information Technology Assenssment. Korea Information Science Society, 23, 7–11(Dig. 9th Annual Conf. Magn. Jpn. p. 301 (1982)) ISSN 1229-6821
5. Lawson, B.: How Designers Think. Architectural Press (1997)
6. SONY, AIBO, http://www.sony.net/Products/aibo/
7. ASADAL, http://selab.postech.ac.kr/realtime/public_html/
8. Rhapsody, http://www.ilogix.com
9. Virtio, http://www.virtio.com

TMO Structuring of a Networked System for Seamless Streaming and Tiled Display of High-Definition Movies

Sheng Liu[1], K.H. (Kane) Kim[1], Sung-Jin Kim[1], Zhen Zhang[1],
Jongho Nang[2], Ki-Seok Choi[2], and Yongbin Kang[3]

[1] Dream Lab, EECS dept., University of California, Irvine
Irvine,CA 92697, USA
{shengl, khkim, sungjink, zhen}@uci.edu
[2] Sogang University, Seoul, Korea
{jhnang}@sogang.ac.kr
[3] Institute for Graphic Interface, Seoul, Korea

Abstract. This paper presents a global-time based approach for realizing high-definition video streaming and highly synchronous tiled display on multiple PC-oriented display nodes. The challenge is to minimize distortion of the temporal relationship among the fragments of video frames played across the display devices. The distortion arises due to the jitter in message transmission delay and the considerably autonomous operations of display nodes. The global-time based coordination approach looked promising as a cost-effective approach for facilitating highly synchronous tiled display and minimizing the collisions between data transmission activities and tile preparation and display activities. The Time-triggered Message-triggered Object (TMO) programming tool-kit, which enables construction of scalable distributed real-time computing programs in the form of networks of high-level, easily analyzable, real-time objects was used because it facilitates efficient practice of the global-time based approach. The results of an experimentation of the approach are also presented.

Keywords: real time, global time, multimedia, HD video streaming, tiled display, jitter, TMO, time triggered, message, object, middleware, distributed, programming, intra-stream synchronization.

1 Introduction

The approach of utilizing PCs, each equipped with a display device, to achieve a large tiled display of a very high-resolution image has been gaining popularity in the past decade. Initially, systems capable of tiled display of static images were built but lately, attempts to handle video-movies started. Video frames forming a movie need to be streamed in timely manners and displayed across multiple display nodes in sufficiently synchronous manners. To achieve high-level *quality of services (QoSs)*, high-precision synchronizations of video streams across multiple display nodes is

R. Obermaisser et al. (Eds.): SEUS 2007, LNCS 4761, pp. 181–191, 2007.
© IFIP International Federation for Information Processing 2007

important. More precisely, the accurate maintenance of the temporal relationship among media units (MUs) such as audio packets and segments of video frames without the loss of RT performance is required [1, 2, 16]. In other worlds, all segments from the same video frame must be displayed "with a high degree of synchrony", i.c., as closely in the time domain as possible. Each video frame, composed of the tile-segments, and corresponding audio packets must also be presented with a high degree of synchrony. Another challenge is to reduce the amount of efforts for designing and implementing the complex application that performs RT video streaming from the source such as a camera, Internet, and a hard disk to the multiple display nodes and high-quality tiled display of a movie.

In this paper, the principle of *global-time-based coordination of distributed actions (TCoDA)* [14] is exploited to form a fundamental and promising approach for meeting the aforementioned QoS (quality-of-service) requirements. As an approach for significantly reducing the design and implementation efforts from that required under the widely practiced low-level programming schemes involving manipulations of threads, thread-priorities, and sockets, the *Time-triggered Message-triggered Object (TMO)* programming scheme was adopted. The scheme backed by an appropriate tool-set (http://dream.eng.uci.edu/TMOdownload/), facilitates easy practice of object and component-oriented (OCO) real-time (RT) distributed programming [3, 5, 6, 7, 8, 9].

To make this paper self-contained, a brief overview of the TMO programming scheme and DirectShow are introduced in Section 2. The TCoDA-based approach for realizing high-quality real-time video streaming services over a tiled display system is discussed in Section 3. The TMO-based implementation for achieving the minimal loss of the temporal relationship among the video data units at all sink nodes are presented in Section 4. Performance measurements discussed in Section 5 have shown that TCoDA is a fundamental and promising approach for distributed real-time multimedia computing. The paper concludes in Section 6.

2 Backgroud

2.1 TMO Scheme

TMO is a natural, syntactically minor, and semantically powerful extension of conventional object structure. As depicted in Fig. 1, the basic TMO structure consists of four parts:

ODS-sec: Object-data-store section. This section contains the data-container variables shared among methods of a TMO. Variables are grouped into ODS segments (ODSSs) which are the units that can be locked for exclusive use by a TMO method in execution. Access rights of TMO methods for ODSSs are explicitly specified and the execution engine analyzes them to exploit maximal concurrency.

EAC-sec: Environment access capability section. These "gate objects" provide efficient call-paths to remote object methods, real-time multicast and memory replication channels (RMMCs) (Kim et al. 2005), and I/O device interfaces.

SpM-sec: Spontaneous method section. These are time-triggered methods that become alive at specified times.

SvM-sec: Service method section. These provide service methods which can be called by other TMOs.

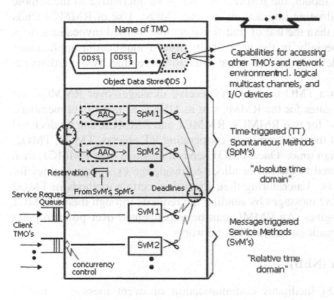

Fig. 1. Basic TMO Structure ([5])

Major features are summarized below.

1) Distributed computing component: The TMO is a distri-buted computing com-ponent and thus TMOs distri-buted over multiple nodes may interact via remote method calls. To maximize the concurrency in execution of client methods in one node and server methods in the same node or different nodes, client methods are allowed to make non-blocking service requests to service methods. In addition, TMOs can interact by exchange of messages over Real-time Multicast and Memory-Replication Channels (RMMCs) [12]. In any place within a TMO, all time references are global time references except where specified explicitly and differenetly.

2) Clear separation between two types of methods: The TMO may contain two types of methods, time triggered (TT) methods (spontaneous methods or SpMs), which are clearly separated from the conventional service methods (SvMs). The SpM executions are triggered when the RT clock reaches time values determined at the design time. On the contrary, SvM executions are triggered by calls from clients that are transmitted by the execution engine in the form of service request messages. Moreover, actions to be taken at real times, which can be determined at the design time, can appear only in SpMs.

Triggering times for SpMs must be fully specified as constants during the design time. Those RT constants as well as related guaranteed completion times (GCTs) of the SpM appear in the first clause of an SpM specification called the autonomous activation condition (AAC) section. An example of an AAC is "for t = from 10 am to 10:50 am every 30 min start-during (t , t + 5 min) finish-by t +10 min" which has the same effect as {"start-during (10 am, 10:05 am) finish-by 10:10 am", "start-during (10:30 am, 10:35 am) finish-by 10:40 am"}.

Executions of SpMs cannot be disturbed by the executions of SvMs because of the execution rule adopted and called the basic concurrency constraint (BCC).

2.2 RMMC

In the TMO programming model, the RMMC scheme is an alternative to the remote method invocation for facilitating interactions among TMOs. Use of RMMCs tends to lead to better efficiency than the use of traditional remote method invocations does in many applications, especially in the area of distributed multimedia applications which involve frequent delivery of the same data to more than two participants housed in different nodes.

In order for methods in a TMO to send and receive messages over RMMCs, the TMO must contain access gates for the RMMCs in its ODS, i.e., as its data members. For example, "access gates" for two RMMCs, RMMC1 and RMMC2, can be declared as data members of each of the three remotely cooperating RT objects, TMO1, TMO2, and TMO3, during the design time. Once TMO1 sends a message over RMMC1, then the message will be delivered to the buffer allocated inside the execution engines for each of the three RT objects. Later during their execution, certain methods in TMO2 and TMO3 can pick up those messages by sending the requests through their RMMC1 gates to their execution engines. An RMMC can be implemented over point-to-point networks as well as over broadcast-enabled bus networks.

2.3 Non-Blocking Buffer (NBB)

The NBB mechanism [18] facilitates communication of event messages from a producer to a consumer without causing any party to experience blocking. Therefore, its application scope includes all conceivable producer-consumer situations. Experiments involving application of this mechanism in building middleware as well as real-time application software confirmed the usefulness of the NBB mechanism.

The producer thread, PROD, owns the circular buffer and can write into the buffer at any time without experiencing blocking and thus is a non-blocking writer of the buffer. There are also two counters: the update counter (UC) and the acknowledgment counter (AC), also called the ack-counter. The two counters are used in ways which ensure that PROD and CONS always access different slots in the circular buffer.

2.4 Direct Show

DirectShow is a multimedia application library produced by Microsoft. It provides a set of APIs which defines various operations for multimedia tasks. Within the framework of DirectShow, the processing of a multimedia task can be divided into a set of steps such as reading the media source, encode/decode, and playback. Each of these steps can be accomplished by a module called a filter. Filters can be connected together through their "input/output" pins so as to form a filter graph that can perform a target multimedia task.

3   Global-Time-Based Approach for HD Video Streaming and Tiled Display

A tiled display system [4, 15, 17] is a cost-effective approach for realizing a large display wall. The combined resolution of a tiled display can easily surpass the resolution of a HD video stream. To utilize a tiled display as an RT HD video stream display, the underlying software system must be able to control the graphic display output of each node to be synchronized so that the user experience a temporally consistent and contextually unified video stream.

Due to the jitters in the network, each video frame in a stream may arrive or may be picked up in different nodes at different times. Also the decompression time taken may be different in different display nodes. Such discrepancies among display nodes may introduce out-of-sync display of different segment of the same video frame. One may make all display nodes wait for a sync message after each decompression process and update the display screen upon receiving the message. However this sync message may arrive or may be picked up in different nodes at a noticeably different times.

With the presence of the global time base of a sub-millisecond precision, one can explain the TCoDA [14], i.e., design all display nodes to render their parts of the video frame at the same instance of global time, e.g., at the target display time = video frame generation + display delay constant. Different applications of the approach have been studied and proof-of-concept systems have been developed [10, 11, 13].

4 TMO-Based HD Tiled Display System

4.1 System Architecture

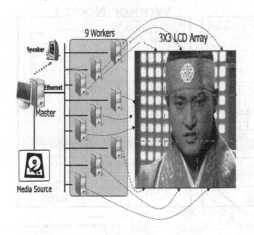

Fig. 2. Architecture of a Tiled Display System

A high-definition video streaming service on a tiled display system consists of one master node and multiple worker nodes, all of which are connected through a LAN. The function of the master node is to retrieve encoded multimedia data from a media source and stream them to the workers with playback timing information embedded. It also takes the responsibility of audio stream playback. The function of a worker is to receive encoded video frames from the communication channel, decode them, and display its assigned tile-segments of video frame that are located on the basis of its unique Worker ID (WID). Fig. 2 illustrates the system architecture.

4.2 Design of the Master Node

The master node includes two software modules: the master filter graph and the master TMO, which are shown in Fig. 3. The master filter graph is an application program built by interconnecting DirectShow library module provided by Microsoft. Each library module is called a filter. This application runs whenever TMOSM running at the top priority-level yields a time-slice of the machine to non-TMO software, which occurs every 3rd time-slice arrives. In the master filer graph, a built-in *source filter* is used for retrieving compressed audio packets and video frames from a media source. Such a media source can be a media file in the local disk or an URL containing a media stream. In the case of audio packets, they are forwarded by the source filter to a local *audio decoder filter* for decoding since the audio stream will be played back in the master node. A customized *grabber filter* is used to grab uncompressed audio packets out of the master filter graph and put them into an output queue. Another grabber filter is used to pull compressed video frames out of the master filter graph into a separate output queue. Inside a *grabber filter*, a callback function is invoked whenever a media frame becomes available from the output pin of an upstream filter. The *audio grabber filter* is connected to the upstream *audio decoder filter* to grab uncompressed audio packets for local playback while the *video grabber filter* is directly connected to the *source filter* to grab compressed video frames for multicast delivery. The output pin of each grabber filter is connected with the input pin of a customized *flow control filter*, which controls the retrieving speed of the source filter (e.g. 30 frames per second); otherwise, the source filter reads media units from the media source as quickly as possible, which necessitates a large buffer to hold all retrieved media data before they can be played back or delivered to worker nodes.

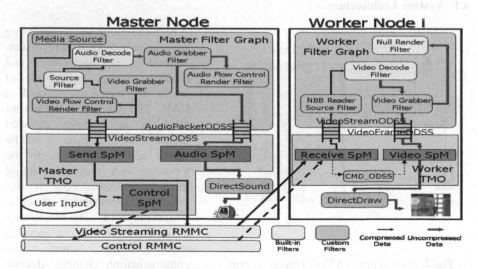

Fig. 3. System Components

Another software module in the master node is the Master TMO, which handles the task of playing back the audio stream and multicasting video stream to all worker nodes. Audio packets and video frames are obtained from the grabber filters in the maser filter graph and need to be picked up by the SpMs in the Master TMO. The grabber filters and the SpMs run in the different thread contexts. An NBB is used to let the grabber filters deposit media data and let the Master TMO SpMs in non-blocking manners. Each NBB is wrapped as a special ODSS in the Master TMO, and its handle is sent to the master filter graph during the system initialization. Two types of ODSS's, namely AudioPacketODSS and VideoStreamODSS are constructed. The *audio grabber filter*, as the writer of the audio NBB, inserts uncompressed audio packets into AudioPacketODSS. Similarly, VideoStreamODSS encapsulates an NBB for holding compressed video frames supplied by the *video grabber filter*.

Besides two ODSS's, the Master TMO contains three SpMs. Audio SpM is used to playback the audio stream. It periodically reads an uncompressed audio packet from AudioPacketODSS and plays it back through Win32 DirectSound APIs. Since an audio packet is played back at the target instant of global time at the beginning of each round of Audio SpM, the intra-stream synchronization jitter is minimized.

Send SpM periodically reads a video frame out of VideoStreamODSS and multicasts it to all workers. In our design, its iteration rate is set to be the same as the frame rate of the media stream being rendered. For example, it runs every 33ms, which means it sends 30 video frames per second. To facilitate video frames to all workers, a video streaming RMMC is constructed. A gate to this RMMC is instantiated during the initialization of the Master TMO. When Send SpM obtains a video frame, it invokes RMMC API Announce() to multicast it out. Since the sizes of compressed video frames are not a constant while an RMMC requires each packet be of fixed size, a video frame needs to be packetized into RMMC packets before being sent out.

The third SpM, Control SpM, runs at the lowest frequency to take user's commands and multicast corresponding control messages, such as "PLAY" and "STOP", to all workers.

4.3 Design of Worker Nodes

Receive SpM in a worker node receives RMMC packets from the video streaming RMMC by calling RMMC API NonBlockingReceiver(), and assembles them if they belong to the same video frame. Then, a complete video frame is inserted into VideoStreamODSS, which is of the NBB type.

Video frames in VideoStreamODSS are read by a customized *source filter*, NBB Reader Source Filter, in the worker filter graph. Its output pin is connected to the input pin of the *video decoder filter*. After being decoded, an uncompressed video frame is sent to the *video grabber filter*. Through the callback function inside the video grabber filter, an uncompressed video frame, the part of a video frame corresponding to the worker's WID, is inserted into the VideoFrameODSS which is of the NBB type. A *null render filter* is added at the end of the worker filter graph by being connected to the output pin of the *video grabber filter* to complete the connection of the worker filter graph. Note that there is no need to use a *flow control filter* on the worker side since the master node has already controlled the media delivery rate.

Similar to Audio SpM, Video SpM periodically gets a video-fame-fragment from VideoFrameODSS and invokes Win32 DirectDraw API to play it back.

4.4 Synchronous Play of the Video Stream in All Worker Nodes

Synchronous play of video stream in all worker nodes is subject to two requirements:

- The play of the video stream starts with a minimal deviation in the time dimension in all worker nodes.

- Video frames are played back with the same rate in all worker nodes.

As mentioned in Section 4.3, periodical executions of Video SpMs in the Worker TMOs meet the second requirement.

Both the master and workers start with certain internal initialization such as starting TMO engine, filter graph construction, initialization of audio/video devices, and registration of SpM and the TMO.

Once these internal initializations are done, Control SpM in the master node waits for user's inputs. After selecting a media source, the user inputs a "PLAY" command. When Control SpM receives this command, it sends a "Play" message to all worker nodes through a control RMMC. Thereafter, it starts the master filter graph and cosequentially, video frames are fetched from the media source and sent to worker nodes through the video streaming RMMC. When a worker node receives the "Play" message through Receive SpM, it starts the worker filter graph and begins to receive video frames from the master node, decode, and buffer them, but not play them back. The purpose for buffering is obvious, to smooth the transmission jitter. The "Play" message also contains an *Initial Play Time (IPT)* to dictate a moment at which all workers shall begin video playback. The value of IPT is saved into the CMD_ODSS in the worker TMO. Video SpM reads its value from the CMD_ODSS and compares it with the current time at the beginning of each round. If IPT is larger than the current time, it fetches the first video frame from VideoFrameODSS to start play.

One critical point is that the Master TMO needs to choose an appropriate IPT before sending out the "PLAY" message so that the Video SpMs on all workers may begin video-playback with a minimal deviation in the time dimension. It means that at least one frame-fragment should be available in the buffer within VideoFrameODSS when IPT arrives. Hence, the duration D from the moment at which a "PLAY" commend is issued, which is denoted as T, to IPT should be no less than the duration from T to the time at which the first frame-fragment is deposited into the buffer within VideoFrameODSS. To tolerate transmission jitters of video frames, D can be increased so that several video frame-fragments buffer within VideoFrameODSS when IPT arrives although it will accompany the cost of larger latency.

$$IPT = T + D$$

To play the first frame-fragment exactly on IPT, one straightforward approach is to let Video SpM continuously compare the current time with IPT. When IPT arrives, the first frame-fragment is played back. However, this polling approach needs to occupy and consume CPU resource extensively only for the time comparisons. A more cost-effeicive approach is to set IPT to the earliest starting time (EST) of the earliest iteration of Video SpM that starts after $(T + D)$ and then to check at the beginning of each iteration of Video SpM if IPT is already past or not. If so, the first frame-fragment will be played immediately. Otherwise, no playback will occur during the current iteration of Video SpM. IPT is thus:

$$IPT = EST + \{ceiling[(T + D) / P]\} * P .$$

where P is the period of Video SpM. In each of the subsequent iterations, a video-frame-fragment is again played at the beginning.

5 Performance Measurement

We ran our tiled display on a 3x3 LCD array. The configuration of each node is, Pentium 2.4G CPU, 512M memory, and Windows XP SP2 OS. Fig. 4 gives a snapshot of our demo.

Two performance attributes were measured. We first measured the difference of playback time across all worker nodes. In particular, a timestamp is taken each time DirectDraw is about to be called to display a video-frame-fragment. Then the playback time difference for each video frame is the maximum difference across all workers. Fig. 5 shows the difference which can be regarded as a measure of how well the workers are synchronized in playing the video. From the figure we can see that,

Fig. 4. Snapshot of Tiled Display on LCD Array

workers' playback times can be pretty well synchronized for the given application. The playback time difference was mostly less than 8ms and did not exceed.

We also measured the latency from the time when a video frame was first extracted from the media source by the master node to the time when a fragment of the video frame was played back by a worker node. On the master node side, a timestamp is

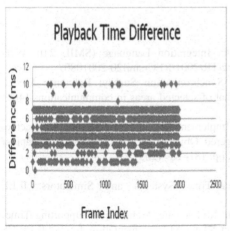

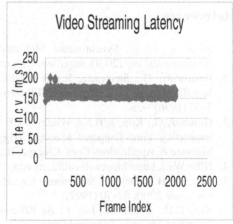

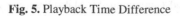

Fig. 5. Playback Time Difference   **Fig. 6.** Transmission Latency of Video Stream

taken whenever a video frame is grabbed by the video grabber filter. On the other hand, for the worker node, a timestamp is taken every time a video-frame-fragment is to be drawn on the screen. The difference of the two timestamps corresponding to the same video frame can be seen as the delay for processing the video frame in the system. Fig. 6 shows that the latency is about the same for different cases of video frames despite the fact that frames of different sizes may take different amount of time in transmission and decoding.

6 Conclusion

Through construction of a global-time-based TMO network, a high-quality high-definition tiled display system was realized. This application case is one demonstration of the global-time-based coordination of distributed actions (TCoDA) as a fundamental and promising approach for distributed multimedia applications. It was also a demonstration that the TMO scheme and its tool-kit enabling relatively easy high-level programming of manipulations of global time-stamps and timely processing of video and other multimedia data reduce the amount of efforts for design and implementation of complex distributed multimedia applications. Our performance measurements have indicated that the TCoDA approach realizes the minimal play jitter in streaming and play of video data.

Acknowledgment

The work reported here was supported in part by the NSF under Grant Numbers 03-26606 (ITR) and 05-24050 (CNS) and under Cooperative Agreement ANI-0225642 to the University of California, San Diego for "The OptIPuter". No part of this paper represents the views and opinions of any of the sponsors mentioned above.

References

1. Ayars, J., et al.: Synchronized Multimedia Integration Language (SMIL 2.0). W3C Recommendation (2001), http://www.w3.org/TR/2001/REC-smil20-20010807
2. Blakowski, G., Steinmetz, R.: A Media Synchronization Survey: Reference Model, Specification, and Case Studies. IEEE Journal of selected areas in communications 14(1), 5–35 (1996)
3. Gimenez, G., Kim, K.H.: A Windows CE Implementation of a Middleware Architecture Supporting Time-Triggered Message Triggered Objects. In: Proc. IEEE CS Computer Software & Applications Conf. Chicago, IL, pp. 181–189 (2001)
4. HIPerWall, http://hiperwall.calit2.uci.edu
5. Kim, K.H.: Object Structures for Real-Time Systems and Simulators. IEEE Computer 30(8), 62–70 (1997)
6. Kim, K.H., Ishida, M., Liu, J.: An Efficient Middleware Architecture Supporting Time-Triggered Message-Triggered Objects and an NT-based Implementation. In: 2nd IEEE CS Int'l Symp. on Object-Oriented Real-time Distributed Computing, St. Malo, France, pp. 54–63 (1999)

7. Kim, K.H.: APIs Enabling High-Level Real-Time Distributed Object Programming. IEEE Computer, 72–80 (2000)
8. Kim, K.H., Liu, J.Q., Miyazaki, H., Shokri, E.H.: A CORBA Service Middleware Enabling High-Level Real-Time Object Programming. In: IEEE CS 5th Int'l Symp. on Autonomous Decentralized Systems, Dallas, pp. 327–335. IEEE Computer Society Press, Los Alamitos (2001)
9. Kim, K.H.: Commanding and Reactive Control of Peripherals in the TMO Programming Scheme. In: 5th IEEE CS Int'l Symp. on Object-Oriented Real-time Distributed Computing, Crystal City, VA, pp. 448–456. IEEE Computer Society Press, Los Alamitos (2002)
10. Kim, S., Kuester, F., Kim, K.H.: A Global-timestamp-based Approach to Construct a Real-time Distributed Tiled Display System. In: EIST-2005, pp. 548–554 (2005)
11. Kim, S., Kuester, F., Kim, K.H.: A Global timestamp-based Approach to Enhanced Data Consistency and Fairness in Collaborative Virtual Environments. ACM Multimedia System 10(3), 220–229 (2003)
12. Kim, K.H, Li, Y., Liu, S., Kim, M.H., Kim, D-II.: RMMC Programming Model and Support Execution Engine in the TMO Programming Scheme. In: 8th IEEE International Symposium on Object-Oriented Real-Time Distributed Computing, pp. 34–43 (2005)
13. Kim, K.H., Liu, S., Kim, M.H., Kim, D.-H.: A Global-Time-Based Approach for High-Quality Real-Time Video Streaming Services. In: 7th IEEE Int'l Symp. on Multimedia, Irvine, CA, pp. 802–810 (2005)
14. Kopetz, H.: Real-Time Systems: Design Principles for Distributed Embedded Applications. Kluwer Academic Publishers, Dordrecht (1997)
15. Renambot, L. and Rao, A.and Singh, R. and Jeong, B. and Krishnaprasad,N. and Vishwanath, V. and Chandrasekhar, V. and Schwarz, N. and Spale, A. and Zhang, C. and Goldman, G. and Leigh, J. and Johnson, A.: SAGE: the Scalable Adaptive Graphics Environment. In: Proceedings of the Workshop on Advanced Collaborative Environments (2004)
16. Steinmetz, R., Engler, C.: Human Perception of Media Synchronization. Technical Report 43.9310, IBM European Networking Center Heidelberg, Heidelberg, Germany (1993)
17. Wallace, G., Anshus, O.J., Bi, P., Chen, H., Chen, Y., Clark, D., Cook, P., Finkelstein, A., Funkhouser, T., Gupta, A., Hibbs, M., Li, K., Liu, Z., Samanta, R., Sukthankar, R., Troyanskaya, O.: Tools and Applications for Large-scale Display Walls. Computer Graphics and Applications 25, 24–33 (2005)
18. Kim, K.H., Clomenares, J., Rim, K.: Efficient Adaptations of the Non-blocking Buffer for event Message Communication. In: 10th IEEE International Symposium on Object-Oriented Real-Time Distributed Computing, Santorini Island, Greece (2007)

Design and Experimental Validation of UAV Control System Software Based on the TMO Structuring Scheme

Hansol Park[1], Moon Hae Kim[1], Chun-Hyon Chang[1], Keechon Kim[1],
Jung-Guk Kim[2], and Doo-Hyun Kim[1,*]

[1] Computer Science Department, Konkuk University, Seoul, Korea
{parkhs, mhkim, chchang, kckim, doohyun}@konkuk.ac.kr
[2] Hankuk University of Foreign studies, Korea
jgkim@hufs.ac.kr

Abstract. The technologies for designing and validating computer-control systems subject to challenging timing and reliability requirements have been advancing slowly. One such type of systems are unmanned aerial vehicle (UAV) control systems. The functional complexity of UAV control systems is steadily increasing. Enabling the design of such complex systems in easily understandable forms that are amenable to rigorous analysis is a highly desirable goal. In this paper, we discuss our experimental application of the Time-triggered Message-triggered Object (TMO) structuring scheme to the design of a UAV control system. The TMO scheme enables high-level structuring together with design-time guaranteeing of accurate timings of various critical control actions with significantly smaller efforts than those required when using lower-level structuring schemes based on direct programming of threads, UDP invocations, etc. An experimental 2-step validation of a UAV control system is also discussed. The first step was to validate the system by use of an environment simulator and then real flight tests were involved only in the second step.

1 Introduction

The technologies for designing and validating computer-control systems subject to challenging timing and reliability requirements have been advancing slowly. One such type of systems are unmanned aerial vehicle (UAV) control systems. Enabling the design of such systems in easily understandable forms that are amenable to rigorous analysis is a highly desirable goal. [5, 6, 8, 10]

The TMO (Time-triggered Message-triggered Object) model formalized earlier by Kim and his collaborators [1, 2] has been found to be a sound real-time object model that can be used for various types of hard and soft real-time distributed computing applications. With the TMO model, both functional and timing behaviors of a system can be specified in explicit and natural easy-to-understand forms.

To support execution of TMOs, several engines have been developed in the form of middleware layered on a few widely used OS platforms. Representative cases are TMOSM [3, also see http://dream.eng.uci.edu] on MS Windows XP Windows CE,

---

* Corresponding Author: New Millennium Hall 1203, School of Internet and Multimedia Engineering, Konkuk University, Kwangjin-Gu, Seoul, 143-701, Korea.

R. Obermaisser et al. (Eds.): SEUS 2007, LNCS 4761, pp. 192–201, 2007.
© IFIP International Federation for Information Processing 2007

and Linux, LTMOS [4] on Linux, and Konkuk TMOSM/Linux on Linux. In the work reported in this paper, we used TMOSM/Linux made by Konkuk University.

In this paper, we propose a TMO-based high-level design and implementation method for the real-time embedded software parts of UAV control systems. The main goal here is to improve the software engineering productivity and the software reliability to a significant extent. Improvements are sought for in various phases of engineering UAV control software such as design, implementation, and testing.

Our UAV control system was validated by use of an environment simulator in the first step. Real flight tests were involved only in the second step. FlightGear was used a virtual flight environment, named Hardware-In-the-Loop (HIL) system, of which components can be replaced by actual hardware without rendering the remainder of the simulator inoperable [7].

In Section 2, as backgrounds, the basic structure of the TMO model, the type of UAVs considered, and the features of FlightGear are described briefly. In Section 3, we present the design of an UAV control system based on the TMO model. In Section 4, our implementation and flight simulation are described. Finally, in Section 5, we conclude with a suggestion for future works.

2 Backgrounds

2.1 TMO Structuring Scheme

We use the TMO model as a fundamental building-block and TMOSM (TMO Support Middleware) as the execution engine for our experiments [2, 3]. TMO is a natural, syntactically minor, and semantically powerful extension of the conventional object(s) [2]. Especially, TMO is a high-level real-time computing object. Member functions (i.e., methods) are executed within specified windows in the domain of global time. Such timing requirements are specified in natural intuitive forms with no esoteric styles imposed.

As depicted in Fig. 1, the basic TMO structure consists of four parts; 1) **Spontaneous Method (SpM)**: A time-triggered (TT) method which is triggered when the real-time clock reaches specific values determined at design time and specified in AAC (Autonomous Activation Condition) as the time-windows for execution. 2) **Method (SvM)**: A method similar to the conventional service method which is triggered by service request messages from clients. 3) **Object Data Store (ODS)**: The set of data members which may be partitioned into ODS segments (ODSSs), each of which is a basic unit of storage that can be exclusively accessed by a certain TMO method at any given time or shared among executions concurrent of TMO methods (SpMs or SvMs). 4) **Environment Access Capability (EAC)**: A list of entry points to remote object methods, logical communication channels, and I/O device interfaces.

2.2 Unmanned Aerial Vehicle (UAV) Control System

An unmanned aerial vehicle (UAV) is an aircraft with no onboard pilot. UAVs can be remote controlled aircrafts (e.g. flown by a pilot at a ground control station), or aircrafts that can fly autonomously with pre-programmed flight plans or dynamically adaptive control systems. Although the UAV control system consists of many components, there are two main components: 1) a ground station component which

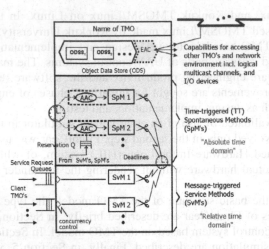

Fig. 1. Structure of TMO model (courtesy of [2, 3])

provides telemetry feedback to the operator and allows him/her to control the aircraft, and 2) an on-board flight system component of the vehicle.

In a UAV, the flight system component (embedded controller) operates some sensors for sensing attitude and position and uses the data in controlling the pose of the UAV on the flight. In our experimental UAV, a gyroscope and a GPS were used to enable precise navigation. In the ground, the operator can monitor the current states of the UAV and issue commands to the running UAV via the ground station component. The ground station component and the UAV flight system component must be connected via communication channels so that they may monitor and command each other.

Our UAV discussed in this paper is designed to fly autonomously with the autopilot. This autopilot requires precise timing of sensor operations. If the timing is badly missed, the UAV would be endangered.

2.3 FlightGear Flight Simulator Project

FlightGear is an open-source flight simulator project which provides flight simulators running on Windows, Linux and Mac platforms. The goal of the FlightGear project is to create a sophisticated flight simulator framework for use in research or academic environments, for the development and pursuit of other interesting flight simulation ideas, as well as for an end-user application. FlightGear provides a multitude of features as follows:

- High Degree of Freedom: FlightGear is open-source.
- Cross Platform: FlightGear runs on many different operating systems.
- Multiple Flight Dynamic Models: Three primary flight dynamics models (FDMs), LarcSim, JSBSim and yasim, are available.
- Moderate Hardware Requirements: Commercial-off-the-shelf (COTS) personal computer components are sufficient for running FlightGear.
- Extensibility: FlightGear can run a simple simulation on a single laptop or drive a sophisticated, realistic, immersive, multi-screen simulation.
- Network Access: A wide variety of external interfaces are available.

3 Experimental System Design and Implementation

3.1 Hardware Architecture

As depicted in Figure 2, the UAV control system consists of a Flight System component, a Ground Station component, and a Communication component. The Flight

System component has three parts, embedded controller, sensors, and actuators. In this project, an RF-Ethernet communication device which used radio frequency for Ethernet protocol was used as the communication component. Flight simulator was set to generate all kinds of sensor data and receive actuator signals for virtual flight control.

3.1.1 Flight System
(1) Sensors
A gyroscope and a GPS receiver were used as the sensors of Flight System. The gyroscope was used to provide attitude data. The gyroscope was set to generate roll, pitch, and yaw data and sends the data to the Embedded Controller, which was connected to the gyroscope via a serial port. The GPS receiver was used to produce geometric location data periodically. The GPS provided NMEA standard location data via a serial port for the Embedded Controller in the Flight System.

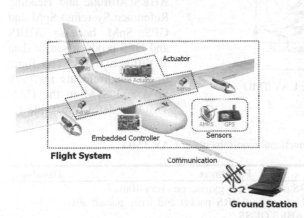

Flight System

Ground Station

Fig. 2. Constitution of UAV Control System

(2) Actuator
A Servo-Actuator that was an actuator of servo motors controlled by PWM (Pulse Width Modulation) signals in the Flight System was assembled by us. The Servo-Actuator was designed to receive servo-control data from the Embedded Controller via a serial port and convert the data to PWM signals and use the signals to control directly-connected servo motors. Atmel's Atmega128 chip was used for the Servo-Actuator and the converting software was newly developed.

(3) Embedded Controller
The Embedded Controller was built using an ARM-based small computer system. This small computer system has a 400 MHz XScale processor, and 64MB of RAM. An extended Serial I/O board is installed in the Embedded Controller to provide four serial ports needed to communicate with the gyroscope and GPS devices. A 64MB built-in NAND flash serves as non-volatile storage and suffices to keep embedded Linux kernel 2.4.18 and UAV controller software based on TMOSM/Linux.

3.1.2 Ground Station
Ground Station is a kind of control unit which monitors the state of the UAV and provides a flight-path to the Embedded Controller in the Flight System. Ground Station supports GUI for monitoring and sends location data which include a flight-path to the UAV. Ground Station uses the RF-Ethernet device for communicating with the UAV.

3.2 Modeling of a UAV Control System Based on TMO Model

As depicted in Fig. 2, the Embedded Controller in the Flight System is connected to Sensor Module, Servo Actuator, and Ground Station. In this section, we present the TMO-structured design of our UAV control system.

3.2.1 UAV TMO : A TMO-Structured Design of the Embedded Controller

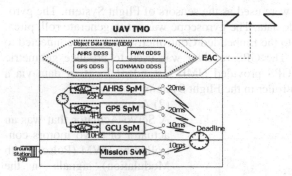

Fig. 3. Design of the UAV TMO

The UAV TMO is a design of the Embedded Controller object in the Flight System. As depicted Figure 3, the UAV TMO has AHRS(Attitude and Heading Reference Systems) SpM and GPS SpM because AHRS and GPS produce sensor data at different rates. The functional requirements for each SpM and SvM in the UAV TMO are defined in Table 1.

Table 1. Functional requirements of UAV TMO

Method Name	Functions	Deadline
AHRS SpM	1. Acquire AHRS packets from gyroscope every 40ms 2. Analyze and parse the AHRS packet and write parsed attitude data to AHRS ODSS 3. Read AHRS data, GPS data, and command data from each ODSS. 4. If GPS data and Command data are empty (initial condition), just use AHRS data. 5. If the current GPS data are not found, produce such data via extrapolation (because GPS internal clock is slower than AHRS). 6. Find flight-path from command data and compare it with the current GPS data. 7. Calculate actuator control signals using PID algorithm to follow given flight-path. 8. Write AHRS, GPS and actuator control data to PWM(Pulse Width Modulation) ODSS.	20ms
GPS SpM	1. Acquire GPS packets every 250ms 2. Analyze and parse the GPs packet and write parsed geometric position data to GPS ODSS	20ms
GCU SpM	1. Read the status data from PWM ODSS every 100ms 2. Send the status data to the Ground Station TMO using a Gate in EAC	10ms
Mission SvM	1. Receive command data from Ground Station TMO 2. Write the command data to COMMAND ODSS	10ms

3.2.2 Ground Station TMO

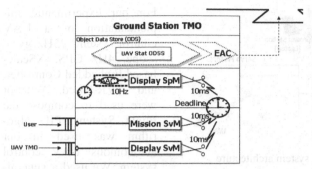

Ground Station TMO includes Display SpM and Display SvM for monitoring and Mission SvM for mission planning as depicted in Fig. 4. The functional requirements for Ground Station TMO are defined in Table 2.

Fig. 4. Design of the Ground Station TMO

Table 2. Functional requirements of Ground Station TMO

Method Name	Functions	Deadline
Display SpM	1. Read all data of the UAV from the UAV State ODSS and Command ODSS every 40ms 2. Send all data to the user application for display	10ms
Mission SvM	1. Read command data which include waypoints of the UAV from the call parameters supplied by the user application 2. Send the data to the UAV TMO in Flight System	10ms
Display SvM	1. Receive the status data of the UAV from Flight System 2. Write the data to UAV State ODSS	10ms

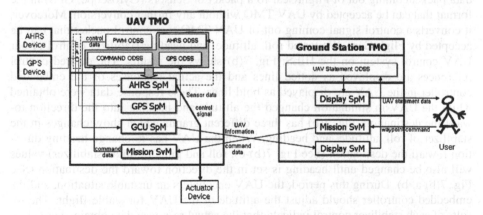

Fig. 5. Interaction of the UAV TMO with the Ground Station TMO

Fig. 5 depicts interactions including data flows between UAV TMO and Ground Station TMO. GCU SpM in UAV TMO requests a service to Display SvM in Ground Station TMO for displaying UAV status data, while Mission SvM in Ground Station TMO requests a service to Mission SvM in UAV TMO for accepting command data.

3.3 Implementation

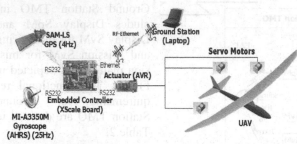

Fig. 6. UAV control system architecture

For our experimental implementation of a UAV control system, 25Hz gyroscope, 4Hz GPS, XScale-based Embedded Controller, and AVR-based Actuator were used to compose the Flight System. PID algorithm was used in our autonomous UAV control system. We used a general-purpose laptop computer as the Ground Station for monitoring the status of the UAV. Fig. 6 presents the hardware structure of the implemented UAV control system. The TMO-structured real-time computing software in both Flight System and Ground Station turned out to be remarkably easier to read, analyze, and maintain in comparison to the initial version of the software that had been designed 4 years ago and composed of threads, sockets, and thread-priorities.

4 Validation

4.1 Step 1: Test with an Environment Simulator

In our experiments, we deployed a hardware-in-the-loop simulator (HILS) centered around FlightGear and depicted in Fig. 7(a). In HILS, a Bridge TMO converts a state data packet coming out of FlightGear to a packet of Sensors (Gyroscope, GPS) in the format that can be accepted by UAV TMO without any further conversion. Moreover, it converts a control signal coming out of UAV TMO to a control packet that can be accepted by FlightGear. We tested roll, altitude, and heading stabilizer control of our UAV control system on the HILS. Fig. 7(b) shows the results. The desired control references are displayed as dotted lines and the actual responses of the embedded controller in the UAV are displayed as bold lines. These response data were obtained while the UAV in simulation changed the altitude and heading into the direction toward the destination. Fig. 7(b) has three different graphs which show changes in the stabilizer of roll, altitude, and heading. When the UAV has to change heading direction toward the destination (See Fig. 7(b)-c), roll and pitch (altitude stabilizer) values will also be changed until heading is set in the direction toward the destination (See Fig. 7(b)-a, b). During this period, the UAV encounters an unstable situation, and the embedded controller should adjust the attitude of the UAV for stable flight. The results of each stabilizer control indicate that the actual response data obtained are close to the desired references for stable flight. By comparing the figures, we can conclude that the exhibited behavior of the simulated Flight System is close to the desired references. These results attest to the accuracy of our embedded control system implemented with the TMO structuring techniques and tools and the usefulness of the hardware-in-the-loop simulator.

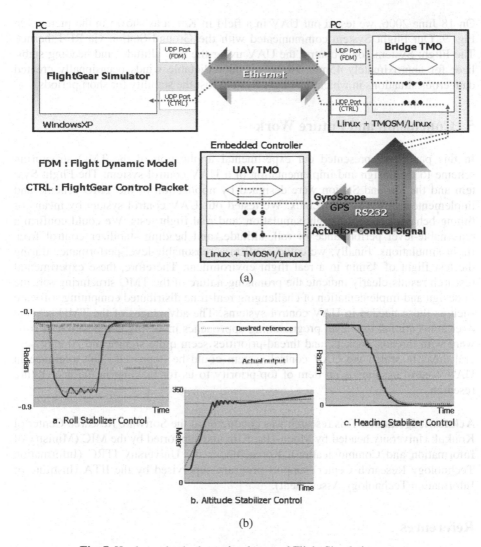

FDM : Flight Dynamic Model

CTRL : FlightGear Control Packet

(a)

(b)

Fig. 7. Hardware-in-the-loop simulator and Flight Simulation output

4.2 Step 2: Real Flight Test

Fig. 8. UAV flight test in Korea on 18 June 2006

On 18 June 2006, we tested our UAV in a field in Korea as shown in the pictures in Fig. 9. Our Flight System communicated with the Ground Station via RF-Ethernet. The Flight System could control the UAV using the roll, altitude, and heading stabilizer for approximately 45min. However, unpredictable winds occasionally created dangerous situations in which the Flight System lost the stability for short periods.

5 Conclusion and Future Work

In this paper, we presented our experimental application of the TMO structuring scheme to the design and implementation of a UAV control system. The Flight System and the Ground Station were designed by application of the TMO scheme and implemented with TMOSM/Linux. We tested our UAV control system by means of timing behavior analysis, flight simulation, and real flight tests. We could confirm a reasonable-level performance of roll, altitude, and heading stabilizer control from flight simulations. Finally, we could confirm a reasonable-level performance during the test flight of 45min in a real flight environment. Therefore, these experimental research results clearly indicate the promising nature of the TMO structuring scheme in design and implementation of challenging real-time distributed computing software such as those needed in UAV control systems. The advantages of the TMO scheme over conventional low-level programming approaches involving composition of software with threads, sockets, and thread-priorities seem quite significant. Among several areas in which the UAV control system could be improved, fault-tolerance in UAV control systems is an item of top-priority to us for tackling in the near future research.

Acknowledgements. This research was conducted at the Software Research Center of Konkuk University headed by Moon-Hae Kim and supported by the MIC (Ministry of Information and Communication), Korea, under the University ITRC (Information Technology Research Center) support program supervised by the IITA (Institute of Information Technology Assessment).

References

1. Kim, K.H.: Object Structures for Real-Time Systems and Simulators, pp. 62–70. IEEE Computer Society Press, Los Alamitos (1997)
2. Kim, K.H.: APIs for Real-Time Distributed Object Programming, pp. 72–80. IEEE Computer Society Press, Los Alamitos (2000)
3. Kim, K.H., Ishida, M., Liu, J.: An Efficient Middleware Architecture Supporting Time-Triggered Message-Triggered Objects and an NT-based Implementation. In: ISORC, pp. 54–63 (1999)
4. Kim, H.J., Park, S.H., Kim, J.G., Kim, M.H.: TMO-Linux: A Linux-based Real-time Operating System Supporting Execution of TMOs. In: ISORC (2002)
5. Koo, T.J., Liebman, J., Ma, C., Sastry, S.: Hierarchical approach for design of multi-vehicle multi-modal embedded software. In: Henzinger, T.A., Kirsch, C.M. (eds.) EMSOFT 2001. LNCS, vol. 2211, Springer, Heidelberg (2001)

6. Koo, T.J., Liebman, J., Ma, C., Horowitz, B., Sangiovanni-Vincentelli, A., Sastry, S.: Platform-based embedded software design and system integration for autonomous vehicles. Proceedings of the IEEE 91(1), 198–211 (2003)
7. Sorton, E.F., Hammaker, S.: Simulated flight Testing of an Autonomous Unmanned Aerial Vehicle Using FlightGear. Institute for Scientific Research Inc., Fairmont, WV AIAA-2005-7083
8. Ippolito, C.: QSS Group, Inc., NASA Ames Research Center, An Autonomous Autopilot Control System Design for Small-Scale UAVs. Internal Report of CMIL in University of Carnegie Mellon: EAV-20051016
9. Lee, E.A.: Embedded Software – An Agenda for Research. UCB ERL Memorandum M99/63 in University of California at Berkeley
10. Matczynski, M.J.: A Distributed Embedded Software Architecture for Multiple Unmanned Aerial Vehicles. Master thesis, EECS, MI

Lifestyle Ubiquitous Gaming:
Computer Games Making Daily Lives Fun

Eiji Tokunaga, Masaaki Ayabe, Hiroaki Kimura, and Tatsuo Nakajima

Department of Information and Computer Science, Waseda University
3-4-1 Okubo Shinjuku Tokyo 169-8555, Japan
Tel&Fax:+81-3-5286-3185
{eitoku,ayabe,hiroaki,tatsuo}@dcl.info.waseda.ac.jp

Abstract. We propose a novel computer gaming style in which users can enjoy games through their daily lives without paying too much attention and time for the games, we call it *lifestyle ubiquitous gaming*. Lifestyle ubiquitous games track human daily activities implicitly and incorporate the tracked activities in their game logics. Then they represent decorated and virtualized those activities on ambient displays. We believe that this gaming style enables not only making their boring and messy daily tasks fun but improving their lazy lifestyle and customs. In this paper, we describe our lifestyle ubiquitous gaming concept and framework, and then we show our two case studies implementing distinguishing scenarios.

1 Introduction

Recent computer game technologies enable us to play games anytime, anywhere and with anyone. The latest portable/non-portable game consoles have significant computing resources and network capabilities, and a lot of games are provided on the cellphone market. On the other hand, the purpose of playing computer games is becoming diverse and expanding. The positive effects of games are being explored in both of academic and industrial research. This is not only for entertainment but also for communication, education, health, business and even military.

In this way it is broadening the consumer base, however, there are still many ordinary people who cannot play computer games even they love playing games. Because current computer games have three significant negative factors to be played by non-gamers: 1) Most of current games require a lot of time to enjoy so that busy people cannot enjoy enough. In particular, massively multiplayer online games require a large amount of time to sufficiently enjoy in their virtual world. 2) Resent games are not only just too hard to enjoy, but also that requires unignorable physical work and psychological barrier to start playing them. We have to turn on the TV and game console, then switch the TV input to which the console is connected to play ordinary console games. Online games might require additional work. Even for mobile games, players must carry slightly heavy mobile game consoles and find appropriate places to play just games. 3) Playing computer games is still considered as socially disgraceful by certain people, even

R. Obermaisser et al. (Eds.): SEUS 2007, LNCS 4761, pp. 202–212, 2007.

by players themselves. Some of Japanese female gamers like to play games using cell phones because other people cannot recognize they are playing computer games. But, it is still slightly strange that a person is giving a steady look into the display of her cell phone, and intensely pushing some buttons.

Therefore, we propose a novel computer gaming style in which gaming features are integrated into our daily lives seamlessly by using sensing technologies. The games extract real-time context and history of everyday activities such as cooking and cleaning. Then, the extracted daily activities are decorated with gaming features and represented in ambient style. Players do no have to be very conscious of how they are and other people are fairly ignorant of what they are doing there. They do not have to take time for games into account, just do daily activities augmented with fun games. They can enjoy and enhance their daily lives by gaming effects with very little efforts. In other words, it makes possible to learn by games for not science or physics but our daily lives. We describe one possible future scenario as follows.

SensPet: Eiji loves to play computer games very much but he is too busy to play recent Hollywood movie-like large-scale games. Nowadays, he is a huge fun of SensPet that is an online virtual fuss-free pet game. SensPet provides a virtual pet that is a virtual counter part of Eiji's daily life. Surrounding sensors in his home or mobile phone is sensing his daily activities, and then extracted contexts automatically influence the growth of his pet. If he cleans his room often, his pet house is always clean and his pet grows up elegant. If he buys fancy clothes, his pet is dressed up and grows up smart. Unlike other virtual pet games that require too much investment to breed, SensPet does not require much time and high skills to enjoy but exciting. If he is smart with daily activities, his pet grows up smart. He is strongly motivated to do the best for his daily life. The vender of SensPet will provide the next version of SensPet that is "SensCity" for intellectual people. . .

We call this kind of gaming style *lifestyle ubiquitous gaimng*. We believe that it enables not only making their boring and messy daily tasks fun but improving their lazy lifestyle and customs. Exploring this novel gaming style leads to establish new outpost for gaming industries. The rest of this paper is structured as follows. Section 2 describes the conceptual framework of lifestyle ubiquitous gaming. We built two lifestyle ubiquitous games on the framework as case studies. Section 3 describes the design and implementation of the case studies. Section 4 discusses some issues and expected exit. Section 5 shows related work and Section 6 concludes this paper with future work.

2   Lifestyle Ubiquitous Gaming Framework

Fig. 1 shows the overview of lifestyle ubiquitous gaming conceptual framework. This framework consists of four stages: *lifestyle tracking, sensor analysis, game logic, lifestyle presentation* enclosing *human daily activities*. These stages transit as a cycle as shown in the figure. We describe about the characteristic of each stage and human daily activities to be used in lifestyle ubiquitous gaming as follows.

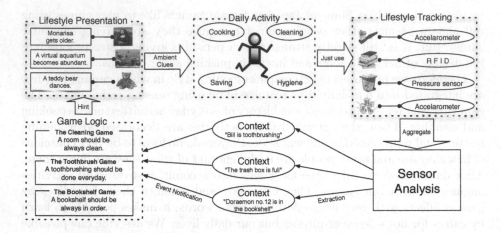

Fig. 1. Lifestyle ubiquitous gaming conceptual framework overview

Lifestyle tracking: In lifestyle ubiquitous gaming, players basically just use daily objects such as a toothbrush, a bookshelf and a kitchen knife in their regular daily lives. Their daily activities using the daily objects are tracked implicitly by sensors embedded in the daily objects[7]. The tracked data is passed to the next stages that use them as input events on the gaming world. In this way, players do not have to very conscious of playing games, and it is very easy to play lifestyle ubiquitous games for even non-gamers such as elderly people.

Sensor analysis: Each tracked data extracted from embedded sensors is often too fine-grained to use in game logics. This stage analyzes the tracked data into *contexts* that are highly abstracted activity information such as "Alice is brushing her teeth" and "The Art of Computer Programming is in the bookshelf".

Game logic: In this stage, goals/idempotents of lifestyle ubiquitous gaming such as making cooking fun and motivating daily cleaning are incorporated with analyzed contexts in game logics. For example, a logic motivating daily cleaning one's own room stores cleaning contexts of player's rooms daily and defines the states of their rooms such as "Alice's room is clean", "Bob's room is dirty" or "Carol's room is not so clean even she often cleans her room". It decides what kind of gaming representation would be shown for making their each cleaning activity fun and motivating them. Then it generates *hints* for achieving the goal/idempotent.

Lifestyle presentation: Unlike in the case of ordinary computer games, too blinging and bright representation would be annoying and disturbing in lifestyle ubiquitous gaming style. In this stage, the hints generated in the game logic stage are represented through daily representation objects such as a fine art, an aquarium and a teddy bear. These objects provide *ambient clues* to achieve goals of the games in restrained ways that do not require too much time and attention to understand. Those goals also mean, in other words, improving players' lives and making their custom better.

2.1 Human Daily Activities

Currently, we have selected four human daily activities to be augmented with games: *cleaning, hygiene, saving, cooking*. We considered possibilities for improvement about the activity and technological implementability to track them.

Cleaning activities: Although cleaning our living environments is necessary to live healthfully, it is boring task for many people. If we can augment the cleaning task with gaming, people who are lazy for cleaning might be decrease. Even for the people who are not lazy, the game would make a part of their daily lives amusing. We can know how clean a room is using dust sensors and movements of cleaners and sweepers.

Hygiene activities: Hygiene activities like tooth brushing and hand washing are obviously quite important for healthy daily lives. But, children and even adults often lazy for doing such hygiene activities. We would like to encourage the continuation of them by presenting the use of hygiene things such as toothbrushes and hand soaps in a virtual gaming world. We can know by whom and when the toothbrushes are used by attaching accelerometers to them[6]. We assume that users will not choose the wrong toothbrush.

Cooking activities Cooking and eating well-balanced meals is one of the most significant ingredients to improve our quality of life. However, managing the balance is not so easy for ordinary people, and its continuation is even more difficult. If we can build a game in which cooking well-balanced meals is connected to positive feedbacks, it might increase mothers motivation to cook well and encourage children to eat wel-balanced meals.

Resource saving activities Saving resources like electricity and water leads to save our money and help natural resources on the earth. But the respective resource saving activities in our daily lives, such as turning off rights and appliances regularly is often very hard to be aware as actually be connected to save resources. If a game can show how the saving activity effects to the overall goal and the total amount of saved resources in a fun way, they might continue to save resources without patience.

3   Case Studies

We built prototype games based on the described conceptual framework to confirm feasibility and effectivity of our lifestyle ubiquitous gaming concept. Currently, we have built two games one is for a kind of hygiene activities: toothbrushing, the another one is for a kind of cleaning activities: arranging a bookshelf.

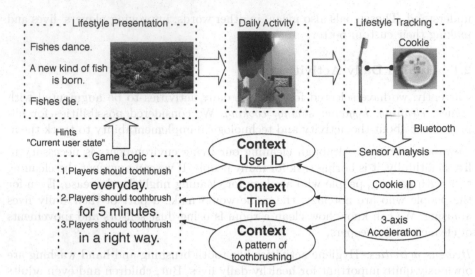

Fig. 2. Toothbrushing connected to breeding tropical fish

3.1   A Virtual Aquarium Improving Toothbrushing Activity

The daily activity in Fig. 2 shows a player toothbrushing, which is a kind of hygiene activities, in front of a virtual aquarium displayed on a micro pc. This game is based on three rules that are *players should tooth brush everyday, players should toothbrush for 5 minutes* and *players should toothbrush in a right way*. It tracks toothbrushing activity and provides *immediate feedback* for encouraging toothbrushing in sufficient time, and *gradual feedback* for encouraging continuance of everyday toothbrushing in a right way.

Fig. 3. Dancing fish and wiping rag while player's toothbrushing

Fig. 4. A spawned egg after player's well-regulated toothbrushing

Immediate feedback: When a player starts toothbrushing, fish in the aquarium dance happily and a rag starts wiping a moss-covered window (Fig. 3). Then, while s/he continues to brush in sufficient time, their dance changes into more

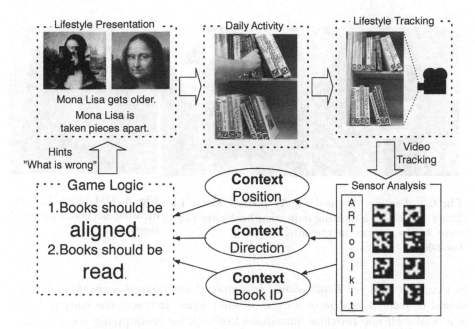

Fig. 5. Mona Lisa breaks up when some books are taken off for a while. She gets older when the bookshelf in a long while.

elegant and the window becomes clean. At last he stops toothbrushing, then fish stop dancing and start to school slowly again.

Gradual feedback If a player succeeded to brush both in morning and night, one of the fish blows an egg in at midnight. The egg hardly catches out initially. If s/he could continue to brush everyday, the incubation ratio increases. If s/he could toothbrush in a right way, such as brushing both of upper and lower teeth, a rare kind of fish might be born (Fig. 4).

Implementation: Fig. 2 shows the overall architecture of this game based on our framework. The toothbrushing activity is tracked by Cookie sensor[12] that is a bluetooth-enabled coin-size sensor node having several kinds of sensors inside. This game uses a 3-axis accelerometer in it. One Cookie is attached to a toothbrush and the sensor analysis module analyzes accelerometer data while a player is toothbrushing. Each Cookie has own unique ID that is used as user ID in this game. Toothbrushing time is recognized by monitoring the difference between maximum and minimum acceleration. Toothbrushing pattern is recognized by monitoring the direction of bristles. Bluetooth connection, context acquisition and event notification are managed by our context acquisition framework[4].

3.2 A Virtual Fine Art Improving Book Arrangement Activity

The second case study is a game encouraging book arrangement activity in a personal bookshelf, which is a kind of cleaning activities. This game is based

Fig. 6. Partly dropped Mona Lisa indicating some books are not in the bookshelf

Fig. 7. Broken Mona Lisa indicating books are not in the order

Fig. 8. Old Mona Lisa indicating no books are read recently

on two rules that are *Books should be arranged and aligned correctly* and *Books should be read at least once a weak or some span.* It tracks the state of books in a bookshelf and provides immediate feedback for encouraging book arrangement and gradual feedback for encouraging reading books. These feedback are represented on a virtual fine art mounted near the bookshelf.

Immediate feedback: When a book is taken off for a while, a piece of Mona Lisa is also taken off. If books are not aligned correctly, the pieces of Mona Lisa are also aligned awkwardly. While the books are arranged correctly in the bookshelf, she smiles peacefully (Fig. 6, 7).

Gradual feedback: If non of the books are not read for a long while, she gets older slowly. Then, when one of the books is read, she gets back her youth and smile. Too old Mona Lisa indicates the books on the bookshelf should be replaced with other ones (Fig. 8).

Implementation: Fig. 5 shows the overall architecture similar in the first one. The positions of books are tracked by using of ARToolkit[10] that is a software library implementing visual tag recognition. A video camera deployed in front of a bookshelf captures visual tags attached to each book. Then, the analysis module calculates their positions, directions, and IDs and notifies them to the game logic. The logic gives hints including information of missing or unaligned books and unread books to the presentation module implemented using Flash.

4   Discussion and Future Work

In this section, we describe some discussions and future work given through designing and implementing prototype games described in case studies.

Immediate feedback vs gradual feedback: We believe lifestyle ubiquitous games should have both of immediate and gradual feedback as described in our case studies. Immediate feedback is useful for notifying players the state of current tracking and making the moment of activities fun. Gradual feedback is appropriate for presenting them the history of tracked activities and encouraging the continuance of daily activities. We expect to observe players' behavior within each feedback result and prospect about relationship between them.

Direct vs indirect metaphor mapping: In our current case studies, the presentations like an aquarium and a fine art have few relevance with the actual activities like toothbrushing and book arrangement. That is because we thought if it is directly connected like the toothbrushing game shows deformed bad teeth, players who are lazy for toothbrushing might not be interested in it. However, that toothbrushing game encourages players who are already interested in toothbrushing more. We expect to build another game that presentation metaphor is directly mapped to the activity and prospect the difference.

User studies: We still have not conducted any formal user studies. We believe that we have to answer two questions: (1) *Is it fun or not? How people accept or reject our gaming concept?* (2) *Can these games really encourage boring daily activities?* For answering the first question, we expect to use think aloud technique and interview with short-term experiments. For the second one, we expect to conduct long-term experiments with following steps. At first, we observe subjects doing particular activities without games several days. Then, we deploy games in their home and observe changes in the activities several days. At last, we remove the games and continue to observe changes. Each observation can be easily done by using sensors embedded in daily objects.

Networking lifestyle ubiquitous gaming: Our prototype games are all stand-alone programs. It is because we thought that it was appropriate to explore lifestyle ubiquitous gaming with building simple games at first step. We identify that networking features can make our games much more fun. For example, competition of virtual aquariums' daily snapshots would make players more competitive. Daily activities on the Web such as blogging and social networking services could be easily integrated with lifestyle ubiquitous gaming like BlogPet[11].

Expected limitations of lifestyle ubiquitous gaming: The final question that we have to explore is "Can lifestyle ubiquitous games become current Hollywood-like large-scale game alternatives?" We expect that even if we could achieve making quite attractive gaming world around lifestyle ubiquitous games, they can hardly become the alternatives for hard core gamers who truly love to play large scale games. But, we can see large movements in which ordinary people leave large scale console games to simple and convenient mobile games around in many parts of the world. We believe that exploring this research makes new alternatives for people who is hesitative about playing computer games.

5   Related Work

Digital Game-Based Learning[14] discussed how learners have changed, how games teach and why they work. [3] and [1] described about *serious games* that are computer and video games that are intended not only entertain users, but have additional purposes such as education and training. As these books shows, the positive effects of games on learning, training, exercising, and medical things are being explored in recent years. However, how integrating gaming features into daily activities effects is not explored.

Several recent gaming projects so-called pervasive gaming[13] have exploited the possibility to combine the world of the game with the physical world. Pirates! [2] allows players to move around in the physical domain and are presented with location dependent games on their PDAs equipped with simple short-range radio frequency proximity sensors. Can You See Me Now?[5] combines a game of tag in a real city in online game-play in a virtual game area by connecting online players' home computers to real runners' handheld computers. These games show positive possibilities and ways to integrate computer games into physical domain, but still they require complicated configuration settings and significant time to enjoy.

FantasyA and SenToy[9] represent an affective control toy. SenToy is a doll including several sensors wirelessly connected to a PC. By using gestures of the doll, it allows players to manipulate the emotions of a synthetic character in the computer game, FantasyA. Physical user interfaces embedded within everyday objects like a SenToy doll would make it easy to entry virtual gaming worlds. But, doll gestures are probably not appropriate for adults and not related to daily activities. We believe that if we can embedded same kind of physical user interfaces of computer games into more common daily activities, that would make more intuitive and easy-to-entry virtual gaming worlds.

Informative art project[8] explores information visualization techniques that use art as inspiration for both their appearance and their role in our surroundings. Its information presentations disappear into the background and enable people to be notified information without too much attention. Lifestyle presentation in lifestyle ubiquitous gaming is a bit similar to informative art in terms of embedding information visualization in daily objects. But our idea includes purposeful movements like making boring tasks fun rather than just showing information.

6   Conclusion

In this paper, we showed a concept and case studies of lifestyle ubiquitous gaming that is a novel computer gaming style embedded in our daily lives. It makes boring daily activities fun and does not require too much attention and time to play. We believe this novel gaming idea can inspire the current game industry and open up new breakthroughs. But, currently this research is in the very early stage so that we still could not verify the effectiveness and feasibility. We are planning to do practical and long-term user studies and build more games exploring the other daily activities: cooking and resource saving.

Acknowledgement

This work is greatly supported by the Microsoft Institute for Japanese Academic Research Collaboration (IJARC) with universities. The authors would like to thank Ying-Qing Xu and Hajime Wada. The prototype games were developed by several students in our laboratory. The authors would like to thank Keisuke Hayashi, Yuri Kuno, Teruhide Kusaka, Hanae Suzuki, Chihiro Takayama and Keita Yamada.

References

1. Bergeron, B.: Developing Serious Games. Charles River Media (2006)
2. Björk, S., Falk, J., Hansson, R., Ljungstrand, P.: Pirates! using the physical world as a game board. In: Interact 2001, IFIP TC.13 Conference On Human-Computer Interaction, Tokyo, Japan (July 2001)
3. Chen, S.: Serious Games: Games That Educate, Train, and Info. Course Technology (2005)
4. Nakajima, T., Kawsar, F., Fujinami, K.: Prottoy: A middleware for sentient environment. In: Yang, L.T., Amamiya, M., Liu, Z., Guo, M., Rammig, F.J. (eds.) EUC 2005. LNCS, vol. 3824, Springer, Heidelberg (2005)
5. Flintham, M., Benford, S., Anastasi, R., Hemmings, T., Crabtree, A., Greenhalgh, C., Tandavanitj, N., Adams, M., Row-Farr, J.: here on-line meets on the streets: experiences with mobile mixed reality games. In: CHI '03. Proceedings of the SIGCHI conference on Human factors in computing systems, Ft. Lauderdale, Florida, USA, ACM Press, New York (2003)
6. Fujinami, K., Kawsar, F., Nakajima, T.: Awaremirror: A personalized display using a mirror. In: The 3rd International Conference on Pervasive Computing, Munich, Germany (May 2005)
7. Fujinami, K., Nakajima, T.: Sentient artefacts: Acquiring user's context through daily objects. In: The 2nd International Workshop on Ubiquitous Intelligence and Smart Worlds, Nagasaki, Japan (December 2005)
8. Holmquist, L.E., Skog, T.: Informative art: information visualization in everyday environments. In: GRAPHITE '03. Proceedings of the 1st international conference on Computer graphics and interactive techniques in Australasia and South East Asia, Melbourne, Australia (2003)
9. Höök, K., Bullock, A., Paiva, A., Vala, M., Chaves, R., Prada, R.: Fantasya and sentoy. In: CHI '03. CHI '03 extended abstracts on Human factors in computing systems, Ft. Lauderdale, Florida, USA, ACM Press, New York (2003)
10. Kato, H., Billinghurst, M.: Marker tracking and hmd calibration for a video-based augmented reality conferencing system. In: IWAR 99. Proceedings of the 2nd International Workshop on Augmented Reality, San Francisco, USA (October 1999)
11. KDDI CORPORATION and WORK@ INC. BlogPet. http://www.blogpet.net/, Last checked: (July 24, 2006)

12. Kimura, H., Tokunaga, E., Okuda, Y., Nakajima, T.: Cookieflavors: easy building blocks for wireless tangible input. In: CHI '06. CHI '06 extended abstracts on Human factors in computing systems, Montréal, Québec, Canada (2006)
13. Magerkurth, C., Cheook, A.D., Mandryk, R.L., Nilsen, T.: Pervasive games: Bringing computer entertainment back to the real world. ACM Computers in Entertainment 3(3) (2005)
14. Prensky, M.: Digital Game-Based Learning. McGraw-Hill Companies, New York (2000)

Speech Recognition System Using DHMMs Based on Ubiquitous Environment

Jong-Hun Kim[1], Un-Gu Kang[2], Kee-Wook Rim[3], and Jung-Hyun Lee[1]

[1] Department of Computer Science & Engineering Inha University
Yonghyun-dong, Nam-gu, Incheon, Korea
jhkim@hci.inha.ac.kr, jhlee@inha.ac.kr
[2] Department of Information Technology Gachon University of Medicine and Science
Yeonsu-dong, Yeonsu-ku, Incheon, Korea
ugkang@gachon.ac.kr
[3] Department of Computer and Information Science
Sun Moon University, Chung-Nam, Korea
rim@sunmoon.ac.kr

Abstract. Most commercialized speech recognition systems that have a large capacity and high recognition rates are a type of speaker dependent isolated word recognition systems. In order to extend the scope of recognition, it is necessary to increase the number of words that are to be searched. However, it shows a problem that exhibits a decrease in the system performance according to the increase in the number of words. This paper defines the context information that affects speech recognition in a ubiquitous environment to solve such a problem and designs a new speech recognition system that demonstrates better performances than the existing system by establishing a word model domain of a speech recognition system.

1 Introduction

The necessity of the interface between humans and machines according to the development of information and communication technologies is required. In particular, speech recognition technologies are necessary to satisfy the natural communication between various devices in ubiquitous environments and most easy interfaces. These speech recognition technologies extract the linguistic information and sound information included in the voice between humans and save the extracted information to transfer it to machine by applying proper practices in order to understand the meaning included in this information.

Types in speech recognition have been developed as an isolated word recognition method that recognizes separately spoken words, continuous pronunciation recognition method that recognizes continuous pronunciations, and voice understanding that recognizes conversational sounds. The final goal of these speech recognition technologies is to understand every voice in all environments. However, the high performance commercial system is mainly represented as a speaker dependant isolated word system.

R. Obermaisser et al. (Eds.): SEUS 2007, LNCS 4761, pp. 213–222, 2007.

Representative commercial speech recognition systems are Voice Scribe 1000 Dragon Dictate by Dragon System, Voice Command by IBM, and Speech Command by Texas Instruments. These systems are speaker dependant isolated word recognitions systems and able to recognize about 1000 words. These systems show certain significant decreases in their performances, such as recognition speed and rate, according to the increase in words.

Therefore, this paper attempts to design a speech recognition system (SRS) using user's context information in speech recognition services. The factors that affect the performance of a speech recognition system will be configured as context information and determined using Ontology. Information can be obtained using the noise measurement, Radio Frequency Identification (RFID) Tag, and RFID Reader, and then accurate context information can be recognized using Ontology Database and inference engine. The system proposed in this study is designed based on Open Service Gateway Initiative (OSGi), which is a type of ubiquitous middlewares, in order to obtain real-time context information and provide the obtained information to applications. Also, the speech recognition algorithm used in this system is a Hidden Markov Models (HMMs) in which this algorithm overcomes the disadvantage in an isolated word speech recognition system and increases the performance by configuring a HMM Domain according to the context. In the results of the test for the user who registered in the system, it showed a high speech recognition rate in a home network system.

2 OSGi

Open Service Gateway Initiative (OSGi) is an organization that establishes standards on the transmission of multi-services that independently home networks and information domestic appliances through access networks by defining network technology and common open architecture structures. OSGi was founded on March 1999, consisted of 15 businesses, and was expanded to include more than 50 software, hardware, and service provider companies.

OSGi is a nonprofit organization that not only defines the API between middlewares and application programs but also plays a role in the separation between specified application programs and middlewares. Standards established by OSGi provide dynamic services for devices with small capacity memories using the platform independence of Java and network mobility of execution codes. In particular, it is an open architecture network technology that can support various network techniques, such as Bluetooth, Home Audio/Video Interoperability (HAVi), Home Phoneline Networking Alliance (PNA), Home Radio Frequency (RF), Universal Serial Bus (USB), Video Electronics Standards Association (VESA), and other networks. It also provides management and connection functions for most products. These include set-top boxes, cable modems, routers, warning systems, power management systems, domestic appliances, and PCs, in which the Java based gateway consists of Java environments, service frameworks, device access management functions, and log services that include the connection technology for these elements when access and new services are required. The OSGi service platform displayed in Fig. 1 consists of the OSGi framework and standard services.

Three major entities of the OSGi are Service, Bundle, and Framework. Service includes Java interfaces that perform specific functions, actually implements objects, and is a component that is accessed through a predefined service interface. A single application can be configured through the cooperation of several services and is able to request services during run-time. Bundle is a functional distribution unit that provides services. Framework is an execution environment that manages the life cycle of the Bundle. Bundle is a service set and a component unit that uses the service registered in service registries. The implementation of Service can be performed physically, distributed, and sent to the Framework through the Bundle in logical units. Bundle exists as JAR files. A JAR file includes more than one service implementation object, resource files, and manifest files. The manifest file represents the service provided by each Bundle and other services that are used to implement Bundle. Finally, Bundle can be implemented or terminated using the Start and Stop function in the Framework.

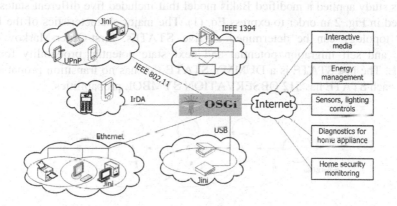

Fig. 1. The Overview of OSGi

3   Domain-Separated Hidden Markov Models (DHMMs)

A pattern recognition method is generally used for speech recognition and is classified as a Dynamic Time Warping (DTW) method that uses a template-based pattern matching and Hidden Markov Model (HMM) method employing a statistical pattern recognition method. HMM is an algorithm that was founded on mathematics. It was introduced in the field of speech signal processing in 1975 and widely applied from isolated word recognition to the spontaneous speech recognition. This algorithm can be classified as a learning and recognition process under the assumption that the time series pattern in speech feature vectors is modeled after the Markov process. In addition, a method that is combined with the HMM is widely used at the present time due to the increase in the amount of calculations even though neural network based methods are also used in speech recognition.

This study applies an HMM that uses a speech recognition algorithm as a pattern recognition method according to the domain. The Baum-welch method is used as a learning method for the HMM. In addition, probability for the HMM is calculated using a Vitervi algorithm.

3.1 HMM Topology

The parameters used in the HMM consist of the transition probability between states, output probability subordinated to states, and initial presence probability of states. The parameter of the HMM can be simply expressed as Eq. (1).

$$\lambda = < A, B, \pi > \tag{1}$$

A : State-transition probability distribution

B : Observation symbol probability distribution

π : Initial state distribution

This study applied a modified Bakis model that included five different states as illustrated in Fig. 2 in order to express Eq. (1). The major characteristics of the HMM model topology can be determined as five STATEs, First-Order-Markov Chain model, and self migration potential and next state potential probability for each STATE. The last STATE is a DUMMY STATE that has no transition probability in which each STATE has 512 OBSERVATION SYMBOL probabilities.

Fig. 2. HMM Topology

Fig. 3 illustrates the internal probability of the "aljip" HMM, a type of computer application words.

파일(F) 편집(E) 서식(O) 도움말(H)

STATE NUM : 5
SYMBOL NUM : 512

TRANSITION :
0.0000000000e+000 9.9905271062e-001 9.4728937603e-004 0.0000000000e+000 0.0000000000e+000
0.0000000000e+000 9.5507871559e-001 4.4479586058e-002 4.4169835501e-004 0.0000000000e+000
0.0000000000e+000 0.0000000000e+000 9.5565827369e-001 4.4334175970e-002 7.5503377021e-006
0.0000000000e+000 0.0000000000e+000 0.0000000000e+000 9.6942863163e-001 3.0571368369e-002
0.000000000e+000 0.0000000000e+000 0.0000000000e+000 0.0000000000e+000 0.000000000e+000

SYMBOL :
1.0000000000e-011 1.0000000000e-011 1.0000000000e-011 1.0000000000e-011 1.0000000000e-011
1.0000000000e-011 1.0000000000e-011 1.0000000000e-011 1.0000000000e-011 1.0000000000e-011
1.0000000000e-011 1.0000000000e-011 6.2799764298e-006 1.2848476230e-005 2.6560503180e-005
1.2843761613e-005 2.1227266131e-007 3.8618702185e-005 1.0000000000e-011 1.0000000000e-011
1.0000000000e-011 1.0000000000e-011 1.0000000000e-011 1.0000000000e-011 1.0000000000e-011
1.0000000000e-011 1.0000000000e-011 1.0000000000e-011 1.6679667102e-004 7.2237814101e-004
6.8729341377e-004 5.0633179316e-004 3.3338170768e-004 7.9427883842e-004 4.4036556549e-004

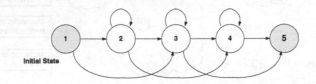

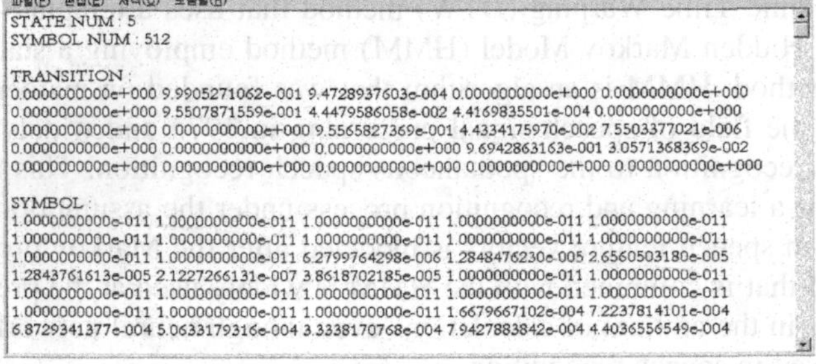

Fig. 3. Five States and 512 Observation Symbols of HMM

3.2 HMM Domain

3.2.1 Context Information Domain

This study configured the HMM domain according to speaker information, utterance location, and used objects. Speaker information and location were verified using RFID sensors installed in user devices and in the home. The state information domain was configured according to the space (Balcony, Bathroom, Bedroom, Guestroom, Kitchen) in the home where detailed configurations were performed in accordance with applied objects (Computer, Television, Radio, Refrigerator, Washing machine, Electric Lamp). State information on the speaker and noise in the Context Manager and Service Manager were transmitted to the Speech Recognition Manager.

3.2.2 Observation Sequence Domain

The speech recognition prototype implemented in this study was based on a word model. The length of the observation sequence produced by the length of the utterance changed because the word model shows the same utterance unit and recognition unit. Therefore, the recognition rate decreased in the application that had HMM topology similar to the isolated word that registered different utterance lengths. Furthermore, recognition speed exhibited a decrease due to the increase in the number of recognition words. The system used in this study configured the domain according to the length of the observation sequence and selected the domain from the HMM of the objective domain using the length information of the observation sequence from the input speech signal.

3.2.3 Syllable Number Domain

This study configured a state information domain, observation sequence domain, and domain for the number of syllables in order to improve the performance of the speech recognition system. Vowels in speech showed a periodical property different from the consonants. Thus, it is possible to improve the performance of the speech recognition system using the domain for the number of syllables through a reliable detection process for vowels. In addition, it is possible to develop a speech recognition system according to the unit of phonemes. The number of syllables can be produced by the analysis of the frequency of isolated words and formant feature extraction data.

4 Speech Recognition System Design

This chapter designed and implemented the speech recognition system (SRS) that was able to recognize correct speech by estimating context information in a Java-based OSGi framework using the context definition.

Fig. 4 presents the diagram of the overall system. The SRS designed in this paper analyzed and suggested various data transferred from context recognition sensors and established it as information to recognize correct speech through a recognition process. In order to perform this process, the SRS consisted of a Context Manager, Service Manager, and Speech Recognition Manager.

The system proposed in this study used an ontology inferencer Jena 2.0 and developed an OSGi gateway using the Knopflerfish 1.3.3, an open architecture source project which implemented a service framework.

4.1 Context Manager

The configuration of context information for the speech recognition system (SRS) consists of user information (sex, age), noise, object, and location information.

User information, nosie, object and location information can be predefined as ontology, and data can be input from sensors. Noise data can be transferred using an OSGi framework and communication from a noise measurement device used in real-time Zigbee communication. User information, use object and location information can be traced using an RFID Tag which is attached to a user.

Table 1 presents the definition of context information as different spaces, such as class 2 for sex, class 5 for age, class 3 for noise, class 6 for object and class 6 for location information, in order to build an ontology model.

In particular, the service area is limited to homes, and the users' location is limited to the Balcony, Bathroom, Bedroom, Guestroom, Kitchen, and Livingroom.

Table 1. Configuration and Definition of Context Information

Sex	Age		Noise		Object	Location
class	num.	class	Num.(dB)	class	class	class
Ma-le	0~7	Infant	20~39	Low	Computer	Balcony
	8~11	Child			Television	Bathroom
	12~17	Young Adult	40~59	Normal	Radio	Bedroom
					Refrigerator	Guestroom
Fem-a le	18~61	Adult			Washing machine	Kitchen
	62~	Old Adult	60~	High	Electric Lamp	Livingroom

The context of the SRS based on the context information used in this study is defined as Web Ontology Language (OWL) that is used on a Semantic Web in order to configure and express exact contexts and various relationships.

The Context Manager transfered data generated by events to a context analyzer and that data was transfered to an OWL inference engine. The OWL inference engine transferred data received from the context manager to the Service Manager in which data was transformed as information using an OWL inferencer including OWL ontology object database.

4.2 Service Manager

The Service Manager consisted of a Bundle Service that provided speech recognition service as a bundle in a Simple Object Access Protocol (SOAP) Service, OSGi framework installed device in order to transfer information received from the OWL inference engine to the SRS, and an Application and Bundle Manager Service that supported the management of the mobility of bundles.

4.3   Speech Recognition Manager

A speech recognition manager extracts observation sequences from the feature extracted voice data and produces the optimum state sequence and probability value by
applying a Viterbi algorithm in the HMM. The HMM that has the largest probability
value in such obtained probability values will be applied to recognize voices. This
system improves the search speed and recognition rate of the HMM according to the
position that is the context information of HMMs and applied objects.

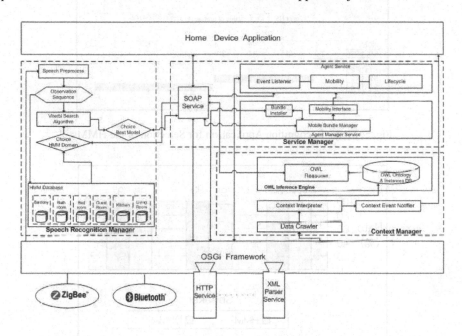

Fig. 4. The Speech Recognition System Using Context Information

5   System Evaluation

In order to test the efficiency of the speech recognition system proposed in this paper,
the test was applied using 50 words that were usually used to control computers and
electronic appliances and recorded in a normal housed hold by three speakers. The
data was sampled by 16kHz and transferred as 16bits using an A/D converter.

The accuracy of the HMM and recognition algorithm was tested on 25 words used
in computer applications. Fig. 5 shows the selection of the word that exhibited the
highest probability among 25 sample words by applying an observation sequence
from the observation sequence used to test the HMM. Fig. 6 illustrates the difference
in recognition rates of the conventional Hidden Markov Models (HMMs) and Do-
main-separated Hidden Markov Models (DHMMs).

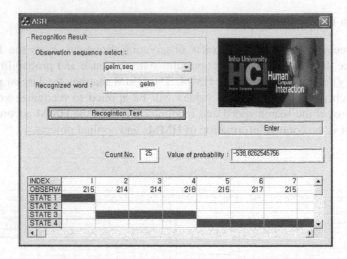

Fig. 5. Model Recognition Application for Selection of the HMMs

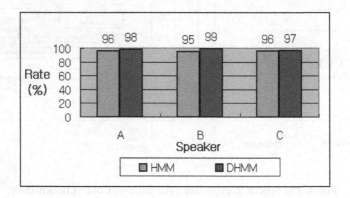

Fig. 6. Speech Recognition Rate of HMM and DHMM

6   Conclusions

Commercial isolated word speech recognition systems used to control the existing application or electronic appliances demonstrate high recognition rates in a limited environment because these systems use only speaker's voices. This was due to the fact that it can't identify the state of utterances and utterance goals of the user. In addition, the searching time of word models will increase, if the number of subject words increased due to the use of a word model. Also, it represents a low recognition rate due to the increase in the number of words.

This study obtains personal information of utterances in a ubiquitous environment and designs a speech recognition system that improves the performance of such a system by investigating utterance goals through the position and applied device. Thus, the context information of utterances was configured in accordance with sex, age, noise, applied object, and position and defined as Ontology. This system configured a word model domain according to the position and object in order to recognize proper information for the applied context information. The actively obtained context information in an OSGi based context recognition manager becomes important information in the selection of a word model domain to recognize voices. In the results of the performance test for the system proposed in this study, it demonstrated a high recognition rate in all positions in a home network environment.

It is necessary to precisely model the given context using various sensors in order to accurately verify the intention of utterances and apply it to a voice recognition system in future. Also, it is necessary to develop a system that has no limitations in noise environments, sex, and age by adding a model, which defines noises, sex, and age.

Acknowledgement

This research was supported by the Ministry of Information and Communication (MIC), Korea, under the Information Technology Research Center (ITRC) support program supervised by the Institute of Information Technology Assessment (IITA).

References

1. Dobrev, P., Famolari, D., Kurzke, C., Millei, B.A.: Device and Service Discovery in Home Networks with OSG. IEEE Communications Magazine 40(8), 86–92 (2002)
2. Rabiner, L.R.: A Tutorial on Hidden Markov Models and Selected Application in Speech Recognition. Proc., IEEE, 77(2), 257–286 (1989)
3. Rabiner, L.R., Levinson, S.E., Sondhi, M.M: On the Application of Vector Quantization and Hidden Markov Models to Speaker Independent, Isolated Word Recognition. The Bell System technical Jounal 62(4) (1983)
4. Weiser, M.: The Computer for the Twenty-first Century. Scientific American 265(3), 94–104 (1991)
5. Brown, P.J., Bovey, J.D., Chen, X.: Context-Aware Application: From the Laboratory to the Marketplace. IEEE Personal Communication, 58–64 (1997)
6. Sohrabi, K., Gao, J., Ailawadhi, V., Pottie, G.: A Self-organizing Sensor Network. In: the Proceedings of the 37 Allerton Conference on Communication, Control, and Computing, Monticello, Illinois (September 1999)
7. Bellavista, P., Corradi, A., Stefanelli, C.: Mobile Agent Middleware for Mobile Computing. IEEE Computer 34(3) (March 2001)
8. Liu, T., Martonosi, M.: Impala: A Middleware System for Managing Autonomic, Parallel Sensor Systems. In: ACM SIGPLAN Symp. Principles and Practice of Parallel Programming (June 2003)
9. Romer, K., Schoch, T., Mattern, F., Dubendorfer, T.: Smart Identification Frameworks for Ubiquitous Computing Application. In: IEEE International Conference on Pervasive Computing and Communication, IEEE Computer Society Press, Los Alamitos (2003)
10. W3C. Web Ontology Language, http://www.w3.org/2004/OWL/
11. Strang, T., Linnhoff-Popien, C.: A Context Modeling Survey. In: UbiComp 1at International Workshop on Advanced Context Modelling, Reasoning and Management, Nottingham, pp. 34–41 (2004)

12. Chen, H., Finin, T.: An Ontology for Context-aware Pervasive Computing Environments. The Knowledge Engineering Review archive 18(3), 197–207 (2003)
13. Chen, H.: An Intelligent Broker Architecture for Pervasive Context-aware Systems. PhD thesis, University of Maryland, Baltimore County (2004)
14. Rodriuez, M., Favela, J.: A Framework for Supporting Autonomous Agents in Ubiquitous Computing Environments. In: CICESE, Ensenada, Mexico (2002)
15. Carroll, J.J., Reynolds, D.: Jena: Implementing the Semantic Web. Recommendations HP Labs, Bristol UK (2005)
16. JADE, Jave Agent Development Framework, http://jade.tilab.com/
17. Want, R., Hopper, A., Falcao, V., Gibbons, J.: The Active Badge Location System. ACM Transactions on Information Systems 10, 91–102 (1992)
18. Gu, T., Pung, H.K., Zhang, D.Q.: An Ontology-based Context Model in Intelligent Environments. In: Proceedings of Communication Networks and Distributed Systems Modeling and Simulation Conference, pp. 270–275 (2004)
19. Bagci, F., Schick, H., Petzold, J., Trumler, W., Ungerer, T.: Support of Reflective Mobile Agents in a Smart Office Environment. In: Proceedings of the 18th International Conference on Architecture of Computing Systems, pp. 79–92 (2005)
20. Dermatas, E., Fakotakis, N., Kokkinakis, G.: Fast Endpoint Detection Algorithm for Isolated Word Recognition in Office Environment. In: Proc., ICASSP-91, Toronto (April 1991)
21. Lee, S., Lee, S., Lim, K., Lee, J.: The Design of Webservices Framework Support Ontology Based Dynamic Service Composition. In: Lee, G.G., Yamada, A., Meng, H., Myaeng, S.-H. (eds.) AIRS 2005. LNCS, vol. 3689, pp. 721–726. Springer, Heidelberg (2005)

Healthcare Information Management System in Home Environment

Chang-Sun Shin[1], Su-Chong Joo[2], and Chang-Won Jeong[2]

[1] School of Information and Communication Engineering, Sunchon National University, Korea
csshin@sunchon.ac.kr
[2] School of Electrical, Electronic and Information Engineering, Wonkwang University, Korea
{scjoo, mediblue}@wonkwang.ac.kr

Abstract. The distributed object group framework (DOGF) enables easier integration of distributed objects to healthcare home applications. This paper describes a healthcare information management system for supporting healthcare home services based on DOGF. The system architecture consists of healthcare database management tool, framework, sensor manager and physical elements such as sensors, devices and appliances. The focus of this paper is on the design and construction of a database system in a framework to support home healthcare services. Healthcare information is organized using database schemes based on the specific types of data collected from various typed-sensors. The database constructed from this information for the purpose of home healthcare services is divided into the base information that uses the real schemes and the context based information that uses the view schemes. To verify the practical use of the healthcare information management system proposed in this paper, we created a prototype healthcare home monitoring service using information, emergency call, and home appliance control. The result of the experimental evaluation shows the comparison of the execution service time of the base information and the context based information in our simulated scenario of a home healthcare application.

Keywords: Healthcare Information Management, Distributed Object Group Framework, Healthcare Home Service.

1 Introduction

Ubiquitous computing strives to develop application environments able to transparently deal with the mobility and interactions of both users and devices. Current research in ubiquitous computing focuses on building infrastructures for managing active spaces, connecting new devices, or building useful applications to improve functionality [1]. But these researches lack of an integrated management of information which is a very important technology in healthcare field, especially for a ubiquitous home healthcare environment. Since existing healthcare information system is usually constructed independently, there is no interconnection to support total business area such as doctor, nurse, patient and environments. That is, the current focus of healthcare information management is still on patient records. Also, a

R. Obermaisser et al. (Eds.): SEUS 2007, LNCS 4761, pp. 223–232, 2007.

large number of healthcare related applications are available that effectively support specific needs but are isolated or incompatible. Ad hoc solutions to interface various components are expensive and time-consuming because systems use different platforms, programming languages and data formats [2]. In this context the paper introduces the healthcare information management system that supports integrated management of information such as environments, personal health and location based on healthcare home environment. We describe how to design and construct the database scheme for the management of the healthcare information system. Our system is based on the distributed object group framework (DOGF) that enables easy integration of distributed objects to healthcare home applications [3, 4]. We used the timer-triggered message-triggered Object (TMO) scheme and TMO Support Middleware (TMOSM) for interactions between distributed applications. To verify the practical use of the healthcare information management system proposed in this paper, we present a home healthcare monitoring service prototype consisting of emergency call, appliance control, and so on designed for the living space of an elderly person living alone. Also, we present the experimental results comparing the execution time of the base information and the context based information service.

The rest of the paper is organized as follows. The next section describes the architecture of the healthcare information management system. Section 3 presents the database for healthcare application services based on home environments. Section 4 describes the system procedure and the GUI of the healthcare management tool and sensor manager process for stream data from sensors. We present a prototype of the healthcare home services using the healthcare database and the result of the evaluation. Finally, the last section describes the conclusion and future works.

2   Healthcare Information Management System

2.1   System Architecture

Our system uses the object group management for domain grouping in DOGF. The needs of a home healthcare environment are considered. The system consists of related services such as location tracking service, healthcare information and supporting service. To facilitate information collection and sharing in this environment, we adopted the TMO scheme and TMOSM [5] into the development environment of the system that we implemented. The architecture of the system is shown in Figure 1 and is organized in five layers. The physical layer contains hardware infrastructures such as various sensors, devices, machines etc. The healthcare database consists of classification of sensor nodes, collected data from the sensors and user profile data including health indicators, service information and access right privileges as information for security, and view information for supporting the service applications. The framework layer contains components of DOGF to support a logical single view of the system environment by grouping them. That is, the group manager API supports the execution of application of appropriate healthcare home services in an upper layer by using the input information obtained from the individual or grouped physical devices through the sensor manger in the lower layer. The tool layer consists of distributed programming developing-tool (DPD-Tool) [6] and healthcare database management tool (HDM-Tool).

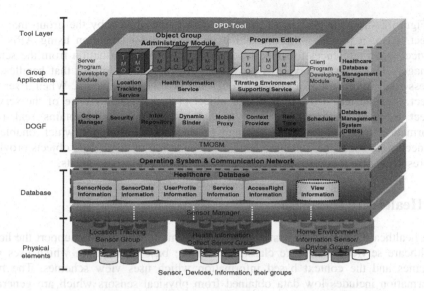

Fig. 1. The architecture for Healthcare Information Management System

2.2 The Interaction of System Components

The functionality of the proposed system is illustrated in Figure 1. We defined the interaction of components which include the distributed application, database, sensors and components of framework.

Fig. 2. Process of Grouping Distributed Objects for Healthcare Home Service

Figure 2 show the process of grouping distributed objects by the group manager object. Also, it provides the interaction of distributed application using APIs and service object references to support collecting real time information from the sensor manager. The security service is provided through security object that handles the access right information of clients through the healthcare database. When a service object is replicated, a dynamic binder object provides the reference of the service object using a binding algorithm. A distributed application obtains real time information from sensor nodes through service object reference which enables a connection to healthcare database. And, the interaction of distributed objects provides the results for the requested service through the framework components.

3   Healthcare Database

The healthcare database is constructed by using this information to support the home healthcare services which are classified into the base information which uses real schemes and the context based information which uses view schemes. The base information includes low data obtained from physical sensors which are generally relevant such as location, personal health, environment, and the user profile. And, the context based information that is produced and fused by using the based information. This context based information might be obtained using various view schemes according to the requirements of a particular healthcare application service. In Figure 3, the base information scheme consists of 14 tables.

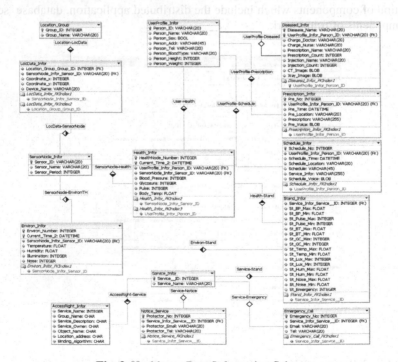

Fig. 3. Healthcare Base Information Scheme

Figure 4 shows the context based information scheme for healthcare applications. It used the healthcare applications which enable to easily apply the services.

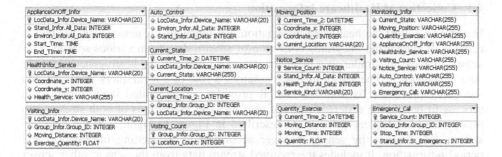

Fig. 4. Healthcare Context Information Scheme

The context based information constructed using materialized view is saved to service schema and managed using the view scheme. This approach allows server and client program developers to develop healthcare application much faster. The healthcare management tool provides the user interface for managing information directly from healthcare database which is described in the next section.

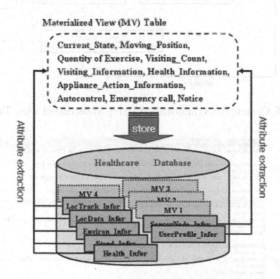

Fig. 5. Context Based Information Using Materialized View Table

4 Procedure for Healthcare Information Management System

In this section, we present the procedure of our system which consists of three main processes: 1) collection of healthcare information by the sensor manager,

2) management of information by the healthcare database management tool and
3) development of a healthcare application.

4.1 Collection of Healthcare Information

In order to collect the healthcare information, we developed a sensor manager that is
capable of supporting integrated collection of stream data from various sensors. Our
sensor manager is similar to a mediator wrapper approach for heterogeneous sensor
data management. The sensor manager assumes a role of a local query translator and
the query processor for the database. It provides an integrated input stream data
process to handle the different types of sensors. The procedures of both stream data
process and local query process are described in Figure 6. Figure 7 is the result of
stream data process by sensor manager according to the setting information and
period information. It includes the received stream data from the sensor, other sensor
specific information and collected and processed into an insert query in the database.

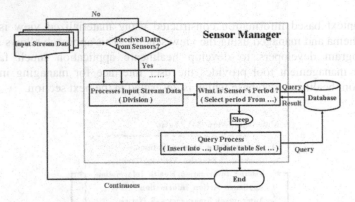

Fig. 6. Context Based Information Using Materialized View Table

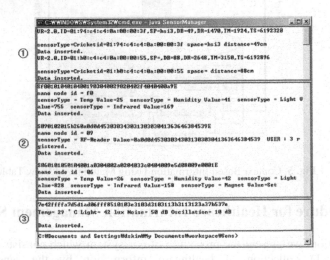

Fig. 7. Execute Results of Stream Data Process by Sensor Manager

Typically, sensors are physically distributed in different locations in different rooms of a building. They are heterogeneous in various ways to handle the diverse types of data such as temperature, localization, luminosity; they have various capacities of computing and storage such as different rates of data delivery (e.g. two measurements per second, a measurement by occurrence of an event) etc. In the current work, we classify according to period of different rates of data delivery. The period information of sensor is managed by the database which controls one or more sensor stream data. The associated methods are matched with the specific to a sensor stream data to enable easier manipulation.

4.2 Management of Healthcare Information

The healthcare database management tool (HDMT) handles the management of the healthcare information through an interface to the healthcare database. This includes the database creation and management tasks such as to display the DB List and table data, the query execution by SQL and search of plan by user, write SQL, dictionary information management, and so on. In addition, it provides the functions to handle context based information to generate the view tables. We implemented the user interface using a GUI-window screening panel according to these functions. The panel consists of five-tabbed display with for Table, Query, DB information and Context based information for management of healthcare database.

Figure 8 shows the execution screens for database management in HDMT. The figure shows are results corresponding to given commands such as user written SQL statements, table properties and interface buttons. Data from various sources must be

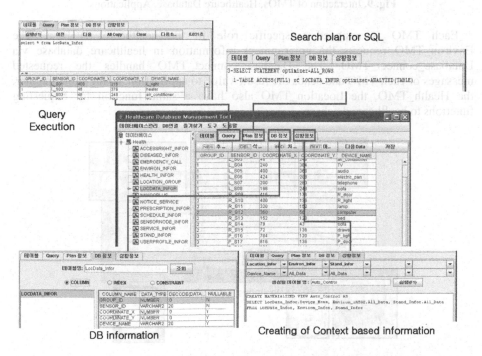

Fig. 8. GUI for Healthcare Database Management Tool

stored in and retrieved from DBMS, because it must always be possible to use data on the basis of diverse criteria. HDMT manages the collected information using ordinary DBMS and provides the upper layers convenient means to access it.

4.3   Executing Results of Healthcare Home Service

To verify the practical use of the proposed system, we show a prototype of a home healthcare monitoring service using information (classified as either base or context based information), emergency call, home appliance control. In this section we describe the results of our evaluation. Figure 9 shows the relationship of the distributed applications with TMO objects and healthcare database.

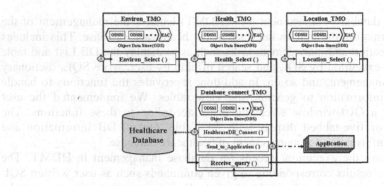

Fig. 9. Interaction of TMOs, Healthcare Database, Applications

Each TMO is assigned a specific role in the healthcare database. The Environ_TMO requests the environment information in healthcare database via Database_connect_TMO. The Database_connect_TMO handles the requested messages of each TMO and sends the result value to application. In the same manner, the Health_TMO, the Location_TMO also have a same function for requesting functions to healthcare database.

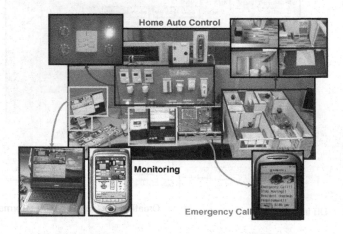

Fig. 10. Physical Environment for Healthcare Home Services

Figure 10 shows the physical environments for healthcare home services reflecting a real world scenario. It is based on elements shown in Figure 9. From these environments, we verify the functionality of the healthcare home services we designed and constructed. The home healthcare services are provided through home healthcare monitoring devices which enable location tracking, health and environment information for home resident, emergency call as SMS using cell phone and home appliance control based on health, location, standard information specified by user for environments of home such as fan, light, air-conditioner, etc.

We analyzed the service time within which the base information and the context based information is able to process a request and reply with the result in the home healthcare services. Figure 11 shows the average service time.

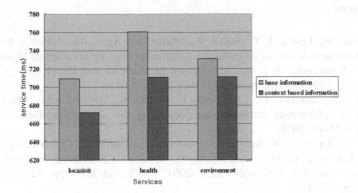

Fig. 11. Average Service Time

The result obtained from this experiment in shown in the graph. For location service the service time difference is 37.4ms; for the health information service, it is 49.5ms; and for home auto control service it is 20.3ms. This evaluation result shows that the context based information could provide a more responsive service for home healthcare.

5   Conclusions and Future Works

Existing healthcare information systems are constructed independently without considering integrated management. The current focus of healthcare information management is still on patient records. A large number of healthcare related applications effectively support specific needs but are isolated or incompatible. And interfaces are expensive and time-consuming because systems use different platforms, programming languages and data formats. To solve this problem we proposed a healthcare information management system. Our research focused on the design of healthcare information management system and the development of a health database based on the framework for supporting home healthcare service. We verified that healthcare related information supporting healthcare home services and the context based information showed better performance than base information at providing the home healthcare services.

Our future work will focus on the applications of different environments for ubiquitous healthcare service and on improving the functionality of our system. We will also address the relevant security issues in the context of this work.

Acknowledgments. This research was supported by the MIC(Ministry of Information and Communication), Korea, under the ITRC(Information Technology Research Center) support program supervised by the IITA(Institute of Information Technology Assessment)" (IITA-2006-(C1090-0603-0047)).

References

1. Rodriguez, M., Favela, J., Gonzalez, V., Munoz, M.: Agent Based Mobile Collaboration and Information Access in a Healthcare Environment. In: Proceedings of Workshop of E-Health: Applications of Computing Science in Medicine and Health Care, Cuernavaca, Mexico, pp. 970–936 (December 2003) ISBN: 970-36-0118-9
2. Spyrou, S.S., Bamidis, P., Chouvarda, I., Gogou, G., Tryfon, S.M., Maglaveras, N.: Healthcare information standards: comparison of the approaches. Health Informatics Journal 8, 14–19 (2002)
3. Shin, C.-S., Jeong, C.-W., Joo, S.-C.: Construction of Distributed Object Group Framework and Its Execution Analysis Using Distributed Application Simulation. In: Yang, L.T., Guo, M., Gao, G.R., Jha, N.K. (eds.) EUC 2004. LNCS, vol. 3207, pp. 724–733. Springer, Heidelberg (2004)
4. Shin, C.-S., Lee, C.-S., Joo, S.-C.: Healthcare Home service System Based on Distributed Object Group Framework. In: Gavrilova, M., Gervasi, O., Kumar, V., Tan, C.J.K., Taniar, D., Laganà, A., Mun, Y., Choo, H. (eds.) ICCSA 2006. LNCS, vol. 3983, pp. 798–807. Springer, Heidelberg (2006)
5. Kim, K.H., Ishida, M., Liu, J.: An Efficient Middleware Architecture Supporting Time-triggered Message-triggered Objects and an NT-based Implementation. In: ISORC'99. Proceedings of the IEEE CS 2nd International Symposium on Object-oriented Real-time distributed Computing, pp. 54–63. IEEE Computer Society Press, Los Alamitos (1999)
6. Jeong, C.-W., Kim, D.-S., Lee, G.-Y., Joo, S.-C.: Distributed Programming Developing Tool Based on Distributed Object Group Framework. In: Gavrilova, M., Gervasi, O., Kumar, V., Tan, C.J.K., Taniar, D., Laganà, A., Mun, Y., Choo, H. (eds.) ICCSA 2006. LNCS, vol. 3983, pp. 853–863. Springer, Heidelberg (2006)

Effective Appliance Selection by Complementary Context Feeding in Smart Home System

Taek Lee, Jiyong Park, and Hoh Peter In*

Department of Computer Science and Engineering, Korea University,
Seoul, 136-713, Republic of Korea
{comtaek, jayyp, hoh_in}@korea.ac.kr

Abstract. Smart Home System (SHS) is one of popular applications in ubiquitous computing, which provides convenient services for a user with user-friendly intelligent system interfaces. Among them, voice recognition is a popular interface. However, voice command statements given by users are often too unclear and incomplete for the devices in SHS to understand the original user intention. So, the devices become complicated and have no idea about whether to work or not. Therefore, we should make sure the proximate selection for the devices which will be eventually targeted and operated following user intention. In this paper, we propose an effective method to make a decision in electing a promising target device among candidates by taking advantage of complementary context feeding around user environment in SHS even with initial incomplete interface information. The proposed method is based on Bayes theorem using the way of empirical statistic inference.

Keywords: Smart home, Situation-aware computing, HCI, Bayes Theorem.

1 Introduction

Ubiquitous computing has a motto to inject intelligent functionality into all of the objects in environment so that they can deliver any service useful and convenient to a user by making the objects collaborating organically with each other. In the similar manner, Smart Home System, which is our prototype application, aims to maximize user convenience by supporting the home appliances in working intelligently satisfying user service requirements. Thus, even for heterogeneous appliances, it should be always guaranteed for them to collaborate and deliver eventually user-friendly services to a user without any confusion in their running conditions. Under our definition, intelligent functionality means that with the minimum interaction costs a user can be served with high satisfaction level originally required. To implement such intelligence, Human Computer Interaction researches, especially multimodal interface area [10], have been getting matured so far. Among them, speech recognition area has been significantly developing since the past decades so that many of commercial products supporting a voice command recognition function have been

---

* Corresponding author.

R. Obermaisser et al. (Eds.): SEUS 2007, LNCS 4761, pp. 233–242, 2007.
© IFIP International Federation for Information Processing 2007

emerged to market. However, regardless of its attractiveness, voice recognition interface is not so popularly used in practical system implementation. The reason is not because of its technical unstableness but because of the following reasons.

- *Users often use incomplete syntax of voice command statement.* Assuming easy working, users tend to consciously or unconsciously use incorrect voice command structures instead of giving complete syntax of commands to a machine. If such commands are given to SHS, we can not expect the appliances to work correctly. For instance, if a voice command not having any explicit target just like 'Turn On!' is given, the system becomes very complicated whether to turn on an audio or to turn on a lamp.
- *Users sometimes use commands not reserved in system manual.* We can not expect that users will always give the system a command statement consisting only of reserved words in system instruction manual.

Therefore, for better understanding, SHS requests more clear and complete interface expression from user. If impossible to expect it from a user, SHS needs other alternative hint information to catch the point of user intention. In this paper, we will take advantage of user contextual information aggregated in running environment to complement the poor primary interface information (i.e. an incomplete voice command). The proposed SHS has ability to train and improve itself by updating a knowledge database. Our proposed method is based on Bayes theory, which plays an important role in understanding user intention with incomplete interface information. When it works, it uses statistics of context (or situation) information stored in the knowledge database.

Basically, intelligent functionality of appliances depends on the system environment deployed. Thus, it is necessary to train and optimize them for user-friendly services. To do so, our proposed SHS identifies the context attributes of situation information relevant to user preferences and then interprets them as a user intention to activate an appliance targeted.

The rest of the paper is organized as follows: Section 2 explains the overview of Smart Home System and Section 3 presents our proposed appliance selection method based on Bayes theorem. Section 4 shows evaluation results of an experiment to which our proposed method was applied. Section 5 introduces related work and the pros and cons of our approach. Finally, we conclude the paper in Section 6.

2   Situation Awareness in Smart Home System

SHS uses user contexts gathered from system environment to complement the incomplete primary interface information (i.e. voice command). To do so, we need to extract more high level of situation information from several of the user-related contexts which are just clues embedding less of implication in their nature. In this section, first of all, we perceive the difference of *context* and *situation*, and then give an idea about how to utilize their different definitions and apply them to materializing SHS.

2.1 Situation Awareness

Situation is a set of past context attributes and/or actions of individual devices which are relevant to determine future device actions. *Context* is any instantaneous, detectable, and relevant condition of the environment or the device. Situation aware interface definition language (SA-IDL [4], [5]) is a tool to materialize and utilize the situation awareness concept. SA-IDL consists of context tuple, action tuple and derived context as Table 1 [6].

Table 1. SA-IDL Model

Action := (*Time, Device, State, StateValue*)
Context := (*Timestamp, Device, State, StateValue*)
$A := \{x \mid x \text{ is an } Action\}$
$C := \{x \mid x \text{ is a } Context\}$
DerivedContext := $P(C) \rightarrow \{true, false\}$
Situation := (*DerivedContext*, $P(C)$, A)

DerivedContext is a kind of function to determine whether a given context set holds or not in the application environment eventually resulting in true or false. In section 3, we propose a detail method which can be used in implementing the concept of *DerivedContext* function.

2.2 Appliance Selection Using Situation Awareness

To complement an incomplete primary interface (i.e. a voice command given by a user), we propose a prototype, Smart Home System (Fig. 1) using not only explicit primary interface information but also context information just like playing a role of additional implicit complementary interfaces.

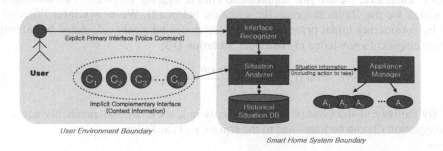

Fig. 1. Overview of Smart Home System

Firstly, Interface Recognizer interprets a given voice command and pass the recognized but not now dependable information to Situation Analyzer. Situation Analyzer produces an Action Tuple including a target appliance of information and its action to take. Situation Analyzer conducts reasoning process with the primary interface information passed by Interface Recognizer, context information gathered from user environment, and statistic information extracted from Historical Situation DB. Appliance Manager receives the Action Tuple from Situation Analyzer. Finally, Appliance Manager distributes a control message to the corresponding appliance supposed to work.

3   The Proposed Appliance Selection Method

We call the appliances being on standby, namely, candidates because they will be potentially designated as targets by an Action Tuple come from Situation Analyzer. Therefore, Situation Analyzer is responsible for making a decision of which candidate must be elected with some justification. In this section, we present a solution approach based on Bayes theorem.

3.1   Selection Problem Interpretation Using Bayes Theorem

When primary interface information, a voice command, is given from a user in SHS, appliance candidates likely to be selected are temporary determined. Let us define the n candidates with set $A = \{ a_1, a_2, a_3, ..., a_n \}$, where the element a_i is a binary random variable whose value is 'on' or 'off'. Hence, $P(a_i='on')$ means the probability of that the i th appliance will work in SHS when a voice command is given. Context set C consists of *Context Tuple* elements like $C = \{ c_1, c_2, c_3, ..., c_m \}$. They can be observed and captured from user environment. Ultimately, in a given selection problem, all of what we have to do for finding a solution is to select a particular a_i making k and the conditional probability $P(a_i='on' \mid C)$ maximized in a solution set S like (1).

$$S = \{\exists a_i \in A \mid maximize(k + P(a_i ='on'|C))\} \tag{1}$$

The constant k means the average success rate of the voice recognition technology used in SHS. Therefore, we don't try to improve k because it is out of focus in this paper. Therefore, we are just supposed to find a_i making $P(a_i='on' \mid C)$ maximized. For that, we use Bayes theorem, the equation below (2). We newly infer $P(a_i='on' \mid C)$ by considering initial prior probability which can be easily calculated by referring to the empirical knowledge in Historical Situation DB.

$$P(a_i ='on'|C) = \frac{P(C|a_i ='on')}{P(C)} \cdot P(a_i ='on') \tag{2}$$

By the way, if the *Context Tuple* elements in a set C are independently occurred, the equation (2) can be translated to the equation (3) as follows.

$$P(a_i ='on'|C) = \frac{P(a_i ='on') \prod_{j=1}^{m} P(c_j |a_i ='on')}{P(C)} \tag{3}$$

To find a solution a_i making $P(a_i='on' \mid C)$ maximized, we have to compare all of the right-handed side of the equation (3) for $\forall a_i \in A$. The denominator $P(C)$ is a common factor in the comparison so that it plays a role as a fixed constant and doesn't influence the prioritization procedure. Therefore, the problem we want to solve is conclusively simplified to the question about how to find the a_i making the numerator part of the equation (3) maximized. The answer is explained in the next sub section with taking a practical example.

3.2 Selection Problem Resolution

Table 2 is a piece of training data used in our SHS prototype. Thus, we can assume set A and C are respectively set A = { 'audio', 'heater', 'cooler', 'stove', 'lamp'} and set C = { 'user tracking', 'time', 'temperature'} in Table 2. The more variant and plentiful training data are given, the more Situation Analyzer is trained well and work effectively in inferring some situation.

Table 2. Samples of fifteen records in Historical Situation DB

Tid	Primary Interface	Historical User Context Set associated with Situation			Derived Target & Action Information	
	PI:voice	c_1:tracking	c_2:time	c_3:temperature	Target	Action
1		bed→bed	morning	10℃	a_1:audio	play classic
2		door→heater	afternoon	-8℃	a_2:heater	run in high
3		bed→kitchen	morning	33℃	a_4:stove	-
4		bed→bed	morning	40℃	a_3:cooler	run in high
5		door→heater	afternoon	10℃	a_2:heater	-
6		door→cooler	afternoon	30℃	a_1:audio	play dance
7		door→heater	afternoon	45℃	a_3:cooler	-
8	Turn On!	door→cooler	night	57℃	a_3:cooler	sleep mode
9		table→bed	night	23℃	a_1:audio	play jazz
10		door→cooler	afternoon	29℃	a_5:lamp	-
11		bed→bed	morning	-10℃	a_2:heater	-
12		door→kitchen	night	5℃	a_5:lamp	lamp door
13		bed→kitchen	afternoon	12℃	a_4:stove	-
14		table→cooler	morning	38℃	a_3:cooler	-
15		door→table	night	20℃	a_5:lamp	lamp table

To solve the equation (1) dealing with selecting problem of our interesting target appliance, first of all, we have to identify which contexts are helpful and related to our problem solving and then know the conditional probability $P(C \mid a_i='on')$ before calculating $P(a_i='on' \mid C)$. When calculating $P(C \mid a_i='on')$, if the element values of the set C are categorical attributes, we can calculate $P(C \mid a_i='on')$ by just counting the number of cases holding the condition $a_i='on'$. However, if the element values are continuous attributes and they follow the normal distribution, we can utilize the Gaussian distribution PDF whose parameters are μ and σ like the equation (4) below.

$$P(C = c_j \mid A = a_i) = \frac{1}{\sqrt{2\pi}\sigma_{ij}} \exp^{-\frac{(c_j-\mu_{ij})^2}{2\sigma_{ij}^2}} \tag{4}$$

The variables that we have to know in the equation (4) are just μ_{ij} (the average of the c_j element values for a given particular a_i) and σ_{ij}^2 (the variance of the element values).

For instance, under the assumption of Table 2, if the current context information captured from a user is $C=\{c_1='door{\rightarrow}cooler',\ c_2='afternoon',\ c_3='43\,°C'\}$, each equation (3) value of candidate appliances can be eventually calculated as following Table 3.

Table 3. Conditional probabilities that each appliance will be targeted for a given C

$P(a_1='on'\mid C) = (P(C\mid a_1='on')\ /\ P(C))\ *\ P(a_1='on') = 0.000408375*\alpha*0.2 = 0.0816*10^{-3}*\alpha$

$P(a_2='on'\mid C) = (P(C\mid a_2='on')\ /\ P(C))\ *\ P(a_2='on') = 0*\alpha*0.2 = 0$

$P(a_3='on'\mid C) = (P(C\mid a_3='on')\ /\ P(C))\ *\ P(a_3='on') = 0.00284375*\alpha*0.27 = 0.76781*10^{-3}*\alpha$

$P(a_4='on'\mid C) = (P(C\mid a_4='on')\ /\ P(C))\ *\ P(a_4='on') = 0*\alpha*0.13 = 0$

$P(a_5='on'\mid C) = (P(C\mid a_5='on')\ /\ P(C))\ *\ P(a_5='on') = 0.00042471*\alpha*0.2 = 0.0849*10^{-3}*\alpha$

In Table 3, α means $1/P(C)$. If we compare each one with one other probability value, the priority order is as follows.

$$a_3 = 0.76781*10^{-3}*\alpha > a_5 = 0.0849*10^{-3}*\alpha > a_1 = 0.0816*10^{-3}*\alpha > a_2 > a_4$$

Conclusively, it has been discovered that our interesting final solution is a_3 since $a_3=0.7678125*10^{-3}*\alpha$ has the highest value than the others. The zero cases of a_2 and a_4 happened because no matched situation data was in Table 2 (i.e. Historical Situation DB). To avoid zero probability calculation, we can use the way of Laplace Correction [2]. In the same manner with the calculation procedure for selecting a target so far, inferring an action to take for given contexts can be conducted as well.

Coming back to the system viewpoint of working flow, we can see that the final result inferred is reformed to *Situation Tuple* format as explained in the section 2.1 and then delivered to *Appliance Manager*.

4   Experiment and Evaluation of the Proposed Method

4.1   Experiment Environments

We applied our proposed method, Bayes Theorem Approach (BTA), to implementing Situation Analyzer in Fig. 1. Through the experiment, we aimed at testing the validation of BTA and appealing its effectiveness by comparing it with a popular existing approach, Rule Based Approach (RBA).

In implementing the experiment, for capturing user movement context, we used AR Toolkit [8]. It is very useful to perceive user identity as well as user 3D tracking because it provides developers with different figures of recognizable marks. For implementing voice recognition functionality, we used Microsoft speech SDK 5.1 [9]. Finally, we gathered more context information from the system environment or the Internet, such as time and temperature.

First of all, to test and find the initial success or failure rate (k) of the primary interface, voice command, we asked three users participated in the experiment to speak any possible type of a voice command with conceiving intention to point some different five appliances such as audio, heater, cooler, stove, and lamp in the test space under assumption of fifteen categorical scenarios. Before starting the experiment, they obviously didn't know which type of voice command is desirable and effective to make the intended appliance work correctly. Through the way, they could give a command to SHS without any bias. For evaluation, we used a criterion, the number of successes over all trials, to measure the degree of user satisfaction for a service, which is called success rate.

4.2 Experiment Result and Evaluation

As you can see in Fig. 2, the success rate (k) of the primary interface was 70% because of some incomplete (arbitrary so not valid) command sentences and environmental noise. The next experiment was to reduce the failure rate by implementing and applying RBA to Situation Analyzer. RBA could improve the 66.6% portion of the failure cases (30%) which were not quite recognized when we had used only voice recognition interface. After all, we could improve the original success rate from 70% up to 89.8% by adding 19.8% of success cases in the case of RBA. However, BTA could more improve it up to 94%. The reason why RBA failed was because there were no rules to check some exceptional situations or sensitive values hanging in a threshold boundary of relation operation. For instance, the rule "*if PI='on' AND c_1=? →cooler AND c_3>45 ℃ then Action=(now, cooler, power, on)*" could not recognize the case Tid 4 in Table 2 as the situation the cooler should be activated following user intention. On the other hand, BTA could work better effectively than RBA not because an exactly matched situation data (just like a rule in RBA) had already existed in Historical Situation DB but because Situation Analyzer referring to Historical Situation DB had been already trained by user preferred similar situation data before that time.

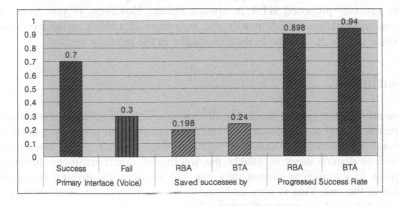

Fig. 2. Experiment Results for given scenarios

5 Related Work

Since introducing the paradigm of Ubiquitous Computing, many of applications addressing or utilizing context (or situation) awareness have been emerged. Especially, to solve interoperability problem between devices in their working, interface definition languages were presented in [4], [5], [6]. To make a decision for whether to be a particular situation or not from a given context set, it uses rule based determination (i.e. Rule Based Approach). In many cases, RBA is very useful and easy to abstract and formalize intangible situation concept. So, it has been used in implementing a situation-aware middleware [6]. However, it has still disadvantages. Table 4 is for pros and cons of RBA and BTA which we proposed in this paper.

Table 4. Rule Based Approach vs. Bayes Theorem Approach

	RBA	BTA
Pros	• Easy update of a rule set if necessary • Light computation and high performance • Easy implementation	• Flexibility for dynamic user preference and habit change • Self training mechanism by feeding user feedbacks
Cons	• Inflexibility against noise input data or a sensitive value in the boundary of a rule threshold • No self-training mechanism	• Need for abundant training data • High computation cost to implement it when having many context attributes
Application conditions	• When implementing it on devices having low computation power for lightness and assuming distributed running environment of devices	• When implementing it on a centralized server system having high computation power and storage capacity.

As you can see in Table 4, each approach has its own pros and cons. Therefore, we can not say our proposed BTA is always better. However, if you have enough conditions to implement BTA, it will give you more flexibility in inferring situation information as you can see the evaluation results in the previous section.

6 Conclusion

In home automation system space, the diverse intelligent appliances can suffer from incompleteness and ambiguousness of interface information given by a user. So, the appliances sometimes malfunction against the original user intention. The malfunctions disturb users to satisfy the intelligent functionality appliances could have given to themselves so that they can not avoid in controlling the appliances manually at the end. That is very undesirable to users expected somewhat automatic working. That is why we are still using a legacy controlling system such as pressing buttons or using a remote controller even though we have very matured commercial products having voice recognition functionality in the recent times.

In this paper, we proposed a prototype of Smart Home System architecture and especially a Bayes theorem based algorithm to be adopted by Situation Analyzer. Our proposed study aims at complementing a poor primary user interface with situation information embedding user intention for the purpose of providing a user-friendly service. Our proposed method, of course, can sometimes recommend a wrong advice because it is impossible for a computer system to perfectly predict user intention. However, for permanent improvement, our approach can take the user feedbacks utilized to fatten and evolve the Historical Situation DB. Situation Analyzer using the DB has high flexibility for dynamically changed user preferences.

Despite the advantages of the proposed study, there are still disadvantages which should be improved in the future as follows:

- *Need for reliable training data.* Through diverse case studies, we need to collect high quality of training data before fully operating SHS. Data collecting, analyzing, and managing processes must be simplified and organized well in practical implementation.
- *Heavy computation.* The proposed method requires many multiplication computations of float numbers to calculate and analyze probability values. Therefore it is not so light to implement the method in small devices having low computation power in SHS so that centralized intelligent system architecture is better choice than that of distributing the computation responsibilities to thick client devices. Hence, we have an idea to combine the advantages of the RBA used in SA-IDL and BTA proposed here in order to present a hybrid method not only suitable to a centralized system but also scalable to small devices in the future.

In addition to complementing future works above, we have a plan to test and check computation overhead in implementing the proposed BTA and compare it not with RBA but with other existing probabilistic methods for better improvement of our research.

Acknowledgments. This work was supported by the 2nd Brain Korea 21 Project in 2007.

References

1. Tan, P.-n., Steinbach, M., Kumar, V.: Introduction to Data Mining. Pearson Addison Wesley, London (2006)
2. Han, J., Kamber, M.: Data Mining - concepts and techniques, 2nd edn. Morgan Kaufmann, San Francisco (2006)
3. Schilit, B., Adams, N., Want, R.: Context-Aware Computing Applications. In: Proceedings of the 1st International Workshop on Mobile Computing Systems and Applications, pp. 85–90 (1994)
4. Chae, H., Kim, T., Lee, D., Peter, H.: Conflict Resolution Model Based on Weight in Situation Aware Collaboration System. In: FTDCS2007. IEEE 11th International Workshop on future Trend of Distributed Computing System (expected publication date - March 2007)

5. Yau, S.S, Wang, Y., Huang, D.: H. P, Situation-aware Contract Specification Language for Middleware for Ubiquitous Computing. In: the proceeding of the Ninth Future Trends of Distributed Computing Systems, pp. 93–99 (May 2003)
6. Yau, Y.W., Karim, F.: Developing Situation Awareness in Middleware for Ubicomp Environments. In: Proc. 26th International Computer Software and Applications Conference, pp. 233–238 (2002)
7. Wang, Y.: An FSM Model for Situation-Aware Mobile Application Software Systems. In: Proceedings of the 42nd annual Southeast regional conference (2004)
8. 3D tracking: AR Toolkit, http://www.hitl.washington.edu/artoolkit/
9. Microsoft speech SDK 5.1, http://www.microsoft.com/downloads
10. Oviatt, S.L.: Multimodal interfaces. In: Jacko, J., Sears, A. (eds.) The Human-Computer Interaction Handbook: Fundamentals, Evolving Technologies and Emerging Applications, ch. 14, pp. 286–304. Lawrence Erlbaum Assoc., Mahwah, NJ (2003)

Vector Graphic Reference Implementation for Embedded System

Sang-Yun Lee[1] and Byung-Uk Choi[2]

[1] Dept. of Electronical Telecommunication Engineering, Hanyang University, Seoul, Korea
`syllee@etri.re.kr`
[2] Division of Information and Communications, Hanyang University, Seoul, Korea
`buchoi@hanyang.ac.kr`

Abstract. We propose the reference implementation with software rendering of OpenVG for the scalable vector graphic hardware acceleration, which the Khronos group standardizes. We present the design scheme that enables EGL and OpenVG to be ported easily in an embedded environment. Moreover, we describe the background of selection of an algorithm, and the mathematical function adopted for the performance improvement, and we propose the optimum rendering method. We present displaying of vector image on a screen through the OpenVG implemented using software rendering method. And, we present the test result of the CTS which is compatibility test tool. And we show the performance comparison against the Hybrid corp.'s reference implementation.

Keywords: OpenVG, EGL, Scalable Vector Graphic, Embedded System, Software Rendering.

1 Introduction

Recently, the demand for the applications using the vector graphics technology has increased [1]. Particularly, in areas such as SVG viewer, hand-held guidance service, E-Book reader, game, scalable user interface, and etc, the vector graphics technology is widely applied. OpenVG™ is a royalty-free, cross-platform API that provides a low-level hardware acceleration interface for vector graphics libraries such as Flash and SVG [2].

Currently in development, OpenVG is targeted primarily at handheld devices that require portable acceleration of high-quality vector graphics for compelling user interfaces and text on small screen devices while enabling hardware acceleration to provide fluidly interactive performance at very low power levels. OpenVG is the standard constituted by the Khronos group. And the version 1.0 was released at July 2005 for the first time [3].

When the standard needs to be verified, or when the OpenVG application needs to be operated through an emulator in advance, or when there is a no hardware supporting OpenVG, it is necessary to have the reference implementation (RI) operating in the software rendering mode. Additionally, it takes much time until the special-purpose hardware supporting OpenVG is produced. The RI also can reduce the cost.

R. Obermaisser et al. (Eds.): SEUS 2007, LNCS 4761, pp. 243–252, 2007.

Besides, as embedded devices and CPU's performance is improved, the possibility of being replaced with the software rendering is high.

In this paper, we propose the OpenVG reference implementation which can be easily ported to the various embedded devices by using the software rendering method. And, we show that our RI is more excellent than the existing RI in the performance aspect.

2   Design of OpenVG and EGL Engine

2.1   System Architecture

The system architecture of the OpenVG RI proposed in this paper is shown in Fig. 1.

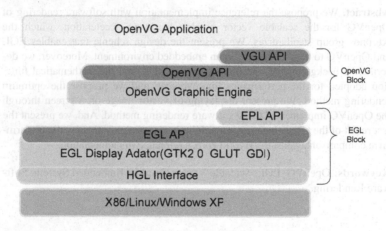

Fig. 1. The system architecture

The OpenVG RI is composed of Embedded Graphics Library (EGL) block and OpenVG block. EGL is an interface between rendering APIs such as OpenGL|ES or OpenVG (referred to collectively as client APIs) and an underlying native platform window system [4]. EGL provides mechanisms for creating rendering surfaces onto which client APIs can draw, creating graphics contexts for client APIs, and synchronizing drawing by client APIs as well as native platform rendering APIs [5]. We designed so that, through the EGL Display Adapter, the client API could access the windowing system of the native platform.

In the EGL standard, the Embedded Platform Library (EPL) API is not included. However, it is necessary in order to implement client API, and must be ported according to a system. The API includes, for example, the functions of returning the frame buffer from Surface, the memory allocation, memory releasing, and etc. Hardware Graphic Library (HGL) interfaces performs the function of connecting EGL to the native graphics system. EGL is itself the standard which is made to abstract the hardware system. However, it is necessary to have the separate porting layer like HGL so that EGL can be ported to the different native platform window systems through the minimum overhead. The OpenVG API is 2D vector graphics library and the VGU

API is 2D vector graphics utility API of the high level. The OpenVG graphic engine provides the core functions that the OpenVG API and the VGU API need.

2.2 Structure of the EGL Engine

The block structure of the EGL engine is shown in Fig. 2.

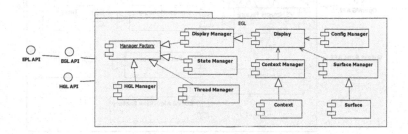

Fig. 2. Structure of the EGL Engine

The Display Manager creates and manages the display object which takes charge of displaying graphics. The State Manager stores the error value generated when the functions executed. The Thread Manager provides the functions for avoiding the race condition in which several processes or the threads try to access EGL at the same time. As to these three modules, however, only one object can be generated. The Manager Factory enables them to have the uniqueness in three modules.

2.3 Structure of the OpenVG Engine

The block structure of the OpenVG engine is shown in Fig. 3. The OpenVG engine provides the OpenVG API which applications can use and the Context Sync API which EGL can use. The Context Sync API provides synchronization between the VGContext generated in the OpenVG internally and the Context generated in EGL. The elements that need synchronization include creation and termination of a context, the current setup status, and etc. The VG State Manager stores and manages the error value generated during the execution of OpenVG. The VG Context Manager, the Paint Manager, the Image Manager, and the Path Manager create and manage the VG Context object, the Paint object, the Image object, and the Path object respectively. The VG Manager Factory performs the role of guaranteeing that these objects operate with singleton. The Rasterizer performs the function of drawing on the frame buffer provided by the surface of EGL with data combined of Path, Image, and Paint information.

2.4 Requirement for Designing the OpenVG/EGL Engine

OpenVG can operate not only on a desktop personal computer but also on a server. But it was developed to be mainly used in the embedded devices. In an embedded

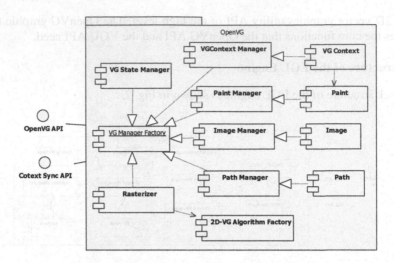

Fig. 3. The Structure of the OpenVG Engine

environment, there are always porting issues, because of wide variety of not only the hardware, but also the platforms and software. Therefore, we must consider porting issues at as early as the architecture design phase, if we want to easily port once developed OpenVG to the various embedded devices. That is, the porting layer must exist so that the part to be modified according to the environmental change can be minimized. In addition, EGL and OpenVG must be loosely coupled.

Generally, in an embedded environment, the performance of a CPU is lower and the size of the memory is restrictive. Therefore, algorithms must be selected in such a way that the selected algorithms produce optimum performance and at the same time use as low memory and power as possible.

3 Novel Features of OpenVG Reference Implementation

3.1 Mathematical Function

In the operation process of drawing each graphic object of OpenVG, the use of the mathematical function is frequent. The method of calculating the mathematical function is classified into two ways. Firstly, it is the method of referring to the table value having the value calculated in advance. The second is the method of calculating the Taylor series of the finite order [6]. The former case consumes big amount of memory, whereas the latter takes longer time to execute.

The Hybrid RI [7] adopted the later case. And as a result, it induced the performance degradation of the mathematics functional operation [8]. However, we adopted the table-look-up method and sought the performance improvement.

3.2 Sort Algorithm

In the OpenVG, sorting is used in the tessellation based rendering algorithm. That is, the vertex passing the scan line is arranged to the abscissa order. Or there is case where it arranges several scissoring rectangles. In the Hybrid RI, the bubble sort algorithm was adopted. But we adopted the merge sort algorithm, in this paper. The merge sort has a complexity of $O(N \log N)$, whereas the bubble sort has a complexity of $O(N^2)$.

3.3 Improved Raster Rendering Algorithm

A rendering refers to the operation of drawing the vector graphics object in the display [9]. There are the vector rendering mode in which the vector graphics object is

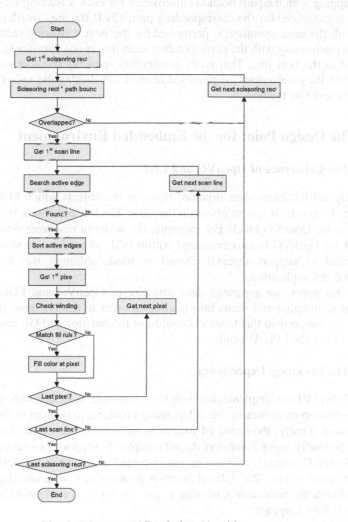

Fig. 4. The proposed Rendering Algorithm

drawn every time, and the raster rendering mode in which objects are drawn by calculating the color of each pixels of an image [10], [11], [12].

The raster rendering has an advantage in comparison with the vector rendering in the various aspect. Firstly, the raster rendering has a lower complexity than the vector rendering according to increasing of the number or area of Path. Secondly, the calculation for applying the Fill Rule is made altogether in the vertex drawing step. Thirdly, the mathematical calculation for vertex drawing is unnecessary because Vertex is not directly drawn. But it spends much time, because this method calculates all the parts which are not in fact displayed in a screen [13].

In this paper, we propose the improved rendering algorithm in order to solve this problem. Fig. 4 shows the improved raster rendering algorithm proposed in this paper.

The procedure of the proposed rendering algorithm is as followings: (1) If the area overlapping with the path bound is discovered for each scissoring rectangle, the pixel color is calculated for the corresponding part; (2) If the area overlapping is not discovered, the same operation is performed for the next scissoring rectangle; (3) If the vertex intersecting with the corresponding scan line is not discovered, the scan line is moved to the next line. That is, by remarkably reducing the area visited in order to calculate the pixel value, the proposed method can display the vector graphics faster than the existing method.

4   The Design Point for the Embedded Environment

4.1   The Coherence of OpenVG and EGL

The Hybrid RI shares data structure between the objects which EGL and OpenVG create. Therefore, it has an effect on the other block if one block is modified among EGL or the OpenVG block. For example, the waste of resources occurs, because the object for OpenVG is also generated within EGL when the data structure of EGL is expanded to support OpenGL|ES and is used, although we develop only the OpenGL|ES application.

In this paper, we separated data structure of OpenVG and EGL and concealed each data structure and status information, in order to resolve these problems. Moreover, we designed so that OpenVG could use the function of EGL engine through the EGL API or the EPL API call.

4.2   The Language Dependency

The Hybrid RI was implemented with C++ language. C++ language is very powerful in the desktop environment, but it has many problems to be used in the embedded environment. Firstly, the speed of executing the inheritance or the virtual function is slow. Secondly, some compilers do not completely support C++ language. Therefore, we adopted C language that can be easily ported to an embedded device and the execution speed is fast. We defined function pointers in C structure that processes and manipulates the information, in order to provide for object-oriented concept supported easily in C++ language.

4.3 The Singleton Pattern Design

There is an object in which several copy creations are not allowed among an object. Each Factory in the EGL block, and the context Manager, state Manager, image Manager, and algorithm Factory in the OpenVG block are those objects. We introduced the singleton pattern for the guaranteed uniqueness of an object. If we design without the singleton pattern, each module has to recognize this object and avoid creating them. Or, these objects have to be registered in the global variables storage and used. However, existing code has to be modified to be ported to other platforms, because it is different in the structure of the global variables storage according to platforms.

5   Implementation and Experimental Results

5.1   Implementation

We verified whether our design method could be easily adapted to the embedded environment by implementing EGL and OpenVG and porting them to the various environments. We implemented EGL and OpenVG based on the Windows XP at first. And then, we modified the porting layer and could easily port it to the Linux and the WIPI platform [14]. At first, we implemented EGL for the Windows XP by using the GDI (Graphic Device Interface) in order to access the native windowing system, and then we ported it with the OpenGL Utility Toolkit (GLUT) for the performance comparison with Hybrid RI. There is the advantage of reducing the code amendment too, when it is ported to the Linux if it uses GLUT.

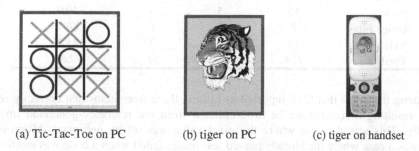

(a) Tic-Tac-Toe on PC   (b) tiger on PC   (c) tiger on handset

Fig. 5. Example of vector graphic displayed using the proposed RI

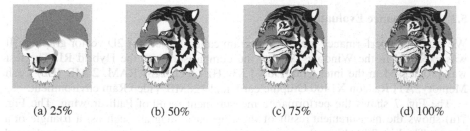

(a) 25%   (b) 50%   (c) 75%   (d) 100%

Fig. 6. The process of drawing tiger

Fig. 5 shows vector graphics displayed on a screen through the proposed RI. Fig. 5(a) shows the image seen in the Tic-Tac-Toe game. Fig. 5(b) shows the tiger image that is the representative image of the vector graphics field. The Tiger image is comprised of 305 paths. Fig. 5(c) shows the tiger image rendered on a celluar phone.

Fig. 6 shows the process of the tiger image being displayed with vector graphics. It shows when of 305 path, 25%, 50%, 75%, and 100% of the path are drawn.

5.2 CTS Test Result

We performed test through the Conformance Test Suites (CTS) 1.0.0, the OpenVG compatibility test tool that the Khronos group distributes [15], in order to verify how our implementing RI adhered to the standard specification. Consequently, the success rate was 73% approximately. Table 1 shows the CTS success rate according to the test item in detail.

Table 1. CTS test result

Item	No. of test	Success	Fail	Success Rate(%)
Parameter	10	8	2	80.0
Matrix	11	11	0	100.0
Clearing	3	3	0	100.0
Scissoring	5	4	1	80.0
Masking	2	2	0	100.0
Path	48	37	11	77.1
Image	10	6	4	60.0
Paint	10	5	5	50.0
Image Filter	3	2	1	66.7
VGU	12	5	7	41.7
Total	114	83	31	72.81

Among the items that CTS reported as failure, there were items that correctly rendered resulting image cannot be differentiated from our reference-generated image visually. This was the case where the pixel value was off by one pixel. Moreover, there was a case where the already passed test image failed when a code was modified in order to pass another failing case. This is grasped that the test image of CTS is not yet stabilized.

5.3 Performance Evaluation

We developed performance measure program called Vgperf for 2D vector graphics. It was executed in the Windows XP for the comparison with the Hybrid RI. The test was progressed in the intel Core Duo 1.83GHz CPU, 2GB RAM, 2 MB (L2) Cash Memory, ATI Radeon X1400 Graphic card, and 128MB Video Ram environment.

The Fig. 7 shows the performance measurement result of Path drawing. The Fig. 7(a) shows the measurement result of drawing basic diagram such as, a triangle or a square. The Fig. 7(b) shows the measurement result of drawing little more complicated

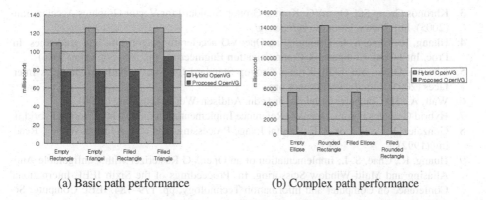

(a) Basic path performance   (b) Complex path performance

Fig. 7. Performance test result

figures like an ellipse or a rounded square. As shown in the figure, the OpenVG RI proposed in this paper is faster than the Hybrid RI 1.3-1.6 times in case of the basic path, 4.6-76 times in case of complicated path.

As to the tiger image, the Hybrid RI took 7.3 seconds and our RI did 3.6 seconds, when the size of the drawing surface was 1,024 x 768.

6 Conclusion

The Flash™ already occupies the market more than 80%, in the vector graphics field. The OpenVG was initiated latter than the Flash, but has been settled as the industry standard. We expect that the OpenVG will expand market occupancy sooner or later, because most of the graphic card companies participate in standardization.

In this paper, we proposed the reference implementation of the OpenVG using software rendering. We showed the possibility of success of the software rendering mode, by showing the proposed RI outperforms the Hybrid RI. Moreover, we could port the proposed OpenVG RI easily to the various platforms due to systematically designing it considering an embedded environment.

The academic research or development case of the OpenVG has been scarcely reported because it is introduced recently. We expect that this paper will become the turning point that it activates the OpenVG research and development.

In the future work, we will enhance the success rate of the CTS and continue to research about the performance improvement by using software rendering mode. Moreover, we have a plan to research of supporting the SVG based on the OpenVG.

References

1. Pulli, K.: New APIs for Mobile Graphics. In: Proceedings of SPIE - The International Society for Optical Engineering, vol. 6074, art. no. 607401 (2006)
2. He, G., Pan, Z., Quarre, C., Zhang, M., Xu, H.: Multi-stroke freehand text entry method using OpenVG and its application on mobile devices. In: Pan, Z., Aylett, R., Diener, H., Jin, X., Göbel, S., Li, L. (eds.) Technologies for E-Learning and Digital Entertainment. LNCS, vol. 3942, pp. 791–796. Springer, Heidelberg (2006)

3. Khronos Group Std. OpenVG, Kronos Grouop Standard for Vector Graphics Accelerations (2005), http://www.khronos.org/openvg/
4. Huang, R., Chae, S.-I.: Designing an OpenVG accelerator: algorithms and guidelines. In: Proc. Int'l Conf. Computer & Communication Engineering, pp. 555–560 (May 2006)
5. Khronos Group Std. EGL, Kronos Grouop Standard for Native Platform Graphics Interfaces (2005), http://www.khronos.org
6. Watt, A.: 3D Computer Graphics, 3rd edn. Addison-Wesley, Reading (2000)
7. Hybrid Graphics Forum, OpenVG Reference Implementation (2005), http://forum.hybrid.fi
8. Gonzalez, R.C., Woods, R.E.: Digital Image Processing, 2nd edn. Addison-Wesley, Reading (1992)
9. Huang, R., Chae, S.-I.: Implementation of an OpenVG Rasterizer with Configurable Anti-Aliasing and Multi-Window Scissoring. In: Proceedings of the Sixth IEEE International Conference on Computer and Information Technology, pp. 179–184. IEEE Computer Society Press, Los Alamitos (2006)
10. Schilling, A.: A new simple and efficient antialiasing with subpixel masks. ACM SIGGRAPH Computer Graphics 25(4), 133–141 (1991)
11. Haeberli, P., Akeley, K.: The accumulation buffer: hardware support for high-quality rendering. ACM SIGGRAPH Computer Graphics 24(4), 309–318 (1990)
12. Doan, K.: Antialiased rendering of self-intersecting polygons using polygon decomposition. In: Proc. 12th Pacific Conf. Computer Graphics and Applications, pp. 383–391 (2004)
13. Harrington, S.: Computer Graphics A Programming Approach, 2nd edn. McGraw Hill, New York (2006)
14. KWISF, Wireless Internet Platform for Interoperability (2006), http://www.wipi.org.kr
15. Huone, Conformance Test Suite for OpenVG (2006), http://www.khronos.org

A QoS Routing Protocol for Mobile Ad Hoc Networks Based on a Reservation Pool

Donghak Pyo[1], Sunggu Lee[1], and Min-Gu Lee[2]

[1] Electrical and Computer Engineering Division
Pohang University of Science and Technology (POSTECH)
San 31 Hyoja Dong, Pohang, Korea
{dhpyo, slee}@postech.ac.kr
[2] Network Control Platform Development Team
BcN Business Unit, Korea Telecom Corporation, Seoul, Korea
bluehope@kt.co.kr

Abstract. Even without possible interference from external radio sources, the problem of guaranteeing quality-of-service (QoS) routing in mobile ad hoc networks (MANETs) is a difficult problem. Difficulties arise because node mobility can cause frequent network topology changes, communication channels can have high error rates, the jitter rate is high and several different applications can be sharing the use of the communication medium. This paper addresses these issues and proposes a new QoS routing protocol for MANETs that combines aspects of a MAC protocol and a path reservation protocol. The proposed QoS routing protocol can be implemented based on any routing method that supports multiple paths (e.g., DSDV, TORA, PDR). The QoS performance of the proposed protocol is verified with simulations conducted using NS-2.

Keywords: Mobile ad hoc network (MANET), quality-of-service (QoS), routing, time division multiple access (TDMA).

1 Introduction

There are many interesting applications that can be supported if quality-of-service (QoS) support can be provided for mobile ad hoc networks (MANETs). Such applications include reliable mobile multimedia services, disaster recovery and real-time identification of mobile objects in a battlefield environment. However, because MANETs typically use electromagnetic-wave-based wireless communication protocols, such as IEEE 802.11 or ZigBee, it can be difficult (or even impossible) to control possible interference from external radio sources. For example, if an ad hoc IEEE 802.11b/g network (named Network A) is created, then other electronic devices using Bluetooth (which uses the same 2.4GHz frequency range) or IEEE 802.11b connections outside of Network A can interfere with communication within Network A. Thus, IEEE 802.11b/g uses a communication protocol based on carrier sense multiple access with collision avoidance (CSMA/CA), which is a protocol that

R. Obermaisser et al. (Eds.): SEUS 2007, LNCS 4761, pp. 253–262, 2007.

inherently cannot guarantee real-time communication. Since, in general, possible interference from external radio sources cannot be controlled, exclusive reservation of communication bandwidth (for a particular application) cannot be achieved, and thus, complete quality-of-service (QoS) support cannot be achieved.

Given the fact that the behavior of external radio sources cannot be controlled, the best that can be hoped for in a MANET environment using wireless links is to create a communication protocol that prevents interference between any two communication channels that strictly adhere to the protocol created. There have been several previous attempts to create such a protocol. However, all previously proposed protocols have drawbacks that limit their usability. Thus, in this paper, a new QoS routing protocol is proposed for use in MANETs.

Let us assume that there is no interference from external radio sources. Even with this restriction, the problem of guaranteeing quality-of-service (QoS) routing in mobile ad hoc networks (MANETs) is a difficult problem. For a given network, sufficient resources must be reserved in order to satisfy the QoS requirements of a particular application. However, in a MANET, node mobility can cause frequent network topology changes, communication channels can become unreliable and have high error rates, the total available bandwidth tends to be lower than in wired networks, the jitter rate is high and several different applications can be sharing the use of the communication medium. In this paper, we propose a new QoS routing protocol that combines aspects of a MAC protocol and a path reservation protocol. First, a MAC protocol based on a multihop TDMA method, adapted to a MANET environment, is used to permit exclusive reservation of network bandwidth resources. Second, a reservation pool method, in which network resources are reserved in advance and placed in a reservation pool, is used to deal with the problem of frequent network topology changes.

The rest of this paper is organized as follows. Section 2 provides an overview of previously proposed QoS routing protocols that can be applied to MANETs. Summaries of the proposed protocols and their drawbacks are described. Next, a new QoS routing protocol that overcomes these drawbacks is described in Section 3. Simulation results are presented in Section 4. Finally, the paper concludes with concluding remarks in Section 5.

2   Related Work

In [1], Lin and Liu proposed a QoS routing method for MANETs built on top of the Direct Sequence Distance Vector (DSDV) routing algorithm. To overcome a potential hidden terminal problem, Lin and Liu propose the use of a code division multiple access (CDMA) technique applied on top of a time division multiple access (TDMA) method. [1] proposes a systematic method for computing the link bandwidth and path bandwidth available to a virtual circuit. Code and time slot resources are reserved for primary and secondary paths that meet the pre-specified bandwidth constraints for a given virtual circuit request. If a link in the primary path becomes disconnected due to node movement or other reasons, the virtual circuit is switched to the secondary path. This method has the drawback of requiring the reservation of valuable network resources for a backup path that may not be used. In addition, the need to implement CDMA over TDMA results in a complex system that may not be appropriate for use in applications with low-performance processors such as wireless sensor networks.

The Ticket Based Probing (TBP) protocol is an alternative QoS-aware routing protocol proposed by Chen and Nahrstedt [2]. Tickets are used for arbitration – the holder of a ticket is given permission to search for a path. Two types of tickets are used: yellow and green. A yellow ticket indicates a preference for paths with shorter delays. A green ticket indicates a preference for lower-cost paths. Flow control is implemented by limiting the number of yellow and green tickets allocated to the network. A localized path repairing scheme is provided to deal with mobile nodes. Three levels of path redundancies are provided in TBP. In the first level of path redundancy, multiple routing paths are established for a single message stream (a separate copy of each data packet is sent only each path). With the second level of path redundancy, multiple routing paths are established, but data packets are only sent along one primary path. The other paths are backup paths that are only used if the primary path becomes disconnected. However, note that the presence of backup paths has an adverse affect on other message streams since valuable network resources have to remain reserved for the backup paths. In the third level of path redundancy, a secondary path is only established when the primary path fails. Such a method will result in a long recovery time – this may result in a temporary failure to meet prespecified QoS requirements.

A method referred to as "Stateless Wireless Ad hoc Networks (SWAN)" is also proposed as a QoS routing protocol for MANETs [3]. The term "stateless" in the name of this method refers to the fact that per-flow or aggregate state information does not need to be stored at each node. This method instead relies on feedback information obtained from the network. When a circuit needs to be established, a probe packet is sent towards the destination. Upon observing a probe packet, each intermediate node marks its bandwidth in the packet header if its own available bandwidth is detected as the bottleneck bandwidth. Upon receiving the probe packet, the destination node replies to the source node with the bottleneck bandwidth value. The source node initiates a rerouting procedure if the bottleneck bandwidth is insufficient to support the necessary level of QoS. This type of route discovery process may incur a large amount of control overhead and a long delay. In addition, false admission is possible because forward reservation is not being used.

In [4], Shih et. al. propose another TDMA-based routing protocol meant to support QoS routing in MANETs. This method, referred as a Distributed Slots Reservation Protocol (DSRP), is designed to be an improvement over Lin and Liu's method [1] based on using CDMA over TDMA. In order to obviate the need for implementing CDMA on top of TDMA, and thereby complicating the system implementation, reasoning about possible conflicts due to hidden terminal and exposed terminal problems is used to determine the set of time slots that can be used by a given node without fear of running into conflicts with other transmitting nodes. This reasoning is implemented in a set of algorithms executed at each node. Route maintenance is implemented by executing a new route discovery phase when a link breakage is detected. Due to this dynamic route maintenance mechanism, however, route recovery may take a long time and QoS requirements may not be met as a result.

3 Proposed QoS Routing Protocol

The QoS routing protocol proposed in this paper overcomes the problems of high complexity, waste of network resources, and/or slow recovery from link breakage observed with the previously proposed MANET QoS routing protocols. There are two aspects to the proposed routing protocol. First, a multi-hop TDMA method is used to provide a simple method of allocating time slots to communication channels such that no two transmitting nodes conflict with each other. Second, a reservation pool method, based on [5], is used to deal with the problem of frequent network topology changes. The following subsections present the assumptions used in the proposed protocol and the above two aspects of this protocol.

3.1 Assumptions

Before delving into the details of the proposed method, let us briefly outline the assumptions being made in this paper. First, it is assumed that external radio interference, if any, will not adversely affect the real-time performance of the proposed routing protocol. Of course, since we cannot control the behavior of all external devices that emit radio waves, it is possible for a wireless communication channel to become disrupted for a short time interval. However, in such a case, we are assuming that appropriate forward error correction techniques can be used to automatically make corrections to the data as it is received at each intermediate node. If external radio interference is of a sufficiently long duration, then no routing protocol will be capable of providing real-time communication guarantees. Thus, we are simply assuming that such is not the case.

Second, a separate clock synchronization mechanism is assumed. Several such clock synchronization mechanisms, including the beacon-based method used in the IEEE 802.11 protocol, are available for use in MANET environments. A clock synchronization mechanism is necessary in order to use TDMA to coordinate the transmission and reception of packets over a wireless communication medium, which is of a broadcast nature by default. The granularity of the clock synchronization method used will determine the duration of the guard time required between adjacent time slots in our TDMA scheme.

Third, as in [1], the only QoS parameter of interest will be assumed to be the bandwidth available to a given virtual circuit between a source node and a destination node. Thus, other possible QoS parameters such as end-to-end latency, signal-to-interference ratio and packet loss rate are not considered in this paper. This assumption is made because bandwidth guarantees are the most critical factor for typical real-time applications. Consideration of other possible QoS parameters will be left as future work.

3.2 Multihop TDMA

Suppose that a given source node wishes to send a sequence of data packets, with certain QoS guarantees, to another node in the MANET. Then the source node can send out probe control packets in order to find a path to the destination node and to reserve appropriate network resources along that path. A set of reserved network channels from the source node to the destination node, using the path found, will form a virtual circuit that can be used to subsequently send out the data packets requiring QoS guarantees. A key requirement of this type of procedure is the capability of reserving network resources. If link bandwidth is considered as the primary network resource of interest, then a method is required to partition the total available bandwidth on a given link and to reserve portions of the total available link bandwidth. A natural way to achieve this is to use TDMA on that link. However, since end-to-end QoS guarantees will be required for the virtual circuit to be created, a multihop TDMA protocol will be required for a MANET environment.

Let us first consider the partitioning of the time available for communication on a single link of a given MANET. For this purpose, time can be partitioned into superframes, with a superframe partitioned as shown in Figure 1. Although this structure appears similar to the frame structure used in [1] and [3], it is actually slightly different because each slot in the control phase is allocated to a specific node in our network (there are as many control phase slots as there are nodes) and each slot in the data phase is used to partition the link bandwidth available for sending data packets. Thus, the idea is that a node can use the control phase slot allocated to it to request allocation of a data phase slot for its exclusive use when sending data packets to a specific neighboring node. Although such a method limits the size of the MANET that can be supported, it is nevertheless a simple and low-overhead method that can be used with appropriately-sized MANETs.

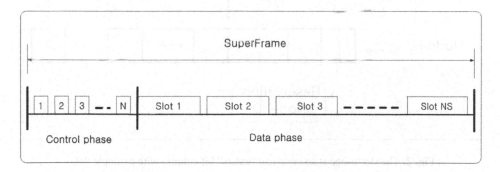

Fig. 1. The structure of a superframe used for bandwidth reservation on a single link

When using the above type of superframe structure, care must be taken to ensure that nodes that are two or fewer hops away from each other do not attempt to use the same data slot. Unless handled properly, such a conflict can result in a so-called "hidden terminal" problem, which is the reason that [1] uses CDMA on top of TDMA. To ensure that there are no potential conflicts with two different packets, received at the same time at an intermediate node, from two different nodes, slot usage information can be exchanged between neighboring nodes.

In particular, each node can maintain a two-dimensional slot-usage state table. This state table only needs to contain information about the data slots being used by neighbors and the neighbors of neighbors. Thus, each node informs its neighbors of the data slots that it has reserved. Those neighbors then pass on this information for one more hop. Figure 2 shows the format of the state table used with example data entries. Node mobility is taken into account by maintaining an "exists" bit that is set when a neighboring node moves into the radio range of the current node; the "exists" bit for a particular node is reset when that node moves out of the radio range of the current node. When making a data slot assignment request, a node only needs to refer to the data slot usage of those nodes with the "exists" bit set to one.

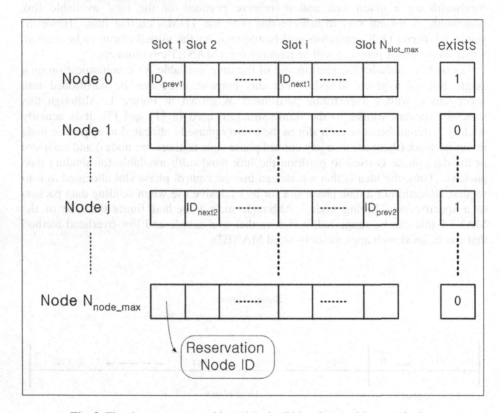

Fig. 2. The slot-usage state table and "exists" bit column with example data

By maintaining appropriate state information, of a manageable size, at each node, the time slots that can be utilized by a given node without conflicting with other nodes can be determined in a much simpler method than that used in [4]. In the example data shown in Figure 2, which could be a slot-usage state table stored at node 0, node 0 is receiving data from a node with ID number ID_{prev1} using slot 1 and sending data to node ID_{next1} using slot i. Node j, which is a neighboring node in the radio range of node 0, is sending data to node ID_{next2} using slot 2 and receiving data ID_{prev2} using slot N_{slot_max}. Since node 0 knows the slots being used by its neighboring nodes (this information is stored in its slot-usage table), node 0 can avoid those slots when reserving bandwidth for a new channel to another adjacent node. Thus, if node 0 wishes to communicate with node 1 after node 1 moves into the radio range of node 0 (which will result in the "exists" bit for node 1 being changed from a 0 to a 1), then it can reserve any slot except the slots 0, 1, i and N_{slot_max}.

3.3 Reservation Pool Method

Suppose that a virtual circuit is created by reserving network resources along a primary path. Data packets requiring QoS guarantees can be sent using such a virtual circuit. However, since a MANET environment is assumed, nodes can move around. Thus, in order to maintain a virtual circuit with the required QoS, path maintenance will be required to switch over to alternate paths or to repair the current primary path when link breakage occurs in the primary path. This problem was handled in different ways by the previous QoS methods surveyed in Section 2. However, as noted there, methods that reserve network resources for a backup path in advance can waste precious network resources if the backup path is not needed, while methods that search for a new path when the primary path breaks can require long path recovery times.

The solution proposed in this paper is to maintain a pool of network resources, reserved in advance and shared by all virtual circuits that may require such resources. If a potential link breakage in a primary path is detected (based on detection of current node movements and estimates of future node movements), path maintenance is initiated. This is done by searching the reservation pool for a set of channels (a channel is a link and its associated data slot reservation, which together creates a communication pathway with a guaranteed bandwidth) that can be used to form a detour path with the required level of QoS. If such a set of channels are found, those channels are removed from the reservation pool and the primary path is modified to use the detour path. If the channels for such a detour path are not found in the reservation pool, control packets are sent out to search for a detour path. In both cases, the primary path is modified to use the detour path *before* the link breakage occurs, if possible.

By using a reservation pool as described above, path recovery will be much quicker than if new network resources have to be found every time a link breakage occurs. Also, since the resources in the reservation pool can be shared, there is much less waste of precious network resources. This solution is based on a method previously presented by two of the authors in [5]. Potential link breakage can be detected using a novel link stability estimation model and method presented in [7]. That paper also discusses other link stability estimation methods presented in the literature. Interested readers are referred to these papers for details on these methods.

4 Simulation Results

In order to evaluate the performance of the proposed QoS routing protocol, computer simulations were conducted using the NS-2 (Version 2.26) simulator [8]. Although simulations were performed using various sets of parameters, in this section, results are only shown for a representative set of environment and protocol parameters since results for other sets of parameters were similar. The simulation environment considered consists of 30 mobile hosts roaming about in a $1500 * 500 \text{ m}^2$ area according to the Random Waypoint model [8]. Hosts move around with a random uniform speed (with maximum speeds ranging from 0 ~ 20 m/s) and an initial randomly chosen direction (with random direction changes). Each mobile host has the same transmission range of 250m. A transmission rate of 2 Mbps is used. The superframe used in the simulations consists of control and data phases as shown in Figure 1. The slot time for each frame in the control phase is set to 1.2 ms and the total number of slots in the control phase is set to 30, which is also the total number of mobile hosts. The slot time of each frame in the data phase is set to 5ms and the total number of slots in the data phase is set to 16. Therefore, the total length of a superframe is 116ms = (30*1.2) + (16*5). Pseudo Distance Routing (PDR) is used as the underlying routing protocol [5]. The source-destination pair for a "call" (a virtual circuit connection) is chosen according to a uniform random distribution. For each call, traffic is generated with bandwidth requirements of 1, 2 or 3 slots (denoted as QoS1, QoS2 and QoS3, respectively) chosen in a uniform random manner. The total simulation time is set to 250 seconds.

In the first set of experiments, we consider the call setup time and bandwidth as the metrics of performance for the proposed protocol. The call setup time is the time required to reserve all of the slots in a path to the destination. Figure 3 shows the simulation result for call setup time versus node mobility. We compare call setup time while varying the number of hops in the path. When the node mobility is low, the number of probing messages used by the routing protocol (PDR) is small. The queuing time before transmission of the control packet is short. However, when the node mobility increases, the number of probing messages is also increased. Thus, the call setup time also increases. As shown in Figure 3, call setup time increases in direction proportion to the number of hops in the path.

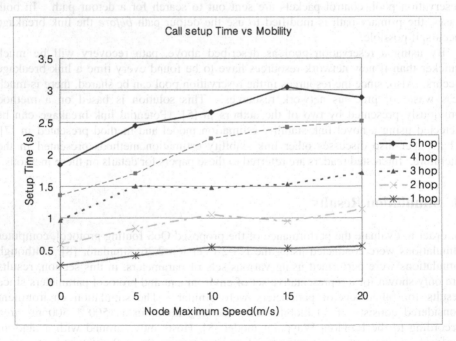

Fig. 3. Call Setup Time vs Mobility

In the second set of experiments, the average throughput was measured for connections with different QoS requirements. As was done in [1], we assumed that each mobile host can request a connection to a destination node with different throughput requirements. The three types of throughput levels that can be requested, QoS1, QoS2 and QoS3, use 1, 2 and 3 slots, respectively, in the data phase of a superframe (refer to Figure 1). Each data packet size is assumed to be 1000 bytes long and the average interarrival time of packets is set to 30 milliseconds. If path reservation is successful, the source node sends 30 data packets to its destination. Figure 4 shows the throughput with various mobility levels. Overall, the average throughput of QoS1 is 67.0Kbps, QoS2 is 125.5Kbps and Qos3 is 183.7Kbps. These simulation results show that the proposed QoS protocol can be used to provide different levels of throughput to circuits with different QoS flow requirements in a consistent, predictable manner.

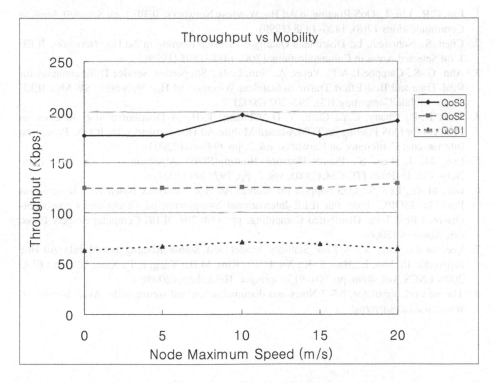

Fig. 4. Throughput vs Mobility

5   Conclusion

This paper has presented a new QoS routing protocol for MANET environments. It has been shown that all previously proposed QoS routing methods for MANETs have drawbacks that limit their usage. The QoS routing protocol presented in this paper gets around these drawbacks by using a multihop TDMA protocol and a reservation pool of network resources. The multihop TDMA protocol presented uses a superframe structure and a slot-usage table stored at each node in order to provide a simple method of allocating time slots to communication channels such that no two transmitting nodes conflict with each other. A backup reservation pool method is used to enable fast recovery when a primary path becomes disconnected because of links that break due to mobile nodes. The performance of the proposed QoS routing protocol is verified with NS-2 simulations. The simulation results show that this protocol can be used to provide different levels of throughput to circuits with different QoS requirements in a highly stable and predictable manner in MANET environments.

References

1. Lin, C.R., Liu, J.: QoS Routing in Ad HocWireless Networks. IEEE J. on Selected Areas in Communications 17(8), 1426–1438 (1999)
2. Chen, S., Nahrstedt, L.: Distributed Quality-of-Service Routing in Ad Hoc Networks. IEEE J. on Selected Areas in Communications 17(8), 1488–1505 (1999)
3. Ahn, G.-S., Campbell, A.T., Veres, A., Sun, L.-H.: Supporting Service Differentiation for Real-Time and Best-Effort Traffic in Stateless Wireless Ad Hoc Networks (SWAN). IEEE Trans. Mobile Computing 1(3), 192–207 (2002)
4. Shih, K.-P., Chang, C.Y., Chen, Y.-D., Chuang, T.-H.: A Distributed Slots Reservation Protocol for QoS Pouting on TDMA-based Mobile Ad Hoc Networks. In: ICON. Proc. 12th International Conference on Networks, vol. 2, pp. 660–664 (2004)
5. Lee, M.-G., Lee, S.: Pseudo-Distance Routing(PDR) Algorithm for Mobile Ad-hoc Networks. In: Proc. ITC-CSCC2005, vol. 2, pp. 797–798 (2005)
6. Lee, M.-G., Lee, S.: QoS Support for Mobile Ad-Hoc Networks Based on a Reservation Pool. In: ISORC. Proc. 9th IEEE International Symposium on Object and Component-Oriented Real-Time Distributed Computing, pp. 194–204. IEEE Computer Society Press, Los Alamitos (2006)
7. Lee, M.-G., Lee, S.: A Link Stability Model and Stable Routing for Mobile Ad-Hoc Networks. In: Sha, E., Han, S.-K., Xu, C.-Z., Kim, M.H., Yang, L.T., Xiao, B. (eds.) EUC 2006. LNCS, vol. 4096, pp. 904–913. Springer, Heidelberg (2006)
8. The network simulator, NS-2 Notes and documentation and source code. Available: http://www.isi.edu/nsnam/ns/

Exact Schedulability Analysis for Static-Priority Global Multiprocessor Scheduling Using Model-Checking*

Nan Guan[1], Zonghua Gu[2], Qingxu Deng[1], Shuaihong Gao[1], and Ge Yu[1]

[1] Department of Computer Science and Engineering
Northeastern University, Shenyang, China
[2] Department of Computer Science and Engineering
Hong Kong University of Science and Technology, Hong Kong, China

Abstract. To determine schedulability of priority-driven periodic tasksets on multi-processor systems, it is necessary to rely on utilization bound tests that are safe but pessimistic, since there is no known method for exact schedulability analysis for multi-processor systems analogous to the response time analysis algorithm for single-processor systems. In this paper, we use model-checking to provide a technique for exact multi-processor scheduability analysis by modeling the real-time multi-tasking system with Timed Automata (TA), and transforming the schedulability analysis problem into the reachability checking problem of the TA model.

1 Introduction

For single-processor systems, there are mainly two approaches to schedulability analysis: *utilization bound tests* and *response time analysis*. Take fixed-priority Rate Monotonic (RM) scheduling for example. The well-known Liu and Layland utilization bound test [1] states that a taskset with N tasks is schedulable if the total utilization does not exceed $N(2^{1/N}-1)$. This is a sufficient but not necessary condition, and rejects some tasksets that are schedulable. In fact, all utilization bound tests are necessarily pessimistic. Lehoczky *et al* [2] presented response time analysis, a polynomial-time algorithm for calculating a task's Worst-Case Response Time (WCRT) by performing processor demand analysis when the task and all other higher-priority tasks are initially released at time 0, the *critical instant*. A task is schedulable if its WCRT is less than its deadline, and the taskset is schedulable if all tasks are schedulable. This is a necessary and sufficient condition for schedulability.

Multiprocessor (MP) systems are drawing a lot of attention recently, with industry trends such as multi-core processors and Multiprocessor Systems-on-a-Chip (MPSoC), hence real-time scheduling and schedulability analysis for MP systems become an important research area. MP scheduling algorithms can be

* This work is partially supported by National Basic Research Program of China (973 Program) under Grant No.2006CB303000 and the Cultivation Fund of the Key Scientific and Technical Innovation Project, Ministry of Education of China, under Grant No.706016.

R. Obermaisser et al. (Eds.): SEUS 2007, LNCS 4761, pp. 263–272, 2007.

classified into three categories, (no migration, restricted migration and full migration) based upon the permissible degree of inter-processor migration [3].

No migration (partitioned) scheduling with a given task allocation to processors is similar to single-processor scheduling and can be addressed with existing techniques, but restricted and full migration scheduling brings serious challenges to schedulability analysis. For these task models, an analogous algorithm for WCRT calculation does not exist, since there may not be a *critical instant* as in single-processor scheduling. Traditionally, there are two methods to determine the schedulability of MP systems: *utilization bound tests*, which is safe but pessimistic, and *simulation*, which is unsafe, since it only explores one execution trace, not exhaustive exploration of the state space. For simulation, a widely adopted convention is to set all task release offsets to be zero. However, in contract to single-processor scheduling, it is not necessarily true that this is the worst case situation that maximizes task response times for MP scheduling, hence simulation sometimes gives the wrong result, i.e., determine a taskset to be schedulable even though it is not.

In view of the drawbacks of utilization bound tests and simulation, it would be valuable if we could have a method for exact schedulability analysis without the pessimism of the utilization bound tests. In this paper, we provide an exact method for static-priority MP schedulability analysis without any pessimism by transforming the schedulability problem into reachability analysis problem of Timed Automata. In addition to exact schedulability analysis of periodic tasksets, model-checking has an additional benefit of being able to handle non-periodic tasksets. In classic scheduling theory, real-time tasks are usually assumed to be periodic, and sporadic tasksets are treated as periodic ones using the minimum inter-arrival time as the task period, which results in pessimistic analysis results. But with model-checking, we can model the external environment that triggers the taskset in a precise manner, thus avoiding the pessimism of the strict periodic taskset assumption.

We make a number of simplifying assumptions in this paper. We assume that tasks are assigned static priorities, and they are independent from each other without precedence relationships and data sharing. Each task has a fixed execution time instead of a range of possible execution times. Although it is not difficult to relax these assumptions in our modeling framework, we make these assumptions for the sake of clarity of presentation.

This paper is organized as follows. We first discuss related work in Section 2. We present the TA model for restricted migration in Section 3 and for full migration scheduling in 4. We present performance evaluation results in Section 5. Finally, we draw conclusions in Section 6.

2   Related Work

2.1   Utilization Bound Tests

For EDF-based MP scheduling, several authors have presented utilization bound tests. Goossens et al [5] presented a test assuming that tasks have relative deadlines equal to the period. Baker [6] presented another test that can handle relative deadlines less than or equal to the period. Baker [7] extended [6] to include tasks with post-period deadlines, and showing that EDF-US[1/2], which gives higher priority to tasks with utilizations above $1/2$, is optimal. Bertogna et al [8] presented an improved test, and showed that it is incomparable to [6], and each test can accept tasksets that the other test rejects. For tasksets with different timing characteristics, they have different performance in terms of acceptance ratio.

For fixed-priority MP scheduling, Andersson [9] proved that the utilization guarantee for any static-priority MP scheduling algorithm, cannot be higher than $(m+1)/2$ for an m-processor platform. This conclusion places a theoretical upper bound of the utilization bound test for MP scheduling, and highlights the inherent pessimistic natural of the schedulability bound tests. For full-migration static priority scheduling, Andersson [9] defined a periodic taskset with constrained deadlines [1] to be a light system on m processors if it satisfies the following properties: (1)$\sum_{i=1}^{N} \frac{C_i}{T_i} \leq \frac{m^2}{3m-2}$, (2) $\frac{C_i}{T_i} \leq \frac{m}{3m-2}$, for $1 \leq i \leq N$, and showed that any periodic task system that is light on m processors is schedulable on m processors with preemptive RM algorithm.

Baruah [17] proved a similar result with the conclusion that a taskset, with all deadlines equal to periods, is guaranteed to be schedulable on m processors with RM scheduling if $C_i/T_i \leq 1/3$ for $1 \leq i \leq N$ and $C_i/T_i \leq m/3$. The group of tests consist of three tests with complexity of $O(N^3)$, $O(N^2)$ and $O(N)$ respectively.

Baker [10] presented a group of efficiently computable schedulability tests for fixed-priority scheduling of periodic tasksets with arbitrary deadlines on a homogeneous MP system. They improve upon Andersson's utilization bound tests by relaxing the assumptions of rate monotonic priorities and deadline being equal to period. For the special case when deadline equals period and priorities are rate monotonic, any set of tasks with maximum individual task utilization u_{max} and minimum individual task utilization u_{min} is feasible if the total utilization does not exceed $m(1 - u_{max})/2 + u_{min}$. We will compare our approach to the utilization bound tests in Andersson [9] and Baker [16] in Section 5.

2.2 Formal Methods for Schedulability Analysis

TIMES [4] is a tool for schedulability analysis of periodic or sporadic tasksets on a single processor. It uses Extended Timed Automata with asynchronous processes to model the real-time taskset, and UPPAAL [12] as the analysis engine. Fersman [10] showed that, for fixed-priority scheduling on a single processor, the schedulability checking problem can be transformed into reachability analysis on TA using only two extra clocks in addition to the clocks to describe task arrival times. This observation greatly reduces the state space and improves scalability of model-checking, since the state space increases sharply with the number of real-time clocks. However, TIMES is only applicable to single-processor systems, while we extend its approach to handle MP scheduling in this paper.

---

[1] The deadline of a periodic task is constrained if its relative deadline is equal to its period.

ACSR-VP [11] stands for Algebra of Communicating Shared Resources with Value Passing, a real-time process algebra used to model and solve the schedulability analysis as well as priority assignment problems. UPPAAL does not have parametric analysis capability of ACSR, so it can be used for schedulability analysis but not for priority assignment. Conceptually, we could have used ACSR-VP to model and solve the MP schedulability problem instead of UPPAAL. It is not our purpose to compare strengths and weaknesses of different modeling formalisms and tools, so we leave this as possible future work.

3   TA Model for Restricted Migration Scheduling

We have two alternatives approaches for building the TA model. The first one is to model all the tasks within a single model. This approach requires two clocks in each task automaton, one for accumulation of execution time in order to know when a job finishes execution, and the other one for testing if a task has missed its deadline. With this approach, $2N$ clocks are involved if there are N tasks.

We take advantage of these restrictions to reduce the number of clocks. Since a high-priority task will never be delayed by low-priority tasks, we model and check schedulability of each task one by one in decreasing order of priority, similar to the approach of TIMES. When we are checking schedulability for a task T_i, T_i is called the *task under analysis*, and all other tasks with higher priority than T_i are called the *background tasks*. The tasks with lower priority than T_i do not need to be modeled. We need to use one clock in the TA modeling each background task to accumulate its execution time, and use two clocks in the TA modeling the task under analysis. Therefore, the maximal number of clocks is $N + 1$, and model-checking needs to be performed for at most N times. Since the state space of timed automata grows drastically with the number of clocks, this alternative is superior to the first one.

As discussed earlier, model-checking is done for each task in decreasing order of priority, and only the tasks with higher priority than task i are modeled in S when task i is the task under analysis. The automaton S is the parallel composition of one task automaton $v - task$ modeling the task under analysis(Fig. 1(a)), i

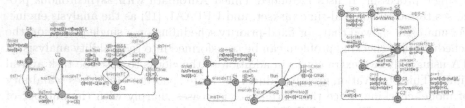

(a) TA modeling the task under analysis

(b) TA modeling the background task

(c) TA modeling the scheduler

Fig. 1. TA model for restricted migration scheduling

task automata $non - v - task$ modeling each background task (Fig. 1(b)), where i is the number of the tasks with higher priority than the task under analysis, and one automaton $scheduler$ modeling the scheduler (Fig. 1(c)). In Fig. 1(a), the task automaton is initially in location $Idle$. When the $scheduler$ automaton issues an event $executeT!$, each task automaton checks to see if this command is meant for itself. If yes ($exeT == i$), then it goes into location Run; otherwise ($exeT! = i$), it goes back to location $Idle$. When task i is in location Run, some other jobs with higher priority may be allocated to its processor and preempt it ($Run \rightarrow C2 \rightarrow Run$). As shown in Fig. 2, when task i is preempted, $r[i]$ is updated, and task i finishes execution when $c[i] == r[i]$. At this time, clock $c[i]$ is reset, and the variable $r[i]$ is updated when $c[i] == Cmax$, where $Cmax$ denotes the maximum execution time of the tasks. When the job of task i is finished, it updates the relevant variables and sends an event $finish!$ to inform the scheduler of its termination($Run \rightarrow C5 \rightarrow Idle$). The automaton $v - task$ models the task under analysis. In contrast to $non - v - task$, $v - task$ resets the clock d and goes into location $Ready$ when a job is released. In the location $Ready$ and Run, when the condition $d == D[i]$ is satisfied, the task has missed its deadline and goes into the $Error$ location.

The automaton $scheduler$ maintains the system state, allocates and schedules released jobs. When a task is released, an event $release!$ sent by T, and the transition $Init \rightarrow C1$ with $release?$ is taken. The value of $rlsT$ updated by T shows which task the released job belongs to. Then we check to see which processor is idle and record it ($p = PrmptW()$). If there is at least one idle processor ($p >= 1$), then the released job is allocated to it. After updating the relevant variables ($C1 \rightarrow C4$), an event $executeT!$ is issued ($C4 \rightarrow Init$) to inform the corresponding task to start execution. If there is no idle processor ($p == 0$), then the scheduler checks to see if there is any running job with lower priority than the newly-released job. If not, then the released job goes into the wait state ($C2 \rightarrow Init$); otherwise, the newly-released job ($C2 \rightarrow C3$) preempts the lower-priority job.

When a job finishes execution, an event $finish!$ is issued by $non - v - task$ or $v - task$, and the transition $Init \rightarrow C5$ with $finish?$ is taken. The value $fshP$ records which processor the finished job has been running on. If all jobs allocated to this processor have finished execution ($rn[p] == 0$), then the scheduler wakes up the waiting task with the highest priority if the wait queue is non-empty.

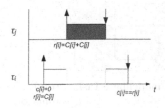

Fig. 2. Execution scenario for tasks i and j with $Prio(j) > Prio(i)$

4   TA Model for Full Migration Scheduling

In contrast to restricted migration scheduling, a preempted job can resume execution on any available processor using full migration scheduling. Due to inherent limitations of the model-checking technology (we are not aware of any model-checkers that can handle fractional numbers.), we can only handle tasksets with integer task attributes. We can safely assume that a task's period and deadline to be integers, since it does not make a lot of sense to assign a non-integer period or deadline to a task from a real-time scheduling perspective, and it is almost never done in industry practice. However, it is possible for a task's execution time and deadline to be non-integers. We can round up the execution time to the nearest integer for schedulability analysis. We believe this is not a major limitation in practice. We can prove the following theorem (proofs omitted due to space limitations):

Theorem 1. *To determine schedulability of a periodic taskset whose attributes are all integers, it is sufficient to only consider task release times at integer time instants, which only produce execution traces in which all scheduling events (task release, preemption, blocking and finish) happen at integer time instants.*

Theorem 1 implies that the expressiveness of discrete time formalism is adequate for the purpose of schedulability analysis if we accept the limitation that all task attributes must be integers. Using the discrete time approach has the additional benefit of making it easier to model preemptive scheduling, since using a continuous time formalism would require a stopwatch mechanism to keep track of each task's execution time when it is preempted and resumed [13]. However, it is not necessarily true that using a discrete time approach always yields a smaller state space than using the continuous time approach, if there are long durations of time intervals within which no significant events happen.

Fig. 3(a) shows the automaton that generates periodic clock ticks. $TICK$ is a constant denoting granularity of clock ticks. When $oc == TICK$, the transition on edge $T \rightarrow T$ is taken, and all discrete clocks are incremented by 1 in the function $UpdateClock()$, which means that one digital clock tick has passed. Unlike continuous time clocks, the integer variable representing a discrete clock can be

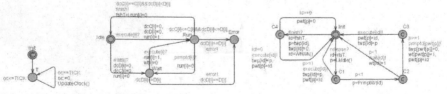

(a) TA modeling the periodic clock tick   (b) TA modeling a task   (c) TA modeling the scheduler automaton

Fig. 3. TA model for full migration scheduling

paused or restarted. We use $dcC[i] = dcC[i] + run[i]$ to update $dcC[i]$ and in $UpdateClock()$. Setting $run[i] = 0$ pauses the discrete clock $dcC[i]$, and setting $run[i] = 1$ resumes it. Since the discrete clocks can be paused and resumed, we can model the time behavior of each task separately rather than accumulating the computing time of the jobs preempted it. As shown in Fig. 3(b), when the automaton is in location Run, if $dcC[i] == C[i]$, then task i has finished execution. When it is in location Run or $Wait$ and $dcD[i] == D[i]$, then task i has missed its deadline, and we determine the taskset to be unschedulable.

In contrast to restricted migration, the full migration scheduler maintains a global wait queue, in which all the ready jobs are waiting. As shown in Fig .3(c), when a job is released, the scheduler checks to see if there is an idle processor $(p = LkIdle())$. If yes $(p >= 1)$, the job starts executing on it immediately $(C1 \rightarrow Init)$. Otherwise, the scheduler checks to see if there is any running job can be preempted $(p = PrmptW(id))$. If yes $(p >= 1)$, the newly-released job preempts the running job $(C2 \rightarrow C3 \rightarrow Init)$. Otherwise, the released job waits $(C2 \rightarrow Init)$. When some job is finished on a processor, the scheduler checks to see if there are any waiting jobs $(id = WhWk())$. If yes $(id! = 0)$, the job with highest priority starts executing, otherwise the processor remains idle.

5   Performance Evaluation

We compare the schedulability analysis results of our method with classical methods. The model-checking experiments were run on a server with four AMD Opteron 844 (1.8GHz) CPUs and 8GB RAM running Fedora Linux. We use a utility program *memtime* developed by the UPPAAL group to record peak memory usage and running time of the model-checker. To our best knowledge, there is no known utilization bound test for the static-priority restricted-migration scheduling, so we only consider the case of full-migration scheduling in the following experiments.

We generated 200 tasksets, each consisting of 5 tasks running on 2 processors. Each task's period is chose randomly in the range of $[8, 20]$, and a task's execution time is the product of its period with a random value in the range of $[0.1, 0.5]$, rounded to the nearest integer. In the experience, 64 tasksets are accepted by Baker's test [16], 98 accepted by Andersson's test, 154 accepted by our method and 157 accepted by simulation in which all task release offsets are 0. We can see that the utilization bound tests in Baker and are indeed pessimistic and rejects a large number of tasksets that are actually schedulable. The acceptance ratio using simulation with zero task release offset is slightly larger than that using model-checking, as several tasksets are determined to be schedulable using simulation, but are in fact unschedulable since the worst-case response time for a task is maximized with some tasks have non-zero release offsets.

Next, we evaluate the performance and scalability[2]. Fig. 4 shows how the worst-case peak memory size and running time of UPPAAL increase with the

---

[2] Since the performance results are similar for restricted and full-migration scheduling, we only show the data for full-migration scheduling to give the reader a general idea of model-checking performance.

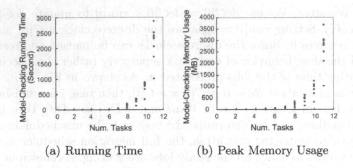

(a) Running Time   (b) Peak Memory Usage

Fig. 4. UPPAAL performance for full-migration scheduling on 2 processors

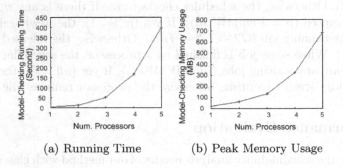

(a) Running Time   (b) Peak Memory Usage

Fig. 5. UPPAAL performance for full-migration scheduling of 6 tasks

number of tasks with a fixed number of processors (2), and Fig. 5 shows how
they increase with the number of processors with a fixed number of tasks (6).

We use a taskset with 6 tasks to show how model-checking complexity grows
with scaling-up of taskset parameter values. The task parameters (period, deadline and execution time) in the first group are integer multiples of those of the
original taskset, and the parameters in the second group are the integer multiples plus 1. A taskset in the second group are "pathological" in the sense that

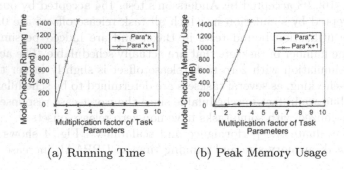

(a) Running Time   (b) Peak Memory Usage

Fig. 6. UPPAAL performance for full-migration scheduling with different scale factors
of task parameters

task periods are relatively prime to each other, so the taskset has a very large hyper-period. The state space for a taskset in the second group grows up much faster with the scale factor than that for a taskset in the first group, which is confirmed by Fig. 6, where we can see that UPPAAL's performance deteriorates quickly with the increase in scale factor for the second group, while it stays more or less constant for the first group. On the other hand, adding 1 to each task's scaled execution time while scaling up its period and deadline has a negligible impact on performance. We can also see that UPPAAL handles long time durations gracefully as long as they are integer multiples of each other. In industry practice, task periods are typically assigned to be integer multiples of each other, thus making the model-checking approach more practically relevant.

6 Conclusions

In this paper, we use model-checking to provide an exact method to schedulability analysis of periodic tasksets on multi-processor systems, in order to overcome the pessimism of schedulability bound tests. As we can see in Section 5, the main limitation of the model-checking is state-space explosion, which limits the size of the problem that can be handled. This is especially problematic for real-time model-checkers like UPPAAL must handle continuous real-time clocks. As part of our future work, we plan to experiment with other modeling formalisms such as ACSR-VP [11], and compare their performance and scalability.

HW task scheduling on a FPGA shares many similarities with global task scheduling on identical multi-processors [3], where all processors in the system have identical processing speed and different task invocation instances may run on different processors. But it is actually a more general and challenging problem since a HW task may occupy a different area size on the FPGA while a SW task always occupies one and only one CPU. Some authors [14][15] have derived utilization bound tests for FPGA scheduling. We plan to apply model-checking to develop a schedulability analysis tool for FPGAs.

References

[1] Liu, C., Layland, J.W.: Scheduling Algorithms for Multi-Programming in a Hard Real-Time Environment. Journal of the ACM 20, 46–61 (1973)
[2] Lehoczky, J.P., Sha, L., Ding, Y.: The Rate Monotonic Scheduling Algorithm: Exact Characterization and Average Case Behavior. In: IEEE Real-Time Systems Symposium (RTSS) (1989)
[3] Carpenter, J., Funk, S., Holman, P., Srinivasan, A., Anderson, J., Baruah, S.: A Categorization of Real-Time Multiprocessor Scheduling Problems and Algorithms, Handbook of Scheduling: Algorithms, Models and Performance Analysis, Chapman and Hall/CRC (2004)
[4] Amnell, T., Fersman, E., Mokrushin, L., Pettersson, P., Yi, W.: TIMES: a Tool for Schedulability Analysis and Code Generation of Real-Time Systems. In: FOR-MATS. International Workshop on Formal Modeling and Analysis of Timed Systems (2003)

[5] Goossens, J., Funk, S., Baruah, S.K.: Priority-Driven Scheduling of Periodic Task Systems on Multiprocessors. Real-Time Systems 25 (2003)

[6] Baker, T.P.: Multiprocessor EDF and Deadline Monotonic Schedulability Analysis. In: IEEE Real-Time Systems Symposium (RTSS), pp. 120–129 (2003)

[7] Baker, T.P.: An Analysis of EDF Schedulability on a Multiprocessor. IEEE Trans. Parallel Distrib. Syst. 16, 760–768 (2005)

[8] Bertogna, M., Cirinei, M., Lipari, G.: Improved Schedulability Analysis of EDF on Multiprocessor Platforms. In: Euromicro Conference on Real-Time Systems (ECRTS), pp. 209–218 (2005)

[9] Andersson, B., Baruah, S.K., Jonsson, J.: Static-Priority Scheduling on Multiprocessors. In: IEEE Real-Time Systems Symposium, pp. 193–202 (2001)

[10] Fersman, E., Mokrushin, L., Pettersson, P., Yi, W.: Schedulability analysis of fixed-priority systems using timed automata. Theor. Comput. Sci. 354(2), 301–317 (2006)

[11] Kwak, H.-H., Lee, I., Philippou, A., Choi, J.-Y., Sokolsky, O.: Symbolic Schedulability Analysis of Real-Time Systems. In: IEEE Real-Time Systems Symposium (RTSS) (1998)

[12] The UPPAAL Model-Checker, http://www.uppaal.com

[13] Cassez, F., Larsen, K.G.: The Impressive Power of Stopwatches. In: Palamidessi, C. (ed.) CONCUR 2000. LNCS, vol. 1877, pp. 138–152. Springer, Heidelberg (2000)

[14] Danne, K., Platzner, M.: An EDF Schedulability Test for Periodic Tasks on Reconfigurable Hardware Devices. In: ACM SIGPLAN/SIGBED Conference on Languages, Compilers, and Tools for Embedded (LCTES) (2006)

[15] Guan, N., Gu, Z., Deng, Q., Liu, W., Yu, G.: Improved Schedulability Analysis of EDF Scheduling on Runtime Partially Reconfigurable Hardware Devices. In: WDPRTS 2007 (2007)

[16] Baker, T.P.: An Analysis of Fixed-Priority Schedulability on a Multiprocessor. Real-Time Systems 32(1-2), 49–71 (2006)

[17] Baruah, S.K., Goossens, J.: Rate-Monotonic Scheduling on Uniform Multiprocessors. IEEE Trans. Computers 52(7), 966–970 (2003)

Soft Real-Time Task Response Time Prediction in Dynamic Embedded Systems

Cássia Yuri Tatibana, Carlos Montez, and Rômulo Silva de Oliveira

Universidade Federal de Santa Catarina, Pós-Graduação em Engenharia Elétrica,
Caixa Postal 476,
Florianópolis-SC, 88040-900, Brazil

Abstract. The hardware infrastructure that provides the support of ubiquitous embedded computing may be shared by different applications. Many of those applications have real-time requirements, where events from the environment require the reaction of the computing system. The meeting of deadlines is hindered by the fast system dynamics. At the same time, the embedded system must deal with overload situations. In this paper we assume that an embedded application receives aperiodic requests with soft deadlines. Other unknown applications are executed simultaneously. The goal of this paper is to discuss algorithms to estimate the probability of a deadline to be met. The prediction of a deadline miss at the request arrival allows actions for damage control.

1 Introduction

The accelerated growth of the use of embedded systems in a huge diversity of products, towards the implementation of ubiquitous systems in different environments, creates the demand for an always larger diversity of applications. In this context, physical and financial constraints will require the sharing of the hardware infrastructure (processors, memory, network, etc) that provides the support of ubiquitous embedded computing among different applications, at different times. Although nowadays most embedded systems are developed through co-design of the hardware and of the software, in the future the infrastructure embedded in the environment will need to support the download and the execution of applications designed much before or after the hardware was designed.

Many embedded system and ubiquitous system applications have soft real-time requirements, where events in the environment generate the need of a reaction from the computing system. Most of the time, those timing requirements are not critical.

In this context, the meeting of timing requirements is hindered by the dynamics of the system (applications are started and finished at any moment), by the lack of knowledge about internal characteristics of the other applications (worst-case computation time, types of existent threads, etc), and by resource constraints. At the same time, the need for autonomy requires embedded systems to deal with overload situations without the aid of human supervision.

R. Obermaisser et al. (Eds.): SEUS 2007, LNCS 4761, pp. 273–282, 2007.

In this paper we consider the situation where an embedded application receives requests from clients that can be physical devices (by hardware interrupts), tasks in other processors (by messages) or tasks in the same processor. Such requests are accompanied by a soft deadline, in an explicit way (for example, a data field in the received message) or in an implicit way (all request of that type always have the same deadline). The application is capable of working with a pre-defined group of request types, that is to say, it implements a pre-defined group of services. There is a local thread pool responsible for serving those requests. It is used at the most a single thread for each service type, in order to reduce the overhead associated with context switching and synchronization mechanisms. Other applications of unknown nature are executed simultaneously.

Requests arrival is aperiodic, characterizing the system as dynamic and subject to overloads. Deadlines are necessarily not critical. During overload there is the formation of request queues for one or more of the supported services. However, the occurrence of an overload in the processor doesn't affect the requests generation directly. That is because requests are generated due to external events and they are not subject to control flow.

The objective of this paper is to discuss algorithms to predict the probability of meeting a deadline, in dynamic systems that are not controlled by the algorithm and there is limited information about the state of the system. The prediction of a deadline missing must be made at the arrival of the service request, since it will allow actions of damage control, such as the signaling of alarms (timing exception), the use of an alternative computer or the use of some mechanism for load reduction (admission control).

The remaining of the paper is organized as follows: section 2 presents some of the related work, section 3 describes the problem, section 4 has the proposed approach, an example application is described in section 5 and section 6 contains the final remarks.

2 Related Work

Most of the real-time scheduling theory considers systems where no deadline may be missed.On the other hand, there are applications that tolerate the eventual miss of a deadline, as long as it doesn't happen too often. Several works present schedulability tests that include the possibility of eventual misses of deadlines. For example, Tia et al. [11] present Probabilistic Time Demand Analysis, which was extended by Diaz et al. [5]. Gardner et al. [7] present Stochastic Time Demand Analysis. Other stochastic analysis methods are the one presented by Manolache [10] for uniprocessor systems and the one presented by Leulseged et al. [9] for multiprocessor systems. Also, the Real-Time Queuing theory presented by Lehoczky [8] can provide stochastic guarantees for system with a high traffic load. Several results have been presented requiring a specific scheduler, such as those by Abeni [1] for reservation based systems, and the Statistical Rate Monotonic Scheduling by Atlas et al. [2].

Some works in the literature deal with the response time of aperiodic tasks. In [3] the existence of periodic tasks is assumed, whose hyper-period is analyzed, the moments of idle processor are identified and these moments form the base of the analysis, which is better when the computation time of the aperiodic task is small compared to the hyper-period. In [4] it is supposed FCFS as the scheduling policy, for tasks whose control flow is described by a probabilistic graph. The service requests are characterized by a probabilistic distribution. In [6] it is supposed that each application can be characterized by a workload that expresses the amount of resources (processor, disk and network) necessary for that application. The modeling of the system is base on this demand description. The estimate of the latency average is used in [12] to predict the response time of a new request sent to a HTTP server. It combines the average and variance of previously observed latencies into a single metric.

3   Problem Description

Consider an embedded computer where several programs execute simultaneously and a program is capable to accomplish a certain group S of services, $S = \{S_1, S_2, \ldots, S_{ns}\}$, where ns is the number of services supported by the program. The execution of a service may correspond to the execution of a single or several software functions, or even the interaction with physical devices.

Along the execution of this program, aperiodic requests arrive for the execution of its services. We will call task the execution of a service. Without loss of generality, we can number the requests in the growing order of their arrival instants, being T_1 the first received request. Each task T_k is characterized by the request of a specific service S_k, $S_k \in S$, and by a relative deadline D_k.

All service requests are executed according to the scheduling algorithm of the program and of the underlying operating system. Tasks whose response time is bigger than the deadline are executed to the end. This avoids the occurrence of internal inconsistency in the data structures of the program. Also, requests for the same service are always executed in the order of arrival. The scheduling among different services may vary.

We want an algorithm that, at the arrival of task T_k, it determines the probability of deadline D_k of task T_k to be met, i.e., $P(R_k \leq D_k)$, where R_k is the response time associated with the execution of T_k. As an additional constraint, the algorithm has to be implemented at the application level, it can not depend of specific support from the underlying operating system.

It is necessary to define the metric used to compare the quality of the response time predictions done by several algorithms in a given system. In this work we use the relative error rate $E(z)$ observed for each considered algorithm, where z indicates the algorithm used. This rate supplies a measure valid only for a given system and a given pattern of request arrivals, but it allows a comparison among different algorithms.

At each arrival of a task T_k in the system, each response time prediction algorithm z under evaluation calculates the probability $P_k(z)$ of this task to meet its deadline, $0 \leq P_k(z) \leq 1$. Task T_k is executed and its effective response time R_k is measured.

The relative error $E_k(z)$ is the error associated with the prediction of the response time done by algorithm z for the task T_k, it is defined as:

$$E_k(z) = \begin{cases} 1 - P_k(z) & \text{case} \quad R_k \leq D_k \\ P_k(z) & \text{case} \quad R_k > D_k \end{cases}$$

The value of E_k is necessarily between 0 and 1. The situations below illustrate the behavior of this metric:

- The algorithm z determines that there is a chance of 80% for task T_k to meet its deadline, $P_k(z) = 0.8$, and it meets its deadline, we have the relative error $E_k(z) = 1 - 0.8 = 0.2$;
- The algorithm z determines that there is a chance of 80% of task T_k to meet its deadline, $P_k(z) = 0.8$, but the task misses its deadline, we have the relative error $E_k(z) = 0.8$;
- The algorithm z determines that there is a chance of 50% of the task T_k to meet its deadline, $P_k(z) = 0.5$, and in this case we will have $E_k(z) = 0.5$ independently of the task meeting $(1 - 0.5)$ or not (0.5) its deadline.

The relative error rate of a given algorithm z is defined as:

$$E(z) = \frac{\sum_{\text{all } k} E_k(z)}{n_k}$$

4   Proposed Approach

A simple approach is to use the response time of tasks in the past to predict the probability of meeting the deadline of a task that arrives. So, the program history should be maintained with the response time of each task executed before, for each service of the program. The history can be used as the PMF (Probability Mass Function) of the random variable R_k, and a simple inspection of the history supplies the probability $P(R_k < D_k)$ of task T_k. However, this simple approach has some disadvantages. Due to the fast system dynamics, only recent response times are important to predict the response time of a new task. Besides, the task type may have not been requested for a long period, and the prediction algorithm has no data to work.

In fact, the complete history contains the PMF of the response time of invocations of a given service, observed on long periods of time. In order to decide about the probability of the next execution of this service to meet its deadline, it is necessary the PMF of this next activation. The PMF of the next request for service S depends on the current state of the system, which is defined by several factors, such as: (i)The parameters supplied in the call of the service; (ii) The current value of the permanent variables of the program; (iii) The computer load due to the other tasks of that application; (iv) The size of the queues associated with services of this program; (v) The computer load due to other applications;

(vi) Changes in the relative demand for the several resources in the system, what affects the many services differently.

The number of possible system states is huge, if not infinite. However, it is possible to merge those states, according to some properties that are easy to measure and capable of indicating the response time approximately to be expected in the next execution of the requested service.

A form of attacking the problem is to use, to predict the response time of a service S_1, not only the old executions of S_1, but also the historical data about old executions of all the services supported by the program. We assume that an overload in the node will increase the response time of all the services, and not only of S_1. Besides, the response time of S_1 may be influenced by the current state of the permanent variables of the program (size and content of the data structures of the program). Thus, the recent behavior of all the services can be used for the calculation of the response time prediction.

An analysis of the crossed correlation among the response times of the several services supported by the program would allow the identification of which services are important for the estimate of the response time of which services. Assuming that the program implements n_s services, it would be necessary n_s^2 correlation studies, including the auto-correlations. Such analysis would need to be done continually, given the non stationary nature of the considered system. For example, a variation in the size of a data structure of the program may change the correlation between two specific services. The processing cost of this solution is prohibitive for many systems.

4.1 Approach Description

The approach proposed in this paper tries to merge all the possible system states in just two: normal and high loaded. Initially the system is in state normal. At the moment a task T_k finishes, its response time R_k is compared with the average response time R_s associated with service S. The new state of the system is defined as State Normal, in case $R_k \leq R_s$, or State High Loaded, in case $R_k > R_s$.

The value R_s is defined as a running average. It is updated whenever a task concludes the execution of service S. The new value of R_s is denoted by $R_s(i+1)$ and it is given by:

$$R_s(i+1) = \alpha \times R_k + (1 - \alpha) \times R_s(i)$$

where $R_s(i)$ is the previous value of R_s, R_k is the last response time observed for service S and α is a constant between 0 and 1. The purpose of keeping R_s as a running average is twofold: to discard old response time values and to reduce the computing cost, since R_s is used by the prediction algorithm every time a new request for service S arrives.

A record of historical data is maintained with the recent response times of each method, together with the information on the system state at the moment of the arrival of that request. In fact, there are two historical records, one with the response times observed with the system in normal state, and another observed with the system in high-load state.

Whenever a new request arrives for service S, the historical data specific for service S response times is used. It is considered only that response time that was observed in the past, when the system was in the same state that it is now. By using this historical record as a PMF, the conditional probability of the task meeting its deadline can be calculated, given that the system is identified as in a given state, that is to say, $P(R_k \leq D_k|\text{system state})$. A simple inspection of the historical record supplies this information.

The historical record is implemented as a circular list, with a finite size. Only the last T conclusions of each service type are maintained in the record. The size T depends on the kind of system, this will be discussed in the next section.

5   Example Application

An application was implemented as a proof of concept for the approach proposed in this paper. Since the objective of the proposed approach is to deal with dynamic systems, whose behavior of the operating system and of the other applications is unknown, the application was implemented in Java and executed on a desktop computer using Windows XP, together with other programs. The availability of Java in the versions Micro-Edition (J2ME) and Real-Time (RTSJ) will increase its use in embedded and ubiquitous systems.

The program to be analyzed is composed by 7 types of services. Simple and quite common functions were used: insert in a list at the end, sequential search and delete from the list, calculation of average through a complete scan of the list, calculation of standard deviation through two complete scans of the list, binary search in a sorted array, generation of two square matrices with pseudo-random numbers and finally the multiplication of two square matrices. The Java class Vector was used for the implementation of the list. The list starts empty and it grows along the execution of the program. The matrix used by the generation service and by the multiplication service has a random size between 50x50 and 100x100, defined at each new arrival of the task of matrix generation. It is important to observe that this variation in the parameters of this service also generates a variation in the computing effort associated with the service. The Java Garbage Collector execution was not controlled neither requested.

Except for the requests for the matrix multiplication, all the others are generated with intervals between arrivals that follow an uniform distribution, within the following intervals: 10mS to 20mS for Insert; 10mS to 40mS for Remove; 10mS to 45mS for Average Computation; 10mS to 45mS for Standard Deviation Computation; 10mS to 20mS for Binary Search; 30mS to 70mS for Matrix Generation.

The matrix multiplication is always requested by the service of matrix generation. Therefore, the interval between arrivals of the requests of matrix multiplication is approximately equal to the interval between arrivals of the requests for matrix generation.

As an additional disturbance in the system, a Java thread was included that generates two matrices of size 100x100, then it makes their multiplication. This thread doesn't use the service queue mentioned before, but it implements its own functionality. This extra load is activated once approximately every 4 seconds. It does not represent a disturbance controlled by the program.

Regarding the priorities of the Java threads, it is important that the request service load does not interfere with the requests generation. So, the threads "source" receive the highest priority, the thread "extra load" has an intermediary priority and the threads "server" have the lowest priority. The scheduling policy among the 7 threads of type "server" is described together with the experiment results, in the next section.

The deadlines for the requests were chosen in a way to be spread along the interval of values observed as their response times. For all the service types, the values of the deadlines were randomly generated, with uniform distribution, inside of an interval defined by 1 millisecond and approximately twice the value of the response time average for that service. Each experience lasted 60 seconds, but the data about the quality of the predictions were collected only during the final 40 seconds. A value of 0.01 was used for α.

5.1 Experiment Results

For each experiment, the relative error rates obtained for each tested algorithm are shown. In each experiment, the following algorithms are considered:

- ALWAYS: it always indicates that the deadline will be met;
- NEVER: it always indicates that the deadline will be missed;
- SOSO: it always indicates a probability of 0.5 of meeting the deadline;
- SAMELAST100: it uses a single history record, size 100 for each service type;
- SAMELAST30: it uses a single history record, size 30 for each service type;
- SAMELAST3: it uses a single history record, size 3 for each service type;
- SAMELAST1: it uses a single history record, size 1 for each service type;
- DUALLAST100: it uses a history record with annotation about the system state, with size 100 for each service type;
- DUALLAST30: it is similar to DUALLAST100, size 30 for each service type;
- DUALLAST3: it is similar to DUALLAST100, size 3 for each service type;
- DUALLAST1: it is similar to DUALLAST100, size 1 for each service type.

A first group of experiences used scheduling COLABORATIVE among the threads that the program uses for servicing the requests. When concluding the servicing of a request, the server thread yields the processor to the next server thread, in a circular way. Results are presented in Table 1.

The algorithms ALWAYS and NEVER present a relative error rate close to 0.5, it indicates that around half of the service requests missed their deadlines during the experiment. This was expected because of the way the deadline values were generated. The algorithm SOSO presents a relative error rate of exactly 0.5.

Two conclusions can be easily noticed from the Table 1. Firstly, the modeling of the system state in two levels brings benefits, because the relative error rate of the algorithms DUALLAST are always smaller than those of the algorithms SAMELAST. Secondly, it can be observed that the size of the response time log is not important. A record with only 3 entries was enough to obtain similar

Table 1. Results with colaborative scheduling

Algorithm	Error rate	Algorithm	Error rate
ALWAYS	0.594		
NEVER	0.406		
SOSO	0.500		
SAMELAST100	0.257	DUALLAST100	0.205
SAMELAST30	0.256	DUALLAST30	0.206
SAMELAST3	0.258	DUALLAST3	0.204
SAMELAST1	0.258	DUALLAST1	0.244

results to a record with 100 entries. That is explained by the PMF of the task response times, which presents an enormous tail to the right. Table 2 shows, for each service, the average response times, their standard deviation and their medians. The fact that the average is so much larger than the median indicates the concentration of values to the left of the curve and the existence of some very big values to the right of the curve.

A second group of experiences was done, now using fixed priorities among the threads that service the requests. Lower priority was defined for threads associated with requests "Remove", "Double scan" and "Matrix multiplication." Table 3 shows the results.

A third group of experiences was done with the same program described before, in the same conditions of the first group of experiences, but now executing simultaneously in the computer an anti-virus program, making a complete scan of the main disk. The program anti-virus represents an additional load to the system. The results were very similar to those of Table 1.

An important question is to know if the relative error rate keeps constant for all the services, or the algorithm makes better predictions for one service than for another. Table 4 shows the relative error rate of the algorithms SAMELAST3 and DUALLAST3, in the conditions of the first experiment, according to each service type. It can be noticed that, although difference exists in the quality of the predictions for the different service types, the prediction of DUALLAST3 is always better than the prediction of SAMELAST3.

Table 2. Statistics about response times

Service type	Average (uS)	Standard dev. (uS)	Median (uS)
Insert	900.1	4814.7	44.0
Remove	1099.4	4186.9	219.0
Scan	941.3	4659.1	126.0
Double scan	948.9	4056.0	184.0
Binary search	862.0	4540.4	36.0
Matrix generation	3173.6	6540.7	2090.0
Matrix multiplication	9408.4	7262.8	7827.0

Table 3. Results with priority scheduling

Algorithm	Error rate	Algorithm	Error rate
ALWAYS	0.699		
NEVER	0.301		
SOSO	0.500		
SAMELAST100	0.255	DUALLAST100	0.216
SAMELAST30	0.253	DUALLAST30	0.216
SAMELAST3	0.249	DUALLAST3	0.210
SAMELAST1	0.251	DUALLAST1	0.272

Table 4. Relative error rate by service type

Service Type	Number of Tasks	SAMELAST3	DUALLAST3
Insert	2421	0.317	0.225
Remove	1501	0.176	0.172
Scan	1384	0.226	0.193
Double scan	1377	0.097	0.080
Binary search	2430	0.328	0.225
Matrix generation	803	0.279	0.279
Matrix multiplication	803	0.332	0.298

6 Conclusions

In this paper we considered algorithms to predict the probability of a deadline to be met, in dynamic systems that are not controlled by the algorithm, which has only limited information on the state of the system. The early prediction of a deadline miss allows actions of damage control, such as the signaling of alarms, the use of an alternative computer or some load reduction mechanism.

The relative error rate was defined as the metric to be used for the comparison among different algorithms. Considering the existence of processing and memory limitations, we looked for algorithms that don't demand a great computing power. The paper proposed the use of an algorithm based on the record of previous response times, maintained separately according to the system state being Normal or High-Loaded. The implementation of an example showed the feasibility of the approach and also that the records used don't need to be big.

An open question is how to integrate, in the definition of the system state, the state of the service request queues. The service request queues are an excellent indication of sudden overload, even when this fact doesn't still shows itself in the response times of the services, because the requests are still being serviced. Another important subject is the size of the record to be maintained. The record of response times represents a time window to the past. Since the requests are aperiodic, a record of fixed size represents a time window with variable size.

References

1. Abeni, L., Buttazzo, G.: Stochastic Rate Monotonic Scheduling. In: WPDRTS'01. Proceedings of the 9th International Workshop on Parallel and Distributed Real-Time Systems (April 2001)
2. Atlas, A., Bestavros, A.: Statistical Rate Monotonic Scheduling. In: RTSS'98. Proceedings of the 19th IEEE Real-Time Systems Symposium, Madrid-Spain, pp. 123–132 (December 1998)
3. Binns, P.: Statistical Estimation of Aperiodic Response Times when Scheduled on top of Static Timelines. In: PARTES'04. 1st International Workshop on Probabilistic Analysis Techniques for Real-Time and Embedded Systems (2004)
4. Chu, W.W., Leung, K.K.: Task Response Time Model and Its Applications for Real-Time Distributed Processing Systems. In: Proceedings of the Real-Time Systems Symp., pp. 225–236 (December 1984)
5. Diaz, J.L., Garcia, D.F., Kim, K., Lee, C.G., LoBello, L., Lopez, J.M., Min, S.L., Mirabella, O.: Stochastic Analysis of Periodic Real-Time Systems. In: RTSS'02. Proceedings of the 23rd IEEE Real-Time Systems Symposium, Austin-USA, pp. 289–300 (December 2002)
6. Ferdean, C., Makpangou, M.: Exploiting Application Workload Characteristics To Accurately Estimate Replica Server Response Time. In: Proceedings of DOA (2005)
7. Gardner, M.K., Liu, J.W.: Analyzing Stochastic Fixed-Priority Real-Time Systems. In: Proc. of the 5th International Conference on Tools and Algorithms for the Construction and Analysis of Systems (March 1999)
8. Lehoczky, J.P.: Real-Time Queuing Theory. In: RTSS'96. Proc. of 17th IEEE Real-Time Systems Symposium, Los Alamitos-USA, pp. 186–195. IEEE Computer Society Press, Los Alamitos (1996)
9. Leulseged, A., Nissanke, N.: Probabilistic Analysis of Multi-processor Scheduling of Tasks with Uncertain Parameter. In: Proc. of the 9th International Conference on Real-Time and Embedded Computing Systems and Applications (February 2003)
10. Manolache, S.: Schedulability Analysis of Real-Time Systems with Stochastic Task Execution Times. Licentiate Thesis No. 985, Dept. of Computer and Information Science, IDA, Linköping University, Sweden (December 2002)
11. Tia, T.S., Deng, Z., Shankar, M., Storch, M., Sun, J., Wu, L.C., Liu, J.S.: Probabilistic Performance Guarantee for Real-Time Tasks with Varying Computation Times. In: RTAS'95. Proc. of the 1st IEEE Real-Time Technology and Applications Symposium, Chicago-USA, pp. 164–173. IEEE Computer Society Press, Los Alamitos (1995)
12. Vingralek, R., Breitbart, Y., Sayal, M., Scheuermann, P.: Web++: A System For Fast and Reliable Web Service. In: Proc. of the USENIX Annual Technical Conference Monterey, California-USA (June 1999)

Transparent and Selective Real-Time Interrupt Services for Performance Improvement

Jinkyu Jeong[1], Euiseong Seo[1], Dongsung Kim[1], Jin-Soo Kim[1],
Joonwon Lee[1], Yung-Joon Jung[2], Donghwan Kim[2], and Kanghee Kim[3]

[1] Dept. of CS, Korea Advanced Institute of Science and Technology
[2] Electronics and Telecommunications Research Institute
[3] Samsung Electronics Co.
{jinkyu, ses, dskim}@calab.kaist.ac.kr, {jinsoo, joon}@cs.kaist.ac.kr
{jjing, dhkim76}@etri.re.kr, kang.hee.kim@samsung.com

Abstract. The popularity of mobile and multimedia applications made real-time support a mandatory feature for embedded operating systems. However, the current situation is that the overall performance is significantly degraded due to the real-time support. This paper suggests a novel scheme to minimize the performance degradation in embedded operating systems with real-time support. Especially, we propose transparent and selective real-time interrupt services which transparently monitor the system and postpone interrupt handling that are not relevant to real-time tasks. The proposed scheme was implemented on the Linux 2.6 kernel and the experimental results show that our scheme improves the throughput by up to 86% for Hackbench benchmark while providing almost the same scheduling latency compared to the previous work.

Keywords: Real-time, Scheduling algorithm, Interrupt handling, Embedded operating systems, Latency, Throughput.

1 Introduction

Due to the digital convergence phenomenon [1], consumer electronics devices, such as cell phones, PDAs (Personal Digital Assistants), and PMPs (Portable Media Players), run many sophisticated applications beyond their original purposes. For example, a typical cell phone is equipped not only with the phone tasks for calling and SMS (Short Message Service), but also with PIMS (Personal Information Management System), still pictures management system, and simple games. The number of these extra applications, as well as the size and the complexity of the individual application, will continue to grow rapidly in the near future.

Pure real-time operating systems are not adequate for those consumer electronics devices because of its limited functionality and the lack of generality. As a result, more general embedded operating systems, such as Windows CE and Embedded Linux, are becoming widely used in the area of portable embedded systems.

Many tasks in portable embedded systems are time sensitive [2] or require prompt response to external stimuli. Notable examples include call processing

R. Obermaisser et al. (Eds.): SEUS 2007, LNCS 4761, pp. 283–292, 2007.

tasks in PDAs or video streaming tasks in PMPs. To make these real-time tasks run harmoniously with other normal tasks, a certain level of real-time support is essential in embedded operating systems. In spite of this requirement, many embedded operating systems which are rooted in general-purpose operating systems do not fully support the real-time constraint.

Recently, Ingo Molnar has proposed a Linux kernel patch called *Complete Preemption* [3] for the improved real-time support in embedded devices. Although Complete Preemption is quite effective in improving the responsiveness of the system [4], the problem is that the system throughput is notably degraded due to the real-time support. We find that the excessive context switching between tasks to provide prompt response to real-time tasks is the main source of the performance degradation.

To resolve this problem, we propose a novel scheme to minimize context switching without sacrificing the responsiveness of the system. The proposed scheme suppresses the preemption by normal tasks so that only the interrupts associated with real-time tasks are rapidly serviced. The interrupts associated with real-time tasks are transparently identified by the system, thus requiring no manual intervention. The proposed scheme was implemented in the Linux kernel 2.6 and evaluated using various benchmarks. Our result shows that the proposed scheme improves the throughput up to 86% for Hackbench benchmark on VIA C3 embedded board.

The rest of the paper is organized as follows. The following section reviews the previous work for real-time support. Section 3 explains Complete Preemption in detail and analyzes the source of performance degradation. Section 4 discusses the proposed scheduling policy of real-time and normal tasks. Section 5 shows the evaluation results compared to the existing solutions in the aspects of scheduling latency and throughput. The final section summarizes our work and concludes the paper.

2 Related Work

Although widely used in embedded systems, Linux is hardly classified into real-time operating system (RTOS) since it does not support full preemption and priority inheritance. Two approaches, sub-kernel and preemptible kernel, are proposed to make Linux support real-time applications.

RTLinux [5] from FSMLabs and RTAI [6] are the representative examples of the sub-kernel approach [7]. The kernel is divided into core-kernel and sub-kernel. When some real-time tasks exist, the core-kernel executes those real-time tasks. Otherwise, the control is transferred to the sub-kernel and normal tasks are executed. In the sub-kernel structure, the scheduling latency of real-time tasks becomes lower than tens of microseconds. However, the sub-kernel approach has a disadvantage that only normal tasks can fully exploit the features provided by the Linux kernel.

A preemptible kernel [8] denotes the kernel which can be preempted either at certain preemption points or everywhere inside the kernel. For example, RED

Linux [9] inserts preemption points in the kernel, while Timesys Linux/RT [10] supports full kernel preemption. The Linux kernel 2.6 also supports kernel preemption originally developed by the preemptible kernel project [11]. In the preemptible Linux kernel, the kernel can be preemptible if it is not in critical sections, which enhances the responsiveness of real-time tasks. Unlike the sub-kernel approach, real-time tasks can make full use of kernel features. The scheduling latency, however, becomes more or less unstable.

Ingo Molnar's Complete Preemption [3,4] makes preemption possible even when the kernel is in critical sections using mutex-based spin locks. ISRs (Interrupt Service Routines) are also made preemptible by implementing them as kernel threads. Consequently, the scheduling latency of real-time tasks is further reduced below tens of microseconds. This means that a real-time task can react to interrupts more quickly. The priority inheritance mechanism is also implemented. Thus, Ingo Molnar's modified Linux kernel meets all the functionalities of RTOS [12].

The performance of Complete Preemption was under investigation by previous studies [13,14]. The evaluation results show that Complete Preemption was quite effective in real-time support because of its outstanding scheduling latency. However, our study reveals that Complete Preemption decreases the system throughput considerably due to many preemption points. The next section investigates Complete Preemption in more detail.

3   Linux Complete Preemption

In the preemptible Linux kernel, preemption is not possible inside critical sections due to synchronization. Consequently, a long scheduling delay for a real-time task is inevitable because the scheduling of the real-time task is postponed until the lock is released. Ingo Molnar's Complete Preemption replaced almost all the spin locks in the kernel with mutex-based spin locks. Using mutex-based spin locks, the real-time task can preempt any tasks even if those tasks are in a critical section. Other tasks trying to enter the critical section are enqueued in the waiter list of the lock. ISRs can be also preempted by real-time tasks in Complete Preemption since they are implemented using kernel threads. As a result, almost all the kernel codes are preemptible by real-time tasks. Complete Preemption also provides the priority inheritance mechanism which further enhances the responsiveness of real-time tasks.

One of the problems in Complete Preemption is that it sacrifices the system throughput in favor of shorter scheduling latency. Our preliminary study reveals that PREEMPT-RT, the Linux kernel patched using Complete Preemption, degrades the throughput considerably. Figure 1 shows the execution time of Hackbench [15] 50 and the number of context switchings during the benchmark tests on Pentium 2.4GHz machine. As shown in the figure, PREEMPT-RT takes about five times of the execution time compared to the Vanilla Linux kernel.

The significant decrease in the throughput is mainly due to excessive context switchings. In PREEMPT-RT, almost all kernel codes are preemptible by any

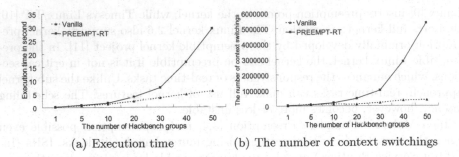

(a) Execution time   (b) The number of context switchings

Fig. 1. Hackbench results of Vanilla and PREEMPT-RT

interrupt even though the interrupt has nothing to do with real-time tasks. Unnecessary context switchings not only waste CPU cycles but also incur hidden costs such as TLB (Translation Lookaside Buffer) flush and cache misses.

4 Transparent and Selective Real-Time Interrupt Services

PREEMPT-RT provides fast and stable scheduling latency. However, allowing a lot of preemption points adversely affects the overall performance since only real-time tasks need to preempt other normal tasks. In the following subsections, we describe our scheme to selectively service interrupts that are associated with real-time tasks.

4.1 Suppressing the Preemptions by Normal Tasks

In Linux, all tasks are classified into two classes, a real-time class and a normal class. The Linux scheduler is based on the priority scheduling and tasks in the real-time class have always higher priorities than normal tasks.

PREEMPT-RT allows any task whose priority is higher than the currently running task to acquire the CPU even if the current task is in a critical section. This helps to reduce the scheduling latency for real-time tasks. However, the problem is that normal tasks are also able to preempt other normal tasks due to Complete Preemption. Since normal tasks are not so sensitive to the scheduling latency, context switchings from a normal task to another normal task take up the CPU cycles unnecessarily with additional overhead such as TLB flush and cache misses.

To remedy this problem, our scheme suppresses the preemptions caused by normal tasks as much as possible. Any higher-priority normal task does not preempt the current normal task immediately. Instead, the execution of the current normal task is guaranteed until the end of its time quantum in order to avoid frequent context switchings between normal tasks. Note that real-time tasks still can preempt other tasks for the minimal scheduling latency.

In our implementation, when the Linux scheduler is invoked due to the change in the runnable task set, the scheduler first chooses the next task based on the Linux scheduling algorithm. If the next task is in the real-time class, the scheduler performs the preemption immediately. If not, however, the previous task is resumed to run until the end of the remaining time quantum, thus suppressing the preemption.

4.2   Selective Handling of Real-Time Interrupt Threads

Because ISRs are implemented as kernel threads in PREEMPT-RT, they are scheduled by the Linux scheduler with their own priorities just like the other tasks. These interrupt threads are treated as real-time tasks. An interrupt thread can cause many context switchings, because it is able to preempt other tasks with the real-time priority.

In the proposed scheme, we basically treat interrupt threads as normal tasks. Although they have real-time priorities, we do not allow them to preempt other normal tasks in order to avoid the situation that the execution of a normal task is interrupted by non-critical interrupts.

The previous scheduling policy, however, may increase the scheduling latency considerably when some interrupt thread triggers a real-time task. Therefore, there should be a mechanism that we can somehow differentiate interrupt threads according to their relevance to real-time tasks. If we know a specific interrupt is associated with real-time tasks, we can set a special RT flag in the task structure of the corresponding interrupt thread. The RT flag indicates that the corresponding thread triggers a real-time task, hence it should be scheduled urgently.

Now the scheduling algorithm presented in Section 4.1 is modified as follows to deliver one or more predefined interrupts fast to real-time tasks. When the next candidate task is an interrupt thread, the Linux scheduler first checks whether the RT flag is marked in the task structure or not. If the RT flag is not set, the preemption is suppressed as explained in Section 4.1. On the other hand, if the RT flag is set, the interrupt thread is scheduled immediately to make the scheduling latency for real-time tasks short and stable.

4.3   Transparent Association of Interrupts with Real-Time Tasks

The selective handling of real-time interrupt threads is effective to achieve the short and stable scheduling latency for real-time tasks while minimizing unnecessary context switchings between normal tasks. In the previous subsection, we assume that interrupts associated with real-time tasks are specified in advance by application developers. Often this assumption is reasonable in many real-time systems since real-time tasks are usually associated with specific sensors and actuators. However, it is annoying for application developers to specify the associated interrupts every time since they may not be familiar with hardware details. Annotating the source code with a special system call not only lowers the application portability but also makes the application dependent on the hardware configuration on which it is running. Sometimes, it may not unclear which are right interrupts for the real-time tasks and the association may even change over time for complex real-time applications. In this subsection, we propose a way to transparently discover the relationship between real-time tasks and interrupts without any hints from application developers.

In PREEMPT-RT, a task is waken up in the function `try_to_wake_up()` when it is called by an interrupt thread. This means that if a real-time task is awakened by an interrupt thread, we can transparently identify those interrupts that are associated with real-time tasks without adding any kernel interface. The identified interrupt handler is marked with the RT flag in the task structure and the RT flag is later used by the Linux scheduler as described in Section 4.2.

In the Linux kernel, a part of interrupt handling can be delayed to *bottom halves*. The kernel thread called the *soft-irq* thread is usually used to perform the remaining work left by the interrupt handler. Since the PREEMPT-RT kernel also follows the same structure, the relationship between real-time tasks and interrupt threads may not be correctly recognized in `try_to_wake_up()` function if real-time tasks are waken up by bottom halves. We pay special attention to this case so that the original interrupt can be associated with the real-time task although the real-time task is awakened by the soft-irq thread.

The RT flag in the interrupt thread is removed when the associated real-time task either terminates or voluntarily turns into the normal task. Even though a real-time task terminates, some interrupt thread can be still marked with the RT flag since two real-time tasks may share the same interrupt. In this case, the RT flag is not removed until all the real-time tasks that share the interrupt terminate. Similarly, a single real-time task may be triggered by more than one interrupts, in which case all the interrupts are marked with the RT flag.

5   Evaluation

In real-time systems, the scheduling latency is one of the most important factors [13]. The overall throughput under limited computing resources is also an important characteristic of the system. Accordingly, the following two metrics are major concerns of our evaluation:

- **Latency.** The scheduling latency is the time between the event time and the start time of the task. In real-time systems, a stable scheduling latency must be guaranteed in various environments.
- **Throughput.** The throughput denotes the total amount of work that can be done in the given interval. In real-time systems, it is desirable to achieve the throughput as high as possible, while guaranteeing the predictable scheduling latency.

We describe our evaluation methodology in Section 5.1. Section 5.2 and Section 5.3 present our experimental results in detail.

5.1   Methodology

In this paper, we evaluate the following four Linux kernels:

- **Vanilla kernel.** The standard Linux kernel. Tasks are not preemptible while in the kernel.

- **Preemptible kernel.** The Linux kernel. Tasks are preemptible in the kernel area except critical sections.
- **PREEMPT-RT kernel.** The Linux kernel modified with Ingo Molnar's Complete Preemption.
- **Selective IRQ kernel.** The Linux kernel which implements the proposed scheme.

Note that our work was not compared to traditional real-time operating systems, such as QNX and VxWorks, because those RTOSes are limited in their functionality. The MontaVista Linux is largely similar to the Preemptible kernel.

We used an open source benchmark called *Realfeel* [16,13,17,18] to measure the scheduling latency. We have also used two benchmark programs, *Hackbench* [15] and *Tbench* [19] to evaluate the throughput of the system. Hackbench and Tbench are executed as normal tasks. The experiments are performed on a 1GHz Nehemiah C3 Core VIA board with 256MB of RAM and a 40GB, 5400RPM IDE disk drive.

5.2   Latency

We generate a 256Hz stream of interrupts using Realfeel to measure the scheduling latency. The total 30 million interrupts are sampled by Realfeel, which run as a real-time task. To see how the scheduling latency is affected by other normal tasks, we give various stresses to the kernel. First, we executed two benchmark programs, Hackbench and Tbench, together with Realfeel (denoted as *light load*). To give heavier stress, one CPU bound task and one I/O bound task are added to two benchmark programs (denoted as *heavy load*). The CPU bound task is a matrix multiplication program and the I/O bound task is an FTP program that downloads ten 700MBytes files.

Figure 2 shows the scheduling latency under two types of system loads. The x-axis represents the scheduling latency in milliseconds and the y-axis the percent of the samples. In Figure 2(a), Selective IRQ shows the similar distribution of the scheduling latencies to that of PREEMPT-RT under the light load. Specifically, in both kernels, all samples are scheduled within 100 microseconds. Under the heavy load, the percent of the samples that have long scheduling latencies is

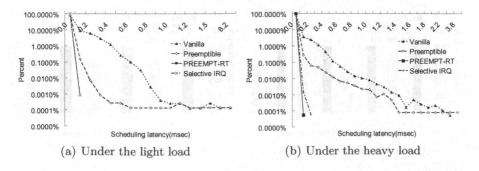

(a) Under the light load   (b) Under the heavy load

Fig. 2. The distribution of the scheduling latencies with 256Hz RTC interrupt

increased in case of the Vanilla kernel and the Preemptible kernel as shown in Figure 2(b). Selective IRQ and PREEMPT-RT still have very stable latencies even under the heavy load. The maximum scheduling latency is measured to be less than 100 microseconds in both PREEMPT-RT and Selective IRQ.

5.3   Throughput

To observe the basic throughput without real-time tasks, we ran two benchmark programs mentioned in Section 5.1 while the system is idle. The next evaluation simulated a realistic workload, where the real-time task Realfeel is run simultaneously with other two benchmark programs. Recall that the scheduling latency of Realfeel in the latter case is already shown in Section 5.2.

Figure 3(a) and (b) present the benchmark results without other interfering tasks. All the values in the figure are normalized to the value of the Vanilla kernel. In Figure 3(a), the x-axis and the y-axis denote the number of Hackbench groups and the relative throughput of Hackbench respectively. PREEMPT-RT drops the throughput about 30% compared to the Vanilla kernel. The Preemptible kernel has the similar throughput to the Vanilla kernel but, as we have already seen in Section 5.2, it fails to provide the stable scheduling latency. Selective IRQ improves the Hackbench throughput by up to 40.3% compared to PREEMPT-RT as the number of Hackbench group increases.

Hackbench generates a considerable number of context switchings when many Hackbench groups run concurrently. The Selective IRQ improves the throughput

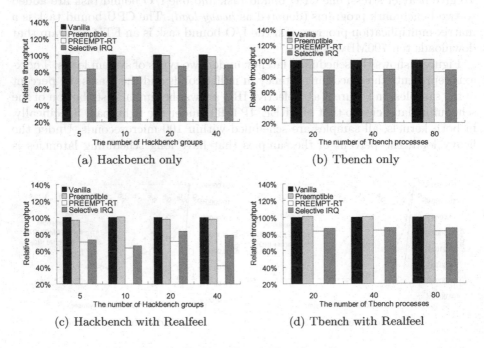

(a) Hackbench only

(b) Tbench only

(c) Hackbench with Realfeel

(d) Tbench with Realfeel

Fig. 3. Hackbench and Tbench results

because the proposed scheme intends to suppress unnecessary preemptions among normal tasks.

Figure 3(b) depicts the results of Tbench. The x-axis illustrates the number of Tbench tasks and the y-axis denotes the relative bandwidth of Tbench normalized to the result of the Vanilla kernel. This result also indicates that PREEMPT-RT achieves only 85% of the throughput of the Vanilla kernel. Selective IRQ enhances the throughput by up to 3.2% compared to PREEMPT-RT.

Figure 3(c) and (d) show the results of Hackbench and Tbench when a real-time task Realfeel is running together. From Figure 3(c), we can observe that the throughput of PREEMPT-RT becomes even worse with the presence of a real-time task. However, the proposed Selective IRQ scheme consistently shows the better throughput compared to PREEMPT-RT. Especially in Hackbench, PREEMPT-RT degrades throughput about 58% and Selective IRQ improves throughput up to by 86% compared to PREEMPT-RT. In Figure 3(d), the enhancement of the bandwidth under Selective IRQ is also increased from 3.2% to 4.6%.

6   Conclusion

In this paper, we proposed a novel scheme to improve the performance of embedded operating systems with real-time support. The performance degradation was mainly caused by a lot of preemption and scheduling points. Kernel-threaded interrupt service routines also contribute to the decrease in the performance. Excessive preemption and scheduling points yield many context switchings among tasks. The increased TLB flush and cache misses following the context switching are the direct sources of the performance degradation.

In the proposed scheme, the number of context switchings is reduced by the following two methods. First, we suppress the kernel preemptions caused by normal tasks as much as possible. Second, interrupts that are not relevant to real-time tasks are delayed. In order to provide prompt response to real-time tasks, our scheme transparently selects the interrupts that are related to real-time tasks and boosts them selectively. Consequently, the proposed scheme improves the system throughput significantly while exhibiting almost the same scheduling latency for real-time tasks.

Our work was implemented in the Linux 2.6 kernel. The experimental results show that the scheduling latency was below tens of microseconds. Moreover, the throughput is enhanced by 40% compared to Complete Preemption when there is no real-time task. If there is a real-time task, the throughput is increased by up to 86%. We plane to optimize our scheme further to achieve better response time and throughput.

Acknowledgments. This research was funded by the MIC(Ministry of Information and Communication), Korea, under the ITRC(Information Technology Research Center) support program supervised by the IITA(Institute of Information Technology Assessment) (IITA-2006-C1090-0603-0020). This work was

292   J. Jeong et al.

also supported by DSRC(Defense Software Research center) and the Korea Science and Engineering Foundation(KOSEF) grant funded by the Korea government(MOST) (No. R01-2006-000-10724-0)

References

1. Yoffie, D. (ed.): Completing in the Age of Digital Convergence. Harvard Business School Press (1997)
2. Abeni, L., Goel, A., Krasic, C., Snow, J., Walpole, J.: A measurement-based analysis of the real-time performance of linux. In: IEEE Real-Time and Embedded Technology and Applications Symposium, p. 133. IEEE Computer Society Press, Los Alamitos (2002)
3. Molnar, I.: Complete preemption (2005), http://people.redhat.com/mingo/realtime-preempt/
4. Heursch, A.C., Grambow, D., Horstkotte, A.: Steps towards a fully preemptable linux kernel. In: Workshop on Real-time Programming (2003)
5. Yodaiken, V.: The rtlinux manifesto. In: Proceeding of The 5th Linux Expo (1999)
6. Mantegazza, P., Dozio, E.L., Papacharalambous, S.: Rtai:real time application interface. Linux Journal (2000)
7. Dankwardt, K.: Real time and Linux, Part 3: Sub-kernels and benchmarks. Embedded Linux Journal 9, 33–37 (2002)
8. Mercer, C.W., Tokuda, H.: Preemptibility in real-time operating systems. In: IEEE Real-Time Systems Symposium, pp. 78–88. IEEE Computer Society Press, Los Alamitos (1992)
9. Wang, Y.C., Lin, K.J.: Enhancing the real-time capability of the linux kernel. In: IEEE Real Time Computing Systems and Applications, IEEE Computer Society Press, Los Alamitos (1998)
10. Oikawa, S., Rajkumar, R.: Linux/rk: A portable resource kernel in linux (1998)
11. Love, R.: The linux kernel preemption project, http://kpreempt.sourceforge.net/
12. Beneden, B.V.: Comp.realtime: Frequently asked questions (faqs) (version 3.6) (2004), http://www.faqs.org/faqs/realtime-computing/faq/
13. von Hagen, W.: Real-time and performance improvements for the 2.6 linux kernel. Linux Journal (2005)
14. captain@captain.at: Linux real time patch review - vanilla vs. rt patch comparison (2006), http://www.captain.at/howto-linux-real-time-patch.php
15. Russell, R.: Hackbench, http://lkml.org/lkml/2001/12/11/19
16. Hahn, M.: Realfeel. www.brain.mcmaster.ca/~hahn/realfeel.c
17. Webber, A.: Realfeel test of the preemptible kernel patch. Linux Journal (2002)
18. Williams, C.: Which is better – the preempt patch, or the low-latency patch? both! Linux Devices (2002)
19. Tridgell, A.: Dbench, ftp://samba.org/pub/tridge/dbench/

An Approach for Energy-Aware Management in Ubiquitous Home Network Environment

Hyung-Soo Mok[1], Sung-Yong Son[2], Jun Hee Hong[2], and Sanghoon Kim[3]

[1] The Department of Electrical Engineering,
Konkuk University, Gwangjin-Gu, Seoul, 143-701, Korea
hsmok@konkuk.ac.kr
[2] Power IT Research Center,
Kyungwon University, Seongam-Si, Gyeonggi-do, 461-701, Korea
{xtra, hongpa}@kyungwon.ac.kr
[3] The Department of Electrical and Electronics Engineering,
Kangwon National University, Chuncheon-Si, Gangwon-do, 200-701, Korea
kshoon@kangwon.ac.kr

Abstract. This research studies energy-aware managemen strategies in ubiquitouse home network environment. Always-on connectivity is essential to establish home networks, and it induces more energy consumption. In this work, a methodology is prosposed to achieve energy saving in overalls without harming the quality of services. Energy management technology used in wireless sensor network is expanded to information appliances, usage patterns and dependecy tree are applieds to design the management system, and the effect in energy saving is analyzed.

Keywords: Energy-Aware, Home Network, Ubiquitous, Information Appliances.

1 Introduction

Home network systems that have been rapidly deployed in Korea change the definition of "home" by expanding its meaning to the cyber world with the anytime and anywhere connectivity. They can check house security from outside in real time by connecting home network systems remotely with PCs, mobile phones, and telematics equipments. Even they can see and talk with the visitors who drop by during their absence. To enable these services the network needs to guarantee always-on connectivity to the internet, and every device at home must be ready to respond to the commands that may come from outside. Although these home network systems bring convenience to users, they increase energy consumption additionally. Considering world-wide tendency in energy saving due to the shortage of energy resources and the necessity of CO_2 reduction, home network systems need to consider energy efficiency to be widely deployed.

Many efforts have been made to reduce energy consumption in various aspects by developing energy efficient materials and chip sets, varying CPU clocks and voltages,

R. Obermaisser et al. (Eds.): SEUS 2007, LNCS 4761, pp. 293–300, 2007.

optimizing communication speed or powers, and controlling software processes, etc. Calhoun tried to reduce standby power with dynamic voltage scaling [1]. Frequency scaling is also considered in addition to voltage [2]. Dynamic power management is a common approach for embedded systems and wireless sensor networks by entering to the sleeping mode during not working [3, 4]. The approach is especially useful when a device needs to work occasionally. Energy-aware system, routing and protocol designs are also widely performed researches [5,6,7,8,9]. Although many efforts have been conducted to reduce energy consumption for specific technology or individual device, the approach from the whole system viewpoint is insufficient.

Reducing standby power is an important and urgent issue for home appliance industry. Standby power means power dissipated while not performing the main function of a device. The power may be used only for waiting incoming commands or to accomplish side functions such as a clock and alarm. Reducing standby power under 1W for home appliances is becoming a world-wide trend. However, it is difficult to define standby status in home network systems because always-on connectivity is a prerequisite for them. Since the devices should be ready to work, there is a limitation in cutting down the standby power.

It is important that energy saving in home network systems should not harm the quality of services. The quality can be divided into two view points. One is the resulting service quality induced from the activity of a home network system. For example, to control the humidity of a home environment, there are few different ways to achieve the goal. They may turn on an air conditioner, activate a dehumidifier, turn on a heater or open a window to reduce the humidity. Such an approach is not considered in this work. The other view point is whether the system can respond to a command appropriately within an expected time. To solve this problem, home network devices are classified into groups based on their allowed latency. Then, an operation strategy is proposed to reduce energy consumption.

2 System Configurations

Figure 1 shows an example of typical home network systems, which consists of control devices, sensor devices, information appliances, data devices and AV devices. In general, control and sensor devices use relatively low electric power because they are designed for a single purpose and do not require high computing performance. Information and AV devices consume much higher energy than control and sensor devices because of their complex and advanced service nature. There are many different ways in connecting these devices to a home network system, and it is difficult to determine a single standard configuration because the environment is different case by case. A network medium is selected for each device based on the functional characteristics and industry trends in this research. For sensor nodes, battery-powered Zigbee is mostly selected. Since control devices usually require relatively high electric power when it works, AC power is directly supplied to the devices when needed while using Zigbee for communication. A low speed PLC is used for information appliances, and Ethernet is used for data and AV devices.

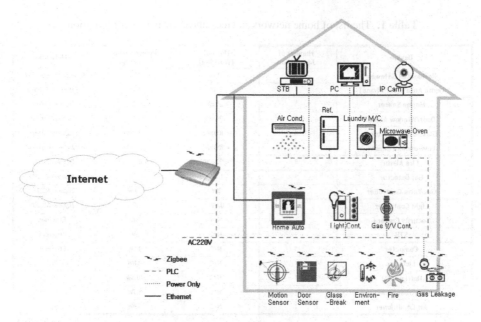

Fig. 1. A ubiquitous home network system configuration which consist of control devices, sensor devices, information appliances, data devices and AV devices

Table 1 shows the power consumption of each device in a ubiquitous home network system used in this research. Ubiquitous sensor network-based devices consume small amount of energy as well as power that ranges 25~1,500mW depending on their functions. On the other hand, information appliances consume high standby power when compared to home appliances without network connectivity. The electric power of home appliances used for normal operation (air conditioning, heating, washing, etc.) is not considered in this work because they are too big ranging 300~1,500W to see the effect of communications. The residential gateway and the home auto (door phone) use high standby power since they should work as communication and control hubs to accept incoming events and data.

The life of battery-powered devices has been regarded as one of the most critical issues because it is directly related to their maintenance. Therefore, efficient system design has been studied in many ways. Dynamic power management is a key approach in ubiquitous sensor networks to maximize the life of sensor nodes. To reduce power consumption, devices go to sleep mode during idle time. Much work has been done exploiting sleep state and active power management [3, 4].

High power consuming devices are essential to connect to the power line directly to obtain enough energy to perform their main functions. The ease of energy acquirement put the energy saving issues of those home network devices in the dead angle so far. Control devices with their own power suppliers are in the similar situation. Not enough efforts are made for those devices compared to battery-powered wireless devices. In this work, energy saving mechanism used for battery-powered wireless device is adopted.

Table 1. The list of home network devices and their power consumption

Device	Number of Installation	Normal (Working)	Power Saving (Waiting)	Network
Residential Gateway	1	15W	12W	Ethernet/Zigbee/PLC
Home Auto (Door Phone)	1	22W	15W	Ethernet/Zigbee
Motion Sensor	3	< 25 mW	< 0.1 mW	Zigbee/Battery
Door/Window Alarm	4	< 90 mW	< 0.1 mW	Zigbee/Battery
Glass-Break Detector	4	< 100 mW	< 0.1 mW	Zigbee/Battery
Environment Sensor	4	< 100 mW	<0.1 mW	Zigbee/Battery
Fire Alarm	3	< 30 mW	< 0.1 mW	Zigbee/Battery
Gas Detector	1	1.5W	1.5W	Zigbee/AC220V
Gas Valve Controller	1	3W	1.0W	Zigbee/AC220V
Light Controller	5	0.9W	0.9W	Zigbee/AC220V
Security Camera	1	12W	8W	Ethernet
STB	1	N/C	8W	Ethernet
Computer	1	N/C	2.3W	Ethernet
Laundry	1	N/C	8.8W	PLC
Refrigerator	1	N/C	10.6W	PLC
Microwave oven	1	N/C	5.7W	PLC
Air Conditioner	1	N/C	3.8W	PLC

N/C : Not Considered

3   System Analysis and Results

The functions of devices used in home networks are classified into 4 basic types depending on the nature of data that they generate or use. Event sources generate urgent signals that should affect to other home network systems immediately. Event sinks accept data generated from event sources, so they should be always ready to get data transferred from other nodes. Information sources generate data that may be important but not urgent, and information sinks accept data generated from information sources. The types can be represented as the latency sensitiveness in their services. Although devices developed to perform a singe function are easy to determine their types, some devices are difficult to be classified into a category because they may perform complex functions. Table 2 shows an example of types and corresponding devices.

Table 2. An example of device type classfications for home network devices

Type	Devices	Latency Sensitiveness
Event Source	Motion Sensor, Door/Window Alarm, Glass-Break Detector, Fire Alarm, Gas Detector	High
Data Source	Environment Sensor	Low
Event Sink	Gas Valve Controller, Light Controller	High
Data Sink	Laundry, Refrigerator, Microwave oven, Air Conditioner	Low
Data Hub	Residential Gateway, Home Auto	High

In real life, the device types can vary depending on the status of home, which is determined from given situations. The status can be represented with life modes such as *Stay*, *Going-out*, and *Sleeping*. In each mode, the types of devices can be differently defined. For example, a motion detector is important in *Sleeping* and *Going-out* modes to monitor unexpected intrusions. However, it may generate false alarm by the interference from the movements of family members in *Stay* mode. Therefore, the detector would be better to be used to collect and analyze life patterns in the mode. Although a light control needs to respond to commands immediately in *Stay* and *Sleeping* mode, slow response would not make a serious problem in *Going-out* mode. For that reason, the types of devices should be determined for each mode to set up appropriate power management strategies. Table 3 shows an example of devices and their types for given life modes.

Table 3. The types of devices corresponding to life modes

Device	Stay	Sleeping	Going-out
Residential Gateway	ESource, Esink, Dsource, Dsink	ESource, Esink, Dsource, Dsink	ESource, Esink, Dsource, Dsink
Home Auto (Door Phone)	Esource, Esink, Dsource	Esource, Esink, Dsource	Esource, Esink, Dsource
Motion Sensor	N/U	Esource	Esource
Door/Window Alarm	N/U	Esource	Esource
Glass-Break Detector	N/U	Esource	Esource
Environment Sensor	Dsource	Dsource	Dsource
Fire Alarm	Esource	Esource	Esource
Gas Detector	Esource	Esource	Esource
Gas Valve Controller	Esink	Dsink	Dsink
Light Control	Esink	Esink	Dsink
Security Camera	N/U	N/U	Dsink
STB	Dsource	Dsink	Dsink
Computer	Dsource	Dsink	Dsink
Laundry	Esink	Dsink	Dsink
Refrigerator	Esink	Dsink	Dsink
Microwave oven	Esink	Dsink	Dsink
Air Conditioner	Esink	Dsink	Dsink

N/U : Not Used

Battery-powered sensor nodes are energy efficient enough compared to other devices in this case. They generally consume less than 100mW and 0.1mW for working modes and power save modes, respectively, as shown in Table 1. When considering the standby powers of information appliances and IP devices that range 2~10W, the electric power used by sensor nodes are negligible. This does not mean that there is no room to be improved in energy management for sensor networks, but more efforts are required for other devices to reduce energy consumption. The home network system used in this work as it is consumes 2,019Wh per day. The electric energy is mostly used by IP devices and information appliances, which amounts 1,109Wh and 693.6Wh, respectively. Although IP devices spend 54% of entire energy, it is difficult to reduce the power consumption of IP devices because they serve as an event and data sink of the system providing network connectivity to the entire system. To receive all events and data generated by other devices without missing, some nodes should be awake all the time. Residential gateways and home auto devices usually do the work in home networks. Though other IP devices such as computers, STBs, and security cameras generally provide complex services, their roles are limited in home networks. Reducing energy consumptions of IP devices is an important issue because they use more than 50% of entire energy.

Information appliances are found to consume more energy than expected when comparing with home appliances which recently tend to be designed to use less than 1W for standby power. By using efficient network communication modules, it is possible to reduce the energy consumption for information appliances. In this example, the energy consumption becomes to 1,747Wh per day, and it is 13% in overall, and 30% without IP devices less than the original amount.

Then, sleeping mechanism is added to remove unnecessary energy waste. Except for some emergency cases, devices can provide the equivalent services without losing the service quality with small amount of response delay. Not to miss incoming events or commands, the devices can contact a service hub right after waking up, and check up incoming signals. Since latency is allowed to a certain degree except for the event sink devices, sleeping can be an effective tool in energy saving as proved in battery-powered wireless devices.

To analyze the energy consumption of the home network system, 3 life patterns are designed as shown in Fig 2. In pattern A, all family members stay outside during daytime. Pattern B and C represent families who spend more time at home than ones with pattern A.

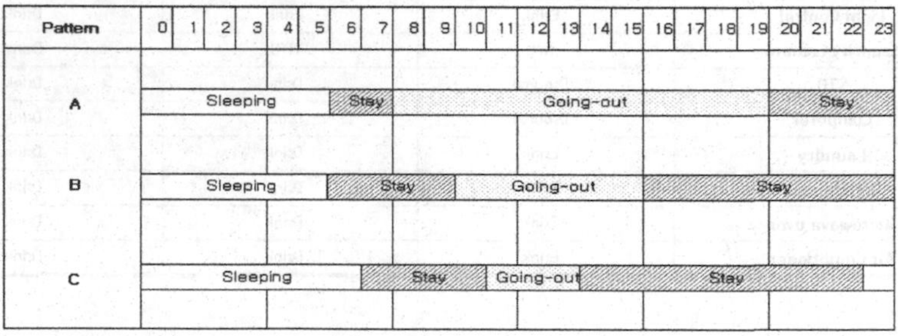

Fig. 2. Three life patterns are designed to analyze the power consumption of a home network system

Figure 3 shows the result of energy used in the home network system after applying two strategies for life pattern A. For the first step, efficient communication modules are applied to information appliances and control devices. This mainly decreased the energy used by information appliances. In the second step, the sleeping mechanism is applied and the energy consumption is decreased 31% of the original amount using 1,390Wh. Without considering IP devices, 70% of the original amount is diminished. The energy consumptions for life pattern B and C are obtained as 1,426Wh and 1,438Wh, respectively.

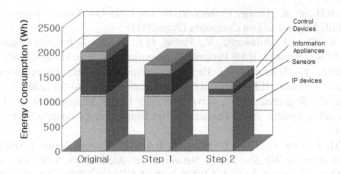

Fig. 3. The energy consumption per day of the selected home network system is shown. In step 1, network communication nodes are improved to be power efficient, and sleeping mechanism is added in step 2 for a life pattern *A* in Figure 2. Most reduction occurs in control devices and information appliances in this work.

Dependency trees among devices in a home network system are useful to make energy management policies. For example, VCR, STB, and DVD are usually dependent on TV, and monitors, printers and scanners are hardly used without computers. By using the relations, a hierarchical energy management can be designed.

4 Conclusions

In this work, a home network system is modeled and analyzed to figure out energy consumption characteristics. Since external electric power is provided to most devices in home networks, no much work has been done to save energy so far. Especially, IP devices and information appliances have much to be improved. Energy efficient hardware and sleeping mechanisms which are used for battery-powered wireless devices are expanded to other home network devices. Device types are classified for each life mode to reduce unnecessary communications, and the possibility of energy saving is shown.

References

1. Calhoun, B.H, Chandrakasan, A.P.: Standby Power Reduction Using Dynamic Voltage Scaling and Canary Flip-Flop Structures. IEEE Journal of Solid-State Circuits 39(9), 1504–1511 (2004)
2. IBM and MotaVista Software: Dynamic Power Management for Embedded System. Ver.1.1, IBM and MotaVista (November 19, 2002)
3. Brock, B., Rajamani, K.: Dynamic Power Managent for Embedded Systems. In: IEEE International System-On-Chip (SOC) Conference, pp. 416–419. IEEE Computer Society Press, Los Alamitos (2003)
4. Sinha, A., Chandrakasan, A.: Dynamic Power Management in Wireless Sensor Networks. IEEE Design and Test of Computers 19(2), 62–74 (2001)

5. Calhoun, B.H., et al.: Design Considerations for Ultra-low Energy Wirelss Microsensor Nodes. IEEE Transactions on Computers (June 2005)
6. Sohrabi, K., Gao, J., Ailawadhi, V., Pottie, G.J.: Protocols for Self-Organization of a Wireless Sensor Network. IEEE Personal Communications 7(5), 16–27 (2000)
7. Raghunathan, V., Schurgers, C., Park, S., Srivastava, M.B.: Energy-Aware Wireless Microsensor Networks. IEEE Personal Communications 7(2), 40–50 (2002)
8. Schurgers, C., Raghunathan, V., Srivastava, M.: Power Management for Energy-aware Communication System. ACM Transactions on Embedded Computing Systems 2(3), 431–447 (2004)
9. Heo, J., Yi, S., Park, G., Cho, Y., Hong, J.: EAR-RT: Energy Aware Routing with Real-Time Guarantee for Wireless Sensor Networks. In: Alexandrov, V.N., van Albada, G.D., Sloot, P.M.A., Dongarra, J.J. (eds.) ICCS 2006. LNCS, vol. 3991, pp. 946–953. Springer, Heidelberg (2006)

On-Chip Bus Architecture Optimization for Multi-core SoC Systems[*]

Cheng-Min Lien[1], Ya-Shu Chen[1], and Chi-Sheng Shih[2]

[1] Department of Computer Science and Information Engineering
[2] Graduate Institute of Networking and Multimedia
National Taiwan University, Taipei, Taiwan 106
cshih@csie.ntu.edu.tw

Abstract. With the significant driving force from the application domains, modern embedded systems are designed over heterogeneous multi-core SoC platforms. When more and more functions are integrated into one system, the designs of embedded systems have become more and more complicated. In particular, most of embedded multimedia applications are data intensive. Performance bottleneck are often caused by inappropriate bus architecture design within the system. In this paper, we present the algorithms for bus architecture optimization in MFASE. The algorithm takes the workloads in the system and their timing behavior requirements into account. The goal is to minimize the number of buses in the system without violating timing requirements. We prove that the minimzation problem is NP-hard and develop a heuristic algorithm. We evaluate the algorithm with extensive simulations. The performance results show that the algorithm reduce up to 80% of the bus cost and performs as well as optimal exponential algorithm does.

1 Introduction

Traditional system-level chip design aims at designing reliable single function systems or distributed embedded systems. Thanks to modern SoC platform, a multiple function system can be integrated onto a single chip. However, the design complexity exponentially grows as the number of functions on one chip increases. Traditional design approach is not suitable for such systems. Without proper system-level performance analysis tool and design tool, engineers rely on their experience of designing single function systems to design multiple function systems. The results are usually over-allocated resources such as bus, memory and processing elements. In addition, traditional design tools focus on the correctness of the systems. Timeliness of the systems is left for the application engineers and is ignored during system-level chip design. Traditional design method leads to great programming overhead and is not suitable for designing multi-function SoC systems.

[*] This work is supported in part by a grant from Academia Sinica Thematic program and part by a grant from the NSC program NSC 96-2752-E-002-008-PAE.

R. Obermaisser et al. (Eds.): SEUS 2007, LNCS 4761, pp. 301–310, 2007.
© IFIP International Federation for Information Processing 2007

The design of SoC can become very complex due to the variety of software and hardware system blocks that need to be integrated. Mobile phone is one example. As the market gets more competitive, more and more features such as motion video capability and audio playback are integrated in mobile phones. A new challenge is how to find a communication architecture between the cost and performance trade-off efficiently for the mobile phone venders. It is because that if all processing elements are on one bus, the execution of every processing element becomes sequential. The application may be fail due to the bus contention. To solve the problem, we can use multi-bus architecture to increase the parallelism of the system.

Figure 1 shows an example of multi-bus architecture which are connected through a bus bridge to exchange data between them. Each bus subsystem has two MPC755s [1] and a memory block. Both bus systems in Figure 1 can operate at the same time without bus contention. In this way, the system performance will increase. On the other hand, the cost of the

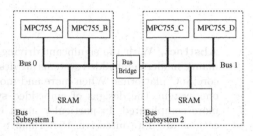

Fig. 1. An example of multi-bus architecture

system also increases because of additional bridge, memory and bus routing for bus subsystems.

In last few decades, many researches have focused on the SoC communication system-level synthesis problem [2,3]. In the paper, we are concerned with the bus architecture synthesis for SoC platform. We use a directed acyclic graph (DAG) to describe the software property including bus transaction, transaction time, precedence constraint and timing constraint. We also demonstrate that the proper selection of the communication architectures which based on multi-bus. For this, we schedule the bus transactions of input software for the different architecture and select one.

There are numerous advantage for conducting system level co-synthesis such as shortening the design time, manufacture cost, die size and power dissipation [4,5]. The researches in system level co-synthesis address on two main issues. The first issue is to optimize the selection and mapping of the system's functional blocks onto a set of processing elements (PE), like CPUs, digital signal processors (DSPs) and application-specific cores, etc [6,7]. The second issue is to optimize the communication architecture between the processing elements [8,9,10,11]. The separation between computation and communication enables the system designers to explore the communication architecture independently of processing elements selection and mapping. The focus of this paper lies on the second problem of the system level co-synthesis design.

The targeted issue in this paper is to systematically determine on-chip bus architecture so as to minimize chip cost subject to the real-time performance constraints. The algorithm is a greedy algorithm. It starts with a most expensive architecture to conduct the feasibility test for the given task set. When the real-time performance constraints are not met, the algorithm terminates. Otherwise, the algorithm iteratively evaluates the design and reduces the number of buses on the chip. It terminates when the real-time performance constraints cannot be met. In this paper, we use a more practical model for the SoC bus design. Both high-level bus transactions as well as the effect of shared memory accesses are considered.

The remainder of this paper is organized as follows: In Section 2, we present related work in on-chip bus communication synthesis and formally define the problem. A two steps heuristic algorithm was proposed for on-chip bus communication architecture synthesis in Section 3. Section 4 presents the performance evaluation results for the developed algorithms. Finally, Section 5 summaries the paper.

2   Background and Formal Model

Our work is related to several on-chip bus synthesis researches. In [10], Lahiri et al. presented an algorithm to find a communication architecture after the system has been partitioned. They focused on how to use a set of bus architectural templates to connect processing elements. To do so, the algorithm assumes that the bus topology is given. In this paper, we relax this assumption. Specifically, we are interested in how to synthesis the bus topology when the bus transactions are given based on system-level design analysis. In [9], Kim et al. presented the problem for finding the on-chip bus topology and the allocation of shared memories. The proposed exploration technique is a three steps algorithm. In the first step, they use a static performance estimation technique, proposed in [8], to quickly evaluate each candidate design and prune the design space. The second step is to scatter communication traffic in conflict on a bus into different buses to reduce conflict and maximize concurrency. For this purpose, the algorithm selects a processing element one at a time, allocates it to a new bus, and produces different share memory allocation. This step is time consuming, when the number of processing elements are large. The last step determines the priorities of each processing elements.

In [11], Pandey et al. formulate the problem from a different perspective. The given input is a hardware communication lifetime interval graph (CLTI.) In CLTI, it is assumed that the computation time for each processing element is a constant but the bus transaction time, depending on the bus width, is not a constant. The contribution of the paper is to find an optimal bus width which minimizes the bus contention, and then to optimize the on-chip bus topology. Unfortunately, many bus protocols such as AMBA only support fixed bus width. Hence, this approach is only applicable for custom designed bus architecture.

In the following, we define the terms used in this paper and define the problem of interests. *Processing element*, denoted by PE_k where k is no less than 0, is a CPU, DSP, or an ASIC in the system. A *Task* is a sequence of works such as computation and file access to complete certain function. Tasks are denoted by

T_1, T_2, etc. When a task needs to send or retrieve data from other components in the system such as memory or processing elements, it triggers a bus access request. When the bus is free, the task occupies the bus to send or retrieve data. Otherwise, it may wait till the request is granted by bus arbitrator. Namely, a *bus transaction* is a data transmission over bus by a task to other devices in the system. The bus transactions for task T_i are denoted by $BT_{i,1}$, $BT_{i,2}$, etc. In this paper, we assume that the execution of a bus transaction cannot be interrupted. A bus transaction fails when it is interrupted during its execution. A bus transaction is defined by two parameters: requesting PE and bus transaction interval. *Requesting PE* is a processing element on which the task starts the bus transaction, and *bus transaction interval* is the amount of time needed to complete the transaction. Bus transaction interval for bus transaction $BT_{i,j}$ is denoted by $BI_{i,j} \in \mathbb{Z}^+$. We assume that the length of all bus transaction intervals are known *a priori*. It is because the HW/SW partitioning result has given. *Precedence constraint* is the execution order of bus transactions. A bus transaction cannot start until all of its preceding bus transactions complete.

Bus transaction graph, denoted by $BTG = (V, E)$ where V and E is the set of vertex and edges, is a labeled directed acyclic graph. A vertex, denoted by $v_{i,j}$, represents bus transaction $BT_{i,j}$; A directed edge from $v_{i,j}$ to $v_{i,k}$, denoted by $e_{i,j,k}$, represents that bus transaction $BT_{i,j}$ is the preceding bus transaction for bus transaction $BT_{i,k}$.

While designing a system-on-chip, we are often interested in a set of tasks. Hence, we can present all the bus transactions for the set of tasks by a set of bus transactions. *Common relative deadline* for a set of bus transactions, denoted by $D \in \mathbb{Z}^+$, is the maximum allowable response time for any of the bus transactions. The set of bus transactions meet its timing constraint when all the bus transactions complete before the common deadline. The rationale of meeting timing constraint is to assure that the tasks can meet their real-time performance requirements. Example for the real-time performance requirements are the playback rates for multimedia player and sampling rate for audio recorder.

Local memory for a bus transaction means that the memory and requesting PE are on the same bus; *Remote memory* for a bus transaction menas that the memory and requesting PE are not on the same bus. Hence, when the bus transaction is executed, it will occupy at least two buses to access the memory. *Shared memory*, denoted by $SM_{i,j,k}$, represents a region of memory space for the data communication between bus transactions $BT_{i,j}$ and $BT_{i,k}$. When the bus transaction $BT_{i,j}$ is executing, the bus connected to the shared memory space is reserved for bus transaction $BT_{i,j}$ to access (i.e. read or write) the shared memory space. *Bridge* connects two buses such as AMBA AHB bus so that a processing element on one bus can access the memory on another bus. We assume that the bridges are programmable and can be set as open or close during the run-time. If a bridge is open, the two buses connected by the bridge can be simultaneously reserved by different PE in the same time. On the other hand, the two buses are linked together, they will be regard as one bus and simultaneously reserved by the same PE.

Communication architecture is based on multi-bus architecture. Every bus connects at least one processing element and exactly one memory. The different buses which are connected by bridges can be reserved by different processing elements concurrently. The more buses brings more concurrency and higher cost.

The bus architecture synthesis problem is defined as following.

Definition 1. *Given a set of bus transaction graphs* $G = \{BTG_1, BTG_2, ...BTG_N\}$ *and their common deadline D. The problem is to determine a communication architecture with the minimal number of buses subject so that the timing constraint is met.*

In the following, we use an example to illustrate the problem defined in Definition 1. Figure 2 shows the set of bus transaction graphs: BTG_0 and BTG_1. There are six bus transactions. The color and label of each vertex represent its requesting PE and bus transaction interval. For instance, $BT_{0,0}$ and $BT_{1,1}$ are requested by processing element PE_0 for 3 time units. In addition, bus transaction $BT_{1,1}$ and $BT_{1,2}$ can start only after bus transaction $BT_{1,0}$

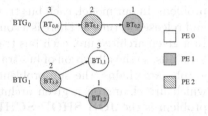

Fig. 2. An example of bus transaction graphs

completes, due to the precedence constraint. Figure 3 shows a communication architecture for the bus transaction graphs shown in Figure 2. This architecture uses two buses to connect three processing elements. The processing elements PE_0 and PE_2 are allocated on bus B_0 and PE_1 is allocated on bus B_1. The shared memory $SM_{0,0,1}$ and $SM_{1,0,2}$ is allocated on memory M_0. The shared memory $SM_{1,0,1}$ and $SM_{0,1,2}$ is allocated on memory M_1.

Given the communication architecture, we can find the bus transaction schedules. Figure 4(a) illustrates the schedule without shared memory. Figure 4(b) illustrates the schedule with shared memory. The blocks in the schedules represent the bus reservations. There are two kinds of bus reservations which caused by local memory access and shared memory access. For example, block $BT_{0,0}$ is a local memory access, so bus 0 is reserved for the temporary files I/O when bus transaction $BT_{0,0}$ is executing in the time interval 0 to 3. $SM_{1,0,1}$

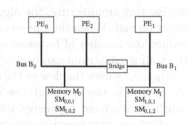

Fig. 3. An example communication architecture for BTG_0 and BTG_1

is a shared memory access between $BT_{1,0}$ and $BT_{1,1}$, so bus 1 is reserved for reading input data from the shared memory when bus transaction $BT_{1,1}$ is executing in the time interval 5 to 8. Similarly, bus 1 is reserved for writing output data to the shared memory when bus transaction $BT_{0,1}$ is executing in the time interval 3 to 5.

Our problem is to find a cost effective architecture with a bus transaction schedule which meets the timing constraint. We will show that the sub-problem

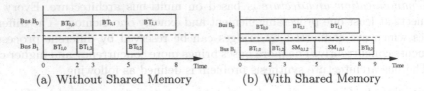

(a) Without Shared Memory   (b) With Shared Memory

Fig. 4. Bus Transaction Schedule Examples

to schedule the bus transaction graphs on a given architecture is a NP-complete problem. In our model, each bus transaction graph is a connected graph in DAG and released at time 0. There is a common deadline for all bus transaction graphs. In a given architecture, each bus transaction is scheduled to the requested PE's local bus, so the allocation of bus transactions are given. If all the bus transaction graphs are chains, the sub-problem is to schedule the bus transaction graphs which are chains on a given architecture. The special case of the scheduling problem is the **JOB SHOP SCHEDULING**[12] which is NP-complete. The special case of the sub-problem is a NP-complete problem, so the hardness of the problem we want to solve in this paper is also NP-complete at least.

3   On-Chip Bus Synthesis Algorithms Design

In this section, we present the heuristic to find near optimal bus architecture, *Greedy Bus Architecture Synthesis Algorithm (GBASA.)* The GBASA algorithm is an iterative algorithm and consists of three major steps. GBASA algorithm starts with the bus architecture in which each processing element is connected to one dedicated bus to conduct the feasibility analysis. If there is no feasible schedule for this architecture, the algorithm stops because the timing constraint will never be met. When the timing constraint can be met, the algorithm continues to reduce the number of buses so as to reduce the cost. The algorithm stops when the timing constraint can barely be met.

Figure 5 shows the flow of the proposed algorithm. In the first step, the algorithm synthesizes a most expensive architecture in which every processing element has its dedicated bus. The second step revises the initial architecture by scheduling the bus transactions. If the timing constraint cannot be met, the algorithm terminates and returns no feasible architecture. Otherwise, the third step chooses a pair of buses and merging them into one bus to reduce the cost. In order to shorten the finish time of the bus transaction graphs, the pair of buses which cause less effect

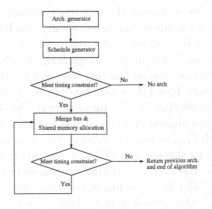

Fig. 5. Flow of GBASA Algorithm

to the finish time of the schedule is merged. After merging the bus pair, the algorithm returns to the second step to revise the architecture. If the timing constraint can be met, the third step tries to reduce cost again. On the contrary, the algorithm returns the last feasible architecture and terminates. In the following, we present the algorithm step by step.

Initial Communication Architecture Generation. The algorithm first adds processing elements to the initial communication architecture, and one memory and one dedicated bus for every processing element. Then, the algorithm checks every edge in the bus transaction graphs for examining the communications between processing elements. If there are bus transactions between any two processing elements, the algorithm adds a bridge between two dedicated buses. After this initiation, we will have a communication architecture with high concurrency and cost. It is because we

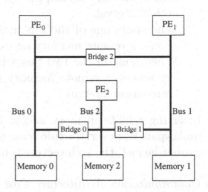

Fig. 6. The initial architecture

use as many memories and buses as we can. Again, take Figure 2 as the input of the algorithm. The algorithm *Initial Architecture Generator* generates the initial architecture which has three PEs with its own bus and memory. After initializing PE, bus and memory, we add a bridge for a pair of buses, if the two PEs on the two buses have to communicate to each other. The output of the algorithm is shown in Figure 6.

Architecture Evaluation. In the second step, the algorithm first conducts the feasibility test and considers the share memory allocation later.

To efficiently generate a schedule which has a short makespan, we use a heuristic instead of exhaustive search. Observing the given task set, we know that each bus transaction has its own release time[1], deadline, and is non-preemptive. The scheduling policy is to schedule the bus transaction which has longer residual execution time. The residual execution time of a bus transaction is the summation of all the successors' execution times. The rationale is that longer residual execution time implies that there are more bus transactions to be completed before the common deadline. We use the value to determine the importance of bus transactions. The time complexity of *Longest Successors' Execution Time First Algorithm* is $O(n^2)$. The algorithm is similar to the Least Slack Time First algorithm [13]. The difference is that each bus transaction does not have equal release time but has common deadline. When the requesting PEs for two consecutive bus transactions are located on different buses and need to exchange data, share memory is the most common mechanism to do so. However, more than one bus may be occupied to access a remote share memory. Hence, which memory

---

[1] Only the first bus transaction for every BTG, $BT_{i,1}$ for $i \geq 0$, has the same release time.

on one of the two buses is used for a share memory determine the makespan and cause deadline miss. After a feasible schedule is found in the above step, the algorithm determines the use of share memory. Three cases are considered:

- When both the schedule of the two buses have available time intervals for remote memory access, the algorithm selects the one with shorter bus transaction interval.
- When only one of the bus have available time interval for remote memory access, a remote memory access is inserted to the bus.
- When none of the two buses has available time intervals for remote memory access, a remote memory access is inserted to the bus for shorter bus transaction interval.

Inserting remote memory access in the first two cases does not prolong the makespan. However, the third case prolongs the makespan. If the timing constraint cannot be met, the architecture is not feasible and the algorithm terminates.

Communication Architecture Cost Down.
When the timing constraint is still met, the GBASA algorithm continues to reduce the number of buses in the design. The algorithm selects one of the bridges if there is any to remove. Two metrics, overlap time and precedence number, are used. The *overlap time* of a bridge is the sum of time intervals during which the two buses are occupied simultaneously. The *precedence number* of a bridge is the number of bus transactions to be removed due to

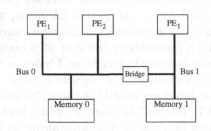

Fig. 7. The example architecture after one iteration

the remote memory access between the bus pair. First, we choose a set of bridges which have the same shortest overlap time. In the second step, we choose a bridge which has the largest precedence number. The rationale is that we merge the two buses which have less bus contention. By merging the bus pair, we can also reduce the additional bus transaction caused by shared memory access. By using this algorithm, we merge the bus pair bus B_0 and B_2. Figure 7 shows the new architecture after bridge remove. The new architecture will be evaluated by Step 2 for further cost down.

4   Performance Evaluations

We evaluate the performance of the GBASA algorithm by extensive simulations and compare its performance with the exponential branch and bound algorithm. Two metrics, *optimality* and *timing overhead time*, are measured to evaluate the performance. *Optimality* is the ratio of the number of buses selected by the GBASA algorithm to that selected by branch and bound algorithm. *Timing overhead* is the amount of time that the two algorithms take to complete their designs.

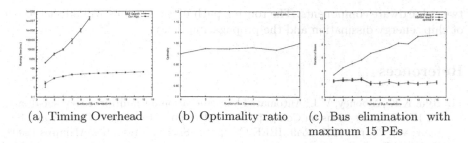

(a) Timing Overhead   (b) Optimality ratio   (c) Bus elimination with maximum 15 PEs

Fig. 8. Evaluation Results

The software environment of the experiments is *Ubuntu Linux Distribution* and *GNU GCC 4.0*. The hardware environment is a machine equipped *Intel Pentium III* 800 MHz and 128MB RAM. We evaluate our algorithm in different types of bus transaction graphs including DAG, tree and chain in order to simulate different types of applications. The transaction time are uniformly distributed in the range of 10 to 70. We compare the result of the GBASA algorithm to the worst case architecture and the optimal case architecture.

Figure 8(a) shows the timing overhead of the GBASA algorithm and B&B algorithm. The confidence interval of each data point in the figure is no less than 95%. The x-axis is the total number of bus transactions. The y-axis is the running time in milliseconds. As shown in the figure, the timing overhead of B&B search-based algorithm exponentially increases with the number of bus transactions. On the other hand, the timing overhead of GBASA algorithm slowly increases. Figure 8(b) shows the optimality of the GBASA algorithm. The figure shows that the GBASA algorithm performs as well as the branch and bound algorithm. Figure 8(c) shows how many redundant buses the GBASA algorithm eliminates, comparing to the worst design. A worst design is the one in which every processing element has its dedicated bus and memory. Figure 8(c) shows the results when there are 15 PEs. The results show that the GBASA algorithm performs as well as an optimal results and eliminates up to 80% of the buses from the worst design.

5 Conclusion and Future Work

In this paper, we presented a solution for on-chip bus synthesis for a system-on-a-chip (SoC) such that the communication cost if minimized subject to real-time performance constraints. We developed a three stages heuristic, GBASA algorithm, to synthesize on-chip bus design and shorten the makespan simultaneously. Performance evaluation results show that the GBASA algorithm reduces the run-time overhead and derive near-optimal solutions. For the future work, we can extend the communication architecture to the multi-layer bus architecture. It is because the multi-layer bus architecture can also provide higher concurrency. Another research direction is the routing path of the on-chip bus. The complex of SoC is still growing up. There will be more complex connection between hardware components. The routing path of on-chip bus will affect the size of chip, energy dissipation and the propagation delay.

References

1. Ryu, K.K., Mooney, V.J.: Automated bus generation for multiprocessor soc design. In: IEEE Transactions on Computer-Aided Design of Integrated Circuits and Systems, vol. 23, pp. 1531–1549. IEEE Computer Society Press, Los Alamitos (2004)
2. Wolf, W.H.: An architectureal co-synthesis algorithm for distributed, embedded computing systems. IEEE Transactions on Very Large Scale Integration Systems 5, 218–229 (1997)
3. Yen, T.Y., Wolf, W.: Performance estimation for real-time distributed embedded systems. IEEE Transactions on Parallel and Distributed Systems 9, 1125–1136 (1998)
4. Zhang, Y., Ye, W., Irwin, M.J.: An alternative architecture for on-chip global interconnect: Segmented bus power modeling. In: The Thirty-Second Asilomar Conference on Signals, Systems and Computers, November 1–4 1998, vol. 2, pp. 1062–1065 (1998)
5. Liveris, N.D., Banerjee, P.: Power aware interface synthesis for bus-based soc designs. In: Proceedings of the Design, Automation and Test in Europe Conference and Exhibition, Feburary 16–20, 2004, vol. 2, pp. 864–869 (2004)
6. Shirvaikar, M., Estevez, L.: Digital camera with jpeg, mpeg4, mp3 and 802.11 features. In: Workshop Presentation, Embedded Systems Conference, San Francisco, USA (2002)
7. Rim, M., Jain, R., Leone, R.D.: Optimal allocation and binding in high-level synthesis. In: Proceedings. 29th ACM/IEEE Design Automation Conference, 1992, June 8–12, 1992, pp. 120–123. IEEE Computer Society Press, Los Alamitos (1992)
8. Kim, S., Im, C., Ha, S.: Schedule-aware performance estimation of communication architecture for efficient design space exploration. In: First IEEE/ACM/IFIP International Conference on Hardware/Software Codesign and System Synthesis (October 1–3, 2003)
9. Kim, S., Im, C., Ha, S.: Efficient exploration of on-chip bus architectures and memory allocation. In: CODES+ISSS '04. Proceedings of the 2nd IEEE/ACM/IFIP international conference on Hardware/software codesign and system synthesis, pp. 248–253. ACM Press, New York (2004)
10. Lahiri, K., Raghunathan, A., Dey, S.: Design space exploration for optimizing on-chip communication architectures. IEEE Transactions on Computer-Aided Design of Integrated Circuits and Systems 23, 952–961 (2004)
11. Pandey, S., Glesner, M., Muhlhauser, M.: Performance aware on-chip communication syhthesis and optimization for shared multi-bus based architecture. In: ACM 17th Symposium on Integrated Circuits and Systems Design, ACM Press, New York (2005)
12. Garey, M.R., Johnson, D.S.: Computers and Intractability. W. H. Freeman and Company, New York (1979)
13. Dertouzos, M.L., Mok, A.K.: Multiprocessor online scheduling of hard-real-time tasks. IEEE Transactions on Software Engineering 15(12), 1497–1506 (1989)

An Effective Path Selection Method in Multiple Care-of Addresses MIPv6 with Parallel Delay Measurement Technique*

Jungwook Song, Heemin Kim, and Sunyoung Han**

Department of Computer Science and Engineering, Konkuk University
1 Hwanyang, Gwangjin, Seoul 143-701, Korea
{swoogi, procan, syhan}@konkuk.ac.kr

Abstract. In the Ubiquitous Society, there will be many types of mobile access network surrounding us and we can access the Internet anytime anywhere. At that time, mobile device can select several links from surrounded mobile access networks and access the Internet with multiple interfaces. We have already Mobile IPv6 protocol that supports mobility and try to extend to support multiple Care-of Addresses registration. But, we don't have any solution for selecting effective path. The effective path has many advantages such as reducing communication overhead. In this paper, we propose that effective path selection method in Multiple Care-of Addresses Mobile IPv6 environment with 'Parallel Delay Measurement' technique. With our technique, we can make down average packet delay.

1 Introduction

In the Ubiquitous Society, there will be many types of mobile access network surrounding us and we can access the Internet anytime anywhere. Nowadays, we can see that many types of devices keep contact to the Internet while moving their location. And there are many types of mobile access network services such as HSDPA(High Speed Downlink Packet Access), IEEE 802.16e mobile WiMAX(WIBRO in KOREA), and IEEE 802.11 Hotspots. HSDPA and mobile WiMAX are supporting high speed movement of mobile devices and IEEE 802.11 Hotspots support connection to the Internet in many public areas.

The network layer protocol is very important as the mobile access network. We have already standardized mobility support protocol that is Mobile IPv6[1]. According to the current Mobile IPv6 specification, a mobile node may have several care-of addresses, but only one, termed the primary Care-of Address, can be registered with its Home Agent and the Correspondent Nodes. However, for matters of cost, bandwidth, delay, etc., it is useful for the mobile node to get Internet access through multiple access media simultaneously, in which case multiple active IPv6 Care-of Addresses would be assigned to the mobile node. So,

---

* This research was supported by the 'Seoul R&D Program'.
** Corresponding author.

R. Obermaisser et al. (Eds.): SEUS 2007, LNCS 4761, pp. 311–318, 2007.

IETF(Internet Engineering Task Force) Monami6 Working Group try to extend exists Mobile IPv6 protocol standard to support multiple Care-of Addresses registration[2].

Many type of Adapters for mobile access network will become more cheaper and smaller. So, the Mobile devices can access multiple link to the Internet with multiple adapters and register multiple Care-of Addresses with MCoA-MIPv6(Multiple Care-of Addresses Mobile IPv6). Not the less, there is no proper solution for selecting effective path(link) to the Home Agent or the Correspondent Nodes. There are many disadvantages cause of non-effective path.

In this paper, we propose the solution for selecting effective path in MCoA-MIPv6 using 'Parallel Delay Measurement' technique. With our method, the Mobile Node and its Home Agent and the Correspondent Nodes can select effective path and we can reduce the communicating overhead.

The rest of the paper is organized as follows. Section 2 describes the path selection problem of MCoA-MIPv6. Section 3 describes the 'Parallel Delay Measurement' technique. Section 4 shows the result of analysis and concluding remarks are in Section 5.

2   Path Selection Problem of MCoA-MIPv6

2.1   Current Problem

The Mobile Node can have multiple interfaces and many types of mobile access network can be overlapped. So, it is needed that multiple Care-of Addresses registration for effectiveness and redundancy. Fig. 1 shows two sample configurations in the middle of overlapped mobile access networks.

Let's assume the CoA1(mobile access network associated with the Care-of Address1) has biggest bandwidth, minimum cost and minimum delay(different from one-way delay or round trip time to the Home Agent or to the Correspondent Nodes), it is natural that MN(Mobile Node) chooses CoA1 as the prime link to access the Internet, and it is reasonable in case (a) of Fig. 1. But in case

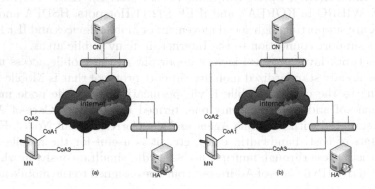

Fig. 1. Sample Configuration

(b) of Fig. 1, we can easily guess that CoA2 is better than CoA1 when MN communicating with CN(Correspondent Node) and CoA3 is better than CoA1 when MN communicating with HA(Home Agent).

There are no functions that can measure whole path quality of communication parties in the MCoA-MIPv6, and they are actually needed. The Mobile Node just grades links and sets priority values to the Binding Unique Identifier sub-option and the Correspondent Node refers to this priority values for selecting effective path of communication. That priority values represent only link specific characters, but communicating parties actually need path specific characters.

2.2   Current Implementations of MCoA

The SHISA is an implementation of Mobile IPv6 which supports MCoA. The WIDE project had developed two different Mobile IPv6 through the KAME project (KAMEMIP) and through the internetCAR project(SFCMIP). They finally decided to work together for single implementation (called SHISA) in the WIDE project on spring 2004. The SHISA support RFC3775, RFC3776, RFC3963, RFC4584, draft-wakikawa-mobileip-multiplecoa-05 and draft-momose-mip6-mipsock-00[3,4,5].

The NEPL NEMO Platform for Linux is the NEMO(NEtwrok MObility) implementation based on the MIPL2 architecture. This is another implementation of supporting MCoA[6,7].

3   Parallel Delay Measurement Technique

In this section, we describe the 'Parallel Delay Measurement' technique for effective path selection in MCoA-MIPv6. We can measure one-way delay with addition of the Binding Timestamp sub-option to the MCoA-MIPv6[2]. From this one-way delay and exist priority values of the Binding Unique Identification sub-option, we can select effective path and reduce communicating overhead. And we also can be adapted to variation of link status through binding refreshment mechanism of MIPv6. Some modification to MCoA-MIPv6 are required to support parallel delay measurement technique.

3.1   Binding Timestamp Sub-option

To measure one-way delay, the Mobile Node must add timestamp information to its own Binding Update message. If needed, the Binding Timestamp sub-option is included in the Binding Update, Binding Acknowledgement, and Binding Refresh Request messages. Fig. 2 shows the format of the Binding Timestamp sub-option that we newly define in this paper. When the Mobile Node sends Binding Update message with the Binding Unique Identifier sub-option and the Binding Timestamp sub-option, the Priority/Status field in the Binding Unique Identifier sub-option can be set to specific value from the MCoA-MIPv6 or set to zero for entrusting selecting path to the Correspondent Node.

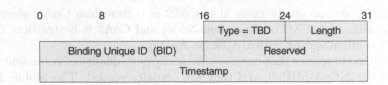

Fig. 2. Binding Timestamp sub-option

- Type
  Type value for Binding Timestamp sub-option will be assigned later.
- Length
  8-bit unsigned integer. Length of the option, in octets, excluding the Type and Length fields. This field must be set to 4.
- Binding Unique ID (BID)
  The BID which is assigned to the binding carried in the Binding Update with this this sub-option. BID is 16-bit unsigned integer. A value of zero is reserved[2].
- Reserved
  8 bits reserved field. Reserved field must be set with all 0.
- Timestamp
  32-bit unsigned integer. This value can be retrieved from normal C library function.

3.2 Parallel Binding Update

In MCoA-MIPv6, the Mobile Node has multiple interfaces and has multiple links to the Internet. So, the Mobile Node has multiple Care-of Addresses and sends the Binding Update messages to the Home Agent and to the Correspondent Nodes per each care-of address[2]. In our method, when the Mobile Node sends the Binding Update messages, it sends all binding information of all Care-of Addresses simultaneously as possible. The Timestamp field in the Binding Timestamp sub-option must be set as the value of the Binding Update message creation time. So, all Timestamp values are slightly different. When the Mobile Node receives the Binding Refresh Request message, it must send all binding information of each Care-of Address at the same time with Binding Timestamp sub-option.

And, when sending Binding Update messages, the Mobile Node sets all TTL(Time To Live) value of the IPv6 header belong the Binding Update messages as the same value. From this small technique, we can easily measure the difference of the hop count of each path.

3.3 Selecting Effective Path on the Home Agent and the Correspondent Node

In MCoA-MIPv6, the Mobile Node determines priorities of each Care-of Address and sends that to the Home Agent and the Correspondent Nodes with the Binding Unique Identifier sub-option[2]. In our method, priorities are synthetically determined by the Mobile Node, the Home Agent and Correspondent Nodes. Whenever the Home Agent receives the Binding Update message with Binding Unique Identifier sub-option and Binding Timestamp sub-option, gets its own timestamp at that time and calculates difference between the Binding Timestamp and its own timestamp. This difference value is the one-way delay. The Home Agent could get minimum one-way delay and gives higher priority value to that binding information. It is not need global timestamp or absolute one-way delay, we need just relative one-way delay. We could assume that relatively small one-way delay means small packet delay. The Correspondent Nodes determine priorities same as the Home Agent.

Because the Mobile Node sets all TTL values as the same value, we can easily measure the difference of the hop count of each path. When the Home Agent receives Binding Update messages, retrieves final TTL values from messages and decides maximum and minimum final TTL value. The smaller final TTL value means the bigger hop count and the bigger final TTL value means the smaller hop count. Thus, the maximum final TTL value means the shortest path.

From these two factor, one-way delay and final TTL value, we could calculate new priority value P_{NEW} as following equation.

$$P_{NEW} = \alpha P_{MN} + \beta \Delta TTL - \gamma Delay$$

P_{MN} means the priority value from the Mobile Node, ΔTTL means difference between final TTL value and minimum final TTL value and $Delay$ means the one-way delay value. α, β and γ are positive weight values that will be determined with real experiment.

3.4   Selecting Effective Path on the Mobile Node

When the Home Agent and Correspondent Node receive the Binding Update message and if that is correct, they send the Binding Acknowledgement

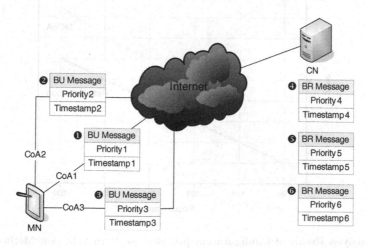

Fig. 3. Parallel Delay Measurement

message[2]. At that time, in our method, they send the Binding Acknowledgement messages with Binding Timestamp sub-option. Then the Mobile Node receives the Binding Acknowledgement messages, calculates one-way delay and determines priorities.

Fig. 3 shows brief sequence of the parallel delay measurement technique.

❶ ~ ❸ MN sends the BU messages to CN with priorities and Timestamps.
❹ ~ ❻ CN replies BR messages to MN priorities and Timestamps.

4 Analysis

To analyze effectiveness of our method, we consider two cases of one scenario. The scenario is that the Mobile Node has three network connection and exchange one thousand messages with the Correspondent Node through the highest priority path. We take the 'tic-toc' model as exchanging messages, the Mobile Node sends a 'tic' message and the Correspondent Node receives 'tic' and reply with a 'toc' message. This is one sequence and repeat five hundred times. Totally they exchange one thousand messages.

The first case of the scenario, the Correspondent Node is plain IPv6 node, therefore the Mobile Node and the Correspondent Node can't optimize the routing path of packets. The second case of the scenario, the Correspondent Node is MIPv6 enabled node, therefore the Mobile Node and the Correspondent Node can optimize the routing path of packets.

And, we consider two network configurations as shown in Fig. 1. We assume that the average delays of each link as follows: CoA1 → 2ms, CoA2 → 3ms, CoA3 → 5ms and internet cloud → 10ms. We don't need to consider the other

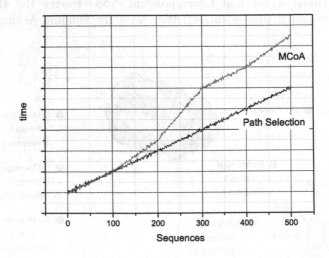

Fig. 4. Analysis Result of Configuration (a). Because Path Selection Method always could select better path, its performance is better.

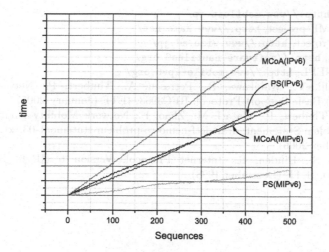

Fig. 5. Analysis Result of Configuration (b). Even if the Correspondent Node is not MIPv6 enabled, the path selection(PS) method is better.

link, because other link will any affect to the result. The delays of each link can be changed suddenly while exchanging messages, because the Mobile Node can moving. We assume that delays of each link rotate when after exchanging every 100th message. Fig. 4 and Fig. 5 show the results.

5   Concluding Remarks

In this paper, we proposed an effective path selection method in MCoA-MIPv6 with 'Parallel Delay Measurement' technique. To measure one-way delay, we defined new sub-option called the Binding Timestamp sub-option and through one-way delay, we could maximize the efficiency of communication between the Mobile Node and the Home Agent or the Correspondent Nodes.

We are building NGN(Next Generation Network) for the Ubiquitous Computing environment. The NGN has huge bandwidth compared with the present Internet. But, if hundreds of or thousands of application services for Ubiquitous Network are deployed, it will become crowded same as the present situation. So, we need the solution that maximize the utilization of the network. We believe that our method can contribute to increasing effectiveness of the network usage. We need more researches on context adaptive measurement method.

References

1. Johnson, D., Perkins, C., Arkko, J.: Mobility Support in IPv6: RFC3775, IETF (June 2004)
2. Wakikawa, R., Ernst, T., Nagami, K.: Multiple Care-of Addresses Registration: draft-ietf-monami6-multiplecoa-01.txt, IETF Draft (October 2006)

3. SHISA, http://www.mobileip.jp/
4. The KAME project, http://www.kame.net/
5. WIDE Project, http://www.wide.ad.jp/
6. Nautilus, http://software.nautilus6.org/
7. MIPL, NEPL, http://www.mobile-ipv6.org/
8. Devrapalli, V., Wakikawa, R., Petrescu, A., Thubert, P.: Network Mobility (NEMO) Basic Support Protocol: RFC3963, IETF (January 2005)
9. Ng, C., Thubert, P., Watari, M., Zhao, F.: Network Mobility Route Optimization Problem Statement: draft-ietf-nemo-ro-problem-statement-03.txt, IETF Draft (September 2006)
10. Deering, S., Hinden, R.: Internet Protocol, Version 6 (IPv6) Specification: RFC2460, IETF (December 1998)

Self-organizing Resource-Aware Clustering for Ad Hoc Networks

Tales Heimfarth, Peter Janacik, and Franz J. Rammig

Heinz Nixdorf Institute, University of Paderborn
Fuerstenallee 11, 33102 Paderborn, Germany
{tales,pjanacik,franz}@uni-paderborn.de

Abstract. This paper proposes an efficient heuristic for solving the *minimum-intracommunication clustering* problem in energy- and resource-constrained ad hoc networks. The heuristic organizes the network in clusters aiming to minimize a given cost function. The function used measures the total communication cost between all nodes within the cluster, keeping a minimum amount of resources per cluster.

The clusterhead selection of the proposed heuristic is based on the division of labor encountered in social insects. The idea is that each node has probabilistic tendencies to assume a determined role in the network. For example, nodes with good connectivity and high energy level are good candidates for being clusterheads. The probability of assuming a determined role is based on a node's fitness for the specific role and the actual *necessity* (reflected by stimulus) of the role in the current network context. After becoming clusterhead, a node starts recruiting members in order to reach a minimum amount of resources that have to be available in the cluster. The procedure is based on a membership fitness function that evaluates the suitability of a node for the cluster.

The realized simulations demonstrate that the proposed heuristic performance was about in average 25% inferior to the global optimum.

1 Introduction

Wireless ad hoc networks enable a myriad of novel applications ranging from human-embedded sensing to ocean data monitoring. Given current hardware limitations of wireless nodes, e.g. commercial off-the-shelf sensor nodes, approaches for the management of ad hoc networks have to be designed to function using only a low amount of resources and communication overhead.

In general, there are two heuristic design approaches for management of ad hoc networks at different levels (e.g. topology control, network layer, application). The first method is to have all nodes maintain knowledge of the network and manage themselves. This encurse a large amount of overhead. An alternative is to *clustering* the nodes, identifying a subset of nodes, and vest them with the extra responsibility of being a leader (clusterhead) of certain nodes in their proximity. The aim of this approach is to reduce communication and memory overhead.

In this paper, we present a new heuristic to organize an ad hoc network into clusters. Our proposal addresses the problem of partitioning the nodes of the

R. Obermaisser et al. (Eds.): SEUS 2007, LNCS 4761, pp. 319–328, 2007.

network in multi-hop groups with a guaranteed minimum amount of resources q in each one of them. This kind of clustering is useful in various scenarios. An example is the operating system (OS) we are currently developing in our research group, called NanoOS [1].

NanoOS is a small distributed OS for sensor networks. In order to provide more functionality on hardware constrained nodes, we are distributing the OS and application services among the nodes of the network. We use the heuristic presented here to organize the network in clusters. After this, each OS and application instance (a set of services) is distributed inside one cluster. We set the resource requirement (q) to the worst-case resource utilization of one instance of the OS and application. Therefore, it is guaranteed that each cluster has enough resources for an instance of our distributed OS.

This paper is organized as following: Section 2 reviews the state-of-the-art in clustering algorithms for ad hoc networks. Section 3 describes the proposed architecture, before Section 4 discusses simulation results. Finally, Section 5 presents the conclusions.

2 Related Work

There are several clustering algorithms that aim to find the *Maximum independent set* (MIS) of a network modeled as an undirected graph. This is often combined with the *dominance* property, which means that the following properties should be satisfied: independence (no two clusterheads can be neighbors) and dominance (every ordinary node has at least a clusterhead as direct neighbor). There are several algorithms that satisfy these properties ([2,3,4,5,6]). Different from our approach, they result in a 1-hop distance to the clusterheads of clusters.

Several approaches have been proposed for multi-hop clustering with different construction objectives. Here we have the *Max-Min D-Cluster Formation* [7] that aims to construct the cluster with nodes at most d hops away from the clusterhead.

Other heuristics that pursue different objectives are the *Budget Approach* [8] which tries to divide the ad hoc network in a set of clusters whose size is close to a given one. Beyond this, the *Upper and under bound approach* [9] works with superior and inferior size limits. It tries to construct clusters that respect these limits. Nevertheless, the approach allows a small overlap among the clusters.

In contrast to above heuristics, our clustering algorithm pursues a different objective: all clusters should posess a minimum amount of resources (i.e., the under bound limit is not given by a size in nodes, but by an amount of resources), and we try to minimize the internal cluster communication cost. This will be discussed in detail in the next sections.

3 The *Minumum-Intracommunication Clustering* Problem

In this section, a formal definition of our clustering problem (we call it *minumum-intracommunication clustering*) is described.

The ad hoc network is modeled by an undirected graph $G = (V, E)$, where V is the set of wireless nodes and an edge $\{u, v\} \in E$ if and only if a communication link is established between nodes $u \in V$ and $v \in V$. Each node $v \in V$ has a unique identifier (ID_v).

For each link, a weighting function attributes a positive weight $w : E \rightarrow [0, 1]$ that represents the quality of a wireless link. In the work [10], we presented a method to estimate the quality of a wireless link based on our combined metric. We call this metric *virtual distance* and smaller values represent better connection links. We define for each edge not in the graph $(\{u, v\} \notin V)$, $w(u, v) = \infty$.

For each node, an additional weighting function r is responsible to characterize the amount of resources available in the node. $r : E \rightarrow \Re^*$. This models the resource capacity of the node.

We aim to create multihop clusters with a minimum amount of resource per cluster minimizing the intra-cluster communication cost.

The considered optimization problem is modeled as follows:

Input: A graph with weighted nodes and links (G, w, r) and a resource requirement $q \in \Re^*$ that must hold in each cluster

Constraints: For every input instance (G, w, r, q), $\mathcal{M}(G, w, r, q) = \{C_1, C_2, .., C_k | C_k$ is the kth cluster configuration, where the following proprieties holds $\}$

$C_k = \{c_{k1}, c_{k2}, .., c_{k(nk)}\}$ is the kth possible cluster configuration of the graph, where $k = \{1, 2, .., n\}$ (n is the number of possible configurations, nk is the number of clusters in the kth configuration, $nk = \#C_k$)

$c_{ki} = \left\{v_{ki}^1, v_{ki}^2, .., v_{ki}^{\#c_{ki}}\right\} \in Pot(V)$ is the ith cluster of the kth configuration,

where v_{ki}^j is the jth element of the cluster c_{ki}

For each configuration C_k, $k = 1, 2, .., n$, the following proprieties must hold:

1. $\bigcup_{i=1,2,..,nk} c_{ki} = V$ (cluster definition constrain)
2. $\bigcap_{i=1,2,..,nk} c_{ki} = \emptyset$ (no overlapping constraint)
3. Let $P(u, v) = \left\{p_1^{(u,v)}, p_2^{(u,v)}, .., p_m^{(u,v)}\right\}$ be the set of all possible paths between nodes u and v. $p_h^{(u,v)} \in Pot(E)$ is the hth possible path where $p_h^{(u,v)} = \{\{u, x_1^h\}, \{x_1^h, x_2^h\}, .., \{x_{g-1}^h, x_g^h\}, \{x_g^h, v\}\}$, $x_f^h \in V$, $f = 1, 2, .., g$, $g \in I\!N$

   For each $\{u, v\} \in E \wedge u, v \in c_{ki}$, $i = 1, 2, ..., nk$, $\exists p_h^{(u,v)} \in P(u, v) | x_f^h \in c_{ki}$ for $f = 1, 2, .., g$. (Connectivity constraint)
4. $\sum_{j=1}^{\#c_{ki}} r(v_{ki}^j) \geq q$, for each $i = 1, 2, ..., nk$ (minimum amount of resource per cluster)

Costs: For every cluster configuration $C_k = \{c_{k1}, c_{k2}, .., c_{k(nk)}\} \in \mathcal{M}(G, w, r, q)$, the cost is $cost(C_k, (G, w, r, q)) = \sum_{i=1}^{nk} \sum_{u,v \in c_{ki}} D_{c_{ki}}(u, v) \cdot (\alpha \cdot r(u) + (1 - \alpha))$, where $D(u, v)$ is the virtual distance between $u, v \in V$. $D_{c_{ki}}(u, v)$ is the virtual distance between u, v using the shortest path that includes just links that are inside the cluster c_{ki} (sum of the link weights of the shortest path inside the cluster) . $\alpha \in [0, 1]$ controls how much the amount of resources influences the distance metric. For $\alpha = 0$, just the distances between cluster members are incorporated into the metric; $\alpha = 1$ means that nodes with n times more resources have an n times stronger influence.

$$PCost(p_h^{(u,v)}) = w(u, x_1^h) + \sum_{f=1}^{g-1} w(x_f^h, x_{f+1}^h) + w(x_g^h, v)$$

$$D(u,v) = PCost(p_h^{(u,v)}), \text{ where } PCost(p_h^{(u,v)}) = \min\left(PCost(p_b^{(u,v)})\right) \text{ for}$$

$$b = 1, 2, .., m \; D_{c_{ki}}(u,v) = PCost(p_h^{(u,v)}), \text{ where } p_h^{(u,v)} \in P(u,v)|x_f^h \in c_{ki}$$

and $PCost(p_h^{(u,v)}) = \min\left(PCost(p_b^{(u,v)})\right)$ for $b = 1, 2, .., m$

Goal: *Minimum* (i.e. $min\{cost(C_k, (G, w, r)) \mid \text{for } k = 1, 2, .., n\}$)

It is important to note that we are trying to minimize the sum of the link costs over all clusters. In each cluster, this cost is given by the sum of the link costs from every node to all other ones.

4 Emergent Clustering

The heuristic presented aims to find good clustering configuration in a network with a low amount of mobility. It reacts by stronger changes through re-execution.

4.1 Clusterhead Selection

In the initial state, all nodes of the network are ordinary nodes, i.e., there is no cluster structure in the network. The variable $state_v$ describes the actual state of a node v ($state_v \in \{CH, Me, Nm\}$) and c_i is set of the current members of the cluster $i \in \mathbb{N}$. For the sake of simplicity, we define that $clusterID = i$. Initially, for $i = 0, 1, .., n$, $c_i =$. The response function $T_{\theta_{CH_v}}(s_{CH_v}) = \frac{s_{CH_v}^\beta}{s_{CH_v}^\beta + \theta_{CH_v}^\beta}$ is responsible for the transition from an ordinary (Nm) node $v \in V$ to clusterhead. θ_{CH_v} is the threshold of the node v to become clusterhead and s_{CH_v} is the stimulus of v to assume the clusterhead role.

The threshold indicates how appropriate a node is for a role. Smaller θ_{CH_v} means that the node v is very well suited to carry out the role of a clusterhead. The definition of the threshold can be seen in (1).

$$\theta_{CH_v} = k_1 \left(\frac{\sum_{u \in Ngb_{Nm}(v)} w(u,v)}{\#Ngb_{Nm}(v)}\right) + k_2(1 - E_v) + k_3 \left(1 - \frac{\#Ngb_{Nm}(v)}{Max\_Nm}\right) \quad (1)$$

Where $E_v \in (0, 1)$ describe the energy level of the node v, such that 1 means the battery is full and 0 that it is depleted. Let $Ngb(v)$ be the set of nodes that are directly connected with v, i.e. $u \in Ngb(v)$ iff $\{u, v\} \in E$. A node u is in the set $Ngb_{Nm}(v)$ iff $u \in Ngb(v)$ and $state_u = Nm$. This means that $Ngb_{Nm}(v)$ is the set of neighbors of v that do not yet belong to any cluster.

The idea of this threshold function is that nodes with high energy level and high connectivity are good candidates for becoming elected as clusterhead. The energy is an important factor because clusterheads assume administrative (among other) tasks within the cluster and have a special status in the network. Good connectivity comes from the greedy assumption that starting a cluster from well-connected nodes will result in a relatively small clustering cost.

The stimulus function is given (for $k_1 + k_2 = 1$) by $s_{CH_v} = k_1 \frac{t_{elapsed}}{t_{required}} +$ $k_2 \left(1 - \frac{Ngb_{Me}(v) + Ngb_{CH}(v)}{Ngb(v)}\right)$. The elapsed time is $t_{elapsed}$ and $t_{required}$ is the maximum running time of the algorithm.

A node u is in the set $Ngb_{Me}(v)$ iff $u \in Ngb(v)$ and $state_u = Me$. Similarly, $u \in Ngb_{CH}(v)$ iff $u \in Ngb(v)$ and $state_u = CH$. With simple words, $Ngb_{Me}(v)$ is the set of neighbors of v that are members of some cluster. $Ngb_{CH}(v)$ is the set of neighboring nodes that are already clusterheads.

The underlying idea is that nodes that are not belonging to any cluster for a longer period of time and nodes without clusters in their vicinity should have a higher stimulus to become clusterhead. With the response function given by $T_{\theta_{CH_v}}(s_{CH_v})$, spontaneously, some nodes will start to change the role to clusterhead based on the stimulus function. When a node decides to be clusterhead, it selects a random *ClusterID*.

4.2   Members Selection

Influencing parameters. During membership selection by the clusterheads the following paramenters help to evaluate the suitability of a node b:

1. *The distance to the closest node already in the cluster*: This parameter helps to reduce the communication cost within the cluster. It is given by $D_{c_i}^b = min\{w(b,e) | e \in Ngb(b) \cap c_i\}$, i.e., the smallest vertice weight that is adjacent to node b and to a member of the cluster c_i. If a node is not directly connected to a cluster member, $D_d^{c_i} = \infty$.

2. *The distance to the clusterhead*: This parameter is responsible for shaping the cluster in order to constrain its diameter.

3. *Connectivity to nonmembers*: This parameter is important when there is a lot of resources still missing in the cluster. Given by $Cn_{Nm}^b = \sum_{e \in Ngb_{Nm}(b)} (1 - w(b,e))$, i.e., the sum of the "proximity" $(1 - w(b,e))$ of the set of the neighbors of b that have nonmember status. Figure 1 illustrates the effect of this term.

4. *Connectivity to members of the cluster*: This parameter helps to reduce the communication cost within the cluster. It is given by $Cn_{c_i}^b = \sum_{e \in \{Ngb(b) \cap c_i\}} (1 - w(b,e))$ where c_i is the current set of members of the cluster $i \in I\!N$.

5. *The resource availability of the node*: Aim of communication cost reduction based on the idea that nodes with higher resource availability will reduce the cost of the cluster to a greater extent since fewer of them are needed.

These aspects will be explicitly or implicitly considered by the *Membership-Select* algorithm presented here.

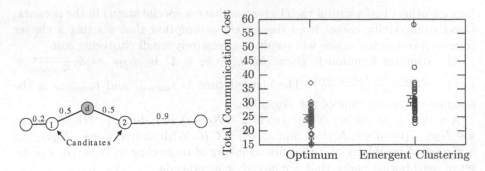

Fig. 1. Example of two candidates with different neighborhood

Fig. 2. Resulting communication cost of a randomly-placed wireless network using the signal strength as link metric. For this trial, $q = 3$ was used.

Membership-Select algorithm. For the membership selection, we use the $state_v$ variable describing the actual state of a node v with an additional state: the deciding (Dd) state $(state_v \in \{CH, Me, Nm, Dd\})$. Let Δq be the amount of additional resources needed by a cluster in order to fulfill the requirement q at a certain point of time. The *Membership-Select* algorithm is an incremental process, i.e., at beginning, the cluster has just the clusterhead (CH) node and during the clustering process, more and more nodes are added until the cluster achieves an appropriate size ($\sum_{v \in c_i} r(v) \geq q$). At the beginning of the clustering process of the cluster i, just one node belongs to the cluster: the clusterhead. We will call it node h_i ($h_i \in c_i, state_h = CH$). When a node becomes part of the cluster (including the clusterhead), immediately a message is broadcasted to the neighboring nodes signalizing the new status and requesting new members (Call_Members message). Each nonmember and deciding node d ($status_d \in \{Nm, Dd\}$) that receives this message changes its state to deciding ($status_d = Dd$).

Deciding nodes are the potential new members of the cluster. Nevertheless, not all nodes are the best choice to be included into the cluster. In order to privilege nodes potentially contributing to a low global cluster cost, each node b in the decision state estimates its own fitness value $0 \leq Fitness^b_{c_i} \leq 1$. This value will be defined later. $Fitness^b_{c_i}$ describes the suitability of the inclusion of node $b \in V$ into the cluster c_i.

At this point, the node b waits using a delay which is proportional to the $1 - Fitness^b_{c_i}$ value. When the waiting time has elapsed, the node sends a Membership_Request message to the clusterhead, informing it that it is willing to be included into the cluster. Now the clusterhead, based on Δq and the availability of resources of the candidate, can decide whether the node will be accepted as member. If accepted, the clusterhead includes the new node in a table with all members of the cluster. A message is sent back to the node confirming/refusing the entrance into the cluster. When receiving the response message, the requester changes its status accordingly ($state_b = Me$, if accepted and $state_b = Nm$ if refused). If accepted, this new status is broadcasted immediately

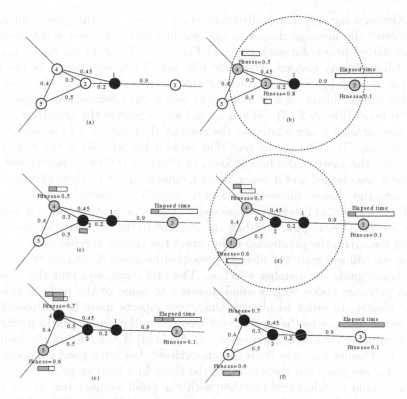

Fig. 3. Example of member selection in a partial network. All nodes have unitary amount of resource ($r(b) = 1, b \in V$) and $q = 3$.

$$Fitness_{c_i}(v) =$$
$$= \begin{cases} 1 - \left(k_1 \cdot D_{c_i}^v + k_2 \cdot min\{\frac{D(v, Clusterhead_{c_i})}{Max\_dist}, 1\} + \\ +k_3 \cdot min\{\frac{Cn_{Nm}^b}{Max\_connect}, 1\} + k_4 \cdot min\{\frac{Cn_{c_i}^b}{Max\_connect}, 1\} + \\ +k_5 \frac{r(v)}{q}\right) & \text{if } r(v) < q \\ 0 & \text{if } r(v) \geqslant q \end{cases}$$

Fig. 4. Definition of the fitness function

in a message calling for new members (**Call_Members**) to the neighborhood of b, starting the process again.

When $\Delta q \leqslant 0$, i.e., the cluster is complete, all additional receiving requests will be rejected.

Consider the example depicted in Figure 3. We colored the nodes according the *state*; white nodes are nonmembers, black nodes members (or clusterhead, i.e. *status* $\in \{Me, CH\}$) of the cluster c_i being formed and gray members are deciding nodes.

In Figure 3 (a), the initial state with a one member cluster (clusterhead, selected by the response function) is shown. The clusterhead broadcasts the

Call_Members message transmitting its state (3 (b)). At this point, all nodes
that receive the message change to the deciding state. A timer is set based on
the calculated fitness for each node. In Figure 3 (c), the programmed time of
node 2 has already elapsed. The node now asks for membership. As the total
resource request (q) is not satisfied by the current cluster size, the node 2 is
included in the cluster. Now it also broadcasts a Call_Members message to the
neighborhood (Figure 3 (d)). When node 4 and 5 receive the broadcasted message, they start a timer related to the computed fitness $(1 - Fitness_{c_i}(4)$ and
$1 - Fitness_{c_i}(5))$. Due to the fact that node 4 has already a timer, just the
timer with the shortest deadline is kept. In Figure 3 (e), the programmed time
of node 4 has elapsed and it requests for membership. It receives permission to
enter into the cluster. Since the cluster is already complete, node 4 does not
broadcast a new Call_Members message. Finally, the waiting time for nodes 5
and 3 is over. They request membership, but due to the fact that the cluster has
enough resources, the permission to integrate the cluster is refused.

Now we will integrate the already presented heuristic hints (see Section 4.2)
that should guide the member selection. The first point says that the heuristic
should privilege nodes with a small distance to some of the nodes inside the
actual cluster. In order to observe that, two aspects must be addressed: (1)
Include the distance to the next cluster member in the fitness function with the
aim of reducing communication costs. (2) An implicit behavior of the heuristic
makes that nodes far away from the clusterhead, but with good connection to
the cluster are penalized since starting the timer in a later stage.

This should be addressed together with the point number two in our influence parameters list: the distance to the clusterhead. This point is aided by the
implicit behavior of algorithm. The two aspects are important for reducing the
cluster cost. Nodes near to the cluster are suitable because the connection cost is
smaller, nevertheless, to keep clusters with smaller diameter also helps to reduce
the total cost.

The distance to clusterhead is also addressed by two points: (1) Including the
distance to the clusterhead in the fitness function. (2) Implicit behavior of the
heuristic. To show that we can reuse the example shown in Figure 3. The fact
that nodes near to the clusterhead started the timer earlier implicitly helps to
get small diameter clusters.

Analyzing these two different requisites, the following method was created in
order to penalize the distance to the clusterhead and reward the distance to
the cluster (i.e. the distance to the closest node in the cluster). We will now
count the rounds that the algorithm has already executed. Using the example
presented in Figure 3, (b) represents the first round of the algorithm and (d) the
second one. Each time that a new member was selected and made a broadcast
to the neighborhood, the variable $round_v, v \in V$ is increased.

We define the waiting time of a node v to request to be included in the
cluster c_i as $WaitingTime_{c_i}^v = k \cdot (1 - Fitness_{c_i}(v)) \cdot \frac{1}{\kappa \, round_v + (1-\kappa)}$, where
$v \in V, \kappa \in [0,1], k \in \Re*$ and $0 \leq Fitness_{c_i}(v)) \leq 1$. It uses the fitness function
and the current round to calculate the waiting time.

Using this equation, for bigger rounds, the time that should be waited is shortened. With the κ parameter, the amount of reward given to the distance to the cluster versus penalization of distance to clusterhead can be controlled.

The fitness function that takes into account all points presented in the Section 4.2 is presented in Figure 4 (for $\sum_{i=1}^{5} k_i = 1$), where $k_1, ..., k_5$ define how each of the terms influences the fitness metric. It is important to remark that $0 \leq Fitness_{c_i}(v) \leq 1$. For two nodes $v, u \in V$ and $Fitness_{c_i}(v) < Fitness_{c_i}(u)$ means that the node v is less suitable for the cluster c_i than the u. Max_dist describes the minimum distance to the clusterhead that should be considered the maximum penalty, $Max\_connect$ is the same for the connection measurements. We should remark that for nodes with more resources than required, the fitness is always 0 because they should form a cluster with one member.

5   Simulation and Results

We implemented our emergent clustering heuristic using Shox [11], a Java-based wireless ad hoc network simulator. As input, we generated 40 instances of the problem with 13 nodes in a field of 25m by 25m. These instances were generated by random selection of the nodes' position.

Our link metric used the received signal strength (RSSI) that was calculated using the free space model for an isotropic point source in an ideal propagation medium. The limits of the RSSI were determined using two thresholds, having the meaning of maximum signal ($w = 0.1$) strength and no signal ($w > 1$). We adjust the radio power in order to achieve a maximum transmission range of 10m. The $RSSI$ was the only metric used to calculate the $virtual\ distance$. In our simulation, we adjust several parameters of the described equations such that every part of the equation has the same weight. In order to calculate the optimum cost of a problem instance, we model our $minimum\text{-}intracommunication$ $clustering$ as an integer linear programming problem and for each generated instance, we solve it using the lp_solve program.

Figure 2 shows the results of the 40 runs for our distributed heuristic and the respective optimal solution. The picture also shows the confidence interval of the obtained average. The average communication cost of the emergent clustering was 30.72 with a standard deviation of 6.07. The optimum solution has a mean of 24.42 with a standard deviation of 4.26.

6   Conclusion

In this paper, we introduce a useful clustering problem and develop an efficient heuristic to solve it. The heuristic is based on the response functions derived from the division of labor in social insects. On the basis of the response function, the most suitable nodes in terms of connectivity, energy and resources are selected for the clusterhead role. After emerging spontaneously, each clusterhead starts gathering members for the clusters until a resource requirement q is satisfied. The membership candidates are evaluated using a fitness function taking into consideration their distance to the cluster and its clusterhead, connectivity and resource availability. After evaluating those items, a node delays its response by a time related to its fitness. Therefore, the higher fitness nodes announce themselves earlier, having higher priority for entering the cluster.

Using simulations in the Shox network simulator, we show that our approach performs well in average. It uses just local information and it is capable of starting in an unorganized ad hoc network, finding a cluster configuration that is in average just 25% above the optimum one. Further, the proposed emergent clustering approach obtains a performance of at least 1.5 times the optimal for 60% of the test cases. There are no test cases with a performance inferior to 2 times the optimum result.

Our results demonstrate once again that a principle from natural systems can be successfully transferred to an efficient algorithm for ad hoc networks solving a problem which is NP-complete in good aproximation.

References

1. Heimfarth, T., Danne, K., Rammig, F.J.: An os for mobile ad hoc networks using ant based hueristic to distribute mobile services, 77 (2005)
2. Baker, D., Ephremides, A.: The architectural organization of a mobile radio network via a distributed algorithm. IEEE Transactions on Communications 29(11), 1694–1701 (1981)
3. Baker, D.J., Ephremides, A., Flynn, J.A.: The design and simulation of a mobile radio network with distributed control. IEEE J. on Selected Areas in Communications SAC2(1), 226–237 (1984)
4. Gerla, M., Tsai, J.T.-C.: Multicluster, mobile, multimedia radio network. Wirel. Netw. 1(3), 255–265 (1995)
5. Basagni, S., Chlamtac, I., Farago, A.: A generalized clustering algorithm for peer-to-peer networks. In: Degano, P., Gorrieri, R., Marchetti-Spaccamela, A. (eds.) ICALP 1997. LNCS, vol. 1256, Springer, Heidelberg (1997)
6. Heinzelman, W., Chandrakasan, A., Balakrishnan, H.: An application-specific protocol architecture for wireless microsensor networks. IEEE Transactions on Wireless Communications 1(4), 660–670 (2002)
7. Amis, A., Prakash, R., Vuong, T., Huynh, D.: Max-min d-cluster formation in wireless ad hoc networks. In: INFOCOM 2000. Nineteenth Annual Joint Conference of the IEEE Computer and Communications Societies. Proceedings. 26-30 March 2000, vol. 1, pp. 32–41 (2000)
8. Krishnan, R., Starobinski, D.: Message-efficient self-organization of wireless sensor networks. In: Proc. IEEE Wireless Communications and Networking Conference, New Orleans, USA, IEEE Computer Society Press, Los Alamitos (2003)
9. Bannerjee, S., Khuller, S.: A clustering scheme for hierarchical control in wireless networks. In: Proc. IEEE INFOCOM, Anchorage, Alaska, IEEE Computer Society Press, Los Alamitos (2001)
10. Heimfarth, T., Janacik, P.: Ant based heuristic for os service distribution on ad hoc networks. In: BICC 2006. 1st IFIP International Conference on Biologically Inspired Cooperative Computing, IFIP International Federation for Information Processing, Boston, MA, USA, vol. 216, pp. 75–84. Springer, Heidelberg (2006)
11. http://shox.sourceforge.net (Accessed on Jannuary 28, 2006)

Intelligent Context-Awareness System Using Improved Self-adaptive Back Propagation Algorithm[*]

Sang-Hun Eo[1], Wei Zha[2], Byeong-Seob You[1], Dong-Wook Lee[1],
and Hae-Young Bae[3]

Dept. of Computer Science & Information Engineering, Inha University
[1]{eosanghun, subi, dwlee}@dblab.inha.ac.kr,
[2]zhazhago@hotmail.com,
[3]hybae@inha.ac.kr

Abstract. Since the context plays a significant role in ubiquitous computing environment, many researches have studied about context-awareness system to improve the performance. An efficient learning mechanism is in importance of context-aware system, but there are seldom algorithms focused on convenience of systems by elaborating the learning mechanism with user's context information. As one of the most adaptable algorithm, Back Propagation provides us favorable inference capability. In this paper, we concentrate on improving the predict ability and reducing the system workload by proposing improved self-adaptive back propagation algorithm. The middleware we proposed improves the predicate capability. Thus, the overall performance becomes better than other systems. By adding system cache to middleware, it is possible for the context-aware system to act faster and improve the workload efficiency. Experiments show that there is an obvious improvement in overall performance of the context-awareness systems.

1 Introduction

According to the definition in [1], "Context is any information that can be used to characterize the situation of an entity". If a system uses context to provide the relevant information and/or services to its clients, it is context-aware. However, the relevancy depends on the user's task[1]. Context-awareness system collects, analyses and utilizes context. It is necessary for system to be context-awareness in ubiquitous environment[2].

As the popularity of sensor network and mobile terminal, mobility has become the main data source of context-aware environment. To provide better service to mobile users and avoid information flood, the context-awareness systems should be proactive according to the changing environment[3]. This requires context-aware systems to have the ability to learn users' environment and to predict users' behavior pattern. Most of the current computing systems are capable to process the users' explicit input and output

[*] This research was supported by the MIC (Ministry of Information and Communication), Korea, under the ITRC (Information Technology Research Center) support program supervised by the IITA (Institute of Information Technology Assessment).

R. Obermaisser et al. (Eds.): SEUS 2007, LNCS 4761, pp. 329–338, 2007.

the result. But they are not aware of users' status[4], for example, where is the user, what the user is doing, when the user does it, who is beside the user, and etc. Some of them focus on providing a uniform model to context, and some of them focus on providing an interface for different applications and distribute context, and some of them focus on how to manage context. But none of these systems can satisfy the requirement of ubiquitous computing environment completely, especially for the mobile user.

In this paper, we propose a new middleware for by using an advanced learning mechanism of context-aware systems. Back Propagation(BP) algorithm[10] is chosen as the basic learning mechanism due to its ability of learning relationships in complex data sets. The standard BP algorithm has limitations that it is too slow to provide the output in a short time. We introduced a dynamic momentum parameter added on the original BP algorithm with the view to make the BP algorithm avoid oscillations and respond instantly. The parameter value is calculated with reference to the LMS(Least Mean Square) between the obtained output and the desired output. By experiment, we prove that by using the improved BP algorithm in the proposed middleware, the system can precisely be proactive according to the users' changing environment.

This paper is organized as follows: in section 2, we briefly review the related work, previous context-awareness systems and the idea of primordial BP algorithm. In section 3, we propose an advanced learning mechanism SABPA (Self-Adaptive Back Propagation Algorithm) and an intelligent middleware for context-awareness system. In section 4, we make a comparison for the proposed middleware. The conclusion and future work are given in section 5.

2 Related Works

Most of the existing contxt-awareness systems have a common deficiency, that is, limitations in proactive and adaptation to the changing environment for the lack of learning mechanism. In [5], Dey et al. introduced their context toolkit system. The system aims to provide balanced touch to different kinds of applications through the distributed context and gives the idea how to achieve better performance, it is crucial for context-awareness systems to adopt proactive behaviors and the key point lies in finding user patterns. However, due to distinct characteristics of individual user behavior, user patterns are diversely different. Therefore, learning is considered as an efficient way to get the pattern.

In this chapter, our learning mechanism and improved BP algorithm for robust context-awareness systems are introduced. But it does not consider proactive and learning mechanisms. Roman et al. developed the Gaia context-awareness system to manage context[6]. This system throws light on assisting mobile applications to be developed and implemented in active spaces and supports mobile applications in a limited area. But it still lacks the ability of learning and proactive through the users' environment. A. shehzad et al. emphasized on interactivity among applications[7]. They proposed a context model in the purpose of having a common understanding of the contextual information but no proactive functions was mentioned. S.S.Yau et al. proposed the adaptive and object-based middleware RCSM in 2004[8]. This context-awareness system is designed for the mobile networks. So, it supports the mobile users and adapts to users' changing environment. In addition, this system supports using some specific contextual information to trigger corresponding actions. However, this system also lacks the ability of learning to proactive. H. Park et al. included context inference, learning, event triggering module of their middleware for the purpose of deal with various context[9]. In learning module, they listed some possible algorithms for learning but no material solutions.

For the robust context-awareness system, we chose BP algorithm as one of the most appropriate solution. From [10], a basic BP algorithm contains 3 layers: input layer, hidden layer and output layer. Input sample is processed step by step in terms of hidden units through input layer. Then it is transmitted to output layer after passing through all the hidden units. During this process, the state of units of each layer influences the next layer. After comparison of present output to expected output, the results are transferred to BP module if they are not matched. During the BP process, error signals are transmitted through original forward path but in converse direction, and weight value is modified by each unit in each hidden layer on the expectation of the minimized error signals.

3 Context-Awareness System Using SABPA

To achieve better performance, it is crucial for context-awareness systems to adapt proactive behaviors and the key point lies in finding user patterns. However, due to distinct characteristics of individual user behavior, user patterns are diversely different. Therefore, learning is considered as an efficient way to get the pattern.

In this chapter, our intelligent context-awareness middleware and advanced learning mechanism SABPA for robust context-awareness systems are introduced.

3.1 Learning Middleware

We propose a new middleware that uses learning mechanism to provide useful context in context-awareness system. As shown in fig.1, we generally divide our middleware into three layers, namely, context source layer, context processing layer and context delivery layer. User and sensors can be the context sources (i.e. context can either come from user input or detected by the sensors).

Context Pre-process Module. Deals with the original context from users and sensors. Since the raw data are in variety of forms and expressions. It is necessary to convert the context into normalized forms which are easy for the system to process. Some context is aggregated to a higher level. We take GPS data for example; following is one data tuple of GPS:

*$GPGGA, 170647, 3726.4905, N, 12627.1471, E, 1, 03, 1.27, 2.7, M, -34.4, M, a*41*

We need to separate following information from this tuple:

Time = 17:06:47
Longitude- Latitude = (37° 26' 49.05", 126° 27' 14.71")
Altitude = 2.7m

And further, it (37° 26' 49.05", 126° 27' 14.71") is changed to specific location such as "Incheon International Airport" by Gauss projection. After that, useless data are abandoned here and essential context is sent to System Cache and stored in the context DB. The context DB stores the historical context including input context and the context predicted by the system.

Dynamic Adaptive Module. Between learning mechanism and context DB keeps the learning network up-to-date. The trigger event of update is controlled here, when new arrival context accounts for certain percent of the total context, the old learning mechanism network can not predict accurately. We need to go on training our network to improve the accuracy. The Dynamic Adaptive module will continue training network with the new context in DB when the trigger event happened, until the error rate is within the default value.

Context DB. Inside the Dynamic Adaptive Module is the database of our middleware. It maintains and provides the data for training and update. Preprocessed data are sent here to store, when the trigger event happened, Dynamic Adaption Model will send message to ask Context DB provide the corresponding data to Learning Mechanism for training. After training, it is possible to categorize the new coming context to the already known classification and conclude the user pattern. By adjusting the default error rate, the accuracy can be controlled in an acceptable range. The structure of network such as number of hidden layers and nodes of each layer depends on applications specifically.

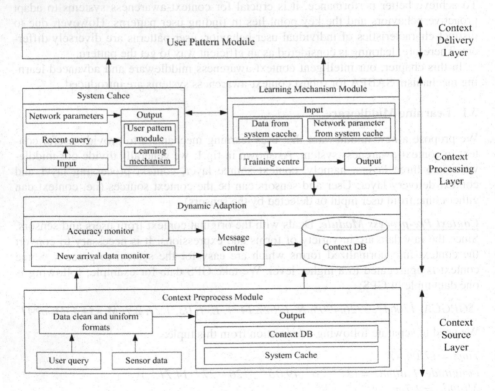

Fig. 1. Middleware for learning mechanism

System Cache. Makes context awareness system possible to response faster. Users would not change their habits suddenly; the maintaining of the latest input context and their options will dramatically improve the response time. These recorded options can be provided rapidly without computing when users repeat their queries. Also, the cache stores the parameters of learning network for different users (users use learning networks respectively, because each user is different individual), which makes it possible to support multiple users and response in a short time. Learning network, a background process that mines users' patterns, needs to be trained before using.

User Pattern Module. Stores the most recently query result. When the recently query is matched in System Cache, the corresponding answer can be provided directly from here. Learning Mechanism is the algorithm chosen for learning. In our research, an improved BP algorithm SABPA is introduced and will be discussed in next section

3.2 SABPA (Self-adaptive BP Algorithm)

The motivation of using BP algorithm is its ability of learning relationships in complex data sets which can not be easily perceived by humans. It has the ability to modify the output according to the changing of user context. It doesn't require the whole network rebuild when new context comes.

However, standard BP algorithm has two drawbacks. First, learning speed is slow. Traditional BP network can not provide fast response. Second, there are oscillations during learning. These problems cause its low efficiency. We have to improve the original BP algorithm so that it can be suitable for our proposing middleware. From [10], the formula for update weight in BP is

$$\Delta\omega_{ij}(t+1) = -\eta \partial E(t+1) / \partial\omega_{ij}(t) + \alpha\omega_{ij}(t)$$

Where η is the constant learning rate, which is usually chosen $0<\eta<1$ to guarantee that the weights space do not overshoot the minimum of the error space. α is momentum, which drastically affects the learning speed.

Table 1. SABPA algorithm

---

1. Initial η, $\omega(0)$, expect error ε and set k=1.

2. Set $\alpha(0) = \dfrac{E(\omega(t))}{\|\nabla E(\omega(t))\|^2}$, $\alpha = \alpha(0)$.

3. If $E(-\eta g(\omega(t)) + \alpha\omega(t)) - E(\omega(t)) \leq -\dfrac{1}{2}\alpha\|\nabla E(\omega(t)\|^2$

   go to step 5; otherwise, set k=k+1 and go to step 4

4. Set $\alpha = \alpha(0)/m^{k-1}$ and go to step 3.

5. Set $\omega(t+1) = -\eta g(\omega(t)) + \alpha\omega(t)$ and $\alpha = \alpha(0)\dfrac{E(t+1)}{E(t)}$

6. If $E(-\eta g(\omega(t)) + \alpha\omega(t)) \leq \varepsilon$, then terminate; otherwise begin recursion.

m in step 4 is reduction factor. The choice of m value is not critical for successful learning, we choose m =0.5 in our algorithm.

E is the batch error measure defined as the sum-of-squared-differences error function over the entire training set

$$E = \sum_{k-1}^{m} E_k = \sum_{k}^{m} \sum_{t}^{q} (y_t^k - c_t^k)^2 / 2$$

By defining $g_i(\omega)$ as the gradient of $E(\omega)$ with respect to the ith variable ω_i, and $g(\omega)=(g_1(\omega),\ldots,g_n(\omega))$, the whole weights update can be written as

$$\omega(t+1) = -\eta g(\omega(t)) + \alpha\omega(t)$$

Also, $g(\omega)$ defines the gradient $\nabla E(\omega)$ of the sum-of-squared-differences error function E at ω.

Large values of momentum can accelerate the learning process but the drawback result is oscillations during learning. On reverse, smaller values of momentum decelerate the learning process. Normally, the momentum α is fixed before training. Here, we propose a strategy for dynamic adjusting momentum α ,called SABP (Self-adaptive BP Algorithm). This strategy makes the BP network faster and avoids oscillations. The basic idea is, check $E(t+1)$ every time. If $E(t+1) > E(t)$, which means learning is too slow, we should accelerate the learning process by increasing α. If $E(t+1) < E(t)$, which means learning is too fast, oscillations may occur, we should reduce the learning process by decreasing α . The proposed algorithm SABPA is illustrated in table 1.

When $E(-\eta g(\omega(t)) + \alpha\omega(t)) - E(\omega(t)) \leq -\frac{1}{2}\alpha\|\nabla E(\omega(t)\|^2$, which means

learning is a little fast, it is advantageous to slow down the learning process. Due to $\frac{E(t+1)}{E(t)} < 1$, then $\alpha(t+1) < \alpha(t)$. The learning process is decelerated.

When $E(t+1) > E(t)$, that means learning is too slow. It is necessary to increase the learning speed. Due to $\frac{1}{m^{k-1}} > 1$, then $\alpha(t+1) > \alpha(t)$ learning process is accelerated.

By dynamically adjusting momentum every time, SABPA avoids oscillations during learning and also accelerates the learning process.

3.3 Learning Steps

Because of the variety of raw data, some preparatory work needs to be done before learning, which are collection and cleaning of each user context, and storing them in context DB to train BP network. The raw data are first sent to Context Preprocess model which will clean the data and generate them to suitable format or higher level to make them available for proposed Learning Mechanism. Preprocessed data will be sent to Context DB which maintains all the necessary data for training and updating our network. According to different situation, diverse BP network (difference in number of hidden layers and nodes of each layer) will be constructed. The training of BP network for each user should continue until the desired error rate is reached. Meanwhile the parameters of BP network for each user are stored in system cache respectively.

When user inputs query or sensors detect changing of environment, the context is sent to context pro-process module where contexts are converted into normalized forms and some context is aggregated to a higher level. The essential contexts are selected to be stored in the context DB and sent to the system cache. If the context information already exists in system cache, the output can be provided directly by system cache as it stores the recently queries and answers. Otherwise, the cache selects parameters of BP network according to the specific user and sends to BP network Learning Mechanism Model. In Learning Mechanism Model, BP network learns these contexts, categorize them to already known classification to fetch the user pattern and sends the results to both output and system cache for repeated queries. Fig 3 shows the learning steps.

The dynamic adaptation module is in charge of the update of SABPA network. When the accuracy of SABPA network decreases or new context takes up certain percent of the total context, this module sends messages to both Context DB and Learning Mechanism Model to manage them goes on training SABPA network until it matches the expected error rate. Thus, the accuracy is guaranteed.

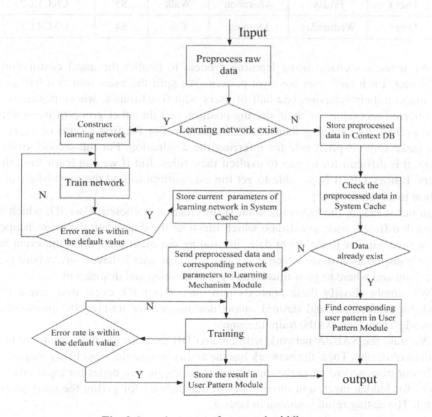

Fig. 3. Learning steps of proposed middleware

4 Implementation

We choose GPS system as the symbol of context-awareness system to implement our learning middleware. A basic BP network is generated by the Neural Network Toolbox for MATLAB for the learning process which contains three layers: input layer, hidden layer, and output layer). A user environment context DB which contains three months' context information is provided for training.

Table 3. Sample of training data set. Since the raw data is in variety of forms, we clean and normalize them to following forms.

Input					Desired Output
User ID	Date	Time	Mode	From	To
User1	Monday	Morning	Bus	S1	C3,C4,C1
User2	Monday	Afternoon	Car	S1	C2,C1,C5
User1	Tuesday	Evening	Car	S3	C2,C3,C4
User3	Friday	Afternoon	Walk	S5	C6,C1,C2
User3	Wednesday	Morning	Car	S4	C5,C4,C5

We made a scenario using learning process to predict the usual destination of GPS user. Each GPS user has own pattern. We split the users into two halves depending on their behavior, one half of users with fixed routes, whose positions can be inferred accurately by their starting position and the other group of users with a high probability changing their routes frequently. For the first groups of users, we can make some explicit rule for inferring the destination. For the second group of users, it is difficult for human to explicit their rules. But if we can learn from these users' history DB, it is possible to get the user pattern to find the most likely destination in a high accuracy.

In our scenario, the following context information is chosen: User ID, which distinguish different user; event date which illustrate the date when the event happens; event time, similar to the event date, illustrating the exact time when the event happens; transportation mode which gives the way how user behaves, say, where is the user from and where to go is illustrated by start position and destination.

We simply classify these contexts into input (User ID, event date, event time, mode, start position) and desired output(destination) for training the proposed BP network. Table 3 shows the training sample.

We train the SABPA network with context DB until we get the output within the desired error rate. Then, the network has the ability to give the most likely output.

In our case, according to the input context we create five nodes for input layer, six nodes for hidden layer, and three nodes in output layer for giving the most possible result. The testing result is shown in table 4.

Table 4. Testing result. By using test data of table 3, our learning network output the most likely three destinations and their probability respectively

Input					Output	
User ID	Date	Time	Mode	From	To	Probability
User 1	Monday	Morning	Car	S1	C1	60%
					C3	87%
					C4	74%
User 3	Friday	Afternoon	Walk	S1	C1	85%
					C2	64%
					C5	84%
User 1	Tuesday	Evening	Car	S3	C2	77%
					C3	80%
					C6	88%
User 4	Monday	Morning	Bus	S5	C2	91%
					C5	65%
					C6	46%
User 2	Thursday	Evening	Car	S4	C1	87%
					C3	69%
					C5	77%

5 Performance Evaluations

After building the learning network for context-awareness system, it is possible for the GPS system to predict the future location of a GPS user. Benefit from this ability, more information can be provided to the users without any query, such as weather, traffic jam, the shortest path. At the same time, workload is obviously reduced. Fig 4 shows the comparison of workload among systems.

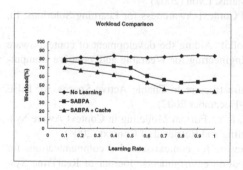
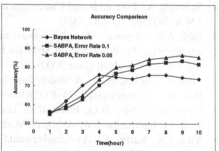

Fig. 4. The workload comparison between the system using learning and without learning

Fig. 5. The accuracy comparison between using Bayes and Backpropagation

Besides BP, other algorithms such as Baye's theorem are widely used. For GPS systems, Bayes could also be adopted as a satisfying learning mechanism. But BP is superior to Bayes on the control of prediction accuracy. Furthermore, when the new context accounts for some percent of the total context, Bayes network requires rebuilding rather than improvement on the current network. Fig 5 shows the accuracy comparison between Bayes and BP with different learning rates.

6 Conclusion and Future Work

In this paper, we propose an intelligent learning middleware of context-awareness systems and using SABPA (Self-adaptive BP Algorithm) as learning mechanism for context recommend in ubiquitous computing environment. Different from standard BP, we improved it to become suitable for the proposed middleware regardless of its slowness. Using this middleware in our scenario, context-awareness systems evidently reduce the workload and provide better service. Through the tests, we proved that our middleware and SABPA performs far beyond just acceptable.

Future work in this are includes how to select the essential context for learning. Training a BP network is CPU-cost computing. Schedule management for training and user service is also important. In addition, the proposed SABPA is not yet completely optimized. More effective algorithm should be discovered for better performance.

References

1. Dey, A.K., Abowd, G.D.: Towards a better understanding of context and context-awareness. Technical Report GIT-GVU-99-22, Georgia Institute of Technology, College of Computing (June 1999)
2. Ranganathan, A., Campbell, R.H.: A Middleware for Context-Aware Agents in Ubiquitous Computing Environments. In: ACM/IFIP/USENIX International Middleware Conference (2003)
3. Byun, H.E., Cheverst, K.: Harnessing context to support proactive behaviours. In: ECAI2002 Workshop on AI in Mobile Systems, Lyon (2002)
4. Schmidt, A.: Potentials and Challenges of Context-Awareness for Learning Solutions. In: LWA 2005, pp. 63–68 (2005)
5. Dey, A.K., Abowd, G.D.: The context toolkit: Aiding the development of context-aware applications. In: Workshop on Software Engineering for Wearable andPervasive Computing, Limerick, Ireland (June 2000)
6. Roman, Manuel, et al.: A Middleware Infrastructure to Enable Active Spaces. In: IEEE Pervasive Computing, pp. 74–83 (October-December 2002)
7. Shehzad, A., Ngo, H.Q., Pham, K.A., Lee, S.Y.: Formal Modeling in Context Aware Systems. In: International Workshop on Modeling and Retrieval of Context (2004)
8. Yau, S.S., Karim, F.: An adaptive middleware for context-sensitive communications for real-time applications in ubiquitous computing environments. Journal of RealTime Systems 26(1), 29–61 (2004)
9. Park, H.: A middleware of context-awareness for ubiquitous computing middlewares. In: International Conference on Information Systems, vol. 00, pp. 369–374 (2005)
10. Kumar, S.: neural networks. McGraw-Hill Education, New York (2005)

Towards an Artificial Hormone System for Self-organizing Real-Time Task Allocation

Uwe Brinkschulte, Mathias Pacher, and Alexander von Renteln

Institute for Process Control, Automation, and Robotics
University of Karlsruhe (TH), Germany
{brinks, pacher, renteln}@ira.uka.de

Abstract. This article presents the concept of an artificial hormone system for a completely decentralized realization of self-organizing task allocation. We show that tight upper bounds for the real-time behavior of self-configuration can be given. We also show two simulation results using the artificial hormone system demonstrating the operation of the artificial hormone system under different workloads.

1 Introduction

Today's computational systems are growing increasingly complex. They are build from large numbers of heterogeneous processing elements with highly dynamic interaction. Middleware is a common layer in such distributed systems, which manages the cooperation of tasks on the processing elements and hides distribution to the application. It is responsible for seamless task interaction on distributed hardware. As shown in figure 1, all tasks are interconnected by the middleware layer and are able to operate beyond processing element (PE) boundaries like if they would reside on a single hardware platform. To handle the complexity of today's and even more tomorrow's distributed systems, self-organization techniques are necessary. Such a system should be able to find a suitable initial configuration by itself, to adapt or optimize itself to changing environmental and internal conditions, to heal itself in case of system failures or to protect itself against attacks. Middleware is a good place to realize such self-X features (self-configuration, self-optimization, self-healing) by autonomously controlling and adapting task allocation. Especially for self-healing, it is important that task allocation is decentralized to avoid single points of failure.

This work presents an artificial hormone system for task allocation to heterogeneous processing elements. In the following, we will present our approach in detail and we will discuss several properties considering real-time aspects induced by the hormone system.

2 Using an Artificial Hormone System to Obtain Self-X-Properties

For task allocation, three types of hormones are used:

Eager value: This hormone determines, how well a PE can execute a task. As higher the hormonal value, as better the task executes on the PE.

R. Obermaisser et al. (Eds.): SEUS 2007, LNCS 4761, pp. 339–347, 2007.

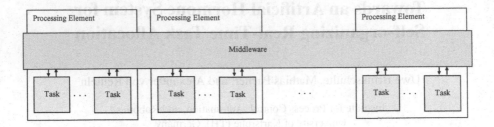

Fig. 1. Middleware in a distributed system

Suppressor: A suppressor represses the execution of a task on a PE. Suppressors are subtracted from eager values. Suppressors are e.g. used to prevent duplicate task allocation or to indicate a detoriating PE state.

Accelerator: An accelerator favors the execution of a task on a PE. Accelerators are added to eager values. The accelerators can be used to cluster cooperating tasks in the neigborhood or to indicate an improved PE state.

The following figure 2 sketches the basic control loop used to assign a task T_i to a processing element. This closed control loop is executed for every task on every processing element. It determines based on the level of the three hormone types, if a task T_i is executed on a processing element PE_γ or not. The local static eager value $E_{i\gamma}$ indicates how well task T_i executes on PE_γ. From this value, all suppressors $S^{i\gamma}$ received for task T_i on PE_γ are subtracted and all accelerators received for task T_i on PE_γ are added. The result of this calculation is a modified eager value $Em_{i\gamma}$ for task T_i on PE_γ. The modified eager value is sent by the middleware to all other PEs in the system and compared to the modified eager values $Em^{i\gamma}$ received from all other PEs for this task. Is $Em_{i\gamma}$ greater than all received eager values $Em^{i\gamma}$, task T_i will be

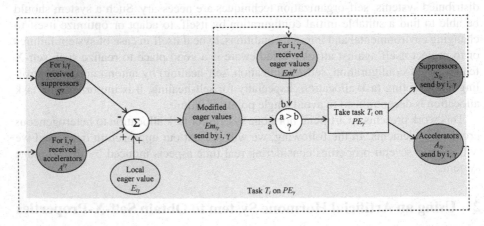

Notation: $H^{i\gamma}$ Hormone for task T_i executed on PE_γ

$H_{i\gamma}$: Hormone from task T_i executed on PE_γ. Latin letters are task indices, Greek letters are processing element indices

Fig. 2. Hormon based control loop

taken by PE_γ (in case of equality a second criterion, e.g. the position of a PE in the grid, is used to get an unambiguous decision). Now, task T_i on PE_γ sends suppressors $S_{i\gamma}$ to all other PEs to prevent duplicate task allocation. Accelerators $A_{i\gamma}$ are sent to neighbored PEs to favor the clustering of cooperating tasks. This procedure is repeated periodically.

It should be emphasized in this point that the strength of the different types of hormones is initially set by the applicants who want to influence the task allocation. In section 3.1 we show the task allocation process based on the hormone values in detail.

The described approach is completely decentralized, each PE is responsible for its own tasks, the communication to other PEs is realized by a unified hormone concept. Furthermore, it realizes several self-X properties:

- The approach is **self-organizing**, because no external influence controls the task allocation.
- It is **self-configuring**, an initial task allocation is found by exchanging hormones. The self-configuration is finished as soon as all modified eager values become zero meaning no more tasks wants to be taken. This is done by sending suppressors which have to be chosen strong enough to inhibit an infinite task assignment.
- The **self-optimization** is done by offering tasks again for re-allocation. The point of time for such an offer is determined by the task respectively the PE itself. It can be done periodically or at a point of time where the task or the PE is idle.
  In this context it is simple to handle the entrance of a new task in the system: At first, all processing elements have to be informed about their hormone values for the new task. Then, the task is allocated as described for self-optimization.
- The approach is **self-healing**, in case of a task or PE failure all related hormones are no longer sent, especially the suppressors. This results in an automatic reassignment of the task to the same PE (if it is still active) or another PE.

In addition, the self-configuration is **real-time** capable. There are tight upper time bounds for self-configuration which we will present in the next sections.

3   Dynamics of the Artificial Hormone System

In the this section, the dynamics of the artificial hormone system and the conditions and rules for its correct working will be presented. Figure 3 shows the cyclic sequence of sending the hormones followed by the task allocation. The sequence starts with "send hormones" (S) to create the knowledge base for the first decision. At least the eager

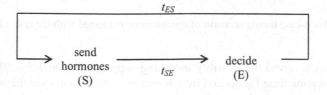

Fig. 3. Hormon cycle

values need to be available. After sending the hormones and waiting the time t_{SE}, a decision (E) on the task allocation, based on the received hormones, is taken. This process is repeated after a waiting time of t_{ES}.

3.1 Dynamics of Task Allocation

Let PE_γ be a processing element willing to run a task T_i. We need to distinguish three cases:

Case 1: All eager values of all processing elements for task T_i are constant and spread over the whole system. Thus, the system is in a steady state and all PEs make their decisions based on up-to-date and constant values. Then, PE_γ can allocate a task if it has the highest eager value, respectively, with equal eager values, a higher priority.

Case 2: The eager value of processing element PE_γ for task T_i decreases (e.g. by suppressor influence). In this case, PE_γ may allocate the task T_i if the decreased eager value is still sufficient. All the other PEs will not allocate the task, as they know either the old or the new eager value of PE_γ which wins with both values.

Case 3: The eager value of the processing element PE_γ for task T_i increases (e.g. by accelerator influence). This case is critical if PE_γ becomes the winner by the increased eager value, because other PEs might not yet know it and therefore decide wrongly. Thus, PE_γ may only allocate the task T_i after the new eager value has successfully been submitted to all PEs and until PE_γ itself has possibly received a suppressor from another PE_δ ($\gamma \neq \delta$), which allocated the task T_i based on the old, lower eager value of PE_γ.

The question, however, is how long the waiting times should be chosen? Figure 4 shows the worst-case scenario in which PE_δ allocated the task T_i just before it has received the new eager value from PE_γ. PE_γ must not come to a decision

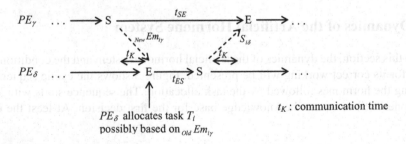

Fig. 4. Worst-case timing scenario of the hormone exchange with the task allocation

until it has received the possibly incoming suppressor from PE_δ. Therefore, the communication time t_K needed by a hormone to be spread over the whole system is very important to be known. Knowing t_K we present a rule for the task allocation with increased eager values as well as conditions for the times t_{ES} and t_{SE}.

Rule: If a processing element PE_γ gets able to allocate a task T_i only based on an increased eager value, then it has to delay it's decision to the next communication cycle to ensure the transmission of the increased eager value and to wait for possible suppressors for the same task from other PEs. This comes true if (follows directly from figure 4):

$$t_{SE} \geq t_{ES} + 2t_K$$

The cycle time t_{Cycle} defines as follows:

$$t_{Cycle} = t_{SE} + t_{ES}$$

Of course the cycle time should be minimized, thus:
1) t_{ES} should be as small as possible, ideally 0.
2) $t_{SE} \geq t_{ES} + 2t_K$, ideally with $t_{ES} = 0$: $t_{SE} \geq 2t_K$

3.2 Self Configuration: Worst Case Timing Behavior

Figure 5 shows the precise cycle of the hormone distribution and interpretation based on figure 3. First of all, the hormones (eager values, suppressors and accelerators) for all the tasks which PE_γ is interested in are emitted by PE_γ.

After waiting the time t_{SE}, the decision for a task T_i (PE_γ is interested in) will be taken. Afterwards i is incremented and the next cycle starts ($t_{ES} = 0$). In this way the hormones for all the relevant tasks are emitted in each cycle and the decision for exactly one task will be taken. This allows the hormones to take effect. If the allocation decisions for all tasks would take place in parallel, the emitted accelerators would not have any impact (as all tasks would already be allocated in the first cycle).

$$t_{ES} = 0$$

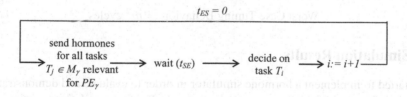

Fig. 5. Cycle of the hormone distribution and the decision making for a PE_γ

Let's assume that all m tasks have to be distributed on all PEs and all PEs are interested in all tasks.

We introduce a further assumption to simplify the scenario: Let all eager values be constant, i.e. there are no accelerators and suppressors. Then all tasks have been inspected and allocated after m cycles and it follows:

$$\text{Worst-case time behavior} = m \text{ cycles}$$

In the following we remove the simplifying assumption of constant eager values, i.e. we allow accelerators and suppressors. Now some tasks might not have been allocated

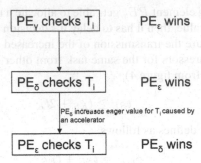

Fig. 6. Accelerator caused delay of the task allocation

after m cycles. This can be caused by accelerators and suppressors, see fig. 6. Let's assume three PEs checking one after another the possibility to allocate the task T_i. While PE_γ and PE_δ are checking PE_ϵ is the winner. After PE_δ has checked, it increases its eager value caused by a received accelerator. If afterwards PE_ϵ checks its status, PE_δ is the winner now. However, PE_δ has already checked its status regarding task T_i and will not repeat this check within the the next m cycles.

So at worst case task T_i will not be checked again until a complete cycle of all other tasks, thus after m cycles. Afterwards the same scenario could occur again.

However, the maximal number of cycles is limited: A change of the eager value by suppressors or accelerators only takes place if a task has been allocated somewhere in the system (Assumption: Monitoring accelerators and suppressors are constant during the initial self-configuration). It follows that in each allocation cycle at least one task will be allocated. Thus, in the case of a variable eager value we get the following worst case timing behavior for the self-configuration:

$$\text{Worst Case Timing Behavior} = m^2 \text{ cycles}$$

4   Simulation Results

We started to implement a hormone simulator in order to evaluate and demonstrate the behavior of our artificial hormone system approach. The first simulations confirmed the worst-case time bound for self-configuration. We also registered that the accelerators have to be smaller than the suppressors to get a stable task allocation. The reason is that if a task is scheduled, accelerators will be submitted to the neighbor cells to allocate cooperating tasks nearby (see section 2). If these accelerators are stronger than the suppressors (which prevent the task from being allocated onto another processing element) the task allocation will not be stable. The reason is that the modified eager values will continuously increase.

In the first configuration we have chosen a grid of 64 processing elements with 64 tasks to be distributed. The tasks were grouped in 8×8 cooperating tasks. Assuming light-weight tasks, the suppressors indication processor were chosen weak. Therefore it is possible that several tasks can run on one processing element. Figure 7 shows the simulation result. Coopearting tasks were scheduled right next to each other which would

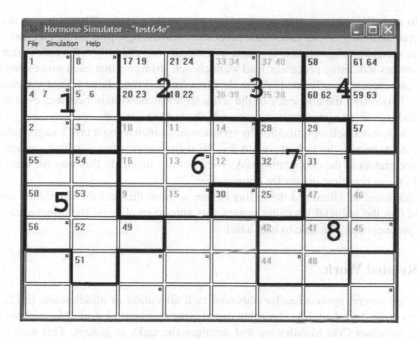

Fig. 7. 64 tasks in eight groups, weak suppressors

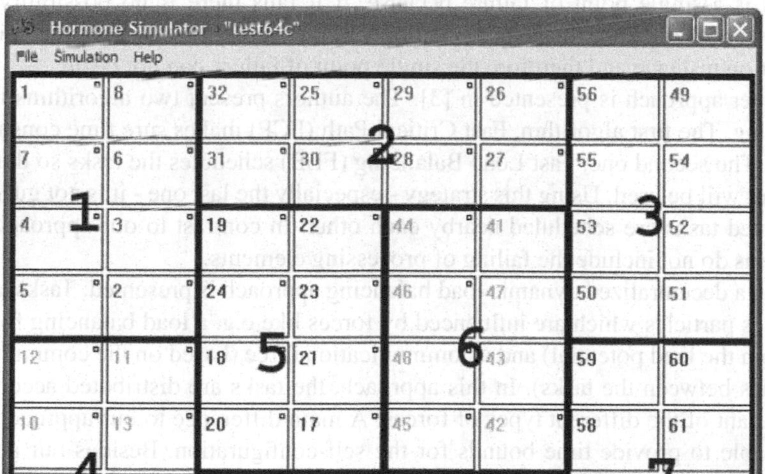

Fig. 8. 64 tasks in eight groups, strong suppressors

lead to a small communication overhead in a real-world scenario. These clusters are not scattered at all and several tasks were scheduled onto a single processing element.

The second configuration is the same as the first one - the only difference is that the suppressors indicating processor load were chosen strong so that each processing element can execute exactly one task. As shown in figure 8 the related tasks form clusters again. This shows the efficiency of the artificial hormone system because, even under full load it is able to form entire clusters which are not scattered.

We also tested self-optimization by spontaneously increasing a task's eager value of a PE. As expected, the task moved to this PE if the eager value was high enough and the accelerators of the cooperating tasks were not too strong. In this way we were also able to move complete organs for optimization.

In addition, we simulated the failing of one or more PEs and the simulation results shows that the artificial hormone system was able to re-allocate the affected tasks if there were enough PEs able to take a task.

5   Related Work

There are several approaches for clustered task allocation in middleware. In [2], the authors present a scheduling algorithm distributing tasks onto a grid. It is implemented in the Xavantes Grid Middleware and arranges the tasks in groups. This approch is completely different from ours because it uses central elements for the grouping: The Group Manager (GM), a Process Manager (PM) and the Activity Managers (AM). Here, the GM is a single point of failure because, if it fails there is no possibility to get group information from this group anymore. In our approach there is no central task distribution instance and therefore the single point of failure can not occur.

Another approach is presented in [3]. The authors present two algorithms for task scheduling. The first algorithm, Fast Critical Path (FCP) makes sure time constrains to be kept. The second one, Fast Load Balancing (FLB) schedules the tasks so that every processor will be used. Using this strategy - especially the last one - it is not guaranteed that related tasks are scheduled nearby each other. In contrast to our approach, these algorithms do not include the failing of processing elements.

In [1], a decentralized dynamic load balancing approach is presented. Tasks are considered as particles which are influenced by forces like e.g. a load balancing force (results from the load potential) and a communication force (based on the communication intensities between the tasks). In this approach, the tasks are distributed according to the resultant of the different types of forces. A main difference to our approach is that we are able to provide time bounds for the self-configuration. Besides our approach covers self-healing which is absolutely not considered by this decentralized dynamic load balancing.

6   Conclusion and Further Work

We presented an artificial hormone system to allocate tasks to processing elements within a processor grid. The assignment is completely decentralized and holds self-X-features. Furthermore, we showed that we can guarantee tight upper bounds for the real-time behavior of the artificial hormone system for the self-configuration. We started testing the presented algorithms using a hormone simulator which confirmed the theoretical results so far.

As ongoing work, we will investigate additional quality properties of the artificial hormone system i.e. if it is possible to find time bounds for self-optimization and self-healing. We will also investigate if we can guarantee stability of the task assignment. Another question in this scope is how to find an optimal task assignment and is the artificial hormone system able to find it (if it exists)?

References

1. Heiss, H.-U., Schmitz, M.: Decentralized dynamic load balancing: The particles approach. In: Proc. 8th Int. Symp. on Computer and Information Sciences, Istanbul, Turkey (November 1993)
2. Cicerre, F.R.L., Bittencourt, L.F., Madeira, E.R.M., Buzato, L.E.: A path clustering heuristic for scheduling task graphs onto a grid. In: MGC05. 3rd International Workshop on Middleware for Grid Computing, Grenoble, France (2005)
3. Radulescu, A., van Gemund, A.J.C.: Fast and effective task scheduling in heterogeneous systems. In: IEEE Computer - 9th Heterogeneous Computing Workshop, Cancun, Mexico, IEEE Computer Society Press, Los Alamitos (2000)

On Self-aware Delay Time Based Service Request Optimization for Gateway Stability in Autonomic Self-healing Systems

Junaid Ahsenali Chaudhry[1], Yonghwan Lee[2], Seungkyu Park[1], and Dugki Min[2],*

[1] Graduate School of Information and Communication, Ajou University,
Woncheon-dong, Paldal-gu, Suwon, 443-749, Korea
{junaid,sparky}@ajou.ac.kr
[2] School of Computer Science and Engineering, Konkuk University,
Hwayang-dong, Kwangjin-gu, Seoul, 133-701, Korea
{Yhlee,dkmin}@konkuk.ac.kr

Abstract. The benefits of component-based service composition are immense however due to their exponential complexity; their real time implementation is a big challenge. In hybrid networks i.e. ubiquitous zone-based networks (u-Zone Networks), the high intensity of service requests can effect drastically on the performance stability of service gateways. In this paper, we present a self-aware service request optimization algorithm for autonomic self-healing systems. We propose when a service request is received and the system is found in the overload state where it can not entertain more service requests, instead of imposing denial of service, the gateway would evaluate the workload of the worker thread at the gateway and reschedule the service request by deferring it. According to our simulation result, the proposed delay time algorithm, if implied, enable gateways with more stability in order to process high flux of service request loads even beyond the saturation point.

1 Introduction

The enormous management [1] cost is the trade-off of countless anticipated reimbursements by distributed networks i.e. u-Zone networks. The u-Zone networks carry the features of cluster-based Mobile Ad-hoc NETworks (MANETs) i.e. high heterogeneity, mobility, dynamic topologies, limited physical security, limited survivability, and low setup time [2] along with the support of high speed mesh backbones [3]. Autonomic Computing (AC) presents a novel solution for management costs in the form of self-management [4] but because of lack of standardization activities and demarcation of functional specifications, self-management is not a straight forward solution. Several network management solutions proposed in [5, 6, 7, 8] are confined strictly to their respective domains i.e. either mesh network or MANETs.

---

* Corresponding author.

R. Obermaisser et al. (Eds.): SEUS 2007, LNCS 4761, pp. 348–357, 2007.

In u-Zone networks, due to such a wide variety of clients, it is not worthwhile to devise separate management solutions for each client. Rather we suggested that dividing the problem domain into sub domains [9]. The component-based solutions can be applied after dividing the problems into sub-domains. A component based self-healing solution is proposed in [10]. The dynamic service composition carries exponential complexity [11] so transaction thrashing can take place. The term thrashing generally describes "a phenomenon where an increase of the load results in decrease of throughput (or another-related performance measure)" [12]. So it is integral to provide a mechanism for preventing the thrashing in dynamic component integration systems. We use the delay time-based peak load control scheme in order to prevent the transaction trashing caused by enormous number of service request in u-Zone-based hybrid networks. This complexity may be the biggest hindrance in real-time implementation of autonomic solutions in real time environments.

Although there has not been much published work on service request management in self managing networks, we propose a time delay based peak load control mechanism for the self healing engine proposed in [11]. As the complexity of the solutions made by dynamic composition from components can be exponential [11], it is critical to provide incremental, low cost and time efficient solutions. The worker pattern [8], connecter-accepter model [16], reactor [15] and proactive [21] approaches are effective in combination but not cost effective in real life applications. The use of the Peak Load Control (PLC) mechanism manages the service requests at the gateway. Depending on the load on the host gateway, the service requests are evaluated and deferred to avoid Denial of Service (DoS). We assign time stamps to the service requests for "*fairness*" in their scheduling. We show the simulation result for proving the stability of performance. According to our experimental results, the proposed delay time algorithm can stably control the heavy overload after the saturation point and has significant effect on the controlling peak load.

In section 2 we discuss related work. The system architecture follows in section 3. In section 4 we discuss self-aware service request optimization mechanism. In section 5 we describe the simulation results along with their significance. In section 6 we conclude the paper and discuss future work.

2 Related Work

In this section we compare our research with related work. Since there has not been any research work published for controlling the service request load control in autonomic self healing networks, we can compare our scheme on the bases of autonomic self-management functions only. However the use of the self-aware PLC mechanism in self-healing networks remains uniqueness in the area.

The Robust Self-configuring Embedded Systems (*RoSES*) project [13] aims to target the management faults using self configuration. It uses graceful degradation as a means to achieve dependable systems. In [14] the authors propose that there are certain faults that can not be removed through configured of the system, which means that RoSES does not fulfill the definition of self management as proposed in [18]. The *HYWINMARC* [3] uses cluster heads to manage the clusters at local level but does not explain the criteria of their selection. The specifications of Mobile Code Execution

Environment (*MCEE*) are absent. Moreover the use of intelligent agents can give similar results as discussed above in the case of [8, 15, 16, and 21]. To enforce management at local level, the participating nodes should have some local management entity. We compare the Autonomic Healing-based Self-management ENgine (*AHSEN*) with the other architectures. The comparison reveals that entity profiling, functional classification of self management entities at implementation level, and assurance of the functional compliance is not provided in the schemes proposed. Moreover the self monitoring at node's local level courtesy *NFM* not only gives a node its self awareness but also uses the shared medium to the minimum. In very dynamic hybrid networks these functionalities go a long way in improving the performance of the self management system.

3 System Architecture

In hybrid wireless networks, there are many different kinds of devices attached with the network. They vary from each other in their power, performance etc. One of the characteristics not present in the related literature is the separate classification of the client and the gateway architectures. Figure 1 shows the client and gateway self-management software architectures.

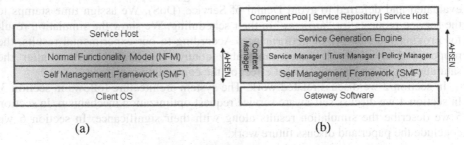

Fig. 1. The AHSEN architectures of client (a) and gateway (b)

The *Normal Functionality Model (NFM)* is a device dependent ontology that is downloaded, along with *SMF*, on the device at network configuration level. It provides a mobile user with an initial default profile at gateway level and device level functionality control at user level. The client *SMF* constantly *tracks* the user activities and sends them to the *SMF* at the gateway. The *SMF* at gateway directs the *track* requests to the context manager which updates the related profile of the user. The changes in service pool, trust manager, and policy manger are reported to the *Context Manager (CM)*. The *CM* consists of a *Lightweight Directory Access Protocol (LDAP)* directory that saves its sessions at predetermined time intervals in the gateway directory. The *Policy Manager (PM)* and *Service Manager (SM)* follow the same registry based approach to enlist their resources. The presence of *NFM* provides decision based reporting unlike the ever-present *SNMP*. The Trust Manager uses the reputation-based trust management scheme in public key certificates [10]. The trust factor is typically decided on trustee's reputation to mitigate risks involved in interaction with unknown and potentially malicious users. We desist providing more details on AHSEN architecture here. For a more detailed description of the architecture shown in figure 1, please refer to [10].

In [3] the authors classify self management into individual functions and react to the anomaly detected through *SNMP* messages. The clear demarcation of *self-** functions is very difficult due to the original mapping of faults onto management functions is not defined. Considering the overlapping nature of faults, it is more fertile to target the problems, which can be either atomic or complex, with atomic, vaguely categorized solutions that either combine at run time to make complex 'healing policies' or work independently in the shape of components [12]. The service generation engine is a rule-based engine embedded into AHSEN for template based service generation from components, the details of which are not within the scope of this paper.

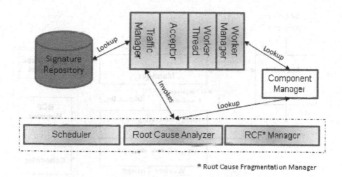

Fig. 2. Architecture of Self Management Framework (SMF)

The Root Cause Analyzer is the core component of the problem detection phase of healing. The State Transition Analysis based approaches [21] might not be appropriate as *Hidden Markov Models (HMMs)* takes long training time along with exhaustive system resources utilization. The profile based Root Cause Detection might not be appropriate mainly because of the vast domain of errors expected. Considering this situation, we use the meta-data obtained from *NFM* to trigger *Finite State Automata (FSA)* series present at the Root Cause Analyzer. In the future we plan to modify *State Transition Analysis Tool* [21] in lines of on fault analysis domains. After analyzing the root-cause results from the *RCA*, the *RCF* manager in cooperation with the Signature Repository and Scheduler search for the already developed solutions else it arranges a time slot based scheduler for plug-ins. The traffic manager directs the traffic towards different parts of *AHSEN*.

4 Self-aware Service Request Optimization

The *Traffic Manager* receives Simple Object Access Protocol (*SOAP)* requests from many devices within a cluster and redirects them to all the other internal parts of *SMF*. Figure 3 shows the structure of delay time-based peak load control. The

Acceptor thread of the *Traffic Manager* receives a *SOAP* request (service request) and then puts it into the *Wait Queue*. The *Wait Queue* contains the latest context of the gateway load. If the gateway is in saturated state, the service request is handled by the self-aware sub module. The figure 4 is the pseudo code of self-aware sub-module in *WorkerManager's* Delay Time Algorithm. Let a service request (SR_1) arrives at the gateway. At first the SR_1 is checked if it contains the *comebacktime* stamp (for fair scheduling). If the *comebacktime* is 'fair' (that is the service request is returned after the instructed time), it is forwarded to the *Wait Queue* else it is accessed against the work load of the *Worker Manager*. The *Acceptor* is updated about the latest status of the Worker Manager. The Acceptor evaluates the intensity of current workload (how long it will take to free resources) and adds *buff* (buffer is the time to give some extra room to gateway) to the time. The aggregate time is assigned to SR_1 and the service request is discarded.

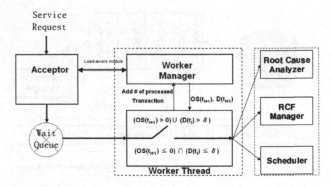

Fig. 3. The Structure of Delay Time-Based Peak Load Control in AHSEN

When the system is ready to accept the service request, the *Traffic Manager* get a *Worker Thread* from a thread pool and run it. The *Worker Thread* gets the delay time and the over speed from the *WorkerManager*. The admission to other internal parts SMF is controlled by the *Worker Thread* that accepts the arriving requests only if the over speed $OS(t_{i+1})$ at the time t_{i+1} is below zero and the delay time $D(t_i)$ at the time t_i is below the baseline delay δ. Otherwise the requests have to sleep for the delay time calculated by the *WorkerManager*. After the *Worker Thread* sleeps for the delay time, the *Worker Thread* redirects the requests to the Root Cause Analyzer, the *RCF* Manager, and the Scheduler. Finally, the *Worker Thread* adds the number of processed transaction after finishing the related transaction.

The figure 4 is the pseudo code for the *WorkerManager's* delay time algorithm. After sleeping during interval time, the *WorkerManager* gets the number of transactions processed by all *Worker Threads* and the maximum transaction processing speed configured by a system administrator. And then, the *WorkerManager* calculates the TPMS (Transaction per Milliseconds) by dividing the number of transactions by the maximum transaction processing speed and calculate the over speed $OS(t_{i+1})$ that means the difference of performance throughput at the time t_{i+1} between the TPMS and the maximum transaction processing speed during the configured interval time. If the value of the over speed is greater than zero, the system is considered as an overload state. Accordingly, it is necessary to control the overload state. On the contrary, if the value of the over speed is zero or less than zero, it is not necessary to control the transaction processing speed. For controlling the overload state, this paper uses the delay time algorithm of the *WorkerManager*. The Figure 6 describes the formulas for calculating the delay time.

```
0-  Let a service request SR₁ arrives at Acceptor
1-  Check SR₁.comebacktime
2-  If (SR₁.comebacktime='fair') // check the virtual queue
        a.  Wait Queue ← Send SR₁
3-  Acceptor ← Send current_context(worker_Manager_Status_Update)
4-  If (current_context!='overloaded')
        a.  Wait queue ← Send SR₁
5-  else
        a.  While (current_context='overlaoded')
                i.   delaytime= Calculate
                     (intensity_of(current_context)+buff
                ii.  Set SR₁.comebacktime ← delaytime
               iii.  Dismount SR₁
6-  While run_flag equals "true" do
7-  get interval time for checking load
8-  sleep during the interval time
9-  get the number of transactions processed during the interval time
10- get the configured maximum speed
11- TPMS := number of transactions / interval time
12- over speed := TPMS - the configured maximum speed
13- If over speed >0 then
        a.  get the previous delay time
        b.  if previous delay time = 0
                i.   previous delay time := 1
        c.  get the number of active worker thread
        d.  new delay time:= over speed / number of active worker *
            previous delay time
14- else
        a.  get current delay
        b.  if current delay > δ
                i.   new delay time := current delay * β
        c.  else
                i.   new delay time := 0
        d.  end if
15- end if
16- end while
```

Fig. 4. The Pseudo code for Self-Aware module and WorkerManager's Delay Time Algorithm

If the over speed $OS(t_{i+1})$ is greater than zero, the first formula of the Figure 6 is used for getting a new delay time $D(t_{i+1})$ at the time t_{i+1}. The $N(t_{i+1})$ means the number of active *Worker Threads* at the time t_{i+1} and $D(t_i)$ means the delay time at the time t_i. If the $D(t_i)$ is zero, $D(t_i)$ must be set one. If the $OS(t_{i+1})$ is below zero and the delay time $D(t_i)$ at the time t_i is greater than the baseline delay δ, The $D(t_{i+1})$ is calculated by applying the second formula of the Figure 6. On the contrary, if the $D(t_i)$ is below the baseline delay, $D(t_{i+1})$ is directly set zero. In other word, because the state of system is under load, the delay time at the time t_{i+1} is not necessary. Accordingly, the *Worker Thread* can have admission to other internal parts *SMF*. The baseline delay is used for preventing repetitive generation of the over speed generated by suddenly dropping the next delay time in previous heavy load state. When the system state is continuously in state of heavy load for a short period of time, it tends to regenerate the over speed to suddenly increment the delay time at the time t_i and then suddenly decrement the delay time zero at the time t_{i+1}. In other words, the baseline delay decides whether next delay time is directly set zero or not.

The β percent of the second formula of the Figure 5 decides the slope of a downward curve. However, if the delay time at the time t_i is lower than the baseline delay. The new delay time at the time t_{i+1} is set zero. Accordingly, when a system state becomes the heavy overload at the time t_i, the gradual decrement by β percent prevents the generation of repetitive over speed caused by abrupt decrement of the next delay time.

$$D(t_{i+1}) := \begin{cases} \dfrac{OS(t_{i+1}) * D(t_i)}{N(t_{i+1})}, if(OS(t_{i+1})) > 0 \\[3mm] D(t_i) * \beta, if((OS(t_{i+1})) \le 0 \cap (D(t_i) > \delta)), \\[3mm] 0, if((OS(t_{i+1})) \le 0 \cap (D(t_i) \le \delta)) \end{cases}$$

Fig. 5. A Mathematical Model for Delay Time Calculation

Once the service request is received by the worker thread the analysis of the cause of anomaly starts. As proposed in [18] the faults can be single root cause based or multiple root cause based. We consider this scenario and classify a *Root Cause Analyzer* that checks the root failure cause through the algorithms proposed in [19]. After identifying the root causes, the *Root Cause Fragmentation Manager (REF Manager)* looks up for the candidate plug-ins as solution. The *RFC manager* also delegates the candidate plug-ins as possible replacement of the most appropriate. The scheduler schedules the service delivery mechanism as proposed in [20]. The processed fault signatures are stored in signature repository for future utilization.

5   Simulation Results

In order to prove performance stability of the self-aware PLC-based autonomic self-healing system, we simulated the self-aware delay time algorithm of the *WorkerManager*. As for load generation, the *LoadRunner 8.0* tool is employed. The delay time and over speed are used as a metric for simulation analysis. The *maximum speed*, δ and β for delay time algorithm are configured 388, 100ms, and 0.75 respectively. Figure 6 shows the result of simulation for describing the relationship between the over-speed and the delay time after the saturation point.

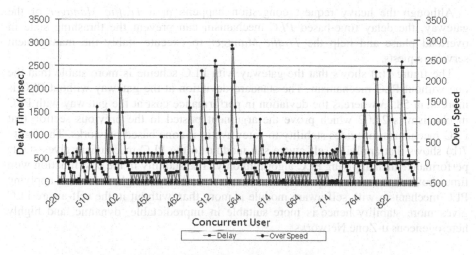

Fig. 6. The Simulation Results Proving the Effect of Delay Time Algorithm

The experimental results prove that the proposed delay time algorithm of the *WorkerManager* has an effect on controlling the over-speed. As the number of concurrent users is more than 220 users, the over-speed frequently takes place. Whenever the over-speed happens, each *Worker Thread* sleeps for the delay time calculated by the *WorkerManager*. As the higher over-speed takes place, each *Worker Thread* sleeps for the more time so that the over speed steeply goes down. Although the over speed steeply goes down, the delay time does not steeply goes down due to the baseline delay value δ. As the baseline delay value is set 100 ms in this experiment, the delay time gradually goes down until the 100 ms. As soon as the delay time passes 100 ms, the next delay time is directly set zero. The result of simulation in figure 7(a) shows that the over-speed does not happen until zero delay time due to the slope of a downward curve. However, As soon as the delay time passes zero, the over speed again occurs and the next delay time controls the over speed.

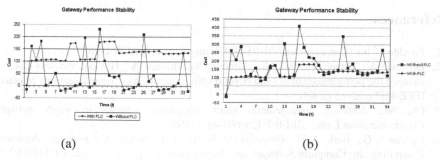

(a)   (b)

Fig. 7. The Simulation Results for Gateway Performance Stability using WorkerManager's Delay Time Algorithm

Although the heavy request congestion happens in a *Traffic Manager* of the gateway, the delay time-based *PLC* mechanism can prevent the thrashing state in overload phase and help the *Traffic Manager* to execute stably the management service requests.

The figure 7(a) shows that the gateway with PLC scheme is more stable than the one without PLC mechanism. The standard deviation at the gateway without PLC is more than 58.23 whereas the deviation in performance cost at the gateway with PLC mechanism is 24.02 which prove the argument posted in the previous section that PLC mechanism provides stability to gateways in u-zone based networks. The figure 7(b) shows that applying self-aware sub module to the PLC mechanism gives stable performance than applying PLC algorithm only. The stability in the cost function with time shows that the cost is predictable over time scale. Although the cost of applying PLC mechanism with self-aware module is more than without it, the self-aware PLC gives more stability hence is more suitable in unpredictable, dynamic, and highly heterogeneous u-Zone Networks.

6 Concluding Remarks and Future Work

In this paper, we propose a self-aware delay time based service request optimization algorithm for gateway stability in ubiquitous networks. We apply the scheme in autonomic self-healing based systems. As there is large variety of clients trying to access the same set of services it is highly probable that a service that works optimally for a certain type of client may prove terminal for another type of client. So we propose to decrease the granularity and name them *components* and join them dynamically. We identify that because of exponential complexity among dynamic service composition systems, their real time implementation is not easy. For this reason, we propose a self-aware delay time based algorithm that gives more stability to the gateway than some of the solutions proposed.

In future we aim to test this scheme in more complex situations and at mutually dependent services. We aim to improve the root cause analysis algorithms so that the exact situation at the client end could be sorted out. The performance of self-aware enabled PLC algorithm is yet to be tested in the presence of multiple users.

References

1. Firetide ™ Inc (Last accesses:(01-01-2007), http://www.firedide.com
2. Doufexi, A., Tameh, E., Nix, A., Armour, S., Molina, A.: Hotspot wireless LANs to enhance the performance of 3G and beyond cellular networks. Communications Magazine, IEEE 41(7), 58–65 (2003)
3. Oh, M.: Network management agent allocation scheme in mesh networks. Communications Letters, IEEE 7(12), 601–603 (2003)
4. Cybenko, G., Berk, V.H., Gregorio-De Souza, I.D., Behre, C.: Practical Autonomic Computing. In: Computer Software and Applications Conference, 2006. COMPSAC '06. 30th Annual International, vol. 1, pp. 3–14 (September 2006)

5. Chaudhry, S.A., Akbar, A.H., Kim, K.-H., Hong, S.-K., Yoon, W.-S.: HYWINMARC: An Autonomic Management Architecture for Hybrid Wireless Networks. Network Centric Ubiquitous Systems (NCUS 2006) (2006)
6. Richard, B.: Network Management. Concepts and Practice: A Hands-on Approach Pearson Education, Inc. (2004)
7. Kishi, Y., Tabata, K., Kitahara, T., Imagawa, Y., Idoue, A., Nomoto, S.: Implementation of the integrated network and link control functions for multi-hop mesh networks in broadband fixed wireless access systems. In: Radio and Wireless Conference, 2004 IEEE, 19-22 September 2004, pp. 43–46 (2004)
8. Yong-Lin, S., DeYuan, G., Jin, P., PuBing, S.: A mobile agent and policy-based network management architecture. In: Proceedings, Fifth International Conference on Computational Intelligence and Multimedia Applications ICCIMA 2003, 27-30 September 2003, pp. 177–181 (2003)
9. Chaudhry, J.A., Park, S.: A Novel Autonomic Rapid Application Composition Scheme for Ubiquitous Systems. In: Yang, L.T., Jin, H., Ma, J., Ungerer, T. (eds.) ATC 2006. LNCS, vol. 4158, Springer, Heidelberg (2006)
10. Chaudhry, J.A., Park, S.: Using Artificial Immune Systems for Self Healing in Hybrid Networks. In: Encyclopedia of Multimedia Technology and Networking, Idea Group Inc. 2006 (to appear)
11. Turing, A.M.: On Computable Numbers, with an Application to the Entscheidungs Problem. Proceedings of the London Mathematical Society 2(42), 230–265 (1936)
12. Denning, P.J.: Thrashing: Its Causes and Prevention. In: Proc. AFIPS FJCC 33, pp. 915–922 (1968)
13. Shelton, C., Koopman, P.: Improving System Dependability with Alternative Functionality. In: DSN04 (June 2004)
14. Morikawa, H.: The design and implementation of context-aware services. In: Proceedings of IEEE saint-w 2004, pp. 293–298. IEEE Computer Society Press, Los Alamitos (2004)
15. Schmidt, D.C.: Reactor: An Object Behavioral Pattern for Concurrent Event Demultiplexing and Event Handler Dispatching. In: Coplien, J.O., Schmidt, D.C. (eds.) Pattern Languages of Program Design, pp. 529–545. Addison-Wesley, Reading (1995)
16. Schmidt, D.C.: Acceptor and Connector: Design Patterns for Initializing Communication Services. In: Martin, R., Buschmann, F., Riehle, D. (eds.) Pattern Languages of Program Design, Addison-Wesley, Reading (1997)
17. Trumler, W., Petzold, J., Bagci, F., Ungerer, T.: AMUN – Autonomic Middleware for Ubiquitious eNvironments Applied to the Smart Doorplate Project. In: International Conference on Autonomic Computing (ICAC-04), May 17-18, 2004, New York (2004)
18. Gao, J., Kar, G., Kermani, P.: Approaches to building self healing systems using dependency analysis. In: Network Operations and Management Symposium, 2004. NOMS 2004. IEEE/IFIP, 19-23 April 2004, vol. 1, pp. 119–132 (2004)
19. Chaudhry, J., Park, S.: On Seamless Service Delivery. In: Wang, L., Jiao, L., Shi, G., Li, X., Liu, J. (eds.) FSKD 2006. LNCS (LNAI), vol. 4223, Springer, Heidelberg (2006)
20. Hu, J., Pyarali, I., Schmidt, D.C.: Applying the Proactor Pattern to High-Performance Web Servers. In: Proceedings of the 10th International Conference on Parallel and Distributed Computing and Systems, IASTED (October 1998)

Algorithmic Skeletons for the Programming of Reconfigurable Systems

Florian Dittmann

Heinz Nixdorf Institute, University of Paderborn
Fuerstenallee 11, 33102 Paderborn, Germany

Abstract. Reconfigurable hardware such as FPGAs combines performance and flexibility, two inherent requirements of many modern electronic devices. Moreover, using reconfigurable devices, time to market can be reduced while simultaneously cutting the costs. However, the design of systems that beneficially explore the reconfiguration capabilities of modern FPGAs is cumbersome and little automated. In this work, a new approach is described that starts from a very high level of abstraction, so-called *algorithmic skeletons*, and exploits the additional information of this level of abstraction to beneficially execute on reconfigurable devices. Particularly, the approach focuses on dynamic run-time reconfiguration on partially reconfigurable FPGAs. As a first introduction to this approach, we consider stream parallelism paradigms including their composition.

1 Introduction

Flexibility and performance are demanding requirements of modern computing systems. Reconfigurable devices offer these requirements as they compute in parallel while still being adaptable (e. g. [1,2]). However, these benefits are cumbersome to explore, particularly, if dynamic reconfiguration shall be exploited. Despite an increasing number of modern FPGAs providing partial run-time reconfiguration—two core requirements for dynamic reconfiguration—methods that allow to exploit these additional flexibilities are rarely found. Nevertheless, some work has been done that proofs the benefit of fine grain granularity and high adaptability of FPGAs, e. g. in [3,4,5,6,7,8].

To eventually exploit the potentials, the cumbersome details of partial run-time reconfiguration should be transparent. We therefore need to offer dynamic reconfiguration on a high level of abstraction to easily gain the benefits of partially reconfigurable systems. These benefits are most likely if the design is done in an FPGA aware manner, i. e., close to the technical (hardware) characteristics of the FPGAs. As the latter is challenging for the application oriented designer, we propose to raise the level of abstraction by using so-called *algorithmic skeletons*. Algorithmic skeletons are programming templates that guide designers to efficiently implement algorithms by separating the structure from the computation itself. In reconfigurable systems, partial run-time reconfigurability thus becomes transparent for the algorithms.

As an introduction to the concept, we show how stream parallelism of applications executed on FPGAs can be abstracted using algorithmic skeletons. On basis of the abstraction, a run-time reconfiguration manager can successfully combine the execution of several—also different—skeletons on one FPGA during the same time.

R. Obermaisser et al. (Eds.): SEUS 2007, LNCS 4761, pp. 358–367, 2007.

This work is organized as follows: In the next section, we review related work. Section 3 formulates the problem, while Sect. 4 conceptually describes the proposed solution. In Sect. 5, we refine the concept proposed by detailing three skeletons of the stream parallel computing paradigm. Dynamic reconfiguration by virtue of algorithmic skeletons is discussed in Sect. 6. Finally, we conclude and give an outlook.

2 Related Work

In the literature, we find some works on designing reconfigurable systems on a higher level of abstraction than hardware description languages (HDLs). Most of these works do not target partial run-time reconfigurable systems. Additionally, the models proposed assume the designer to have reasonable knowledge of the system under development.

The work of DeHon et al. [9] on design patterns for reconfigurable systems is a sophisticated approach on providing canonical solutions to common and recurring design challenges of reconfigurable systems and applications. The authors intend on providing a mean to crystallize out common challenges of reconfigurable system design and the typical solutions. However, their work focusses more on providing a layer of abstraction to the reconfigurable systems community than to application engineers.

Some years earlier, SCORE (Stream Computations Organized for Reconfigurable Execution) was proposed in [10]. The approach focusses on providing a unifying compute model to abstract away the fixed resource limits of devices. Therefore, the resources are virtualized, which can ease the development and deployment of reconfigurable applications. Again, the addressees of the SCORE approach are mainly reconfigurable computing engineers.

Modern languages for embedded systems like SystemVerilog or SystemC also aim at raising the level of abstraction. These approaches can be seen as extended HDLs that introduce design principles to the hardware world, such as re-use, polymorphism, etc. For example, SystemC as language to model dynamic reconfigurable hardware is used in [11]. However, the languages are often used for simulation only and the generation of executable code is challenging.

Further approaches propose an operating systems for reconfigurable systems or FPGAs, respectively, e. g. [7,12,13,14]. These approaches focus on providing the reconfigurable fabric to tasks via the abstraction layer of the operating system. The benefit of these approaches can be a predictable behavior of the executed task. Operating systems, however, seldom consider structure and behavior of the algorithms to be computed.

Finally, in low-level hardware design, [15] focus on a high-level hardware description called hardware skeletons. Considering the idea of separation of structure from the algorithm, this approach is closest to our work. Moreover, the authors motivate their work similar to us, i. e., an increase of abstraction in order to open the field of hardware design to a broader audience. However, the amount of skeletons is very limited and they are still very low-level and will often be too far away from algorithm designers. Moreover, we do not find the paradigm of reconfigurability in their work.

To summarize, all these abstracting approaches barely consider partial run-time reconfiguration and therefore lack the possibility to make the cumbersome details of reconfigurable systems transparent to the application designer.

3   Problem Definition

The design of applications for the execution on partially run-time reconfigurable systems is twofold. On one hand, FPGAs fundamentally are hardware that can be programmed and whose configuration may change over time. Therefore, we need a firm background in hardware design, including communication and I/O requirements. We also have to respect the critical path information, clock skew, etc. Moreover, partially reconfigurable FPGAs require to consider the modification of hardware over time.

On the other hand, the application design is driven by achieving high performance and short time to market. Designers therefore explore the theory behind applications and search for algorithms that server the problems best. Moreover, they try to abstract from the execution platform, mostly due to reasons of programmability and portability. Partial run-time reconfiguration becomes a feature that should be beneficially for the performance of the algorithm. The details of hardware and FPGAs thereby are of secondary focus, as development takes place more in the terms of the software world, even if special requirements of embedded systems are respected.

Synthesis from behavioral problem description to reconfigurable hardware targets this issue. However, in the domain of partial run-time reconfigurable hardware, automatic synthesis still lacks good results. Furthermore, if iterative design due to performance evaluation is required, or portability is an issue, we require a more suitable design methodology that supports designers on a high level of abstraction.

4   Problem Solution

We propose to use algorithmic skeletons as bridge between circuit design and application development for FPGAs. Algorithmic skeletons therefore are offered as a library that is used by the algorithms of the application under development. The usage of algorithmic skeletons constrains the design of algorithms to a set of templates. However, we can extract valuable information for dynamic reconfiguration from these templates.

4.1   Algorithmic Skeletons

Algorithmic skeletons were introduced by Cole [16]. They separate the structure of a computation from the computation itself. Originally, the application domain of algorithmic skeletons are parallel machines or cluster computers. In particular, the skeletons free the programmer from the implementation details of the structure, such as how to map it to the available processors. By providing a structured management of parallel computation, they can be used to write architecture independent programs, shielding application developers from the details of a parallel implementation.

Algorithmic skeletons are similar to higher order functions of functional languages for conventional imperative languages. Concerning design space exploration, skeletons and their level of abstraction enable to explore a variety of parallel structurings for a given application. A clean separation between structural aspects and the application specific details is realized by virtue of algorithmic skeletons. Thanks to the structural information provided, static and dynamic optimization of implementations is possible.

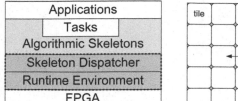
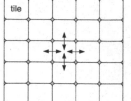
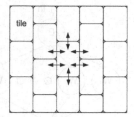

Fig. 1. Layer model   **Fig. 2.** Two run-time execution environments

The purpose of every skeleton is to abstract a pattern of activities and their inter-actions. They provide a means of implementation, which separates them from design patterns. The latter are mostly used during the design phase and offer only orientation for the final implementation. Due to their proximity to a run-time environment, algorithmic skeletons allow us to exploit the performance offered by the processing system.

Consequently, there has to be a balance between generality (allowing re-use for different architectures and user kernels) and specificity (for efficient implementation and interfaces to the user kernels). There also is the so-called trap of universality, i. e., providing a skeleton that is generic in itself and can be used if no other skeleton might fit. Such a skeleton would increase the complexity of a run-time environment. In order to avoid this trap, there is usually the restriction of the acceptable input for a system to a set of valid algorithmic skeletons only, see also [17,18]. In case of modern FPGAs, we can also overcome this gap by exploiting soft or hard core CPUs. These general purpose processors can execute any algorithm due to their Turing completeness.

4.2 Application in Reconfigurable Systems

Reconfigurable computing on FPGAs basically is similar to processing on parallel systems, as execution of algorithms on hardware like FPGAs also means processing in parallel. When reconfiguring FPGAs, we usually define exchangeable regions and apply different modules to these regions. Several such regions can be marked on the same FPGA. These regions are comparable to the nodes of a computing cluster. The inter-module communication, so still a challenging research area, enables various ways of data exchange. Thus, we see broad similarities to parallel computing in the sense of algorithmic skeletons. We can distribute applications into the regions as it is done in the parallel computing domain. For efficient execution and beneficial exploitation of the capabilities, both systems need structure, which is provided by algorithmic skeletons.

Therefore, we use algorithmic skeletons as means of abstraction for partial run-time reconfiguration of FPGAs. The skeletons provide a seminal method to abstract reconfigurable fabrics on a high level. We combine the skeletons into a library. As a first introduction to this new concept, we detail stream parallelism in the next section.

We abstract the general concept by virtue of a layer model, see Fig. 1. Applications, which built the top layer, are described by a set of tasks. These tasks must be implemented using algorithmic skeletons. An execution environment that executes the tasks

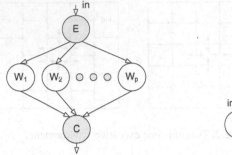

Fig. 3. Farm parallelism   **Fig. 4.** The pipeline paradigm

on an FPGA accepts the tasks described by a set of skeletons only. The set of skeletons is processed by a dispatcher that is deeply connected to its execution environment.

4.3 Execution Environment

Concerning the practical realization of a suitable run-time environment for the execution of the set of skeletons on an FPGA, we consider a tiled system. As we focus on homogenous FPGAs in this work, each tile comprises similar logic resources. However, we still consider two different tile arrangements: the first being a purely quadratic organization, while the second one offers more direct communication possibilities due to an underlying hexagonal structure (see Fig. 2).

Xilinx Virtex 4 devices support the proposed execution environments as they support 2D style partial reconfiguration. Furthermore, on these devices, the external communication, i. e. the I/O pads, is separated and not part of a slice. With the advances in FPGA design, more sophisticated run-time environments are possible.

5   Stream Parallelism

Stream parallelism may be the closest idea of parallel computing that matches the ideas of execution on FPGAs [19]. Stream computation can be described as applying $f : \alpha \to \beta$ on a stream of input values $a_1, a_2, \ldots$. The idea is to exploit the parallelism within the computation of f on different (and unrelated) elements of the input stream. As an example, we can consider a vision system that explores images. The images enter the system abstracted as a stream and must be handled differently.

5.1   Farm Paradigm

An algorithm that computes the same f on all of the elements of a stream $a_1, a_2, \ldots$ exploits the farm paradigm. The computations $f(a_1), f(a_2), \ldots$ can be executed in parallel using a pool of parallel processing modules. Figure 3 depicts the concept. The major characteristic to observe is that the functions can be executed independently of each other as they are all operating on a different data set.

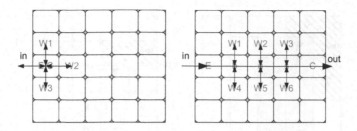

Fig. 5. Two possible execution schemes of applications using the farm skeleton

As an application example, we can assume a stream of two video channels that should be output alternatingly to one single channel. However, the switch between the two channels should not be abrupt but smoothly, i. e., a fading between the two channels. We thus have a function f that is applied on a stream of three input values $\langle x_1, y_1, c_1 \rangle, \langle x_2, y_2, c_2 \rangle, \ldots$, while x_1 and y_1 denote the two video streams and c_1 the dominance of the one stream over the other (an increasing/decreasing number of e. g., 8 bit width). Both streams arrive at the node E which distributes the single images to the worker processes $W_1, W_2, \ldots, W_n$ adding the number c_i. These functions can be computed independently of each other in different worker nodes W_i. The results then are propagated to the combining node C that forwards the stream to the video screen.

If we describe our algorithm using a skeleton for the farm paradigm, the structure of the application is given. Thus, we know how to execute the algorithm on the execution device. First, we can derive a meaningful placement of the algorithm that serves both the requirements of the farm and the characteristics of the FPGA. Figure 5 shows how the skeleton can be mapped in two different ways. In the left approach, we use the same tile for the input and output of the nodes. However, if we rely on direct communication links only, the number of possible worker tiles is limited. Therefore, the right approach of Fig. 5 spans the farm skeleton over the whole width of the FPGA.

Dynamic run-time reconfiguration is needed if the amount of worker modules should be adapted during run-time. External stimuli therefore could be a requirement to adapt the quality of service, etc. Further details are discussed in Sect. 6.

To summarize the farm skeleton, a structural concept is given that allows to distribute workers of an application on different tiles of a partially and run-time reconfigurable FPGA. The execution of the workers including their reconfiguration is part of the run-time environment and its dispatcher. However, by describing an application on basis of the farm skeleton, the number of workers is not set. Depending on the resources available, a different quality of service can be realized. The optimal solution, i. e., a solution that avoids the blocking of workers, etc. due to overload conditions, must be derived carefully by evaluating the execution times of the function f and the distribution time of the initial node E.

5.2 Pipeline Paradigm

The pipeline paradigm comprises a composition on n functions $f_1 \ldots f_n$ such that

$$f_1 : \alpha \to \gamma_1, \ldots, f_i : \gamma_{i-1} \to \gamma_i, \ldots, f_n : \gamma_{n-1} \to \beta \qquad (1)$$

Figure 4 shows the concept as a graph.

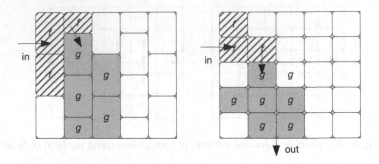

Fig. 6. Two realizations of a pipeline with different area requirements

As an example within our image processing environment, we consider a scenario of a stereo vision system. We receive the input of two cameras $\langle x_1, y_1 \rangle, \langle x_2, y_2 \rangle, \ldots$ and want to extract valuable information out of the system. We therefore compute the composition of two functions $f \circ g$. Function g will result in a combination of the two images, having the pixel combined into the means $(g(\langle x_i, y_i \rangle) = z_i)$, while f will produce the histogram on the resulting image z_i. The functions f and g can be executed in parallel each on a subsequent data set, thus exploiting pipeline parallelism.

In Fig. 6, we depict two possible realizations assuming the second function f to consume more area than function g. Here we can see that different stages can consume more area than available on one single tile by simply combining tiles. The dispatcher of the run-time environment may react on the different requirements of the functions within the pipeline. If enough area is available, the dispatcher may also built up a second pipeline in parallel in order to increase the throughput of the systems.

Describing a problem using the pipeline skeleton, we can further exploit the characteristics of stream processing. As the stages of the pipeline get activated in sequence, we can decrease the reconfiguration latency of the overall system. We successively load the bitstreams of the pipeline stages in their order given. After reconfiguring the first stage, this stage may start its execution before the complete pipeline is loaded. The same holds for the subsequent stages. Thus, the fastest possible response time can be guaranteed. Additionally, if less area than required by the stages is available, we may apply hardware virtualization. Therefore, only parts of the overall pipeline are loaded on the FPGA at the same time. These parts may also perform block processing of a block of input sets in order to hide the reconfiguration overhead, which is still in the range of milliseconds on modern FPGAs.

A further approach to improve the behavior of a pipeline streaming algorithm is to identify the bottleneck stage. In order to reduce the impact of this stage, we can provide a functionality to map this stage on a tile comprising of specific computation resources (assuming a heterogenous FPGA). Alternatively, we might provide critical stages in different implementation variants that can be tested in a design space exploration that explores different implementations of the pipeline skeleton. We then select the combination of these stages that offer the best overall performance.

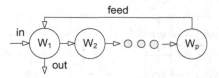

Fig. 7. Stream iterative paradigm

5.3   Stream-Iterative Paradigm

In the stream-iterative paradigm, we have a number of functionally equivalent stages. This number of stages may depend on the input values and is generally unknown before execution. We can view the stream-iterative paradigm as a tail recursive function f that comprises of a finite result x if a boolean function $c(x)$ computes true, or a recursive call $f(g(x))$ otherwise. We can compute such a problem in parallel by a pipeline including a stage for each recursive call of f. Figure 7 depicts the concept. In order to implement such an unbounded pipeline on an FPGA with limited resources available, we emulate the unbounded pipeline by folding it on a chain of processes of a fixed length.

As an example, we can consider again a stream of images that are processed by a filter in each of the stages. The processing will go on until no further refinement of the image is possible and the final result is sent to the output.

6   Dynamic Reconfiguration

The above presented paradigms can be composed to built more complex parallel structures. In Fig. 8, we show how different skeletons can be executed on the same FPGA, exploiting a multi task environment. Depending on the specific needs (quality of service, etc.) of the applications behind the skeletons, we can react and dynamically adapt the purpose and organization of the tiles of our execution environment.

Such a dynamic reconfiguration means the adaptation of a device during run-time. In particular, the amount and shape of tasks that shall be executed on a run-time environment are not known at design time. When realizing such a behavior without any abstracting layers on top of an FPGA, we would have to cope with fragmentation and on-line routing issues that can be tremendously challenging.

The implementation of applications by virtue of algorithmic skeletons enables a sophisticated and dynamic execution of tasks on FPGAs. The run-time environment allows us to load tasks which are available on the basis of algorithmic skeletons onto the FPGA. As the usage of algorithmic skeletons enforces the applications to be well-formed, we thereby can prevent fragmentation of the devices and guarantee communication requirements. Additionally, the quality of service may be considered.

In the example depicted in Fig. 8, we first assume a scenario where a farm skeleton is executed in the left side of the FPGA and a stream-iterative skeleton occupies the right side of the FPGA. The former one can use four worker tiles, while the latter has eight worker tiles on its dispose. At some point in time, a new application requests to enter the system. We can decrease the pipeline of the stream-iterative skeleton, thus freeing

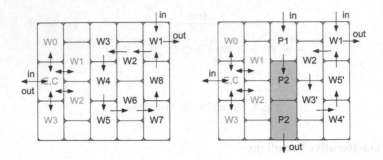

Fig. 8. Combination of different skeletons

area in the middle of the FPGA. This area is then used to execute a new application that ist implemented referring to the pipeline skeleton.

In the example, the execution environment is fixed, as it provides the computational resources and the communication for its set of skeletons. The dispatcher accepts a set of skeletons only. On basis of the information of the skeletons, we can take care of connections, etc. The combination of dispatcher and specific run-time environment allows us the execution of a set of skeletons. We can execute any algorithm on this run-time environment irrespectively of its behavior and size, as long as the algorithm can be implemented by virtue of some of this environment's skeletons. If the area requirements exceed the size of the FPGA, we can apply hardware virtualization as described above. As a drawback, we only serve applications which are implemented as skeletons that the execution environment supports.

The design of applications by virtue of algorithmic skeletons allows us to react on changing needs of the whole system and of a single application of the system. In particular, if the quality of service must be increased, we can demand additional resources.

7 Conclusion

In this work, we have introduced algorithmic skeletons for dynamic reconfigurable computing. Algorithmic skeletons separate structure from the behavior of an algorithm. By providing a library of skeletons to implement applications for reconfigurable systems, we can beneficially explore partial run-time reconfiguration of reconfigurable fabrics. Therefore, solutions, i.e., hardware realizations, of the skeletons are applied to various applications. We have introduced the field of stream parallelism comprising of the farm, pipeline and stream-iterative paradigm. In general, the approach is a hopeful mean to provide an interface between the hardware platform (FPGA) and applications. Moreover, additional benefits are possible if a composition of skeletons is used.

We currently broaden the library of algorithmic skeletons to offer also data prallelism. Furthermore, we want to consider heterogeneous FPGAs, as the additional resources of such fabrics facilitate improved solutions for specific applications that we hope to also cover by algorithmic skeletons. As a final outlook, also coarse-grain reconfigurable devices as execution environments may be taken into account.

References

1. DeHon, A., Wawrzynek, J.: The case for reconfigurable processors (1997)
2. Compton, K., Hauck, S.: Reconfigurable Computing: A Survey of Systems and Software. ACM Computing Surveys 34(2), 171–210 (2002)
3. Ganesan, S., Vemuri, R.: An Integrated Temporal Partitioning and Partial Reconfiguration Technique for Design Latency Improvement. In: DATE '00. Proceedings of the IEEE Design, Automation and Test in Europe, Paris, France (2000)
4. Diessel, O., ElGindy, H., Middendorf, M., Schmeck, H., Schmidt, B.: Dynamic Scheduling of Tasks on Partially Reconfigurable FPGAs. IEE Proceedings – Computer and Digital Techniques (Special Issue on Reconfigurable Systems) 147(3), 181–188 (2000)
5. Horta, E.L., Lockwood, J.W., Taylor, D.E., Parlour, D.: Dynamic hardware plugins in an FPGA with partial run-time reconfiguration. In: DAC '02. Proceedings of the 39th conference on Design automation, pp. 343–348. ACM Press, New York (2002)
6. Li, Z., Hauck, S.: Configuration prefetching techniques for partial reconfigurable coprocessor with relocation and defragmentation. In: FPGA '02. Proceedings of the 2002 ACM/SIGDA tenth international symposium on Field-programmable gate arrays, pp. 187–195. ACM Press, New York (2002)
7. Steiger, C., Walder, H., Platzner, M.: Operating systems for reconfigurable embedded platforms: Online scheduling of real-time tasks. IEEE Trans. Comput. 53(11), 1393–1407 (2004)
8. Danne, K., Bobda, C., Kalte, H.: Run-time Exchange of Mechatronic Controllers Using Partial Hardware Reconfiguration. In: Cheung, P.Y.K., Constantinides, G.A. (eds.) FPL 2003. LNCS, vol. 2778, Springer, Heidelberg (2003)
9. DeHon, A., Adams, J., DeLorimier, M., Kapre, N., Matsuda, Y., Nacimi, H., Vanier, M.C., Wrighton, M.G.: Design patterns for reconfigurable computing. In: FCCM, pp. 13–23 (2004)
10. Caspi, E., Chu, M., Huang, R., Yeh, J., Wawrzynek, J., DeHon, A.: Stream computations organized for reconfigurable execution (score). In: Grünbacher, H., Hartenstein, R.W. (eds.) FPL 2000. LNCS, vol. 1896, pp. 605–614. Springer, Heidelberg (2000)
11. Antti Pelkonen, K.M., Cupák, M.: System-Level Modeling of Dynamically Reconfigurable Hardware with SystemC. In: Proceedings of International Symposium on Parallel and Distributed Processing (Reconfigurable Architectures Workshop), pp. 174–181 (April 2003)
12. Brebner, G.J.: A Virtual Hardware Operating System for the Xilinx XC6200. In: Glesner, M., Hartenstein, R.W. (eds.) FPL 1996. LNCS, vol. 1142, pp. 327–336. Springer, Heidelberg (1996)
13. Danne, K.: Operating Systems for FPGA Based Computers and Their Memory Management. In: ARCS 2004.Organic and Pervasive Computing, Workshop Proceedings. GI-Edition Lecture Notes in Informatics (LNI), vol. P-41, Köllen Verlag (2004)
14. Walder, H., Platzner, M.: A Runtime Environment for Reconfigurable Hardware Operating Systems. In: Becker, J., Platzner, M., Vernalde, S. (eds.) FPL 2004. LNCS, vol. 3203, pp. 831–835. Springer, Heidelberg (2004)
15. Benkrid, K., Crookes, D.: From application descriptions to hardware in seconds: a logic-based approach to bridging the gap. IEEE Trans. VLSI Syst. 12(4), 420–436 (2004)
16. Cole, M.I.: Algorithmic Skeletons: Structured Management of Parallel Computation. Pitman/The MIT Press, London, UK/Cambridge, Massachusetts, USA (1989)
17. Cole, M.: Bringing skeletons out of the closet: a pragmatic manifesto for skeletal parallel programming. Parallel Comput. 30(3), 389 406 (2004)
18. Rabhi, F.A., Gorlatch, S.: Patterns and Skeletons for Parallel and Distributed Computing. Springer, Heidelberg (2002)
19. Pelagatti, S.: Structured development of parallel programs. Taylor & Francis, Inc., Bristol, PA, USA (1998)

A Framework for Supporting the Configuration and Automatic Integration of Heterogeneous Location Sensors

Yoo Chul Chung, Yangwoo Ko, Youngrock Cha, and Dongman Lee

Information and Communications University
{chungyc, newcat, u00cha, dlee}@icu.ac.kr

Abstract. We propose a framework that supports user-friendly configuration of a new location sensor system and its integration with a location manager. The proposed framework abstracts the diversity of heterogeneous sensor technologies using adapters that provide a common interface to the location manager. Configuration of a location sensor system requires information provided by the vendor of the location sensor system, so we propose a configuration protocol with which a newly deployed location sensor system can provide and obtain configuration options and parameters. An integration protocol is proposed as well so that a newly deployed sensing system can be integrated as part of an existing location manager. In order to verify the efficiency of the proposed framework, we measured configuration time with our framework and against manual configuration. Experimental results show that the proposed framework reduces configuration time significantly.

Keywords: location management, location service, location sensors, configuration, integration, coordinate mapping, transformation matrix, adapter.

1 Introduction

In ubiquitous computing environments, smart objects interact with each other and users [7]. In these environments, the location of a user is an important piece of information about the user. Smart objects decide what services to provide to specific users based on this information.

As location sensors become cheaper, users may start deploying a variety of location sensor systems in order to obtain higher accuracy using sensor fusion and to provide diverse methods for obtaining locations. In order to deploy a new location sensor system, sensor-specific coordinates need to be transformed into reference coordinates used by the location manager. Manually configuring the sensor system to support this, as is done in MiddleWhere [3] and LORE [11], requires significant effort and skill. In addition, location sensor systems may be added, moved, or removed according to the needs of the users. Therefore, a ubiquitous computing environment must be able to simplify the work required for configuring and integrating diverse location sensor systems.

R. Obermaisser et al. (Eds.): SEUS 2007, LNCS 4761, pp. 368–377, 2007.

Many of the current location sensor systems [8, 9, 10] require careful configuration and calibration to work properly, so manual integration of heterogeneous location sensor systems may be comparatively insignificant additional work. However, we expect that location sensor systems will become increasingly self-configuring and self-calibrating in the near future [1, 2, 6], so the effort required for manual integration may become increasingly unacceptable.

Our research introduces a framework for supporting the configuration and integration of location sensor systems with a minimum of user interaction. Each location sensor system includes an adapter, which connects to the location manager using a standard interface that abstracts the underlying sensor technologies. It also transforms a local coordinate specific to a location sensor system to a reference coordinate usable by the location manager. As a result, the framework makes it easy for users to deploy a location sensor system. Experimental results from deploying Ubisense [10] on top of a WLAN-based location sensor system show that the proposed framework reduces configuration time significantly, although manual configuration still results in higher accuracy.

The rest of this paper is organized as follows. Section 2 examines related work. We then describe the design and implementation of our framework in Section 3. We describe experimental results with a sample application based on our implementation in Section 4, and conclude the paper in Section 5.

2 Related Work

[1] and [2] propose techniques for sensor localization in a large-scale sensor network which consists of a very large number of nodes. Each sensor node has the ability to estimate distance to nearby nodes. Based on this information, each sensor node knows where it is in a common frame of reference. This sensor localization is attained in real-time without the need for human intervention. However, their work assumes the use of only a single homogeneous location sensor system.

[6] also proposes sensor localization techniques for Cricket. Initially there is no coordinate system in each node. Sensor nodes gather to form a local cluster, where each cluster has its own coordinate system. Coordinate transforms can then be computed between overlapping clusters to stitch them into a global coordinate system. As in [1] and [2], this approach cannot be applied to heterogeneous location sensor systems because they assume all nodes are Cricket nodes. In contrast, our work supports the integration of heterogeneous location sensor systems which cannot directly interoperate with each other and where each system can have their own coordinate system.

MiddleWhere [3] and LORE [11] are location managers which are able to integrate multiple location sensor systems. These systems acquire locations of objects from multiple location sensors and fuse the sensor data by using a variety of algorithms. Their focus is on producing more accurate locations and representing locations in various forms. Each location sensor system uses an adaptor to transparently integrate with the location manager. MiddleWhere and LORE require the manual configuration of each adapter, while our work overcomes this limitation by proposing a framework which eases configuration and automates the registration of heterogeneous location sensor systems with a location manager.

3 Approach

Our framework introduces several components required for configuring and integrating location sensor systems. We also define a protocol between the components that the vendors of location sensor systems can take advantage of.

3.1 Overview

When a location sensor system is deployed, the adapter for a location sensor broadcasts its existence, which is detected by the configurator. The configurator responds to the notification and replies with its own reference to the adapter. The adapter, the configurator, and the location manager then interact with each other to configure the location sensor system and integrate it with the location manager. We envision that the vendors of location sensor systems may implement an adapter for their sensor system in order to take advantage of our framework. The adapter should include sensor-specific information such as accuracy, precision, communication mode, type and reporting rate.

However, for a ranged location sensor system, which covers an area or a volume, the configuration of the adapter cannot be done completely automatically. A location sensor system will typically use a coordinate system that is independent of that used by the location manager, especially if the location sensor system is self-calibrated. This means that we must be able to transform a coordinate in the sensor-specific coordinate system to that in the reference coordinate system used by the location manager. Since such transformations are done on physical coordinates and separate location sensor systems cannot directly know how their coordinate systems are different from each other, the configuration required to support such transformations cannot be done purely in software.

The actual transformation of coordinates is done using a transformation matrix and a displacement vector as in Equation (1). The transformation matrix represents the scaling and rotation of the coordinate systems, while the displacement vector represents the displacement of the origins between the sensor-specific coordinate system and reference coordinate system. Also, (x, y) is a sensor-specific coordinate in the newly deployed coordinate system, while (x', y') is a reference coordinate in the location manager for the same physical location. In the rest of the paper, we will simply refer to both the transformation matrix and the displacement vector together as the "transformation matrix."

$$\begin{pmatrix} a & b \\ c & d \end{pmatrix} \begin{pmatrix} x \\ y \end{pmatrix} + \begin{pmatrix} e \\ f \end{pmatrix} = \begin{pmatrix} x' \\ y' \end{pmatrix} \quad (a,b,c,d,e,f \text{ are constants}) \tag{1}$$

In order to actually configure the transformation matrix, the framework collects coordinates from both the newly deployed location sensor system and the location manager for the same physical location. This is done by providing sensor tags to a user from the newly deployed location sensor system and the location sensor system already integrated with the location manager. The location sensor systems detect location based on these sensor tags. A user then moves as the framework directs him to while carrying both tags. As the user moves around, coordinates from both location

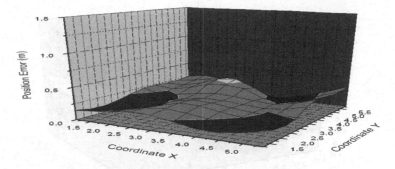

Fig. 3. Error distribution when manually configured

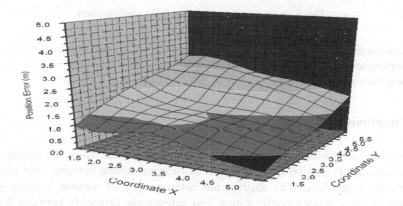

Fig. 4. Error distribution with guideless configuration

When comparing the error distributions between the different configuration methods, we see that manual configuration is the most accurate with a maximum error of 25cm, guided configuration is next with a maximum error of 2.5m, and guideless configuration is the least accurate with a maximum error of 3m. Manual configuration is much more accurate because the most of the error comes from only Ubisense, which has an error of 25cm. Guideless and guided configuration are not only affected by errors in Ubisense, but also by errors in the WLAN-based system, which has an error of 3m. The errors resulting from the use of our framework is within the limits of the error of the WLAN-based system.

We also measure how the error changes in guided configuration when varying the number of locations from which coordinates are gathered and the number of samples gathered at each location. At least eight mappings are required to halve the measured errors. We also found that it is much more important to gather coordinates from more distinct locations than gathering more samples from each location. This suggests that the user should move in a large region covered by both location sensor systems instead of limiting movement to a small region, since moving around in a large region would result in more locations from which coordinates can be gathered.

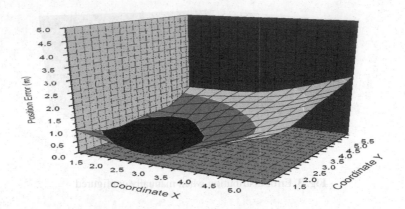

Fig. 5. Error distribution with guided configuration

From the experimental results in this section, we can see that our framework makes the deployment and integration of new location sensor systems with an existing location manager much easier.

5 Conclusion

The goal of our research is to build a location manager that eases the configuration and automates integration of heterogeneous location sensor systems. Our proposed framework uses adapters to abstract the heterogeneity of various location sensor systems. It also defines configuration and integration protocols between location system components, which vendors of location sensors can take advantage of for easing the deployment of their sensors.

The proposed framework significantly reduces the amount of time and effort required to deploy a new location sensor system. One of the methods supported simply requires two button presses on a PDA and random movement of the user in between the button presses, while another provides a user interface with a map viewer to guide the movement of the user.

We have implemented the proposed framework in the Active Surroundings environment and successfully tested the deployment of a Ubisense location sensor system on an existing WLAN-based location sensor system. Our results show that the proposed framework is much easier to use compared to manual configuration, with accuracy being constrained only by the underlying sensor technologies.

Further issues that need to be studied are techniques for reducing errors, especially when accurate sensors are being deployed in an environment with existing inaccurate sensors, and a mathematical analysis of how errors in the underlying sensors affect the final results. We also plan to use the Active Surroundings location manager developed in this work to investigate how multiple location managers can cooperate with each other with the goal of providing more extensive location services.

Acknowledgments. This research is supported by the Ubiquitous Computing and Network Project, the Ministry of Information and Communication 21st Century Frontier R&D Program in Korea.

References

1. Brooks, A., Williams, S., Makarenko, A.: Automatic online localization of nodes in an active sensor network. In: IEEE 2003 International Conference on Robotics and Automation, vol. 5, pp. 4821–4826. IEEE Computer Society Press, Los Alamitos (2003)
2. Efrat, A., Forrester, D., Iyer, A., Kobourov, S.G., Erten, C.: Force-Directed Approaches to Sensor Localization. In: ALENEX. 8th Workshop on Algorithm Engineering and Experiments, pp. 108–118 (2006)
3. Ranganathan, A., Al-Muhtadi, J., Chetan, S., Campbell, R., Dennis, M.: MiddleWhere: A Middleware for Location Awareness in Ubiquitous Computing Applications. In: ACM/IFIP/USENIX 5'th International Middleware Conference, Toronto, Ontario, Canada (October 18th - 22nd, 2004)
4. Jiang, C., Steenkiste, P.: A hybrid location model with a computable location identifier for ubiquitous computing. In: Borriello, G., Holmquist, L.E. (eds.) UbiComp 2002. LNCS, vol. 2498, Springer, Heidelberg (2002)
5. Lee, D., Han, S., Insuk Park, S.K., Lee, K., Hyun, S.J., Lee, Y.H., Lee, G.H.: A Group-Aware Middleware for Ubiquitous Computing Environments. In: ICAT 2004 (November 2004)
6. Moore, D., Leonard, J., Rus, D., Teller, S.: Robust distributed network localization with noisy range measurements. In: SenSys '04. Proceedings of the Second ACM Conference on Embedded Networked Sensor Systems, Baltimore, MD (November 2004)
7. Saha, D., Mukherjee, A.: A Paradigm for the 21st Century. IEEE Computer, 25-31, (March 2003)
8. Yousief, M.A.: HORUS: A WLAN-based indoor location determination system, Ph.D. dissertation, University of Maryland, College Park, MD (2004)
9. Priyantha, N.B., Chakraborty, A., Balakrishnan, H.: The cricket location-support system. In: Procedddings of MOBICOM 2000, Boston, MA, pp. 32–43. ACM Press, Boston (2000)
10. UbiSense, http://www.ubisense.net/
11. Chen, Y., Chen, X.Y., Rao, F.Y., Yu, X.L., Li, Y., Liu, D.: LORE: An infrastructure to support location -aware services, vol. 48(5/6) (September/November 2004)

Searching Visual Media Service Providers Using ASN.1-Based Ontology Reasoning

Youngkun Min, Bogju Lee, and Yunmook Nah

Department of Computer Engineering, Dankook University
Hannam Dong, Youngsan Ku, Seoul, Korea
{minyk, blee, ymnah}@dankook.ac.kr

Abstract. Information retrieval is one of the most challenging areas in which the ontology technology is effectively used. Among them, image retrieval using the image metadata and ontology is the one that can substitute the keyword-based image retrieval. In the paper, the retrieval of visual media such as the art image and photo picture is handled. It is assumed that there are more than one service providers of the visual media, and also there is one central service broker that mediates the user's query. Given the user's query the first step that must be done in the service broker is to get the list of candidate service providers that fit the query. This is done by defining various ontologies such as the service ontology and matching the query against the ontology and providers. A novel matching method based on the ASN.1 is proposed in the paper. The experiment shows that the method is more effective than the existing tree-based or interval-based methods.

1 Introduction

Image retrieval from the web is an important research issue. The technology has been is improved from the exact query matching and content-based retrieval using general features such as colors, textures, shapes of the images, to the semantic content-based retrieval using concepts, semantics, categories and spatial relationships of images. To accomplish the semantic content-based retrieval the ontology is effectively used.

There are several researches on the image retrieval using the ontology in distributed environment. They include the Finnish Museums on the Semantic Web [1] at Finland HIIT (Helsinki Institute for Information Technology), Semantic Annotation of Image Collections [2] at University Amsterdam Computer Science, and SIMILE Project [3] from W3C, HP, MIT Libraries, and MIT CSAIL. Research goal at HIIT is a web portal site for heterogeneous databases that have different table schema and retrieval method. For the goal they need unification of data. So they build syntactic interoperation using XML-schema and use RDFS-RDF for semantic relation. The site supports view-based image retrieval for more useful user-interface to end user, and recommended services for intelligent service. In University Amsterdam Computer Science, they perform the research on describing images using the existing ontology such as WordNet. They are focusing on building ontology for images and describing metadata. The goal of SIMILE project is to develop a system to integrate distributed

R. Obermaisser et al. (Eds.): SEUS 2007, LNCS 4761, pp. 378–383, 2007.

images that a person or community has. It provides the service search with ontology and schema metadata for user.

In this paper, it is assumed that there are multiple image providers and single central broker in a distributed environment. The broker accepts and answers the user's query. The provider's services are classified into the service ontology. Each provider has its own provider-specific service ontology and the broker has the union of all the providers' service ontology. Given a user's query, the broker needs to find the most appropriate providers that answer the query quickly and effectively.

The existing query matchmaking methods include the well-known CMU's matchmaking method [4] and the interval-based matchmaking which is proposed by the Swiss Federal Institute of Technology [5]. In this paper we suggest a new matchmaking method based on the ASN.1 scheme. The experiment shows that our method is more effective than the tree-based (CMU's matchmaking) and the interval-based method.

Section 2 describes the two existing matchmaking methods. Section 3 introduces our service ontology and the ASN.1-based matchmaking method. Section 4 shows the experimental result and finally Section 5 gives the conclusion.

2 Existing Matchmaking Methods

As in the figure 1, there are four matchmaking patterns between query service Q and library service S. "Exact" pattern means the library service S is matched to query service Q. "Plug in" means library service S is plugged in the query service Q. "Subsume" means the library service S is subsumed within the query service Q. "Failed" means there is no relationship between the library service S and the query service Q. Order of matchmaking estimation pattern is firstly "Exact", secondly "Plug In", thirdly "Subsume", and finally "Failed", so the "Failed" has the lowest estimation pattern [6].

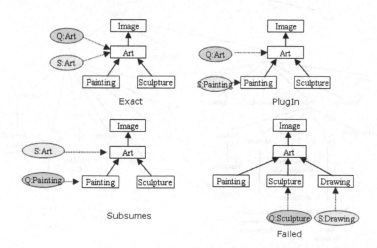

Fig. 1. Matchmaking estimation patterns

Interval-based matchmaking method is suggested by Swiss Federal Institute of Technology, any class in multi-inheritance layer can be symbolized into interval and tree. The interval is included in other intervals but not overlapped. They use two standards for setting up interval values. One is parent-child relationship and the other is child-child relationship. In parent-child relationship, interval is determined at between 0 and 1. Child node is assigned unique key from parent node and interval with key-dependence function. Namely, parent-node is assigned global interval, child-node interval that is connected it is there into parent-node's global interval [5].

In the visual media service ontology, for example, Visual Media is represented by <0, 1>. Then its children Video and Image are represented by <0, 0.5> and <0.5, 1>. Image's children Art, Medical, and Photo are represented by <0.5, 0.6>, <0.6, 0.7>, <0.7, 0.8>. So Art domain is sub-domain of the Visual Media domain since <0.5, 0.6> (Art) is included by <0, 1> (Visual Media). Also, Art domain has no inclusion relationship with Video domain since <0.5, 0.6> (Art) has no overlap with <0, 0.5> (Video).

This method, however, has problems in that there cannot be more than ten children since it uses the floating point number. Also the number of digits increases as the tree depth increases.

3   Visual Media Service Ontology and ASN.1-Based Matchmaking

Visual media service ontology is defined and used as a part of HERMES Visual Media Retrieval System [7]. As described in Section 1. The broker accepts and answers the user's query. Each provider has its own provider-specific service ontology and the broker has the union of all the providers' service ontology. Given a user's query, the broker needs to find the most appropriate providers that answer the query quickly and effectively.

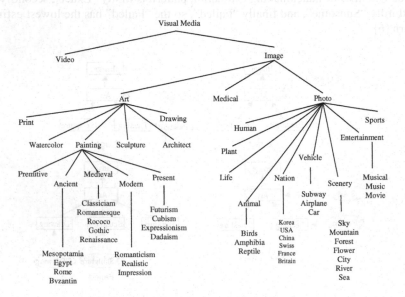

Fig. 2. The visual media service ontology

Visual media service ontology provides a whole classification domain for the provider's services. Figure 2 shows the service ontology which is used in the paper. Note that this is the union of all the providers' service ontology.

Now we explain the ASN.1-based matchmaking. ASN.1 standard [8], made by ISO, is the common abstract grammar to define data at distributed environment. All services have unique service ID's and we know easily the relationship between super-concept (parent) or sub-concept (child). This method has no limitation in terms of the number of children. Figure 3 shows the service ontology with ASN.1.

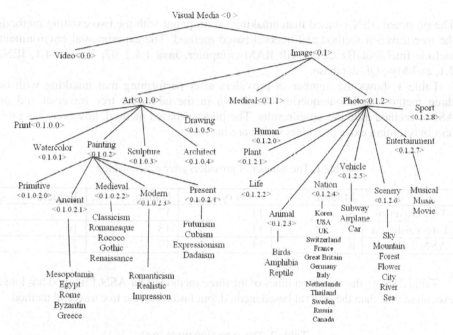

Fig. 3. The visual media service ontology with ASN.1

In this scheme, the root node Visual Media is represented by <0>. Its children Video and Image are represented by <0.0> and <0.1> respectively. Image's children Art, Medical, and Photo are represented by <0.1.0>, <0.1.1>, and <0.1.2> respectively. As for Print, Watercolor, Painting, Sculpture, Architecture, and Drawing which are Art's children, the numbers are given by adding numbers after <0.1.0>. So Print has <0.1.0.0>, Watercolor has <0.1.0.1>, Painting has <0.1.0.2>, Sculpture has <0.1.0.3>, Architecture has <0.1.0.4>, and Drawing has <0.1.0.5>. Suppose Q is the query domain ID, P is the provider service domain ID. Then the method determines the Exact, Plug In, and Subsume as follows.

Exact: Q = P
Plug In: Q = prefix(P)
Subsume: prefix(Q) = P
Failed: None of above

Plug In, for example, if P is <0.1.0.2.3> (Modern) and Q is <0.1.0.2> (Painting), then since "0.1.0.2" (Painting) is a prefix of "0.1.0.2.3" (Modern), they have Plug In relationship. To effectively perform the matching, the provider services and their ID's are listed in a table. When the query is given it is matched against the table entries one by one. Exact, Plug In, Subsume, Failed are determined. The matched providers are listed in this order.

4   Experimental Results

The proposed ASN.1-based matchmaking is compared with the two existing methods, the tree traversal method and interval-based method. The experimental environments include Intel 3.0GHz CPU, 1GB RAM computer, Java 1.4.2_07, Tomcat 4.1, JENA 2.1, and My-SQL database.

Table 1 shows the number of providers after performing matchmaking with the three methods and four queries. As shown in the table, the tree traversal and our ASN.1 method give the same results. The interval-based method, however, has problem in returning extra providers which are incorrect.

Table 1. The number of providers after matchmaking

	Modern	Scenery	Nation	Vehicle
Tree traversal	8	11	17	7
Interval-based	8	11	13	10
ASN.1-based	8	11	17	7

Table 2 shows the execution times of the three methods. Our ASN.1 method has longer execution time than the interval-based method, but faster than the tree traversal method.

Table 2. The execution times (ms)

	Modern	Scenery	Nation	Vehicle
Tree traversal	18.9	20.3	25.2	22.3
Interval-based	6.5	4.87	7.14	3.87
ASN.1-based	19.6	17.4	15.3	14.6

As shown in the table 1 and 2, ASN.1-based method is slower than the interval-based method, but more accurate than the interval-based method and faster than the tree traversal method, our method is more effective than the two other methods.

5   Conclusions

In the paper, we designed a service ontology which is used in retrieving visual media. To effectively find the service providers when the query is given, a novel ASN.1-based matchmaking method is proposed. The proposed method is compared with existing methods in terms of accuracy and speed. The experimental result shows that the method is more effective that the existing methods. The ASN.1-based method can be used in any other domain.

Acknowledgements

This work was supported by grant No. R01-2003-000-10133-0 from the Basic Research Program of the Korea Science and Engineering Foundation.

References

1. Hyvonen, E., Junnila, M., Kettula, S., Saarela, S., Salminem, M., Syreeni, A., Valo, A., Viljanen, K.: Publishing Collections in the Finnish Museums on the Semantic Web Portal. In: Museums and Web Conference (MW 2004) (March 31 - April 1, 2004)
2. Hollink, L., Schreiber, G., Wielemaker, J., Wielinga, B.: Semantic Annotation of Image Collections. In: KCAP'03. Workshop on Knowledge Markup and Semantic Annotation, Florida (October 2003)
3. Semantic Interoperability of Metadata and Information in unLike Environments, http://simile.mit.edu/
4. Paolucci, M., Kawamura, T., Payne, T.R., Sycara, K.P.: Semantic Matching of Web Services Capabilities. In: Proceedings of the First International Semantic Web Conference on the Semantic Web, pp. 333–347 (2002)
5. Constantinescu, I., Faltings, B.: Efficient Matchmaking and Directory Services. In: Proceedings of the IEEE/WIC International Conference on Web Intelligence (2003)
6. Choi, W., Yang, J., Choi, J., Cho, H., Cho, H., Kim, K.: Service Discovery Algorithm Using Ontoly Herarchy Relationship. The Korean Information System 30(1) (2003)
7. Kwon, E., Nah, Y.: Extended Query Processing using Image Metadata Mapping in Distributed and Heterogeneous Environments. In: SIGDB-KISS, pp. 250–257 (2005)
8. The ASN.1 Consortium, http://www.asn1.org/
9. The DARPA Agent Markup Language Homepage, http://www.daml.org
10. Protégé Ontology Editor and Knowledge Acquisition System, http://protege.stanford.edu/overview/

SharedSpace Based Service Discovery Mechanism and Its Implementation for Ubiquitous Environments

Sangdo Park, Junhyeong Kim, and Paul Barom Jeon[*]

Communication and Networking Lab.,
Samsung Advanced Institute of Technology
Nongseo Giheung Yongin Gyeonggi 446-712, Korea
{sdpark, skykimjh, paul.barom.jeon}@samsung.com
http://www.sait.samsung.com

Abstract. We propose a new service discovery method based on Shared-Space concept. SharedSpace is a virtual community space for service registration and sharing, which is similar to a chat room in a chat system. Any user[1] can freely create a SharedSpace and register his/her services. Others can join the created SharedSpace as members and register their services. All registered services can be shared by the SharedSpace members as if they are in a single network. Detailed mechanism is designed and implemented with Obje middleware in order to validate our scheme.

1 Introduction

Advances in networking and computing technology have progressed to a point of real ubiquitous computing environments. Consequently, researchers come to show interest in complex usage scenarios as well as ad-hoc connectivity issues [1]. Various connectivity technologies have been discussed so far, but are not able to cover all scenarios satisfactorily yet even though most of the issues can be resolved[2].

Early ubiquitous network's usage scenario mainly focused on connectivity issues among nodes that compose ubiquitous network. Network-enabled devices such as camera phone, MP3 player, Portable Media Player (PMP), etc., are increasing explosively and various solutions are presented also in reply. On the other hand, a tendency to separate contents and devices occurs because it causes several inconvenience to carry hundreds of GB multimedia contents. This means that ubiquitous computing environments require connectivity among nodes over the network boundary as well as inside the network [3].

Before connecting nodes, one should achieve service/component discovery first. Conventional service discovery methods can be classified into two categories: multicast and directory server based methods. However, multicast based

---

[*] Corresponding author.
[1] In this paper, user is defined as a person who is connected to a server. Participant is an user joining a SharedSpace and clinet is a program run by the user.

R. Obermaisser et al. (Eds.): SEUS 2007, LNCS 4761, pp. 384–388, 2007.

service discovery can't find services beyond network boundary. Note that listing up available services instead of querying a specified service, will give users more flexibility to compose a desirable service under *ad hoc* ubiquitous environments.

Therefore, in this paper, a new service discovery method that can be utilized in ad hoc ubiquitous network environments is proposed. The proposed method delegates mDNS[4] to discover services on the local network. Whereas, for service discovery beyond network boundary, a new concept of *SharedSpace* similar to a chat room in a chat system is suggested.

2   Service Discovery Using ShardSpace

SharedSpace is a kind of tiny database(DB) on the public network server(Shared Space Server). It can contain device and service information that are registered by participants authorized to access the shared space. As people open a chat room, any participant can create a SharedSpace. Participants can upload device and service information as people talk to other persons. We can imagine that a participant joins the SharedSpace and sends some information on service and devices available locally. Once a new information is uploaded, this information can be transferred to all participants. As devices or services are not available any more, participants can get rid of the information from the SharedSpace. Similar to general discovery systems, uploading and deleting information are dynamically performed depending on local network environments. Figure 1 shows an example of SharedSpace that contains information about services and devices.

To get information about services, user should connect to the Shared Space Server first using client application. Client application can be run on any network device. As user connects to server, it receives the list of SharedSpaces created before. Every SharedSpace has *Title* for identification. Authentication and authorization to enter the SharedSpace can be adapted to the user for access control. On entering the SharedSpace, user can get current service information registered before. All participants can upload local service information and participants inside the SharedSpace should be notified about it. For some reason, service may not be available on any moment. So, users should be able to revoke services on the SharedSpace. Revoked services should also be notified to all participants belonged to the same SharedSpace.

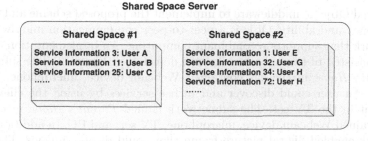

Fig. 1. An example of Shared Space

If there is no adequate SharedSpace, user can generate a new one with an identification. New identification should be announced to all users connected to server for potential joining. Similarly, SharedSpace can be removed from Shared Space Server if it is not used any more. For proper operation, SharedSpace should be equipped with server and user functionality. Server should be able to create DB for each SharedSpace. Optionally, server can authenticate and authorize users to offer access control. On the other side, user functionality gives user to connect to server and to generate UI for selecting SharedSpace as well as to achieve service discovery on local network utilizing multicast discovery method such as mDNS.

The proposed method has following features: First, it is not restricted to only two participants. Through one SharedSpace, more than two users can upload services to support abundant service pool. Moreover, even though the number of services increase, clients don't need to know each service description a priori. Participant should only select a SharedSpace he/she wants to join. Secondly, user can join more than two SharedSpaces simultaneously. Naturally, a participant can use some services provided separately by other SharedSpace. Although same services are provided by more than two subnetworks, participant can identify each using context information such as subnetwork name, location, etc. Finally, sharing service information only within SharedSpace enables a natural access control.

The mechanism can discover various services inside and outside of the local network without specific service descriptions. However, it should solve how a client could select the proper SharedSpace to participate in among many available SharedSpace. That is users in each subnetwork should be concerned with service directly(user-in-the-loop) and users should agree on the title of the SharedSpace. In other words, the proposed method requires that each subnetwork should have at least one client, for the services to be registered and become accessible. We can assume that user is controlling the client because proposed mechanism targets ubiquitous computing environment. If there is no user in a subnetwork, we can distribute a nominal client to register services on a fixed network to a specific SharedSpace. Also, we assume that the SharedSpace's title acquisition issue can be solved by using side communication channels such as internet messenger, e-mail, voice communication etc.

3   Practical Implementation

We utilized Obje [5] middleware to implement the proposed scheme and validate its efficiency and ability. Obje is a peer-to-peer communication middlware over IP network that supports recombinant computing. An implementation example which consisted of two subnetworks was depicted in Figure 2. The subnetwork named *My Home* in the left contained Webcam device, microphone, TV set, and PC. An user could discover and utilize services by using the client agent immanent in the TV set. The subnetwork named *Parent's Home* in the right also contained Webcam device, microphone, TV set, and PC. In addition, it had a network-enabled digital picture frame that could display images. The access point (AP) bridges wired and wireless networks together.

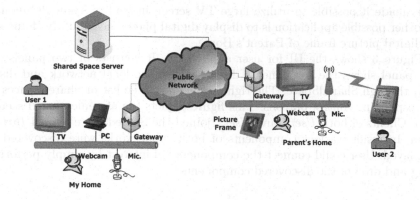

Fig. 2. Network Configuration

Following example scenarios were studied. User 2 with a PDA connected to Parent's Home network forming a new ubiquitous environment. Once the network was formed, the client inside the PDA searched for available services on the local network. The discovered available services were provided to user 2. At the same time, the client gained access to the Shared Space Server, obtained the list of SharedSpaces and joined the *Birthday Plan* generated by user 1 on My Home. Then, user 2 got service references of My Home as well as Parent's Home. After gathering the service references of both subnetworks, the client sent them to the Obje middleware. Then, Obje presented specific information of the service. Finally, user 2 connected TV, Webcam, microphone, and speaker of My Home to Webcam, TV, speaker, and microphone of Parent's Home respectively by using the Obje user interface and performed video conference with user 1.

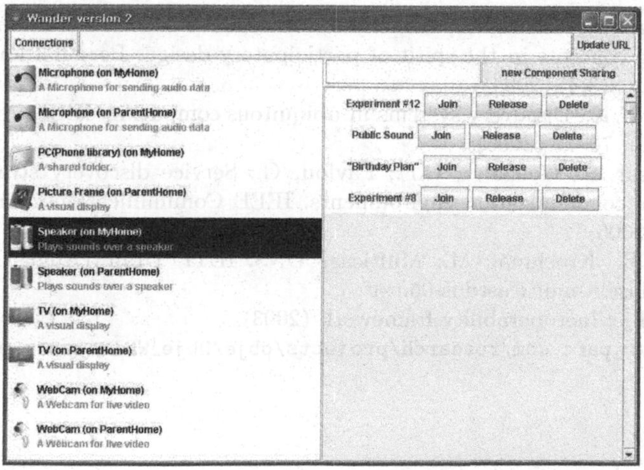

Fig. 3. User Interface

This made it possible to utilize large TV screen instead of small PC monitor. Another possible application is to display digital photos saved in My Home's PC to digital picture frame of Parent's Home.

Figure 3 shows the UI for user application. It consists of two panels. The left panel shows the components discovered on the local network and discovered through SharedSpace. The right panel shows the list of SharedSpaces and corresponding control buttons. This figure depicts the aforementioned scenario also. Clients of both *User1* and *User2* joined the SharedSpace named *Birthday Plan*. In result, various components of both subnetworks were discovered and displayed. User could connect the components of interest by simply performing drag and drop of the discovered components.

4   Conclusion

In this paper, we described a process of performing service discovery mutually for the clients when they belong to different subnetworks. *SharedSpace* concept was used to hold service information on the server. Clients were to register local services they discovered to the SharedSpace each. All service information of the subnetworks could be shared among clients that joined the SharedSpace. Authorization and authentication on the server enabled ordinary control of the accesses to the services without any additional complex process. We validated out proposed scheme by implementing a video conference application with modified Obje middleware. The proposed method offers a simple guide of how services can be discovered by various application scenarios under ubiquitous computing environments in the future.

References

1. Stromberg, H., Pirttila, V., Ikonen, V.: Interactive scenarios-building ubiquitous computing concepts in the spirit of participatory design. Personal and Ubiquitous Computing 8(3-4) (2004)
2. Edwards, W.K.: Discovery systems in ubiquitous computing. IEEE Pervasive Computing 5(2), 70–77 (2006)
3. Sivavakeesar, S., Gonzalez, O.F., Pavlou, G.: Service discovery strategies in the ubiquitous communication environments. IEEE Communications Magazine 44(9), 106–113 (2006)
4. Cheshire, S., Krochmal, M.: Multicast DNS. IETF Draft (August 2006) draft-cheshire-dnsext-multicastdns-06.txt
5. PARC: Obje: Ineroperability framework (2003), http://www.parc.com/research/projects/obje/Obje_Whitepaper.pdf

A Study of Developing Virtual Prototyping by Using JavaBean Interface Tool and SystemC Engine*

Husni Teja Sukmana, Jeong B. Lee, Jong Il Kim, Young J. Jung, Jin B.Kwon,
Kee W. Rim, and Young R. Lee

Sun Moon University, Dept. of Computer Science,
Asan, Chungnam, 336-708, South Korea
husniteja@yahoo.com, jblee@sunmoon.ac.kr, rumpet0@empal.com,
yjjung.kr@gmail.com, jbkwon@sunmoon.ac.kr, rim@sunmoon.ac.kr,
yrlee@sunmoon.ac.kr

Abstract. SystemC is a popular open source library in C++ for developing embedded system design, from the abstract System Level Design until the accurate Register Transfer Level Design. SystemC simulation, however, runs in console mode (text-based), thus making it difficult for user to interact with the simulation. To extend the capabilities of SystemC simulation, it is necessary to create Graphical User Interface. In this paper we recommend to use RapidPLUS tool for making the interface for embedded system prototype to reduce time to market. We also propose the connectivity between RapidPLUS and SystemC by using socket communication that attached in JavaBean RapidPLUS object

Keywords: SystemC, Embedded System, RapidPLUS, Simulation, Socket, virtual prototyping.

1 Introduction

In process to making the good embedded system products, usually we are not only faced with quality but also must deal with time. The average time to market constraint has been reported as having shrunk to only 8 month [1]. There are many ways to reduce time to market; one is by using prototyping such as real and virtual prototyping.

In this paper we want to suggest how to manage these problems by providing a suitable environment. The environment that we propose will use the SystemC as a simulation engine along with RapidPlus as a tool for making the interface.

SystemC can be used to make a virtual prototyping, where virtual prototyping is one way to speed up the development process [3]. However, SystemC fails to provide a graphical user interface (GUI). It only supports text-based console application. As a feedback with a user during simulation, the user only can use printf or cout[5,6].

---

* This research was supported by Ministry of Information and Communication, Korea, under the ITRC (IT Research Center) support program supervised by Institute of Information Technology Assessment.

R. Obermaisser et al. (Eds.): SEUS 2007, LNCS 4761, pp. 389–393, 2007.

To handle this weakness, we use RapidPLUS to build the system interface. Rapid-Plus is one of good tool for making interface prototypes. It is a comprehensive software package for the generation of simulation and prototypes of embedded systems [7]. Furthermore, to connect both of them, we propose to use the socket mechanism.

We also want to show an example how to make an interface in RapidPlus. In the previous research, we have implemented the SystemC in company with Java as a GUI. This paper does not show how to implement the connectivity between SystemC and RapidPLUS instead of just show how the RapidPLUS can be communicate with SystemC. The implementation still not yet finished, however we are still doing to implement.

The paper is organized as follows: Section 2 describes the related work, and Section 3 presents the system environment. In Section 4, we describe out the RapidPlus testing, and in Section 5 we conclude our work.

2   Related Works

Many researchers have been worked to improve the ability of SystemC. We can look some of example in [5, 6]. The architecture, as given in the Figure 1, is comprised of three main parts: SystemC, Java and CommunicationLib.

In SystemC terminology, the processes are methods. It recognizes two kinds of processes, SC_METHOD and SC_THREAD. For utilization of these processes, specific port and signal must be set. Because of this procedure, processes will be triggered during data transmission by changes of signal and port. Declaration of the process and the sensitive are registered in constructor (SC_CTOR) which is included in the module. Child module initialization and interconnection will be declared in constructor. Of these circumstances, SC_MODULE, SC_THREAD, SC_METHOD and SC_CTOR are macros in SystemC.

SystemC also has own mechanism to connect modules which consists important role due to number of dependant modules. Single module port is responsible to input data (SC_IN) and pairs for output data (SC_OUT), but others can be responsible to input and output data. Single SC_OUT can receive more than one SC_IN.

2.1   Client Side

For the Client, Java Swing was used to develop the Television Simulation for GUI application. This is due to Object Oriented enhancement and provision of various libraries. The Television Simulation can be divided into input and output modules. Input modules are used to input data from users via push buttons or text field. Received inputs conveys to SystemC through CommuLibrary API. Output modules receive data from SystemC through the SCJLib API which enables interface manipulation to help users to understand how the server operates.

2.2   SCJLib API

SCJLibrary is an API for bridging SystemC (server) and GUI simulation (Java Swing). Integration between server (back end) and client (front end) are very important for the users, due to user friendly interaction and efficiencies.

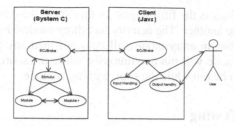

Fig. 1. The Server (SystemC) and The Client (Java) System Architecture

There are three main classes in this library. SCJBroker class is responsible to provide connection between server and client (see figure 1), and each part must have only one instance of this class. SCJOutput class is used to send data from client to server. Unlike the SCJBroker class, it has only one instance in each part, whereas SCJOutput class must instantiate for each number of data variations for delivery. In simulation using SCJLib API, at least one instance of SCJOutput should be created.

3 System Environment

The new environments for the recommendation system will changes client side. Besides using the Java as an Interface, the new system will apply to use the RapidTools. The detail of RapidTools will be emphasized in this section. However, before we give details about the RapidTools, Figure 2 presents our new suggestion for the new system architecture.

There are six stages that be used to track the RapidPLUS progress. First, we will use the Object Layout to create the application's user interface. This is very important stages since the market sales record condition depend on the interface.

The object, JavaBean, plays the basic rule for communicate to the SCJLib. The JavaBean acquire data from the other objects properties such as position of frame object or the value of the buttons and than send data to the SystemC. On the other hand, the respond data from SystemC will traverse to the JavaBean object, and they will give back to the other RapidPLUS Objects.

The second until the fourth stages are to define the modes and their transition, including the triggers. The modes can be illustrated as a state machine. They will transfer from one mode to others mode by waiting the triggers. The triggers can be event or condition triggers.

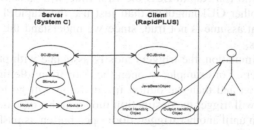

Fig. 2. The New System Architecture, SystemC as a Server, RapidPlus as a Client

Defining the activities is the fifth stages. In this stage the data from among the objects transfer each one another. The activity has three modes. Entry mode, mode, and exit mode. All activities in entry mode will be confirmed any time the source is accessed. The mode's mode will run continuously while the source is read. In contrast, the exit mode just can be run while the source exits its mode.

4 RapidPLUS Testing

Since RapidPLUS can be applied for creating the good embedded system interface, the following section will give an example how to use and test the RapidPLUS tool. The example will utilize the six stages that have been mention in the last section.

We made an elevator simulation where it contains some function such open and close door, running up, running down and automatic waiting time. Figure 3 depict the elevator interfaces that build in RapidPLUS.

4.1 Adding Object

There are some objects that must be integrated in order making the runtime simulation. As a normal elevator, the button objects must have the floors button, open and close door button. Furthermore, the bitmap picture objects have been chosen to illustrate the exact car door and car wall.

Figure 3 represent all the graphical objects for our runtime testing elevator. In addition, we also should insert some non graphic objects such as timers.

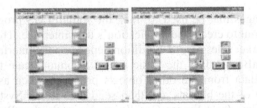

Fig. 3. The elevator in Runtime Test: (a) show the idle time, (b) show the automatic open and close door

4.2 Insert Triggers, Actions and Activities

Most developers who run RapidPLUS the first time will said that better to work in Java coding or another GUI language than just use the RapidPLUS tool. We, however, can prove that assume is not true, since we understand the behavior of trigger, action and activities.

Simply in our simulation, the triggers mostly associate with press button in, press button out and timers. For example, to open the door from idle time, we should press the door open button and than the button in condition will go to the activity mode. The activity mode will trigger the destination mode, in this case door open. Door open will keep door open until another trigger, door open button, is push out. The stage will continuo to another destination, close door.

The actions are similar to activities, but they take place only during transitions. We utilize some actions along with internal transitions

5   Conclusion

RapidPLUS is one tool for designing interface easily than using the traditional write code. It contains many objects that can be used for making interface design. In our experience, RapidPLUS can be used as the client side for making virtual prototyping along with SystemC as server side.

As a conclusion, this paper studied about the ability of RapidPLUS as a tool for making virtual prototyping in order to reduce time to market. In addition we propose to use the SystemC as an engine instead of direct to use hardware description language, because the time to market is our constraint. This paper are still implementing, however, the prototyping interface have been build with elevator example. Furthermore, the next research may deal to create the communication library and systemC engine.

References

1. Vahid, F., Givargis, T.: Embedded System Design: A Unified Hardware/Software Introduction, 1st edn. John Wiley & Sons, Chichester (2002)
2. SystemC 2.0 User Guide, SystemC.org, http://www systemc.org/
3. Simulation Based Design Center of Univ. of New Orleans. Primer on Virtual Prototyping, http://www.gcrmtc.org/sbdc/protoprimer print.html
4. Sukmana, T., Satria, H., Kwon, J.B., Lee, J.B., Kee, W.: User-level Virtual Prototyping for Television Simulation using SystemC and Java GUIHusni
5. "RapidStart 8.0", pp. 1, e-SIM. Ltd. (2004)

Configurable Virtual Platform Environment Using SID Simulator and Eclipse*

Hadipurnawan Satria, Baatarbileg Altangerel, Jin Baek Kwon, and Jeongbae Lee

Department of Computer Science, Sun Moon University
Kalsan 100, Tangjeong, Asan, Chungnam, South Korea
hadi198@yahoo.com, a_bbileg@yahoo.com, jbkwon@sunmoon.ac.kr,
jblee@sunmoon.ac.kr

Abstract. For designing and testing embedded software, simulation tools have been used to keep pace with the rapid development of customized hardware parts. SID is a framework for building computer system simulations and SID is made for debugging, testing and verifying embedded software. Though, it is difficult for developers to use SID for their work. In this work, we developed an integrated virtual platform environment based SID simulation framework for a simulator engine and Eclipse for development platform. The proposed system avoids users to manually write the configuration file, and aids loading and connecting components on the fly. We also developed an image file builder and an automation tool for running SID simulation with GDB debugger. Furthermore, users can also monitor/probe the status of all the active components in the target virtual platform during the simulation

Keywords: embedded software, development tools, virtual platform, full system simulator.

1 Introduction

Nowadays, embedded system products are found everywhere and are becoming more and more advanced. To keep up with the market competition, the products must be more sophisticated and feature rich, but manufacturers also require a shorter time to market. Nevertheless, the improvements to the design and testing tools have not kept pace with the rapid development of customized hardware parts. Simulation tools have been designed to help close the gap and meet the needs of embedded software developers. The simulation of the target environment or virtual platform enables embedded software developers to analyze and test their software, even in the absence of the physical hardware.

From the perspective of full system simulation and emulation, there are number of software systems that support a wide rage of devices[1][3][4][5][6][7][8][9]. However, SID is specifically made for debugging, testing and verifying embedded

---

* This research was supported by Ministry of Information and Communication, Korea, under the ITRC(IT Research Center) support program supervised by Institute of Information Technology Assessment.

R. Obermaisser et al. (Eds.): SEUS 2007, LNCS 4761, pp. 394–398, 2007.

software. Since our work focuses on an environment for building embedded hardware simulators with simulated components, SID is a better fit for our work.

Although SID is a well-designed framework and environment of building a new virtual platform, it is difficult for embedded software developers to use SID for their work. To use it for an actual development, the users should configure a target platform by editing a configuration file with a text editor, run the virtual platform by typing a command in console, write and build a binary image to be run on the target, run a debugger such as GDB, and load and run the binary image to the active virtual platform. Since each step is manually done with independent tools, the users of today who get used to user-friendly user interface should endure considerable inconvenience. Therefore, it is desirable to integrate the tools and automate the usage procedure with graphical user interfaces.

In this work, we developed an integrated virtual platform environment based SID simulation framework for a simulator engine and Eclipse[2] for development platform. Eclipse is an open source development environment having extensible architecture, where the environment can be extended by adding plug-ins. Thus, our system is developed as Eclipse plug-ins. The proposed system avoids users to manually write the configuration file, and aids loading and connecting components on the fly. We also developed an image file builder and an automation tool for running SID simulation with GDB debugger. Furthermore, the users can also monitor/probe the status of all the active components in the target virtual platform during the simulation.

2 Background

2.1 SID Simulation Framework

In SID, a simulation is comprised of a collection of loosely coupled *components*. Simulated systems may range from a CPU's instruction set to a large multi-processor embedded system. SID defines a small component interface which serves to tightly encapsulate them. Components may be written in C++, C, Tcl or any other language to which the API is bound. C++ is the main language used, and for additional language a special component, a *bridge*, is required. During simulation start-up, components are instantiated, interconnected, and configured as necessary to represent some specific system. SID is suitable for consideration as an integration platform for other simulators by interconnecting models from different simulators, as has been done with Bochs[1], and also with a live Verilog system.

The components and their relationships are described in a configuration file, therefore required to run a simulation. The configuration file describes all components to be loaded and which component connected to which component. The SID simulator engine loads the components and connects them according to the configuration file. The SID framework provides a few ways for components to communicate with each other, i.e. pin, bus, attribute and relation mechanisms. All of these communication mechanisms may also be set up in the configuration file. Although there is an auto-configuration file builder for some typical target boards, in general users have to manage the configuration file content for new target platform by editing the file.

2.2 Eclipse Platform

The Eclipse[3] platform is designed for building integrated development environments (IDEs) as an open source project. One of the key benefits of the Eclipse Platform is realized by its use as an integration point. Building a tool or application on top of Eclipse Platform enables the tool or application to integrate with other tools and applications also written using the Eclipse Platform. The Eclipse Platform is turned in a Java IDE by adding Java development components (e.g. the JDT[5]) and it is turned into a C/C++ IDE by adding C/C++ development components (e.g. the CDT[2]). It becomes both a Java and C/C++ development environment by adding both sets of components. Eclipse Platform integrates the individual tools into a single product providing a rich and consistent experience for its users [4].

Eclipse platform has a plug-in architecture, where a plug-in is the smallest unit that can be developed and delivered separately. Plug-ins are coded in Java. Each plug-in has a plug-in manifest declaring its interconnections to other plug-ins. The interconnection model is simple: a plug-in declares any number of named extension points, and any number of extensions to one or more extension points in other plug-ins.

3   Architecture

In this section, we describe the overall architecture of our system, which the modules implementing the functions mentioned above are developed as plug-ins over Eclipse platform. Fig. 1 shows the architecture.

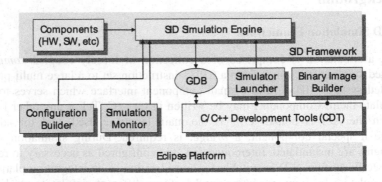

Fig. 1. Overall Architecture

As shown the figure, the architecture is based on SID framework and Eclipse platform, and includes CDT that is a set of plug-ins for IDE for C/C++. CDT consists of an editor, building tools such as compiler and linker, a debugger front-end connecting to GDB, etc. We extended it by adding two plug-ins, the binary image builder and the simulator launcher, to cooperate with SID. And, the configuration builder and the simulation monitor are plugged directly in Eclipse platform.

CDT does not support a cross-development environment. An embedded software development environment should provide the cross-development environment, where an image file built in a host is run on the target system. That is why the *binary image builder* was developed. It provides the cross-development environment to CDT with GNU cross toolchains, e.g., arm-elf-gcc, arm-elf-as, etc. Therefore, users can build an image file to be run on a virtual target platform with the binary image builder.

The SID simulator requires a configuration file that describes the target platform. Basically, the file should be manually edited by a developer. In order to eliminate the troublesomeness, the *configuration builder* automatically generates a configuration template file for a target platform by checking the components to be used and inserting some values such as memory addresses on a GUI.

CDT has a debugger user interface interacting GDB. And, SID has a built-in component that performs the equivalent function of a GDB remote stub. Hence, CDT can load and debug an image on the virtual platform through GDB. The *simulator launcher* activates the virtual platform described by the configuration file selected when a debugging session begins.

SID also provides a built-in but experimental system monitor written in Tcl/Tk, to monitor a running simulation. The system monitor lists the components in the active virtual platform, showing specific component attributes such as pins, registers, etc. Since our system is based on the Eclipse framework, the system monitor should also be made to an Eclipse plug-in, which must be written in Java. However, SID cannot support components written in Java directly without a Java bridge component. Instead of developing the bridge component, we connected the simulation monitor plug-in and SID over a socket communication.

4 Implementation

The simulation monitor is implemented by interacting between the SID simulator and the Eclipse plug-in. Thus, it is implemented in two parts, one as SID component and another as an Eclipse plug-in.

The configuration builder is implemented as a new file wizard along with SID file types. Using the wizard, users can choose the target processor, e.g., ARM, and they can also select the components of the target platform SID supports many kinds of components, we currently only provide some of most important components on this wizard. The configuration builder generates a configuration template file according to the user's choice. Then the user can edit the template manually for a finer configuration.

The binary image builder provides the cross-development environment to CDT with GNU cross toolchains, e.g., arm-elf-gcc, arm-elf-as, etc. In CDT, the set of the tools and their settings to be used for build process is determined by selecting "Build Target." Thus, we add new build targets for ARM processor. By this way, the binary image file can be successfully built with the default tools and build settings. Users can also further modify the build settings as needed.

CDT has a debugger user interface interacting GDB. And, SID has a built-in component that performs the equivalent function of a GDB remote stub. The simulator launcher activates the virtual platform described by the configuration file selected when a debugging session begins. Eclipse has a general debug configuration window, where users can select different kinds of debug configuration template. After they choose the proper template, they can configure the debugger based on that template. We implemented the "C/C++ Virtual" configuration template for GDB debugging session with the virtual platform. In this configuration, the users can select an SID configuration file describing a target machine. The simulator launcher activates the virtual platform on SID when the debugging starts, and also deactivates it when the debugging stops.

5 Conclusion

In this work, we developed an integrated virtual platform environment based SID simulation framework for a simulator engine and Eclipse for development platform. Our system is developed as Eclipse plug-ins. The proposed system avoids users to manually write the configuration file, and aids loading and connecting components on the fly. We also developed an image file builder and an automation tool for running SID simulation with GDB debugger. Furthermore, users can also monitor/probe the status of all the active components in the target virtual platform during the simulation.

References

1. The Bochs IA-32 Emulator Project, http://bochs.sourceforge.net
2. Eclipse C/C++ Development Tools (CDT), http://www.eclipse.org/cdt/
3. Eclipse Platform, http://www.eclipse.org
4. Eclipse Platform Technical Overview (2006), http://www.eclipse.org/articles/Whitepaper-Platform-3.1/eclipse-platform-whitepaper.pdf
5. Eclipse Java Development Tools (JDT), http://www.eclipse.org/jdt/
6. Magnusson, P.S., Christensson, M., Eskilson, J., Forsgren, D., Hallberg, G., Hogberg, J., Larsson, F., Moestedt, A., Werner, B.: Simics: A Full System Simulation Platform. IEEE Computer 35(2), 50–58 (2002)
7. PearPC: PowerPC Architecture Emulator, http://pearpc.sourceforge.net
8. QEMU: A Generic and Open Source Processor Emulator, http://fabrice.bellard.free.fr/qemu
9. System, S.I.D.: Simulator, http://sourceware.org/sid
10. SimOS: The Complete Machine Simulator, http://simos.stanford.edu
11. SkyEye: An Embedded Simulation System, http://www.skyeye.org
12. Witchel, E., Rosenblum, M.: Embra: Fast and Flexible Machine Simulation. ACM SIGMETRICS Performance Evaluation Review 24(1), 68–79 (1996)

An Energy-Efficient *k*-Disjoint-Path Routing Algorithm for Reliable Wireless Sensor Networks

Jang Woon Baek[1], Young Jin Nam[2,*], and Dae-Wha Seo[1]

[1] School of Electrical Eng. & Computer Science, Kyungpook National University
[2] School of Computer & Information Technology, Daegu University
[1] {kutc, dwseo}@ee.knu.ac.kr, [2] yjnam@daegu.ac.kr

Abstract. Wireless sensor networks are subject to sensor node and link failures due to various reasons. This paper proposes an energy-efficient, *k*-disjoint-path routing algorithm that adaptively varies the number of disjoint paths (*k*) according to changing data patterns and a target-delivery ratio of critical events. The proposed algorithm sends packets through a single path (*k*=1) under no occurrence of critical events, whereas it sends through *k* disjoint paths (*k*>1) under the occurrence of critical events, where *k* is computed from a well-defined fault model and the target delivery ratio. Note that the proposed algorithm detects the occurrence of critical events by monitoring changing data patterns. Our simulations reveal that the proposed algorithm not only guarantees the target delivery ratio as much as a multi-path routing algorithm, but also makes energy consumption and average delay as low as a single-path routing algorithm.

Keywords: Wireless sensor networks, data variation, disjoint-path routing.

1 Introduction

According to advances in MEMS, wireless communication, and digital electronics technology, wireless sensor networks have been widely deployed to monitor and control physical environments [1]. Wireless sensor networks typically consist of a large number of sensor nodes which can observe physical phenomena, process sensed information, and communicate with other nodes. Since sensor nodes are equipped with limited battery power, low-power consumption is very crucial in wireless sensor networks [2]. It is believed that power consumption is dominated by the costs of transmitting and receiving messages [3]. It is known that in-network aggregation can save a significant amount of energy by reducing the number of transmitted messages over wireless sensor networks [4]. Sensor nodes with in-network aggregation can combine data from their child nodes and their locally-collected data before sending a message to their parent nodes. Typically, in-network aggregation employs a single-path routing algorithm with a tree topology for energy saving [4, 10]. However, if any node on a single routing path fails, the data packet cannot be delivered to the base

---

* Corresponding author.

R. Obermaisser et al. (Eds.): SEUS 2007, LNCS 4761, pp. 399–408, 2007.
© IFIP International Federation for Information Processing 2007

station. Actually, individual sensor nodes are highly vulnerable to failures caused by battery drain, outside damages, or security attacks [5].

Multi-path routing algorithms have been proposed for the reliable event delivery in wireless sensor networks [6-8]. Basically, this breed of routing algorithms constantly employs m disjoint paths, where m is generally determined in an ad-hoc manner. With a larger m, the multi-path routing algorithms require more nodes to participate in the event transmission. In result, more energy is consumed, and the overall traffic in the wireless sensor network is increased, thus resulting is a higher possibility of congestion and worse load balancing [9]. Another breed of routing algorithms for reliable event delivery is the path-repair routing algorithm that forwards data along a single path and repairs paths in the presence of failures in order to achieve a higher delivery ratio with low-energy consumption [9, 10]. Path-repair routing algorithms, however, usually generate additional latency in the search for alternative paths. If some packets arrive after a timeout especially during in-network aggregation, the aggregation process excludes these packets. To make matters worse, if packets encompass any critical events, packet loss poses serious problems for sensor applications.

This paper proposes an energy-efficient k-disjoint-path routing algorithm for in-network aggregation over wireless sensor networks. The key of the proposed algorithm is to adapt the number of disjoint paths (k) according to the changing data patterns and the target delivery ratio of critical events, such as fires and poisonous gas leaks, etc. The proposed algorithm configures $k=1$ if the variance of the received data (data variation) from children is lower than a pre-defined threshold, whereas it sets $k>1$ if data variation is higher than the pre-defined threshold, where k is determined by the target delivery ratio. Note that the proposed algorithm detects the occurrence of critical events by monitoring data variation. Since sensor nodes usually collect non-critical events that have less important information and little effect on aggregation results, the proposed algorithm spends a large portion of its lifetime operating like the single-path routing algorithm. As a result, the proposed algorithm consumes much less power than multi-path routing algorithms. After detecting the occurrence of critical events, the proposed algorithm begins to work like a k-disjoint-path routing algorithm in order to meet target delivery ratios.

The remainder of this paper is organized as follows. Section 2 provides background information on multi-path routing and path-repair algorithms. Section 3 offers a detailed description of the proposed algorithm, and Section 4 compares the performance of the proposed algorithm with that of exiting routing algorithms. Finally, concluding remarks are presented in Section 5.

2   Background

Data collection from wireless sensor networks typically uses a single-path routing algorithm with tree topology for energy saving [4, 11]. Wireless sensor networks have a relatively short radio range and may be deployed into a large geographical coverage area, i.e., the route between a source node and a base station is likely to consist of a large number of hops. As a result, the success probability of the single-path routing becomes very low. There are two different methods to maintain routing paths in the presence of node failures: multi-path routing algorithms and path-repair algorithm.

Multi-path routing algorithms have shown higher resilience to node failure both theoretically and experimentally comparing with the single-path routing [6-8]. The construction of disjoint multi-path is described in [7]. In this approach, multiple copies of data are sent along different paths, allowing for resilience to failures of a certain number of paths. For instance, the same data packet along *m* disjoint paths can increase the delivery ratio in approximate proportion to *m*, as compared with the single-path routing algorithm. A smaller value of *m* can save energy, but it is less likely to meet a target delivery ratio. On the other hand, a larger value of *m* is more likely to guarantee a target delivery ratio, whereas it not only causes higher energy consumptions, but it also creates more traffic for the packet delivery. Note that more traffic implies higher collisions in wireless channels and longer back-off delays for transmission.

Path-repair algorithms are proposed to overcome the problems of multi-path routing algorithms [9, 10]. In the face of path failure, a notification is sent to the source node, which is responsible for finding an alternative path and resending the packet. However, this kind of a source-initiated path-repairing approach is inefficient, especially when a failure occurs in many hops away from the source node. To decrease long-path recovery time and unnecessary energy consumption of source-initiated path-repairing approaches, local-node-based path-repair algorithms have been proposed [10]. These algorithms detect packet loss with implicit acknowledgements [9]. In the presence of path failure, a sensor node searches for an alternative node among a list of neighbor nodes, and it immediately sends the packet stored in its local cache to the alternative node. These algorithms, however, still make additional latency while discovering alternative paths.

3   The Proposed Algorithm

To begin, we assume that data aggregation is performed periodically in a wireless sensor network. The key of the proposed algorithm is to vary the number of disjoint paths (*k*) according to the changing data patterns and the target delivery ratio of critical events. Note that the routing algorithm operates at each sensor node in a distributed manner.

The proposed algorithm exploits the following characteristics of sensor readings in order to detect critical events. First, as time passes, there is little change in sensor readings from wireless sensor networks. Second, there is little change in sensor readings from physically-adjacent sensor nodes in a wireless sensor network. Third, in the presence of critical events, such as earthquakes or forest fires, there is significant change in sensor readings from a wireless sensor network. By using the first two characteristics, the proposed algorithm maintains single-path routing (*k*=1) when a variance of the received data from children is lower than a pre-defined threshold because there are not any critical events. As a result, it can consume energy dramatically compared with the multi-path routing algorithms. The proposed algorithm, however, employs the k-disjoint path (k>1) when the variance becomes higher than a pre-defined threshold in order to meet a target delivery ratio of critical events.

The occurrence of a critical event can be detected by monitoring data variation. For example, a sharp change in the light intensity, an unusual sound matching a certain signature and a very high temperature in the same region within a specified time interval implies an explosion event [12]. In building risk monitoring, if the variation of data collected by acceleration and strain sensors of sensor node is large, we can infer that an abnormal symptom of building is generated [13]. In the earthquake detection, a sensor node can detect the event using an earthquake detection algorithm triggered on significant seismic or acoustic signal [14]. From theses examples, we can see that data variation is important to detect the occurrence of critical events. The information on detected critical events has to be reliably transferred to the base station.

The threshold of data variation is set by using maximum data variation in a normal condition without occurrence of critical events. The normal data variation can be empirically obtained by running iterative experiments. Data variation depends on the location of sensor node from the point of event occurrence. We can change the threshold of data variation according to the characteristics of sensor applications.

The proposed algorithm computes the minimum number of disjoint paths (k>1), say k', between a sensor node and its final destination (a base station) in the presence of critical events to meet a given target delivery ratio. Presently, it uses a simple fault model, where each sensor node can be faulty independently with the probability of f in a wireless sensor network. Fig. 1 shows a packet-transmitting model through k disjoint multiple paths at a sensor node located N hops away from the base station. The probability that no duplicated packet is delivered to the base station, $P_{fail}(N)$, is calculated as $P_{fail}(N) = (1 - (1 - f)^N)^k$. Therefore, the probability that at least one single copy of the packet is delivered to the base station can be computed as $P_{succ}(N) = 1 - P_{fail}(N)$. Given a target delivery ratio, $P_{succ}(N) = \alpha$, the minimum number of disjoint paths denoted by k' can be computed as

$$k' = log(1 - \alpha) / log(1 - (1 - f)^N). \tag{1}$$

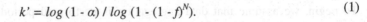

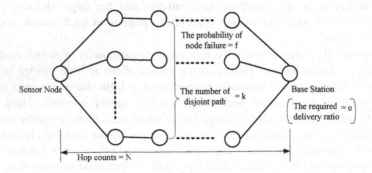

Fig. 1. Packet-transmitting model through k disjoint paths

```
procedure PATH_INITIALIZATION()
    // N = {n| node(n)}, all sensor nodes
    // Pn = {pi}i=1, ..., M, parent list of node(n)

    foreach sensor node(n) ∈ N do
        receive queries from its parents;
        initialize a parent list Pn ;
        compute the number of disjoint path k' to meet
                          the target delivery ratio(α);
        construct k' disjoint paths to the base station;
        pick k' parents and its primary parent;
    end

end PATH_INITIALIZATION

procedure DATA_TRANSMISSION()
    n ← node_id;
    packetn ← sensing critical or non-critical events;

    repeat
        packetchild(n) ← receive(nodechild(n));
        packetn ← data_aggregation(packetn, packetchild(n));
        update data variation(dvn) at noden;
        check threshold conditions and update Timeoutn
    until Timeoutn has expired

    if (critical event occurred) then
        send packetn to each of the k' parents;
    else
        send packetn to the primary parent;
    endif

    sleep until the next period;
end DATA_TRANSMISSION
```

Fig. 2. The operational behavior of the proposed algorithm

The operational behavior of the proposed algorithm is described in Fig. 2. We assume that there exits a set of sensor nodes denoted by N, where each sensor node is denoted by a $node_n$. We denote the parent nodes and the child nodes of a $node_n$ by $node_{par(n)}$ and $node_{child(n)}$, respectively. The first step of the proposed algorithm (**PATH_INITIALIZATION**) is to construct a minimum number of disjoint paths between each sensor node to the base station. This is done in order to meet a given target delivery ratio of critical events. A sensor node receives multiple queries from its parent nodes ($node_{par(n)}$) and initializes its parent list (P_n) and data aggregation parameters including a target delivery ratio (α) and a data variation threshold (DV). Next, the proposed algorithm calculates the minimum number of disjoint paths (k') by using Eq.(1) and constructs k' disjoint paths from the $node_n$ to the base station as follows. The $node_n$ sends duplicate requests including information of *source ID*, *sender ID, hop counts,* and *request ID* to k' parents that are randomly selected from the parent list. Note that the request ID is unique during toward the base station. When a node at a lower hop count receives the request, it stores the path information unless it has received the same request ID. Otherwise, it returns the NACK message to the request sender. Then, the sender delivers the request message to another parent. By repeating this process at each node in a wireless sensor network, the base station can receive the request messages through k' disjoint paths. The base station returns acknowledgements to the $node_n$ through each of the reverse paths for the confirmation of the path setup. Finally, path initialization chooses k' parents for k'-disjoint-path routing and a primary parent is selected from the k' parents.

The next step in the proposed algorithm (**DATA_TRANSMISSION**) is to transmit sensed data to the base station. The $node_n$ waits for packets ($packet_{child(n)}$) from the child nodes, and fulfills partial aggregation; the $node_n$ checks the threshold condition of data variation during a timeout (T_n), which is configured by the adaptive timeout scheduling scheme [10]. If data variation (dv_n) at $node_n$ is within DV, which means that critical events have not occurred, the proposed algorithm sends a packet to its primary parent (single-path routing). If the data variation is larger than DV, which means that critical events have occurred, the proposed algorithm sends a packet to each of the k' parents in the parent list (k'-disjoint-path routing). When the transmission is completed, the $node_n$ sleeps until the next period.

4 Performance Evaluations

This section evaluates the performance of the proposed algorithm via simulations. We implemented the proposed k-disjoint-path algorithm in the ns-2 network simulator [16]. We compared the proposed algorithm with a single-path routing algorithm [4], a multi-path routing algorithm [7], and a path-repair routing algorithm [9]. The performance metrics encompass the average dissipated energy, the event delivery ratio, and the average delay.

Table 1. Simulation parameters

Parameters	Values
Number of nodes	100
Transmission Range	50m
Physical Link Bandwidth	1Mbps
MAC Layer	802.11
Transmit Energy	14.88mW
Receive Energy	12.50mW
Data Collection Period	1 sec.
Critical Event Injection	50 sec.
Data Variation Threshold	5%
Probability of A Node Failure (f)	0.1

4.1 Simulation Environment

Table 1 shows the parameters used in our experiments. Each simulation begins by deploying 100 sensor nodes randomly in a 1000-by-1000 grid. All the sensor nodes remain static after being deployed. The radio range of each node is set to 50 meters. The bandwidth of each physical link is 1Mbps. We employ an 802.11 MAC-layer protocol, where the transmission and reception energy consumption is set to 14.88 and 12.50mW [15]. Each simulation runs for 1,000 seconds, and the sensor application collects sensed data every one second through the wireless sensor network. Critical events are randomly injected into sensor nodes in the wireless sensor network. The threshold of data variation to detect the critical events is set to 5 percents. In normal environments, the data variation of temperature is lower than 5% at the reasonable reporting period. We assume that each node can be faulty independently with the probability ($f=0.1$), and the sensor application demands the target delivery ratio of 0.9 ($\alpha=0.9$).

4.2 The Average Dissipated Energy

The average dissipated energy represents the average of the total dissipated energy at each node when the simulation completes. Table 2 summarizes the average dissipated energy of the proposed algorithm and the other routing algorithms with $f=0.1$ and $\alpha=0.9$. The number of the disjoint paths, 5-disjoint path, for the multi-path routing algorithm is obtained from Eq.(1). The proposed algorithm is observed to consume 43% more energy than the single-path routing algorithm. However, it consumes much less energy than the multi-path routing algorithm by 110% and even the path-repair routing algorithms by 47%. Recall that the path-repair routing algorithm generates additional packets to find an alternative routing path.

Table 2. A comparison of the average dissipated energy with the different routing algorithms: The single-path algorithm, the multi-path (5-disjoint path) algorithm, the path-repair algorithm, and the proposed algorithm, where $f=0.1$ and $\alpha=0.9$

Routing Schemes	Single-path	Multi-path	Path-repair	Proposed
Dissipated Energy (J)	1.013	2.616	1.822	1.239
Improvement (%)	158.0	-	43.5	110.0

4.3 The Event Delivery Ratio of Critical Events

The event delivery ratio of critical events represents the ratio of the number of the critical events received at the base station to the total number of critical events injected at sensor nodes. Fig. 3 depicts the results of the event delivery ratio of critical events with the different routing algorithms. While the single-path routing algorithm cannot guarantee the target delivery ratio of 90%, the multi-path and the proposed routing algorithms can meet the target ratio. Interestingly, the path-repair provides only the event delivery ratio of 82% that is slightly lower than the target ratio. Additional experiments show that the multi-path routing algorithm with three disjoint paths cannot meet the target ratio, whereas four disjoint paths can barely guarantee the target ratio.

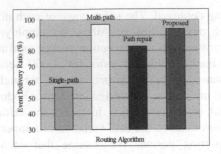

Fig. 3. A comparison of the event delivery ratio of critical events with the different routing algorithms (max. 10-hop distance between the sensor node and the base station): The single-path algorithm, the multi-path (5-disjoint path) algorithm, the path-repair algorithm, and the proposed algorithm, where f=0.1 and α=0.9

4.4 The Average Delay

The average delay represents the average latency required to transmit a critical event from a sensor node to the base station. Fig. 4 shows the average delay measured with each routing algorithm. The proposed algorithm has about 15% longer average delay compared with the single-path routing algorithm making the shortest average delay. However, the average delays of the path-repair routing algorithm and the multi-path routing algorithm are higher than that of the proposed algorithm by 22% and 37%, respectively. Again, the path-repair routing algorithm requires a considerable amount of time to search an alternative path and retransmit the packet. The multi-path routing generates more traffic by sending a packet along multiple-disjoint paths. As a result, it causes higher collisions in wireless channels and longer back-off delays for transmission.

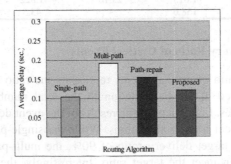

Fig. 4. A comparison of the average delay with the different routing algorithms (max. 10-hop distance between the sensor node and the base station): The single-path algorithm, the multi-path (5-disjoint path) algorithm, the path-repair algorithm, and the proposed algorithm, where f=0.1 and α=0.9

5 Concluding Remarks

This paper proposed an energy-efficient k-disjoint-path routing algorithm that can vary the number of disjoint paths (k) according to changing data patterns and a target delivery ratio of critical events. The proposed algorithm operates as in the single-path routing algorithm ($k=1$) if the data variation is lower than a pre-defined threshold under no occurrence of critical events in order to consume less energy. On the other hand, it works like a multi-path (k-disjoint path) routing algorithm ($k>1$), if data variation is higher than the pre-defined threshold in order to meet the target delivery ratio under the occurrence of critical events. The value of k is obtained from the well-defined fault model and a target delivery ratio. Our simulation showed that the proposed algorithm guaranteed the target delivery ratio as much as the multi-path routing algorithm, whereas the single-path and path-repair routing algorithms could not meet the target ratio. Compared with the single-path routing algorithm, the proposed algorithm should a slight increase in the average dissipated energy and the average delay by 18% and 15%, respectively. The multi-path routing algorithm and the path-repair algorithm, however, consume more energy than the proposed algorithm by 110% and 47%, respectively. In future work, we plan to apply more complex fault models to the current routing algorithm for reliable wireless sensor networks.

Acknowledgments. This research was in part supported by the MIC(Ministry of Information and Communication), Korea, under the ITRC(Information Technology Research Center) support program supervised by the IITA(Institute of Information Technology Assessment) (IITA-2006-C1090-0603-0045).

References

1. Levis, P., Madden, S., Gay, D., Polastre, J., Szewczyk, R., Woo, A., Brewer, E., Culler, D.: The Emergence of Networking Abstractions and Techniques in TinyOS. In: First USENIX/ACM Symposium on Networked Systems Design and Implementation, ACM Press, New York (2004)
2. Akyildiz, I., Su, W., Sankarasubramaniam, Y., Cayirci, E.: Wireless sensor networks: A survey. Computer Networks 38 (2002)
3. Yao, Y., Gehrke, J.: Query Processing for Sensor Networks. In: Proceedings of CIDR (2003)
4. Madden, S., Szewczyk, R., Franklin, M., Cullera, D.: Supporting Aggregate Queries Over Ad-Hoc Wireless Sensor Networks. In: Proceedings of WMCSA (2002)
5. Deng, J., Han, R., Mishra, S.: A Robust and Light-Weight Routing Mechanism for Wireless Sensor Networks. In: Proceedings of DIWANS (2004)
6. Ye, F., Zhong, G., Lu, S., Zhang, L.: GRAdient Broadcast: A Robust Data Delivery Protocol for Large Scale Sensor Networks. Wireless Networks 11 (2005)
7. Ganesan, D., Govindan, R., Shenker, S., Estrin, D.: Highly-Resilient, Energy-Efficient Multipath Routing in Wireless Sensor Networks. Mobile Computing and Communication Review 4(5) (2001)

8. Karlof, C., Li, Y., Polastre, J., ARRIVE,: Algorithm for Robust Routing in Volatile Environments. Technical Report, UCB//CSD-03-1233 (2003)
9. Ortolani, M., Gatani, L., Re, G.: Robust Data Gathering for Wireless Sensor Networks. In: Proceedings of ICON (2005)
10. Tian, D., Georganas, N.: Energy Efficient Routing with Guaranteed Delivery in Wireless Sensor Networks. In: Proceedings of WCNC (2003)
11. Baek, J., Nam, Y., Seo, D.: ATS-DA: Adaptive Timeout Scheduling for Data Aggregation in Wireless Sensor Networks. In: Proceedings of ICOIN (2007)
12. Li, S., Lin, Y., Son, S., Stankovic, J., Wei, Y.: Event Detection Services Using Data Service Middleware in Distributed Sensor Networks. Telecommunication Systems 26 (2004)
13. Kurata, N., Spencer, B., Ruiz-Sandoval, M.: Application of Wireless Sensor Network Mote for Building Risk Monitoring. In: Proceedings of INSS (2004)
14. Werner-Allen, G., Wieskowski, P., Welsh, M.: Demonstration: Real-Time Volcanic Earthquake Localization. In: Proceeding of SenSys (2006)
15. Boukerche, A., Pazzi, R., Araujo, R.: A Fast and Reliable Protocol for Wireless Sensor Networks in Critical Condition Monitoring Applications. In: Proceedings of MSWiM (2004)
16. VINT: The Network Simulator NS-2 (2005), http://www.isi.edu/nsnam

Supporting Mobile Ubiquitous Applications with Mobility Prediction and Soft Handoff

Marcello Cinque[1] and Stefano Russo[1,2]

[1] Dipartimento di Informatica e Sistemistica
Universita' degli Studi di Napoli Federico II
Via Claudio 21, 80125 - Naples, Italy
{macinque, sterusso}@unina.it
[2] Laboratorio ITEM "Carlo Savy"
Consorzio Interuniversitario Nazionale per l'Informatica
M.S. Angelo, Via Cinthia - 80125 Naples, Italy

Abstract. The increasing success of mobile-enabled embedded devices is stressing the need for software architectures facing mobility-related issues. This paper proposes a simple yet effective mobility management scheme to ease the development of mobile ubiquitous applications. The scheme seamlessly handles handoff events and provides ubiquitous applications with both location-awareness and mobility prediction support. An implementation prototype has been developed on real-world Bluetooth enabled devices. Experimental results are then obtained from the prototype, showing the effectiveness of the proposed scheme.

1 Introduction

Mobility management has widely been recognized as one of the most challenging problems for a seamless integration of embedded, mobile devices (MDs) into the physical world. Such integration is an important step towards the ubiquitous view of computing, where computation resources are spread into small devices which pervasively interact each other "all the time and everywhere" by means of wireless communication infrastructures [1].

One of the key aspects of mobility management is the handling of handoff procedures, i.e., the set of operations that need to be performed to guarantee a MD to be connected with one or more wireless Access Points (APs) while it roams across the ubiquitous environment. Specifically, a handoff procedure is composed of two basic steps: i) the *initiation*, which detects and triggers a handoff event from the old AP to a new one, and ii) the *decision*, where a new AP is selected among the available ones.

Several handoff management schemes have been proposed over the last years, addressing different flavors of wireless networks, from cellular networks, to the wireless Internet. However, when facing mobility-related issues for ubiquitous environments, several new challenges arise which are not generally supported by current software architectures for ubiquitous applications.

R. Obermaisser et al. (Eds.): SEUS 2007, LNCS 4761, pp. 409–418, 2007.

First, to achieve the "all the time and everywhere" view of mobility, handoff management should provide high connection availability to each MD. Second, ubiquitous devices typically offer limited computation and storing capabilities, and rely upon batteries. The mobility management support should thus take into account MDs and APs constrained resources by managing the handoff in a lightweight fashion. Third, ubiquitous applications would greatly benefit from a handoff management architecture able to provide mobility prediction. The ability of predicting both the handoff event and the next MD location enables to implement proactive resource allocation schemes which can have a significant impact on the overall performance.

Connection availability and mobility prediction can be obtained by implementing "soft" handoff procedures, where the MD is always connected to more than one AP, in order to minimize unavailability periods and to oversee the movements. However, this type of strategy may involve unacceptable resource consumption at both MD and AP sides.

This paper addresses these problems by proposing a novel, hybrid approach to handoff management, which requires the MD to be connected to a single AP, while guaranteeing soft handoffs and providing mobility prediction. The novel contribution, namely "Octopus", is a lightweight handoff scheme which extends our previous Last Second Soft Handoff Scheme (LSSH) [2,3]. In particular, even if LSSH provides soft handoffs while reducing unavailability periods (please refer to [2] for a quantitative evaluation), it presents the drawback of long decision periods, which may in turn degrade the accuracy of the location awareness support. Moreover, LSSH does not embody mobility prediction schemes.

The novel handoff scheme has been implemented and integrated in a mobility management architecture, running over Bluetooth wireless networks. Experimental results have been run on the actual implementation, demonstrating how the novel mobility prediction support offered by Octopus can significantly improve the decision latency and the location accuracy.

2   Related Work

Handoff strategies can be classified as reactive and proactive. Reactive strategies, such as [4,5], look for other available APs only after the current AP signal is lost.On the other hand, proactive strategies continuously monitor channel conditions and start communication-level handoff before losing current AP signal, at the cost of higher battery consumption. Several criteria are based on the Receiver Signal Strength Indicator (RSSI) [6,7,8,9].Some of them, such as [6,9] are based on a fixed threshold mechanism, that is, the handoff is initiated when the RSSI falls below a certain threshold. It is simple to argue how this kind of initiation leads to a poor availability. Indeed, noisy environments and shadowing problems can lead to transient RSSI degradations, which do not strictly require any handoff. Fore this reason, other solutions use a more complicated RSSI processing, such as fuzzy controllers [7], or mobility prediction [8].We can further distinguish two types of handoff: hard handoff, where the MD is connected to only one AP at time, minimizing signaling overhead but increasing latency and packet losses;

and soft handoff that activates the new data path to the destination AP before client disconnection from the origin AP [10]. It is worth noting that none of the mentioned solutions is able to answer to the needs outlined in previous section.

3   Handoff Management and Mobility Prediction

3.1   The LSSH Scheme

The LSSH scheme is a hybrid approach that tries to exploit the advantages of both hard and soft solutions. The initiation phase takes place using uniquely the information about the AP currently in use, as in hard handoff, and only in the decision phase multiple connections are established, as in soft handoff.

LSSH initiation. The initiation phase can be performed using diverse sets of information and techniques, such as broken link recognition and AP monitoring through RSSI or other measures and metrics. Our solution is RSSI based, for several reasons: i) it allows the handoff to be proactive, ii) the RSSI parameter is often already provided by the wireless interface, without performing intrusive measures, and iii) RSSI is an indication of the device position with respect to APs; this helps to achieve load balancing on APs depending on device distribution in the environment. Furthermore, locationing techniques can be implemented. According to the LSSH scheme, the initiation has to be performed using only the RSSI of the AP in use. It is thus crucial to carefully discriminate transient signal degradations, from permanent ones. Indeed, transient signal degradations can trigger unnecessary handoff procedures. To this aim, the LSSH scheme adopts the α-count mechanism due to the clear and simple mathematical characterization, the thorough analysis already conducted, and the minimal computational complexity which properly answers lightweight needs [11]. The α-count function $\alpha^{(L)}$ is a count and threshold mechanism. It takes the L-th measured RSSI as an input, then $\alpha^{(L)}$ is incremented by 1 as the current RSSI falls below the threshold S_{RSSI}. Similarly, $\alpha^{(L)}$ is decremented by a positive quantity dec if the L-th measured RSSI is greater than the S_{RSSI}. A handoff is triggered as soon as $\alpha^{(L)}$ becomes greater than a certain threshold α_T. The function $\alpha^{(L)}$ is thus defined as follows:

$$\alpha^{(L)} = \begin{cases} \alpha^{(L-1)} + 1 & \text{if } RSSI^{(L)} < S_{RSSI} \\ \alpha^{(L-1)} - dec & \text{if } RSSI^{(L)} \geq S_{RSSI} \text{ and } \alpha^{(L-1)} - dec > 0 \\ 0 & \text{if } RSSI^{(L)} \geq S_{RSSI} \text{ and } \alpha^{(L-1)} - dec \leq 0 \end{cases} \quad (1)$$

In our previous work we outlined how the values of α_T, dec and S_{RSSI} parameters can be tuned in order to achieve a trade-off between early and late handoffs.

LSSH decision. During the decision phase, the MD sequentially connects to all the neighboring APs of the old AP. The decision is then taken by evaluating the RSSI of all the links to the neighbors and by choosing the best AP among them. Let $\{ng_1, ..., ng_n\}$ be the set of neighbors. During the scanning, the scheme keeps track of the best visited AP, let say ng^*. When it connects to ng_i, if the

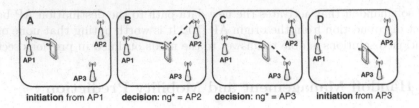

Fig. 1. The LSSH scheme

RSSI of ng_i is greater than the ng^* one, then $ng^* = ng_i$. At the end of the scanning, the resulting ng^* is selected as the new AP. It is simple to argue that such sequential scanning may require long decision latencies. As for locationing issues, we assume that a mobile device is in a zone x when it is attached to a AP covering the zone x. Being the RSSI strictly related with the distance between antennas, the scheme enforces devices to be connected to the closest AP. However, even if pathological situations can lead to the selection of a wrong AP, poor values of the signal strength, which are measured on the selected AP, will eventually result in the initiation of a new handoff, thus correcting the error.

For more information on the LSSH scheme, please refer to our previously published work [2]. Figure 1 summarizes the LSSH scheme in the simplistic case of three APs.

3.2   The Novel *Octopus* Scheme

The Octopus scheme has been introduced to overcome LSSH's main drawbacks, that is, long decision periods, which may affect the locationing accuracy, and the lack of a mobility prediction support able to predict with reasonable anticipation the next AP the device is going to be connected to.

The basic idea behind Octopus is the same of LSSH, i.e., exploiting the advantages of both hard and soft handoff. The main difference lays in the decision phase, which is anticipated and concurrently performed with the initiation. During its normal operation, the MD monitors only one connection, as in hard handoff (panel A in figure 2). When a handoff event becomes probable, the MD starts to monitor its neighboring APs, as in soft handoff. Specifically it connects,

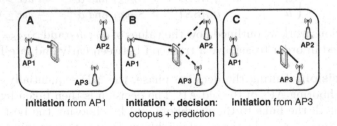

Fig. 2. The Octopus scheme

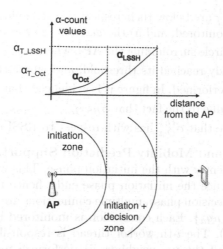

Fig. 3. The zones defined by the Octopus scheme and their relationship with $\alpha_{LSSH}^{(L)}$ and $\alpha_{Oct}^{(L)}$ functions

i.e., concurrently attaches "tentacles", to all them, hence the name "octopus" (panel B). During this phase, the device still keeps using the old AP. In addition, thanks to the multiple, concurrent connections, it can predict the AP it is going to be shortly connected to. Finally, when the handoff event is triggered, the MD can quickly decide the next AP, and release connections (panel C).

Octopus Initiation. Differently from the LSSH scheme, the Octopus initiation is based on two α-count functions, which are evaluated concurrently on the same RSSI signal. The first function, called $\alpha_{LSSH}^{(L)}$ and based on $\alpha_{T_{LSSH}}$, dec and $S_{RSSI_{LSSH}}$ parameters, has the same purpose of the LSSH α-count: it triggers the handoff event as soon as $\alpha_{LSSH}^{(L)}$ becomes greater than $\alpha_{T_{LSSH}}$. The second function, called $\alpha_{Oct}^{(L)}$ and based on $\alpha_{T_{Oct}}$, dec and $S_{RSSI_{Oct}}$ parameters, triggers the anticipated decision phase as soon as $\alpha_{Oct}^{(L)}$ becomes greater than $\alpha_{T_{Oct}}$. Since the decision phase has to be triggered before the handoff event, it results:

$$\alpha_{T_{Oct}} = \frac{\alpha_{T_{LSSH}}}{K_T}, \ K_T \geq 1 \tag{2}$$

In other terms, the threshold on the $\alpha_{Oct}^{(L)}$ (for the anticipated decision) has to be lower than the threshold on $\alpha_{LSSH}^{(L)}$ (for the initiation). The value of the K_T constant tunes the earliness of the anticipated decision phase: the bigger K_T, the earlier the decision phase will be undertaken. Similarly, it has to be:

$$S_{RSSI_{Oct}} = K_S \cdot S_{RSSI_{LSSH}}, \ K_S \geq 1 \tag{3}$$

that is, $\alpha_{Oct}^{(L)}$ has to be less tolerant to RSSI degradations than $\alpha_{LSSH}^{(L)}$.

Figure 3 depicts how the octopus scheme defines two "zones" surrounding every AP: i) the pure *initiation* zone (the first circle surrounding the AP), where both $\alpha_{LSSH}^{(L)}$ and $\alpha_{Oct}^{(L)}$ are below their respective thresholds and where only the source AP RSSI is monitored, and ii) the *decision+initiation* zone (between the first and the second circle surrounding the AP), where $\alpha_{LSSH}^{(L)}$ is below its threshold, while $\alpha_{Oct}^{(L)}$ already reached its threshold, and where the monitoring of the neighboring APs is performed. In figure it is evidenced that $\alpha_{Oct}^{(L)}$ increases faster than $\alpha_{LSSH}^{(L)}$. This is due to the fact that $S_{RSSI_{Oct}} \geq S_{RSSI_{LSSH}}$, or equivalently, to the lower tolerance that $\alpha_{Oct}^{(L)}$ has with respect to RSSI degradations.

Octopus Decision and Mobility Prediction Support. The decision phase is performed concurrently with the initiation phase. This way, the final decision is already available once the initiation phase ends, hence reducing the decision latency. During the decision phase, multiple connections are created to the neighboring APs $\{ng_1, ..., ng_n\}$. Each connection is monitored by a separate worker thread (the tentacle). The i-th worker thread is responsible to periodically i) read the RSSI level of the ng_i neighbor, ii) perform a moving average of the current reading with past readings (in order to filter out transient degradation phenomena), and iii) store the moving average in a shared structure. A manager thread (the octopus itself) periodically evaluates the best neighbor ng^* by getting the RSSI average of all neighbors from the shared structure. Once the $\alpha_{LSSH}^{(L)}$ triggers the handoff event, the current best neighbor ng_* is selected as the next neighbor. Consequently, all the worker threads are stopped and all the connections to other neighbors are dropped. If the decision cannot be made (e.g., the device movements are too fast to let the octopus create all the needed connections), the LSSH decision is performed as a back up mode.

The manager thread owns the information about the best neighbor during all the decision phase. The best neighbor can of course change during the decision phase, due to natural MD movements. In other terms, the manager thread "follows" device movements and it is thus able to know in advance, i.e., prior to the handoff execution, which is the device direction and hence the next AP that will be likely selected. Therefore, the octopus decision scheme naturally holds precious mobility prediction information, that can be easily provided to applications as soon as the decision phase starts, that is, while the device lays in the *initiation+decision* zone.

4   Experimental Results

This section shows the effectiveness of the novel Octopus scheme as compared to the LSSH scheme. In particular, the main objectives of the experiments are: (i) to show how Octopus practically eliminates the decision latency, and (ii) to demonstrate that Octopus obtains better location accuracy as compared to LSSH. To follow such objective, two are the parameters that need to be measured: the decision time, both with Octopus and with LSSH, and the location estimate accuracy, which can be measured in terms of the percentage of location errors, both with Octopus and with LSSH. The percentage of location errors can be evaluated as:

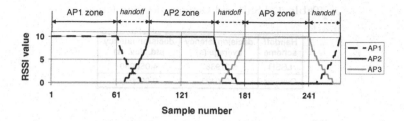

Fig. 4. RSSI reference traces, registered at a 1 m/s speed

$$\% \ of \ location \ errors = 100 \cdot \frac{N_{wl}}{N_{req}} \tag{4}$$

where N_{wl} is the number of times that the handoff management scheme (either LSSH or Octopus) returns a wrong location information with respect to the actual device location, and N_{req} is the total number of location requests. This parameter is particularly sensible to the device speed. The faster the device, the more is likely that the location estimate is wrong. In other terms, the faster the device, the less the handoff management scheme is able to follow device movements and to choose the right AP. Our experiments evidence how the Octopus scheme is more robust to device movements than the the LSSH scheme.

4.1 Prototype and Experimental Setting

The Octopus scheme has been implemented and integrated in a preexisting mobility management architecture, which is thoroughly described in our previous work [3]. Please refer to our web site: www.mobilab.unina.it/Prototypes.htm if you wish to download the last release of CLM and NCSOCKS including the Octopus scheme. Current implementation has been sufficiently tested only on Bluetooth wireless networks. Experimental results have been thus conducted over such networks.

In order to perform the above mentioned measures, we set up a simple testbed composed of three Bluetooth antennas acting as APs and one roaming, Bluetooth-enabled MD. In order to let each AP have two neighbors, we adopted a triangular topology. This way, every handoff procedure requires a decision between two APs. The distance between the antennas is set to 15 meters. Since we adopted Class 2 Bluetooth devices (with 10 meters transmission range), the overlapping zone between every couple of APs is set to 5 meters. To ease the measurement process at different device speeds, we adopted emulated RSSI readings by exploiting RSSI reference traces. The reference traces have been obtained by measuring actual RSSI values while the MD was moving around the testbed with a 1 m/s speed. The resulting traces are shown in figure 4. The emulated reading takes place by reading the RSSI value from the registered trace, rather than from the channel. To emulate different speeds, the reading from the traces is performed with different sampling periods. The sampling period is inversely proportional to the device speed. To exemplify, the double the sampling period, the half the emulated speed.

416   M. Cinque and S. Russo

Table 1. LSSH and Octopus decision latency

Handoff scheme	decision latency average (s)	decision latency std. dev. (s)
LSSH	5.279387	4.056980
Octopus	0.000137	0.000012

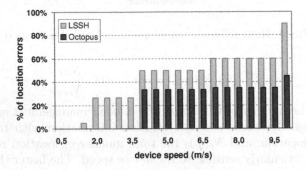

Fig. 5. LSSH and Octopus location accuracy as a function of the device speed

4.2 Results

Table 1 reports the decision latency we obtained with both LSSH and Octopus, with a 1 m/s speed. Due to its anticipated decision strategy, Octopus practically eliminates the decision latency. In particular, Octopus leads to a 99.99% improvement for the decision latency, which only accounts for the time spent by the manager thread to stop all worker threads and to return the last best neighbor estimate. In addition, as confirmed by the standard deviation latency estimates, the Octopus decision latency is by far more predictable than the LSSH decision latency. It is worth mentioning that the high decision latency value obtained for LSSH is particularly influenced by the Bluetooth technology, which involves relatively long connection set-up times.

As for the location accuracy, figure 5 shows the percentage of location errors as a function of the device speed. As expected, the percentage of location errors increases with the device speed. However, the figure clearly shows how Octopus outperforms LSSH by exhibiting a better robustness with respect to device fast movements. Specifically, Octopus starts to exhibit errors (about 30% errors on the total number of location estimates) when the MD speed approaches 4 m/s (e.g., the average speed of a running human being). On the other hand, LSSH starts to deliver wrong estimates even for relatively slow speeds, around 2 m/s. This is basically due to the long decision latency. For relatively high speeds, e.g. from 6 m/s to 10 m/s, Octopus roughly exhibits half the errors of LSSH.

As a last result, table 2 shows the Octopus decision latency as a function of the speed. From a certain speed on (e.g. 5 m/s), the decision latency starts to assume higher values. Fast movements may indeed induce the Octopus decision to fail: for instance, the Octopus fails to establish all the needed connections

Table 2. Octopus decision latency as a function of the device speed

Speed (m/s)	Sampling period (s)	No. of connections	Average latency (s)	
			Initiation	Decision
0,5	2	7	85,415200	0,000144
1	1	14	43,633162	0,000137
2,5	0.4	33	17,945656	0,000144
5	0.2	51	9,955675	0,365707
7,5	0.13333	54	10,061330	0,626858
10	0.1	55	9,859646	1,383985

on time. In these cases, the basic LSSH back-up scheme is adopted, leading to longer decision latencies. However, it is worth noting that performances are good for human walking/running speeds, that is, from 1 m/s up to 4 m/s. This means that the Octopus scheme can be successfully adopted in all those scenarios where the ubiquitous infrastructure "moves" at a human speed, e.g., wearable and portable devices embedded into human activities. However, it is worth recalling that the actual measures are relative to a Bluetooth-based scenario, where the results are partially influenced by long connection set-up times. Hence, the actual numbers (and the speed at which Octopus can successfully operate) depends on the adopted wireless technology. Besides actual numbers, we can reasonably claim that the improvement introduced with Octopus is valid in general terms.

5   Conclusions

This paper presented the driving ideas behind Octopus, a novel mobility prediction and soft handoff support for mobile ubiquitous applications. The novel scheme builds upon a previously proposed scheme, namely LSSH, and improves it by eliminating the need for time-consuming decision periods. This result has been made possible by the integration of mobility prediction, which also leads to the improvement of the locationing accuracy. Such improvements have been quantitatively demonstrated by means of experimental results on a real-world prototype.

Future efforts will concern a thorough evaluation of the Octopus scheme for other widely adopted wireless technologies, such as Wi-FI and ZigBee.

Acknowledgments

This work has been partially supported by the Italian Ministry for Education, University, and Research (MIUR) in the framework of the PRIN project "COMMUTA : Mutant hardware/software components for dynamically reconfigurable distributed systems", and in the framework of the "COSMIC" project "Centro di ricerca sui sistemi Open Source per le applicazioni ed i Servizi MIssion Critical". Authors are grateful to Gabriele Piantadosi and Daniele Zagordi for the precious help they profused in the implementation of the Octopus prototype and related experimental results.

References

1. Saha, D., Mukherjee, A.: Pervasive computing: A paradigm for the 21st century. In: IEEE Computer, pp. 25–31. IEEE Computer Society Press, Los Alamitos (2003)
2. Cinque, M., Cotroneo, D., Russo, S.: Achieving All the Time, Everywhere Access in Next-Generation Mobile Networks. ACM-SIGMOBILE Mobile Computing and Communication Review (MC2R) 9(2), 29–39 (2005)
3. Cinque, M., Cotroneo, D., Russo, S.: Mobility Management and Communication Support for Nomadic Applications. In: Meersman, R., Tari, Z. (eds.) On the Move to Meaningful Internet Systems 2005: CoopIS, DOA, and ODBASE: OTM Confederated International Conferences, Lecture Notes in Computer Science. LNCS, vol. 3760, pp. 882–900. Springer, Heidelberg (2005)
4. Baatz, S., Frank, M., Gopffarth, R., Kassatkine, D., Martini, P., Scheteilg, M., Vilavaara, A.: Handoff support for mobility with IP over Bluetooth. In: Proc. of the 25th Annual IEEE Conf. on Local Computer Networks (LCN 2000) (2000)
5. Tourrilhes, J., Carter, C.: P-handoff: A protocol for fine grained peer-to-peer vertical handoff. In: Proc. on the 13th IEEE Int. Symposium on Personal, Indoor and Mobile Radio Communcations (PIMRC '02) (2002)
6. George, M.L., Kallidukil, L.J., Chung, J.M.: Bluetooth handover control for roaming system applications. In: Proc. of the 45th Midwest Symposium on Circuits and Systems. MWSCAS-2002 (2002)
7. Bianchi, G., Blefari-Melazzi, N., Holzbock, M., Hu, Y.F, Jahn, A., Ray, E, Sheriff, R.E.: Design and validation of QoS aware mobile internet access procedures for heterogeneous networks. Mobile Networks and Applications, Special Issues on Mobility of Systems, Users, Data and Computing 8(1), 11–25 (2003)
8. Bellavista, P., Corradi, A., Giannelli, C.: Mobility Prediction for Mobile Agent-based Service Continuity in the Wireless Internet. In: Karmouch, A., Korba, L., Madeira, E.R.M. (eds.) MATA 2004. LNCS, vol. 3284, Springer, Heidelberg (2004)
9. Chung, S.-H., Yoon, H., Cho, J.-W.: A Fast Handoff Scheme For IP over Bluetooth. In: Proc. of 2002 Int. Conf. on Parallel Processing Workshops (ICPPW'02) (2002)
10. Saha, D., et al.: Mobility support in IP: a survey of related protocols. IEEE Network, 9(6) (2004)
11. Bondavalli, A., Chiaradonna, S., Di Giandomenico, F., Grandoni, F.: Threshold-based mechanisms to discriminate transient from intermittent faults. IEEE Transanction on Computers 49(3), 230–245 (2000)

Event-Driven Power Management for Wireless Sensor Networks*

Sang Hoon Lee[1], Byong-Ha Cho[1], Lynn Choi[1], and Sun-Joong Kim[2]

[1] School of Electrical Engineering
Korea University, Anam-Dong, Sungbuk-Ku, Seoul, Korea
{smile, sntblue, lchoi}@korea.ac.kr
[2] RFID/USN Research Group, Telematics•USN Research Division
ETRI, Daejeon, Korea
kimsj@etri.re.kr

Abstract. In this paper we propose event-driven power management techniques for wireless sensor networks. To accomplish this we model a sensor network application as a set of application-specific events that the application may contain. Events are first classified into scheduled and non-scheduled events. These events are further classified according to the size and the locality of the data, and the real-time characteristics of the event. For scheduled events we propose schedule-driven power control and global coordination. For non-scheduled events we propose source-driven and sink-driven power control for both lower energy consumption and higher performance. Experimentation results confirm that the event driven power management can substantially save energy compared to existing low energy sensor network protocols while it can meet the performance required by the application.

1 Introduction

Energy efficiency has been one of the key issues in implementing wireless sensor networks. Although a wide variety of sensor network protocols have been proposed [4, 5, 7, 10], the existing low-energy protocols are protocol-specific in a sense that they do not collaborate with the power management functions of upper or lower layers, limiting their scope. For example, when a source node reports an event to a sink, not only the nodes on the communication path but also all the other idle nodes repeatedly wake up unnecessarily. Furthermore, the busy nodes on the communication path still employ the periodic wake up and sleep during the event processing, which would substantially degrade the network performance. This can be attributed to the fact that each node decides its power management action without knowing its context, i.e. the state of the application or the characteristics of the on-going event.

In this paper, we investigate ways of exploiting the application-level information to further improve the energy efficiency of networking protocols. To accomplish this,

* This work was supported by the research commissioned by the Electronics and Telecommunications Research Institute.

R. Obermaisser et al. (Eds.): SEUS 2007, LNCS 4761, pp. 419–428, 2007.
© IFIP International Federation for Information Processing 2007

we characterize the sensor network events by using the following classification parameters: the event timing, the size and the locality of the report data, and the real-time characteristics of the event. A sensor network application is then modeled as a set of application-specific events that the application may contain.

Sensor network events are largely classified into scheduled and non-scheduled events. For scheduled events we propose *schedule-driven power control* and *global coordination*. For non-scheduled events we propose *source-driven* and *sink-driven power control*. With these event-driven power management (EPM) techniques, all the nodes on the communication path fully wake up during the event processing while all the non-participating nodes may not need to wakeup at all. This is controlled by each event source, i.e. a source node in the case of source-driven event, a sink node in the case of sink-driven event, and a report timer in the case of a scheduled event. The full duty-cycle operation during the event processing can not only reduce the message delay but also can reduce the time spent on idle listening by increasing the interval of the periodic wakeup during an idle state. Our detailed simulation results show that the energy savings achieved by EPM range from 29% to 94% depending on the application scenarios. Furthermore, EPM can also reduce the average message delay by up to 98% by employing the full duty-cycle operation on demand.

2   Application Model

2.1   Event Classification

In this work we define an event as an incident where a report needs to be sent to the sink. An event may occur due to a sensing activity by a sensor node, a query generated by a sink, or a local report timer at a sensor node since all of these activities may generate a report to the sink. Thus, an event is always associated with the generation of a report. However, a sensing activity can be performed regardless of the report. In this sense a sensing is regarded as a means to recognize an event.

We can classify events based on the following parameters: the timing of the event, the data characteristics of the report, and the real-time characteristics of the event. When an event is scheduled at a specific time, the event is called a *scheduled event*. Scheduled events are further classified into periodic and non-periodic events. *Periodic events* generate reports at every constant interval, such as hourly, daily, weekly, or monthly. *Non-periodic events* occur at predetermined times but not periodically. When an event occurs non-deterministically, the event is called a *non-scheduled event*. Non-scheduled events are classified into source-driven and sink-driven events. *Source-driven events* are asynchronous events that are triggered by a sensing activity at a sensor node, i.e. a source. *Sink-driven events* are triggered by a query sent by a sink and is considered as another type of non-scheduled asynchronous events.

Events can be further classified according to the size and the redundancy characteristics of the data that are reported. Depending on the size of the data events can be classified into *single data events* and *burst data events*. A single data event requires a report of a small data item such as the temperature or humidity, leading to the generation of a few data packets. On the contrary, a burst data event requires a report of a large data such as images or videos, leading to the generation of a packet stream. The redundancy characteristics of the data are closely related with the locality characteristics of the event. When an event can be detected by multiple sensor nodes nearby, the event is classified as a *spatial locality event*. For this type of event, only a single source needs to report the event. If a node detects multiple consecutive events but there exist a significant redundancy among the data reports, the events can be classified as a *temporal locality event*. In this case the node can summarize or aggregate the data before sending out a report. This locality characteristic of an event determines the type of aggregation that can be performed for the event.

The real-time characteristic of an event is related with the latency tolerance characteristics of an application for the event. The events with hard or soft deadlines are classified as a *real-time event* since the deadline must be met by the network. Events that can tolerate a considerable latency are classified as a *non-real time event*.

Table 1. Event classification factors

Event class	Non-scheduled event	Sink-driven non-scheduled event	NS_{Sink}
		Source-driven non-scheduled event	NS_{Source}
	Scheduled event	Periodic event	$S_{Periodic}$
		Non-periodic event	$S_{Non-periodic}$
Data characteristic	Data size	Single data	D_{Single}
		Burst data	D_{Burst}
	Data redundancy	Spatial locality	$DR_{Spatial}$
		Temporal locality	$DR_{Temporal}$
		Spatial & temporal locality	$DR_{Locality}$
		No locality	$DR_{No-locality}$
Latency tolerance	Real time		L_{Real}
	Non-real time		$L_{Non-real}$

2.2 Application Model

Table 1 shows our event classification parameters and their corresponding notations. Using the notation an event can be classified as a tuple, {event type, data size, data redundancy, latency tolerance}. Table 2 classifies the major event types of several well-known sensor network applications according to our classification parameters. For example, the most common event of volcanic monitoring application is classified as a source-driven, non-scheduled, single-data, real time event since the volcanic alarm must be reported within a limited delay. However, this application may have a periodic report of regional temperature and its image on an hourly basis, suggesting that it may include a periodic scheduled, burst-data, non-real time event. Thus, a sensor network application in general can be viewed as a set of different event classes rather than a single event class.

2.3 Application State

An application state can be specified by the type of event that the application is currently processing. Figure 1 shows the state transition diagram of a general sensor network application that has all three different event classes, i.e. scheduled event,

Table 2. Event classification of several well-known sensor network applications

Applications	Event class
Great Duck Island Project [6]	{ $S_{Periodic}$, D_{Single}, $DR_{Temporal}$, $L_{Non-real}$ }
James Reserve Extensible Sensing System [3]	Climate: { $S_{Periodic}$, D_{Single}, $DR_{Temporal}$, $L_{Non-real}$ }
	Wildlife: { $S_{Non-periodic}$, D_{Single}, $DR_{Spatial}$, $L_{Non-real}$ }
Volcanic monitoring [8]	{ NS_{Source}, D_{Single}, $DR_{No-locality}$, L_{Real} }
CORIE [2]	{ $S_{Periodic}$, D_{Single}, $DR_{Temporal}$, $L_{Non-real}$ }
FabApp [5]	{ $S_{Periodic}$, D_{Single}, $DR_{No-locality}$, $L_{Non-real}$ }
CodeBlue [1]	Monitoring: { $S_{Periodic}$, D_{Single}, $DR_{No-locality}$, L_{Real} }
	Alert: { NS_{Source}, D_{Single}, $DR_{No-locality}$, L_{Real} }
Traffic pulse technology [9]	{ $S_{Periodic}$, D_{Single}, $DR_{Temporal}$, L_{Real} }

source-driven event, and sink-driven event. On a deployment, the application starts from the initial state. In the initial state the self-organizing nature of the network requires all the network setup functions to be completed such as the routing path setup and the global time synchronization. After the setup process is complete, the application goes to the idle state and is ready to process any event. During this idle state, a node may need to wake up to detect a non-scheduled event. As discussed, the sensing activity is not regarded as an event and is processed locally by each node. Depending on the event source, i.e. the report timer, query, or an asynchronous event triggered by a sensing activity, the application goes to the corresponding state that handles the particular event class. Sometimes, another event may occur during the processing of an event. We assume that each event is processed in order. Thus, after the first event is completed, the application goes back to the idle state, and immediately makes a transition to process the second event.

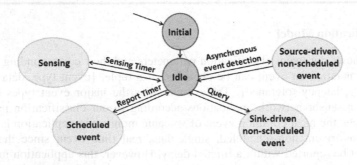

Fig. 1. Event-driven state transition diagram of an application

3 Event-Driven Power Management Techniques

3.1 Application-Specific Protocol Customization

The parameters of a networking protocol must be customized according to the performance requirements of a target application during the network design stage. We call this process *protocol customization*. The application characteristics that can influence the protocol customization include the size of the network field, the maximum tolerable latency for each event class, and the size of data types. In addition, the network designer must consider the physical characteristics of the sensor node.

3.2 Event-Driven Dynamic Power Management

3.2.1 Scheduled Events

For a scheduled event, a node needs to wake up only during the scheduled report period. Thus, the usual periodic wakeup and sleep employed by an existing MAC protocol can be completely eliminated if there are no other event classes in the application. The wakeup and sleep of a node can be controlled precisely by the report timer since the report schedule is prescheduled. This is called the *schedule-driven power control*. Both periodic and non-periodic events can be handled by the same technique. To meet the delay requirement of the event, the wakeup time must account for the worst-case communication delay, which can be computed by using the protocol customization procedure described in Section 4.2. A node must wake up if it is on the communication path from a source to a sink. If a single node is generating a report, all the nodes in the path from the source to the sink must wake up. All the non-participating nodes may not need to wake up at all. Thus, the idle listening can be completely eliminated if a node is not participating. This is called a *single-source event*. If multiple nodes are generating reports, the event is called a *multiple-source event*. In this case the worst-case communication delay must consider the delay due to the contention. If all the nodes in the network are generating reports, the scheduled event is called a *global event*.

In the case of a global event, all the nodes may start transmitting the report messages simultaneously. This is called *parallel transmission*. Although this might reduce the message delivery latency for each node, this may cause a significant delay in the MAC layer due to the contention caused by simultaneous transmissions. An alternative approach is that each node waits until it combines the messages from all of its descendants in the routing tree. If the event has a spatial locality, an aggregation can also be applied and the size of the report message can be further reduced. This is called *global coordination*. This technique reduces the number of transmissions by reordering the transmissions in the sensor field.

3.2.2 Source-Driven Non-scheduled Events

A node cannot predict the timing of a source-driven non-scheduled event. In addition, a node may not determine how many sources are participating in such an event. Thus, neither the global coordination nor the schedule-driven power control can be applied. Instead, a node must periodically wake up to check if such an event has occurred.

For the source-driven events, we can apply the *source-driven power control*. In this scheme, a source detecting an event can notify the occurrence of the event to all the nodes in the routing path from the source to the sink by sending a *wakeup signal* to the sink. After receiving the signal, a node must fully wake up to process the message. This full wakeup not only reduces the message delivery latency but also can increase the cycle time of the periodic wakeup and sleep during an idle state. If the event has a spatial locality, multiple sources can report the same event. Thus, a node must wake up as long as there is an active wakeup signal from any of its descendants. After the report is complete, then each source can send a *sleep signal* to request the nodes on the routing path to go back to an idle state. The RTS packet [10] can be used as a wakeup signal since the destination address field of the packet can be used to designate the recipient to wake up. In addition, the fragment flag of the normal data packet header can be used as a sleep signal since a source node can indicate if the current packet is the last data packet of a message by setting this flag.

3.2.3 Non-scheduled Sink-Driven Events

A sink node may generate a sink-driven event by sending a query. Like a source-driven event, a sensor node must check the occurrence of a sink-driven event by employing a periodic wakeup since it cannot predict the timing of such an event.

For the sink-driven events, we can apply the *sink-driven power control*. In this scheme, the sink node sending a query can notify the occurrence of the event to the sensor field. Thus, the query itself is considered as a wakeup signal and all the nodes receiving the query must wake up to process the query message. The sink sends a sleep signal after it receives all the report messages, signaling the completion of the query processing. Thus, a separate power down message is needed to implement the sink-driven power control.

4 Experimentation and Results

To evaluate both the energy efficiency and the network performance of EPM, we have implemented all the proposed EPM techniques in the NS-2 simulator framework. As a baseline routing protocol, we used the virtual sink rotation (VSR) routing [4] which is able to support multiple mobile sinks using the tree-based routing topology. Such a tree-based routing protocol is used since the global coordination assumes a tree-based topology. In addition, we use S-MAC [10] as an underlying MAC protocol, which assumes a periodic wakeup. We have implemented the schedule-driven, source-driven, and sink-driven power control to the underlying S-MAC protocol.

We use two metrics: average dissipated energy and average message delay. The *average dissipated energy* measures the ratio of total dissipated energy per node in the network to the number of distinct events seen by sinks. This metric computes the average work done by a node in delivering useful sensor data to the sinks. The *average message delay* measures the average latency observed from the time when an event is detected to the time when the last packet has arrived at the sink.

4.1 Benchmarks and Network Configurations

We use seven application scenarios as benchmarks as shown in Table 3. Applications 1 through 4 are a single event class application. Application 1 consists of a scheduled, non-real time, single data event class with spatial locality and simulates a climate monitoring system. Application 2 has the same event class as the application 1 but without locality. Application 3 consists of a non-scheduled, source-driven, hard real time, burst data event class and simulates an intrusion detection system with a camera. Application 4 is an example of a non-scheduled sink-driven, soft real time, burst data event class. This application can be viewed as a wildlife animal tracking system. Applications 5, 6, and 7 are various combinations of these single-event classes.

Table 3 also shows the characteristics of the network configurations used for the simulation. A 100-node sensor field is generated by placing the nodes in a 10x10 grid. A sink node is located at the center of the field. The size of a MAC packet is 200 bytes. A sensor node spends 33mW, 15mW, and 0mW at transmit, receive/idle, and sleep mode respectively. This is consistent with previous studies [10].

Table 3. Benchmarks and network configurations used for the simulation

	App. 1 (scheduled)	App. 2 (scheduled)	App. 3 (source-driven)	App. 4 (sink-driven)	App. 5	App. 6	App. 7
Report period	1 hour		-		App. 1+ App. 3	App. 2 + App. 4	App. 2 + App. 3 + App. 4
Data size	32B		64KB				
Aggregation	no	yes	no	no			
latency tolerance	1 hour		10 minutes	30 minutes			
Network Top.	10 * 10 grid						
Num. of nodes	101 nodes (100 sensor nodes + 1 sink node)						
MAC packet size	200 bytes						
Routing protocol	VSR						
MAC protocol	S-MAC						
Power Cons.	Tx: 31mW, Rx/Wakeup: 15mW, Idle: 0mW						

4.2 Protocol Customization

At the network design stage, the network designer must determine the sleep and wakeup schedule of each node which can guarantee the maximum tolerable latency. For a MAC protocol employing a periodic wakeup and sleep, such as S-MAC, the sleep and wakeup schedule can be expressed by the node's cycle time (t). A *cycle* is defined as the periodic interval, which consists of an active period and a sleep period [7]. The *cycle time t* should be long enough to accommodate a single data packet transaction, i.e. the sequence of SYNC, RTS, CTS, DATA and ACK packets. This is called the *minimum cycle time (t_{min})*, which can be calculated from the size of each packet, the contention window size for each packet, the transmission delay, and the RF transmission parameters of a given node. To derive the maximum cycle time permitted by the application, the longest path length in the network (N), the maximum tolerable latency for each event class (L), and the size of a message (S) need to be considered. Assuming that there is no other traffic, the latency of a single packet over N hops [10] under both S-MAC and EPM can be given by

$$\text{single-packet message delay under S-MAC / EPM} = N*t \qquad (1)$$

If multiple packets are transmitted consecutively on the same path, each packet needs to be separated at least 3 hops apart to avoid collision [10]. All the packets except the first one suffer from this additional delay for a multi-packet message. The delay of a multi-packet message assuming zero traffic can be given by

$$\text{multi-packet message delay under S-MAC} = N*t + 3(S-1)*t \qquad (2)$$

While the multi-packet message delay of S-MAC can be expressed by (2), the message delay of EPM is lower, because a node works at the full duty-cycle after receiving the first packet. The multi-packet message delay of EPM can be given by

$$\text{multi-packet message delay under EPM} = N*t + 3(S-1)*t_{min} \qquad (3)$$

Since the message delay must be smaller than L, the cycle time t can be derived from the equations (1) through (3). Table 4 shows the derived cycle times and the corresponding duty-cycles for our benchmarks under S-MAC and EPM. For applications 5, 6, or 7, the cycle time must be determined by the event class which requires the lowest latency. Note that the cycle time is not applicable to EPM for scheduled events since it does not employ the period wakeup and sleep for such events. However, due to the distributed clock synchronization required by S-MAC, each node wakes up at least every 30 seconds even under EPM.

Table 4. The cycle times and the duty cycles of S-MAC and EPM derived for our benchmarks

	App. 1	App. 2	App. 3	App. 4	App. 5	App. 6	App. 7
S-MAC	15s(1%)	15s(1%)	0.6s(25%)	1.8s (8%)	0.6s(25%)	1.8s(8%)	0.6s(25%)
EPM	N.A.	N.A.	48s(0.3%)	288s(0.05%)	48s(0.3%)	288s(0.05%)	48s(0.3%)

4.3 Simulation Results

Figure 2 shows the average dissipated energy and the average message delay for each event class in our benchmarks. For the scheduled events, EPM eliminates unnecessary wakeup during an idle state, reducing the energy consumption by up to 39% compared to S-MAC. Note that the global coordination is only effective for application 2 but the additional energy savings are relatively small. The average message delay of EPM is substantially smaller than that of S-MAC since each node can act with full performance during the event processing. For the source-driven event, the much higher duty cycle (25%) required by the S-MAC substantially increases the idle listening compared to EPM, which has a duty cycle of only 0.3%. As a result, an idle node with S-MAC requires 36.5 times more energy and a busy node with S-MAC requires 2.4 times more energy compared to EPM in this simulation. The average message delay of EPM is smaller than the maximum tolerable latency since the clock synchronization requires each node to wake up more frequently than that required for the tolerable latency. Like the source-driven power control, the sink-driven power control increases the network performance and reduces the energy consumption for the sink-driven event. EPM can eliminate 92% of the idle listening energy in S-MAC.

Figure 3 shows the case for multiple-event class applications. In the figure we only show the result of EPM assuming global coordination. As show in Figure 3(a) EPM can successfully eliminate up to 94% of the per-node dissipated energy compared to S-MAC. Since the event class with the minimum tolerable latency determines the cycle time of a node, usually a non-scheduled real-time event plays a dominant role in determining both the dissipated energy and the message delay of an application.

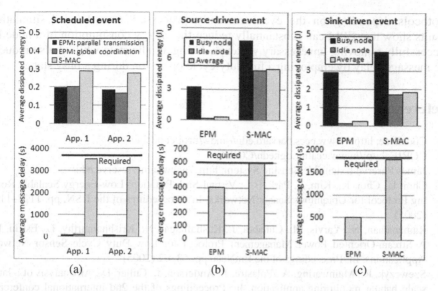

Fig. 2. Average energy consumption and average message delay (a) for a scheduled event, (b) for a non-scheduled source-driven event, and (c) for a non-scheduled sink-driven event

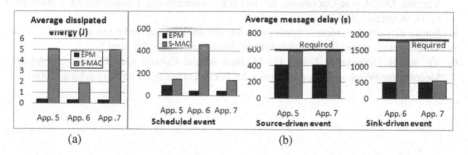

Fig. 3. (a) The average energy consumption for applications with multiple event classes. (b) The average message delay for applications with multiple event classes.

Figure 3 (b), (c), and (d) compares the average message delay of both S-MAC and EPM for a scheduled, source-driven, and sink-driven events respectively. Scheduled events have lower delay compared to single-event cases since the protocol is customized to meet the lowest latency required by the non-scheduled events.

5 Conclusion

In this paper we explore ways of exploiting the application state information at runtime to efficiently manage the energy and the performance of the networking protocols. To accomplish this we model a sensor network application as a set of application-specific events and propose various event-driven power management (EPM) techniques. EPM dynamically controls the operating mode of the protocols depending on the event currently processed. Our detailed simulation results show that EPM can substantially reduce the energy consumption of a node by successfully removing unnecessary wakeups during an idle state while it also reduces the message delay by employing a full duty-cycle operation during a busy state.

References

1. CodeBlue: http://www.eecs.harvard.edu/~mdw/proj/codeblue/
2. CORIE: http://www.ccalmr.ogi.edu/CORIE/
3. James Reserve Extensible Sensing System: http://www.jamesreserve.edu/
4. Choi, L., Choi, K., Kim, J., Park, B.J.: Virtual Sink Rotation: Low-Energy Scalable Routing Protocol for Ubiquitous Sensor Networks. In: Proceedings of the USN, pp. 1128–1137 (2005)
5. Ramanathan, N., Yarvis, M., Chhabra, J., Kushalnagar, N., Krishnamurthy, L., Estrin, D.: A Stream-Oriented Power Management Protocol for Low Duty Cycle Sensor Network Applications. In: Proceedings of the EmNets, pp. 53–62 (2005)
6. Szewczyk, R., Mainwaring, A., Polastre, J., Anderson, J., Culler, D.: An analysis of a large scale habitat monitoring application. In: Proceedings of the 2nd international conference on Embedded networked sensor systems, pp. 214–226 (2004)
7. Lee, S.H., Park, J.H., Choi, L.: Traffic-adaptive Sensor Network MAC Protocol through Variable Duty-Cycle Operations. In: The IEEE International Conference on Communications (to appear, 2007)
8. Sensor network for volcanic monitoring: http://www.eecs.harvard.edu/~mdw/proj/volcano
9. Traffic pulse technology: http://mobilitytechnologies.com/index.html
10. Ye, W., Heidemann, J., Estrin, D.: Medium Access Control with Coordinated Adaptive Sleeping for Wireless Sensor Networks. In: IEEE Transactions on Networking (2004)

Time Synchronization in Wireless Sensor Network Applications

Y.S. Hong and J.H. No

Department of Computer Engineering, Dongguk University, Seoul, Korea
{hongys, jhno}@dgu.ac.kr

Abstract. In most sensor network applications, events are time stamped with node's local time. However, energy is highly constrained resource in sensor networks. The purpose of this paper is to present a time-synchronization algorithm for sensor networks that aims at reducing the computation and communication energy expended by the algorithm. We use MAC-layer time stamping and estimate the clock drift rate and the offset in order to obtain high precision performance. Our algorithm works in two steps. In the first step, a spanning tree is built in the sensor network. In the second step, all nodes in the network synchronize their clocks to their parent nodes. We analyze and implement our time synchronization algorithm on Berkeley MicaZ platform and show that it can synchronize a pair of neighboring motes to an average accuracy of around one microsecond with communication complexity of $O(\log n)$.

Keywords: time synchronization, sensor network, wireless communication.

1 Introduction

Applications such as environmental monitoring deploys a sensing network consisting of a large number of sensor nodes with limited energy resource. These sensor nodes need to maintain local clocks in order to time-stamp events. Due to the severe resource constraints in sensor nodes, the traditional time synchronization algorithms for distributed systems should be reevaluated for the sensor network. Register clocks used in wireless sensor networks, even initially synchronized with a standard clock, gradually deviate from each other over a period of time. Due to the unavoidable deviation of local clocks, network-wide time synchronization can be achieved by synchronizing clocks.

This paper proposes a time synchronization algorithm for the wireless sensor network. This approach is based on the accumulated time information in order to estimate the clock drift rate and the clock offset of sensor nodes. Our algorithm works in two steps. In the first step, a hierachical structure is built in the sensor network. Finally, all nodes in the network synchronize their clocks to their parent nodes.

This paper is organized as follows: Section 2 briefly describes existing time synchronization algorithms. In Section 3, we present the proposed time synchronization algorithm in detail and analyze the proposed algorithm. In Section 4, we

R. Obermaisser et al. (Eds.): SEUS 2007, LNCS 4761, pp. 429–435, 2007.

describe implementation and results from the experiment. The paper concludes in Section 5.

2   Approaches to Time Synchronization Schemes

Clock synchronization algorithms have been extensively studied in the past to ensure that the deviation between clocks remains bounded. Most clock synchronization algorithms try to guarantee on the maximum clock deviation by deterministic algorithms. Probabilistic clock synchronization algorithm is based on a remote clock reading to read the clock at a remote node with a minimum error [2]. Another probabilistic approach used the time transmission protocol to estimate the time at a remote node. In the time transmission protocol, a sequence of clock synchronization messages containing the transmitting node's time-stamp are sent to the target node [1]. The target node estimates the time on the transmitting node's clock based on the time-stamps on the synchronization messages and the message delay statistics. An approach to synchronize clocks via OS- or middleware architecture mechanism tried to reduce the scheduling delay [10]. The Network Time Protocol have been widely used to synchronize clocks in the internet domain.

In wireless sensor networks, however, nondeterminism in transmission time caused by the Media Access Control(MAC) layer of radio stack can introduce unexpected delay at each hop. In the Reference Broadcast Synchronization(RBS) algorithm [5], a reference message is broadcasted. The receiver nodes record their local time and exchange the recorded time between neighboring nodes. In this approach, additional message is necessary to communicate the local time-stamp between nodes. The Timing-sync Protocol(TPSN) [6] first creates a hierachical structure in the network and then performs pair-wise synchronization between parent and children nodes. Each node synchronize its local time to its reference node by exchanging two synchronization messages with its parent node. The Flooding Time Synchronization Protocol(FTSP) [12] synchronizes the time of a sender by exchanging a single time-stamp message between the sender and the receivers.   Ideas from these protocols were used and enhanced in the proposed time synchronization protocol.

3   Time Synchronization Using the Accumulated Time Information

Our algorithm works in two steps. The first step of the algorithm is to create a spanning tree in the sensor network by broadcasting a *make-tree* packet starting from a root node. After a spanning tree is created, the root node initiates the synchronization stage by broadcasting a *sync* packet.

Our algorithm makes the following assumptions.

(a) There are n sensor nodes in the network and each sensor node has a unique identifier.

(b) Each sensor node maintains a 16-bit register as a clock that is triggered by a crystal oscillator.

(c) The clock drift rate between two physical clocks is bounded.

(d) Delays of successive synchronization message are independent of each other.

The time synchronization messages are periodically broadcasted by the sensor nodes at the same level in the tree structure.

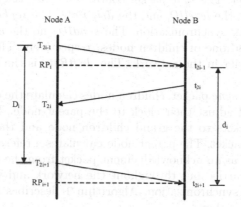

Fig. 1. Message exchange for time synchronization

Figure 1 shows the message exchange between node 'A' and node 'B' for time synchronization. Here, T_{2i-1}, T_{2i} and T_{2i+1} represent the time measured by local clock of node 'A'. t_{2i-1}, t_{2i} and t_{2i+1} represent the time measured by local clock of node 'B' . At time T_{2i-1}, 'A' sends a *sync* packet to 'B' . Node 'B' receives the packet at t_{2i-1}. At time t_{2i}, 'B' sends back an acknowledgement packet to 'A'. Node 'A' receives the packet at T_{2i}. These time variables satisfy following equations:

$$T_{2i-1} + p = at_{2i-1} + b$$
$$T_{2i} = at_{2i} + b + p \tag{1}$$

Here p, a, and b denote the propagation delay, the clock drift rate and the clock offset between the nodes respectively. Node 'B' can calculate the clock drift rate, the clock offset and the accumulated time information M_i as:

$$M_i = (T_{2i+1} - T_{2i-1}) - (t_{2i+1} - t_{2i-1}) \tag{2}$$

$$\approx (D_i + d_i) \cdot \frac{\sum_{k=1}^{i}(D_k + d_k)}{\sum_{k=1}^{i}(D_k - d_k)} \tag{3}$$

$$a = \frac{T_{2i+1} - T_{2i-1}}{T_{2i+1} - T_{2i-1} - M_i} \tag{4}$$

$$b = \frac{(T_{2i+1} + T_{2i-1}) - a(t_{2i+1} - t_{2i-1})}{2} \tag{5}$$

Knowing the clock drift rate and the clock offset, node 'B' can synchronize to node 'A'. The proposed protocol reduces the jitter of interrupt handling by maintaining the accumulated time information M_i in each node.

The message exchange for the time synchronization at the sensor network begins with the root node of level 0. The time synchronization starts by broadcasting a *sync* packet. The *sync* packet contains 5 fields: the *refTimeStamp*, the *sendID*, the *childID*, the *levelID*, and the *driftRate*. The *refTimeStamp* contains the reference time for synchronization. The *sendID* and the *childID* contain the ID of the sender and one of children nodes, respectively. The *levelID* contains the level of the sender in the network. The *driftRate* is the estimated value of the clock drift.

On receiving this *sync* packet, children nodes calculate the clock drift rate and the clock offset and adjust their clock to the parent node. The children nodes broadcast *sync* packets to the grand children node and the parent node will overhear the *sync* packet. The parent node calculates a reference time-stamp by utilizing the packet as an acknowledgement packet from the child node.

This process is carried out throughout the network and we can achieve the network-wide time synchronization. Algorithm 1 describes the proposed time synchronization algorithm.

Algorithm 1. Time synchronization

Step 1. Create a spanning tree.

   Assign level number to each sensor node by

   broadcasting a *make-tree* packet

Step 2. Synchronize to the parent node

   The root node initiates time synchronization

      by broadcasting a *sync* packet

   Repeat

      On receiving the *sync* packet, children

      nodes at the same level calculate

      the clock drift rate and the clock offset

      and broadcast a *sync* packet

   until all sensor nodes are synchronized.

Let us analyze the communication complexity of the Algorithm 1. Step 1 takes $O(log\ n)$ message exchanges. Step 2 also takes $O(log\ n)$ message exchanges. Hence, The communication complexity of Algorithm 1 will become $O(log\ n)$.

Table 1 shows communication complexities for RBS, TPSN, FTSP and the proposed algorithm.   If the resynchronization period is T seconds, then each node sends 1 message per T seconds in the proposed protocol. Each node sends 2 messages per T seconds in TPSN, 1.5 message per T seconds in RBS and 1 message per T seconds in FTSP [12].

Table 1. Communication complexities

Time synchroniztion Algorithm	Communication Complexity
RBS	$O(n^2)$
TPSN	$O(n)$
FTSP	$O(n)$
Proposed Algorithm	$O(logn)$

Since the proposed protocol employs a single broadcast message, it does not compensate for the propagation delay which is less than 1 microsecond for up to 300 meters.

There may be failures in sensor nodes or links. This situation may arise, when a level i node does not receive any *sync* packet from any neighbor at level *i-1*. When a node does not receive new *sync* packet for *TimeOut* number of resynchronization periods, it starts the root election process to select a new root node. In addition, when a new node is introduced to the network, the root election process will be needed in order to build a new spanning tree in the network.

4   Implementation

The proposed algorithm is implemented in the platform of Berkeley motes. Figure 2 shows the system for evaluating the time synchronization scheme described here.

The test system consists of four Berkeley MicaZ motes running Tiny OS 1.1.14. Three motes were used for time synchronization test and one of the motes was designated as a data collector connected to a PC running Windows XP in order to record the measured data. One of three motes was designated as the parent node and was responsible for broadcasting the synchronization message after every 10 seconds. The parent node was broadcasting time-stamped synchronization message to children nodes. The time-stamps were recorded on children nodes and the clock drift rate and the clock offset were calculated based on the accumulated time information. The synchronization error between a pair of motes is the absolute value of the difference of the recorded time-stamp and the corrected time-stamp.

The synchronization error from the experiment is summarized in Table 2. The results are obtained after averaging over 100 independent runs. The average and maximum time-stamping errors were 0.81 microsecond and 1.72 microsecond.

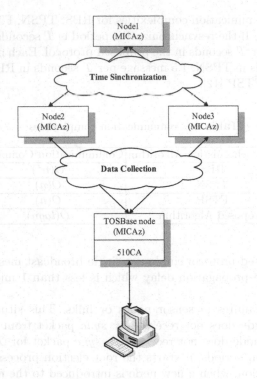

Fig. 2. Test environment

Table 2. Synchronization error from the experiment

	Synchronization error
Mean	0.81
Maximum	1.72
Variance	0.65

5   Conclusion

We have presented a time synchronization protocol for wireless sensor networks.
The protocol uses the accumulated time information in order to estimate the clock
drift rate and the offset. We have tested our protocol on the Berkely MicaZ platform with four motes. The measurements indicate that the synchronization error
is in the range of one microsecond with communication complexity of $O(logn)$.

We plan to extend our experiment to the multi-hop networks of motes.

Acknowledgments. This research was supported by the MIC(Ministry of Information and Communication), Korea, under the ITRC(Information Technology
Research Center) support program supervised by the IITA(Institute of Information Technology Assessment).

References

1. Arvind, K.: Probabilistic Clock Synchronization in Distributed Systems. In: IEEE Trans. On Parallel and Distributed Systems, 5th edn, pp. 474–487 (1994)
2. Cristian, F., Fetzer, C.: Probabilistic Internal Clock Synchronization. In: Proc. of thirteenth Symposium on Reliable Distributed Systems, pp. 22–31 (October 1994)
3. Dai, H., Han, R.: TSync: A Lightweight Bidirectional Time Synchronization Service for Wireless Sensor Networks. Mobile Computing and Comm. Review 8, 125–139 (2004)
4. Dam, T.V., Langendoen, K.: An Adaptive Energy-Efficient MAC Protocol for Wireless Sensor Networks. In: The First ACM Conference on Embedded Networked Sensor Systems (Sensys03), Los Angeles, CA, USA, pp. 171–180 (2003)
5. Elson, J.E., Girod, L., Estrin, D.: Fine-Grained Network Time Synchronization using Reference Broadcasts. In: Proc. 5th Symp. Op. Sys. Design and Implementation, Boston, vol. 36, pp. 147–163 (2002)
6. Ganeriwal, S., Kumar, R., Srivastava, M.: Timing Sync Protocol for Sensor Networks. In: ACM SenSys, Los Angeles, CA, pp. 138–149 (2003)
7. Greunen, J.V., Rabaey, J.: Lightweight Time Synchronization for Sensor Networks. In: Proc. 2nd ACM Int'l. Conf. Wireless Sensor Networks and Apps, San Diego, CA, pp. 11–19 (2003)
8. Hong, Y.S., No, J.H.: Clock Synchronization in Wireless Distributed Embedded Applications. In: IEEE Workshop on Software Technologies for Future Embedded Systems, pp. 101–104. IEEE Computer Society Press, Los Alamitos (2003)
9. IEEE Computer Society. IEEE 802.15.4: Wireless Medium Access Control (MAC) and Physical Layer (PHY) Specifications for Low-Rate Wireless Personal Area Networks (LR-WPANs) (2003)
10. Kim, K.H(K.), Im, C., Athreya, P.: Realization of a Distributed OS Component for Internal Clock Synchronization in a LAN Environment. In: Proc. of the fifth IEEE Symposium on Object-Oriented Real-Time Distributed Computing, pp. 263–270 (2002)
11. Kopetz, H., Ochsenreiter, W.: Clock Synchronization in Distributed Real-Time Systems. IEEE Transactions on Computers C-36(8), 933–939 (1987)
12. Maroti, M., Kusy, B., Simon, G., Ledeczi, A.: The flooding time synchronization protocol. In: Proc. 2nd international conference on Embedded networked sensor systems, pp. 39–49 (2004)
13. Mills, D.L.: Internet time synchronization: the Network Time Protocol. IEEE Transactions on Communications 39, 1482–1493 (1991)
14. Mock, M., Nett, E., Frings, R., Trikaliotis, S.: Clock Synchronization for Wireless Local Area Networks. In: Proc. of the 12th Euromicro Conference on Real-Time Systems, Stockholm, pp. 183–189 (2000)
15. Romer, K.: Time Synchronization in Ad Hoc Networks. In: ACM MobiHoc '01, Long Beach, CA, pp.173-182 (October2001)
16. The TinyOS Project, http://webs.cs.berkeley.edu/tos

GENSEN: A Topology Generator for Real Wireless Sensor Networks Deployment

Tiago Camilo, Jorge Sá Silva, André Rodrigues, and Fernando Boavida

Department of Informatics Engineering, University of Coimbra
Polo II, Pinhal de Marrocos, 3030-290 Coimbra, Portugal
{tandre, sasilva, arod, boavida}@dei.uc.pt

Abstract. Network Simulators are important tools in network research. As the selected topology often influences the outcome of the simulation, realistic topologies are required to produce realistic simulation results. The topology generator presented in this document, GenSeN, was created based on the authors' knowledge from several experiences. GenSeN is a tool capable of generating realistic topologies of wireless sensor networks and, additionally, auto-configuring important characteristics of sensor nodes, such as energy parameters. The tool was validated by comparison with real deployment strategies and experiences.

Keywords: Wireless Sensor Networks, Simulators, Sensor Node Deployments.

1 Introduction

Due to technology advances in telecommunications, microprocessors and monitoring, it is now possible to design networks with special features, such as Wireless Sensor Networks (WSNs) [1]. Such networks have specific requirements such as reduced energy availability, low memory and reduced processing power. A WSN consists of a number of sensors (e.g. from ~10 up to ~10000) spread across a geographical area. Each sensor is equipped with a wireless communication system, and some level of intelligence for signal processing and networking of the data.

Although they can be considered ad hoc networks, WSNs are in fact quite distinct from these networks in the deployment phase. In typical ad hoc networks, devices are mobile and their location is a random factor, since users of such equipment normally cannot predict the place and time where the network will be stable. On the other hand, in WSNs the deployment phase is critical and may require careful planning, due to the singular characteristics of sensor nodes. As the authors demonstrated [2], the correct distribution of sensor devices over the target monitoring area affects the entire WSN deployment, from the choice of the correct sensor nodes, to the correct network protocol, and the architecture/topology to use. When a WSN solution is designed, it is important to define the main evaluation criteria that, in the end, will be used to validate the obtained results. Lifetime, latency, fault-tolerance, scalability and precision are some of the parameters used to evaluate WSN solutions.

R. Obermaisser et al. (Eds.): SEUS 2007, LNCS 4761, pp. 436–445, 2007.
© IFIP International Federation for Information Processing 2007

In optimal conditions, where radio interference does not exist, the terrain is plane and no obstacles are present, the most effective deployment strategy would be the grid strategy, where all devices are in range and evenly placed to cover the whole monitoring area. However, due to their vast applicability, WSNs are commonly deployed in unusual locations, where human accessibility is limited (e.g. inside a volcano). In such environments it is necessary to place sensor nodes using different strategies (e.g. dropping sensor nodes from a plane). Therefore, it becomes crucial to develop the necessary tools to study such variables in a simulation environment, before the tests in the final environment begin. In [13] the authors identified some research issues / directions that influence the WSN MAC layer development. One of them was the need to improve the simulation tools with better representations of the reality (namely better radio models that account for terrain, antenna location, foliage types, etc). This paper, based in data from [2,8], tries to address some of these problems by developing a new WSN topology generator for Network Simulator 2 (NS-2).

The remainder of this paper is organized as follows: Section 2 presents the related work regarding topology generators. Special focus is given to the topo_gen, which is the only specific tool that covers WSNs. Section 3 identifies the main problems regarding the deployment of WSN and presents six different deployment strategies. In Section 4 the GenSeN is introduced. Special attention is given to the input and to the output parameters of the generator. Results taken from the topology generator are discussed in Section 5. Finally, conclusions and future work are addressed in the last section.

2 Related Work

The development of topology generators that emulate real environment features is a problem that attracted and still attracts the attention of the scientific community. Nowadays there are a number of competing approaches to the construction of random network topologies, for wired and wireless environments.

One of the most popular generators available is BRITE [3]. It is a flexible tool that supports flat router and hierarchical topologies, allowing the configuration of several important parameters such as bandwidth and delay.

GT-ITM [4], another topology generator, focuses on reproducing the hierarchical structure of the topology of the Internet.

Finally, the Inet [5] is a network generator aiming to reproduce the connectivity properties of Internet topologies, assigning node degrees from a power-law distribution.

However, the referred approaches are specially designed to build well known Internet network topologies, which present significant differences when compared to WSNs.

The Topo_gen [11] is a topology generator designed by the ISI Laboratory for Embedded Networked Sensor Experimentation, which intends to be a tool to generate random sensor node locations. Although it was originally designed to be used in directed diffusion experiments, it is an adaptable tool that can be easily ported to support other protocols. Topo_gen has some configurable parameters such as map dimensions, source and sink count. It allows the creation of topology files for NS-2 and EmSim [12]. Nonetheless, this topology generator does not take in account real sensor network placements, since it only allows random or cluster node distribution. Characteristics such as sensor node deployment strategies are not covered.

3   Wireless Sensor Network Deployment

WSNs differ from typical ad hoc networks by requiring a deployment phase, in contrast with ad hoc networks, which are known to group spontaneously and move in a random way. Sensor nodes are normally placed in special environments without guarantee of position. This is why the deployment phase in a WSN project is extremely important to the final experiment output. Due to its characteristics, the WSN can be deployed in environments where the accessibility by humans is difficult, and where ambient conditions can significantly vary.

The minimal number of sensor nodes required to monitor a specific area (A), is provided by Equation 1, where r represents the sensing range of each sensor node [6].

$$NS = \frac{2A.\pi}{r^2\sqrt{27}}$$ (1)

However, this approach considers that all nodes have the same monitoring capabilities, which means that it cannot be applied to WSN with different types of sensor nodes. Moreover, it does not take into account the existence of obstacles, such as trees or walls.

As mentioned before, in order to optimize sensor node placement, sensor nodes must be deployed as a grid, where all devices are meticulously and evenly spaced according to their monitoring/transmitting range. Such method minimizes the number of nodes needed to monitor a specific area, with full phenomenon coverage. However, such scenario can only be applied when ideal radio environment characteristics are present (i.e. no radio interference exists, the terrain is flat and there is no vegetation). Moreover, sensor nodes deployment is often made in inhospitable locations, where it becomes impossible to deploy a uniform distribution. In places such as the ocean bed, it is not feasible to deploy sensor nodes in a grid arrangement. On the other hand, applications such as monitoring a cyclone require a fast deployment phase, since this kind of phenomenon is not predictable, and it is necessary to distribute sensor nodes as quick as possible to maximize the coverage area, connectivity, etc.

For this reason, it is necessary to consider different deployment strategies, which could be used in inhospitable areas or could be more suitable to different sensor network applications. Therefore the authors suggested six different deployment strategies in a previous piece of work [2], each one listed below:

- **Grid:** In this strategy it is important to create a network of sensors similar to the one illustrated in Fig. 1, where each sensor device is evenly separated from neighboring devices by r, which is the communication/monitoring range of each sensor. An operator is responsible to place each sensor facing up (antenna point up). A ribbon-metric is used so that the sensor location is determined as exactly as possible;

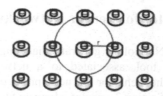

Fig. 1. Sensor nodes placed as a grid

- **One-by-One:** This strategy consists in deploying each sensor individually, but without using metrics tools. The operator is responsible to throw each node using only his knowledge regarding the average distance between nodes, not relying on the node position;
- **Two-by-two:** The only difference between this strategy and the previous one, is the fact that the operator, in this case, throws sensor nodes in pairs;
- **Three-by-three:** The technique is similar to that in the one-by-one and two-by-two strategies, but in this case the operator drops the sensor nodes in groups of three elements;
- **Cliff:** In this strategy the operator drops the nodes from a higher point, more precisely from a 10 meters crag. Such strategy intends to simulate a WSN experiment were the phenomenon is located far bellow the operator, or even to simulate the deployment from inside a helicopter;
- **Propellant:** In this final strategy the sensors are spread in the area to monitor through the help of a propellant. All sensors are spread at the same time. The propellant is calibrated to send the sensors nodes to the middle of the monitored area.

The different deployment strategies were compared using a real WSN implementation [8]. In a 60 m2 monitoring area (6 per 10 meters), a set of Embedded Sensor Board (ESB) sensor devices from the ScatterWeb [9] platform were used. The environment was strategically chosen: plain, dry and with no natural or human made obstacles. Each sensor was placed at ground level. For each strategy, the deployment time, cost and network connectivity were analyzed. By dividing the rectangle area in 15 squares the authors found the average node location per square, on each deployment strategy; the results can be found in [2]. From this study it was possible to conclude that the best results were obtained by the grid strategy, since it leads to an optimal node distribution, (each of the 15 regions was covered by one node). Strategies such as cliff and propellant, which have reduced deployment time, tend to concentrate the nodes in the center of the scenario, decreasing the area covered by the sensors.

Another important difference in WSN deployment is the fact that it is not possible to guaranty the correct node (antenna) orientation, contrary to normal ad hoc networks behaviour. When a node is spread (e.g. by a propellant), depending on the device (the ESB permits six different antenna orientations), it can be facing different positions: antenna up, antenna down, etc. As presented in [2], such characteristic can be crucial for WSNs, since a bad sensor node position can decrease the radio range by 30%.

4 GenSeN: A Generator for Sensor Networks

The need for a realistic WSN topology generator has long been recognized by sensor network researchers. Such tool, associated to a network simulator, is the first instrument to understand the behavior of new protocol prototypes. The existing approaches, as described in Section 2, are not adequate to the WSN characteristics (ad hoc network topology generators), or do not contemplate realistic node distribution (TopoGen).

The GenSeN is a topology generator built in C++ that is specifically designed to work with NS-2 [7]. It is based on real WSN deployments performed by the authors, and described in Section 3. This generator has the capability to simulate the behaviour of the presented deployment strategies: grid, one-by-one, two-by-two, three-by-three, cliff, and propellant. It presents several input parameters which are used to characterize each sensor node (Fig. 2).

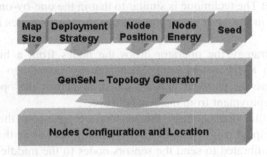

Fig. 2. GenSeN – Topology Generator Architecture

As output, GenSeN provides a tcl format file containing the configuration of each sensor and also its position in the monitoring area.

The following sub-chapters provide a detailed explanation on the input and output parameters provided by GenSeN.

4.1 GenSeN Input

GenSeN provides variable input parameters, each one used in the characterization of each sensor device. As illustrated in Fig. 2 the first parameter to be introduced is the monitoring area dimension. Unfortunately NS-2 does not yet provide a tridimensional scenario. For this reason only x and y parameters are used.

In the next step it is necessary to choose which will be the deployment strategy to use in the sensor distribution. The user has the following options:

```
1 - Grid (You need to set the distance)
2 - Random (DEFAULT)
3 - One-by-one
4 - Two-by-two
5 - Three-by-three
6 - Propellant
7 - Cliff
```

The user has the possibility to choose any of the deployment strategies presented in the previous section, plus the random node distribution, which is in fact the default option. This latter option will randomly distribute the sensors throughout the defined monitoring area. Such option should be used in case the user does not know which deployment strategy will be used in the final WSN implementation. In the grid alternative the user must set the minimal distance between the nodes. Such distance should be set to the smallest of two distances: the radio range and the sensing scope. The node locations are determined by the probabilistic rules learnt from [2].

Regarding the node position, GenSeN enables the user to configure the number of possible node orientations (regarding the antenna). The user should select how many possible positions the sensor node device will have. As an example, the device used in [2], the ESB, only supports four possible orientation-stages, contrary to the Mica family (Mica2, Micaz), which presents only two. As default, only one position is considered:

```
1 - One Position (DEFAULT)
2 - Two Positions
3 - Three Positions
4 - Four Positions
```

GenSeN will randomly choose the node position, which then will affect the transmitting and receiving energy for each node. Due to restrictions in NS-2, it is not possible to specify different radio propagation conditions in the same simulation. Therefore, it was necessary to emulate such capability. This was achieved by modifying the levels of transmitted energy in each node, although all the nodes have the same transmitting range.

In terms of energy configuration, GenSeN allows to set the following parameters: initial energy, idle energy, transmitting energy and receiving energy. Moreover, it supports the configuration of four different levels of energy, meaning GenSeN can generate different initial energy levels per sensor node. To allow such behavior, the user needs to choose one of the following options:

```
1 - All nodes with same energy (DEFAULT)
2 - Two energy levels
3 - Three energy levels
4 - Four energy levels
```

For each node, GenSeN will randomly choose the initial energy based on the option (initial energy) provided by the user.

In each iteration, GenSeN generates different results when compared to previous iterations, since its random factors are associated to a variable seed. However, the generator enables the user to configure its own seed, allowing debugging operations. Finally, it is also possible to specify the final *tcl* output file.

4.2 GenSeN Output

GenSeN is NS-2 based, meaning it was created to produce a WSN topology which can be used in a simulation experience in this simulator. As such, GenSeN outputs two tcl script files. One of the files saves the information regarding the nodes location (*x* and *y*), which is created as result of the chosen deployment strategy. The second file outputs the node configurations, namely the energy parameters of each individual node.

Finally, GenSeN calculates the estimated time required to perform the deployment of the entire sensor network which, once again, depends on the deployment strategy chosen by the user. These values are based on the ones achieved by the authors in [8].

5   Results

In order to study the behaviour of GenSeN, this section presents the results produced by this topology generator, and briefly validates them with the results achieved by the authors in [2].

The main goal of this study is to compare the node distribution for the different deployment strategies. Using a monitoring area of 6000 m2 (100 m per 60 m), a total of 32 sensor nodes were spread using seven deployment strategies: grid, random, one-by-one, two-by-two, three-by-three, cliff, and propellant, as described in Section 3. The environment area was virtually cut into 16 equal squares, each one with 375 m2. The number of nodes distributed on each square was registered and it is illustrated in figures 3-9. Since there are 32 sensor nodes, it would be expected that the best solution were to deploy 2 devices per region. Such result was achieved only by the grid strategy (Fig. 3). This solution presents the best results in terms of connectivity and sensing coverage.

Fig. 4 presents the results produced by the random distribution of nodes. This technique is the most used by the scientific community when simulating new protocols. However, the results are not very encouraging, since there exist enormous differences in terms of area coverage per device, and it also does not really reflect a real deployment strategy.

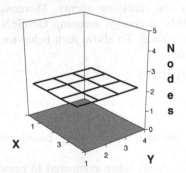

Fig. 3. Nodes per region for the Grid Deployment Strategy

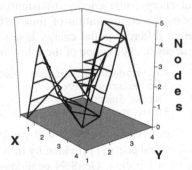

Fig. 4. Nodes per region for the Random deployment strategy

On the other hand, the solution presented in Figure 5, shows a better placement when compared to that of Figure 4. In Figure 5 the maximum numbers of nodes per square is 3, and all the squares are covered by at least one device.

Fig. 6 and Fig. 7 present the two-by-two and three-by-three strategy deployments, respectively. These strategies lead to poorer results when compared to the one-by-one strategy. In the case of the three-by-three strategy, one of the square areas ends up with no devices at all. On the other hand, a single region ends up with 5 devices.

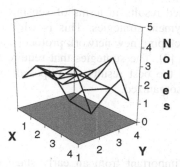

Fig. 5. Nodes per region for the One-by-one deployment strategy

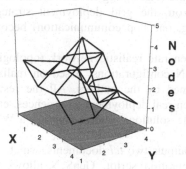

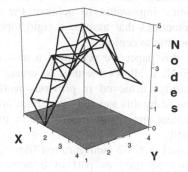

Fig. 6. Nodes per region for the Two-by-two deployment strategy

Fig. 7. Nodes per region for the Three-by-three deployment strategy

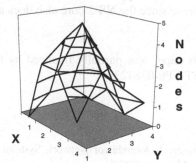

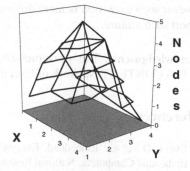

Fig. 8. Nodes per region for the Cliff deployment strategy

Fig. 9. Nodes per region for the Propellant deployment strategy

Finally, Fig. 8 and Fig. 9 show the worst sensor distribution results, mainly due to the characteristics of the used strategies. It is notorious that there is an excessive node density in the centre of the environment area, contrary to the edges, where several regions without sensor nodes exist.

Looking at the presented results in terms of sensing coverage, there is a huge difference between deployment strategies. This is why it is important to consider realistic models when developing new network protocols. All the results are coherent with the ones achieved in [2]. The strategies that require human intervention in the monitoring area achieved the best results, as opposed to the last two approaches where the nodes appear disorganized.

6 Conclusions

In a WSN project, it is important from an early stage to define the deployment strategy to use. Decisions such as which architecture to use or what kind of nodes to deploy, have to be in consonance with the deployment strategy. As an example, in an environment where the human presence is not safe (e.g. biological contamination) it becomes impossible to achieve the results from the grid deployment strategy. Architectures that assume a rigid topology (e.g. one hop communication) become impossible to deploy.

In this paper we presented a new tool to generate realistic network topologies, GenSeN. It allows the user to create new WSN configurations, based on realistic knowledge achieved in previous work performed by the authors. All the results produced by this topology generator are based on real deployment experiences; each placement strategy reflects some of the possible solutions when preparing a WSN scenario.

Based in NS-2 configuration files, GenSeN outputs two *tcl* documents, which can directly be used as part of a network configuration script. GenSeN allows the specification of several parameters, such as different energy levels.

As future work, it would be important to extend the supported deployment strategies. Solutions such as water environment are crucial for certain sensor network applications. Another important extension would be the support of 3D environments. However such extension is more difficult to achieve since the NS-2 core also does not support such feature.

Acknowledgments. The work presented in this paper was partially financed by the IST FP6 CONTENT Network of Excellence (IST-FP6-0384239).

References

1. Estrin, D., et al.: Embedded, Everywhere: A research Agenda for Network Systems of Embedded Computers. National Research Council Report (2001)
2. Camilo, T., Rodrigues, A., Sa Silva, J., Boavida, F.: Lessons Learned from a Real Wireless Sensor Network Deployment. In: Proceedings of the Workshop on Performance Control in Wireless Sensor Networks, co-located with Networking 2006 - 5th International IFIP-TC6 Networking Conference, Coimbra, Portugal (2006)
3. Medina, A., Lakhina, A., Matta, I., Byers, J.: BRITE: Universal Topology Generation from a User's Perspective (User Manual) BU-CS-TR-2001-003 (April 2005)
4. Calvert, K., Doar, M., Zegura, E.: Modeling Internet Topology. EEE Transactions on Communications , 160–163 (1997)

5. Jin, C., Chen, Q., Jamin, S.: Inet: Internet Topology Generator. Technical Report Research Report CSE-TR-433-00, University of Michigan at Ann Arbor (2000)
6. Slijepcevic, S., Potkonjak, M.: Power efficient organization of wireless sensor networks. In: ICC, Helsinki, Finland (June 2001)
7. The USB/LBNL Network Simulator – ns2 (2006); http://www.isi.edu/nsnam/ns
8. Camilo, T., Rodrigues, A., Silva, S.J, Boavida, F.: Redes de Sensores Sem Fios, considerações sobre a sua instalação em ambiente real. In: Wireless Sensor Networks – some Considerations on Deployment in Real Environments), CSMU2006 - Conferência sobre Sistemas Móveis e Ubíquos, Guimarães, (Portugal) (June 2006) (in Portuguese)
9. Scatterweb; (2006), http://www.scatterweb.com/ESB/
10. CrossBow (2006), http://www.xbow.com
11. I-LENSE Topology Generator (topo_gen) http://www.isi.edu/ilense/software/topo_gen/topo_gen.html (2005)
12. Arroyo, D., Lee, B., Yu, C.: EMSim: An Extensible Simulation Environment for Studying High Performance Microarchitectures. In: SCI2002: International Conference Challenges Ecoinformatics (2002)
13. Ali, M., Saif, U., Dunkels, A., Voigt, T., Römer, K., Langendoen, K., Polastre, J., Uzmi, J.: Medium Access Control Issues in Sensor Networks. In: ACM SIGCOMM Computer Communication Review (April 2006)

Energy-Aware Routing for Wireless Sensor Networks by AHP

Xiaoling Wu, Jinsung Cho, Brian J. d'Auriol, and Sungyoung Lee*

Department of Computer Engineering, Kyung Hee University, Korea
{xiaoling,dauriol,sylee}@oslab.khu.ac.kr, chojs@khu.ac.kr

Abstract. Wireless sensor networks (WSNs) are comprised of energy constrained nodes. This limitation has led to the crucial need for energy-aware protocols to produce an efficient network. In this paper, we propose an energy
aware geographical multipath routing scheme for WSNs. The distance to the
destination location, remaining battery capacity, and queue size of candidate
sensor nodes in the local communication range are taken into consideration for
next hop relay node selection, and Analytical Hierarchy Process (AHP) is applied for decision making. Simulation results show that this scheme can extend
the network lifetime longer than the original geographical routing scheme
which only considers distance to the destination location. Moreover, the proposed scheme can reduce the packet loss rate and link failure rate since the
buffer capacity is considered.

Keywords: Sensor networks, AHP, routing, lifetime, energy.

1 Introduction

Wireless sensor networks (WSNs) are expected to be widely employed in various
applications such as medical care, military, environmental monitoring and industry
since they have high flexibility, low production costs, and scalability [1]. The sensor
nodes can sense the physical environment in various modalities, including acoustic,
temperature, seismic, and infrared, etc. In WSNs, there exist some challenges, for
example,

- The routing path (link) failure may happen during data transmission because of
  collision, node dying out (no battery), node busy, or other accidents. Some applications require real time information and data, which means retransmission
  is not possible. This motivates us to design a multipath routing scheme for
  wireless sensor networks.
- There exists energy constraint in WSNs because most sensors are battery operated. This motivates us to consider energy aware routing.

Many routing protocols have been developed for ad hoc networks, which can be
summarized into two categories: table-driven (e.g., destination sequenced distance

---

* Corresponding author.

R. Obermaisser et al. (Eds.): SEUS 2007, LNCS 4761, pp. 446–455, 2007.
© IFIP International Federation for Information Processing 2007

vector [2], cluster switch gateway routing [3]) and source-initiated on-demand (e.g., ad hoc on-demand distance vector routing [4], dynamic source routing (DSR) [5]). In [6], Lee and Gerla propose a Split Multipath Routing protocol that builds maximal disjoint paths, where data traffic is distributed in two roots per session to avoid congestion and to use network resources efficiently. A Multipath Source Routing (MSR) scheme is proposed in [7], which is an extension of DSR. Their work focuses on distributing load adaptively among several paths. Nasipuri and Das [8] present the On-Demand Multipath Routing scheme which is also an extension of DSR. In their scheme, alternative routes are maintained, which can be utilized when the primary one fails.

In sensor networks, location is often more important than a specific node ID. For example, in sensor networks for target tracking, the target location is much more important than the ID of reporting node. Therefore, some location-aware routing schemes have been proposed for WSNs. A greedy geographic forwarding with limited flooding to circumvent the voids inside the network is proposed in [9], and some properties of greedy geographic routing algorithms are studied in [10]. Jain et al [11] proposes a geographical routing using partial information for WSNs.

In this paper, we propose an Analytical Hierarchy Process (AHP) based Energy-aware Geographical Multipath Routing (AE-GMR) scheme for WSNs, and compare with Geographical Multipath Routing (GMR) scheme.

The rest of the paper is organized as follows. We define the basic assumptions and state the problems in section 2. The third section presents the proposed AHP based AE-GMR scheme. Section 4 evaluates and analyzes the performance of the proposed method. Finally, we draw the conclusion and discuss future work in section 5.

2 Problem Statements

In this paper, we also investigate the multipath routing problem and propose an AHP based Energy-aware Geographical Multipath Routing (AE-GMR) scheme. In the existing geographical routing approach (e.g., [11]), the path selection doesn't consider the remaining battery capacity of each node, which is a very important factor for energy efficiency and network lifetime. In our AE-GMR, we consider *distance to the destination*, *remaining battery capacity*, and *queue size* of each sensor node. Our scheme is a fully distributed approach where each sensor only needs the above three parameters, and we use AHP to handle these three parameters in the AE-GMR.

A. Energy Model

We adopt the same radio model as stated in [12] with $\varepsilon_{fs} = 10pJ/bit/m^2$ as amplifier constant, $E_{elec} = 50nJ/bit$ as the energy being dissipated to run the transmitter or receiver circuitry. It is assumed that the transmission between the nodes follows a second-order power loss model. The energy cost of transmission for common sensor nodes at distance d in transmitting an l-bit data is calculated as:

$$E_T(l,d) = lE_{elec} + l\varepsilon_{fs}d^2 \qquad (1)$$

and to receive the message, the radio expends:

$$E_R(l) = lE_{elec} \qquad (2)$$

and the energy for data aggregation is set as $E_{DA} = 5\ nJ/bit$.

B. Design Criteria

In our AE-GMR design, we set up three criteria for node selection, and they are:

1) Distance to Destination: Distance of a node to the destination. The geographical location of destination is known to the source node (as in [11]), and the physical location of each sensor node can be estimated easily if the locations of three sensor nodes (within a communication range) are known in wireless sensor network. The node with shorter distance to the destination is preferred to be selected.

2) Residual energy: Remaining battery of the sensor node. The initial energy is predefined. In addition, the energy consumption for transmission and reception can be calculated using Eq. (1) and Eq. (2).

3) Queue size: It indicates the buffer capacity at the node. This parameter helps avoid packet drops due to congestion at the receiver.

The optimized node selection in multipath routing is a multiple factors optimization problem and can be achieved using the AHP approach which is introduced in the next section.

3 Node Selection in Multipath Routing by AHP

In our AE-GMR for M-path routing, the source node select M nodes in its communication range for the first hop relay. Assume there are N $(N > M)$ nodes in its communication range, nodes that are farther to the destination node than the source node are not considered. Choosing M nodes from remaining eligible nodes is based on AHP (as will be described in detail). Starting the second hop, each node in the M-path selects its next hop node also using AHP.

The Analytical Hierarchy Process (AHP) [13] is a multiple criteria decision-making method which decomposes a complex problem into a hierarchy of simple sub problems (or factors), synthesizes their importance to the problem, and finds the best solution. In this paper, AHP is used to determine the nodes which are eligible to be selected as next hop relay. It is carried out in three steps:

Step 1: Collect information and formulate the next hop routing nodes selection problem as a decision hierarchy of independent factors.

Step 2: Calculate the relative local weights of decision factors or alternatives of each level.

Step 3: Synthesize the above results to achieve the overall weight of each alternative node and choose the nodes with largest weight as the eligible next hop relay nodes.

A. Structuring Hierarchy

The goal of the decision "Next hop relay node selection" is at the top level of the hierarchy as shown in Fig. 1. The next level consists of the decision factors which are called criteria for this goal. At the bottom level there exist the N alternative sensor nodes to be evaluated.

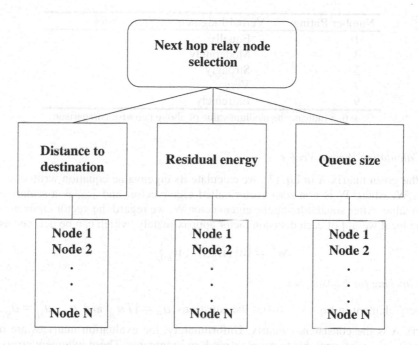

Fig. 1. AHP hierarchy for next hop relay nodes selection

B. Calculating Local Weights

Local weights consist of two parts: the weight of each decision factor to the goal and the weight of each nominee to each factor. Both of them are calculated with the same procedure. Taking the former as an example, we describe the procedure as the following three steps.

1) Making Pairwise Comparison

The evaluation matrices are built up through pairwise comparing each decision factor under the topmost goal. The comparison results are implemented by asking the questions: "Which is more important? How much?" and they may be presented in square matrix A as

$$A = \left(a_{ij}\right)_{n \times n} = \begin{pmatrix} a_{11} & a_{12} & \hbar & a_{1n} \\ a_{21} & a_{22} & \hbar & u_{2n} \\ \hbar & \hbar & \hbar & \hbar \\ a_{n1} & a_{n2} & \hbar & a_{nn} \end{pmatrix}, \tag{3}$$

where a_{ij} denotes the ratio of the ith factor weight to the jth factor weight, and n is the number of factors. The fundamental 1 to 9 scale can be used to rank the judgments as shown in Table 1.

Table 1. A fundamental scale of 1 to 9

Number Rating	Verbal Judgment of Preferences
1	Equally
3	Moderately
5	Strongly
7	Very
9	Extremely

2, 4, 6, 8 indicate the medium value of above pairwise comparison.

2) Calculating Weight Vector

For the given matrix A in Eq. (3), we calculate its eigenvalue equation written as AW = λ_{max}W, where W is non-zero vector called eigenvector, and λ_{max} is a scalar called eigenvalue. After standardizing the eigenvector W, we regard the vector element of W as the local weight of each decision factor approximately, which can be denoted as:

$$\mathbf{w}_j^T = \{w_1, w_2, \hbar\ , w_n\} \tag{4}$$

3) Checking for Consistency

If every element in Eq. (3) satisfies the equations $a_{ij} = 1/a_{ji}$ and $a_{ik} \cdot a_{kj} = a_{ij}$, the matrix A is the consistency matrix. Unfortunately, the evaluation matrices are often not perfectly consistent due to people's random judgments. These judgment errors can be detected by a consistency ratio (CR), which is defined as the ratio of consistency index (CI) to random index (RI). CI can be achieved by

$$CI = (\lambda_{max} - n)/(n-1), \tag{5}$$

where

$$\lambda_{max} = (1/n)\sum_{i=1}^{n}(AW)_i / W_i . \tag{6}$$

The *RI* is given in Table 2 [14]. When $CR \leq 0.1$, the judgment errors are tolerable and the weight coefficients of the global weight matrix W_j are the weights of decision factor under the topmost goal. Otherwise, the pairwise comparisons should be adjusted until matrix A satisfies the consistency check.

Table 2. Random index

n	1	2	3	4	5	6	7	8	9	10	11
RI	0	0	0.58	0.90	1.12	1.24	1.32	1.41	1.45	1.49	1.51

C. Calculating Global Weights

From above steps, we can obtain not merely the weights of decision factors towards the topmost goal from W_j but also the weights of alternative nodes towards each factor. If there are four candidate nodes in the communication range, all the four weight matrixes of alternatives under three factors construct a 4×3 matrix, denoted as $W_{n_i/j}$, $i=1, 2, ..., 4, j=1, 2, 3$.

The global weight of each senor node can be achieved through multiplying the local weight by its corresponding parent. So the final weight matrix in the symbol of W_{n_i} is calculated as

$$W_{n_i} = W_{n_i/j} \cdot W_j, \tag{7}$$

where the final weight of each alternative is calculated as

$$W_{n_i} = \sum_{j=1}^{3} W_{n_i/j} \cdot W_j. \tag{8}$$

The larger the final weight of node, the higher the probability of node which is eligible to be selected. Thus, the M nodes with the largest weight are selected as the next hop relay nodes in multipath routing.

In this paper, we assume that each sensor node keeps a table which has some information about its neighbor nodes: locations, battery level, and queue size. The table is updated periodically by the locally-broadcasted information (beacon) from each neighbor node. We define a time interval T, during which the three parameters (locations, battery level, and queue size) do not change very much. This time interval T is the shortest time duration that a sensor node will send another beacon. Each sensor examines itself the status of the three parameters in every period T, and if a certain parameter has changed above a threshold, it will locally broadcast a beacon.

D. Path Set Up

In the route discovery phase, the source node uses AHP model to evaluate all eligible nodes (closer to the destination location) in its communication range based on the parameters of each node: distance to the destination, remaining battery capacity, and queue size. The source node chooses the top M nodes based on the local weight that this node will be selected. The source node sends a Route Acknowledgement (RA) packet to each desired node, and each desired node will reply using a REPLY packet if it is available. The structure of RA and REPLY is summarized in Table 3. If after a certain period of time, the source node did not receive REPLY from some desired node, it will pick the node with highest weight among the remaining $N-M$ ndoes. In the second hop, the selected node in each path will choose its next hop node using the same process. As illustrated in Fig. 2, node B needs to choose one node from four eligible nodes C, D, E, and F based on their three parameters, and sends RA packet to the selected node and waits for REPLY. If the top one node is unavailable (for exmaple, selected by another path), then the top second node will be selected. Consequently, M paths can be set up.

Table 3. RA and REPLY message structure

Type	Desired Node ID	Self Node ID	Dest_X	Dest_Y	Src_ID

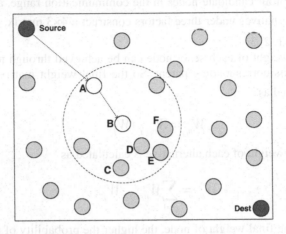

Fig. 2. Illustration of next hop node selection

4 Performance Evaluations

4.1 Simulation Environment

In order to evaluate the nodes selection in multipath routing by AHP, we have used J-Sim [15] as the simulation environment. 60 sensors are randomly deployed in an area of 100m x 100m. The source and destination sensors are set as 2J initially, and 5 couples of source and destination nodes are communicating at the same time in this network. All the other sensors have initial energy of 0-2J. The buffer capacity of each sensor node has been taken as 5 packets with packet length 512 bit and bit rate 9.6kb/sec. The time interval T is set as 10s in our simulation. The source node select $M=3$ nodes in its communication range for the first hop relay. From the second hop, each node along the 3 paths selects only one node toward its next hop.

In AHP modeling, the matrix A is determined as follows according to Section 3:

$$
A = \begin{matrix} \alpha \\ \beta \\ \gamma \end{matrix} \begin{array}{ccc} \text{Distance} & \text{Residual} & \text{Queue} \\ \text{to Dest} & \text{energy} & \text{size} \\ (\alpha) & (\beta) & (\gamma) \end{array} \begin{bmatrix} 1 & 2/1 & 3/1 \\ 1/2 & 1 & 2/1 \\ 1/3 & 1/2 & 1 \end{bmatrix}
$$

where the three criteria are denoted by α, β and γ respectively.

The computed eigenvector W = [0.5396 0.2970 0.1634]. It indicates the local weight of the distance to destination, remaining battery capacity, and queue size, respectively, so that we can see clearly that the distance to destination is the most important criterion, and queue size is the least. According to Eq. (6), we can get the eigenvalue λ_{max} = 3.0093. Consequently, consistency ratio can be calculated as CR= 0.0047 < 0. 1, thus matrix A satisfies the consistency check.

Each sensor node determines the weight matrixes of alternatives under three factors and then gets global weight based on its specific situation. Its eligibility as next hop relay node can be finally decided by the AHP hierarchy model.

4.2 Simulation Results

We compare our AE-GMR against the geographical multipath routing (GMR) [11] scheme where only distance to the destination is considered. In Fig. 3, we plot the simulation time versus the number of nodes dead. It shows that when 50% nodes (30 nodes) die out, the network lifetime for AE-GMR has been extended about 40%. In

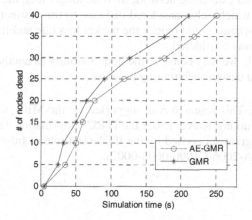

Fig. 3. Lifetime comparison

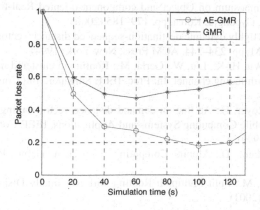

Fig. 4. Simulation time vs. packet loss rate

Fig. 4, we compare the packet loss rate of these two schemes. Packets are dropped either due to insufficient buffer capacity at the receiver or because of the lack of energy needed to transmit the packet. Observe that our AE-GMR outperforms the GMR with about 20% less packet loss resulting in greater reliability. The average latency during transmission (end-to-end) is 422.16ms for our AE-GMR and 407.5ms for GMR, and link failure rate for AE-GMR is 6.24%, but for GMR is 10.42%.

5 Conclusion and Future Work

In this paper, we proposed an energy aware geographical multipath routing scheme for WSNs. Three factors contributing to the next hop relay node selection are considered and they are the distance to the destination location, remaining battery capacity, and queue size of candidate sensors in the local communication range, respectively. Analytical Hierarchy Process (AHP) was applied for optimal decision making. We evaluated the efficiency of our proposed scheme and the simulation results showed that this scheme could extend the network lifetime longer than the original geographical routing scheme which only considered distance to the destination location. Moreover, the proposed scheme could reduce the packet loss rate and link failure rate since the buffer capacity was considered.

In the future work, we may consider the node mobility as another factor for routing decision making and design such routing protocol.

Acknowledgments. This research was supported by the MIC (Ministry of Information and Communication), Korea, under the ITRC (Information Technology Research Center) support program supervised by the IITA (Institute of Information Technology Advancement) (IITA-2006-C1090-0602-0002).

References

1. Wu, X., Heo, H., Shaikh, R.A., Cho, J., Chae, O., Lee, S.: Individual Contour Extraction for Robust Wide Area Target Tracking in Visual Sensor Networks. In: Proc. of 9th IEEE International Symposium on Object and component-oriented Real-time distributed Computing (ISORC), Gyeongju, Korea, pp. 179–185 (2006)
2. Bhagwat, C.P.: Highly dynamic destination-sequenced distance vector routing. In: Proc. of ACM SIGCOMM, pp. 234–244. ACM Press, New York (1994)
3. Chiang, C.-C., Wu, H.-K., Liu, W., Gerla, M.: Routing in clustered multihop mobile wireless networks with fading channel. In: Proc. IEEE Singapore Intl Conference on Networks (1997)
4. Perkins, C.E., Royer, E.: Ad hoc on demand distance vector routing. In: Proc. 2nd IEEE Workshop o Mobile Computing Systems and Applications, IEEE Computer Society Press, Los Alamitos (1999)
5. Johnson, D., Maltz, D.: Mobile Computing. Kluwer Academic Publishers, Dordrecht (1996)
6. Lee, S.J., Gerla, M.: Split Multipath Routing with Maximally Disjoint Paths in Ad Hoc Networks. ICC (2001)

7. Wang, L., Shu, Y.T., Dong, M., Zhang, L.F., Yang, W.W.: Multipath Source Routing in wireless Ad Hoc Networks. In: Canadian Conference on Electrical and Computer Engineering, vol.1, pp. 479–483 (2000)
8. Nasipuri, A., Das, S.R.: On-Demand Multipath Routing for Mobile Ad Hoc Networks. In: IEEE ICCCN, pp. 64–70. IEEE Computer Society Press, Los Alamitos (1999)
9. Finn, G.G.: Routing and addressing problems in large metropolitanscale internetworks. USC ISI Report ISI/RR-87-180 (1987)
10. Xing, G., Lu, C., Pless, R., Huang, Q.: On Greedy Geographic Routing Algorithms in Sensing-Covered Networks. In: Xing, G., Lu, C., Pless, R., Huang, Q. (eds.) ACM International Symposium on Mobile Ad Hoc Networking and Computing (MobiHoc), Japan (2004)
11. Jain, R., Puri, A., Sengupta, R.: Geographical routing using partial information for wireless sensor networks. In: IEEE Personal Communications, pp. 48–57 (2001)
12. Heinzelman, W.B., Chandrakasan, A.P., Balakrishnan, H.: An Application-Specific Protocol Architecture for Wireless Microsensor Networks. IEEE Transactions on Wireless Communications 1(4), 660–670 (2002)
13. Saaty, T.L.: The Analytic Hierarchy Process. NY, McGraw Hill (1980)
14. Song, Q.Y., Jamalipour, A.: A network selection mechanism for next generation networks. In: IEEE Int. Conf. Communication (ICC), vol.2, pp. 1418–1422 (2005)
15. J-Sim, http://www.j-sim.org/

A Wireless System for Real-Time Environmental and Structural Monitoring*

Valerio Plessi[1], Filippo Bastianini[2], and Sahra Sedigh[1]

[1] Department of Electrical and Computer Engineering
[2] Center for Infrastructure Engineering Studies
University of Missouri-Rolla
Rolla, MO 65409-0040
{vp427,fbroptic,sedighs}@umr.edu

Abstract. Accurate real-time monitoring of structural health can result in significant safety improvements, while providing data that can be used to improve design and construction practices. For bridges, monitoring of water level, tilt, displacement, strain, and vibration can provide snapshots of the state of the structure. Real-time measurement and communication of this information can be invaluable in guiding decisions regarding the safety and remaining fatigue life of a bridge.

This paper describes the real-time data acquisition, communication, and alerting capabilities of the Flood Frog, an autonomous wireless system for remote monitoring. Battery power and utilization of the GSM cellular network result in a completely wireless system. Coupled with the low cost of the device, the elimination of cables allows deployment in locations where autonomous monitoring is hindered by cost or infeasibility of installation. The first prototype of the system was deployed in Osage Beach, MO in November 2006.

1 Introduction

Early warning and advanced preparation for emergency are two of the most effective lines of defense against natural disasters such as floods, earthquakes, and hurricanes. The impact of catastrophic events, including the recent hurricanes Katrina and Rita, underscores the limits of established early warning systems, especially with regard to rapidly evolving situations. Environmental monitoring, which refers to measuring and recording parameters such as temperature, humidity, salinity, water level, acoustic emission and pollution for a selected site, enables early detection of potentially disastrous events. Timely provision of information facilitates recovery efforts and aids in the containment of aftereffects.

Structural monitoring is another important issue, as periodic collection of information about the health of a structure, such as a bridge or a building, can prevent sudden breakdown, save money, and most importantly, protect human lives. In this context, changes in tilt, displacement, strain and vibration can serve as warnings for impending structural damage or even collapse. Regardless of the phenomenon being monitored, the information should be collected and communicated with resolution and frequency sufficient to enable accurate and timely knowledge of the situation.

* This research was supported in part by the United States Department of Transportation.

In monitoring applications, one major challenge is the infeasibility of installing the necessary devices in remote areas or hostile environments. As an example, low water bridges, which are prone to flooding, are typically located in rural areas that lack accessible power and communication lines. The problem is further exacerbated by the costs associated with digging trenches and drawing the wires needed for a wired system. Physical installation challenges have been addressed in our previous work [1].

The aforementioned challenges underscore the necessity of a novel monitoring system that is less costly, more dependable, and more flexible in terms of locations where it can be installed. Furthermore, for a broad range of environmental and structural phenomena, there is a critical need for autonomous real-time acquisition and communication of data.

The solution proposed in this paper is a wireless embedded system, termed the *Flood Frog*. The ultra-low power design of the system enables several years of operation with a standard battery pack. The data is acquired using embedded sensors, then aggregated, processed, and reported by the device. In batch production, the device can be manufactured for less than $300 per unit, which is orders of magnitude less than existing solutions, the majority of which have to be embedded in a structure at the time of construction. The wireless nature of the system makes it more robust, and eliminates the considerable cost of drawing cables to the site. The savings achieved in installation and maintenance costs facilitate large scale deployment of the system.

The design of the Flood Frog is general, and includes an onboard digital signal processing unit with an embedded A/D converter (ADC), which allows the use of digital or analog sensors. Communication is completely wireless and uses the existing GSM cellular infrastructure. Despite being battery-powered, the device acquires and communicates data in real time. The first prototype of the system was deployed in Osage Beach, MO in November 2006, and has been communicating accurately since, as validated by data provided by the United States Geological Service (USGS).

Recent years have witnessed the development of a number of platforms for wireless sensor networks (WSNs), including motes manufactured by Intel and Crossbow. Our device is not intended to serve as a mote. It is an autonomous embedded system with an onboard power source, long-range communication capability, considerable computing power, data storage, embedded sensors, and an embedded signal conditioner that can support a wide range of additional sensors, such as load cells, or strain and displacement gauges. Furthermore, our system supplies multi-purpose software that enables the plug-and-play addition of other sensors. The simplicity of this software leads to more dependable operation than that of motes with complex operating systems. Encapsulation of the system in a rugged waterproof and dustproof case further increases the dependability. Utilization of a general-purpose mote for structural monitoring would require considerable effort in software and hardware development, with the end result being a more expensive system that is inferior in terms of unattended field life, long-range communication, computing power, and sensor support.

The remainder of this paper is organized as follows. Section 2 presents relevant research in real-time monitoring systems. Sections 3 and 4 describe the hardware and software of the system, respectively. The prototype and field test are discussed in Section 5. Section 6 concludes the paper.

2 Related Work

Accurate monitoring of structures and their surrounding environment is an area of critical need, and the development of embedded systems for this purpose has been of interest to the research community. This section presents several relevant studies.

In FloodNet [2], wireless sensor nodes deployed in a river bed are used to collect data that is later used for flood prediction. The system does not operate in real time, as the main purpose is collection of data to be fed to a simulator. A related system, described in [3], also uses a WSN to collect data for flood prediction, but carries out the computation locally, using a grid-based approach.

A study performed by the Meteorological Development Laboratory of the US National Weather Service is described in [4]. The approach taken involves the processing of current radar information and monitoring of precipitation to predict flood. Other studies, presented in [5] and [6], use satellite and microwave images to monitor floods. The main disadvantage of such approaches is the prohibitively high cost of acquiring radar and satellite data. Moreover, the predictions are not made in real time, and are subject to human error.

Another flood monitoring device is described in [7], which describes a flash flood alerting system that uses a WSN to track a flood as it evolves. This system is still in the conceptual design phase, and as of the date of this publication, a prototype does not appear to be under development. Two predictive flood monitoring systems are presented in [8] and [9]. In both studies, measurement of the extent and distribution of flooding during severe weather conditions is utilized to generate maps for future analysis and prediction. IN4MA [10] manufactures commercial systems for monitoring rainfall and river levels in order to minimize the damage caused by flooding. The data collected is communicated over the GSM network. In contrast to the Flood Frog, which has been designed to be easily expanded by wireless nodes to create a local WSN, the IN4MA device can only operate as a standalone unit. Campbell Scientific [11] is another company that develops monitoring systems for flood and other environmental phenomena. They offer precipitation, wind speed, soil moisture and water quality measurement through a set of modular devices. The cost of a complete system is orders of magnitude higher than that of our proposed system.

A wireless environmental monitoring system is presented in [12]. It describes the design and implementation of a reactive and event-driven network for monitoring soil moisture. The study presents data about the field life of the device; the maximum duration is approximately one month, whereas the Flood Frog can operate for several years on a standard battery pack. A similar system is presented in [13]. This study introduces the "Sensor Web," which is a platform that combines in situ and remote sensing to collect information about the environment. One significant difference between this project and our work is their use of satellites as a means of long-range communication, which is very costly and incapable of frequent updates. Low power consumption has not been addressed for the system, which again constrains unattended operation.

The study in [14] presents a wireless strain sensing system for structural health monitoring. This system shares a number of features with the Flood Frog, but is limited to strain sensing and does not allow for the addition of other sensors. Another structural monitoring system is presented in [15], where a wireless base station and several sensor nodes are deployed in a building. The system is not capable of long-range communication and requires periodic inspections for data collection. An improvement to this system is presented in [16]. The communication range of this system is still limited, as it cannot utilize the cellular phone system, and the field life of less than one year is considerably shorter than that of our system.

An important difference between the work proposed in this paper and other existing systems is that the Flood Frog has been designed as a general-purpose monitoring system that can be customized for various applications. Data acquisition, communication and alarm generation occur in real time for all monitored phenomena. Considering the high power consumption typically associated with real-time operation, the ultra-low power consumption of the system is a significant achievement.

The studies mentioned above demonstrate the wide range of applications that can benefit from a device such as the Flood Frog. Each application presents different requirements, from site monitoring to collection of data for forecasting.

3   Hardware Implementation and Features

In the context of this paper, *monitoring* refers to continuous evaluation of the quantities under consideration. If the data is acquired, and any necessary alarms are generated within acceptable time limits, *real-time monitoring* has been accomplished. The specific time limits imposed depend on the monitored phenomena, and can range from seconds to hours, based on the urgency of subsequent countermeasures. For example, closing a bridge in case of flooding should happen within an hour, while the inspection needed to investigate excessive strain on the bridge can occur within several days without compromising the safety of the structure.

The structural and environmental phenomena monitored by the Flood Frog generally evolve slowly. Quantities such as temperature, humidity, water level, tilt, displacement, and strain vary slowly; therefore, a sampling period on the order of seconds or minutes will suffice.

Flash flooding is an example of a critical situation well-suited to the monitoring and alerting capabilities of the Flood Frog. According to the National Oceanic and Atmospheric Administration [17], flash floods can occur within a few minutes of excessive rainfall, dam or levee failure, or sudden release of water held by an ice jam. For such phenomena, a sensor sampling period of minutes can easily provide for real-time monitoring, with prompt alarm generation whenever a threshold is exceeded.

In contrast, the monitoring of vibration makes real-time operation more challenging, as it is a rapidly-evolving event. The Flood Frog incorporates additional hardware to enable timely acquisition of such data. Signal conditioning is carried out to reduce the amount of data communicated over the GSM network, resulting in a significant decrease in power consumption.

The device has been designed to overcome the limitations of current monitoring systems, including high cost, high power consumption, extensive use of cabling and lack of real-time data acquisition and communication capabilities. The low cost of the Flood Frog facilitates installation in areas where monitoring has been rendered infeasible due to the associated cost. Ultra-low power consumption enables the use of batteries instead of traditional power lines, while reducing the cost of installation and allowing deployment in locations that are off the power grid. Wireless communication through an existing infrastructure such as the GSM cellular network greatly increases flexibility and ease of installation.

To avoid frequent battery replacements and allow several years of unattended field life, the Flood Frog utilizes hardware and software mechanisms for reducing power consumption. These techniques include event-driven execution, code optimization, switching off hardware peripherals when not in use, and varying the clock frequency used based on the circumstances.

The device includes onboard sensors for water level, temperature, acceleration, tilt, and vibration. Flood detection is carried out by a magnetic switch used to sense the position of a magnetic floater in the water. The actual level of the water is measured by a capacitive sensor. Acceleration and tilt are sensed with a MEMS three-axis accelerometer that supplies three analog signals, one for each direction. Lastly, vibrations are captured by a piezoelectric sensor. Excluding the magnetic sensor, which is a simple on/off switch, all other sensors are analog, and therefore their output needs to be digitized. This is accomplished by the internal ADC of the onboard microcontroller unit (MCU). Several additional analog channels have been included to allow the addition of sensors such as load cells, strain gauges and motion potentiometers.

4 Software Implementation and Features

The Flood Frog is an embedded device built from the ground up, and its unique requirements necessitated the development of a custom real-time operating system (RTOS). We chose not to use an off-the-shelf RTOS to keep the software as simple as possible, implementing only necessary features. The main requirements for the software are real-time functionality, compact code, reliability, efficiency, and power-awareness. In developing the software, the main objective was to create the smallest and least complex OS capable of carrying out all required operations within specified time constraints.

The software design takes into account the limited energy available to the device by reducing computation and keeping the device in sleep mode for as long as possible. This can be achieved by writing efficient code and by manipulating the hardware capabilities, e.g., placing the peripherals in "off" state when they are not in use. Disabling the peripherals poses a significant challenge in view of the real-time capabilities of the Flood Frog, as the device may not be able to access available resources immediately. The challenge is to find the best tradeoff between power consumption and the monitoring duty cycle, while meeting timing constraints.

The powerful onboard computational unit eliminates the need for multitasking. The MCU has a 16-bit 30-MIPS processor, which is more powerful than an Intel 80486 (20-MIPS) chip. Sequential operation results in greater dependability, due to the relative ease of troubleshooting a single flow of execution. The only task that may require a fast real-time reaction is the vibration alarm; in that case, the device is switched on as quickly as possible in order to avoid loss of information.

The Flood Frog can be used in either time-driven or event-driven fashion. As a time-driven device, the data collected by the sensors is recorded periodically, and the device remains in sleep mode unless it is recording data or an exception occurs. The recorded data is compared with preset thresholds, and alarms are triggered as necessary. In event-driven mode, the device wakes up in response to specified events, the occurrence of which is detected by the sensors. An interrupt is configured for each event, and causes a wake up of the device and the activation of its interrupt service routine (ISR). The current prototype of the system provides ISRs for timer, flood, and vibration interrupts.

Vibrations occur suddenly, and can happen during the long sleep periods when data cannot be recorded. To overcome this problem, once vibration is detected, the analog signal is immediately sent into an analog delay line that provides enough lag to allow the sampling circuit to be switched on. Meanwhile, the MCU senses the vibration interrupt and invokes the appropriate ISR, which immediately wakes up the Flood Frog. In case the oscillation exceeds the specified threshold (e.g., during an earthquake), an alarm is triggered. This technique allows real-time monitoring of sudden phenomena such as vibration with limited battery power.

To maintain autonomy, the device must retain minimal functionality even when in sleep mode. As a result, the software must run continuously, but the system should be kept in low-power mode whenever possible. In the event of an exception (e.g., math, stack, or oscillator errors) or other failure, a complete hardware and software reset (i.e., reboot) of the device may be necessary for returning it to a safe and predictable state.

Figure 1 depicts the software state diagram of the device. The software execution flow has a single entry point, where the software begins initial operation and to which the software returns in the event of system reset. The source of each system reset is determined immediately and flagged in an internal register.

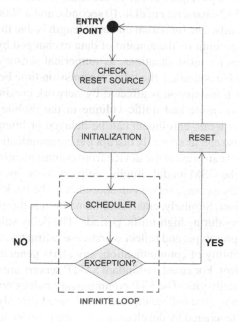

Fig. 1. Software state diagram

At the entry point to the software, after the reset source is determined, an initialization routine is performed to prepare the various hardware components for operation. A complete execution cycle of the infinite loop is comprised of two phases: the sleep period and the scheduler check.

The first task of the infinite loop is to place the device in sleep mode. When its sleep timer expires (i.e., every 1 second) the device wakes up and updates the internal clock and counters. Other interrupts (e.g., flood, vibration) may also wake up the system and demand immediate service.

The task queue is implemented as an array where ready processes are placed, ordered by priority, with the highest priority being assigned to vibration, as it requires a rapid response. If the scheduler stack is not empty, the first task is popped and executed; when it is completed, the next task, if any, is popped. If the queue is empty, the device is returned to sleep mode. This design results in a very simple and computationally efficient execution flow.

In real-time monitoring, it is important to communicate the data in a timely manner. As explained in Section 1, we utilize the existing GSM network infrastructure to increase flexibility and ease of installation, while meeting delay constraints. The Flood Frog is equipped with a worldwide-compatible quad-band GSM module, which allows GPRS data transfer of 8-24 kbps upstream and 24-48 kbps downstream, and provides SMTP and FTP capabilities, in addition to email. The GSM module is the main source of power consumption in the Flood Frog, therefore it is normally kept off. The communication time is dictated by the GSM network.

In order to communicate, the GSM module needs to be switched on and enrolled in the network. These two steps require about 15 seconds. After enrollment, an SMS can be sent in 5 seconds, a 512-character email in 10 seconds, and a 5000-character text file, through FTP, in 20 seconds. The limitation on email length is due to the particular GSM module used. There is no limit on the amount of data exchanged by FTP. A text file of 5000 characters suffices for most situations, as numerical sensor data is compact. In case a 10000-character file is needed, the total transmission time becomes 27 seconds.

Timing of the GSM transmission is affected by network conditions such as signal strength, electromagnetic noise and traffic volume in the mobile cell and the entire network. If the signal is weak, enrollment can be delayed or interrupted, while external electromagnetic noise can temporarily disrupt the communication. Traffic is also an issue, as a congested cell can prevent the device from communicating. Successful transmission of an SMS by the GSM module implies delivery to the message server, and not to the final recipient; this message server can sporadically be backlogged, delaying delivery to the final recipient. Similarly, email communication is through an SMTP server, which can delay delivery during high-traffic periods. The delay values discussed above were measured on the prototype, and reflect worst-case estimates.

To increase the reliability of communication, any alerts generated are sent by SMS to more than one recipient. For email, redundant SMTP servers are used to diminish the probability of delayed deliveries. The FTP communication does not have this problem, as once the connection is established, the file is delivered directly to the final server. This advantage can be leveraged by developing a PC application that constantly checks for the presence of new files.

Assuming no unusual delays in communication, delivery of an alarm composed of SMS, email and FTP, takes a total time of 50 seconds from when the device exits sleep mode. This is a very good result, mainly because the first alarm, sent by SMS, is most likely received after 20 seconds, and the second alarm, which is sent by email, after 30 seconds. Considering that even for severe flash floods the water takes several minutes to reach a dangerous level [17], our device is satisfying real-time constraints.

A large amount of data can be sent by FTP in a relatively short period of time. Once an alarm is received by SMS and/or email, the data uploaded to the FTP server can provide a complete picture of parameter trends in the period before the alarm, allowing analysis of the situation. Implementing the aforementioned PC application would provide an additional means of triggering alarms in real time.

5   Prototype and Field Test

In its first field study, the Flood Frog was installed on Bridge A6531 in Osage Beach, MO in November 2006. The objective was to detect flooding and measure water level, temperature, battery level, and tilt of the structure along three axes. The case chosen for the prototype is 7.5x5x4 inches and completely sealed, with the exception of a small perforation for the water level probe. The entire system is enclosed in the case and operates wirelessly. The flood sensor is implemented as a floater inside a hollow vertical pipe affixed to the pier; the position of the floater indicates the water level. In order to communicate this information to the device, a magnet is embedded inside the floater and magnetic switches are installed inside the case.

The case design is depicted in Fig. 2. Figure 3 shows the device, circled in red, affixed to the pier. The yellow cable is the probe used to measure the water level. Since being installed, the Flood Frog has delivered a daily heartbeat message through SMS and email and has uploaded the acquired data to the FTP server. The water level data has been validated with values published by the USGS, and is accurate within 10%, which is an acceptable result given the margin of error of the USGS values.

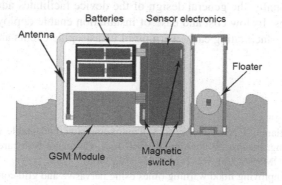

Fig. 2. Block diagram of the Flood Frog

Fig. 3. Installation on Bridge A6531 in Osage Beach, MO

6   Conclusions

This paper describes an autonomous real-time device for environmental and structural monitoring. The device incorporates embedded sensors, is battery-powered and communicates using the GSM/GPRS cellular phone network, eliminating the need for cables of any type. The data collected, any alarms triggered, and software anomalies are automatically reported to designated recipients through SMS messages, email, and FTP file upload. The specific application discussed is flood monitoring, for which the device meets real-time constraints on data acquisition and communication.

   The cost reduction achieved by the Flood Frog has the potential to expand the practice of structural health monitoring to a significantly higher number of existing and new structures. This improvement will increase safety and reduce the cost of operations by facilitating real-time monitoring, which in turn yields a more efficient maintenance schedule. Additionally, the general design of the device facilitates adaptation to alternative applications. Its low cost and ease of installation enable deployment in a broad range of locations, facilitating early warning of catastrophic events and potentially reducing casualties.

References

1. Plessi, V., Bastianini, F., Sedigh-Ali, S.: An autonomous and adaptable wireless device for flood monitoring. In: Proc. 30th Annual IEEE Int'l. Computer Software and Applications Conference (COMPSAC06), vol. 2, pp. 378–379 (2006)
2. Roure, D.D.: Improving flood warning times using pervasive and grid computing, http://envisense.org/floodnet/ingenia/ingenia.htm
3. Hughes, D., et al.: GridStix: Supporting flood prediction using embedded hardware and next generation grid middleware. In: Proc. IEEE Int'l Symp. World of Wireless, Mobile and Multimedia Networks (WoWMoM) (2006)

4. NOAA - National Weather Service: Flash flood monitoring and prediction (FFMP) (March 2006) http://www.nws.noaa.gov/mdl/ffmp/index.htm
5. Galantowicz, J.F.: High-resolution flood mapping from low-resolution passive microwave data. In: Proc. IEEE Int'l. Geoscience and Remote Sensing Symposium (IGARSS '02), vol. 3, pp. 1499–1502 (2002)
6. Temimi, M., et al.: Near real time flood monitoring over the Mackenzie River basin using passive microwave data. In: Proc. IEEE Int'l. Geoscience and Remote Sensing Symposium (IGARSS 04), vol. 3, pp. 1862–1865 (2004)
7. Castillo-Effen, M.: Wireless sensor networks for flash-flood alerting. In: Proc. 5th IEEE Int'l. Caracas Conference on Devices, Circuits and Systems, Dominican Republic, pp. 142–146 (2004)
8. Dellepiane, S., et al.: SAR images and interferometric coherence for flood monitoring. In: Proc. IEEE Int'l. Geoscience and Remote Sensing Symposium (IGARSS '00), pp. 2608–2610 (July 2000)
9. Shao, Y., et al.: Chinese SAR for Yangtze River flood monitoring in 1998. In: Proc. IEEE Int'l. Geoscience and Remote Sensing Symposium (IGARSS 00), pp. 2495–2497 (2000)
10. IN4MA Remote Monitoring Solutions: Wireless outstations for flood warnings, http://www.in4ma.co.uk
11. Campbell Scientific, Inc.: ALERT flood warning (2001), http://www.campbellsci.com/flood-warning
12. Cardell-Oliver, R., et al.: A reactive soil moisture sensor network: design and field evaluation. In: Int'l J. Distributed Sensor Networks, pp. 149–162 (2005)
13. Delin, K.A., et al.: Sensor Web for spatio-temporal monitoring of a hydrological environment. In: Proc. 35th Lunar and Planetary Science Conf. (2004)
14. Arms, S.W., Townsend, C.P.: Wireless strain measurement systems - applications and solutions (2003)
15 Lynch, J.P., et al.: Advanced wireless structural monitoring: Past, present and future. The John A. Blume Earthquake Engineering Center (28) (2001)
16. Wang, Y., Lynch, J.P., Law, K.H.: A wireless structural health monitoring system with multithreaded sensing devices: Design and validation. Structure and Infrastructure Engineering - Maintenance, Management and Life-Cycle Design & Performance 3(2), 103–120 (2007)
17. National Oceanic and Atmospheric Administration (NOAA) and National Weather Service (NWS): Flash floods: a preparedness guide (1992), http://www.nws.noaa.gov/om/brochures/ffbro.htm

Integrated Notification Architecture Based on Overlay Against DDoS Attacks on Convergence Network*

Mihui Kim, Jaewon Seo, and Kijoon Chae

Dept. of Computer Science and Engineering, Ewha Womans University, Korea
{mihui,seojw}@ewhain.net, kjchae@ewha.ac.kr

Abstract. The distributed denial of service (DDoS) attack that is one of the most threatening attacks in the wired network has been already extended in the wireless mobile network, owing to the appearance of DDoS attack tool against mobile phone. In the future, the latent threats for the converged form of DDoS attack should be resolved for the induction of successful convergence network. However, because of the current problems in defending against converged DDoS attacks on convergence network, such as the absence of a converged defense, research on cooperation architecture between defense processes is critical. In this paper, we analyze possible converged attacks, thus we propose a scalable and dynamic notification architecture based on overlay routing against DDoS attacks in consideration of the capacity of each node. A main feature of this architecture is the speedy notification of attack detection to each highest defense system in the network of the attack agents as well as in the victims. Thus it makes it possible not only to fast defense at the network of victims but also to identify attack agents. We analyzed the overhead for constructing our hierarchical overlay, simulated the transmission rate and speed of detection notification, and found a marked improvement using our defense compared to general routes.

1 Introduction

Recently, the International Telecommunication Union-Telecommunication (ITU-T) standardization sector recognized "next generation network" (NGN) factors in the telecommunication industry, including the need to converge and optimize the operating networks and the extraordinary expansion of digital traffic. Among other research topics such as quality of service (QoS), interoperability, generalized mobility, and service capabilities and architecture, security issues are as crucial to the NGN as they are to today's network environment. In Korea, a broadband convergence network (BcN) is being created to provide seamless and

* "This research was supported by the MIC(Ministry of Information and Communication), Korea, under the ITRC(Information Technology Research Center) support program supervised by the IITA(Institute of Information Technology Advancement)" (IITA-2006-C1090-0603-0028).

R. Obermaisser et al. (Eds.): SEUS 2007, LNCS 4761, pp. 466–476, 2007.

secure, quality-guaranteed broadband multimedia service, which includes converged communication, broadcasting, and Internet access. Because of security threats and defense problems in this converged environment, security is thus a main area of research.

A converged network is characterized by factors such as host heterogeneity, dynamic topology, and scalability, and services that are provided should consider these characteristics. Although each network has existing security systems, they are insufficient to defend against converged attacks on the nodes of other networks, such as a short message service (SMS) Flooder attack. This was the first DDoS attack tool on computers in a wired network directed at mobile phones. The attack commanded all infected Microsoft Outlook software to send SMS messages to a certain victim's mobile phone, to inundate it. In a converged attack, the victims and the attack agents are located in different types of networks. Because of the power of the converged attack and the damage it could cause, the converged DDoS attack may be the most threatening of the various attacks in a converged network, that is in a ubiquitous environment. In addition, because of the open network structure of ubiquitous environments, it is easy to access the communication network, raising the imminent possibility of hacking and the dissemination of the virus. In the case of a converged attack, the defense systems on each network should collaborate to provide a fast defense. Therefore, a systematic integrated defense system is needed, but until now has been lacking because of the difficulty in gathering information and distributing it in a heterogeneous environment [1].

In this paper, we design an overlay structure for notification of converged DDoS attacks on converged networks. Most defenses against DDoS attack consists of detection, identification of attack agents, and filtering of attack traffic. However, our overlay structure is mainly used for notification of the detection of an attack. Both defense systems in the networks of victims and attack agents are notified, making possible not only fast defense in the network of victims but also the identification of attack agents. This overlay has hierarchical structure like the hierarchy of the most networks, such as wired network, NEMO (NEtwork MObility) network, and hierarchical sensor networks. The each overlay of networks is connected through the overlay nodes with multiple interfaces, for example, Ethernet and wireless LAN interfaces. Also, each overlay is composed in consideration of the capacity of the each node. This structure pursues the following design goals and we will confirm the performance by simulation and analytical results.

- **Speedy notification of attack detection** to each highest defense system in the network of attack agents, as well as victims.
- **Scalable and dynamic defense structure** of overlay in consideration of the capacity of each node

This paper is divided into five sections. In Section 2, we explain the threats of DDoS attacks on converged networks. We introduce in Section 3 our integrated notification architecture. And next, we evaluate our mechanism in various views, and explain the analysis of simulation results. Finally, a brief conclusion is presented.

2 Threats of DDoS Attacks on Converged Networks

Convergence could be considered from three viewpoints: user services convergence, device convergence and network convergence. Among them, network convergence implies consolidation of the network to provide different user services, with telecom-grade quality of service, to several access types with an emphasis on operator cost efficiency. In this paper, we mainly consider the network convergence. The characteristics of converged network are as follows, and the converged network services should consider these characteristics.

- **Host heterogeneity** Nodes may vary widely in their capacities in terms of CPU power, memory, or network bandwidth.
- **Dynamic topology** Nodes may join and leave to a network at any time by mobility or by node redeployment. The system must be able to efficiently maintain a dynamic topology.
- **Scalability** The system must be able to scale to very large nodes in converged networks.
- **Convergence** Results of management service can be properly linked and merged.

In future ubiquitous environments, the following converged DDoS attacks are likely. We therefore need to design integrated defense service against these potential converged attacks.

(1) Wired network → Mobile network

For example, SMS Flooder is a DDoS attack tool against mobile telephones that has already emerged in wired networks. Because most mobile devices have extremely limited functionalities and bandwidth, a host with a powerful capacity in the wired network could easily break down the mobile network.

(2) Mobile network → Wired network

Most mobile networks are interconnected with a wired network, to allow the connection of distant mobile nodes or to provide mobile nodes with the various Internet services in a wired network. Mobile nodes, for example, a mobile phone using a RFID reader, can severely request these connections to the servers in the wired network, thus threatening the availability of servers.

(3) Sensor network → Mobile network

Numerous technologies exist for mobility support, such as the Mobile Internet protocol (MIP), code division multiple access (CDMA), International Mobile Telecommunications-2000 (IMT-2000), and so on. Network mobility has been realized among these after the foundation of the Network Mobility (NEMO) Working Group (WG) in the IETF. This WG is concerned with managing the mobility of an entire network that changes, as a unit, its point of attachment to the Internet. NEMOs can include a sensor network, for example, a vehicle that includes sensors for its control. In this case, compromised sensors in a NEMO can generate a great deal of sensing information that will congest the NEMO.

(4) Mobile network → Sensor network
Mobile routers or nodes performing as a mobile sink are infected with virus, then can request the sensing information in a sensor network, pretending other mobile sinks. In this case, the flood of request traffic can affect all of the sensor nodes, aggregator nodes, and sink nodes in the sensor network.

(5) Wired network → Sensor network
Static nodes in a wired network can severely request the sensing information to sinks in a sensor network to induce tremendous traffic from sensors.

(6) Sensor network → Wired network
Compromised sensors in the sensor network can transmit the sensing information to the server in the wired network that manages the sensor network, creating sudden traffic that influences the server or the wired network connected to the server.

3   Notification Mechanism Using Overlay

We introduce integrated notification architecture against DDoS attack on converged network using overlay as shown in the figure 1, in order to fast notify the attack detection to both highest defense systems in the network of victims and attack agents, through detouring victims. In figure 1, three overlays are connected through the connection of overlay nodes, and we assume the highest defense system exists at the highest overlay. However, our defense can apply to networks that are different from that of figure 1 if the overlay nodes know the location and overlay level of the defense systems. In the converged network, each hierarchical overlay networks are interconnected by the overlay nodes with multiple interfaces. We also assume secure communication between the highest defense systems and the overlay nodes. We will explain our defense overlay architecture in detail below.

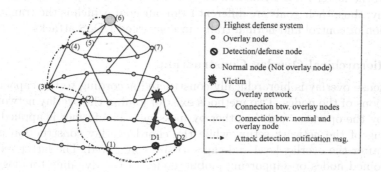

Fig. 1. Basic architecture for our notification

3.1 Chord Overlay Routing

Our defense architecture uses chord overlay routing to transmit the attack detection message and detour normal traffic, before excluding attack agents. The *chord protocol* is a distributed lookup protocol that efficiently locates the node that stores a particular data item. In the N-node chord system, each node maintains information only about $O(\log N)$ nodes, and resolves all lookups via $O(\log N)$ messages to other nodes. The chord maintains its routing information as nodes join and leave the system. A high probability exists that each event will result in no more than $O(\log^2 N)$ messages. The chord protocol resolves the inability of previous methods to scale to a large number of nodes, and is referenced in more than 1000 papers using overlay routing in various fields.

In chord, each node is assigned a numerical ID via a hash function in the range $[0, 2^m\text{-}1]$ for some predetermined value of m. The nodes in the overlay are ordered by these identifiers. The ordering is cyclic (i.e., wraps around) and can be viewed conceptually as a circle, where the next node in the ordering is the next node along the circle in the clockwise direction. Each overlay node maintains a table that stores the identities of other overlay nodes. The ith entry in the table is the node whose identifier equals or, in relation to all other nodes in the overlay, most immediately follows x+2^{i-1} (mod 2^m). When the overlay node receives a packet destined for ID y, it forwards the packet to the overlay node in its table (called a finger table) with the ID that precedes it by the smallest amount.

As other overlay routing applications, the chord protocol has multicasting [2] or attack defense [3,4]. Secure overlay services (SOS) architecture using chord overlay [3] was proposed to proactively prevent DDoS attacks. SOS architecture is geared toward supporting emergency services or similar types of communication and introduces randomness and anonymity into the forwarding architecture, making it difficult for an attacker to target nodes along the path to a specific SOS-protected destination. HOURS [4] using hierarchical overlays achieved DoS resilience in an open service hierarchy, such as a domain name server (DNS), lightweight directory access protocol (LDAP), or public key infrastructure (PKI). However, the former is for the protection of a specific server against a DDoS attack and the latter is for DDoS defense between servers with the specific service hierarchy; thus, their goals are different from our goal, which is the transmission protection of control and normal traffic in converged DDoS attacks.

3.2 Hierarchical Overlay Construction

Our defense overlay is hierarchically constructed according to the capacity and connections of the nodes. Two methods exist of joining the overlay network, one set up by the operator and the other by messages. The former is applied at the beginning of the network setup, while the chord overlay construction method is used after the overlay level and capacity are configured. The latter redeploys newly joined nodes or supporting mobile nodes in the dynamic topology, with the following *join inquiry message (JIM)* and *join response message (JRepM)*. We will explain the latter steps in detail.

A newly joining node n_{new} first sends the *JIM*, including the node's capacity, to neighbor nodes. Neighbor nodes are the upper or lower nodes directly connected to the n_{new}, or in the Ethernet case, the nodes in the broadcast domain. The overlay nodes n_is receiving the *JIM* send *JRepM*s, including their capacity ($Capacity_i$) and overlay Level ($Level_i$). The newly joining node n_{new} waits a specified amount of time for the *JRepM*s, then determines its own overlay level with reference to $Capacity_i$s and $Level_i$s according to table 1, and sends a **join request message (JReqM)** to an overlay node in that overlay level. If no *JRepM*s is received in the specified time period, the node n_{new} sends a *JReqM* directly to the highest defense system.

The join process through the *JReqM* is based on the chord method, but the *JRepM* also includes the connection information (to high, low, and other networks), and if a direct connection to other overlay nodes exists, their overlay level joins information. In the join process, joining overlay nodes should update the information of the upper/lower/other interface successor node, if necessary, so that information can be used in the attack detection notification. The information stored at each overlay node contains the predecessor in the overlay network (used for the join process), the routing table (called the finger table), the high/low_successor directly connected to the higher and lower layer, and the otherif_succcessor directly connected to other type networks. The high/low/otherif_succcessor is the first node directly connected to the higher/lower layer/other network in a clockwise direction in the ring.

The modified join process sets up the predecessor, finger table, and high/low/otherif_successor at node n_{new}, and then updates their information at previously joined overlay nodes, if necessary. The configuration method for the high/low/otherif_successor is as follows. If the already joined overlay nodes n_i receive the *JReqM*, they compare their $high/low/otherif\_successor_i$, and update themselves with those in the *JReqM* when $high\_successor_i > new > i$, $low\_successor_i > new > i$, or $otherif\_successor_i > new > i$. Figure 2 shows an example of an overlay and finger table after the joining of node 6. In this example, the $high\_successor_3$ of node 3 and $otherif\_successors$ are updated. In addition, for a more practical overlay construction, the modified chord can be used to reduce routing latency if IPv6 is used [7].

3.3   Notification of Attack Detection

In our defense structure, we assume that existing distributed detection methods are used. For example, there are a monitoring method for IP address or the change rate of IP/MAC address using the network configuration information at the middle nodes[5], a data mining method[6], and so on. Thus detection mechanism is beyond the research scope of our defense structure.

If overlay nodes detect a DDoS attack, they send an **attack detection message (ADM)** to the highest defense system through hierarchical overlays, that is, to its high_successor using the finger table. To defend against and identify attack agents, the *ADM* includes detection node information (IP address and overlay level), victim information (IP address and overlay level, if it exists), the

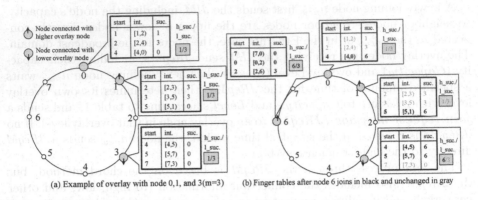

(a) Example of overlay with node 0,1, and 3(m=3)   (b) Finger tables after node 6 joins in black and unchanged in gray

Fig. 2. Example of overlay and finite table after node 6 joins

Table 1. Level decision method of a newly joining node

$if(Capacity_i \leq Capacity_{new} < Capacity_{(i+1)})$	$(Level_{new} = Level_i)$
$elseif(Capacity_1 \geq Capacity_{new})$	$(Level_{new} = Level_1)$
$elseif(Capacity_K \leq Capacity_{new})$	$(Level_{new} = Level_K)$

- $n_i (1 \leq i \leq K$, K: Number of nodes sending $JRepM$)
- $Capacity_i$: Capacity of node n_i (capacities in increasing order, thus $Capacity_i \leq Capacity_{(i+1)}$)
- $Level_i$: Overlay level of node n_i
- $Capacity_{new}$: Capacity of a newly joining node n_{new}
- $Level_{new}$: Determined level of a newly joining nod n_{new}

connection relationship of the detection node and the victim, and information about the neighbors of the detection nodes (connection information of neighbors). The high_successor receiving the ADM also sends its high_successor, and finally the highest defense node receives the ADM, after repeating this transmission through the hierarchical overlay. In the example shown in Figure 1, after overlay nodes D1 and D2 detect a victim, they send the ADM through (1)-(5), and finally the ADM arrives at the highest defense node (6).

In the converged network, hierarchical overlays such as depicted in Figure 1 are constructed for each network, and are connected with each other through the overlay node with multiple interfaces. Each overlay node manages successors that connect to other networks in the finger table. If the converged attack is detected, the attack detection is relayed to the highest defense system (node (8) in Figure 3) in the network of the attack agents as well as in its own network (node (2)). The route (node (1)-(2)) of notification in the network of detection node D follows the pattern described in the previous paragraph. The network of the attack agents is notified; first, the detection node sends the ADM to successors connecting to the network in its overlay layer (node (3)-(5)), then the ADM is routed through the hierarchical overlay (node (6)-(8)). The notification to the highest defense system in the network of the attack agents provides the

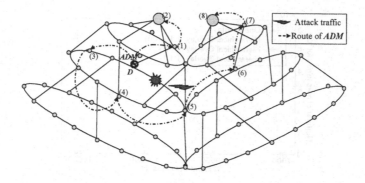

Fig. 3. Attack detection notification in the case of converged attack

information for follow-up measures against the attack agents. The route through this hierarchical overlay makes it possible to randomize the notification route for all detection nodes, in comparison to a direct route between each highest defense system, which can be a point of failure or attack.

4 Evaluation

In this chapter, we attempt to provide an analysis of the advantages and usefulness of our defense architecture. At first, we analyze the construction overhead of hierarchical overlay relative to only one big overlay, and we simulate the detection notification speed in converged DDoS attack on converged network with GloMoSim that provides a scalable simulation environment for wireless and wired network systems[8].

4.1 Overhead of Overlay Construction

We assume that our defense overlay is hierarchically constructed based on node capacity. To provide scalability or heterogeneity, one of the design issues in a converged network, the defense architecture should support a variety of nodes, making the construction of several overlays profitable. Moreover, a small overlay can be favorable for nodes with low capacity, such as the aggregators on the sensor network. Our defense overlay is based on the construction method of chord, thus $O(log^2 N)$ message transmission is required for a node join/leave in N-size

Table 2. Decision method of defense nodes

Construction of one overlay
$\geq$ Construction of β overlays with the different number of nodes
$\geq$ Construction of β overlays with the same number of nodes,
$N \cdot logN \geq \sum_{i=1}^{\beta} \alpha_i \cdot log\alpha_i \geq \beta \cdot N/\beta \cdot log(N/\beta)$

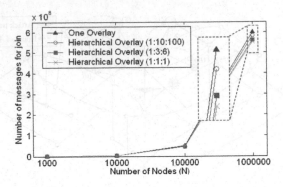

Fig. 4. Comparison for construction overhead

overlay network, and this can be reduced to $O(\log N)$ with practical optimization[3]. The construction overhead of our hierarchical overlays is smaller than
for the construction of one overlay, and the construction overhead of overlays
with the same number of nodes is smaller than that of overlays with a different
number of nodes, as shown in table 2. The bigger the N in an N-node network is,
the larger the overhead difference is, as shown in figure 4. In figure 4, the hierarchical overlay is made with three overlays; for example, a hierarchical overlay
(1:10:100) in a 1000-node network is composed of an overlay with 10 nodes, an
overlay with 100 nodes, and an overlay with 890 nodes.

4.2   Simulation Results

We configured the converged network as in Figure 5 to analyze the influence
on the converged attack. In figure 5, we depict the wired and wireless networks
differently to clearly differentiate them, but they share the same area, and wired
nodes 2, 3, 5, 9, 11, and 15 are the same as the wireless nodes with the same

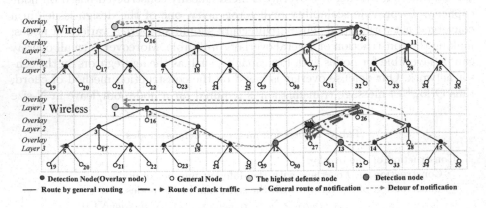

Fig. 5. Simulation network for converged network

respective numbers. We mounted the DDoS attack from the wired node 26, 27 and 27 to wireless node 27, and attack traffic is generated at 1-ms intervals. If overlay nodes detected the converged DDoS attack, they sent five ADMs at 1-s intervals to the highest defense nodes n1 of the networks of both victims and attack agents, through overlay routing.

In results, general routes incur the low transmission rate and long delay of notification to the highest defense system (Wireless, Wl_n1) in comparison with overlay routes like table 3, because the general routes pass via victims. Moreover, the overlay route provides the fast and exact notification to highest defense system (Wired node, Wd_n1) in wired network where attack agents exist, to take immediate follow-up measure such as the identification of attack agents.

Table 3. Key re-distribution message

Node ID	Transmission rate (pkts or %)			Transmission time (sec)		
	General routing	Overlay routing		General routing	Overlay routing	
		Wl_n_1	Wd_n_1		Wl_n_1	Wd_n_1
12	1	5	5	0.436562669	0.019297497	0.037087675
13	0	1	5	-	1.219606000	0.025713102
	10%	60%	100%	0.436562669	0.019297497	0.025713102

5   Conclusion

In this paper, we proposed an integrated notification architecture using hierarchical overlay in consideration of node capacity, in order to interconnect defense systems on each network, and guarantee the speedy notification for attack detection through detour victims. It is especially important to defense possible converged attacks in the future. We constructed hierarchically the overlay in due consideration of the various capacities of nodes and lots of nodes on converged environment, and we extended the chord overlay routing to interconnect overlay layers and hierarchical overlays on different networks. The hierarchical overlays can decrease the overhead for construction in comparison with the construction of a big overlay. In simulation results on converged environment, we gained the fast and high notification rate for the attack detection. Moreover, our overlay route could notify the fast and exact attack detection to highest defense system where attack agents exist, to take immediate follow-up measure.

References

1. Won, Y.: BcN security Issues. In: Proc of Korea Internet Conference (KRNET) (2006)
2. Zhang, Z., Chen, S., Ling, Y., Chow, R.: Capacity-Aware Multicast Algorithms on Heterogeneous Overlay Networks. IEEE Transactions on Parallel and Distributed Systems 17(2), 135–147 (2006)

3. Keromytis, A., Misra, V., Rubenstein, D.: SOS: An Architecture for Mitigating DDoS Attacks. IEEE JSAC 22(1) (2004)
4. Yang, H., Luo, H., Yang, Y., Lu, S., Zhang, L.: HOURS: Achieving DoS Resilience in an Open Service Hierarchy. In: Proc. of DSN, pp. 83–92 (2004)
5. Kim, M., Chae, K.: Detection and Identification Mechanism against Spoofed Traffic Using Distributed Agents. In: Laganà, A., Gavrilova, M., Kumar, V., Mun, Y., Tan, C.J.K., Gervasi, O. (eds.) ICCSA 2004. LNCS, vol. 3043, pp. 673–682. Springer, Heidelberg (2004)
6. Kim, M., Na, H., Chae, K., Bang, H., Na, J.: A Combined Data Mining Approach for DDoS Attack Detection. In: Kahng, H.-K., Goto, S. (eds.) ICOIN 2004. LNCS, vol. 3090, pp. 943–950. Springer, Heidelberg (2004)
7. Xiong, J., Zhang, Y., Hong, P., Li, J., Guo, L.: Reduce Chord Routing Latency Issue in the Context of IPv6. IEEE comm.letters 10(1) (2006)
8. GloMoSim, http://pcl.cs.ucla.edu/projects/glomosim/

Making Middleware Secure on Embedded Terminals

Yoshiharu Asakura, Atsushi Honda, Satoshi Hieda, Hiroshi Chishima,
and Naoki Sato

NEC Corporation
1753, Shimonumabe, Nakahara-Ku, Kawasaki, Kanagawa 211-8666, Japan

Abstract. Recently more embedded terminals have begun to use a
general-purpose OS such as Linux. These terminals can perform various functions, such as downloading applications. Since these applications
maybe malicious, it is necessary to protect terminals against them and to
ensure stability of services provided by the terminals. We have proposed
a security enhanced middleware model for embedded terminals based on
Linux (SEMMETL). The SEMMETL offers client identification, access
control for each application and resource control for each application.
The security enhanced X server (SEN XServer) is an example of our
proposed SEMMETL. By applying the SEMMETL to middleware, we
can enhance the security of embedded terminals and ensure stability.

1 Introduction

Recently more embedded terminals have begun to use a general-purpose OS such
as Linux [1]. These terminals have functions that include downloading content
data and applications. Since the content or applications downloaded may be
malicious, they can have an adverse affect on terminals. Therefore, it is necessary
to protect embedded terminals against such problems and to ensure the stability
of services they provide.

Access control and resource control are functions that ensure the stability of
services provided by terminals. The former is a function to restrict the kinds
of resources that applications can access. The latter is a function to restrict
the amount of resources that applications can consume. Server-type middleware
such as the X Server[1] accepts connections from client applications and provides
services for them. Therefore, middleware needs to identify each client application.

Access control – To implement access control, it is a good idea to introduce a
secure OS such as SELinux[2]. Although a secure OS can control accesses to resources provided by the OS itself, it cannot control accesses to resources provided
by middleware. Therefore, middleware needs access control for its resources.

Resource control – Many embedded terminals have only limited resources.
Server-type middleware allocates resources for client applications to provide services for them. Hence, if one client application consumes a large amount of

---

[1] All trademarks and registered trademarks referenced herein are the property of their
respective owners.

R. Obermaisser et al. (Eds.): SEUS 2007, LNCS 4761, pp. 477–485, 2007.
© IFIP International Federation for Information Processing 2007

resources, other client applications cannot be allocated sufficient resources[3]. Therefore, middleware needs resource control to restrict resource consumption for each client application.

In this paper, we focus on making middleware for embedded terminals based on Linux secure. This is because Linux has become popular in embedded terminals recently. In Sect. 2, we propose a model that enables middleware for embedded terminals based on Linux to enhance security. In this paper, we call this model *Security Enhanced Middleware Model for Embedded Terminals based on Linux* (SEMMETL). In Sect. 3, we give an example of the SEMMETL being applied to the X Server.

2   SEMMETL

The SEMMETL ensures the services provided by an embedded terminal are stable. The SEMMETL is a middleware model that satisfies the following three requirements:

R1: client identification. The SEMMETL must identify each client application.

R2: access control. The SEMMETL must check whether a client application has permission to access resources.

R3: resource control. The SEMMETL must restrict resource consumption for each client application and each kind of resource.

Figure 1 shows middleware to which the SEMMETL is applied. The middleware accepts connections from client applications and identifies client applications to control access and resources. When the middleware receives and processes requests from client applications, the middleware controls accesses to its resources and restricts resource consumption for each client application.

2.1   R1: Client Identification

There are several kinds of connections, such as the Internet domain connections and the UNIX domain connections between the SEMMETL and client applications. In the case of a UNIX domain connection, the SEMMETL can obtain a process ID of a connected client application via a UNIX domain socket[4]. However, the UNIX domain connection can only be utilized for internal communication within a terminal. If the SEMMETL needs to accept connections from outside a terminal, a new reliable communication method to obtain client identifiers is required. For example, labeled IPSec is a candidate for this purpose[5]. This functionality enables terminals to control communication with applications on other terminals based on the security label defined in SELinux. This security label can be used as a client identifier.

After obtaining a client identifier, the SEMMETL performs the following two activities:

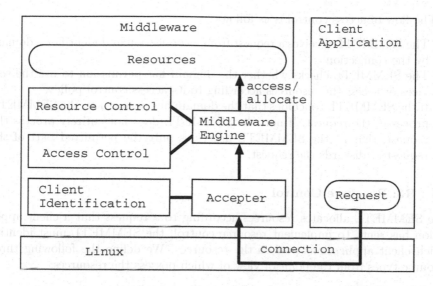

Fig. 1. Middleware to which the SEMMETL is applied

A1: deciding whether the SEMMETL accepts a connection according to a given criteria, e.g. connection types.

A2: classifying the accepted client application into domains according to the client identifier.

To process **A1** and **A2**, the SEMMETL must define rules that specify relations between client identifiers and domains in advance. We call these rules *a domain policy*.

2.2 R2: Access Control

The SEMMETL provides services to client applications and allows access to none or more of its resources depending on the service required. Therefore, the SEMMETL can implement access control at different levels. The SEMMETL implements **AC1** or **AC2** or both of them.

AC1: restricting use of services provided by the SEMMETL

AC2: restricting access to resources provided by the SEMMETL

In **AC1**, the SEMMETL controls whether client applications have permission to use services. In **AC2**, the SEMMETL controls whether client applications have permission to access resources. The SEMMETL must define rules that specify services or resources that client applications have permission to use or access. We call the rules *an access control policy*. To reduce the size of an access control policy, we specify an access control policy in a domain unit. Permission for a client application is given by the domain to which the client application belongs.

The flow of access control is as follows:

1. The SEMMETL receives a request from a connection and identifies a domain by the connection.
2. The SEMMETL checks whether the domain has permission to use the services or access the resources according to its access control policy.
3. If the SEMMETL concludes that the domain has permission, the SEMMETL processes the request. If not, the SEMMETL does not entirely process the request, that is, the SEMMETL processes only the permitted part of the request or discards the request.

2.3   R3: Resource Control

The SEMMETL allocates resources according to a request that a client application has sent. To implement resource control, the SEMMETL must identify which client applications possess the resources. We define the following three resource types from the point of view of which possess the resources:

RT1: The resources possessed by one client application
RT2: The resources possessed by several client applications
RT3: The resources possessed by middleware

The SEMMETL must classify allocated resources into the above three resource types, which are described in more detail below:

RT1. Some kinds of resources are allocated to one client application, that is, the resources are accessed by the client application. In this resource type, we consider that the client application that has sent the request possesses allocated resources. The SEMMETL sums the amount of allocated resources in respective client applications and respective kinds of resources.

RT2. Some kinds of resources are shared and accessed by several client applications. In this resource type, we consider that the domain to which those client applications belong possesses allocated resources or middleware possesses them as a shared resources whichever client application has sent the request. The SEMMETL sums the amount of allocated resources in respective domains and respective kinds of resources or as shared resources.

RT3. The SEMMETL allocates resources to itself to work and manage client applications and no client application can access this resource type. In this resource type, we consider that middleware possesses the allocated resources.

For **RT1** and **RT2**, the SEMMETL must define rules that specify maximum amount of resources in each domain and at each kind of resource. We call the rules *a resource control policy*. The maximum amount of resources a client application has is that of the domain to which the client application belongs.

3   Security Enhanced X Server

The X Server is middleware that provides GUI services to X clients. When an X client sends an X request to the X Server, the X Server allocates and accesses

X resources, such as windows and pixmaps, while the X Server processes the X request. However, as the X Server has no access control and resource control, an X client can access and consume X resources unrestrictedly. Hence, a malicious X client can obstruct services provided by an embedded terminal by accessing X resources iniquitously or consuming a large amount of a resource. In order to protect against these attacks, we use the SEMMETL on the X Server. We call this X Server *the Security Enhanced X Server* (SEN XServer).

We define one concept as "an owner of an X resource" here. We can classify X resources into a non-shared X resource, which is classified as **RT1**, and a shared X resource, which is classified as **RT2**. An example of the former is a window that is allocated to one X client. An example of the latter is a font that is allocated to all X clients. Therefore, we define the owner of a non-shared X resource as the X client that has sent the X request and the owner of a shared X resource as the SEN XServer.

The SEN XServer satisfies the three requirements described in Sect. 2. The policy file is composed of a domain policy, an access control policy and a resource control policy.

3.1 Client Identification in the SEN XServer

The SEN XServer only accepts UNIX domain connections that satisfy **R1**. Since few embedded terminals are required to accept connections outside of terminals, we consider that this restriction is acceptable.

The SEN XServer identifies an X client as follows. The SEN XServer obtains a process ID of an X client via a UNIX domain socket first, and then obtains a full pathname of the X client via a /proc/[process ID]/exe link file. After obtaining the full pathname, the SEN XServer processes **A1** and **A2** as follows. The SEN XServer only accepts the UNIX domain connections as **A1** and classifies the X client into a domain as **A2**. In order to classify the X client into a domain, we specify relations between full pathnames of X clients and domains in a domain policy. If the full pathname is not classified as any domain, the SEN XServer regards the X client as an invalid client and refuses the connection.

3.2 Access Control in the SEN XServer

The X Server defines several kinds of access to each X resource. When the X Server receives an X request from an X client, the X Server accesses none or more X resources to process the X request. To implement access control, the X Server must conclude whether a received X request needs processing, that is, whether the X client that has sent the X request has permission to access necessary X resources. Namely, **AC2** is suitable for the SEN XServer.

We define the kinds of access in respective X resources as a primitive access control unit. We call the primitive access control unit *the operation*. Table 1 shows part of the operation for an X resource. We define operations that an X request needs in respective X requests. That is because the SEN XServer must conclude whether an X client has permission to execute the necessary operations

Table 1. Operations (extract)

operations	explanations
Window:addchild	append a child window to a parent window
Window:destroy	destroy a window
Window:map	display a window on the screen
Drawable:draw	draw on a drawable
Drawable:copy	copy pixels from a drawable
Cursor:assign	relate a cursor to a window

Table 2. Sets of X request and operations for an X resource (extract)

X requests	operations	X resources
CreateWindow	Window:addchild	a parent window
	Drawable:copy	using a drawable
	Cursor:assign	using a cursor
CreatePixmap	nothing	–

for an X resource to process the X request. Table 2 shows part of the sets of the X request and the operations for X resources. We specify operations that domains have permission to execute for an X resource in an access control policy.

The SEN XServer processes an X request only if a domain to which an X client that has sent the X request belongs has permission to execute all operations that the X request needs for an X resource. For example, CreateWindow needs three operations: Window:addchild for the parent window; Drawable:copy for the using pixmap; and Cursor:assign for the using cursor. The SEN XServer checks whether the domain has these three operations for the X resource. If the domain has permission to execute the three operations, the SEN XServer processes CreateWindow.

The SEN XServer processes an X request as follows.

1. Identifying a connection from which the SEN XServer receives the X request.
2. Identifying a domain by the connection.
3. Identifying all X resources.
4. Checking whether the domain has permission to execute all the operations that the X request needs for the X resource.
5. If the domain has permission, the SEN XServer processes the X request. If not, the SEN XServer discards the X request.

3.3   Resource Control in the SEN XServer

The SEN XServer manages X resource usage as a resource control. Since the X Server consumes memory when the X Server creates X resources, the SEN XServer manages memory consumption for each X client. For resource control, we specify the maximum amount of memory in each domain in a resource control policy. We classify the memory types into the following three types as described in Sect. 2.3.

Non-shared memory (RT1): The memory that is consumed when the SEN XServer creates non-shared X resources.

Shared memory (RT2): The memory that is consumed when the SEN XServer creates shared X resources.

Working memory (RT3): The memory that is consumed when the SEN XServer works and manages X clients.

For the non-shared memory, when the SEN XServer creates a non-shared X resource, the SEN XServer adds a given amount of the non-shared memory to the memory consumption of the owner of the non-shared X resource. If memory consumption of an X client exceeds the specified maximum amount of memory, the SEN XServer does not allocate memory to the X client.

For the shared memory and the working memory, since the owner of a shared X resource is the SEN XServer and the working memory is also used for the SEN XServer, the SEN XServer adds a given amount of the shared memory and the working memory to the memory consumption of the SEN XServer.

3.4   The Policy File in the SEN XServer

The policy file is composed of a domain policy, an access control policy and a resource control policy. Hence, the policy file defines the following three elements.

1. Relations between full pathnames of X clients and domains (a domain policy)

   The policy file defines full pathnames of X clients in each domain. The SEN XServer can identify a domain to which an X client belongs by its full pathname.

2. Operations that X clients have permission to execute (an access control policy)

   The policy file defines operations that domains have permission to execute for an X resource. We call a domain that has permission to execute operations *a source domain*. We also call a domain to which an owner of an X resource belongs *a target domain*. The policy file defines operations for a target domain on each source domain.

3. Maximum amount of memory (a resource control policy)

   The policy file defines the maximum amount of memory in each domain per byte unit.

Figure 2 shows an example of a policy file. In this example, the policy file defines 2 domains, the SYSTEM domain and the DOWNLOAD domain. In this policy, /usr/X11R6/bin/xcalc and /usr/X11R6/bin/xclock belong to the SYSTEM domain and /usr/local/bin/dlbrowser and /usr/local/bin/dlmessenger belong to the DOWNLOAD domain. xcalc and xclock can each consume memory up to 2097152 bytes. In the same way, dlbrowser and dlmessenger can also each

```
[SYSTEM 2097152] /usr/X11R6/bin/xcalc /usr/X11R6/bin/xclock
[DOWNLOAD 1048576] /usr/local/bin/dlbrowser
                   /usr/local/bin/dlmessenger

domain SYSTEM {
    {SYSTEM Window:addchild}
    {SYSTEM Drawable:copy}
    {SYSTEM Cursor:assign}
    {DOWNLOAD Window:addchild}
    {DOWNLOAD Drawable:copy}
    {DOWNLOAD Cursor:assign}
}
domain DOWNLOAD {
    {DOWNLOAD Window:addchild}
    {DOWNLOAD Drawable:copy}
    {DOWNLOAD Cursor:assign}
}
```

Fig. 2. An example of a policy file

consume memory up to 1048576 bytes. xcalc and xclock have permission to execute Window:addchild for X resources possessed by the X clients that belong to the SYSTEM and the DOWNLOAD domains. dlbrowser and dlmessenger have permission to execute Window:addchild only for X resources possessed by the X clients that belong to the DOWNLOAD domain. If the SEN XServer receives CreateWindow that uses a drawable possessed by xclock from dlbrowser, the SEN XServer discards CreateWindow because dlbrowser does not have permission to execute Drawable:copy for the drawable possessed by xclock.

4   Conclusion

In this paper, we have discussed a proposed model called the SEMMETL. The SEMMETL enables the enhancing of security of middleware by satisfying three requirements: client identification, access control for each application, and resource control for each application. Moreover, we have given the SEN XServer as an example of the SEMMETL. By applying the SEMMETL to middleware, we can enhance the security of the middleware.

References

1. X.Org Foundation.http://www.x.org/
2. NSA: Security-Enhanced Linux.http://www.nsa.gov/selinux
3. Hieda, S., et al.: Resource Management in Linux for Mobile Terminals. IPSJ Transactions on Computing System 46(SIG3), 1–10 (2005)

4. Wheeler, D.A.: Secure Programming for Linux and Unix HOWTO,
   http://www.linux.org/docs/ldp/howto/Secure-Programs-HOWTO/index.html
5. Jaeger, T.R., et al.: Leveraging IPSec for Mandatory Access Control of Linux Network Communications. Technical Report RC23642 (W0506-109), IBM (June 2005)
6. Kilpatrick, D., Salamon, W., Vance, C.: Securing The X Window System With SELinux. http://www.nsa.gov/selinux/papers/X11_Study.pdf

Dynamic Translator-Based Virtualization

Yuki Kinebuchi[1], Hidenari Koshimae[1], Shuichi Oikawa[2], and Tatsuo Nakajima[1]

[1] Department of Computer Science, Waseda University
{yukikine, hide, tatsuo}@dcl.info.waseda.ac.jp
[2] Department of Computer Science, University of Tsukuba
shui@cs.tsukuba.ac.jp

Abstract. Microkernels and virtual machine monitors are both utilized as platforms for running operating systems. Although there are many similarities in their designs and features, they have opposite advantages and drawbacks. A microkernel based system is highly portable. However, the interface it exposes is inflexible and incompatible with other real hardware interfaces. In contrast, a virtual machine monitor interface is identical to a specific real hardware interface. However, the implementation of virtual machine monitors highly depends on processor architectures and specific hardwares.

In this paper, we present a new model of virtual machine monitor, a flexible dynamic translator constructed on a portable microkernel. Our model offers both high portability and compatibility. Moreover, its flexible interface could be reconfigured to support various types of hardware interfaces. The results of the evaluation show that the performance of our prototype system is unsatisfactory, so we propose some techniques to improve its performance as future work.

1 Introduction

Microkernels and virtual machine monitors (VMMs) have common purpose which is to run operating systems on them. There are many similarities in their designs and features. However, since their primary aims differ from each other, they have opposite advantages and drawbacks in a point of portability and compatibility.

Microkernels started with the redesigning of conventional operating systems. In order to reduce the size and the complexity of a kernel, the number of its functions was minimized and some traditional kernel functionality were moved to the application level. The resulting system realizes a moduled and highly portable structure. Since their interfaces differ from real hardwares interface, there is a drawback that a guest operating system needs to be modified to run on a microkernel.

In contrast, VMMs aim to the reuse of commodity operating systems. Like a microkernel, VMM is a small and simple program running in privileged mode, but provides an interface identical or almost identical to the underlying real hardware. Thus, operating systems can run on VMM without any or with minimum modification. Since its implementation highly depends on a processor architecture and a specific hardware, the portability of itself is low.

R. Obermaisser et al. (Eds.): SEUS 2007, LNCS 4761, pp. 486–495, 2007.

In this paper, we propose a new model of constructing a VMM, which is a flexible dynamic translator constructed on a portable microkernel. The past virtual execution platforms have implemented their interfaces directly on hardware interfaces. They have a hardware dependent, not portable and inflexible interface implementation. In our model the hardware dependent layer is split from the interface implementation. The underlying hardware interface is abstracted by the microkernel, which provides a uniform interface on different architectures to the machine emulator running on it. The machine emulator provides an flexible interface implementation, which enables the execution of unmodified operating systems and can be reconfigured to support different hardware interfaces. We implemented a prototype system by porting an existing portable machine emulator to an existing microkernel, and made some evaluations on its performance.

The next section compares microkernels and VMMs. Section 3 introduces some related work. Section 4 introduces the implementation of our prototype system. Section 5 proposes some applications using our model. Section 6 introduces the results of the evaluation. Section 7 discusses some performance issues and future directions. Finally Section 8 concludes the paper.

2 Microkernel vs VMM

This section compares advantages and disadvantages of microkernels, VMMs, and propose our new virtualization model which integrates the advantages of both of them.

A microkernel is a small operating system supporting only a minimum set of API. Microkernels are used as bases for constructing operating systems. The interface provided by a microkernel is an abstract hardware interface, which is different from any existing hardware interfaces. Therefore, when running an existing operating system on a microkernel, its architecture dependent part must be modified as shown in Figure 1 (a). This is the drawback of the microkernel-based approach. The advantage of using microkernels is their portability. Since a microkernel-based system splits the hardware dependent layer and operating system services, the system could be supported on a different hardware by porting only a part of the microkernel.

A virtual machine monitor is a software that enables multiple operating systems to run on a single hardware by giving the illusion of using a whole hardware to each operating system. The interface provided by a virtual machine monitor is almost identical to a specific existing hardware interface. The advantage to use VMMs is that they do not require the modification of guest operating systems to be run on it. Figure 1 (b) shows the operating system for architecture A running directly on the hardware of architecture A. The operating system could run on the virtual machine monitor without modifying its architecture dependent part as shown on in Figure 1 (c). The drawback of the virtual machine monitor-based approach is strong dependency to the underlying hardware interface. Moreover, the architecture offered by the virtual machine monitor and the interface of the underlying hardware should be the same.

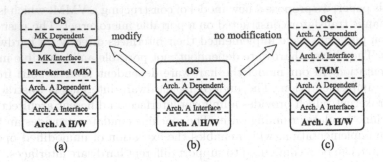

Fig. 1. OS on VMM and a microkernel

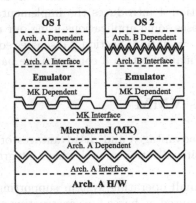

Fig. 2. Machine Emulator on a microkernel

We propose a new virtualization architecture, which has the advantages of both microkernels and virtual machine monitors, the portability and the compatible interface with existing hardware architectures. Figure 2 shows the overview of our model. Flexible machine emulators are running on a portable microkernel. The emulator provides an interface compatible with an existing architecture interface. The emulator on the lefthand side of the figure offers the interface of architecture A, which executes an unmodified operating system. In addition, the emulator could be reconfigured to execute operating systems on various different architectures. The emulator on the lefthand side of the figure is reconfigured to offer the interface of architecture B. The implementation of the emulator depends on the microkernel interface but not the host architecture. The underlying microkernel hides the hardware interface from the emulator and offers a uniform interface. When the underlying hardware changes, only the small architecture dependent part of the microkernel is modified. Therefore the porting cost of the system is decreased dramatically.

3   Related Work

In this section, we introduce an existing machine emulator and some existing virtual machines.

Bochs[6] is a machine emulator which emulates the x86 architecture machine. It has a capability to run guest operating systems built for the x86 architecture without any modifications. The code of Bochs is written in C++, which can be compiled to run on various operating systems. Although it supports a high portability over operating systems, the portability of supporting new hardware platform depends on the host operating system implementation.

Xen[1] is VMM leveraging a virtualization technique called para-virtualization. Using para-virtualization increases the performance of guest operating system, but it requires the modification of guest operating systems to be virtualized. In addition, the implementation of Xen highly depends on the x86 architecture, it has low portability.

VMware Workstation[8] is VMM that can run unmodified operating systems built for the x86 architecture. It runs as an application running on commodity operating systems such as Linux and Windows. It installs VMM running in the privileged level as a device driver in order to use privileged level instructions. This is to increase the performance of running guest operating systems. At the same time it increases the dependency on both the host operating system and the host hardware architecture.

4   Constructing Machine Emulator on Microkernel

4.1   Overview

We implemented a prototype system of our proposed model by porting the QEMU machine emulator[2] to the L4Ka::Pistachio microkernel[9] (L4 for short) with the Kenge[4] environment. The architecture of the prototype system is shown in Figure 3. QEMU, originally running on Linux, is modified to run as an application on L4. Each of QEMU can run a single guest operating system on it. By running multiple QEMU, multiple guest operating systems can run simultaneously on a single hardware. Kenge provides some libraries and servers that facilitate the constructions of applications on L4.

The following subsections briefly introduce QEMU, L4 and Kenge followed by the description of virtual devices.

4.2   QEMU

QEMU is a portable machine emulator, which emulates entire computer interface including CPU, memory and hardware devices. It runs as an application on commodity operating systems such as Linux, Windows, Mac OS X and Free BSD. Since QEMU emphasizes a portability, it supports various processor architectures as the host and the guest architecture. Currently, it supports x86, x86_64, ARM, SPARC, PowerPC and MIPS for the guest architecture, x86,

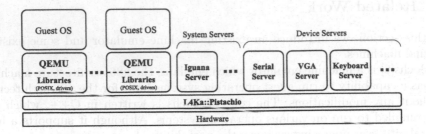

Fig. 3. A machine emulator on a microkernel

x86_64 and PowerPC for the host architecture. In addition, the host and the guest architecture can be different.

In order to provide a virtual CPU running guest programs, QEMU leverages the technique of a dynamic translation. It splits a guest instruction into pseudo microcodes that consists of host instructions. The translation is continued up to the next jump instruction, and the chunk of translated codes is put in a buffer as a unit of translated block (TB). TBs are reused when corresponding codes are executed again. Each microcode is written in the C language that is compiled to native code by GCC on the building stage of QEMU. Since the C codes can be compiled for various architectures by using different compilers, the porting costs are kept low.

QEMU also provides virtual devices that offer interfaces of existing hardware devices. The virtual devices for original QEMU are implemented using functions and libraries of the host commodity operating system. For example, data contained in a virtual hard disk is saved to a file on a host filesystem as a hard-disk image. In addition, the inputs and outputs of a guest operating system for a display, keyboard and mouse are processed using host graphic libraries and window systems. Since these libraries are not supported on L4, we modified the virtual devices to run in the L4 environment. The implementation of virtual devices on L4 is described in Section 4.5.

4.3   L4Ka::Pistachio

L4Ka::Pistachio is a portable microkernel. L4 itself only provides primitive functions to support thread management, address space management and IPC. Facilities supported by modern operating systems are moved to the user level and implemented as servers and libraries. For example, device management is moved to the user level, and implemented as device servers. Applications running on the microkernel interface with device servers to access hardwares.

4.4   Kenge and Iguana

Since L4 offers only primitive functions, we worked on the Kenge environment which helps the development of applications for L4. Kenge consists of a system build environment, libraries and servers, including the Iguana server[3] and some device servers. The libraries provide some POSIX functions, device drivers and some RPC stubs to interact with servers. The detail of device servers is described in the next section.

Iguana is a privileged server which manages resources such as memory, CPU and capabilities to access those resources. It also provides some high-level functions for applications running in L4 to create and delete threads, map and unmap memory regions.

QEMU on L4 uses some POSIX functions provided by these libraries, but not all the POSIX functions used by QEMU are provided by Kenge. Therefore we added some POSIX functions used by QEMU to help the porting.

4.5   Virtual Devices

This section describes the two different models of virtual hardware implementation. The first implementation is the model which virtual devices interact with device servers running beside QEMU and other applications. The second implementation is the model which links virtual devices with device driver libraries which let them directly interact with hardwares.

Device Server. A device server is a special application running on L4 which manages a device I/O to a specific hardware device. Although device servers are running in unprivileged mode, they are given a permission to access hardware devices. Therefore device drivers contained in device server can directly interact with hardware devices.

QEMU interact with device servers through the IPC function provided by L4. When a guest operating system writes to a virtual hardware, it transfers the written data to a corresponding device server using IPC. The device server receives the data, it invokes the device driver function, and perform an actual device output (Figure 4 (a)).

When multiple guest operating systems are sharing a single real device, the device server should arbitrate inputs and outputs. For example, the console server we made, can switch to which QEMU it transfers data, and let multiple guest operating systems to share a single display and keyboard. The drawback of this model is that frequent IPC between a guest operating system and device servers triggers frequent context switch.

Internal Device Driver. The other is the model using device driver library. QEMU, using the module linked to itself, interfaces with hardware directly (Figure 4 (b)). In this model there is no overhead of IPC because the data does not go through the device server, however a real device cannot be shared among multiple guest operating systems. For example, the ported QEMU accesses the VGA device using VGA device driver library. In this case, the guest operating system directly writes to real VRAM.

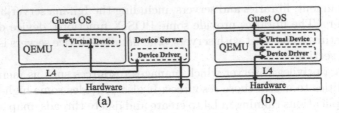

Fig. 4. The implementation of virtual devices

5   Applications Using QEMU on L4

This section propose some applications using our system.

5.1   Emulating Multiple Architectures

The primary use of our system is the reuse of existing operating systems on top of various types of architectures. Since QEMU exposes an interface compatible with existing hardwares, guest operating systems can run on top of it without any modifications. QEMU can run a guest operating system even if the host and the guest architecture are different as shown in Figure 5. The console server splits the monitor into four parts and makes each guest Linux to use one of them.

5.2   Anomaly Detection/Recovery

Alex Ho et al. proposed a taint-based protection using a machine emulator[5]. In normal times, an operating system runs on VMM. When the CPU is executing a code that interacts with data downloaded through the internet, the execution is dynamically switched on to the machine emulator. In this way, it reduces the performance degradation and protect the system from tainted data.

Using our system, we propose a similar system that offers an anomaly detection and recovery (Figure 6). In normal times, applications run directly on L4. When the system finds the symptom of application anomaly, the application is migrated to run on QEMU. QEMU runs the application and analyzes it in detail. When it detects an anomaly, it stops the execution of the application, and if possible, it recovers the application and puts it back to run directly on L4 again. In this way, the system can realize the anomaly detection and recovery with near-to-native performance.

6   Evaluation

In this section, we evaluate the performance of Linux running on QEMU on L4. We used LMbench[7] to measure their performance. LMbench is a cross platform benchmark to measure the performance of operating system primitives. We built LMbench for three different architectures; x86, SPARC and ARM.

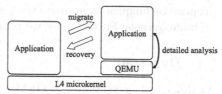

Fig. 5. SPARC, PowerPC, ARM and x86 Linux on the prototype system

Fig. 6. Anomaly detection

Table 1. LMbench measurement result

	x86(Native)	x86	ARM	SPARC
lat_syscall (μsec)	0.2634	3.0967	18.9526	3.0504
lat_ctx (μsec)	0.54	48.10	80.13	83.09
bw_mem rd (MB/s)	9328.49	1051.80	618.39	508.50
bw_mem wr (MB/s)	5509.96	597.21	436.50	379.23
bw_file_rd (MB/s)	1557.27	36.29	45.42	41.47

The measurements were performed on non-virtualized (native) Linux for x86 architecture, virtualized Linux for x86, ARM and SPARC. For non-virtualized and virtualized Linux for x86, we used the same kernel and root filesystem. The machine we used for the measurement is IBM ThinkPad R40, with 1.3GHz CPU and 768MB memory. Dynamic frequency control is disabled for accuracy.

Table 1 shows the result of the measurement. We measured the system call latency, context switch latency, the bandwidth of reading from and writing to the memory, and the bandwidth of reading a file. The first row of the table shows the system call performance. Comparing non-virtualized and virtualized Linux for x86, the performance is decreased by a factor of 11. The second row shows the latency of the context switch. The performance decreased by approximately a factor of 90. The third and forth row show the bandwidth of reading and writing a memory. The throughput decreased by a factor of 10. The memory access speed of programs running on QEMU is the one of the major overhead of QEMU, which we describe in more detail in Section 7.2. The last row shows the bandwidth of reading a file. Comparing non-virtualized and virtualized Linux for x86, the performance is decreased by approximately a factor of 40.

7   Discussion

Running QEMU on L4 realizes the running of multiple operating systems simultaneously on a single hardware, isolation between the guest operating systems with giving them the illusion of using a hardware by itself, and the reuse of operating systems without modification even for the operating system for different architectures. However, as shown in Section 6, the performance of guest operating systems is degraded comparing to native Linux. In this section we propose techniques to improve the performance of dynamic translators running on microkernels. Furthermore we propose future directions of this research.

7.1 Hypercall

As described in Section 4.2, QEMU translates guest codes to host codes with dynamic translation before executing them. The dynamic translation produce two types of overheads, the direct and the indirect. The direct overhead is the processing time of dynamic translation itself. Since every single instruction is translated to corresponding microcodes at the execution time, the execution of a code is significantly delayed. When the guest code is executed again, it is executed without any translation by reusing TB. The indirect overhead derives from the inefficient code contained in TB. Since the guest code is translated to microcode which consists of several host codes, the number of instructions contained in TB is longer than the corresponding original guest code.

In order to reduce these overheads, we propose to implement a *hypercall* by extending an instruction set provided by QEMU. In time of execution an extended instruction is translated to a host instruction which directly calls a QEMU function. For instance, we propose the implementation of efficient device driver for guest operating systems using these extended instructions. We replace the code included in a function exposed by the device driver, say `write()`, with a single extended instruction. When the function is executed, the instruction is translated to a host instruction which directly invokes a function in QEMU which may be a device driver function or RPC stub calling a device server function. In this way, the direct and the indirect overhead of the dynamic translation can be decreased.

7.2 MMU with Map Function

Since many modern processors has MMU, virtual machines and emulators needs to support a function equal to MMU in some fashion.

QEMU provides *software MMU* which emulates MMU only with software function. Software MMU interposes every single memory access done by guest programs running on top of QEMU. When the guest program accesses a memory, software MMU perform a lookup through the page tables constructed by a guest operating system and translates a virtual address to a physical address. Therefore, single memory access expands to multiple memory accesses including the access to page tables. The resulting time for memory access would be factor of ten.

Unlike commodity operating systems, L4 provides APIs to manage address spaces. Using these APIs, an application on L4 can create new address spaces and map memory section into them. We propose the implementation of new virtual MMU which employs L4 APIs. The virtual MMU creates and maps memory regions into the space according to page tables constructed by a guest operating system. A guest program is executed in a separate address space, so it can access memory directly without interposed by software MMU. The implementation should dramatically decrease the overhead of software MMU.

8   Conclusion

In this paper, we proposed the model of running a dynamic translator on a microkernel and implemented the prototype system. We also proposed some sample applications using our model and evaluated the performance.

The model we proposed has a greater flexibility and higher portability than existing VMMs and microkernels. The prototype has shown it by running multiple guest operating systems for different architectures simultaneously on a single hardware. Our model is expected to be useful for the basis for reusing existing operating systems and applications, debugging and a system that requires high degree of security and reliability.

References

1. Barham, P., Dragovic, B., Fraser, K., Hand, S., Harris, T., Ho, A., Neugebauer, R., Pratt, I., Warfield, A.: Xen and the art of virtualization. In: SOSP '03: Proceedings of the nineteenth ACM symposium on Operating systems principles, pp. 164–177. ACM Press, New York (2003)
2. Bellard, F.: QEMU, a fast and portable dynamic translator. In: Proceedings of the USENIX Annual Technical Conference, FREENIX Track (June 2005)
3. Embedded, Real-Time, and Operating Systems. Iguana,
   http://www.ertos.nicta.com.au/software/kenge/iguana-project/latest/
4. Embedded, Real-Time, and Operating Systems. Kenge,
   http://www.ertos.nicta.com.au/software/kenge/
5. Ho, A., Fetterman, M., Clark, C., Warfield, A., Hand, S.: Practical taint-based protection using demand emulation and intel research cambridge. In: Proceedings of the EuroSys 2006, April 18–21 2006, Belgium (2006)
6. Lawton, K.P.: Bochs: A portable pc emulator for unix/x. Linux J., (29), 7 (1996)
7. McVoy, L., Staelin, C.: Lmbench - tools for performance analysis,
   http://www.bitmover.com/lmbench/
8. Sugerman, J., Venkitachalam, G., Lim, B.-H.: Virtualizing I/O devices on VMware workstation's hosted virtual machine monitor. In: Proceedings of the General Track: USENIX Annual Technical Conference, pp. 1–14, Berkeley, CA, USA, 2001. USENIX Association (2002)
9. System Architecture Group. L4Ka:Pistachio microkernel,
   http://l4ka.org/projects/pistachio/

Mesovirtualization: Lightweight Virtualization Technique for Embedded Systems

Megumi Ito and Shuichi Oikawa

Department of Computer Science, University of Tsukuba
1-1-1 Tennodai, Tsukuba, Ibaraki 305-8573, Japan

Abstract. These days, embedded and ubiquitous devices are becoming feature rich, and multiprocessor architectures for those devices are on the horizon. In order to utilize the resources of multiprocessor systems efficiently and securely, virtual machine monitors (VMMs) have been common among servers and desktop systems. The same can be applied if the cost of virtualization becomes much less expensive. In this paper, we introduce *mesovirtualization*, a new lightweight virtualization technique. Mesovirtualization makes VMMs smaller and requires only a few modifications for the guest operating system (OS) source code. We designed and implemented a VMM named Gandalf according to mesovirtualization. Our experimental results show that Linux on Gandalf performs better than Xen-Linux. Therefore, mesovirtualization makes virtualization environments suitable for embedded and ubiquitous devices.

1 Introduction

Expectations for virtualized execution environments to be used in embedded and ubiquitous devices are becoming higher and higher day by day. While the provision of secure and reliable, yet efficient execution environments is a must for those devices, users' desire for using applications of their own choices is rapidly growing. In order to deal with both requirements, safe programming languages, Java for most cases, have been employed. Such a language based solution restricts applicable applications because of its performance limitation.

Servers and desktop systems adopt virtual machine monitors (VMMs) [6] for mostly the same requirements. Figure 1 shows the structure of a VMM with two guest operating systems (OSes). The physical machine underlying the VMM is a host machine. The VMM operates directly on top of the host machine. Guest OSes can use functions of the host machine only via virtual machines (VMs) realized by the VMM. Because the VMM constructs a VM for each guest OS by virtualizing the functions of a host machine, the guest OSes can operate independently for better security and reliability. On the other hand, because there is no intervention needed to execute applications code on a guest OS, the execution performance of applications on the VMM is much better than that of safe programming languages, such as Java.

A major barrier of applying such virtualization to embedded and ubiquitous devices is the limited resources of those devices. Therefore, we propose a new lightweight virtualization technique, *mesovirtualization*, in order to enable virtualization on them. Mesovirtualization does not require a huge VMM as full virtualization and a huge amount

R. Obermaisser et al. (Eds.): SEUS 2007, LNCS 4761, pp. 496–505, 2007.
© IFIP International Federation for Information Processing 2007

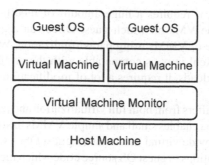

Fig. 1. The Structure of a Virtual Machine Monitor based System

of modifications to the guest OS source code as paravirtualization. Mesovirtualization provides sufficiently virtualized environments for guest OSes with fewer overheads.

This paper describes the design and implementation of a VMM, named Gandalf, which was constructed according to mesovirtualization. It currently operates on x86 processors, and two Linux OSes concurrently run on it as its guest OSes. The code size and memory footprint of Gandalf is much smaller than that of full virtualization. The number of the modified parts and lines shows that the cost to bring up a guest OS on Gandalf is significantly fewer than paravirtualization. Our experimental results show that Linux on Gandalf performs better than XenLinux; thus, Gandalf is an efficient and lightweight VMM that suits resource constraint embedded and ubiquitous devices.

We have done two other studies on Gandalf. First, we applied Gandalf to construct a Linux/RTOS hybrid environment, which enables two OSes, Linux and RTOS, to coexist on Gandalf [10]. Second, we also have an experimental implementation that uses only two protection levels of x86 processors since processor architectures with two protection levels are more common among embedded processors. Those studies also support the high feasibility of Gandalf to be used on embedded and ubiquitous devices. This paper focuses on the rationale of mesovirtualization.

1.1 Related Work

There are two well-known techniques to virtualize a physical environment to support several OSes on the same machine. One technique is full virtualization, and the other is paravirtualization. Each of them has advantages and disadvantages. Full virtualization provides VMs that are identical to a host machine for guest OSes. In this case, guest OSes do not require any modifications because VMMs create VMs which works in the same way as the host machines from guest OSes' point of view. However, in order to virtualize the whole ability of the host machine, VMMs become huge and complicated; thus, the cost to virtualize a physical environment is expensive. IBM VM [2] is one of VMMs using full virtualization. IBM VM implements many of virtualization functions in its proprietary hardware in order to lower the cost of full virtualization.

On the other hand, paravirtualization does not virtualize the whole ability of a host machine, but rather artificially creates VMs which are advantageous to guest OSes for efficiency. VMMs become smaller and simpler; thus, VMs can achieve higher performance. However, it requires a huge amount of modifications to the guest OS source code because the VMs on which guest OSes run are different from the host machine. Xen [1] is one of VMMs using paravirtualization. While the performance of Linux on Xen, called XenLinux, is comparable with the original Linux on a physical machine for some workloads, it requires a lot of modifications to the guest OS source code.

Mesovirtualization differs from both full virtualization and paravirtualization in many ways. Mesovirtualization enables small and simple VMMs to support guest OSes, which makes it possible to provide virtual machines to guest OSes with higher performance. The number of modifications to guest OS source code which mesovirtualization requires is significantly less than paravirtualization. It means that we can use an OS as a guest OS with much few costs.

Pre-virtualization [8] is a new virtualization technique that addresses the cost to bring up an OS on a VMM. It needs much less modifications to a guest OS than paravirtualization, and eases the adoption to a different VMM by having a virtualization module that transforms the standard platform API into the VMM API. Although pre-virtualization shares one of the goals of mesovirtualization, it does not address the code size and memory footprint of a VMM as mesovirtualization does.

The use of virtual machine monitors is not only the way to execute an OS above the processor's most privileged level. Microkernels, such as Mach3 [4] and L4 [5], provides simplified abstractions to run OSes as their applications. More recently, even Linux showed the capability to execute another Linux as its application [3]. The approach of running OSes as applications is close to paravirtualization in terms of the high costs of modifications needed for the guest OS source code.

Partitioning an OS environment into multiple management domains with independent name spaces is also possible. FreeBSD jails [7], Linux VServer, and Solaris containers are the examples. The key difference between those OS partitioning and virtualization is that the OS partitioning has a single kernel shared among multiple domains while virtualization runs multiple kernels, which are not shared. Such sharing of a single kernel makes difficult to maintain predictability required by embedded systems.

1.2   Paper Organization

The rest of this paper is organized as follows. In Section 2 we propose mesovirtualization, a new virtualization technique we introduced to build a lightweight VMM. Section 3 describes the design and implementation of a VMM, named Gandalf, which we built according to mesovirtualization. Section 4 describes the current status of its development, and also shows its evaluation results. Finally, Section 5 concludes the paper.

2   Mesovirtualization

We propose mesovirtualization, a new lightweight virtualization technique to construct a VMM. Mesovirtualization opts to modify a few parts of the guest OS source code in order to enable lightweight configuration of a VMM, but the cost of modifications can be kept as low as possible to make the modifications easily manageable. Therefore, it does not require the complicated work typically needed for full virtualization and paravirtualization. We must configure huge VMMs for full virtualization and modify a huge amount of the guest OS source code for paravirtualization. Mesovirtualization does not require such complicated work, yet it can provide guest OSes with sufficient virtualization environments, in which guest OSes can manage their environments, use processors, memory and devices as if they run on a physical machine.

Mesovirtualization is based on the principle of minimalism. We do not need to virtualize the entire of the host machine to provide identical environments to guest OSes as full virtualization. We do not need to modify many of the guest OS source code to trap into a VMM and to handle it in the VMM as paravirtualization. Mesovirtualization is a technique which supports guest OSes just enough to run it on a VMM. For some parts of the host machine that are considered safe to be dedicated or shared, a VMM does not virtualize these parts and allows guest OSes touch them directly. This rationale keeps a VMM as simple as possible, so that the code size and memory footprint of the VMM small and also the costs of virtualization can be kept cheap; thus, it can be used on embedded and ubiquitous systems, of which computing resources are not as rich as desktop and server systems.

One significant characteristic of mesovirtualization is how a VMM handles sensitive instructions used in guest OSes. While they are emulated by a VMM very much like in full virtualization, only the essentials are emulated. There are some cases that sensitive instructions which are not emulated by a VMM produces unexpected results for a guest OS. Such cases are actually very rare. Rather than having every sensitive instruction changed to trap to a VMM and handled it with hard work, mesovirtualization modifies guest OS source code a little and manages without causing an interrupt to a VMM.

Such a characteristic leads to a lightweight VMM. Because it does not need to virtualize the full ability of the host machine, such a VMM is released from the jobs to spend a number of lines providing exactly the same machine to guest OSes. It also leads to the reduction of VMM's use of processor time, which makes it possible to provide higher performance to guest OSes.

A decrease in the number of modifications of guest OS source code is another characteristic. While it requires just a few modifications concerned to memory management, it does not need to change the most parts, which is required in Xen. Because we modify a few lines of the source code concerned to sensitive instructions rather than change all of them, we can decrease the modifications to the guest OS source code. Such characteristic also reduces the cost to use an OS as a guest OS on a VMM. Although a guest OS must be modified a little before bringing it up on a VMM, the cost of the required modifications is much less than paravirtualization.

3   Design and Implementation

According to mesovirtualization, we designed and implemented a VMM named Gandalf. Gandalf currently operates on x86 processors, and provides virtual machines for

Linux. The next section describes the architectural design of Gandalf, and the following section describes its implementation. The last section shows the modifications we made to the Linux source code.

3.1 Architectural Design

In order to execute guest OSes on a VMM and to make guest OSes not to invade it, it is essential to control the behavior of guest OSes. It can be achieved by combining the following two means. One is to use the ring protection architecture with 4 privilege levels of x86 processors. A VMM can control guest OSes if it has a higher privilege level than guest OSes. The other is the segmentation and paging architecture for memory management. A VMM can manage accesses of guest OSes to memory by setting limitation to the available memory for guest OSes. The VMM decides the physical memory partitions and constructs the first mapping. It also manages the page directory pointer in CR3 register, which implies the base address of the page directory.

An x86 processor employs the ring protection architecture with 4 different privilege levels from Ring 0 to 3. Ring 0 is the most privileged and Ring 3 is the least privileged; thus, guest OSes usually use Ring 0 for kernel and Ring 3 for user processes. In our design, Gandalf uses Ring 0 because it has the strongest privilege in the system so that Gandalf can manage the behavior of guest OSes. Therefore, we changed guest OSes kernel to operate in Ring 1 from Ring 0.

We also modified the segment limit and the privilege level in the segment descriptors of guest OSes, so that the guest OSes do not access the memory for Gandalf and do not use Ring 0 used by Gandalf. Both the segment limit and the privilege level are essential to manage the access to the memory.

Gandalf is in the role of setting up all the memory for itself and guest OSes. It statically partitions the physical memory for itself and guest OSes. It allocates the top most part of the physical memory for itself and the other parts for guest OSes. It changes the start and end addresses of the usable memory for guest OSes to those of the allocated physical memory. Gandalf sets up the first version of the page table using the allocated memory for each OS, and enables paging before booting it. Gandalf maps itself on the top of the virtual memory in every Guest OS's virtual memory space. This first mapping emulates the physical memory; thus, it enables every guest OS starts from the same address as the physical memory. Such provision of the initial mapping reduces the guest OS modifications. In general OSes, they boot with paging disabled and then enable paging during the boot sequence. A guest OS on Gandalf boots with paging enabled in order to make the address of the guest OS look the same as it boots directly on the processor. After guest OSes starts running, they are responsible for the most part of the memory management. Except for setting a new page directory pointer to CR3 register and managing a page fault caused in Gandalf, guest OSes care for the page table.

As far as the memory management is concerned, Gandalf is invoked only to handle general protection faults and page faults after guest OSes starts running. Guest OSes' attempts to execute privileged instructions cause general protection faults, and Gandalf emulates them. There are two cases for page faults. Page faults caused by a guest OS can be handled only by the guest OS; thus, Gandalf simply passes the control back to it. Gandalf handles page faults caused by itself. When guest OSes attempt to set a new page directory pointer to CR3 register of the processor in order to change a page table, a general protection fault is reported because the instructions to write to control registers are privileged instructions. In response to the general protection fault, Gandalf takes control and sets the page directory pointer appropriately.

3.2 Gandalf

Based on the mesovirtualization technique and the architectural design described above, we implemented a VMM named Gandalf. By employing mesovirtualization, Gandalf provides noticeably lightweight virtual environments to guest OSes. As we described in Section 2, Gandalf does not virtualize the entire ability of a host machine. Such a decision decreases the number of the interactions between guest OSes and Gandalf. It enables guest OSes to process most of their jobs without Gandalf's interventions; thus, it leads to the reduction of the virtualization overheads. Since Gandalf targets on a multiprocessor systems, their support is included.

Gandalf first sets up the environment for one guest OS, and builds the environments for the other guest OSes later. It is done during the initialization phase before the first guest OS starts booting. The initialization module has two sub-modules, the setup sub-module and the SMP sub-module. The setup sub-module is executed for every guest OS. On the other hand, the SMP sub-module is executed only once. In the setup sub-module, Gandalf creates an E820 memory map for a guest OS based on the multiboot information, which is a collection of structures containing physical memory map information provided by a boot loader. It changes the start and end addresses of the E820 memory map to the allocated physical memory to the guest OS. The arguments to the guest OS kernel passed from the boot loader are also copied for it. Because the virtual address of the E820 memory map and the arguments used by a guest OS are fixed to static addresses, Gandalf sets up the memory map and the arguments to be placed at the same virtual addresses for every guest OS. Gandalf also relocates each guest OS and its modules to individual memory regions.

In SMP sub-module, Gandalf wakes up the other processors in turn and starts each processor to boot assigned guest OS. In order to wake up the other processors, Gandalf checks the SMP configuration table and sends startup inter-processor interrupts to them.

3.3 Guest OS Modifications

In order to execute guest OSes on Gandalf, we need to modify only a small number of lines of their source code. The cost of such modifications is much less than building a full virtualization VMM or guest OSes' modifications for paravirtualization. The modifications are concerned to three points, the segment descriptor, the judgment of the privilege level, and the memory management. The segment descriptors include the segment limit and the privilege level, which are especially important for Gandalf to manage memory access. The problem on judging the privilege level occurs due to the changes we made in the segment descriptors. There are also some issues in guest OSes memory management because it usually assumes the physical memory is available from the address 0x0.

The first modification is made to the segment descriptors. As we mentioned in Section 3.1, we need to change the value of the segment limit and the privilege level to avoid guest OSes invading Gandalf. We modified the segment limit from `0xffffffff` to `0xfc400000` and the privilege level from 0 to 1 so that guest OSes do not access the Gandalf's memory accidentally or intentionally and interfere with its processing. Either the segment limit or the privilege level in the segment descriptors affects to the management of the memory access.

Secondly, we changed the judging value used to examine the privilege level of the trapped execution in order to decide if it executed in kernel mode or user mode. In order to judge it, guest OSes perform a logical AND operation on the saved privilege level and 3 as shown in the following pseudo code:

```
if (regs->xcs & 3) { /* for user mode */ }
```

In this example, the saved privilege level of the previously executed code segment is stored in `xcs`. The result of the logical AND will be 0 in case the privilege level is 0. In this case the guest OS executed in kernel mode; thus, the code in the braces is not executed. On Gandalf, however, the privilege level of the kernel mode in guest OSes is changed to 1. It changes the result of the logical AND, and leads to taking a wrong action. The result remains to be 0 if the judging value was 2. In order to decide the trapped execution mode correctly, we changed such judging values in guest OSes.

Finally, we modified several parts of the guest OS source code concerned to the physical memory management. We changed the codes in setting up the page table, initializing memory zone sizes, and converting the physical address to/from virtual address. Guest OSes usually assume that the physical memory is available from the address `0x0`, which causes a problem if the memory starts from another address. On Gandalf, every OS except for one are allocated a physical memory region that starts with a different address. In order to deal with this problem, we added a hypercall to guest OSes for the purpose to ask Gandalf the actual start address of the physical memory it allocated. Guest OSes use this address to construct the page table, initialize zone sizes, and convert physical/virtual address.

4   Current Status and Evaluation

In this section, we describe the current status of Gandalf and show its evaluation results. We evaluated the basic cost of modifying a guest OS to boot on Gandalf. We also measured the costs of issuing a null hypercall and processing a privileged instruction, compared with Xen. Finally, we describe the evaluation result using a benchmark.

4.1   Current Status

We implemented Gandalf from scratch on x86 processors and brought up the Linux OS as a guest OS on it. We first used a single processor system for the development, and moved to a dual processor system after the Linux OS on Gandalf started working on a single processor system. Currently, we can have two configurations. One is that a single Linux OS as a guest OS on a single processor system, and the other is that two Linux OSes as guest OSes on a dual processor system.

Table 1. The Costs of Modifications

	Modified parts	Modified lines
Single Linux OS	15 parts	28 lines
Two Linux OSes	28 parts	73 lines

Since a dual processor system configuration has not been matured enough, the quantitative evaluation was performed on a single processor system configuration.

4.2 Qualitative Evaluation

This section presents the cost of modifying the Linux kernel in order to bring it up on Gandalf. The version of the Linux kernel we used is 2.6.12.3. Table 1 shows the number of parts and lines we modified or added to the Linux source code in order to use it as a guest OS. We evaluated the modification cost for two cases. One is when only one Linux OS runs on Gandalf and the other is when two Linux OSes run simultaneously. The former contains the modifications concerned to segment descriptors and the judging value to examine the privilege level. The latter includes the modifications concerned to memory management in addition to the former modifications.

The results show that the cost to modify the Linux source code is obviously very few. Only 28 lines for 15 parts of modifications are enough to run one Linux OS on Gandalf, and it requires no more than 73 lines for 28 parts to modify to execute two Linux OSes simultaneously. In contrast, Xen requires 2995 lines of modifications to use a Linux OS as its guest OS [1], of which cost is more expensive than Gandalf by two orders of magnitude.

Table 1 also shows that the required modifications for the single Linux OS case are fewer than those for the case of two Linux OSes, which includes the changes to deal with different physical memory start address. There can be other OSes, of which kernel architecture allows physical memory starting with various addresses. If we use such an OS as a guest OS, the modifications we added to the parts for memory management in the Linux source code is not required, therefore the cost of modifications will be fewer than the results in Table 1.

Please note that those modifications need to bring up Linux on Gandalf were made at very obvious places in the Linux source code. Although we made those modifications by hand, it should not be too difficult to make necessary modifications semiautomatically.

4.3 Quantitative Evaluation

In this section, we present the quantitative evaluation of Linux on Gandalf. All measurements reported below were performed on the Dell Precision 470 Workstation with Intel Xeon 2.8GHz CPU.[1] Hyper-threading was turned off, so that all measurements were performed on a single CPU.

We first measured the basic performance related to running a guest OS on a VMM. We measured the costs of issuing a hypercall, and processing a privileged instruction.

---

[1] Linux reports this CPU as 2794.774 MHz. We use this number to convert cycle counts obtained from RDTSC instruction to micro seconds for accuracy.

Table 2. Basic Performance Comparisons

	Xen	Gandalf
Null Hypercall	0.43 μ sec	0.37 μ sec
Ignored Privileged Instruction	N/A	0.56 μ sec

Table 2 shows the measurement results obtained from Xen and Gandalf. We used cycle counts obtained from RDTSC instruction for these measurements on both Xen and Gandalf. The all numbers shown were the average costs after repeating 1,000 times. The cost of processing a privileged instruction was measured only for Gandalf since Xen uses only hypercalls to handle requests that are usually handled by privileged instructions.

The results show that the costs of hypercalls on Xen and Gandalf are very similar. Although handling a hypercall on Gandalf is slightly faster, the difference is negligible if we take account of other runtime overheads, which frequently happen during the execution of programs, including cache misses. Since hypercalls use the processor's software interrupt mechanism, there is relatively small room for software implementations to make a difference. It is more interesting that how much processing a privileged instruction takes longer than handling a hypercall. Processing a privileged instruction involves more steps than handling a hypercall. It consists of identifying the instruction address that caused an exception, fetching an instruction from the address, decoding the instruction, and emulating it. The measurement was done with HLT instruction, which is a simple one-byte instruction, and it does not include the emulation cost. In case of processing a longer privileged instruction, it will take longer to decode and fetch an emulating instruction.

Finally, in order to evaluate our mesovirtualization method used for Linux, we ran several programs included in lmbench benchmark suite [9]. Figure 2 (a) and (b) show the results of lmbench programs. We ran the same programs on the original Linux (without virtualization), XenLinux (Dom0), and Gandalf for comparison of performance.

The measurement results show that our mesovirtualization method reduces the runtime costs significantly as a Linux OS on Gandalf outperforms XenLinux in all cases.

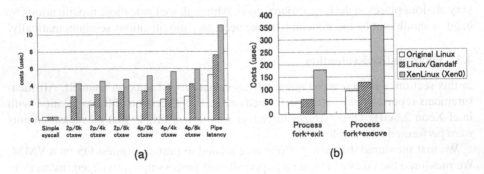

Fig. 2. Linux Performance Comparison

The costs of process fork and exec are even close to the original non-virtualized Linux and significantly better than XenLinux.

5 Conclusion

We introduced mesovirtualization, a new technique that enables lightweight virtualization. It does not require a huge VMM as full virtualization and a huge amount of modifications to the guest OS source code as paravirtualization. Mesovirtualization provides sufficient virtualized environments for guest OSes without complicated work; thus, it makes a whole system more reliable. According to mesovirtualization, we implemented a lightweight VMM, Gandalf. It currently operates on x86 processors and two Linux OSes successfully run on it as guest OSes. The number of the modified parts and lines shows that the cost to modify the Linux source code to bring up Linux OSes on Gandalf is significantly few. The performance evaluations show that the cost for virtualization is also reduced. From the evaluation results, we conclude Gandalf makes virtualization environments suitable for embedded and ubiquitous devices.

References

1. Barham, P., Dragovic, B., Fraser, K., Hand, S., Harris, T., Ho, A., Neugebauer, R., Pratt, I., Warfield, A.: Xen and the Art of Virtualization. In: Proceedings of the 19th ACM Symposium on Operating System Principles, pp. 164–177. ACM Press, New York (2003)
2. Creasy, R.J.: The Origin of the VM/370 Time-Sharing System. IBM Journal of Research and Development 25(5) (1981)
3. Dike, J.: A User-mode Port of the Linux Kernel. In: Proceedings of the 4th Annual Linux Showcase and Conference (October 2000)
4. Golub, D., Dean, R., Forin, A., Rashid, R.: UNIX as an Application Program. In: Proceedings of the USENIX Summer Conference (June 1990)
5. Hartig, H., Hohmuth, M., Liedtke, J., Schonberg, S., Wolter, J.: The Performance of μ-Kernel-Based Systems. In: Proceedings of the 16th ACM Symposium on Operating System Principles, ACM Press, New York (1997)
6. Goldberg, R.P.: Survey of Virtual Machine Research. IEEE Computer (June 1974)
7. Kamp, P., Watson, R.: Jails: Confining the Omnipotent Root. In: Proceedings of the 2nd International System Administration and Networking Conference (May 2000)
8. LeVasseur, J., Uhlig, V., Chapman, M., Chubb, P., Leslie, B., Heiser, G.: Pre-Virtualization: Slashing the Cost of Virtualization. Fakultät für Informatik, Universität Karlsruhe, Technical Report 2005-30 (November 2005)
9. McVoy, L., Staelin, C.: lmbench: Portable Tools for Performance Analysis. In: Proceedings of the USENIX Annual Technical Conference, pp. 279–294 (January 1996)
10. Oikawa, S., Ito, M., Nakajima, T.: Linux/RTOS Hybrid Operating Environment on Gandalf VMM. In: Sha, E., Han, S.-K., Xu, C.-Z., Kim, M.H., Yang, L.T., Xiao, B. (eds.) EUC 2006. LNCS, vol. 4096, pp. 287–296. Springer, Heidelberg (2006)

Building a Customizable User Interface Framework Using Hyperlinks for Smart Devices

Mitsuko Sato, Eigo Okada, and Yukikazu Nakamoto

Graduate School of Applied Informatics, University of Hyogo
1-3-3, Higashi-Kawasaki-cho, Chuou-ku, Kobe 650-0044, Japan
nakamoto@ai.u-hyogo.ac.jp

Abstract. A new customizable user interface for smart devices based on hyperlink associability is presented. Although mobile devices should be easy to use, many current devices have complex and widely varying interfaces. The proposed framework, Hyrax, attempts to improve the menu structure and accessibility of functions while considering user preferences. In Hyrax, the user interface is constructed and customized using hyperlinks for access to application functions. We focus herein on the user interface of a phone and present the customizable menu structure of the phone using XLink defined in W3C and the External Function Interface (EFI) defined in the WAP Forum specifications. To implement the proposed framework, we have developed a design tool to customize the user interface with hyperlinks and a runtime environment, which manages the objects generated by the tool with the hyperlinks, to evaluate the framework.

1 Introduction

Smart devices such as information appliances and mobile devices should be convenient enough to use on a daily basis. However, many products have user interfaces that are difficult to use. For example, with current mobile phones, users are required to navigate a complex menu structure to access even simply functionalities. To overcome this inconvenience, customization mechanisms with greater flexibility are expected to be introduced to allow users to organize functionalities more easily and flexibly according to personal preferences.

Recently more sophisticated mobile phones have the ability to provide user-preferred functionalities. However, the flexibility of such functionalities is limited. Thus, the user interface should be made more customizable and flexible to better handle individual user preferences.

The fixed menu structures of smart devices force users to adapt to the user interface of each device. Mobile phone manufactures often manufacture different types of phones with different menu structures, and users may have difficulty adapting to the different interfaces. Ideally, the menu structure should be the same regardless of how often the user changes phones, that is, the user-preferred menu should be portable. In addition to portability of the menu structure among the same device

R. Obermaisser et al. (Eds.): SEUS 2007, LNCS 4761, pp. 506–515, 2007.

class, portability among different device classes, for example, phone and television, is expected. In this scenario, a user is able to interact with a television in the same menu as a mobile phone according to the user's personal preferences.

In the present paper, the menu structure contains menus for invoking programs as well as menus for calling a function inside the program. In this sense, the menu structure can be used to form an application program framework that determines the structure of applications. Thus, the customizability and flexibility of the menu structure affects the software structure of the device.

Some software vendors utilize XML in implementing phone functions primarily to improve the productivity of phone software [1,2,3,4,5]. Such vendors separate GUI functionalities implemented by XML from phone functionalities. Separating the GUI functionalities gives the following benefits. First, single phone hardware can be utilized for various phones by changing the GUI. Second, the GUI design of the phone can be performed not only by programmers but by web designers as well. Since the number of web designers is larger than the number of programmers, a productivity increase is expected.

In the present study, a customizable user interface framework based on hyperlinks is presented for use with smart devices, particularly smart phones. The proposed user interface framework, Hyrax, attempts to solve the problems of customizability and portability mentioned above. Hyperlinks are widely used throughout the World Wide Web, and can be regarded as a formulation of human associative memory. Thus, hyperlinks are well suited to the improvement of user interface functionality in smart devices. We herein focus on user customizability and framework, which enables customizability by hyperlink structure.

In a previous paper, we described the concept and the design of the hyperlink-based user interface framework [6]. In the present paper, we present design and implementation issues of the hyperlink-based customizable user interface framework.

Section 2 summarizes the requirements for the customizable user interface framework with respect to ease of use. We present a customizable user interface framework to meet these requirements in Sect. 2. To implement the proposed user framework, we have developed a design tool to customize the user interface with the hyperlinks and a runtime environment that manages objects generated by the tool with the hyperlinks. Section 4 and Section 5 present specifications and an evaluation of the design tool and the runtime environment, respectively. Conclusions are presented in Sect. 6.

2   Requirements of a Customizable User Interface Framework in Smart Phones

In the present study, we examine the requirements for a customizable user interface by examining examples of such a customizable menu structure of a smart phone. We can describe the customizability of the user interface as follows:

– To make a menu structure in the smart phone customizable.
– To assign phone functionalities to programmable keys easily and flexibly.

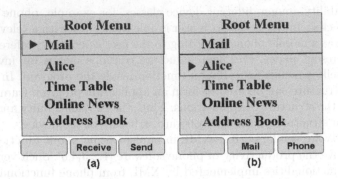

Fig. 1. Example of a customizable user interface

Figure 1 shows an example of a menu structure of a smart phone. The large area is the main screen of the phone, and the two smaller areas are soft keys. The main screen shows the user's preferred menu. We assume that the interface has three programmable keys: two soft keys and one 'select' key, which is used for the default action. The menu shown in Fig. 1(a) is the root menu and contains five items: Mail, Alice, Time Table, Online News, and Address Book. When the first item, Mail, is selected, the programmable keys have two functions: receiving mails of the mail program, which is assigned to the center 'select' key, and change-sending mails, which is assigned to the soft key on the right. Since a user often receives mails, the user assigns this function to one of the programmable 'select' keys on the Mail item in the root menu. This means that the user can initiate the two actions with only one click from the Mail menu. For the user, it is convenient to issue commands with one click, without having to navigate through multiple menus. In Fig. 1, the item 'Alice' appears because the user communicates with Alice frequently. Since the user communicates with Alice mainly by mail, the 'Mail' operation is assigned to the select key (Fig. 1(b)). Since the user also frequently accesses a timetable, an online news service, and an address book, the items Time Table, Online News, and Address Book appear in the root menu.

The framework for the above described customizable menu structure, or user interface, has the following requirements:

F1: Flexible structure and linking between menu items

An item that the user clicks is a functional item or a data item. Clicking a functional item invokes a function, and clicking a data item specifies either actual data or a directory to the data. A menu may contain both functional items and data items. In the example menu shown in Fig. 1(a), Mail is a functional item that invokes the mail function and Alice, Time Table, Online News, and Address Book are data items, each of which has links to the related information.

F2: Enabling multiple operations from one item

A single menu item may have multiple operations. The example menu shown in Fig. 1(a) indicates that when a user chooses to execute Mail program or

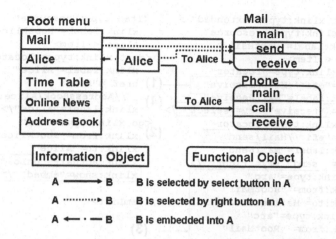

Fig. 2. Object structure for Fig. 1

send a mail to the 'team mate', the user wants to perform the operation by a single click. Moreover, multiple operation functionality for a single item is preferable because the display size of smart devices, particularly smart phones, is limited.

F3: Enabling a customizable menu structure in the usage time

It is preferable for the user to be able to customize the user interface of the smart phone while using the phone. It is because access frequencies to menu items of functional objects and information items in information objects changes in the usage time.

3   Hyperlink-Based Customizable User Interface Framework

In Hyrax, menus are linked by hyperlinks and users select functions by traversing the hyperlink. The menu structure in the user interface functions is constructed in the form of an object structure linking functional and information objects as follows.

Functional objects: Functional objects are program entities that correspond to expected functions and are implemented by sets of functions or methods.
Information objects: Information objects include menu items and links to other information objects or functional objects and are implemented in extensible markup language (XML).

Requirement **F1** is satisfied by implementing an object structure. An object structure provides menu structure for application programs and enables a consistent and unified user interface for the programs. Figure 2 shows an object

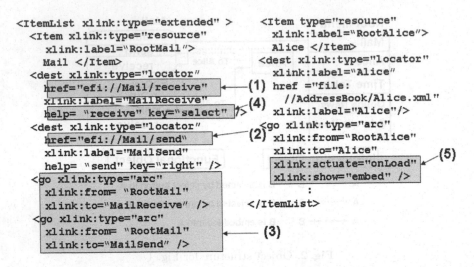

```
<ItemList xlink:type="extended" >          <Item type="resource"
  <Item xlink:type="resource"                xlink:label="RootAlice">
     xlink:label="RootMail">                 Alice </Item>
     Mail </Item>                          <dest xlink:type="locator"
  <dest xlink:type="locator"                 xlink:label="Alice"
     href="efi://Mail/receive"      ←(1)     href ="file:
     xlink:label="MailReceive"        (4)       //AddressBook/Alice.xml"
     help= "receive" key="select" />        xlink:label="Alice"/>
  <dest xlink:type="locator"                <go xlink:type="arc"
     href="efi://Mail/send"      ←(2)         xlink:from="RootAlice"
     xlink:label="MailSend"                   xlink:to="Alice"
     help= "send" key="right" />              xlink:actuate="onLoad"     (5)
  <go xlink:type="arc"                        xlink:show="embed" />
     xlink:from= "RootMail"                            :
     xlink:to="MailReceive" />
  <go xlink:type="arc"                      </ItemList>
     xlink:from= "RootMail"
     xlink:to="MailSend" />         ← (3)
```

Fig. 3. XLink description for Fig. 2

structure to realize menus in the user interface shown in Fig. 1. The information object of the root menu contains four items: Mail, Alice, Time Table, Online News, and Address Book. Operations assigned to soft keys, or selection operations for items, are represented as links between objects in an object structure. The first item, Mail, has two ending objects, which correspond to the two operations 'receive' and 'send' mail functions. The Alice information object has two links to Send Mail and Phone Call and is embedded in the root menu. An embedded object is displayed simultaneously when an object that has a link to the embedded object, the root menu in this case, is displayed.

Figure 3 shows a description of the hyperlink structure in Fig. 2. Links between objects are implemented using XLink [7] because XLink has strong and flexible link mechanisms. The itemList tag denotes a functional or an information object, and the item tag denotes an item contained in the object. The dest tag denotes a remote object that is linked to an object defined by an item tag. An object defined in an item tag or a dest tag has labels with the xlink:label attribute[1] In the arc definition xlink:type="arc" in the go tag of (3), the xlink:from and xlink:to attributes have labels of the starting object and the ending object, respectively. The arc definition specifies a link from the starting object to the ending object.

Function invocation: A link is defined between a menu item and a function invoked from that item and is implemented using the External Functionality Interface (EFI) scheme [8]. In the EFI, a program can access functionalities inside a device through the uniform resource identifier (URI) naming scheme.

---

[1] In this paper, an attribute in the XLink namespace has the xlink: prefix, e.g. xlink:type.

Multiple links between objects: As shown in Fig. 2, the Mail item has multiple links to remote objects. Multiple links enable Requirement **F2** to be satisfied. To implement a multiple-link object, we utilize an *extended* link in XLink. The extended link enables a link that associates an arbitrary number of linked objects. A multiple link is described as follows. Starting and ending objects are declared with the `xlink:type="locator"` and the `xlink:label` attribute. Multiple tags with `arc` values define links between the starting objects and the ending objects. For example, there are two go tags in (3) as multiple links. One is a link to invoke the main service in the mail server, and the other is a link to invoke the Send Mail service in the mail server with Team Mate parameter. Multiple arc definitions realize multiple links in the object structure.

Next, we consider how to deal with multiple implementation-dependent links. In Hyrax, we introduce `key` and `help` attributes for (4) in Fig. 3 to denote a key that is assigned to a link object and a string, shown at the bottom of the main screen to display its functionality.

- `key` attribute: A `key` attribute specifies a programmable key when the linked object is traversed. The value of the attribute is "left", "select," or "right," which denotes the left-hand soft key, the 'select' key of the pointing device, and the right-hand soft key, respectively.
- `help` attribute: A `help` attribute must be used with a `key` attribute. The value of the attribute is displayed at the soft key display area at the bottom of the phone screen to indicate the meaning of the programmable key.

4   User Interface Design Tool: Hyrax Builder

We have developed the Hyrax Builder to design and customize the user interface in a smart phone. The builder manages an object structure and reconfigures the structure by changing the links between functional objects and information objects manually on a PC, according to the preferences of the user. The builder generates object descriptions in the XML format from the object structure with hyperlinks. The main display of the builder is shown in Fig. 4 and contains the following panes:

Main pane (1): The main pane shows an image of the menu of the smart phone. We provide two types of menu layouts: a list layout and a picture layout. The two layouts can be exchanged with the layout change item in the menu. The main pane in Fig. 4 shows the picture layout.

Programmable key pane (2): Help messages for the three programmable keys are displayed in the programmable pane.

Operation pane (3): The user can change the order or location of an item in the main pane using the operation pane.

Object selection pane (4): The user can select an object description file, which represents an information object and a functional object, to appear in the main pane.

Item pane (5): An object description file selected in the object selection pane may contain several items. In an object pane, a list of the items is shown.

(1)

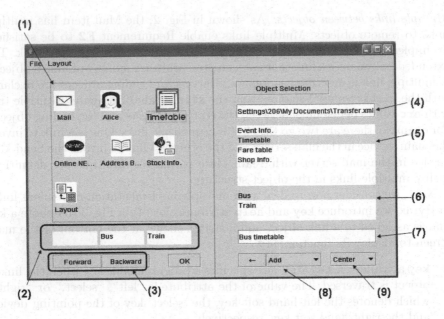

Fig. 4. Hyrax Builder

Destination pane (6): Destinations linked from the item selected in the item pane are shown in the destination pane. The destination includes the items linked from an information object and the provided method names contained in a functional object.

Parameter pane (7): In this pane, the parameters needed for a method invocation are specified.

Set buttons (8) and (9): An item selected in the item pane is set to the selected programmable key in pane (2) with the parameters specified in pane (7).

5   Hyrax Runtime Environment

5.1   Functionalities

The Hyrax runtime environment provides the program execution environment and the framework for a customizable user interface on a target machine. The Hyrax runtime environment loads the object description files and provides such a user interface. Figure 5 shows the runtime environment of Hyrax, which includes a micro browser, a builder, and an execution environment.

Browser: The browser loads the object descriptions generated by the builder and provides functionalities such as XML browsing and XML document management libraries, the application programming interface (API) of which invokes the XML parser and builds the data structure representing the XML

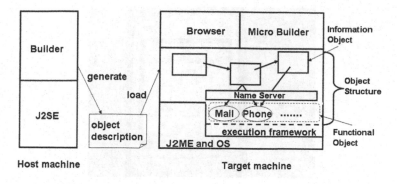

Fig. 5. Architecture of Builder and Hyrax runtime environment

document. The browser handles the manipulation and invocation of objects in the object structure.

Micro Builder: The Micro Builder is a runtime subset version of the Hyrax Builder and manages an object structure and reconfigures the structure by changing the links between functional objects and information objects manually or automatically, according to the preference of the user while using the phone. As an example of automatic reconfiguration, if an object is accessed frequently for communication, the object may be moved closer to an entry object for easier access. The micro builder is required to satisfy Requirement **F3**.

Hyrax Execution Framework: In Hyrax, a functional object has the following requirements. First, a functional object should have a main method that starts the execution of a program. Other methods can be exported from the functional object (from the Server in EFI terminology) and used in the specific service in the EFI scheme.

5.2 Implementation and Evaluation

We have implemented the Hyrax runtime environment, with the exception of the micro builder, in the Java programming language on a PC emulator, which is contained in the J2ME Wireless Toolkit provided by Sun Microsystems, and a smart phone Nokia 6680 as a target machine. The Java runtime environments of both are CLDC 1.0 and MIDP 2.0 [9]. The parser is based on kXML2 (version 2.2.2)[2]. Photographs of a sample program on the Hyrax runtime environment on the target machine are shown in Fig. 6.

In order to evaluate the Hyrax user interface framework in terms of overhead, we develop a program that shows menus and invokes programs directly without the XML document, which is called a direct implementation version. We have measured two response times: the first display time and the redisplay time of the Hyrax browser and the direct implementation version.

---

[2] http://kxml.sourceforge.net/kxml2/

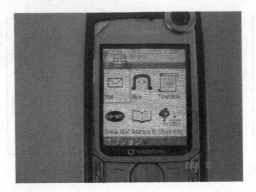

Fig. 6. Picture of sample user interface of Hyrax on a smart phone

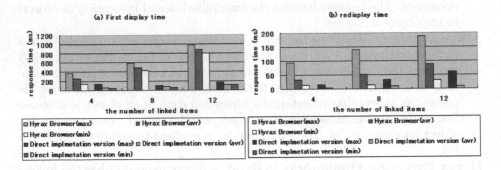

Fig. 7. Evaluation of the display time

First display time : the period of time starting from when the object description of a menu in the memory has been processed and ending when the menu is initially displayed. The result is shown in Fig. 7(a) [3] . The display time and the increasing ratio of the display time in the Hyrax browser are larger than those in the direct implementation version. This is because the browser parses the object description by kXML parser, and links to objects from the menu items, and places the items into the form during the time.

Redisplay time: the period of time for redisplaying the display using the generated form. The result is shown in Fig. 7(b). The redisplay time and the increasing ratio of the response time in the Hyrax browser are also larger because a form in the Hyrax browser has more information. This amount of time is not considered to be lengthy in ordinary usage.

---

[3] In the current implementation, in order to avoid asking for user permission each file access, the browser loads all of the object description into memory. However, this implementation results in larger memory consumption at the start-up time. In order to reduce the memory consumption, we can modify the Hyrax browser, which reads object description files on-demand. The additional file access overhead are 176, 270, and 325 ms for 4, 8 and 12 items, respectively.

Since the Hyrax browser caches a form generated in the first display time and displays in the redisplay time, the menu display time in actual usage becomes the average of the first display time and the redisplay time.

6   Conclusions and Remarks

Hyrax is a hyperlink-based customizable user interface framework for smart devices. The architecture and implementation of Hyrax were presented in the present paper. The user interface realized by Hyrax is readily customizable according to user preferences. We have developed a design tool to customize the user interface with hyperlinks and a runtime environment that manages objects generated by the tool with hyperlinks, and evaluated the framework. We have demonstrated that the features of XLink in W3C and EFI in WAP enable user customization.

In the future, we will examine the customization pattern of the user interface using the builder. Based on this result, we will be able to prepare a template to customize the user interface more easily. Moreover, we should implement the micro builder and evaluate the usability of the customizability.

References

1. Access: Netfront Dynamic Menu (2005) http://www.access-sys-eu.com/fileadmin/user_upload/PDF_documentation ASE_NFDM_2005-02-24.pdf
2. Microsoft: (Windows Automotive 5.0 Datasheet)
   http://www.microsoft.com/windows/embedded/windowsautomotive/about.mspx
3. Qualcomm: (uiOne) http://brew.qualcomm.com/brew/en/about/uione.html
4. UIEvolution (UIEngine), http://www.uievolution.com/products/uiengine.html
5. Acrodea (VIVID UI), http://www.acrodea.co.jp/en/product_vividui.html
6. Nakamoto, Y., Sato, M.: Design of A Hyperlink-based Software Architecture for Smart Devices. In: Proc. 9th IEEE International Symposium on Object and component-oriented Real-time distributed Computing, pp. 261–268. IEEE Computer Society Press, Los Alamitos (2006)
7. W3C: XML Linking Language (XLink) Version 1.0 (2001)
8. Open Mobile Alliance: External Functionality Interface Framework, Candidate Version 1.1 9-Jun-2004 (2004)
9. Riggs, R., Taivalsaari, A., Huopaniemi, J., Patel, M., VanPeursem, J., Uotila, A.: Programming Wireless Devices with the Java2 Platform, Micro Edition, 2nd edn. Addison-Wesley, Reading (2003)

An Efficient Location Index for the Semantic Search of Moving Objects

Dong-Oh Kim, Jung-Su Shin, Hong-Koo Kang, and Ki-Joon Han

School of Computer Science & Engineering, Konkuk University,
1, Hwayang-Dong, Gwangjin-Gu, Seoul 143-701, Korea
{dokim, jssinn, hkkang, kjhan}@db.konkuk.ac.kr

Abstract. In moving object databases, researches on the spatio-temporal access method are very important for the efficient search of moving object location in ITS, LBS, and Telematics. Recently, researches are being made actively on the efficient management of the current location of moving objects and on the estimation of future location using information such as the current location and moving pattern of moving objects. In this paper, we propose Map-Based R-tree(MBR-tree), which is a new current location index structure for indexing the current location of moving objects in an urban area, a 2-dimentional space. MBR-tree is an index which forms the MBR(Minimum Bounding Rectangle) of R-tree nodes using static objects(or fixed objects) on the map. Because moving objects generally moves within a static object, if the MBR is formed using static objects, we can reduce the cost of updating the index of the current location of moving objects. In addition, it shows superior performance in semantic search that searches in a specific building or place (e.g. "Who are in Konkuk university?") rather than in an arbitrary area. Finally, to test the index proposed in this paper, we compared its performance with that of hashing technique and Lazy Update R-tree using various datasets and proved the superiority of its performance.

Keywords: Location Index, Semantic Search, Moving Object, MBR, MBR-tree.

1 Introduction

With the development of location positioning systems such as GPS(Global Positioning System), application systems using the location of moving objects are widely used including ITS(Intelligent Transportation System), LBS(Location Based Service) and Telematics. In addition, a moving object database has emerged to manage the location of moving objects efficiently in application systems. In particular, researches are being made actively on the spatio-temporal access method for the efficient search of moving object location[2,4].

In general, spatio-temporal access methods are divided into past location index, current location index and future location index according to the type of query. Recently, hashing technique[6], Lazy Update R-tree(LUR-tree)[1], etc. have been

R. Obermaisser et al. (Eds.): SEUS 2007, LNCS 4761, pp. 516–526, 2007.
© IFIP International Federation for Information Processing 2007

proposed for the efficient management of the current location of moving objects. However, hashing technique, though its update cost is low, has low search performance due to node chaining that takes place on overflow. LUR-tree improves the update performance of R-tree, which is superior in the search performance, but still has high update load from node reconstruction.

Thus, we propose Map-Based R-tree(MBR-tree), which is a new current location indexing technique for indexing the current location of moving objects(e.g. persons) in an urban area, a 2-dimensional space. MBR-tree is an index that forms the MBR(Minimal Bounding Rectangle) of R-tree[3] nodes using static objects(e.g. buildings) on the map. Because moving objects generally move within a static object, if the MBR is formed using static objects, we can reduce the cost of index update for the current location of moving objects.

In addition, MBR-tree shows superior performance in semantic search that searches in a specific building or place(e.g. "Who are in Konkuk University?") rather than in an arbitrary area. Lastly, to test the index proposed in this paper, we compare its performance with that of hashing technique and LUR-tree using various datasets[7]. According to the results, MBR-tree is superior in the search and update performance and particularly excellent in semantic search.

The structure of this paper is as follows. Chapter 2 reviews related works, examining hashing technique and LUR-tree as well as semantic search. Chapter 3 explains MBR-tree in detail, and Chapter 4 analyzes the results of performance evaluation using various datasets. Finally, Chapter 5 draws conclusions.

2 Related Works

This chapter reviews hashing technique and LUR-tree, whose performance will be compared with that of MBR-tree. In addition, it examines semantic search.

2.1 Hashing Technique

In order to reduce the cost of update, hashing technique uses a location pre-processing module that plays the role of a filter between a database and moving objects reporting their locations[6]. The location pre-processing module synchronizes its own hashing function with the hashing function used in the database and stores the location of moving objects into the database using bucket information obtained by entering the location of moving objects into the hashing function. When moving object location is updated, if new bucket information obtained using the hashing function is the same as existing bucket information, the new information is not reported to the database but is recorded only in the location pre-processing module.

Hashing functions used in hashing technique are composed of an overlap-free space partition function that removes redundant hashing nodes while maintaining constant the number of moving objects managed in the bucket, an augmented space partition function that allows the overlapping of hashing nodes and expands hash nodes to the specified size, a quad-tree hashing function that utilizes quad-tree division to resolve the uneven distribution of moving objects, etc.

Hashing technique improves the scalability and the performance of update because it is possible to do distributed processing of moving objects using multiple location pre-processing modules, but if the number of moving objects managed in a bucket is large, the search performance is lowered due to node chaining on overflow.

2.2 LUR-Tree

LUR-tree is an index that can reduce update cost by improving an update algorithm and, as a result, reducing the number of times of index reconstruction in R-tree[1]. LUR-tree is composed of R-tree for indexing the current location of moving objects and Direct Link for direct reference to leaf nodes of the index where moving objects are stored. Direct Link, which is an auxiliary index that uses the ID of moving objects as the key, refers to the leaf node in R-tree where the moving object of the corresponding ID is stored. Therefore, it effectively reduces the cost of tree search caused by update of R-tree.

In addition, LUR-tree reduces the cost of updating moving objects that travel zigzag using the extended MBR, which extended the MBR value of index nodes. When updating the location of a moving object, LUR-tree can directly refer to the index node containing the corresponding object using Direct Link. Thus, if the new location of the moving object is in the extended MBR of the current extended node, R-tree is not reconstructed and only information in the node is changed and, in this way, the cost of update can be reduced. LUR-tree has lower update cost than R-tree but its search performance is lowered by node redundancy and its update load increases due to node reconstruction.

2.3 Semantic Search

A semantic space can correspond to a physical space expressed with one or more coordinates, and the expression of the semantic space is easily understandable to users. That is, it has a logical name like "Konkuk University" or "National Road No. 13" corresponding to a physical space expressed with coordinates like "15,13,18,17". The semantic space is often used as a search keyword in the database[5]. Figure 1 shows examples of correspondence between physical spaces and semantic spaces.

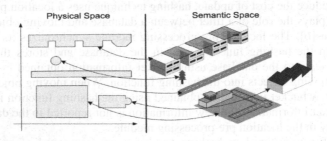

Fig. 1. Correspondence between Physical Spaces and Semantic Spaces

Semantic search is generally used to execute a query which contains semantic spaces in the query condition. Examples of query for semantic search are "Who are in Konkuk University?", "What cars are on the road where car K is running?", "Who are passing by Konkuk University?", etc.

3 MBR-Tree

This chapter explains motivation for MBR-tree proposed in this paper as well as its index structure and data structure. Lastly, it examines the insert, update, delete, and search algorithms of MBR-tree in detail.

3.1 Motivation

Real moving objects do not move in a free space as in Figure 2(a) but their movement is restricted by surrounding environments as in Figure 2(b). That is, the movement of a moving object is restricted by buildings and roads on the map. Thus, if the MBR of nodes in R-tree is formed with the MBR of static objects on the map, the index on the location of moving objects is not updated in case the moving object moves within a static object.

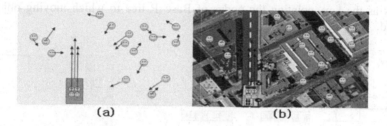

Fig. 2. Movement of Moving Objects

Figure 3 shows differences in insert and update between R-tree and MBR-tree. Figure 3(b) shows the result of inserting O_1 to R-tree in Figure 3(a). In Figure 3(b), R_1 is expanded to minimize the MBR of the node to which O_1 was inserted. Figure 3(f) shows the result of creating the MBR in MBR-tree with static objects in Figure 3(e) and inserting O_1. Because the MBR is fixed in MBR-tree, the index is not reconstructed.

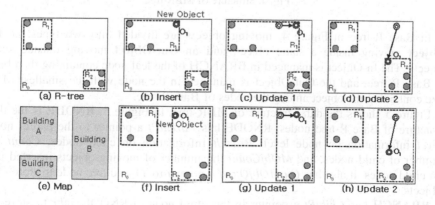

Fig. 3. Insert and Update in R-tree and MBR-tree

In the same way, R-tree is reconstructed as location is updated as in Figure 3(c) and Figure 3(d), but only the location of O_1 is updated in MBR-tree without changing the information of R_2 when updating the location of O_1 within a static object as in Figure 3(g) and Figure 3(h) and, by doing so, it can reduce the cost of update. In addition, because the MBR that manages moving objects uses static objects that have semantic spaces, MBR-tree can be more efficient in semantic search than R-tree.

3.2 Structure of MBR-Tree

Figure 4 shows the overall structure of MBR-tree. MBR-tree is composed of **Base R-tree** and **Quad-tree**. Base R-tree is an index constructing the nodes of R-tree using the MBR of static objects on the map. Quad-tree is an index, connected to Base R-tree, to store the ID and location of moving objects, enabling efficient search even when a leaf node in Base R-tree manages a large number of moving objects. The **Secondary Index** is an auxiliary index for high-speed update using the ID of moving objects as the key, pointing the nodes of Base R-tree to which moving objects are inserted.

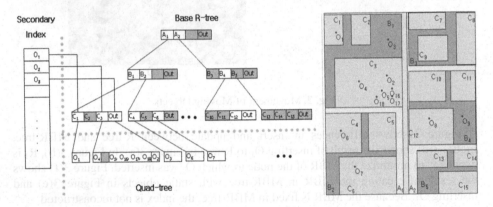

Fig. 4. Structure of MBR-tree

In Base R-tree in Figure 4, moving objects are divided into two types: an **In-Object** moving inside a static object, and an **Out-Object** moving outside static objects. The In-Object is managed in BRANCH of the leaf node containing the object in Base R-tree, and the Out-Object is managed in the node with the smallest MBR size containing the object among the nodes of Base R-tree.

Figure 5 shows the data structure of MBR-tree. In Figure 5, **RNODE** is the data structure of Base R-tree nodes. RNODE has *ParentPt* a pointer to the parent node, *Level* information on node level, *Branch* information on child nodes, *Count* the number of child nodes, and *MObjCount* the number of moving objects inserted into the child nodes. It also has *OutMObjQuad* a pointer to a Quad-tree node to store Out-Objects.

BRANCH has *ChildPt* a pointer to the child node of RNODE, *mbr* to store the MBR of child nodes, and *InMObjQuad* a pointer to a Quad-tree node to store In-Objects. **QUADNODE**, which is the data structure of Quad-tree nodes, has *Count* the number of moving objects stored, *MObj* a pointer to the first moving object, and *ChildPt* a pointer to the child node of Quad-tree. **MOBJECT**, which is the data structure to store information on moving objects, has *Oid* the ID of the object, *Loc* location information, and *NextPt* a pointer to the next moving object.

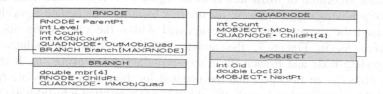

Fig. 5. Data Structure of MBR-tree

3.3 Algorithms

This section examines the insert, update, delete, and search algorithms of MBR-tree in detail.

3.3.1 Insert Algorithm

The insert algorithm of MBR-tree is as in Figure 6. It is executed with input *oid* the ID of a moving object and *loc* the location of the object.

Algorithm : Insert (*oid, loc*)	Algorithm : Update (*oid, new_loc*)
begin	begin
1: [*RNodePt, BranchID*] ← Find_InNode (*loc*)	1: Find [*RNodePt, BranchID*] with *oid* in Secondary Index
2: if (*RNodePt* is not NULL) //Moving Object is In-Object	2: if (*BranchID* is not NULL) // Moving Object is In-Object
3: Insert [*oid, loc*] into *RNodePt.Branch[BranchID].InMObjQuad*	3: if(*RNodePt.Branch[BranchID].mbr* Contained *new_loc*)
4: Insert [*oid, loc, RNodePt, BranchID*] into Secondary Index	4: Update *new_loc* in *RNodePt.Branch[BranchID].InMObjQuad*
else //Moving Object is Out-Object	5: Update *new_loc* in Secondary Index
5: *RNodePt* ← Find_OutNode (*loc*)	else
6: Insert [*oid, loc*] into *RNodePt.OutMObjQuad*	6: Delete (*oid*)
7: Insert [*oid, loc, RNodePt, BranchID*] into Secondary Index	7: Insert (*oid, new_loc*)
end if	end if
8: while (*RNodePt.ParentPt* is not NULL)	else // Moving Object is Out-Object
9: *RNodePt.MObjCount* ++	8: Delete (*oid*)
10: *RNodePt* ← *RNodePt.ParentPt*	9: Insert (*oid, new_loc*)
end while	end if
end	end

Fig. 6. Insert Algorithm   **Fig. 7.** Update Algorithm

The insert algorithm inserts a moving object, distinguishing it between In-Object and Out-Object. As in Figure 6, if the input moving object is an In-Object, the algorithm finds the leaf node in Base R-tree containing *loc* using Find_InNode(loc) function and inserts the moving object into the InMObjQuad of the corresponding branch. If the moving object is an Out-Object, it finds the node with the smallest MBR among Base R-tree nodes containing *loc* using Find_OutNode(loc) function and inserts the moving object into OutMObjQuad. After insertion, it increases MObjCount by 1 from the root node to the node to which the object has been inserted.

3.3.2 Update Algorithm

The update algorithm of MBR-tree is as in Figure 7. It is executed with input *oid* the ID of a moving object and *new_loc* the new location. The update algorithm does not reinsert the moving object to be updated within the same static object into MBR-tree. As in Figure 7, the update algorithm finds the pointer to the corresponding node and Branch ID in the secondary index using *oid*. If the input moving object is an In-Object and the updated location does not deviate from the MBR of the corresponding branch, the object is not reinserted into InMObjQuad but only the location information of the moving object is updated. However, if it deviates from the MBR, the moving object is reinserted. If the input object is an Out-Object, it is reinserted into MBR-tree.

3.3.3 Delete Algorithm

The delete algorithm of MBR-tree is as in Figure 8. It is executed with input *oid* the ID of a moving object.

Algorithm : Delete (*oid*)
begin
1:   Find [*RNodePt*, *BranchID*] with *oid* in Secondary Index
2:   If (*BranchID* is not NULL) // Moving Object is In-Object
3:      Delete In-Object with *oid* in *RNodePt.Branch[BranchID].InMObjQuad*
else // Moving Object is Out-Object
4:      Delete Out-Object with *oid* in *RNodePt.OutMObjQuad*
end if
6:   Delete Moving Object with *oid* in Secondary Index
7:   while (*RNodePt.ParentPt* is not NULL)
8:      *RNodePt.MObjCount* --
9:      *RNodePt ← RNodePt.ParentPt*
end while
end

Algorithm : Search_Window (*RNodePt*, *Rectangle*)
begin
1:   If (*RNodePt.OutMObjQuad* is not Null)
2:      Find Moving Object that inside *Rectangle* in *RNodePt.OutMObjQuad*
end if
3:   If (*RNodePt.Level* is ZERO) // Leaf Node of RNODE
4:   for each *RNodePt.Branch* in *RNodePt*
5:      If (*RNodePt.Branch.mbr* intersects *Rectangle*)
6:         Find Moving Object that inside *Rectangle* in *RNodePt.Branch.InMObjQuad*
end if
end for
else // Internal Node of RNODE
7:   for each *RNodePt.Branch* in *RNodePt*
8:      If (*RNodePt.Branch.mbr* intersects *Rectangle* & *RNodePt.MObjCount* is not ZERO)
9:         Search_Window (*RNodePt.Branch.ChildPt*, *Rectangle*)
end if
end for
end if
end

Fig. 8. Delete Algorithm   **Fig. 9.** Search Algorithm

The delete algorithm accesses the corresponding node using the secondary index and deletes the moving object. As in Figure 8, the delete algorithm finds the pointer to the corresponding node and Branch ID in the secondary index using *oid*. If the moving object is an In-Object, it is deleted from InMObjQuad of the corresponding branch, and if it is an Out-Object, it is deleted from OutMObjQuad of the corresponding node. After deletion, it decreases MObjCount by 1 from the node from which the object has been deleted to the root node.

3.3.4 Search Algorithm

The search algorithm of MBR-tree is as in Figure 9. It is executed with input *RNodePt* a node pointer in Base R-tree and *Rectangle* a window range. The search algorithm retrieves all moving objects included in *Rectangle* among nodes managing moving objects. As in Figure 9, the search algorithm retrieves Out-Object included in *Rectangle* if there are moving objects in OutMObjQuad of input *RNodePt*. Next, it checks if the current node is a leaf node and, if it is, the algorithm retrieves moving objects included in *Rectangle* among In-Objects stored in MObjQuad of the branches. If the current node is not a leaf node, it checks if there are moving objects in its child nodes, and the search algorithm is executed recursively for child nodes.

4 Performance Evaluation

This chapter compares MBR-tree with LUR-tree and hashing technique through evaluating their performance. Performance evaluation was made by comparing update performance, window query performance and semantic search performance in terms of time and memory usage.

4.1 Experiment Environment

Performance evaluation was made using a PC with Intel Pentium4 2.53GHz CPU and 1GB memory. Data used in performance evaluation was generated from City Simulator and GSTD. Figure 10(a) shows the map used in City Simulator and data generated from it, and Figure 10(b) shows data generated from GSTD.

(a) City Simulator   (b) GSTD

Fig. 10. Data Generated from City Simulator and GSTD

In performance evaluation, we used hashing with 144 buckets (12X12) and hashing with 324 buckets (18X18) to compare with MBR-tree. The number of buckets in hashing (12X12) is similar to the number of leaf nodes in MBR-tree.

4.2 Update Performance Evaluation

Update performance evaluation uses trajectory data in which 1000/3000/5000 moving objects move 300 times as generated from City Simulator and GSTD. Figure 11 shows graphs that compare the index update performance according to the number of moving objects.

The results of performance evaluation show that MBR-tree is much superior to LUR-tree in the update performance and not much inferior to hashing, which generally has high update performance.

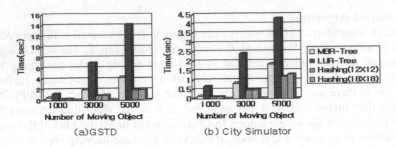

Fig. 11. Update Performance

4.3 Query Performance Evaluation

Query performance evaluation was made using the data of 50,000 moving objects generated from City Simulator and GSTD.

4.3.1 Window Query Performance Evaluation

Figure 12 shows graphs that compare the window query performance according to window size.

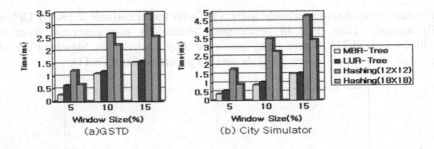

Fig. 12. Window Query Performance

The results of performance evaluation show that the window query performance of MBR-tree is 2.1 times higher than that of hashing on the average and higher than that of LUR-tree based on R-tree, which generally has high window query performance.

4.3.2 Semantic Search Performance Evaluation

Figure 13 is a graph that compares the semantic search performance.

The results of performance evaluation show that the semantic search performance of MBR-tree is 2.1 times higher than that of LUR-tree and 3.4 times higher than that of hashing on the average.

4.4 Memory Usage

Because memory usage is closely related to the number of moving objects regardless of the type of dataset, we use data of 1000/3000/5000 moving objects generated from

GSTD. Figure 14 is a graph that compares the size of memory usage according to the number of moving objects.

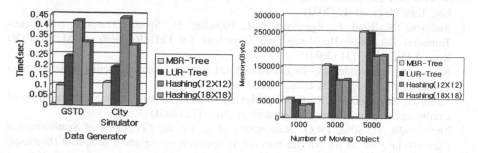

Fig. 13. Semantic Search Performance   Fig. 14. Memory Usage

In the comparison of memory usage, MBR-tree shows a slight difference from LUR-tree in memory usage but uses 1.4 times larger memory space than hashing, which generally uses a small size of memory.

5 Conclusions

This paper proposed MBR-tree that can index location data of moving objects by forming R-tree nodes using the MBR of static objects on the map. MBR-tree reduced update cost and improved the semantic search performance by managing moving objects in the unit of static object.

In the results of performance experiment, hashing showed advantage in memory usage and update speed but was much inferior in the search performance, and LUR-tree showed advantage in the search performance but its update cost was high. MBR-tree reduced update cost effectively compared to LUR-tree while guaranteeing search speed higher than hashing. Particularly in semantic search, MBR-tree showed much higher performance than all the other methods. Accordingly, MBR-tree can have high utility in the environment where search transactions are as important as update transactions and where high semantic search performance is required.

Acknowledgements

This research was supported by the Seoul Metropolitan Government, Korea, under the Seoul R&BD Program supervised by the Seoul Development Institute.

References

1. Kwon, D.S., Lee, S.J., Lee, S.H.: Indexing the Current Positions of Moving Objects Using the Lazy Update R-tree. In: Proc. of the Third International Conference on Mobile Data Management, pp. 113–120 (2002)

2. Inam, O., Matin, A.: A Survey of Indexing Techniques for Moving Object Trajectories. Technical Report, University of Waterloo (2003)
3. Mokbel, M.F., Ghanem, T.M., Aref, W.G.: Spatio-Temporal Access Methods. IEEE Data Eng. Bull. 26(2), 40–49 (2003)
4. Roddick, J.F., Hoel, E., Egenhofer, M.J., Papadias, D.: Spatial, Temporal and Spatio-Temporal Databases: Hot Issues and Directions for PhD Research. ACM SIGMOD Record 33(2), 126–131 (2004)
5. Roth, J.: Novel Architectures for Location-Based Services. Annual Meeting for Information Technology & Computer Science, 5–8 (2004)
6. Song, Z., Roussopoulos, N.: Hashing Moving Objects. In: Proc. of the 2nd International Conference on Mobile Data Management, pp. 161–172 (2001)
7. Theodoridis, Y., Silva, J.R.O., Nascimento, M.A.: On the Generation of Spatiotemporal Datasets. In: Proc. of the 6th International Symposium on Advances in Spatial Databases, pp. 147–164 (1999)

Model-Driven Development of Ubiquitous Applications for Sensor-Actuator-Networks with Abstract State Machines

Sebastian Schuster and Uwe Brinkschulte

Institute for Process Control and Robotics,
Universität Karlsruhe(TH), Kaiserstraße 12, 76128 Karlsruhe
{sschu, brinks}@ira.uka.de

Abstract. The development of applications in the domain of Ubiquitous Computing has to deal with some unique challenges. The target environment consists of very heterogeneous and partly low-power devices. It changes rapidly due to wireless communication and mobile users. We propose to use model-driven development based on Abstract State Machines to deal with these challenges. Applications are defined on high levels of abstraction and efficient implementations tailored to the target platform are automatically generated.

1 Introduction

Mark Weiser's vision of Ubiquitous Computing (UC) [9] describes a world where computers are everywhere and support your everyday life. They relieve you from routine work, which makes UC attractive to many people, as it does to us.

Today, users have to tell the computer what to do and enter information in the way the machine wants it - the main issue Weiser had with the way we use computers. To realize UC, computers and other devices must be enhanced to detect the user's needs and to support him actively.

Wireless sensor networks (WSNs) [3] consist of simple, low power, and cheap sensor nodes, working together to monitor their environment. Thus, they can serve the purpose of detecting the user's actions. By adding nodes with the capabilities to influence their environment, a sensor and actuator network (SAN) can be established and serve as an infrastructure for ubiquitous applications.

SANs will include all kinds of devices from different vendors, ranging from full-featured PCs over PDAs and Smartphones to tiny, low-power sensor nodes and embedded devices tailored to specific needs. Some of these nodes are stationary, and some will be mobile. Different kinds of applications are possible: there will be applications bound to a specific environment, like controlling the lighting based on user presence. Other applications will be bound to a specific user and will control the environment based on the user's preferences, like controlling TV, heating or air condition. Some applications will mainly provide information, e.g. cooking recipes or traffic guidance. All of these applications will run simultaneously and have to share resources. They must possibly interoperate without

R. Obermaisser et al. (Eds.): SEUS 2007, LNCS 4761, pp. 527–536, 2007.

knowing each other. They must adapt themselves in an ever-changing environment, from switching input and output devices when the user moves to showing a very different behavior depending on the current context.

At a first glance, using established development techniques from traditional distributed systems for SANs, like middleware, may seem to be a good idea. For a number of reasons discussed in section 2, this is not feasible for SANs. However, without powerful tools raising software development productivity of ubiquitous applications, there is no chance that Weiser's vision will ever be realized. Ubiquitous applications will stay a toy for the wealthy people instead.

After introducing the major challenges in the area of ubiquitous application development in section 2, we discuss related development tools tailored to ubiquitous applications in section 3. Afterwards, we present our arguments for model driven techniques in this application field in section 4. Furthermore, we sketch our approach to realize a model-driven development process. The work of implementing this approach is in progress. We are optimistic our ideas will prove to be valuable in practice. This paper concludes with a summary in section 5.

2   Challenges

There are a number of challenges to be addressed when developing ubiquitous applications. Obviously, a ubiquitous application is a distributed one. Multiple processes run within the SAN and communicate by exchanging messages. Typical challenges of distributed applications include partial failures, transmission errors, and synchronization. All of these are well researched. Furthermore, solutions to deal with these problems are incorporated in middleware, ready to be reused by the developer. However, what are the challenges that do not allow to transfer existing solutions to the domain of Ubiquitous Computing?

2.1   Efficiency

Since nothing comes for free, the advantages of using a middleware introduce costs. The computation steps done in the middleware consume time and energy, while the necessary code takes memory space and energy. The resources of sensor nodes in computation power, memory space, and energy, are very constrained. This, putting an upper bound on the amount of work that can be done on a sensor node, becomes a challenge of efficiency when using a middleware.

Middleware is supposed to offer flexible solutions to a diverse range of applications. The tailoring to the needs of the application happens mostly at runtime, e.g. when the application feeds parameters to middleware function calls. Selecting the proper middleware functionality according to these parameters takes extra computation steps. Furthermore, many functions are unused, despite taking memory space. One can generally say – with a classical middleware – higher flexibility decreases efficiency (while facilitating reuse). How to deal with this tradeoff for SANs is an open question.

2.2 Heterogeneity and Interoperability

A typical task of middleware is to deal with a heterogeneous system consisting of nodes with different properties. Its goal is to hide the differences from the programmer and make the system look like a homogeneous one, easing software development. When the nodes of the network are not too different in terms of processing power and storage space, this can be achieved by including standard communication protocols, conversion of different data representations etc. within the middleware. In a system with nodes ranging from tiny sensor nodes to full-featured personal computers, with resources differing by orders of magnitudes, this is nearly impossible. However, in the absence of powerful abstractions, programmers would have to write specific code for every kind of node, manually adding functions to make the nodes interoperate. It means resolving problems already solved for traditional distributed systems – surely not the best way to go.

2.3 Dynamics

Traditional distributed applications often assume to run upon a fixed network. Processes communicate directly and reliably – the developer does not see details like network routing or location information. A node unreachable for some reason is treated as a failure and handled by the middleware or the application. However, in ubiquitous environments, users carry nodes around, nodes use unreliable wireless communication, their energy can be exhausted, and the user can interfere with the system in unforeseen ways. Communication failures are common and network connectivity changes rapidly. Since the user should not be bothered to deal with exceptions, self-organizing algorithms that make the system adapt itself to changes autonomously are necessary. These algorithms should be generic and flexible enough to make them available for reuse for a wide range of ubiquitous applications. At the same time, efficiency must be preserved.

2.4 Goals

For a productive development of ubiquitous applications, solutions for efficiently dealing with heterogeneity and the dynamics of the system must be available for reuse. The developer should describe system behavior on a high level of abstraction, hiding differences between nodes and network changes. Applications cannot be custom made for each environment – this would be much too expensive. The developer might not even know the system his application has to run on. Specifying in abstract terms that can be found in any ubiquitous environment is the only way possible. Instead of specifying on the level of individual nodes, stating *node X turn the light on*, the developer must be able to code an equivalent of *turn on the light in the user's room*. Detecting the presence of the user in a room and finding a node with a certain capability – like turning on the light – is something that will happen regularly in ubiquitous applications. Implementing these functions adaptable to different environments once and reusing them is a prerequisite for high development productivity.

However, the target application must not only be adaptable to different environments. People may have different requirements regarding privacy issues or they want their daily life support to be a little different. Applications must be customizable to the varying needs of the users.

3   Related Work

Since the research area of Ubiquitous Computing is quite young, most of the work has been carried out in trying to solve certain problems and not in making these solutions available for reuse. However, two proposals explicitly dealing with some of the identified challenges had a major influence on our work.

The first one is PCOM [8], a component-oriented middleware for pervasive applications. PCOM applications consist of a tree of components, each implementing parts of the application functionality. The actual layout of tree instances is determined by the PCOM middleware at runtime – based on capabilities of the different nodes and requirements of each component given by the developer in some XML-dialect. Thus, the application can also be adapted to changes in the environment. Motivated by the *development-by-composition*-paradigm, components implemented once can be reused in other applications as well. PCOM is built upon another middleware layer, BASE [1], offering communication services in heterogeneous and dynamic environments, relieving the developer from dealing with network routing. BASE and PCOM transfer the traditional approach – using layers of middleware – to the development of ubiquitous applications, explicitly considering highly dynamic and heterogeneous environments. Their memory footprint is about 120-160KB, preventing to use them on sensor nodes. The level of abstraction that can be achieved depends on the available components. Specifying tree composition in some XML-dialect and using general purpose programming languages to implement components without further support is still way off developing applications in terms of the target domain.

An approach motivated by the OMG's Model Driven Architecture (MDA) is described in [7]. The OMG proposes to use models and not code as the primary artifact of software development. While models are widely used in software development, serving as a sketch for the real code, they tend to get out of synch as code development evolves. The resulting code is always a mix of parts dealing with the real business problems and, to a large amount, of parts due to the way these problems have to be solved on a specific platform. Problem domain and realization domain should be clearly separated instead, by describing the application in platform-independent models (PIM) containing application logic only. Afterwards, they are transformed to platform-specific models, enriched with platform details. In the last step, executable code can be generated. These transformations can be performed manually or automatically – the latter one being the preferred way.

In [7] a language with a fancy graphical representation to describe platform-independent models of applications for home automation is defined. The developer describes the behavior of the system using several communicating state machines running in the system. When deploying the application in a target environment, the state machines of the PIM are split up into roles, which can be assigned to nodes of the target system. These roles are transformed to executable code and installed on the target nodes, depending on their capabilities. Our lighting application would consist of two roles, one for detecting the presence of a user, and one for turning on the light. The first one would be installed on all nodes with a motion detector, the second on all connected to the lighting. The system can adapt to changes by activating and deactivating nodes, e.g. roles of failing nodes can be taken over by others. Multiple platforms can be supported by developing the necessary transformers and code generators. The generative model-driven approach allows to generate efficient code specifically tailored to the target nodes, avoiding the overhead of a middleware. At the same time, the roles-based approach can deal with a dynamic system, suggesting a way to deal with the flexibility vs. efficiency tradeoff in classical middleware. Our approach is based on this idea too. The described development method lacks ways of ensuring interoperability. On the highest level, descriptions based on finite state machines can probably be improved with terms more closely resembling the domain of Ubiquitous Computing.

4 Proposed Solution

We propose to use model-driven development to handle the identified challenges. The aim is to combine the advantages of using a middleware, development on a high level, with the generation of code tailored to different platforms for higher efficiency. The functionality provided by a middleware is added by model transformations instead. At the same time, the overhead introduced by a middleware is avoided. Applications can be developed in a coherent way for heterogeneous target environments that include devices as resource-constrained as sensor nodes. When installing an application, it is transformed automatically, taking user preferences and properties of the target environment into account.

While realizing this vision will surely be appreciated, a lot of work lies ahead. The main questions that have to be answered include: How do the models look like? How to define transformations? How to guide them? We present first answers to these questions in the following sections. We are currently at the start of developing and implementing our development process, following a bottom-up approach. Our concept certainly needs further refinements.

4.1 Process Overview

Different kinds of models are involved in the development process: models describing user preferences, models describing the target environment, and models describing the behavior of some entity. At the top-level, the developer implements the application by specifying a platform-independent behavior model, describing how the environment reacts to what the user is doing. On lower levels, the behavior of parts of the system down to individual nodes is specified. Compared to the MDA, we propose to use multiple transformation steps from top-level models to executable code. The available transformations are arranged in a hierarchy, each transformation bridging a smaller gap. Models are transformed along the edges, starting at the highest level of the hierarchy and yielding executable code at the leaves. The direction to take when traversing and how to transform is controlled by the target environment and user preferences – the available devices decide which transformations to take. Wether to add encryption algorithms depends on the user preferences for example.

An extract of the transformation hierarchy is given in figure 1. On the highest level, different modeling languages can be used to describe different kinds of applications. These can be transformed to a language where application functionality is decomposed into distributed roles, dealing with the dynamics of the environment – similar to [7]. Several transformations not shown here add communication and interoperability support or customizations. After that, transformations generate models for different platforms, containing the roles the target node can take. At first, these models will be generated for generic platforms like *Sensor Node* or *PC*, using features offered by all types of sensor nodes or PCs respectively. The generic models are then transformed to models for specific device types, like Mica or Scatterweb ESB sensor nodes. Eventually, executable code can be generated.

An example transformation process is given in figure 2, showing the installation of an application controlling the lighting based on user presence. The transformation processor (a device with less resource constraints like a PC) rec-

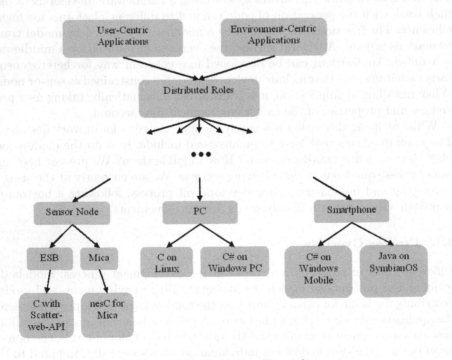

Fig. 1. Transformation Hierarchy

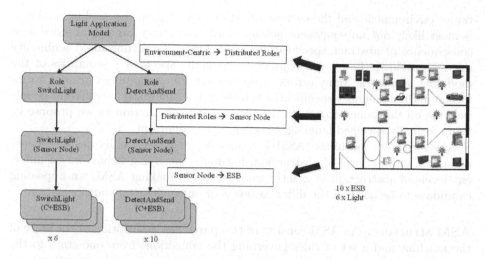

Fig. 2. Example Transformation

ognizes ten Scatterweb ESB [6] sensor nodes able to detect user presence. Six of the nodes can control a light. When transforming to the next role-based modeling layer, it deduces there will be two types of roles necessary. The first (*DetectAnd-Send*) detects user presence and informs the second role (*SwitchLight*) able to control the light. These roles are then converted into models for generic sensor nodes, describing how nodes communicate and activate their roles. In the last step, C-code is generated from these descriptions and flashed onto the nodes.

Composing the transformation chain of smaller transformations facilitates their reuse. Introducing a new type of sensor node only needs a less expensive transformation from the generic platform to the new platform for example. The role-based decomposition of application functionality allows to adapt at run-time. By adding additional roles, e.g. for data conversion, interoperability can be assured. Finally, the generated code is more efficient than a middleware-based approach, leaving out unnecessary features.

4.2   Abstract State Machines as Behavior Models

Models are defined in terms of a modeling language, describing what models look like (syntax) and how to interpret those (semantics). At the top-level, we need expressive languages specific to Ubiquitous Computing. Since ubiquitous applications let the environment support the user, reacting to what the user is doing, this language will feature an event-driven control flow. A language suitable for home automation would offer terms like *Room, Lighting* or *TV*. At lower levels, we need languages to describe roles and the behavior of nodes.

When transforming models, we have to make sure that the resulting model describes a behavior equivalent to the source model. A top-level model that includes an abstract action *Alert the user*, may be correctly transformed to a ringing Smartphone or a message shown on screen of a TV – depending on the target environment and the current situation. Turning on the washing machine is most likely not an equivalent action. While ambiguity can be intended as a consequence of abstract specifications on a higher level, unwanted ambiguity must be avoided. The key is a precise – formally specified – semantics of the modeling languages. Many errors made in software development are due to informal natural language specifications, interpreted differently by different people working on the same project. In a multi-step transformation as we propose it, using formally specified languages is even more important.

Abstract state machines (ASMs) [4] can be used to formally describe every algorithm on any level of abstraction. Formally specifying behaviors on different levels of abstraction is exactly what we need, making ASMs an appealing candidate to be used on the different levels of our multi-step transformation.

ASM structure. An ASM consists of two parts: the description of the state of the machine and a set of rules governing the transitions from one state to the next. The state is described in terms of an algebra – sets with operations and relations. The author of [5] argued that ...*every static mathematic reality can be described as a structure in the sense of mathematical logic....* The rules are made up of conditions guarding the firing of the rule and of updates describing how to change the state of the machine. Starting in an initial state, the machine performs step by step, in each step executing all matching rules and updating the state of the machine in one atomic step.

ASMs for Ubiquitous Applications. The following example shows an excerpt from a high level ASM describing our lighting application.

```
enum Rooms = {Livingroom, Bathroom, Kitchen, Bedroom}
function Light: Rooms -> BOOLEAN
function Occupied: Rooms -> BOOLEAN

rule Main = par
forall room in Rooms do Light(room):=Occupied(room) endforall
endpar
```

A set *Rooms* is defined consisting of the different rooms in the ubiquitous environment. The function *Light* can be used to control the lighting in every room. A function *Occupied* returns true if anybody is in a room. The only rule *Main* states, the lights should be switched according to user presence.

This is a description on a very high level. It contains what could be called the business logic of the application. Since ubiquitous applications are about relieving people from routine tasks, we argue that their business logic is not too complex and compact descriptions on a high level are possible. ASMs can also be used on a lower level to describe the behavior of a role or of a single node. A sensor node can be described in terms of the state of its sensors and functions yielding current sensor values.

In order to use ASMs for behavior descriptions, a vocabulary to describe the ASM states has to be defined at the different levels. At the highest level, there will be sets and functions like the ones shown above. For lower levels, functions showing the state of sensors have to be defined for example. We are currently investigating possible vocabularies for sensor nodes.

Transforming ASMs. The vocabularies of the different levels essentially describe our modeling languages – the terms that can be used to describe the state of system with ASM rules describing the behavior of its entities. How to define the transformations, mapping the abstract function *Occupied* to ASMs describing roles, that observe the motion detection sensor and transmit a message when movements are detected?

The ASM method [2] describes a software development process based on ASMs. According to this method, a developer starts with a high-level ASM describing the application under construction. This ASM is refined stepwise – gradually enriching it with details describing how to implement what was specified on the higher level. Functions can be replaced by additional ASMs computing this function or ASMs can be composed of sub-ASMs. Sequential ASMs can be refined by adding agents, making it a distributed ASM. All of these steps have to be performed manually by the developer. What we need is a way of automating these steps - this would eventually yield our transformation chain.

To establish our approach in practice, an expressive specialized language to describe ASM transformations would be necessary. We are currently considering general purpose languages using established model transformation and code generation patterns only. We first want to investigate how to apply transformations and how to parametrize them. The application of special transformation languages is planned for the future.

5   Summary

We proposed to use model-driven development techniques to deal with the primary challenges of developing ubiquitous applications: high degrees of heterogeneity, the need for efficiency, and high dynamism in ubiquitous environments. Applications are described as high level models independent of a specific platform and are automatically transformed to platform-specific models matching the target environment. The core idea of our approach is to use a chain of transformations with small transformation steps. Building new transformations and including new platforms will be less expensive and reuse is facilitated.

Introducing multiple transformation steps, unwanted ambiguity through specifications given in languages with informally defined semantics becomes an even bigger problem. Therefore, we proposed to use Abstract State Machines to formally describe the behavior on all levels of abstraction. We sketched how ASMs can be used on different levels and why they are suitable for transformations.

The next step will be define vocabularies for ASMs on the different levels. Afterwards we will investigate how transformations can be defined. We plan to implement a complete transformation chain based on ASMs – including decomposition of application functionality and adapting the composition at runtime.

Acknowledgements

Sebastian Schuster is supported by the German Research Foundation (DFG) within the Research Training Group GRK 1194 Self-organizing Sensor-Actuator-Networks.

References

1. Becker, C., Schiele, G., Gubbels, H., Rothermel, K.: BASE - A micro-broker-based middleware for pervasive computing. In: Proceedings of the First IEEE International Conference on Pervasive Computing and Communication (PerCom), pp. 443–451. IEEE Computer Society, Los Alamitos (2003)
2. Börger (Egon), E., Stärk, R.F.: Abstract state machines: a method for high-level system design and analysis. Springer, Heidelberg (2003)
3. Estrin, D., Pottie, G., Girod, L., Srivastava, M.: Instrumenting the world with wireless sensor networks. In: ICASSP 2001 (June 2001)
4. Gurevich, Y.: Sequential abstract-state machines capture sequential algorithms. ACM Transactions on Computational Logic 1(1), 77–111 (2000)
5. Gurevich, Y.: Abstract state machines: An overview of the project. In: Seipel, D., Turull-Torres, J.M. (eds.) FoIKS 2004. LNCS, vol. 2942, pp. 6–13. Springer, Heidelberg (2004)
6. Schiller, J.H., Liers, A., Ritter, H., Winter, R., Voigt, T.: Scatterweb - low power sensor nodes and energy aware routing. In: HICSS 2005 (2005)
7. Ulbrich, A., Weis, T., Mühl, G., Geihs, K.: Application development for actuator- and sensor-networks. In: 4. GI/ITG KuVS Fachgespräch Drahtlose Sensornetze, Zurich, Switzerland (2005)
8. Weis, T., Handte, M., Knoll, M., Becker, C.: Customizable pervasive applications. In: PERCOM '06: Proceedings of the Fourth Annual IEEE International Conference on Pervasive Computing and Communications (PERCOM'06), pp. 239–244. IEEE Computer Society, Washington (2006)
9. Weiser, M.: The computer for the twenty-first century. Scientific American 265(3), 94–104 (1991)

Design and Implementation of Peripheral Sharing Mechanism on Pervasive Computing with Heterogeneous Environment

Wonhong Kwon, Han Wook Cho, and Yong Ho Song

College of Information and Communications, Hanyang University,
Seoul, Korea
{whkwon, hwcho, yhsong}@enc.hanyang.ac.kr

Abstract. As pervasive computing permeate into user's lives, many embedded devices based on Linux exist around the users. In this circumstance, the heterogeneousness of operating systems causes incompatibility problems in sharing peripherals since the users and the devices have a different operating system. In this paper, we propose a USB Cross-platform Extension to share peripherals in a heterogeneous environment via a TCP/IP network. Using our approach, the users can access remote peripherals with different operating systems as if they were attached to a local computer. According to our evaluation results, our approach has some overhead, but sufficient performance for practical usage.

Keywords: Peripheral sharing, Heterogeneous operating system environment, Pervasive computing.

1 Introduction

Recent advances in computing technology have enabled ubiquitous computing environments to permeate users' lives rapidly. In such an environment, a number of embedded devices such as PDA, MP3 player, or cell phone, exist around the users. These devices usually use Linux as their operating system because of its characteristics such as reconfigurability, flexibility, lightweight size, and cheap price. However those who use these devices are more familiar with Microsoft Windows rather than Linux.

The heterogeneousness of operating systems causes incompatibility problems in sharing peripherals between users and embedded devices. For instance, a user who uses Windows may want to access an external storage device in a PDA based on Linux. Also, the user may want to use a speaker connected to a MP3 player or a DVD-RW in home appliances. In these scenarios, if the user's computer and the embedded devices use a same operating system, they can easily share peripherals. If the devices do not use the same operating system, however, they need a way of sharing peripherals in a heterogeneous environment.

R. Obermaisser et al. (Eds.): SEUS 2007, LNCS 4761, pp. 537–546, 2007.

Many peripheral sharing mechanisms have been proposed for heterogeneous environments. For instance, SAMBA [1] is a well-known file and print service protocol between Windows clients and non-Windows servers via a TCP/IP network. Using the SAMBA, a user can access files or printers located at remote machine with a non-Windows operating system. However, traditional approaches including SAMBA depend on specific peripherals. Therefore, these approaches are inappropriate for the recent variety of sophisticated peripherals in pervasive computing. In these circumstances, there is a great need of peripheral-independent sharing mechanism in heterogeneous operating system environment.

In this paper, we propose USB Cross-platform Extension (UCE) to share peripherals in a heterogeneous environment via a TCP/IP network. We assume that all computers and embedded devices are connected together via the network and they have heterogeneous operating systems. In this environment, our approach enables users to access remote USB peripherals with different operating systems as if they were attached to a local machine. USB was chosen because it supports almost all devices including storage, keyboard, speaker, and printer. This characteristic gives peripheral-independence to our approach.

The rest of this paper is organized as follows. Section 2 introduces related work. Section 3 describes the general concepts of Windows USB System and Section 4 explains the USB Cross-platform Extension. Section 5 explains our evaluation results. We conclude this paper in Section 6.

2   Related Works

USB Cross-platform Extension is based on USB over IP technology to provide sharing mechanism in a heterogeneous environment. Takahiro et al. proposed USB/IP [2][3] is a peripheral bus extension over a TCP/IP network in a homogeneous environment. Virtual Host Controller Interface (VHCI) Driver and Stub Driver were added to Linux to extend the peripheral bus via the network. VHCI located at a client-side which required to access remote devices, is responsible for processing enqueued USB Request Block (URB) like legacy USB Host Controller in Linux. When VHCI receives the URBs, they are converted into USB/IP packets and sent to a remote machine. Stub Driver is a new USB Per-Device Driver and located at the remote machine. It decodes incoming USB/IP packets, extracts the URBs and submits them to devices. These new drivers enable users to share a large range of devices over the network without any modification in existing components. This mechanism supports all USB transfer features such as bulk, interrupt, control, and isochronous mode and its I/O performance is sufficient for practical usage.

We extend this mechanism to heterogeneous environment. In the context of our approach, the operating system of a client is Windows instead of Linux in USB/IP. This requires that the VHCI is migrated to Windows for processing URBs and sending them to the remote machine. Therefore, we create UCE Bus in Windows as a new USB bus architecture to extend peripheral bus to other operating systems.

In the next section, we use Windows USB System to explain how UCE is designed and implemented.

3   Windows USB System

Windows supports USB in various ways such as system-provided USB Function Driver (usbhid.sys, usbstor.sys), USB Bus Driver (usbhub.sys), USB Host Controller Driver (usbohci.sys, usbuhcd.sys, usbehci.sys), and USB common library (usbd.sys) to provide convenience for users and developers. Fig. 1 shows the architecture of these drivers in Windows USB System.

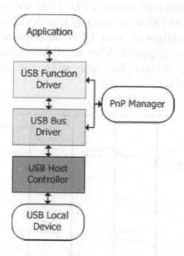

Fig. 1. Windows USB System Architecture

USB Function Driver has the information about specific hardware and provides controlling methods of the hardware to applications. When a device is attached, Windows dynamically loads the appropriate USB Function Driver with the information of the device. While this driver is active, it provides an interface to applications supporting I/O requests and translates these requests to a USB-specific format called URB.

USB Bus Driver manages USB devices that are currently attached and supports self-identifying of newly attached devices. Self-identifying, one of the important features of USB, is where configuring a device automatically occurs without additional steps taken by the user. This driver cooperates its work with PnP (Plug and Play) Manager because managing and self-identifying require various PnP operations. USB Host Controller Driver is responsible for the notification of device attachment. USB Root Hub on this controller sends a message to the USB Bus Driver when a device is arrived.

Fig. 2 shows that how these drivers work together. When a USB device is attached to the host, USB Host Controller Driver senses this attachment and sends a message to USB Bus Driver called Hot-plug Notification in MSDN [4]. If that happens, USB Bus Driver allocates resources for the device and sends a message indicating that a relation of attached devices is changed to PnP Manager using a Windows kernel API called IoInvalidateDeviceRelations(). Because a change of relation is generated when a device is attached or removed, PnP Manager needs to confirm the cause of a change. Therefore, PnP Manager requests a list of devices to USB Bus Driver to identify the changes. USB Bus Driver responds to this message with an updated device list, and PnP Manager recognizes the cause of a change and performs various PnP operations as required. Then the PnP Manager loads the proper USB Function Driver based on previous PnP operations, allocates resources for the device, and starts the device. Even if the USB Function Driver has been loaded, it does not know device-specific information but only general information about the device. For instance, usbhid.sys is system-provided USB Function Driver for a USB keyboard. It has routines for general USB keyboard processes but does not know that how many keys are in the keyboard or which information is displayed on the LED. USB specification [5] provides USB descriptors to USB Function Driver to support this device-specific information. USB Function Driver is self-configured with USB descriptors and performs additional device-specific operations as required. After all of the processes have been completed, the architecture of these drivers for supporting the device is established and applications can use the device.

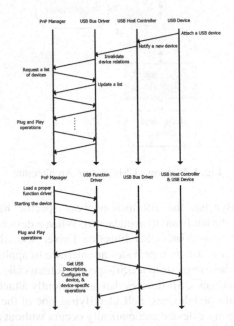

Fig. 2. Initialization process of a local device

4   USB Cross-Platform Extension

USB Cross-platform Extension (UCE) is a peripheral sharing mechanism via a TCP/IP network for heterogeneous environment. In this section, we explain the architecture of UCE and describe UCE Bus which is a main component of our approach.

4.1 UCE Architecture

Using the UCE, a user can use a remote device in heterogeneous operating system as if the device were attached locally and working in the same operating system. It means that UCE provides transparency to the user by hiding a location and an operating system of the device. To achieve this, we attach the device to a local machine not physically but conceptually and we call this "virtual device."

UCE has different device driver architecture than the Windows USB System due to the virtual device. This is because the virtual device has some extraordinary characteristics compared to the local one. Therefore, Windows USB System as we mentioned in Section 3 is not directly applicable to our approach in two ways. First, the virtual device is not a real device. A legacy system sometimes needs to get the information from a device like USB Descriptors. However, the virtual device does not have this information because it only exists conceptually. In addition, the Windows USB Bus cannot receive a notification message indicating that a new device is attached from USB Host Controller because no devices are attached to local machine physically. Second, the real location of the virtual device is not local but remote. Therefore, a remote machine must be accessed via the network but a legacy system does not support this. Because of these problems, a legacy system needs modification supporting the virtual device. Fig. 3 shows our proposed methods.

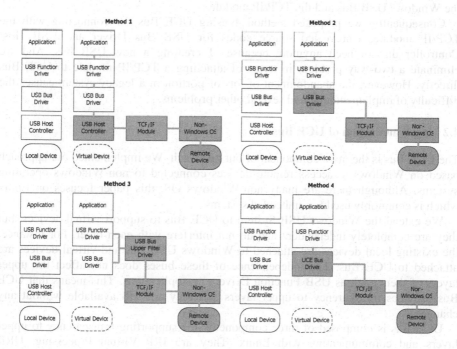

Fig. 3. Design candidates of UCE

Method 1 and 2 are quite a simple and easy to implement compared to others because these methods reuse large portions of the legacy system. For instance, UCE needs a communication module to access a remote device, so we added a TCP/IP module to the legacy system. The TCP/IP module is attached to USB Host Controller in method 1 and USB Bus Driver in method 2. This approach requires less modification to UCE. However, Microsoft does not release source codes for the USB Bus Driver and Host Controller because of their security policies. That is, we cannot modify the USB Bus Driver or Host Controller to add the TCP/IP module. In this respect, these methods are inappropriate for our approach.

Method 3 uses USB Bus Upper Filter Driver to cooperate with the TCP/IP module. Because it is located between USB Function Driver and USB Bus driver, every packet generated from USB Function Driver is arrives in it. If that happens, it has three methods for processing the enqueued packets: passing packets to a lower layer, processing and passing packets, or processing and completing packets. Among these methods, we chose the processing and completing method when USB Function Driver requests the information from a remote USB device. That is, packets are delivered to a remote machine in which a remote device resides and are completed after receiving a response from a remote machine. In other cases such as device initialization or PnP operations, we chose a passing method which is simply transfers packets to the Windows USB Bus. However, this two-way approach has a serious problem. When Windows USB Bus needs information from the device, this approach does not pass the packets to a remotely-attached device because of the lack of connection between the Windows USB Bus and the TCP/IP module.

Consequently, we proposed method 4 using UCE Bus for connecting with the TCP/IP module. Unrevealed source codes for USB Bus Driver and USB Host Controller do not need anymore because of creating a new USB bus. And we eliminate a two-way problem in terms of attaching a TCP/IP module to UCE Bus directly. However, the abandonment of lots of portion in a legacy system causes the difficulty of implementation and several other problems.

4.2 Implementation of UCE Bus

The UCE Bus is the main component of our approach. We implemented our approach based on Windows to access remote devices connected to non-Windows operating systems. Although there are many non-Windows OS, this paper focuses on Linux which is commonly used for embedded systems.

We extend the Windows USB System to UCE Bus to support virtual devices, but they are completely independent and do not interfere with each other. For instance, the existing local devices are attached to Windows USB Bus and virtual devices are attached to UCE Bus. The independence of these buses does not affect the upper layers of them such as USB Function Drivers or applications. This means that UCE Bus provides transparency to upper layers and they are still available without any changes.

UCE Bus is composed of three components for supporting transparency to upper layers and communicating with Linux. They are IRP Virtual Processing, URB Conversion, and the Transport Driver Interface.

IRP Virtual Processing. IRP (I/O Request Packet) is a data structure to communicate between Windows and kernel-mode device drivers. In order to provide transparency to upper layers, UCE Bus handles IRPs like Windows USB Bus. However, we cannot know the behaviors of USB Bus Driver exactly because of its unrevealed source codes, so these IRPs are handled virtually. In order to make this easier, we use USB Bus Upper Filter Driver to analyze behaviors of USB Bus Driver. As we mentioned before, filter driver receives all IRPs which pass through itself. We get these IRPs using WinDBG [6], and make UCE Bus more likely to act as Windows USB Bus. For instance, an IRP named with IRP_MN_QUERY_CAPABILITIES is requested by PnP Manager to get the information of a device such as power status, approval of removing suddenly from a host without ejection process. UCE Bus receives this IRP when the device is enumerated, but before the USB Function Driver is loaded for the device. In most case, USB Bus Driver sets any relevant values in the DEVICE_CAPABILITIES structure and returns it to the PnP Manager. However, UCE Bus does not know the information related to the device because it has a virtual device. Therefore, we handle this IRP virtually based on our analysis of the results with USB Bus Upper Filter Driver. Table 1 shows IRPs handled virtually in UCE Bus.

Table 1. IRPs with IRP_MJ_PNP as a major function code

IRPs
IRP_MN_QUERY_DEVICE_RELATIONS
IRP_MN_QUERY_ID
IRP_MN_QUERY_CAPABILITIES
IRP_MN_DEVICE_TEXT
IRP_MN_QUERY_RESOURCE_REQUIREMENTS
IRP_MN_QUERY_BUS_INFORMATION
IRP_MN_RESOURCES
IRP_MN_QUERY_LEGACY_BUS_INFORMATION
IRP_MN_FILTER_RESOURCE_REQUIREMENTS

URB Conversion. USB Request Block is a packet format used by device drivers related to USB when a driver needs communication with other drivers. Windows and Linux use URB but the structure and data types are different. For instance, URB has pipe information which indicates direction of transfer (host-to-device or device-to-host), type of pipe (isochronous, interrupt, control, or bulk), and endpoint address. Both operating systems have this information but different presentation. The variable that indicates the interrupt type of pipe has a value 3 in Windows and 1 in Linux. To solve this problem, UCE Bus has URB Conversion component to convert URB for Linux Stub Driver. This conversion process is based on USB over IP technique in USB/IP.

Transport Driver Interface. UCE Bus needs to use a TCP/IP network to communicate with Linux. Therefore, we apply Transport Driver Interface (TDI) to UCE Bus. TDI is a kernel-mode network interface in Windows and it supports all transport protocol stacks and is used particularly for a TCP network in our approach.

Fig 5 shows the attachment and initialization of a virtual device. In a legacy case, Windows USB Bus notices the attachment of a device by a message from the USB Host Controller Driver. However, UCE Bus does not have a method of confirming the attachment. In this respect, UCE Bus sends a message to a remote machine to identify available remote devices. Once this process is done, the remaining processes are the same compared with Fig 2 excluding virtually processing IRP and converting URB.

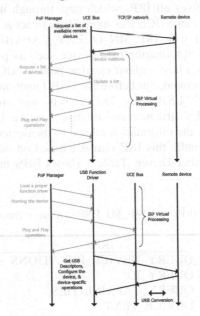

Fig. 5. Initialization process of a virtual device

UCE Bus needs to confirm the type of IRP before using these components. IRP has major and minor function codes to indicate its type. USB Function Driver sends URB to UCE Bus via IRP which has IRP_MJ_INTERNAL_DEVICE_CONTROL in a major function code. In other words, UCE Bus receives general IRP when it receives IRP without IRP_MJ_INTERNAL_DEVICE_CONTROL. Based on this information, UCE Bus activates the IRP Virtual Processing component for general IRP and the URB Conversion component for URB.

IRP Virtual Processing component receives general IRPs related to power management or PnP operation. These IRPs are completed immediately after processing because they are processed virtually in a local machine. This process is simple and does not require much time. However, URB Conversion component receives URBs and most of them need complicated works. For instance, USB Function Driver requests a read operation to an USB storage device. This operation requires serialized I/O and it has a great deal of overhead even if it is processed locally. In our situation, received URBs are not completed after processing because we transmit URBs to a remote machine in addition to the original overhead. Therefore, URBs are pending immediately when they are arrive and are completed after processing with a remote machine.

Once URB is pending, URB Function Driver can request another URB. To handle this, we maintain IRPs in pending IRP queue until they are completed. URB Conversion component checks this queue repeatedly and when IRP is found it starts a process with receiving and sending modules in TDI Client. URB Conversion component and two modules in TDI Client are made by thread for concurrency process.

5 Evaluation

In order to evaluate the performance of our approach, following environment was used as shown in Table 2.

Table 2. Evaluation environment

Client	
CPU	Intel Pentium 4 3.20GHz (dual core)
Memory	1024MB
OS	Microsoft Windows XP Professional
Server	
CPU	Mobile Intel Celeron 2.0GHz
Memory	510MB
OS	Linux 2.6.13

USB has four transfer features which are isochronous, interrupt, bulk, and control. Among these features, we evaluate interrupt transfer mode for human interface devices like mouse or keyboard. Our target device is a SAMSUNG USB SEM-DT35 keyboard. We measured response time which indicates the period of processing enqueued URB. We tested the device when it was attached to local and remote in order to evaluate our approach compared with legacy Windows USB System.

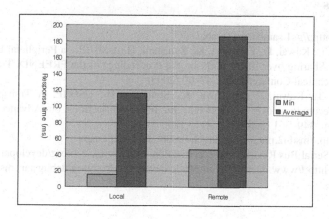

Fig. 6. Evaluation results

First, we evaluated the local device. When URB is generated, it is processed by USB Bus Driver, USB Host Controller Driver, and USB device. And it is completed in reverse direction. Response time in this evaluation includes all of these processes.

According to our measurement, the average response time was 116ms. In second evaluation, the device was attached to a remote machine with Linux. Therefore, generated URB was processed by UCE Bus, TCP/IP network, Stub Driver in Linux, and remote USB device. Average response time was 186ms. As Fig. 6 shows, response time of the remote device was 1.6 times longer than one of the local device. Although performance of UCE was lower than Windows USB System, it is sufficient for practical use.

6 Conclusion

This paper proposed USB Cross-platform Extension that is a peripheral sharing mechanism in a heterogeneous environment via a TCP/IP network. Our approach enables users to access remote USB devices as if they were attached to a local machine using the same environment.

In order to design and implement our approach, we apply UCE to Windows and exploit Linux as the target heterogeneous environment. UCE Bus is a virtual peripheral bus based on Windows and provides virtual attachment and transparency to local machine for accessing remote devices regardless of concerning their location and operating systems. According to our evaluation results, performance of remote USB devices attached to UCE Bus virtually is 1.6 times less than local one, but it is sufficient for practical use.

Acknowledgments. This research work has been supported by Nano IP/SoC Promotion Group of Seoul R&BD Program in 2006 and the Brain Korea 21 Project in 2006.

References

1. SAMBA, http://us1.samba.org/samba/
2. Hirofuchi, T., Kawai, E., Fujikawa, K., Sunahara, H.: USB/IP – a Peripheral Bus Extension for Device Sharing over IP Network. In: the Proceedings of the FREENIX Track: USENIX Annual Technical Conference, pp. 47–60 (2005)
3. Hirofuchi, T., Kawai, E., Fujikawa, K., Sunahara, H.: USB/IP: A Transparent Device Sharing Technology over IP Network. In: IPSJ Transactions on Advanced Computing Systems, pp. 349–361 (2005)
4. MSDN, http://msdn2.microsoft.com/en-us/library/default.aspx
5. Universal Serial Bus Revision 2.0 specification, http://www.usb.org/developers/docs/
6. WinDBG, http://www.microsoft.com/whdc/devtools/debugging/debugstart.mspx

A Review on System Architectures for Sensor Fusion Applications

Wilfried Elmenreich

Vienna University of Technology
Treitlstrasse 3, 1040 Vienna, Austria
wil@vmars.tuwien.ac.at

Abstract. In the literature there exist many proposed architectures for sensor fusion applications. This paper briefly reviews some of the most common approaches, i.e., the JDL fusion architecture, the Waterfall model, the Intelligence cycle, the Boyd loop, the LAAS architecture, the Omnibus model, Mr. Fusion, the DFuse framework, and the Time-Triggered Sensor Fusion Model, and categorizes them into abstract models, generic and rigid architectures. While an abstract model does not guide the designer in the concrete implementation, the generic architectures provide a generic design but leave open several design decisions regarding operating system, hardware, communication system, or database system. Rigid architectures specify at least some of these aspects and therefore provide existing hardware designs, tools, and source code at the cost of flexibility.

1 Introduction

Sensor fusion, *"the combining of sensory data or data derived from sensory data such that the resulting information is in some sense better than would be possible when these sources were used individually"* [1], encompasses a wide variety of different application types (e.g., automation, automotive driver assistance systems, autonomous robots, C^3I (command, control, communications, and intelligence)). An example for sensor fusion applications are current innovations in automotive electronic driver assistant systems [2].

Due to the fact that sensor fusion models heavily depend on the application, there exists no generally accepted model of sensor fusion. According to Kam, Zhu, and Kalata, it is unlikely that one technique or one architecture will provide a uniformly superior solution [3]. Thus, there exist numerous architectures and models for sensor fusion in the literature. In order to use sensor fusion for an application, it is of interest which models and architectures can be used as design patterns.

It is the objective of this paper to review several sensor fusion models and architectures that have been used for sensor fusion. The different approaches will be assessed with respect to their eligibility for real-time applications.

The rest of the paper is structured as follows: The following section briefly describes nine sensor fusion architectures or architectures that have been used to implement sensor fusion applications. Section 3 introduces a classification and discusses the implications of design decisions and design freedom for an implementation. The paper is concluded in Section 4.

R. Obermaisser et al. (Eds.): SEUS 2007, LNCS 4761, pp. 547–559, 2007.
© IFIP International Federation for Information Processing 2007

2   Architectures for Sensor Fusion

2.1   The JDL Fusion Architecture

A frequently referred fusion model originates from the US Joint Directors of Laboratories (JDL). It was proposed in 1985 under the guidance of the Department of Defense (DoD). The *JDL model* [4] comprises five levels of data processing and a database, which are all interconnected by a bus. The five levels are not meant to be processed in a strict order and can also be executed concurrently. Figure 1 depicts the top level of the JDL data fusion process model. The elements of the model are described in the following:

Sources: The sources provide information from a variety of data sources, like sensors, *a priori* information, databases, human input.

Source preprocessing (Level 0): The task of this element is to reduce the processing load of the fusion processes by prescreening and allocating data to appropriate processes. Source preprocessing has later been labelled *level 0* [5].

Object refinement (Level 1): This level performs *data alignment* (transformation of data to a consistent reference frame and units), *association* (using correlation methods), *tracking* actual and future positions of objects, and *identification* using classification methods.

Situation refinement (Level 2): The situation refinement tries to find a contextual description of the relationship between objects and observed events.

Threat refinement (Level 3): Based on *a priori* knowledge and predictions about the future situation this processing level tries to draw inferences about vulnerabilities and opportunities for operation.

Process refinement (Level 4): Level 4 is a meta process that monitors system performance (e.g., real-time constraints) and reallocates sensor and sources to achieve particular mission goals.

Database management system: The task of the database management system is to monitor, evaluate, add, update, and provide information for the fusion processes.

Man-machine interaction: This part provides an interface for human input and communication of fusion results to operators and users.

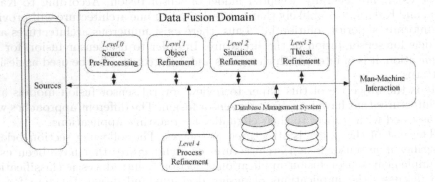

Fig. 1. JDL fusion model (from [4])

The JDL model has been very popular for fusion systems. Despite its origin in the military domain it can be applied to both military and commercial applications. The JDL model also has categorized processes related to a fusion system. However, the model suffers from the following drawbacks:

- It is a data-centered or information-centered model, which makes it difficult to extend or reuse applications built with this model.
- The model is very abstract, which makes it difficult to properly interpret its parts and to appropriately apply it to specific problems.
- The model is helpful for common understanding, but does not guide a developer in identifying the methods that should be used [4] – thus, the model does not help in developing an architecture for a real system.

The basic JDL model has also been improved and extended for various applications. Waltz showed, that the model does not address multi-image fusion problems and presented an extension that includes the fusion of image data [6]. Steinberg, Bowman, and White proposed revisions and expansions of the JDL model involving broadening the functional model, relating the taxonomy to fields beyond the original military focus, and integrating a data fusion tree architecture model for system description, design, and development [7].

2.2   Waterfall Fusion Process Model

The waterfall model, proposed in [8], emphasizes on the processing functions on the lower levels. Figure 2 depicts the processing stages of the waterfall model. The stages relate to the levels 0, 1, 2, and 3 of the JDL model as follows: Sensing and signal processing correspond to source preprocessing (level 0), feature extraction and pattern processing match object refinement (level 1), situation assessment is similar to situation refinement (level 2), and decision making corresponds to threat refinement (level 3).

Being thus similar to the JDL model, the waterfall model suffers from the same drawbacks. While being more exact in analyzing the fusion process than other models, the major limitation of the waterfall model is the omission of any feedback data flow. The waterfall model has been used in the defense data fusion community in Great Britain, but has not been significantly adopted elsewhere [5].

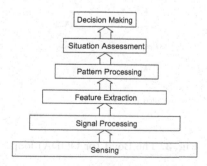

Fig. 2. The waterfall fusion process model (from [8])

2.3   The Intelligence Cycle

Another approach to model a fusion application is to line out its cyclic character. Representatives of such an approach are the intelligence cycle [9] and the Boyd control loop [10].

The *Intelligence Cycle* [9] comprises the following five stages:

Planning and Direction: This stage determines the intelligence requirements.
Collection: Gathering of appropriate information, e. g., through sensors.
Collation: Here the collected information is lined up.
Evaluation: The actual fusion is done and the information gets analyzed.
Dissemination: Dissemination distributes the fused intelligence.

2.4   Boyd Model

Boyd has proposed a cycle containing four stages [10]. This *Boyd control cycle* or *OODA loop* (depicted in figure 3) represents the classic decision-support mechanism in military information operations. Because decision-support systems for situational awareness are tightly coupled with fusion systems [11], the Boyd loop has also been used for sensor fusion. Bedworth and O'Brien compared the stages of the Boyd loop to the JDL [5]:

Observe: This stage is broadly comparable to source preprocessing in the JDL model.
Orientate: This stage corresponds to functions of the levels 1, 2, and 3 of the JDL model.
Decide: This stage is comparable to level 4 of the JDL model (Process refinement).
Act: This stage has no direct counterpart in the JDL model.

The Boyd model represents the stages of a closed control system and gives an overview on the overall task of a system, but the model lacks of an appropriate structure for identifying and separating different sensor fusion tasks.

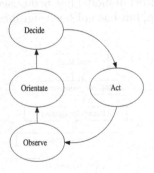

Fig. 3. The Boyd (or OODA) loop

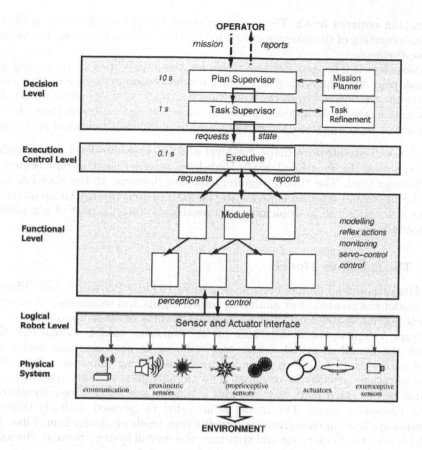

Fig. 4. LAAS Architecture (from [12])

2.5   The LAAS Architecture

The LAAS (Laboratoire d'Analyse et d'Architecture des Systèmes) architecture [12] was developed as an integrated architecture for the design and implementation of mobile robots with respect to real-time and code reuse. Due to the fact that mobile robot systems often employ sensor fusion methods, we briefly discuss the elements of the LAAS architecture (depicted in figure 4).

The architecture consists of the following levels [12]:

Logical robot level: The task of the logical robot level is to establish a hardware independent interface between the physical sensors and actuators and the functional level.

Functional level: The functional level includes all the basic built-in robot action and perception capabilities. The processing functions, such as image processing, obstacle avoidance, and control loops, are encapsulated into separate controllable communicating modules.

Execution control level: The execution control level controls and coordinates the execution of the functions provided by the modules according to the task requirements.

Decision level: The decision level includes the capabilities of producing the task plan and supervising its execution while being at the same time reactive to other events from the execution control level. Depending on the application, the decision level can be composed of several layers that provide different representation abstractions and have different temporal properties.

The LAAS architecture maps low-level and intermediate-level sensor fusion to modules at the functional level. High-level sensor fusion is represented in the decision level. The timing requirements are different at the decision level and the functional level. In contrast to the JDL model, the LAAS architecture guides a designer well in implementing reusable modules as part of a real-time application.

2.6   The Omnibus Model

The Omnibus model [5] has been presented in 1999 by Bedworth and O'Brien. The model was created after analyzing the strengths and weaknesses of existing models and integrates most of the beneficial features of other approaches.

Figure 5 depicts the architecture of the Omnibus model. Unlike the JDL model, the Omnibus model defines the ordering of processes and makes the cyclic nature explicit. It uses a general terminology that does not assume that the applications are defense-oriented. The model shows a cyclic structure comparable to the Boyd loop, but provides a much more fine-grained structuring of the processing levels. The model is intended to be used multiple times in the same application recursively at two different levels of abstraction. First, the model is used to characterize and structure the overall system. Second, the same structures are used to model the single subtasks of the system.

Although the hierarchical separation of the sensor fusion tasks is very sophisticated in the Omnibus model, it does not support a horizontal partitioning into tasks that reflect distributed sensing and data processing. Thus, the model does not support a decomposition into modules that can be separately implemented, separately tested, and reused for different applications.

2.7   Mr. Fusion

Mr. Fusion [13] is a middleware framework supporting data fusion. Mr. Fusion is not exactly tailored to the communication and processing of sensor measurements but aims at data at application level, as for example the output from several network servers.

The architecture consists of two main subsystems, a *fusion core* running a Fusion Virtual Machine (FVM) and a Fusion Status Service (FSS). The communication between the main components is done via CORBA (Common Object Request Broker Architecture). The FVM gathers so-called ballots, i. e., messages from the replicas and evaluates a given policy in order to create an output ballot or an exception. The FSS monitors the output from the fusion core and collects information about value and timing errors for each fusion session into a

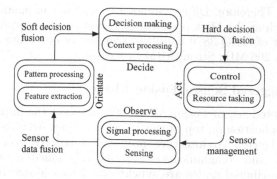

Fig. 5. The Omnibus model (from [5])

database. Information from this database is used by a component named Fusion VM Manager in order to eventually adjust a policy for the FVM.

2.8   DFuse Framework

The DFuse framework for distributed data fusion [14] has been designed to support data fusion applications in heterogeneous ad hoc wireless sensor networks. DFuse models an application as a task graph of data sources, fusion points and data sinks. DFuse assumes data sources to have data available, whenever it is required. If requested data does not arrive at a fusion point in time due to extended computation time or communication failures, the fusion points may perform the fusion over an incomplete set of data.

Figure 6 depicts the two main components of the DFusion architecture, the fusion module implementing the fusion API and the placement module that tries to find a good mapping of the fusion functions within the sensor network. DFuse provides an automatic deployment of applications on the network. An application is launched by passing the task graph and fusion code to a designated root node. The DFuse architecture then performs a distributed algorithm that automatically deploys the application onto the network nodes.

While being a very powerful approach, DFuse requires an underlying hardware and middleware that provides support for timestamping data and a reliable

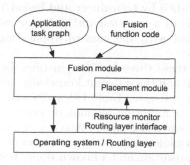

Fig. 6. DFuse Architecture (from [14])

transport layer. Therefore, DFuse cannot be deployed in small wireless sensor architectures such as the Mica platform [15]. Kumar et al. present a case study running on a set of iPAQ 3870 handheld computers providing each at least 32 MB RAM and a 206 MHz StrongARM processor.

2.9   Time-Triggered Sensor Fusion Model

The Time-Triggered Sensor Fusion Model [16] proposes the implementation of a sensor fusion application on top of the Time-Triggered Architecture [17].

The Time-Triggered Architecture proposes a strictly synchronous design, where each task and communication activity is planned *a priori* in a static schedule. All distributed nodes are synchronized to a global time base, which enables the nodes to perform coordinated actions like measurement or actuator settings. Furthermore, the design supports an easy verification of the timing constraints.

The Time-Triggered Sensor Fusion Model describes a set of jobs that represent all necessary activities like measurement, data processing, decision, and actuation. The jobs are represented as vertexes in a distributed graph, whereas each communication activity is represented by an edge between the service providing linking interface (SPLIF) of the job that provides the data and the service requesting linking interface (SRLIF) of the job that receives the data. A physical node may host one or several jobs, thus two logically different tasks may be split up into two jobs but still executed on the same microcontroller subsequently.

The job graph is furthermore structured hierarchically into three levels in order to distinguish between transducers (direct interfaces to the environment), fusion and dissemination activities, and decision activities.

Figure 7 depicts a control loop modelled by the time-triggered sensor fusion model. Interfaces are illustrated by a disc with arrows indicating the possible data flow directions across the interface. Physical sensors and actuators are located on the borderline to the process environment and are represented by circles. All other components of the system are outlined as boxes. The model distinguishes three levels of data processing with well-defined interfaces between them. The *transducer level* contains the sensors and actuators that interact directly with the controlled object. A *smart transducer interface* provides a consistent borderline to the above *fusion/dissemination level*. This level contains fault tolerance and sensor fusion tasks. The *control level* is the highest level of data processing within the control loop. The control level is fed by a dedicated view of the environment (established by transducer and fusion/dissemination level) and outputs control decisions to a *fault-tolerant actuator interface*. User commands from an operator interact with the control application via the *man-machine interface*.

The breakdown into these three levels is justified by the different tasks the three levels have to fulfill and the different knowledge necessary for designing the corresponding hard- and software. Table 1 describes the task and the attributes of the different levels. The following sections describe the three levels in detail.

Prerequisites for implementing an application in the Time-Triggered Sensor Fusion Model are a deterministic time-triggered communication system that supports coordinated task execution and a known upper bound for the computation time of each job in the real-time control loop. Thus, the Worst-Case-Execution

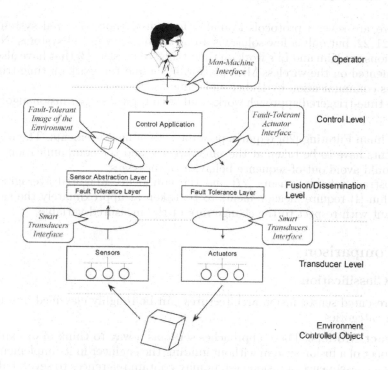

Fig. 7. Data flow in the time-triggered sensor fusion model

Table 1. Properties of transducer, fusion/dissemination, and control level

Level	Task	Implementer	Knowledge
Transducer level	Deliver sensor measurements, instrument actuators	Transducer manufacturer	Internals of sensor/actuator
Fusion/Dissemination level	Gather, process, and represent sensor information; disseminate control decisions to actuators	System integrator	Sensor fusion algorithms, fault tolerance concepts
Control level	Find a control decision, navigation and planning	Application programmer	Mission goals, control theory, decision finding
Operator	Definition of goals	—	Conceptual model of system

Time (WCET) has to be determined for each job, an overview of appropriate methods and tools for WCET estimation can be found in [25].

There are several protocols available for wired time-triggered systems [18, 19, 20, 21, 22] but only a few solutions are available for wireless systems. Notable exceptions are Kim and Li's work on time-triggered tasks [23] that have also been implemented on the wireless Mica platform [15] and the work on time-triggered wireless communication by Huber and Elmenreich [24].

The time-triggered approach works well with typical sensor fusion algorithms, such as:

- Kalman Filtering [26] requires periodic sets of measurements. The measurements have to be taken at the same instant and the communication system should avoid out-of-sequence behavior of messages.
- Abstract reliable sensors [27] and the confidence-weighted averaging algorithm [1] require measurements to be taken at approximately the same instant with respect to the change rate of the measured variable.

3   Comparison

3.1   Classification

The presented sensor fusion architectures can be roughly classified into the following categories:

Abstract Models: These approaches serve as a way to think of or explain an aspect of a fusion system without guiding the engineer in its implementation. As a consequence, a fusion system may contain references to several abstract models. Members of this group are the Waterfall model, the Boyd control loop.

Generic Architectures: A generic architecture gives an outline how to implement an application, but for example does not specify which operating system, hardware, communication system or database should be used. Examples for this group are the JDL model and the Omnibus Model.

Rigid Architectures: These systems guide the engineer well in its implementation, but at the cost that several design decisions have already been taken. While new systems can be realized quickly by taking advantage of existing hardware designs, tools, and source code, the cost of migrating a design from one rigid architecture to another is unnecessarily high. Examples for this group are the LAAS architecture, Mr. Fusion, DFuse, and the Time-Triggered Sensor Fusion Model.

The three categories should not imply a valuation. Abstract models are very important to understand and model the problem statement at the beginning. Using a generic architecture will provide the necessary designer's freedom if a special solution for a special problem is required. On the other hand, selecting a rigid solution will be often the best way to avoid unnecessary re-implementations of already available solutions.

3.2   Real-Time Support

Typically, sensor fusion applications interact with a real environment where it is necessary to fulfill some timing constraints, e.g., for a timely reaction on a particular situation.

For most architectures, especially the abstract and generic ones, it is possible to support real-time behavior, if the implementation of the system is provided with the respective means, like timestamping, deterministic communication, etc. Thus, these architectures neither support nor hinder real-time behavior. However, in order to reduce system complexity such real-time issues should be intrinsic to the architecture.

We will quickly review the rigid architectures regarding this issue:

The LAAS architecture provides real-time support within the functional level by the Generator of Modules (GenoM) [28]. Modules are annotated by the user stating period, delay, and priority properties. GenoM creates the concrete real-time architecture for the application.

Mr. Fusion has been designed at a higher network level, where several sources of indeterminism like possible network delays or unpredictable execution time of the virtual machines jeopardize hard real-time behavior. Therefore, Mr. Fusion is not suited to real-time control applications.

The DFuse framework does not provide predictable timing due to the nature of the underlying wireless communication network. One cannot predict how the heuristic placement algorithm assigns the roles in the networks. Moreover, a wireless transmission may be arbitrary delayed due to inference from other wireless nodes. Therefore, the DFuse framework will not fulfill hard real-time requirements.

The Time-Triggered Sensor Fusion Model is very rigid regarding the timing assumptions and therefore well apt to design real-time fusion applications. However, in applications with soft real-time requirements, the approach still requires a strict analysis and design of the communication schedule. Although this is supported by tools like [29], this strictness comes with some overhead.

4   Conclusion

The large number of proposed sensor fusion architectures makes it difficult for a system engineer to decide which model best fits his or her needs.

While some fusion models are too vague in order to support and guide an implementation, the more concrete models propose different interfaces that do not interoperate with each other. Some systems, especially the ones that stem from the robotic domain are in principle compatible regarding their basic data items and the role of time (that is supporting real-time communication and being implementable on small embedded devices). In contrast, high-level network systems such as Mr. Fusion are tailored to their specific application requirements.

For the future it would be advantageous to elaborate ways that provide interoperation between components of existing fusion architectures instead of creating even more isolated systems anew.

Acknowledgments

This work was supported by the Austrian FWF project TTCAR under contract No. P18060-N04.

References

1. Elmenreich, W.: Sensor Fusion in Time-Triggered Systems. PhD thesis, Technische Universität Wien, Institut für Technische Informatik, Vienna, Austria (2002)
2. Kirchner, A., Obojski, A., Philipps, H., Rotaru, C., Stueker, D., Weiss, K.: Development of an environmental server for advanced driver assistance systems. In: 5th Eur. Congr. and Exhibition on Intel. Transportation Systems and Services (2005)
3. Kam, M., Zhu, X., Kalata, P.: Sensor fusion for mobile robot navigation. Proceedings of the IEEE 85(1), 108–119 (1997)
4. Llinas, J., Hall, D.L.: An introduction to multi-sensor data fusion. In: Proceedings of the International Symposium on Circuits and Systems, vol. 6, pp. 537–540 (1998)
5. Bedworth, M.D., O'Brien, J.: The omnibus model: A new architecture for data fusion? In: Proceedings of the 2nd International Conference on Information Fusion (FUSION'99), Helsinki, Finnland (1999)
6. Waltz, E.: The principles and practice of image and spatial data fusion. In: Proceedings of the 8th National Data Fusion Conference, Dallas (1995)
7. Steinberg, A.N., Bowman, C.L., White, F.E.: Revisions to the JDL data fusion model. In: Proceedings of the 1999 IRIS Unclassified National Sensor and Data Fusion Conference (NSSDF) (May 1999)
8. Markin, M., Harris, C., Bernhardt, M., Austin, J., Bedworth, M., Greenway, P., Johnston, R., Little, A., Lowe, D.: Technology foresight on data fusion and data processing. The Royal Aeronautical Society (1997)
9. Shulsky, A.N.: Silent Warfare: Understanding the World of Intelligence. Brassey's, New York (1991)
10. Boyd, J.R.: A discourse on winning and losing. Unpublished set of briefing slides, Air University Library, Maxwell AFB, AL, USA, (May 1987)
11. Bass, T.: Intrusion detection systems and multisensor data fusion: Creating cyberspace situational awareness. Comm. of the ACM 43(4), 99–105 (2000)
12. Alami, R., Chatila, R., Fleury, S., Ghallab, M., Ingrand, F.: An architecture for autonomy. International Journal of Robotics Research 17(4), 315–337 (1998)
13. Franz, A., Mista, R., Bakken, D., Dyreson, C., Medidi, M.: Mr. fusion: A programmable data fusion middleware subsystem with a tunable statistical profiling service. In: Proceedings of the International Conference on Dependable Systems and Networks (DSN'02), pp. 273–278 (2002)
14. Kumar, R., Wolenetz, M., Agarwalla, B., Shin, J., Hutto, P., Paul, A., Ramachandran, U.: DFuse: A framework for distributed data fusion. In: Proceedings of the Intl. Conference on Embedded Networked Sensor Systems, pp. 114–125 (2003)
15. Hill, J.L., Culler, D.E.: Mica: A wireless platform for deeply embedded networks. IEEE Micro 22(6), 12–24 (2002)
16. Elmenreich, W., Pitzek, S.: The time-triggered sensor fusion model. In: Proceedings of the 5th IEEE International Conference on Intelligent Engineering Systems, Helsinki–Stockholm–Helsinki, Finland, pp. 297–300 (September 2001)
17. Kopetz, H., Bauer, G.: The Time-Triggered Architecture. Proceedings of the IEEE 91(1), 112–126 (2003)
18. Kopetz, H., et al.: Specification of the TTP/A protocol. Research Rep. 61/2002, TU Vienna, Inst. of Comp. Engineering, Vienna, Austria, Version 2.00 (September 2002)
19. TTAGroup. Specification of the TTP/C Protocol V1.1 (2003), Available at http{www.ttagroup.org}

20. Flexray Consortium. *FlexRay Communications System Protocol Specification Version 2.1* (2005), Available at http{www.flexray.com}
21. Hartwich, F., Müller, B., Führer, T., Hugel, R.: Time triggered communication on CAN. In: Proc. of the Intl. CAN Conference, Amsterdam (2000)
22. Kopetz, H., Ademaj, A., Grillinger, P., Steinhammer, K.: The Time-Triggered Ethernet (TTE) design. In: Proceedings of the Intl. Symposium on Object-Oriented Real-Time Distributed Computing (ISORC), pp. 22–33 (May 2005)
23. Kim, K., Li, Y.: Toward easily analyzable sensor networks via structuring of time-triggered tasks. In: Proceedings of the Ninth IEEE Workshop on Future Trends of Distributed Computing Systems (FTDCS'03), pp. 344–351. IEEE Computer Society Press, Los Alamitos (2003)
24. Huber, B., Elmenreich, W.: Wireless time-triggered real-time communication. In: Proceedings of the Second Workshop on Intelligent Solutions for Embedded Systems (WISES'04), Austria, pp. 169–182 (June 2004)
25. Puschner, P., Burns, A.: A review of worst-case execution-time analysis. Journal of Real-Time Systems 18(2/3), 115–128 (2000)
26. Kalman, R.E.: A new approach to linear filtering and prediction problems. Transaction of the ASME, Series D, Journal of Basic Engineering 82, 35–45 (1960)
27. Marzullo, K.: Tolerating failures of continuous-valued sensors. ACM Transactions on Computer Systems 8(4), 284–304 (1990)
28. Fleury, S., Herrb, M., Chatila, R.: Genom: A tool for the specification and the implementation of operating modules in a distributed robot architecture. In: Proceedings of the IEEE/RSJ International Conference on Intelligent Robots and Systems (IROS), Grenoble, France, pp. 842–848 (September 1997)
29. Elmenreich, W., Paukovits, C., Pitzek, S.: Automatic generation of schedules for time-triggered embedded transducer networks. In: Proceedings of the 10th IEEE Conference on Emerging Technologies and Factory Automation (ETFA05), Catania, Italy, vol. 2, pp. 535–541 (September 2005)

Author Index

Lecture Notes in Computer Science

Sublibrary 3: Information Systems and Application, incl. Internet/Web and HCI

For information about Vols. 1– 4295
please contact your bookseller or Springer